HALLMARK Keepsake Ornaments

FIFTH EDITION

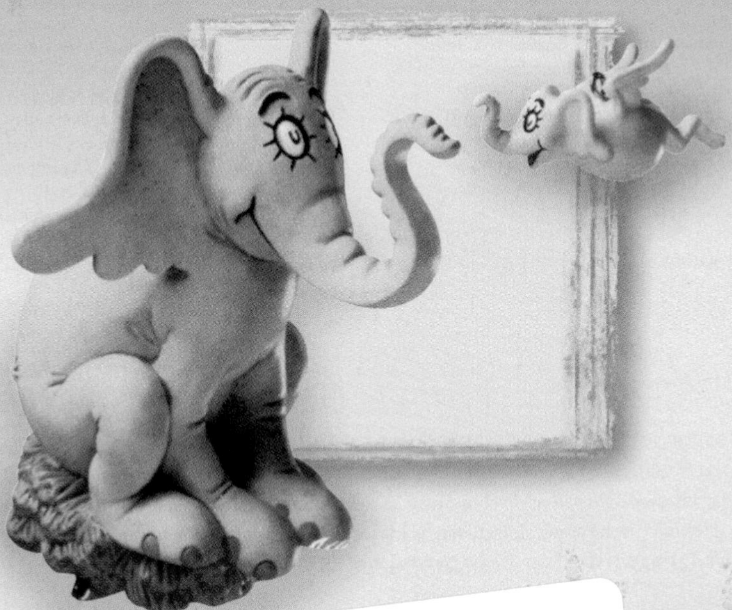

Secondar... & Col...

HALLMARK

Keepsake Ornaments

Front cover (left to right): "Poppy Field" (Magic Ornament, 2001), "Faerie Brilliana" (Frostlight Faeries Collection, 2001) and "Santa Claus with Miniature Panda Bear" (Event Piece, 2001)

Back cover (top to bottom): "Best-dressed Turtle" (Spring Ornament, 1993) and "1955 Murray® Fire Truck" (Kiddie Car Classics, 1992)

First page: "Horton Hatches the Egg™" (3rd in the Dr. Seuss® series, 2001)

EDITORIAL

Managing Editor: Jeff Mahony
Associate Editors: Melissa A. Bennett, Gia C. Manalio, Mike Micciulla, Paula Stuckart
Assistant Editors: Heather N. Carreiro, Jennifer Renk, Joan C. Wheal
Editorial Assistants: Timothy R. Affleck, Beth Hackett, Christina M. Sette, Steven Shinkaruk

PRODUCTION

Production Manager: Scott Sierakowski

ART

Creative Director: Joe T. Nguyen
Assistant Art Director: Lance Doyle
Senior Graphic Designers: Marla B. Gladstone, Susannah C. Judd, David S. Maloney, Carole Mattia-Slater, David Ten Eyck
Graphic Designers: Jennifer J. Bennett, Sean-Ryan Dudley, Kimberly Eastman, Melani Gonzalez, Jim MacLeod, Jeremy Maendel, Chery-Ann Poudrier

R&D

Product Development Manager: Paul Rasid

ISBN 1-58598-153-2

306 Industrial Park Road
Middletown, CT 06457

Table Of Contents

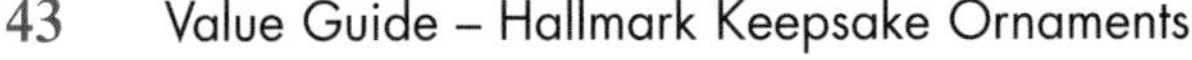

Foreword By Clara Johnson Scroggins

Clara Johnson Scroggins has been collecting Hallmark Ornaments for over 30 years and is widely known to be an expert in the field of ornament collecting. She has written nine books on the subject, serves as a consultant to Hallmark and tours the world to speak at ornament clubs and conventions.

Dear Friends,

We have begun a new era, celebrating 15 years of the Keepsake Ornament Collector's Club, the oldest ornament club in existence. Mark Amren, Keepsake Ornament Collector's Club Manager, has done a remarkable job of bringing the club to this important milestone. The club will celebrate its anniversary this year with the 15th Anniversary Jubilee, which will be held in five cities across America. These events are sure to be filled with great fun and wonderful memories. I hope to see many of you there!

With the new millennium, we also welcome in a variety of different materials, designs and ideas such as the Frostlight Faeries Collection, with its breathtaking fiber optics. As with every new year, we once again have many beautiful and original pieces to help us commemorate all of the important occasions in our lives. The entire Keepsakes Department continues to work diligently to bring us exciting ornaments each year and it is truly amazing that they are able to outdo the remarkable designs of the past for each new holiday season.

Clara

Introducing The Collector's Value Guide™

The holidays are a time for embracing traditions and nothing can capture the spirit of the season quite like a Hallmark Keepsake Ornament. You'll want to make the Hallmark Keepsake Ornaments Collector's Value Guide™ a tradition in your family as well. This full-color handbook, now in its fifth edition, is the ultimate authority on the world of Hallmark Keepsake Collectibles.

Inside this guide's 400-plus pages, you'll find complete information for every Keepsake Ornament, in addition to Spring Ornaments, Merry Miniatures® and Kiddie Car Classics. You'll also find everything you ever wanted to know about collections such as The Dr. Seuss™ Collection, PEANUTS® Gallery and School Days Lunch Boxes. The Collector's Value Guide™ truly is your one-stop source for the world of Hallmark collectibles!

The Value Guide gives you all of the information you need to get the most out of your collection including a color photograph, artist, stock number and updated secondary market value for each piece. You'll also find:

 An exclusive question and answer session with Hallmark artists Joanne Eschrich, Kristina Kline and Dill Rhodus.

 A first look at the brand-new 2001 series as well as a fond farewell to the series that are coming to a close this year.

 Learn how local Hallmark clubs across the country are helping to improve their communities.

 An overview of other Hallmark collectibles.

History Of Hallmark

Joyce Hall, Hallmark's founder and chief executive, remained at the helm of the company until 1966.

Joyce Hall embodies the ultimate rags to riches story. He arrived in Kansas City in 1910 with nothing more than a head full of dreams and a shoebox full of postcards – which he turned into one of the world's most successful companies.

Taking A Gamble

Who could have imagined that Hallmark would start as just a small mail-order business run out of a room in the YMCA? Hall began his empire by sending packages of 100 post-cards with printed invoices to retailers throughout the Midwest. Many retailers returned the cards, but others kept the packages and about one third of the dealers even sent him checks for his work. Within a few months, Hall had earned more than $200 and was on his way to greatness.

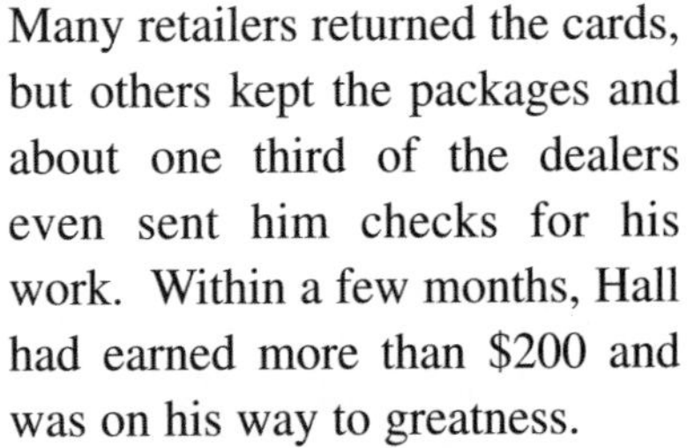

Hall's business continued to grow and by 1915, he had established Hall Bros. and was selling a series of quality holiday cards packaged with envelopes. The introduction of these illustrated greeting cards was an enormous success and the company soon had 120 employees, including Hall's brothers Rollie and Bill (hence, the name, Hall Bros.). By 1923, the company had outgrown its four offices and moved to a new six-story plant.

Why Do We Decorate?

The Christmas Tree tradition is often traced back to Germany, where holiday celebrations once entailed decorating trees with roses, fruits, candies and guilded nuts. Small toys were also nestled within the branches of the tree and along with strings of beads, berries or popcorn.

During the late 1800's, store-bought ornaments, originally made of tin, became popular. Ornaments made of tinsel, wax and even cardboard soon followed. As the artistry of the ornaments increased, molds were made for glass designs.

Word Spreads

The Hallmark name was unveiled only two years after the company made its first big move and, thanks to a 1928 national advertising campaign, Hallmark quickly became associated with quality products. In 1944, the now-familiar company slogan, "When you care enough to send the very best," first appeared and further reinforced the company's reputation with the public.

Hamlet Crowned By Hallmark

In 1953, "Hallmark Hall of Fame" presented Hamlet, which became the first Shakespearean play to be broadcast on national television.

Over the years, Hallmark's products have expanded to include gift wrap and paper party goods. The first "Hallmark Hall Of Fame" television special made its debut on Christmas Eve in 1951. The productions, which still air today, have received more Emmy awards than any other program on television.

The Big Payoff

Company picnics are just one of the employee benefits offered at Hallmark.

Hallmark has the world's largest creative staff within its many branches – and for good reason! Since its early days, the company has prided itself on its employee relations. Company picnics and other events started as early as 1921. In 1956, the company moved to its current three-million-square-foot corporate offices. Today, Hallmark's almost 20,000 employees own approximately one-third of the $3.5 billion corporation and each worker enjoys benefits that go far beyond basic insurance.

The Next Generation

In 1966, Joyce Hall stepped down as Chief Executive Officer and passed the family business on to his son, Donald J. Hall. The younger

Hall made several acquisitions, including jigsaw puzzle manufacturer, Springbok Editions, in 1967 and Crayola Crayon® manufacturer, Binney & Smith, in 1984. He is also responsible for introducing Keepsake Ornaments in 1973.

Crowning Achievement

Hallmark has grown from a one-room company to a global leader in the world of greeting cards.

In Kansas City, Hallmark is king, and not just because its one of the most influential companies in the nation, either. The introduction of the Crown Center, built in 1968, turned Kansas City's downtown area from what was considered by many to be a wasteland into a business and social center that provides the community with jobs and a family-oriented entertainment arena. Crown Center is a massive development perfect for shopping, dining and family fun. The center is continually developing; in fact, plans for further construction and renovations are in the works for the next 20 years.

Hallmark In The Community

Hallmark is known for the extensive amount of work that it does within the Kansas City community. In addition to its involvement with Crown Center, the company takes part in several charity events including the creation of the Kansas City Mayor's Ornaments, the proceeds of which go to the needy. Hallmark's community work doesn't stop in Kansas City, either. The company recently signed on as a sponsor of the 2002 Olympic Winter Games in Sydney, Australia.

This giant corporation may have had its humble beginnings in a small YMCA room with just a few handmade postcard samples, but with Hallmark's commitment to quality products, this family-owned business will continue to grow for centuries to come.

A Closer Look At The Hallmark Line

The introduction of Hallmark Ornaments in 1973 changed the world of collectibles forever. Never afraid to be innovators, Hallmark took the classic glass ball ornament and gave it a new twist – homey and traditional holiday illustrations. Many of these early designs featured works by famous artists like Norman Rockwell, Betsey Clark and Currier & Ives.

Hallmark continues to produce new and unique ornaments today, while using products like plastic, die-cast metal and even paper. And the company has ensured its popularity with collectors by releasing not only traditional ornaments, but also ornaments with current themes. Favorite movies, cartoon characters and popular sports have all joined the ranks.

Keepsake Ornaments

Hallmark Keepsake Ornaments were first introduced in 1973. This collection features everything from traditional blown glass ornaments to handcrafted ornaments made with more unique materials like cloth, wood and porcelain.

Though collectors may have to wait until late summer to begin buying their ornaments, the "Dream Book" is usually available by March. This full-color catalog previews all of the year's upcoming ornaments and gives Hallmark collectors a chance to plan their purchases well in advance.

This booklet provides a sneak peek into the year's line of Keepsake ornaments, which may range from a "Baby's First Christmas" giraffe to a pewter version of "Harry Potter™." Collectible series within the Keepsake line are also featured. These consist of pieces with related themes, such as *Robot Parade* or *Gift Bearers*. One piece (known as an "edition") is added to the series each year until the final edition is announced and the series retires. In addition, many collections are released which are not officially labeled as a series but which share a common theme. Some examples of these "unannounced series," as they are often called, include Mr. Potato Head®, Mickey & Co. and the Child's Age Collection.

Magic Ornaments

Another favorite among collectors are the Magic Ornaments. The term "Magic" is used to describe pieces with special effects, such as light or music. These ornaments were originally introduced as "The Lighted Collection" in 1984. Motion was the next feature to be added, followed by sound in 1989. Select Magic Ornaments also have been grouped into series – nine have been introduced so far. And there's no problem locating Magic Ornaments in the "Dream Book," since they are marked with a special symbol each year.

Crown Reflections

Crown Reflections, a collection based on the traditional blown glass ornaments of yesteryear, was introduced in 1998. Several new pieces were introduced to the line in 1999, including ornaments inspired by the Kiddie Car Classics collection and pop culture phenomenons like Star Trek®. The collection is rounded out with a series of blown glass balls called *Holiday Traditions*.

Li'l Blown Glass

The success of Crown Reflections in 1998 and 1999 inspired a new collection. Li'l Blown Glass features miniature versions of these popular blown glass ornaments and was introduced in 2000. 25 ornaments were in the collection's first release, each representing a traditional holiday image like candy, fruit or "Li'l Roly-Poly Santa."

Laser Gallery

Hallmark took advantage of the latest technological advances in 1999 when it released Laser Creations. Later dubbed the Laser Gallery, these delicate holiday ornaments are made with archival paper which is cut by a tiny, precise laser beam. These patterns are then assembled by hand and the majority come equipped with light clips, so that light can be used to showcase the intricate designs that reflect intriguing shadows.

Frostlight Faeries Collection

New for 2001, the Frostlight Faeries Collection features whimsical flying faeries. Each of the five faeries is painted in a different wintry color and carries a special object which reflects its purpose. And using the technology of fiber optics, each faerie has glowing wings. Other ornaments, like icicles and snowflakes are also available to spice up the collection, as well as a number of accessories like the "Queen Aurora Tree Topper" and a bag of faerie dust. This collection is only being offered through Hallmark Gold Crown® Stores.

Showcase Ornaments

Hallmark looked to religious and folk art themes for these metal and porcelain ornaments introduced in 1993. Originally available only at Hallmark Gold Crown Stores, the line is no longer in production. However, the line's influence can still be seen in many current pieces.

Miniature Ornaments

Second in number only to the Keepsake Ornaments, these pint-sized ornaments sport the same range of classical and pop culture themes as the originals. Measuring from 1/2" to 1-3/4" in size, Miniature Ornaments tend to be released in limited numbers and can be harder to find than their Keepsake brethren. Over thirty-five miniature series have been released over the years.

Other Hallmark Ornaments

In addition to the hundreds of ornaments available to the general public each year, Hallmark releases many special pieces that can only be obtained at retail or club events or through special promotions.

Collector's Club Ornaments – One of the main benefits of belonging to the Keepsake Ornaments Collector's Club is access to exclusive pieces. Some ornaments are presented as a benefit of membership, others are available for purchase exclusively by club members and still others require attendance at special events. Club pieces are often made to complement series in the general Keepsake line.

Premiere Exclusives – The ninth annual Hallmark Gold Crown Keepsake Ornament Premiere is scheduled for July 21, 2001. To celebrate, Hallmark offers premiere exclusive ornaments and figurines that cannot be purchased anywhere else or at any other time. This year's Premiere Ornament is "Santa's Sleigh With Sack And Miniature Ornament," which will be available to collectors who attend the event at their local Gold Crown stores on that day.

Open House and REACH Program Pieces – In past years, the REACH Program has started on the same weekend as the annual Holiday Open House and lasted about three weeks. This year's Open House, occurring at Hallmark Gold Crown stores all over the country, is slated for November 10 and 11, 2001 and will offer the exclusive piece, "Santa Claus With Miniature Teddy Bear."

Special Event Pieces – Several limited edition pieces are crafted by the Keepsake artists for special events throughout the year. These ornaments are then used as prizes and giveaways during the events. Special event pieces could be an ornament from the general line with a new paint scheme or a totally new, never-before-seen piece.

Expo Pieces

Before there were Artist On Tour events, members of the Keepsake Ornament Collector's Club gathered in similar fashion in 1994 and 1995. These events were called Expos and the ornaments which were given to collectors in attendance are now known as Expo Ornaments.

Artists On Tour has been a favorite event with collectors since its start in 1994. During these events, which are held at various locations around the nation annually, collectors have the opportunity to meet their favorite Keepsake artists and have their ornaments signed. This "meet-and-greet" will be replaced in 2001 by the Keepsake Ornament Collector's Club's 15th Anniversary Jubilee which will feature artist signings, raffles and plenty of fun activities at five locations around the nation in August and September.

Spring Ornaments

In 1991 the "Easter Ornaments" line was introduced featuring traditional Easter images like bunnies and colored eggs. However, as the line gained in popularity, new pieces were added with more general springtime themes and as a result, the name of the collection was eventually changed to "Spring Ornaments." The majority of the line was still represented by pastel colors and Easter themes but now other animals and licensed characters, such as BARBIE™ and Peter Rabbit™, have joined the ranks. The Spring Ornament line also contains several series, ranging from *Cottontail Express* to *Vintage Roadsters*.

Merry Miniatures

In 1974, just one year after the first Keepsake Ornaments made their debut, a line of tiny figurines took the collecting world by storm. The first pieces sported simple names such as "Snowman" and "Bunny" but the line quickly became more sophisticated. Soon, more special occasion pieces and familiar characters (like Winnie the Pooh) were added and after that, even backdrops to create scenes were released. Merry Miniatures have often been presented as special pieces for the Hallmark Ornament Premiere and the Gold Crown Open House.

Three new collections have been released for 2001. The "Way To Bees" collection features 12 bees, one for each month of the year, engaging in seasonal pastimes or celebrating holidays. For example, February's "Bee Loving" is a tribute to Valentine's Day while October's "Bee Scary" is a treat for Halloween. The second collection is the Kids! Collection. There are 12 figurines of children in this set, all participating in some of their favorite activities. From "Blade" the hockey player to "Speedy" the soccer player, there's something for everyone in this adorable collection. Finally, there is a whole new "Madame Alexander® Collection" with seven new pieces and a display stand.

Kiddie Car Classics

These highly collectible die-cast metal car models are sure to please any car enthusiast! First introduced in 1992, their popularity has soared and collectors race to the store when the newest pieces are released. With their generous length (approximately 8 inches) the artist has plenty of room to add realistic-looking details like rubber tires, working headlights, movable pedals and a great paint job.

Kiddie Car Classics has several divisions, including the general Kiddie Car Classics, the Mini Kiddie Car Collection, the Sidewalk Cruisers and the Don Palmiter Custom Collection, named after the artist who creates most of the Kiddie Car pieces. The collection also boasts several series including the *Vintage Speedster* series and the *Winner's Circle* collector's series. Adding further collectibility to the line are the many luxury, numbered and limited editions.

The Kiddie Car Classics underwent some major changes in 2001. All cars issued before December 31, 2000 were retired on that date and future releases will be limited to 14,500 pieces. So hurry and get yours today!

Other Hallmark Collections

In the last several years, Hallmark has been creating additional collectible lines. Legends in Flight™ – only available in limited editions of 12,500 since 2001 – celebrates the history of aircraft with scale replicas, while Great American Railways™ takes a similar look at the locomotive. School Days Lunch Boxes™ brings back memories with replicas of tin lunch boxes (each with a matching beverage holder) from the 1950s, '60s, '70s and '80s.

In 2000, three new collections were introduced. To celebrate the U.S. Mint's 50 State Quarters™ program, Hallmark released the American Spirit Collection™ in 2000. The popular double-stamped metal ornaments each comes with an authentic quarter in its center.

Whether you're a beginner to the quarter craze or a die-hard state quarter fanatic who has snapped up every coin so far, Hallmark offered plenty of ways to show off your "American Spirit." The first ten state quarters were released in the inaugural assortment, but look for more to follow.

The Peanuts® Collection was issued to celebrate the 50th anniversary of Peanuts® and to commemorate the ending of the classic comic strip. Many items like framed comic strips, pewter figurines and 6" jointed porcelain figurines were released for this collection in 2000. The 2001 collection additions once again featured everyone's favorite gang – Charlie Brown, Snoopy, Woodstock, Linus and Lucy.

The magical characters of Dr. Seuss left the pages of his books and came to Hallmark where they were turned into products like bookends and coin banks in Hallmark's The Dr. Seuss™ Collection. Everyone's favorites are here like "Hop On Pop™" and "The Cat in the Hat™" with several new releases for 2001.

And There's More!

In addition to their Keepsake Ornaments and collections, Hallmark continues to offer a wide variety of collectibles including stocking hangers, salt and pepper shakers and a collection of figurines designed by Ed Seale known as Tender Touches.

For more information on these other collectibles, see our *Other Hallmark Collectibles* section which begins on page 361.

Spotlight On The Mayor's Ornaments

AP/WWP

Kansas City, Missouri's majestic skyline is a welcome sight to visitors hoping to catch a glimpse of the Mayor's Christmas Tree.

The Kansas City Mayor's Christmas Tree has stood tall in Crown Center Square every holiday season since the 1970s. However, the tradition of putting up and decorating a tree as a symbol of citywide unity has been intact since the first tree was raised in 1908. Sure, lots of cities around the country have Christmas trees, so what makes this one special?

Not only is Kansas City's tree among the largest trees in the nation (it was said to be #1 in height in 1996), but it does big things for the holiday spirit of the town, as well. In conjunction with Hallmark, the tree – and many talented artists – bring much-needed holiday cheer to those less fortunate in the surrounding areas.

Mayor Thomas Crittenton started the tradition of the tree almost a century ago, and was also responsible for the fundraiser that has survived in one form or another into the present day. Hallmark, a company whose name is synonymous with holiday cheer, is the perfect sponsor to help continue the custom.

Every year, a Douglas fir standing 90 to 100 feet is decorated with over 6,000 lights and 1,000 ornaments. The decoration process takes over two weeks and culminates in a tree-lighting and caroling ceremony held close to Thanksgiving.

At The Heart Of It All

Once the season has come to a close and the tree is removed from the plaza, the heart of the trunk is given to the Hallmark Keepsake Studio, where it is then turned into 2,500 laser-cut and dated wooden tree ornaments to commemorate the festive Mayor's Christmas Tree celebration. Usually sold at the Crown Center for between $10 and $15 an ornament, all of the proceeds from the ornament sales go to the Mayor's Christmas Tree Fund which helps nearly 30,000 poor and elderly in Kansas City to have a merry Christmas.

How Many Do You Have?

1981 – Acrylic Star
1982 – Acrylic Tree
1983 – Acrylic Stocking
1984 – Acrylic Bear
1985 – Acrylic Mug
1986 – Wooden Sleigh
1987 – Tree On Oval
1988 – Tree On Triangle
1989 – Shaped Tree
1990 – Tree On Circle
1991 – Pinecone
1992 – Wreath
1993 – Toy Soldier
1994 – Rocking Horse
1995 – Angel
1996 – Locomotive
1997 – Log Cabin
1998 – Teddy Bear
1999 – Snowflake
2000 – Dove

Twenty Years Of Mayor's Ornaments

The first Mayor's Christmas Tree ornament was produced by Hallmark in 1981. These early ornaments were not created using the recycled wood of the Mayor's Christmas Tree. Rather, the ornaments sold from 1981 until 1986 were revised designs of already existing Hallmark ornaments.

The first ornament to be created from wood of the actual Mayor's tree was released in 1987. Since then, a new ornament has been created each year by Hallmark artist Fayrol Unverferth. Wreaths, pine cones, wooden soldiers and angels are just some of the popular designs that have been produced.

Introducing The New Keepsake Series

"Not Quite" Series

In addition to the series which are listed in the "Dream Book" each year, several "unofficial" or "unannounced" series also exist. These phantom series release pieces within a specific theme each year and include the Child's Age Collection, STAR TREK™ and Mickey & Co. among others.

Ever since the *Betsey Clark* series made its debut in 1973, Hallmark has dutifully designed annual additions to many new series. In fact, since the debut of the *Carrousel* and *Thimble* series in 1978, at least one new series has been created every year!

Traditionally, series last for at least three years, but in one case, the first ornament in the series was the last, as well. Do you remember which one? It was the *African-American Holiday BARBIE™*. She made her way onto the scene all dolled up for the holiday season in 1998, but when the 1999 ornaments were released, the follow-up ornament wasn't in the bunch.

However, most series run for more than three years. In fact, one of the most popular Hallmark series is the *Frosty Friends* line. With its grinning Eskimo children bundled up in parkas playing in the winter snow, the line has become one of the most recognizable (and most sought-after) ornament series ever since it was introduced in 1980. The longest-running series to date is *Here Comes Santa*, which, with this year's release, has a total of 23 ornaments. Which ones do you have?

Collectors have found that, over the years, their series ornaments have had the most appreciation in value on the secondary market. Usually the most desirable piece in a series is the initial release.

Although it's hard to tell which series will be big hits for future collectors, it's easy to see that ornaments from the 2001 series will be darlings on every collector's tree!

New Keepsake Series

Kris and the Kringles – For the series' first ornament, Santa and his musically inclined reindeer friends are making plenty of noise to let you know they're on the way! The first ornament in this musical series was sculpted by Keepsake artist Ken Crow. Wonder what antics Santa will be up to next year!

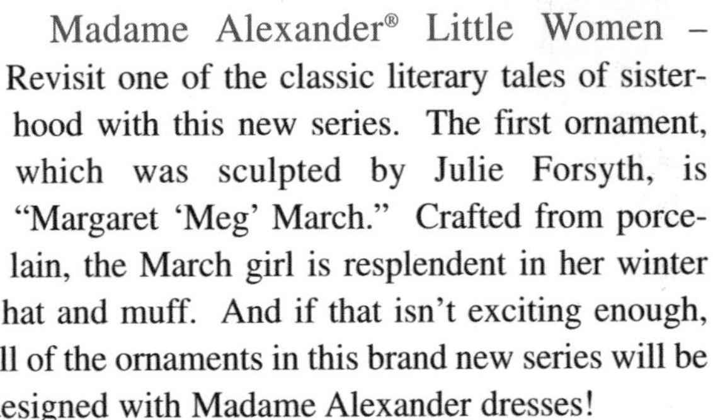

Madame Alexander® Little Women – Revisit one of the classic literary tales of sisterhood with this new series. The first ornament, which was sculpted by Julie Forsyth, is "Margaret 'Meg' March." Crafted from porcelain, the March girl is resplendent in her winter hat and muff. And if that isn't exciting enough, all of the ornaments in this brand new series will be designed with Madame Alexander dresses!

Mistletoe Miss – The first Mistletoe Miss piece, sculpted by Nina Aubé, is wearing a dress of real fabric. And this adorable munchkin doesn't go anywhere without her teddy bear. Future "misses" to be added to this series will also be wearing real fabric dresses and wonderfully painted expressions!

Safe and Snug – This little penguin's guardian made sure that he is warm and cozy and well-prepared for winter in his scarf and earmuffs! The other animals in the forthcoming porcelain series will be sure to warm your heart as well.

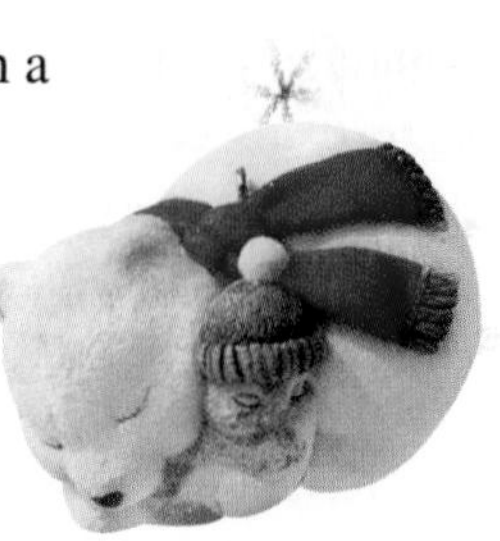

Snowball and Tuxedo – All wrapped up in a warm ball and ready for a nice long nap right through Christmas, Snowball the polar bear and Tuxedo the penguin are cute as can be when they're hanging on your tree. What will these two best friends be up to once the alarm clock goes off? You'll just have to wait until next year to see!

New Miniature Series

Sky's the Limit Miniature Series – Already a Keepsake series, this new miniature series is sure to delight flight enthusiasts young and old! Beginning with "The Flight at Kitty Hawk," the series takes off and promises to deliver ornaments that commemorate all sorts of historical aircraft!

Other Exciting Ornaments For 2001

In addition to these new series, this year's "Dream Book" is full of original designs which are sure to delight Hallmark collectors of all ages. Popular themes of years past, including snowmen, Santas and BARBIE™ have returned for 2001, as well as a few new concepts.

Some of the pieces that are sure be a hit include the huggable "Ready Teddy," the lazy "Snoozing Santa" and "Mickey Mantle," based on the baseball legend. The popular Snowmen of Mitford make their return in "Mitford Snowman Jubilee," a set of 4 adorable snow creatures. "Peggy Fleming" and "Angel of Faith," this year's Cards For The Cure piece, both represent the elements of grace and beauty.

Other Series

In addition to the Keepsake and Miniature series within the line, Hallmark has also released a number of Magic series, which feature pieces with light, sound or motion. One Crown Reflections series has also made its way into the line, featuring decorative blown glass ornaments.

Last Call For Final Editions

Just as 2001 brought some new series to the collection, others will be waving goodbye at the end of the season, so make sure you complete these series while you still can!

Keepsake Series

Favorite Bible Stories – "Daniel in the Lions' Den"

Hockey Greats – "Jaromir Jagr"

Joyful Santa – "Joyful Santa"

Winnie the Pooh and Christopher Robin, Too – "A Story for Pooh"

Miniature Series

Holiday Flurries – "Holiday Flurries"

LIONEL® Norfolk and Western – "Car Carrier and Caboose"

Miniature Harley-Davidson® Motorcycles – "1947 Servi-Car™"

Miniature Kiddie Car Luxury Edition – "1937 Garton® Ford"

The Nativity – "The Nativity"

Seaside Scenes – "Seaside Scenes"

The Wonders of Oz™ – "Toto"

In Their Own Words

Three Hallmark Keepsake Artists recently put down their sculpting tools to talk to CheckerBee Publishing about what goes on behind the scenes at the Keepsake Studio and how their daily lives influence the ornaments we put on our trees! Read on to learn what Joanne Eschrich, Kristina Kline and Dill Rhodus had to say.

Joanne Eschrich

Sculptor Joanne Eschrich is ready to greet collectors at a signing event.

One of Joanne's major contributions to the 2001 ornament line is the brand new Frostlight Faeries Collection. She's also working on more pieces for the line of *Fashion Afoot* shoe ornaments, in addition to the regular line pieces which she creates every year. So how does this artist and mother of two celebrate the holiday season? Well, that's just what we asked her!

CheckerBee Publishing: What was it like to work on this year's Frostlight Faeries Collection? Can we look forward to more of these pieces in the future?

Joanne Eschrich: I loved working on the whole theme and look! It was a true team effort led by Art Director Peggy Sixta. And yes! There are more exciting additions to come!

CP: What was your favorite Frostlight Faeries piece to create?

JE: My favorite Frostlight Faeries piece to create was "The Queen [Aurora] Tree Topper," but also "Floriella," who holds the flower. She's also my daughter's favorite.

CP: Miniature shoes have recently become a hot collectible and your *Fashion Afoot* series is no exception. We've noticed that you have created another shoe this year, "Holiday Shoe." Do you collect shoes (either real or miniature)? And with such a wide variety of designs to choose from, how do you choose which to do?

JE: I love real shoes, hence, I couldn't help but have a fascination for the miniature ones. With the *Fashion Afoot* series, I knew it'd have to be a boot in order to be big enough as a container [for the mouse]. I wanted the first one to be from the same era as [the shoes that] my grandmother had and work up through the decades.

CP: When you originally moved to Kansas City from Massachusetts, did you experience any "culture shock?" How is Kansas City different from the Northeast? Also, what, if anything, do you miss about home and what do you like better about the Midwest?

JE: I come from a large, close family who has always lived on a farm 15 minutes from the ocean – so not only did I miss them tremendously, but I also missed the smell of salt water and the sounds of sea gulls. "Culture shock?" Yes! [When I got to Kansas City,] they couldn't understand my heavy Boston accent! I do like the slower pace and friendly people out here.

> My favorite Frostlight Faerie piece to create was "The Queen [Aurora] Tree Topper," but also "Floriella" who holds the flower. She's also my daughter's favorite.
>
> ***– Joanne on her latest collection, Frostlight Faeries***

CP: What do your daughters think about your job? Are they impressed that their mom creates the holiday decorations that adorn their tree each year?

JE: Jamie, age 8, and Anna, age 4, are thrilled with what I do – especially when I bring my sculpts home sometimes to work on. I love getting their input! On a few occasions, they've brought my original sculpts along with the finished product to "Show and Tell" at school. The kids love it! They also love seeing "Mom" on the box in the stores.

Jaime, age 8, and Anna, age 4, are thrilled with what I do – especially when I bring my sculpts home sometimes to work on. I love getting their input!

– Joanne on her daughters' reaction to Mom's line of work

CP: Who would you say has been the most influential person in your career so far?

JE: This is a tough question, since I can't narrow my list down enough for this interview. But a few on the top of my list are: my sister Laurie, who was always was on top of everything I did; the old masters like Michelangelo, Leonardo and Rodin; and the new masters (my peers) whom I've learned so many different skills from.

CP: This year, you created "Creative Cutter – Cooking for Christmas." Cooking and baking cookies are a holiday tradition in many households. Do you have any holiday traditions to help you celebrate Christmas each year?

JE: I do like decorating sugar cookies with my girls. My Portuguese family tradition was to make Portuguese Sweet Bread called *masa*. Also, my mother is always sure to add the Portuguese sausage *chourico*, which is similar to *chorizo*, to any holiday meal.

CP: Is there any piece that you have not gotten a chance to sculpt that you hope to create in the future?

JE: I have always wanted the chance to create a whole line of faeries, and fortunately, my wish came true. I guess the only other piece I've always wanted to do was a male angel – like Gabriel or St. Michael.

CP: How does it feel to know that your work affects so many Hallmark collectors around the country?

JE: Does it? I certainly hope so! Especially since what I do is for them, the collectors.

CP: How would your fellow Keepsake Artists describe you?

JE: I'm afraid to ask!

Kristina Kline

Kristina Kline greets a collector as she prepares to sign an ornament.

Kristina Kline, the artist behind many of the popular animal and animated character sculptures since 1995, discusses the cartoon characters she loved as a child, the pets that keep her on her toes and what it's like to work as an artist in the Keepsake Studio.

CheckerBee Publishing: At the 25th Anniversary celebration, you and Nello Williams sang a duet about collecting at the Winter Wonderland dinner. Have you always been interested in music? Will we hear your voice again soon?

Kristina Kline: Singing is a fun stress reliever for me, but unfortunately, there are not many opportunities as wonderful as that song was. I usually sing in the car or at home. Sometimes I sing for church, but mostly it's just for my own amusement. I'm grateful to Nello for the opportunity he gave me.

CP: You've sculpted a lot of ornaments featuring children's characters this year – "Pat the Bunny," "Blue and Periwinkle Blue's Clues™" and a piece based on the VeggieTales® characters. Did you have a favorite literary or television character growing up? Who was it and do you plan to (or have you already) sculpted an ornament of this character?

KK: I was a huge Smurfs® fan and I still have some of the little figurines of them. I don't see any future ornament plans for them, but I have noticed they have come full circle and there are Smurfs toys in the stores again.

CP: How did you feel when, as a student at the Kansas City Art Institute, you found out that you had won an internship at the Keepsake Studio?

KK: I was just ecstatic! It was such as thrill and everyone was excited for me.

CP: Several of your pieces, such as this year's "Our First Christmas Together" and "Graceful Reindeer" incorporate an animal theme. Do you have any pets?

KK: I have a great fondness for *all* animals, but cats are my favorite. I have one calico female named Kaylie who is always an endless source of entertainment. She plays a mean game of "hide and seek" and "tag."

CP: When you were growing up, did you dream of becoming an artist? Did you ever imagine that one day you would be sculpting the ornaments that you had on your Christmas tree every year? And how does it feel to accomplish that goal?

KK: I have always wanted to be an artist, but growing up we didn't have Keepsake ornaments, so I never saw sculpting as a possibility. To accomplish my goals as an artist is rewarding and now my tree is full of Keepsake Ornaments.

CP: What types of activities or projects do you like to do in your spare time?

KK: I like to sew various things and I'm always looking for new projects to start. Unfortunately, I have a hard time finishing that projects that I have started before I move on to a new one.

CP: You are the artist behind this year's "A Perfect Christmas!" ornament featuring Arthur™. What would be your idea of a perfect Christmas?

KK: To have my family together for Christmas. My brother and his wife live in Portland so it's been almost 8 years since [the whole family has] been together for Christmas.

CP: How would your fellow Keepsake Artists describe you?

KK: It depends on who you ask.

> I have a great fondness for all animals, but cats are my favorite. I have one calico female named Kaylie who is always an endless source of entertainment.
>
> *– Kristina speaks about her animal inspiration*

CP: What is your favorite part of your job as a Keepsake Studio Artist?

KK: The environment and the comraderie in the studio. A day hasn't gone by that I haven't laughed at some antic or another. You have to keep on your toes. It's fun.

CP: What are your goals for the future?

KK: I just want to be happy, to live each day to the fullest and to learn from my past mistakes so I don't repeat them.

Dill Rhodus at work in the Keepsake Studio.

Dill Rhodus

An avid sports fan, Dill is the innovator behind many of the sports-themed ornaments in the collection. See what he says about working with other sports nuts in the studio and what he does on the weekends to relax after a week of sculpting and designing Keepsake Ornaments.

CheckerBee Publishing: What's it like to work with your wife, fellow sculptor Patricia Andrews, in the Keepsake Studio every day?

Dill Rhodus: We both have been asked that question many times. Trish and I have a wonderful relationship and marriage. We fully support each other on the job and at home with our family. She is a fabulous artist and sculptor. She has helped me greatly to develop my skills as an artist. Plus, we love to be around each other – we are the best of friends. That makes working with each other every day a delight.

CP: In an interview with us two years ago, your wife mentioned that she takes a week off from work to fully decorate for the holidays. What do you do to get into the spirit?

DR: I watch her decorate.

CP: As the sculptor of this year's "All-Sport Santa" and a few baseball and football series, you have admitted that you are the studio's "resident sports nut." Duane Unruh has also sculpted several sports-themed pieces. How do you decide who sculpts what?

I took a poll in the studio once. They mostly said, "short, bald and cute." Although, Duane Unruh said I was a nice guy.

– Dill on what his fellow Keepsake Artists think of him

Is there any office rivalry between sports fans?

DR: No, there isn't any rivalry. The *Football Legends* and *At The Ballpark* series are mine to do. I know very little about hockey, and I'm too short to know much about basketball. Duane and Collin fight over those two series.

CP: Your father was a minor league baseball player. Did you ever have athletic aspirations?

DR: Yes, but unfortunately, I can't hit a curve ball.

CP: You and your wife have a four-acre garden. Do you grow anything special? How do you find the time to work on it between your job and caring for your children?

DR: We really have a four-acre yard with a lot of gardens. [Patricia] Trish is the planner and gardener. I'm just the laborer. She tells me to dig a hole and I do it. On a normal Saturday in the summer, Trish works on the gardens, our two girls swim and I play golf. That's how we juggle our time. It works for me.

CP: We've noticed that you've sculpted many Star Wars pieces over the years. How do you go about sculpting detailed characters such as "Jar Jar Binks™?"

DR: Most of the credit goes to Lucas Films. They give us some really great research for the characters and the ships that we sculpt.

CP: Having worked in the Studio for 15 years, how do you keep coming up with ideas for new pieces?

DR: Everyday life gives us endless ideas. We just have to be aware enough to recognize and remember things we see that tell a story and that will work as an ornament.

CP: Do you have a favorite ornament that you, or maybe another artist, has created? What is it and why is it your favorite?

DR: The way we enjoy ornaments is very subjective. How one person feels about an ornament will probably differ from how I feel about it. It might strike a very nostalgic or warm memory for you but not for me. On just sheer beauty and form, I think this year's "Peggy Fleming" is fabulous. This group of sculptors does so many great ornaments, it's impossible to choose just one alone.

CP: How would your fellow Keepsake Artists describe you?

DR: I took a poll in the studio once. They mostly said, "short, bald and cute." Although, Duane Unruh said I was a nice guy.

CP: Is there any piece that you have not gotten a chance to sculpt yet that you hope to do in the future?

DR: Yes, but I can't say it. I'll give you a hint, though – he's my all-time favorite baseball player.

Everyday life gives us endless ideas. We just have to be aware enough to recognize and remember things we see that tell a story and that will work well as an ornament.

– Dill comments on his daily inspiration

Meet The Hallmark Artists

Now that you've pored over every page of the "Dream Book," and you know exactly which pieces you want to buy (all of them!), meet the artists who created these delights!

Patricia Andrews

Known for her nostalgic sculptures, Patricia lived up to her reputation as the "Barbie Lady," this year with her sculpture of "1950s BARBIE™ Ornament." She is married to fellow Keepsake artist Dill Rhodus.

Nina Aubé

An avid collector of everything from dolls to Hallmark ornaments, Nina has sculpted Keepsakes since 1994. Often inspired by animals, her 2001 creations include "Beginning Ballet" and "Sharing Santa's Snacks."

Katrina Bricker

"This is my dream job!" says Katrina, a sixth-year ornament artist. She enjoys working with licensed properties, such as this year's *Harry Potter*-themed pieces, "Ron Weasley™ and Scabbers™" and "Fluffy™ on Guard."

Robert Chad

Robert especially enjoys sculpting cartoon characters ("Holiday Spa Tweety" and "SCOOBY-DOO™" are new this year). He hopes his pieces will be "passed down through families for generations."

Ken Crow

Originally from California, Ken enjoys puppetry and even has a ventriloquist dummy named Jerry Mahoney. This year, Crow's creations include the club exclusive "Santa Marionette" (a miniature of one of Ken's own, perhaps?), and "Up on the Housetop."

Joanne Eschrich

Joanne, a native of Massachusetts who has been with the Studio since 1996, is the creator of this year's *Frostlight Faeries Collection*. Part of the joy of sculpting for Joanne is imagining that "after I've completed an ornament, it might somehow come to life!"

Julie Forsyth

Julie came to Hallmark in 1978 to sculpt for the Little Gallery line. She re-entered the Keepsake Studio three years ago and has since been creating designs such as this year's "Hagrid™ and Norbert the Dragon™" and the new series piece "Safe and Snug."

John "Collin" Francis

While hard at work at Hallmark (he's one of the first Keepsake sculptors and the first for Merry Miniatures®), John keeps busy creating such ornaments as 2001's "Lazy Afternoon" and "Jaromir Jagr." In his spare time, John prefers to watch the wildlife in his backyard!

Tammy Haddix

When Tammy was five, she knew she wanted to work at Hallmark and she practiced by drawing on her closet walls! She moved on to the Keepsake Studio right out of college in 1996. "Springing Santa" and "Cool Decade" are two of her newest designs.

Kristina Kline

"Gouda Reading" and "Pat the Bunny" are two of Kristina's new ornaments. She's been with the Studio since 1995, when a piece she sculpted for a class won her an internship. Kristina says that her favorite part of sculpting is creating fantasy characters!

Rich LaPierre

Best known as the artist behind the School Days Lunch Boxes, Rich came to Hallmark 16 years ago soon after graduating from college with a degree in cartooning. He has since been designing (and sometimes sculpting) many new ornaments for the Studio.

Tracy Larsen

Tracy started at Hallmark as a greeting card artist in 1987 and made his way to the Keepsake Studio in 1995, where he has been delighting collectors with his ornaments ever since. 2001's "Moose's Merry Christmas" and "Jolly Visitor" are Tracy's!

Joyce Lyle

When Joyce isn't sculpting, she's directing a children's choir and spending time with her family – her husband, daughter and four sons. She is the artist behind the *Wonders of Oz*™ miniature series where this year's piece, "Toto," is a welcome addition!

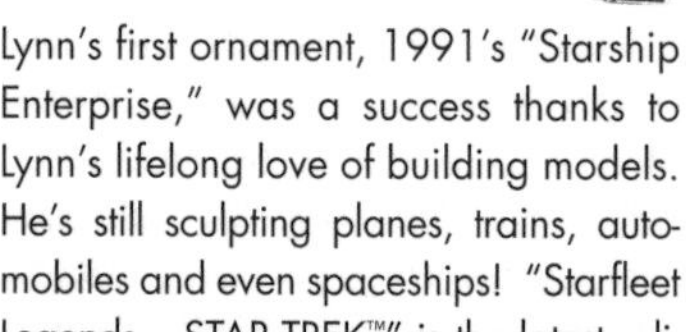

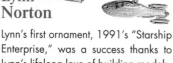

Lynn Norton

Lynn's first ornament, 1991's "Starship Enterprise," was a success thanks to Lynn's lifelong love of building models. He's still sculpting planes, trains, automobiles and even spaceships! "Starfleet Legends – STAR TREK™" is the latest edition to the out-of-this-world collection!

Don Palmiter

If it has wheels, Don will sculpt it! Part of the Hallmark family since he began as an engraver right out of high school, Don is the creator of the Kiddie Car Classics Collection as well as this year's "1947 Servi-Car™" and "1957 XL Sportster®" ornaments.

Sharon Pike

"I'm so glad to be back!" said Sharon after her 4-year absence from the studio due to a broken arm. She designs her own jewelry in her spare time, but while she's in the Studio, she's creating ornaments such as 2001's "Santa's Workshop" and "Grandmother."

Dill Rhodus

Best known for sculpting athletes, Dill's been part of the Keepsake family since 1986. One of his favorite things about ornament sculpting is "the wide range of subjects that I get to work on." This year, Dill sculpted "All-Sport Santa" and the *Collegiate Collection.*

Anita Marra Rogers

While her affection for sculpting animals can be seen in the beloved *Puppy Love* series, Anita is also skilled at creating likenesses of people. She's been with the studio for 14 years and sculpted "Santa's Day Off" and "Raggedy Ann" for the 2001 collection.

Ed Seale

"When someone tells you that . . . a particular ornament has a special personal meaning to them – it leaves you with a wonderful feeling," says Ed, who is now semi-retired from the Keepsake Studio. He is the artist behind the popular *Frosty Friends* series.

Linda Sickman

"The Christmas Cone," "Noche de Paz" and "Old-World Santa" are just three of Linda's newest pieces that bring back memories of Christmases past. Linda has been winning praise from collectors for her pressed tin designs since 1976.

Bob Siedler

Bob entered the Keepsake Studio after showing off the sculptures he had created on his lunch breaks while working in Hallmark's sales department. He gets his inspiration watching people, and his latest ornaments include, "Kiss the Cook" and "Beaglescout."

Sue Tague

"Sculpting really is my favorite form of artistic expression," says Sue, who started as a greeting card artist for Hallmark thirty-five years ago. She's been sculpting for the Studio since 1994 and this year created "Mitford Snowmen Jubilee" and "Godchild."

Duane Unruh

High school athletic coach-turned-ornament designer Duane Unruh has successfully integrated his love of sports and his design talent through his work in the Keepsake Studio. His contributions to this year's line include "Tim Duncan" and "It Had To Be You."

Sharon Visker

For 17 years, Sharon has been designing for Hallmark and she eventually made her way into the field of three-dimensional sculpting. This Colorado native's 2001 pieces include the nostalgic wood toy replicas, "Waggles," "Wiggles" and "Waddles."

LaDene Votruba

LaDene, a Kansas native, has been sculpting for the Keepsake Studio since 1983. This year, she relied on a few of her many interests – reading and antique teapots – to help her create the 2001 designs "Tootle the Train" and "Cozy Home."

Chris Webb

Chris is a classic car enthusiast. He restores and builds automobiles in his spare time and then he sculpts them as ornaments when he's in the studio! For 2001, Chris has crafted the "2001 Jeep™ Sport Wrangler" and "LIONEL® I-400E Blue Comet Locomotive."

Nello Williams

Nello always dreamed of being a Disney animator and now he lives out his dream by sculpting these characters into three-dimensional form for Hallmark. Nello also enjoys composing his own music and created "What a Grinchy Trick!" for 2001.

Hallmark Top Ten

Hallmark ornaments are very popular on the secondary market and many of the classic pieces (and some newer ones, too!) have increased significantly in value. Here are the top ten most valuable ornaments on the secondary market today!

1

Kansas City Santa (1991)
Convention Ornament
No stock number
Original Price: N/C
Market Value: $1,000

2

Santa's Motorcar (1979)
1st in the *Here Comes Santa* series
#900QX1559
Original Price: $9
Market Value: $685

3

Tin Locomotive (1982)
1st in the *Tin Locomotive* series
#1300QX4603
Original Price: $13
Market Value: $660

4

A Cool Yule (1980)
1st in the *Frosty Friends* series
#650QX1374
Original Price: $6.50
Market Value: $645

5

Rocking Horse (1981)
1st in the *Rocking Horse* series
#900QX4222
Original Price: $9
Market Value: $640

6

K.C. Angel (1993)
Convention Ornament
No Stock Number
Original Price: N/C
Market Value: $575

7

Frosty Friends (1981)
2nd in the *Frosty Friends* series
#800QX4335
Original Price: $8
Market Value: $495

8

Truest Joys Of Christmas (1977)
5th in the *Betsey Clark* series
#350QX2642
Original Price: $3.50
Market Value: $450

9

Rocking Horse (1982)
2nd in the *Rocking Horse* series
#1000QX5023
Original Price: $10
Market Value: $440

10

The Bellswinger (1979)
1st in *The Bellringers* series
#1000QX1479
Original Price: $10
Market Value: $415

How To Use Your Collector's Value Guide™

1. **Locate** your piece in the Value Guide. Keepsake Ornaments are listed first in two sections: series (listed in alphabetical order by series name) and general ornaments (listed in reverse chronological order). The general ornaments are grouped in each year as follows (if applicable): Keepsake, Magic, Special Collections, Miniature and miscellaneous. Spring Ornaments, Merry Miniatures and Kiddie Car Classics follow in their own sections.

Hallmark Artist Key

ANDR	Patricia Andrews
AUBE	Nina Aubé
BAUR	Tim Bauer
BISH	Ron Bishop
BLAC	Thomas Blackshear
BRIC	Katrina Bricker
BRWN	Andrew Brownsword
CHAD	Robert Chad
CROW	Ken Crow
DLEE	Donna Lee
DUTK	Peter Dutkin
ESCH	Joanne Eschrich
FORS	Julie Forsyth
FRAL	Tobin Fraley
FRAN	John "Collin" Francis
GOSL	Steve Goslin
HADD	Tammy Haddix
HAMI	Mary Hamilton
JLEE	Julia Lee
JOHN	Cathy Johnson
KLIN	Kristina Kline
LAPR	Rich LaPierre
LARS	Tracy Larsen
LYLE	Joyce Lyle
MAHO	Jim Mahon
MCGE	Diana McGehee
N/A	not available
NORT	Lynn Norton
PALM	Don Palmiter
PATT	Joyce Pattee
PIKE	Sharon Pike
PYDA	Michele Pyda-Sevcik
RGRS	Anita Marra Rogers
RHOD	Dill Rhodus
SCHU	Lee Schuler
SEAL	Ed Seale
SICK	Linda Sickman
SIED	Bob Siedler
TAGU	Sue Tague
UNRU	Duane Unruh
VARI	various artists
VISK	Sharon Visker
VOTR	LaDene Votruba
WEBB	Chris Webb
WILL	Nello Williams

1978 Dodge® L'il Red Express Truck (6th, 2000)
Handcrafted • PALM
1395QX6581 • **Value $22**

2. **Fill** in the price you paid for the piece in the "Price Paid" column. The original retail price is the first 3 or 4 digits of the Hallmark stock number. For example, a piece with stock number 795QX6679 would have a retail price of $7.95. A N/A means that the information is not available.

3. **Record** the current market value of your piece in the "Value" column. "N/E" means the market value is not yet established for that piece.

4. **Add** the values together and transfer the totals from each page to the "Total Value Of My Collection" worksheets, found on pages 348-352. Finally, add these together to find the total value of your collection.

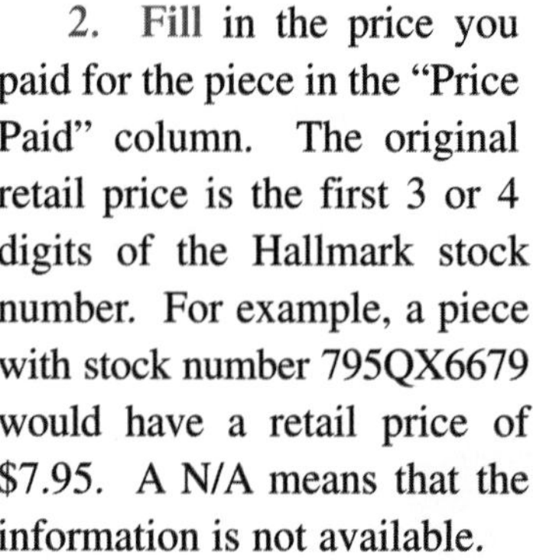
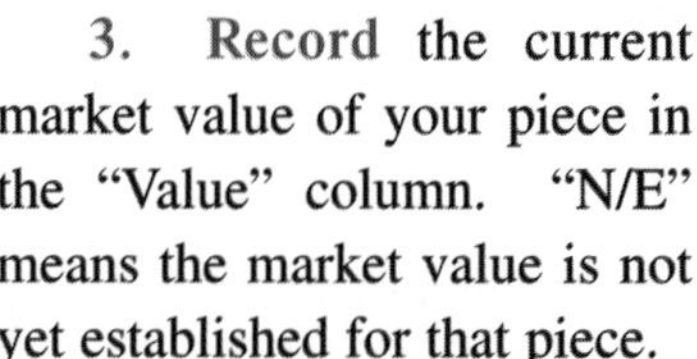

	Price Paid	Value
African-American Holiday BARBIE™		
1.		
All-American Truck		
2.		
3.		
4.		
5.		
6.		
7.	$13.95	$22.00
8.		
All God's Children®		
9.		
10.		
11.		
Art Masterpiece		
12.		
13.		
14.		
At the Ballpark		
15.		
16.		
17.		
Totals	$13.95	$22.00

43

Keepsake Series

There was something for everyone in the 2001 line of Keepsake Series as five new series were introduced featuring everything from the "Little Women" of literary fame to an adorable penguin and polar bear known as "Snowball and Tuxedo." 2001 also bids farewell to 3 retiring series which celebrate their final editions.

1

African-American Holiday BARBIE™ (1st & final, 1998)
Handcrafted • ANDR
1595QX6936 • **Value $28**

2

1956 Ford Truck (1st, 1995)
Handcrafted • PALM
1395QX5527 • **Value $38**

3

1955 Chevrolet Cameo (2nd, 1996)
Handcrafted • PALM
1395QX5241 • **Value $31**

4

1953 GMC (3rd, 1997)
Handcrafted • PALM
1395QX6105 • **Value $27**

5

1937 Ford V-8 (4th, 1998)
Handcrafted • PALM
1395QX6263 • **Value $26**

6

1957 Dodge® Sweptside D100 (5th, 1999)
Handcrafted • PALM
1395QX6269 • **Value $25**

7

1978 Dodge® L'il Red Express Truck (6th, 2000)
Handcrafted • PALM
1395QX6581 • **Value $22**

8

1959 Chevrolet® El Camino™ (7th, 2001)
Handcrafted • PALM
1395QX6072 • **Value $13.95**

9

Christy (1st, 1996)
Handcrafted • N/A
1295QX5564 • **Value $27**

10

Nikki (2nd, 1997, set/2)
Handcrafted • N/A
1295QX6142 • **Value $24**

11

Ricky (3rd & final, 1998)
Handcrafted • N/A
1295QX6363 • **Value $23**

12

Madonna and Child and St. John (1st, 1984)
Bezeled Satin • MCGE
650QX3494 • **Value $20**

13

Madonna of the Pomegranate (2nd, 1985)
Bezeled Satin • MCGE
675QX3772 • **Value $17**

14
Madonna and Child with the Infant St. John (3rd & final, 1986)
Bezeled Satin • MCGE
675QX3506 • **Value $32**

15

Nolan Ryan (1st, 1996)
Handcrafted • RHOD
1495QXI5711 • **Value $40**

16

Hank Aaron (2nd, 1997)
Handcrafted • RHOD
1495QX6152 • **Value $30**

17

Cal Ripken Jr. (3rd, 1998)
Handcrafted • RHOD
1495QXI4033 • **Value $28**

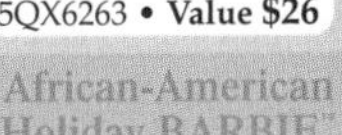

African-American Holiday BARBIE™

	Price Paid	Value
1.		

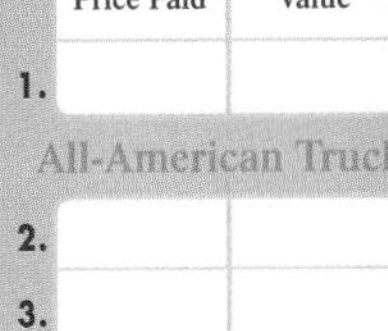

All-American Truck

	Price Paid	Value
2.		
3.		
4.		
5.		
6.		
7.		
8.		

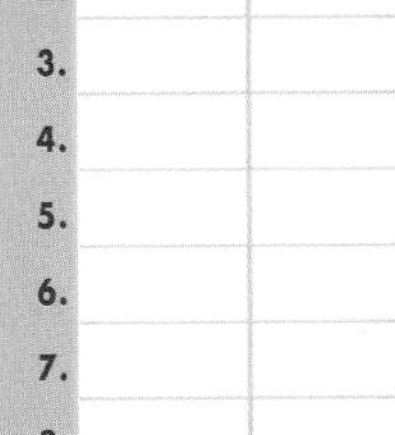

All God's Children®

	Price Paid	Value
9.		
10.		
11.		

Art Masterpiece

	Price Paid	Value
12.		
13.		
14.		

At the Ballpark

	Price Paid	Value
15.		
16.		
17.		

Totals		

Keepsake Series

1

Ken Griffey Jr.
(4th, 1999)
Handcrafted • RHOD
1495QXI4037 • **Value $23**

2

Mark McGwire
(5th, 2000)
Handcrafted • RHOD
1495QXI5361 • **Value $20**

3

Ken Griffey Jr.
(Cincinnati, 2000)
Handcrafted • N/A
1495QX15251 • **Value $23**

4

Sammy Sosa
(6th, 2001)
Handcrafted • RHOD
1495QXI6375 • **Value $14.95**

5
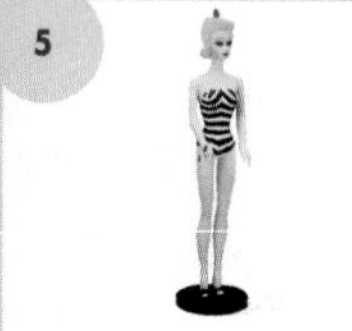
BARBIE™ (1st, 1994)
Handcrafted • ANDR
1495QX5006 • **Value $46**

6

Solo in the Spotlight
(2nd, 1995)
Handcrafted • ANDR
1495QXI5049 • **Value $28**

7

Brunette Debut – 1959
(club edition, 1995)
Handcrafted • ANDR
1495QXC5397 • **Value $65**

8

Featuring the
Enchanted Evening
BARBIE® Doll (3rd, 1996)
Handcrafted • ANDR
1495QXI6541 • **Value $30**

9

Wedding Day 1959-1962
(4th, 1997)
Handcrafted • ANDR
1595QXI6812 • **Value $32**

10

BARBIE™ and KEN™
Wedding Day (complements the series, 1997, set/2)
Handcrafted • ANDR/PALM
3500QXI6815 • **Value $53**

11

Silken Flame™ (5th, 1998)
Handcrafted • ANDR
1595QXI4043 • **Value $29**

12

Gay Parisienne™
BARBIE™ Ornament
(6th, 1999)
Handcrafted • ANDR
1595QXI5301 • **Value $27**

13

Commuter Set™
(7th, 2000, set/2)
Handcrafted • ANDR
1595QX6814 • **Value $25**

14

BARBIE™ in Busy Gal™
Fashion (8th, 2001, set/2)
Handcrafted • RGRS
1595QX6965 • **Value $15.95**

15

Babe Ruth (1st, 1994)
Handcrafted • RHOD
1295QX5323 • **Value $58**

16

Lou Gehrig (2nd, 1995)
Handcrafted • RHOD
1295QX5029 • **Value $23**

17

Satchel Paige (3rd, 1996)
Handcrafted • RHOD
1295QX5304 • **Value $22**

18
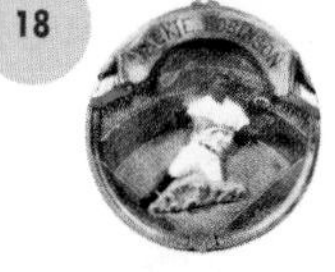
Jackie Robinson
(4th & final, 1997)
Handcrafted • RHOD
1295QX6202 • **Value $25**

	Price Paid	Value
At the Ballpark		
1.		
2.		
3.		
4.		
BARBIE™		
5.		
6.		
7.		
8.		
9.		
10.		
11.		
12.		
13.		
14.		
Baseball Heroes		
15.		
16.		
17.		
18.		
Totals		

1

The Bellswinger
(1st, 1979)
Handcrafted/Porcelain • N/A
1000QX1479 • **Value $415**

2
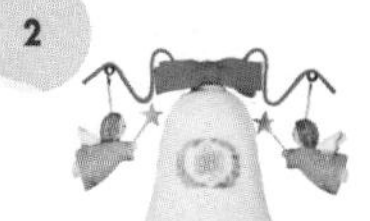
The Bellringers
(2nd, 1980)
Handcrafted/Porcelain • N/A
1500QX1574 • **Value $84**

3

Swingin' Bellringer
(3rd, 1981)
Handcrafted/Ceramic • N/A
1500QX4415 • **Value $98**

4

Angel Bellringer
(4th, 1982)
Handcrafted/Ceramic • DLEE
1500QX4556 • **Value $98**

5

Teddy Bellringer
(5th, 1983)
Handcrafted/Porcelain • N/A
1500QX4039 • **Value $135**

6

Elfin Artist
(6th & final, 1984)
Porcelain • N/A
1500QX4384 • **Value $52**

7

Christmas 1973
(1st, 1973)
Glass • N/A
250XHD1102 • **Value $130**

8

Musicians (2nd, 1974)
Glass • N/A
250QX1081 • **Value $83**

9

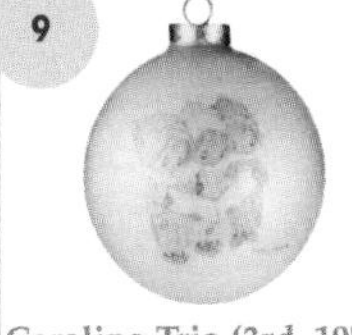
Caroling Trio (3rd, 1975)
Glass • N/A
300QX1331 • **Value $73**

10

Christmas 1976
(4th, 1976)
Glass • N/A
300QX1951 • **Value $112**

11

Truest Joys of
Christmas (5th, 1977)
Glass • N/A
350QX2642 • **Value $450**

12
Christmas Spirit
(6th, 1978)
Satin • N/A
350QX2016 • **Value $62**

13

Holiday Fun (7th, 1979)
Satin • N/A
350QX2019 • **Value $42**

14

Joy-in-the-Air
(8th, 1980)
Glass • N/A
400QX2154 • **Value $32**

15
Christmas 1981
(9th, 1981)
Glass • N/A
450QX8022 • **Value $32**

16

Joys of Christmas
(10th, 1982)
Satin • N/A
450QX2156 • **Value $34**

17

Christmas Happiness
(11th, 1983)
Glass • N/A
450QX2119 • **Value $34**

18

Days are Merry
(12th, 1984)
Glass • N/A
500QX2494 • **Value $34**

19

Special Kind of Feeling
(13th & final, 1985)
Glass • PIKE
500QX2632 • **Value $38**

	Price Paid	Value
The Bellringers		
1.		
2.		
3.		
4.		
5.		
6.		
Betsey Clark		
7.		
8.		
9.		
10.		
11.		
12.		
13.		
14.		
15.		
16.		
17.		
18.		
19.		
Totals		

1

Betsey Clark: Home For Christmas (1st, 1986)
Glass • PIKE
500QX2776 • **Value $35**

2

Betsey Clark: Home For Christmas (2nd, 1987)
Glass • PIKE
500QX2727 • **Value $24**

3

Betsey Clark: Home For Christmas (3rd, 1988)
Glass • PIKE
500QX2714 • **Value $24**

4

Betsey Clark: Home For Christmas (4th, 1989)
Glass • N/A
500QX2302 • **Value $35**

5

Betsey Clark: Home For Christmas (5th, 1990)
Glass • N/A
500QX2033 • **Value $24**

6

Betsey Clark: Home For Christmas (6th & final, 1991)
Glass • N/A
500QX2109 • **Value $28**

7

Betsey's Country Christmas (1st, 1992)
Glass • N/A
500QX2104 • **Value $27**

8

Betsey's Country Christmas (2nd, 1993)
Glass • N/A
500QX2062 • **Value $19**

9
Betsey's Country Christmas (3rd & final, 1994)
Glass • N/A
500QX2403 • **Value $16**

10

Antique Toys (1st, 1978)
Handcrafted • N/A
600QX1463 • **Value $400**

11

Christmas Carrousel (2nd, 1979)
Handcrafted • N/A
650QX1467 • **Value $190**

12

Merry Carrousel (3rd, 1980)
Handcrafted • N/A
750QX1414 • **Value $175**

13

Skaters' Carrousel (4th, 1981)
Handcrafted • N/A
900QX4275 • **Value $92**

14

Snowman Carrousel (5th, 1982)
Handcrafted • SEAL
1000QX4783 • **Value $102**

15
Santa and Friends (6th & final, 1983)
Handcrafted • SICK
1100QX4019 • **Value $52**

16

Cat Naps (1st, 1994)
Handcrafted • RHOD
795QX5313 • **Value $42**

17

Cat Naps (2nd, 1995)
Handcrafted • RHOD
795QX5097 • **Value $26**

18
Cat Naps (3rd, 1996)
Handcrafted • RHOD
795QX5641 • **Value $21**

19

Cat Naps (4th, 1997)
Handcrafted • BRIC
895QX6205 • **Value $19**

20

Cat Naps (5th & final, 1998)
Handcrafted • BRIC
895QX6383 • **Value $20**

Betsey Clark: Home For Christmas

	Price Paid	Value
1.		
2.		
3.		
4.		
5.		
6.		

Betsey's Country Christmas

	Price Paid	Value
7.		
8.		
9.		

Carrousel Series

	Price Paid	Value
10.		
11.		
12.		
13.		
14.		
15.		

Cat Naps

	Price Paid	Value
16.		
17.		
18.		
19.		
20.		

	Price Paid	Value

Totals

1

A Celebration of Angels (1st, 1995)
Handcrafted • ANDR
1295QX5077 • **Value $26**

2

A Celebration of Angels (2nd, 1996)
Handcrafted • ANDR
1295QX5634 • **Value $26**

3

A Celebration of Angels (3rd, 1997)
Handcrafted • ANDR
1395QX6175 • **Value $23**

4

A Celebration of Angels (4th & final, 1998)
Handcrafted • ANDR
1395QX6366 • **Value $24**

5

Christmas Kitty (1st, 1989)
Porcelain • RGRS
1475QX5445 • **Value $31**

6

Christmas Kitty (2nd, 1990)
Porcelain • RGRS
1475QX4506 • **Value $33**

7

Christmas Kitty (3rd & final, 1991)
Porcelain • RGRS
1475QX4377 • **Value $28**

8

St. Nicholas (1st, 1995)
Handcrafted • RGRS
1495QX5087 • **Value $30**

9

Christkindl (2nd, 1996)
Handcrafted • VOTR
1495QX5631 • **Value $28**

10

Kolyada (3rd & final, 1997)
Handcrafted • VOTR
1495QX6172 • **Value $26**

11

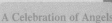

1957 Corvette (1st, 1991)
Handcrafted • PALM
1275QX4319 • **Value $215**

12

1966 Mustang (2nd, 1992)
Handcrafted • PALM
1275QX4284 • **Value $54**

13

1956 Ford Thunderbird (3rd, 1993)
Handcrafted • PALM
1275QX5275 • **Value $39**

14

1957 Chevrolet Bel Air (4th, 1994)
Handcrafted • PALM
1295QX5422 • **Value $33**

15

1969 Chevrolet Camaro (5th, 1995)
Handcrafted • PALM
1295QX5239 • **Value $25**

16

1958 Ford Edsel Citation Convertible (club edition, 1995)
Handcrafted • PALM
1295QXC4167 • **Value $77**

17

1959 Cadillac De Ville (6th, 1996)
Handcrafted • PALM
1295QX5384 • **Value $29**

18

1969 Hurst Oldsmobile 442 (7th, 1997)
Handcrafted • PALM
1395QX6102 • **Value $28**

19

1970 Plymouth® Hemi 'Cuda (8th, 1998)
Handcrafted • PALM
1395QX6256 • **Value $27**

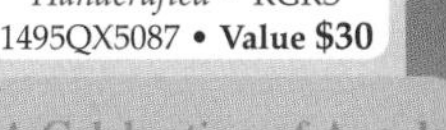

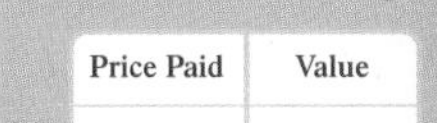

A Celebration of Angels

	Price Paid	Value
1.		
2.		
3.		
4.		

Christmas Kitty

	Price Paid	Value
5.		
6.		
7.		

Christmas Visitors

	Price Paid	Value
8.		
9.		
10.		

Classic American Cars

	Price Paid	Value
11.		
12.		
13.		
14.		
15.		
16.		
17.		
18.		
19.		

	Price Paid	Value
Totals		

1

1955 Chevrolet® Nomad® Wagon (9th, 1999)
Handcrafted • PALM
1395QX6367 • **Value $25**

2

1969 Pontiac® GTO™ – The Judge™ (10th, 2000)
Handcrafted • PALM
1395QX6584 • **Value $22**

3

New!
1953 Buick® Roadmaster™ Skylark™ (11th, 2001)
Handcrafted • PALM
1395QX6872 • **Value $13.95**

4

The Clauses on Vacation (1st, 1997)
Handcrafted • SIED
1495QX6112 • **Value $30**

5

The Clauses on Vacation (2nd, 1998)
Handcrafted • SIED
1495QX6276 • **Value $23**

6

The Clauses on Vacation (3rd & final, 1999)
Handcrafted • SIED
1495QX6399 • **Value $21**

7

British (1st, 1982)
Handcrafted • SICK
500QX4583 • **Value $135**

8

Early American (2nd, 1983)
Handcrafted • SICK
500QX4029 • **Value $51**

9

Canadian Mountie (3rd, 1984)
Handcrafted • SICK
500QX4471 • **Value $32**

10

Scottish Highlander (4th, 1985)
Handcrafted • SICK
550QX4715 • **Value $30**

11

French Officer (5th, 1986)
Handcrafted • SICK
550QX4063 • **Value $30**

12

Sailor (6th & final, 1987)
Handcrafted • SICK
550QX4807 • **Value $30**

13
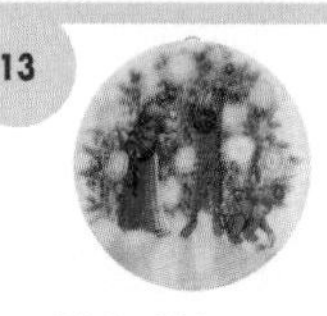
Light Shines at Christmas (1st, 1987)
Porcelain • VOTR
800QX4817 • **Value $72**

14

Waiting for Santa (2nd, 1988)
Porcelain • VOTR
800QX4061 • **Value $48**

15

Morning of Wonder (3rd, 1989)
Porcelain • VOTR
825QX4612 • **Value $29**

16

Cookies for Santa (4th, 1990)
Porcelain • VOTR
875QX4436 • **Value $32**

17

Let It Snow! (5th, 1991)
Porcelain • VOTR
875QX4369 • **Value $27**

18

Sweet Holiday Harmony (6th & final, 1992)
Porcelain • VOTR
875QX4461 • **Value $24**

19

Cool Decade (1st, 2000)
Handcrafted • HADD
795QX6764 • **Value $15**

20

Cool Decade (club edition, 2000)
Handcrafted • HADD
795QX6764 • **Value $25**

	Price Paid	Value
Classic American Cars		
1.		
2.		
3.		
The Clauses on Vacation		
4.		
5.		
6.		
Clothespin Soldier		
7.		
8.		
9.		
10.		
11.		
12.		
Collector's Plate		
13.		
14.		
15.		
16.		
17.		
18.		
Cool Decade		
19.		
20.		
Totals		

1

Cool Decade
(2nd, 2001)
Handcrafted • HADD
795QX6992 • **Value $7.95**

2

Bright Journey
(1st, 1989)
Handcrafted • SICK
875QX4352 • **Value $65**

3

Bright Moving Colors
(2nd, 1990)
Handcrafted • CROW
875QX4586 • **Value $51**

4

Bright Vibrant Carols
(3rd, 1991)
Handcrafted • CROW
975QX4219 • **Value $43**

5

Bright Blazing Colors
(4th, 1992)
Handcrafted • CROW
975QX4264 • **Value $40**

6

Bright Shining Castle
(5th, 1993)
Handcrafted • CROW
1075QX4422 • **Value $32**

7

Bright Playful Colors
(6th, 1994)
Handcrafted • CROW
1095QX5273 • **Value $32**

8

Bright 'n' Sunny Tepee
(7th, 1995)
Handcrafted • ANDR
1095QX5247 • **Value $26**

9

Bright Flying Colors
(8th, 1996)
Handcrafted • CROW
1095QX5391 • **Value $28**

10

Bright Rocking Colors
(9th, 1997)
Handcrafted • TAGU
1295QX6235 • **Value $29**

11

Bright Sledding Colors
(10th & final, 1998)
Handcrafted • TAGU
1295QX6166 • **Value $24**

12

Native American BARBIE™ (1st, 1996)
Handcrafted • ANDR
1495QX5561 • **Value $31**

13

Chinese BARBIE™
(2nd, 1997)
Handcrafted • RGRS
1495QX6162 • **Value $28**

14

Mexican BARBIE™
(3rd, 1998)
Handcrafted • RGRS
1495QX6356 • **Value $27**

15

Russian BARBIE™ Ornament
(4th & final, 1999)
Handcrafted • RGRS
1495QX6369 • **Value $24**

16

The Cat in the Hat
(1st, 1999, set/2)
Handcrafted • WILL
1495QXI6457 • **Value $28**

17

One Fish Two Fish Red Fish Blue Fish™
(2nd, 2000)
Handcrafted • WILL
1495QX6781 • **Value $24**

18

Horton Hatches The Egg
(3rd, 2001, set/2)
Handcrafted • WILL
1495QX6282 • **Value $14.95**

19

Cinderella (1st, 1997)
Handcrafted • CROW
1495QXD4045 • **Value $32**

	Price Paid	Value
Cool Decade		
1.		
CRAYOLA® Crayon		
2.		
3.		
4.		
5.		
6.		
7.		
8.		
9.		
10.		
11.		
Dolls Of The World		
12.		
13.		
14.		
15.		
Dr. Seuss® Books		
16.		
17.		
18.		
The Enchanted Memories Collection		
19.		
Totals		

Value Guide — Hallmark Keepsake Ornaments

1

Walt Disney's *Snow White* (2nd, 1998)
Handcrafted • N/A
1495QXD4056 • **Value $27**

2

Walt Disney's *Sleeping Beauty* (3rd & final, 1999)
Handcrafted • N/A
1495QXD4097 • **Value $26**

3

Fabulous Decade (1st, 1990)
Handcrafted/Brass • SEAL
775QX4466 • **Value $40**

4

Fabulous Decade (2nd, 1991)
Handcrafted/Brass • SEAL
775QX4119 • **Value $43**

5

Fabulous Decade (3rd, 1992)
Handcrafted/Brass • SEAL
775QX4244 • **Value $50**

6

Fabulous Decade (4th, 1993)
Handcrafted/Brass • PIKE
775QX4475 • **Value $24**

7

Fabulous Decade (5th, 1994)
Handcrafted/Brass • SEAL
795QX5263 • **Value $27**

8
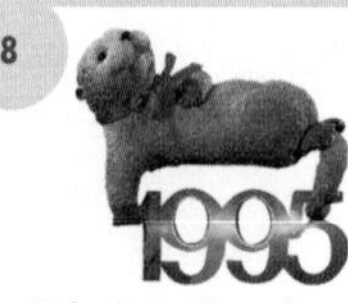

Fabulous Decade (6th, 1995)
Handcrafted/Brass • SEAL
795QX5147 • **Value $22**

9
Fabulous Decade (7th, 1996)
Handcrafted/Brass • SEAL
795QX5661 • **Value $23**

10

Fabulous Decade (8th, 1997)
Handcrafted/Brass • PIKE
795QX6232 • **Value $18**

11

Fabulous Decade (9th, 1998)
Handcrafted/Brass • PIKE
795QX6393 • **Value $28**

12

Fabulous Decade (10th & final, 1999)
Handcrafted/Brass • PIKE
795QX6357 • **Value $28**

13

Fashion Afoot (1st, 2000)
Handcrafted • ESCH
1495QX8341 • **Value $24**

14

Fashion Afoot (2nd, 2001)
Porcelain • ESCH
1495QX8105 • **Value $14.95**

15

David and Goliath (1st, 1999)
Handcrafted • LARS
1395QX6447 • **Value $27**

16
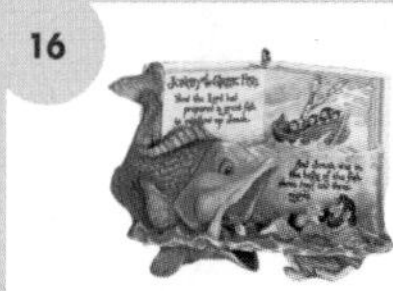
Jonah and the Great Fish (2nd, 2000)
Handcrafted • LARS
1395QX6701 • **Value $21**

17

Daniel in the Lions' Den (3rd & final, 2001)
Handcrafted • LARS
1395QX8122 • **Value $13.95**

18

Joe Montana (1st, 1995)
Handcrafted • RHOD
1495QXI5759 • **Value $50**

19

Joe Montana (Kansas City, 1995)
Handcrafted • RHOD
1495QXI6207 • **Value $100**

20

Troy Aikman (2nd, 1996)
Handcrafted • RHOD
1495QXI5021 • **Value $28**

	Price Paid	Value
The Enchanted Memories Collection		
1.		
2.		
Fabulous Decade		
3.		
4.		
5.		
6.		
7.		
8.		
9.		
10.		
11.		
12.		
Fashion Afoot		
13.		
14.		
Favorite Bible Stories		
15.		
16.		
17.		
Football Legends		
18.		
19.		
20.		
Totals		

1

Joe Namath (3rd, 1997)
Handcrafted • RHOD
1495QXI6182 • **Value $28**

2

Emmitt Smith (4th, 1998)
Handcrafted • RHOD
1495QXI4036 • **Value $27**

3

Dan Marino (5th, 1999)
Handcrafted • RHOD
1495QXI4029 • **Value $25**

4

John Elway (6th, 2000)
Handcrafted • RHOD
1495QXI6811 • **Value $19**

5

Brett Favre (7th, 2001)
Handcrafted • RHOD
1495QXI5232 • **Value $14.95**

6

A Cool Yule (1st, 1980)
Handcrafted • BLAC
650QX1374 • **Value $645**

7

Frosty Friends (2nd, 1981)
Handcrafted • N/A
800QX4335 • **Value $495**

8

Frosty Friends (3rd, 1982)
Handcrafted • SEAL
800QX4523 • **Value $285**

9

Frosty Friends (4th, 1983)
Handcrafted • SEAL
800QX4007 • **Value $325**

10

Frosty Friends (5th, 1984)
Handcrafted • SEAL
800QX4371 • **Value $95**

11

Frosty Friends (6th, 1985)
Handcrafted • SEAL
850QX4822 • **Value $84**

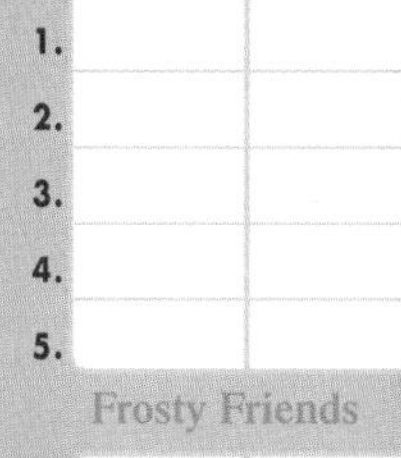

12

Frosty Friends (7th, 1986)
Handcrafted • SIED
850QX4053 • **Value $76**

13

Frosty Friends (8th, 1987)
Handcrafted • SEAL
850QX4409 • **Value $64**

14

Frosty Friends (9th, 1988)
Handcrafted • SEAL
875QX4031 • **Value $70**

15

Frosty Friends
(10th, 1989)
Handcrafted • SEAL
925QX4572 • **Value $65**

16
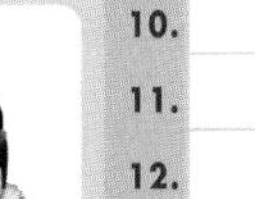

Frosty Friends
(11th, 1990)
Handcrafted • SEAL
975QX4396 • **Value $39**

17

Frosty Friends
(12th, 1991)
Handcrafted • PIKE
975QX4327 • **Value $45**

18

Frosty Friends
(13th, 1992)
Handcrafted • JLEE
975QX4291 • **Value $35**

19

Frosty Friends
(14th, 1993)
Handcrafted • JLEE
975QX4142 • **Value $33**

20

Frosty Friends (complements the series, 1993)
Handcrafted • SEAL
2000QX5682 • **Value $48**

Football Legends

	Price Paid	Value
1.		
2.		
3.		
4.		
5.		

Frosty Friends

	Price Paid	Value
6.		
7.		
8.		
9.		
10.		
11.		
12.		
13.		
14.		
15.		
16.		
17.		
18.		
19.		
20.		
Totals		

1

Frosty Friends
(15th, 1994)
Handcrafted • SEAL
995QX5293 • **Value $34**

2

Frosty Friends
(16th, 1995)
Handcrafted • SEAL
1095QX5169 • **Value $29**

3

Frosty Friends
(17th, 1996)
Handcrafted • SEAL
1095QX5681 • **Value $26**

4

Frosty Friends
(18th, 1997)
Handcrafted • SEAL
1095QX6255 • **Value $25**

5

Frosty Friends
(19th, 1998)
Handcrafted • SEAL
1095QX6226 • **Value $30**

6

Frosty Friends
(20th, 1999)
Handcrafted • SEAL
1295QX6297 • **Value $28**

7

Frosty Friends
(21st, 2000)
Handcrafted • SEAL
1095QX6601 • **Value $15**

8

Frosty Friends
(Premiere, 2000, set/3)
Porcelain/Pewter • SEAL
1895QX8524 • **Value $23**

9

Frosty Friends
(Premiere, green, 2000)
Handcrafted • SEAL
QX6601 • **Value N/E**

10

Husky (club edition, miniature, 2000)
Pewter • N / A
(N / C) No stock # • **Value N/E**

11
New!

Frosty Friends
(22nd, 2001)
Handcrafted • SEAL
1095QX8012 • **Value $10.95**

12

Gift Bearers (1st, 1999)
Porcelain • TAGU
1295QX6437 • **Value $24**

13

Gift Bearers (2nd, 2000)
Porcelain • TAGU
1295QX6651 • **Value $18**

14
New!

Gift Bearers (3rd, 2001)
Porcelain • TAGU
1295QX8115 • **Value $12.95**

15

St. Nicholas (1st, 1989)
Glass • VOTR
500QX2795 • **Value $26**

16

St. Lucia (2nd, 1990)
Glass • VOTR
500QX2803 • **Value $24**

17

Christkindl (3rd, 1991)
Glass • VOTR
500QX2117 • **Value $24**

18

Kolyada (4th, 1992)
Glass • VOTR
500QX2124 • **Value $23**

19

The Magi
(5th & final, 1993)
Glass • VOTR
500QX2065 • **Value $23**

20
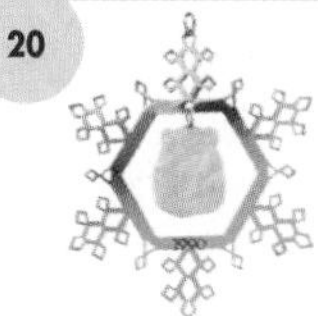
Greatest Story (1st, 1990)
Porcelain/Brass • VOTR
1275QX4656 • **Value $28**

Frosty Friends	Price Paid	Value
1.		
2.		
3.		
4.		
5.		
6.		
7.		
8.		
9.		
10.		
11.		
Gift Bearers		
12.		
13.		
14.		
The Gift Bringers		
15.		
16.		
17.		
18.		
19.		
Greatest Story		
20.		
Totals		

1

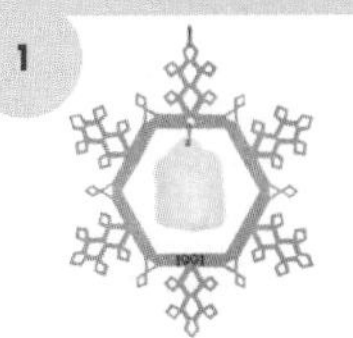

Greatest Story (2nd, 1991)
Porcelain/Brass • VOTR
1275QX4129 • **Value $27**

2

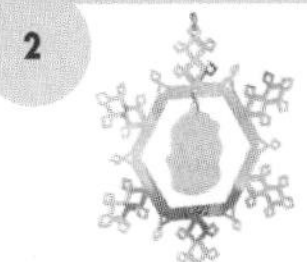

Greatest Story
(3rd & final, 1992)
Porcelain/Brass • VOTR
1275QX4251 • **Value $25**

3

Donald's Surprising
Gift (1st, 1997)
Handcrafted • BRIC
1295QXD4025 • **Value $28**

4

Ready for Christmas
(2nd, 1998)
Handcrafted • N/A
1295QXD4006 • **Value $23**

5

Minnie Trims the Tree
(3rd & final, 1999)
Handcrafted • N/A
1295QXD4059 • **Value $21**

6

Hark! It's Herald
(1st, 1989)
Handcrafted • CROW
675QX4555 • **Value $27**

7

Hark! It's Herald
(2nd, 1990)
Handcrafted • CROW
675QX4463 • **Value $21**

8

Hark! It's Herald
(3rd, 1991)
Handcrafted • RGRS
675QX4379 • **Value $25**

9

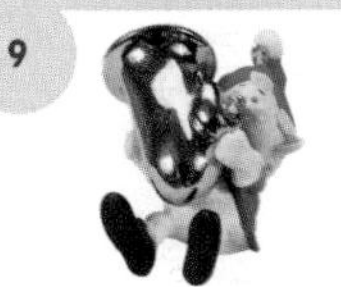

Hark! It's Herald
(4th & final, 1992)
Handcrafted • JLEE
775QX4464 • **Value $21**

10

Heritage Springer®
(1st, 1999)
Die-Cast Metal • PALM
1495QXI8007 • **Value $33**

11

Fat Boy® (2nd, 2000)
Die-Cast Metal • PALM
1495QXI6774 • **Value $22**

12

New!

1957 XL Sportster®
(3rd, 2001)
Die-Cast Metal • PALM
1495QXI8125 • **Value $14.95**

13

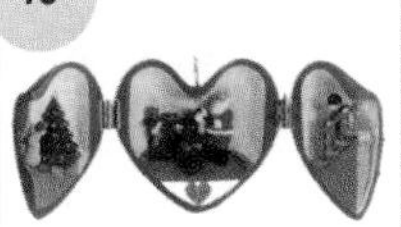

Heart of Christmas
(1st, 1990)
Handcrafted • SEAL
1375QX4726 • **Value $78**

14

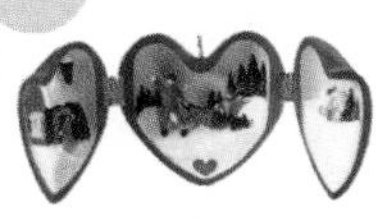

Heart of Christmas
(2nd, 1991)
Handcrafted • SEAL
1375QX4357 • **Value $30**

15

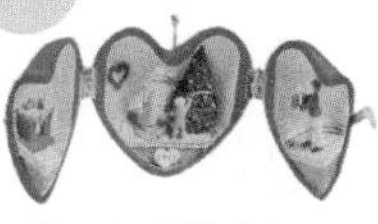

Heart of Christmas
(3rd, 1992)
Handcrafted • SEAL
1375QX4411 • **Value $28**

16

Heart of Christmas
(4th, 1993)
Handcrafted • SEAL
1475QX4482 • **Value $27**

17

Heart of Christmas
(5th & final, 1994)
Handcrafted • SEAL
1495QX5266 • **Value $29**

18

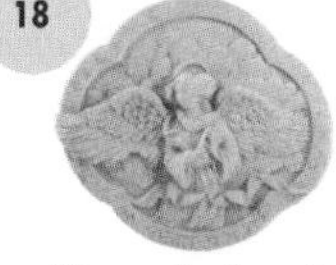

Heavenly Angels
(1st, 1991)
Handcrafted • LYLE
775QX4367 • **Value $27**

19

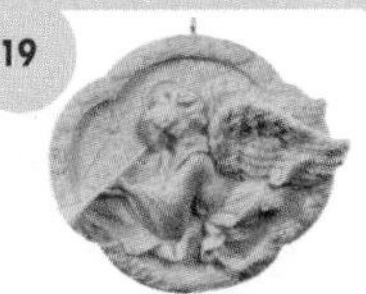

Heavenly Angels
(2nd, 1992)
Handcrafted • LYLE
775QX4454 • **Value $30**

20

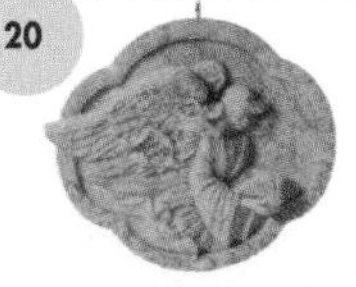

Heavenly Angels
(3rd & final, 1993)
Handcrafted • LYLE
775QX4945 • **Value $21**

	Price Paid	Value
Greatest Story		
1.		
2.		
Hallmark Archives		
3.		
4.		
5.		
Hark! It's Herald		
6.		
7.		
8.		
9.		
Harley Davidson® Motorcycle Milestones		
10.		
11.		
12.		
Heart Of Christmas		
13.		
14.		
15.		
16.		
17.		
Heavenly Angels		
18.		
19.		
20.		
Totals		

1

Santa's Motorcar
(1st, 1979)
Handcrafted • MAHO
900QX1559 • **Value $685**

2

Santa's Express
(2nd, 1980)
Handcrafted • MAHO
1200QX1434 • **Value $225**

3

Rooftop Deliveries
(3rd, 1981)
Handcrafted • MAHO
1300QX4382 • **Value $335**

4

Jolly Trolley (4th, 1982)
Handcrafted • SICK
1500QX4643 • **Value $150**

5

Santa Express (5th, 1983)
Handcrafted • DLEE
1300QX4037 • **Value $300**

6

Santa's Deliveries
(6th, 1984)
Handcrafted • SICK
1300QX4324 • **Value $94**

7

Santa's Fire Engine
(7th, 1985)
Handcrafted • SICK
1400QX4965 • **Value $70**

8

Kringle's Kool Treats
(8th, 1986)
Handcrafted • SIED
1400QX4043 • **Value $75**

Here Comes Santa

	Price Paid	Value
1.		
2.		
3.		
4.		
5.		
6.		
7.		
8.		
9.		
10.		
11.		
12.		
13.		
14.		
15.		
16.		
17.		
18.		
19.		
20.		
Totals		

9

Santa's Woody (9th, 1987)
Handcrafted • CROW
1400QX4847 • **Value $90**

10

Kringle Koach
(10th, 1988)
Handcrafted • CROW
1400QX4001 • **Value $52**

11

Christmas Caboose
(11th, 1989)
Handcrafted • CROW
1475QX4585 • **Value $52**

12

Festive Surrey
(12th, 1990)
Handcrafted • SICK
1475QX4923 • **Value $45**

13

Santa's Antique Car
(13th, 1991)
Handcrafted • SICK
1475QX4349 • **Value $58**

14

Kringle Tours
(14th, 1992)
Handcrafted • SICK
1475QX4341 • **Value $36**

15

Happy Haul-idays
(15th, 1993)
Handcrafted • SICK
1475QX4102 • **Value $35**

16

Shopping With Santa
(complements the
series, 1993)
Handcrafted • SICK
2400QX5675 • **Value $47**

17

Makin' Tractor Tracks
(16th, 1994)
Handcrafted • SICK
1495QX5296 • **Value $56**

18

Santa's Roadster
(17th, 1995)
Handcrafted • SICK
1495QX5179 • **Value $31**

19

Santa's 4 x 4 (18th, 1996)
Handcrafted • SEAL
1495QX5684 • **Value $32**

20

The Claus-Mobile
(19th, 1997)
Handcrafted • TAGU
1495QX6262 • **Value $28**

1

Santa's Bumper Car
(20th, 1998)
Handcrafted • TAGU
1495QX6283 • **Value $25**

2

Santa's Golf Cart
(21st, 1999)
Handcrafted • RHOD
1495QX6337 • **Value $23**

3

Sleigh X-2000
(22nd, 2000)
Handcrafted • WILL
1495QX6824 • **Value $20**

4

New!

Santa's Snowplow
(23rd, 2001)
Handcrafted • UNRU
1495QX8065 • **Value $14.95**

5

Wayne Gretzky
(1st, 1997)
Handcrafted • UNRU
1595QXI6275 • **Value $34**

6

Mario Lemieux
(2nd, 1998)
Handcrafted • FRAN
1595QXI6476 • **Value $27**

7

Gordie Howe®
(3rd, 1999)
Handcrafted • FRAN
1595QXI4047 • **Value $25**

8

Eric Lindros
(4th, 2000)
Handcrafted • FRAN
1595QXI6801 • **Value $24**

9

New!

Jaromir Jagr
(5th & final, 2001)
Handcrafted • FRAN
1595QXI6852 • **Value $15.95**

10

Holiday BARBIE™
(1st, 1993)
Handcrafted • ANDR
1475QX5725 • **Value $178**

11

Holiday BARBIE™
(2nd, 1994)
Handcrafted • ANDR
1495QX5216 • **Value $56**

12

Holiday BARBIE™
(3rd, 1995)
Handcrafted • ANDR
1495QXI5057 • **Value $36**

13

Holiday BARBIE™
(4th, 1996)
Handcrafted • ANDR
1495QXI5371 • **Value $34**

14

Holiday BARBIE™
(5th, 1997)
Handcrafted • ANDR
1595QXI6212 • **Value $31**

15

Holiday BARBIE™
(6th & final, 1998)
Handcrafted • ANDR
1595QXI4023 • **Value $32**

16

Based on the 1988 Happy Holidays® BARBIE® Doll
(1st, club edition, 1996)
Handcrafted • ANDR
1495QXC4181 • **Value $80**

17

Based on the 1989 Happy Holidays® BARBIE® Doll
(2nd, club edition, 1997)
Handcrafted • ANDR
1595QXC5162 • **Value $53**

18

Based on the 1990 Happy Holidays® BARBIE® Doll
(3rd, club edition, 1998)
Handcrafted • ANDR
1595QXC4493 • **Value $44**

19

Based on the 1991 Happy Holidays® Barbie™ Doll
(4th, club edition, 1999)
Handcrafted • ANDR
1595QXC4507 • **Value $50**

20

Based on the 1992 Happy Holidays® BARBIE® Doll
(5th & final, club edition, 2000)
Handcrafted • ANDR
1595QXC4494 • **Value $29**

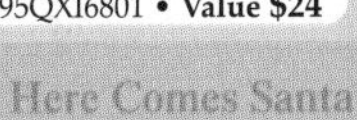

	Price Paid	Value
Here Comes Santa		
1.		
2.		
3.		
4.		
Hockey Greats		
5.		
6.		
7.		
8.		
9.		
Holiday BARBIE™		
10.		
11.		
12.		
13.		
14.		
15.		
Holiday BARBIE™ – Collector's Club		
16.		
17.		
18.		
19.		
20.		
Totals		

1

Celebration BARBIE™ (1st, 2000)
Handcrafted • ANDR
1595QXI6821 • **Value $30**

2

Holiday Celebration BARBIE™ (2nd, 2001)
Handcrafted • ANDR
1595QXI5202 • **Value $15.95**

3

Holiday Heirloom (1st, LE-34,600, 1987)
Crystal/Silver-Plated • UNRU
2500QX4857 • **Value $33**

4

Holiday Heirloom (2nd, club edition, LE-34,600, 1988)
Crystal/Silver-Plated • N/A
2500QX4064 • **Value $33**

5

Holiday Heirloom (3rd & final, club edition, LE-34,600, 1989)
Crystal/Silver-Plated • N/A
2500QXC4605 • **Value $35**

6
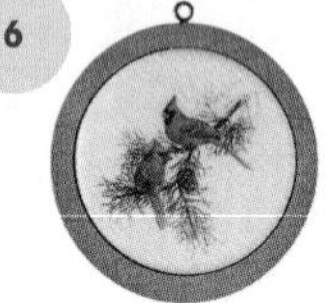
Cardinalis (1st, 1982)
Wood • N/A
700QX3133 • **Value $400**

7

Black-Capped Chickadees (2nd, 1983)
Wood • N/A
700QX3099 • **Value $75**

8

Ring-Necked Pheasant (3rd, 1984)
Wood • N/A
725QX3474 • **Value $33**

9

California Partridge (4th, 1985)
Wood • N/A
750QX3765 • **Value $32**

10
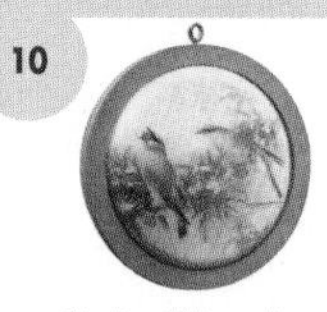
Cedar Waxwing (5th, 1986)
Wood • N/A
750QX3216 • **Value $30**

11

Snow Goose (6th, 1987)
Wood • VOTR
750QX3717 • **Value $27**

12

Purple Finch (7th & final, 1988)
Wood • N/A
775QX3711 • **Value $30**

13

Shaquille O'Neal (1st, 1995)
Handcrafted • N/A
1495QXI5517 • **Value $47**

14

Larry Bird (2nd, 1996)
Handcrafted • N/A
1495QXI5014 • **Value $31**

15

Magic Johnson (3rd, 1997)
Handcrafted • N/A
1495QXI6832 • **Value $30**

16

Grant Hill (4th, 1998)
Handcrafted • UNRU
1495QXI6846 • **Value $26**

17

Scottie Pippen (5th, 1999)
Handcrafted • UNRU
1495QXI4177 • **Value $23**

18

Karl Malone (6th, 2000)
Handcrafted • UNRU
1495QXI6901 • **Value $20**

19

Tim Duncan (7th, 2001)
Handcrafted • UNRU
1495QXI5235 • **Value $14.95**

20

Joyful Santa (1st, 1999)
Handcrafted • CHAD
1495QX6949 • **Value $27**

	Price Paid	Value
Holiday Celebration BARBIE™		
1.		
2.		
Holiday Heirloom		
3.		
4.		
5.		
Holiday Wildlife		
6.		
7.		
8.		
9.		
10.		
11.		
12.		
Hoop Stars		
13.		
14.		
15.		
16.		
17.		
18.		
19.		
Joyful Santa		
20.		
Totals		

1

Joyful Santa (2nd, 2000)
Handcrafted • ANDR
1495QX6784 • **Value $22**

2

New!
Joyful Santa
(3rd & final, 2001)
Handcrafted • ANDR
1495QX8152 • **Value $14.95**

3

Murray® "Champion"
(1st, 1994)
Die-Cast Metal • PALM
1395QX5426 • **Value $70**

4

Murray® Fire Truck
(2nd, 1995)
Die-Cast Metal • PALM
1395QX5027 • **Value $32**

5

Murray® Airplane
(3rd, 1996)
Die-Cast Metal • PALM
1395QX5364 • **Value $28**

6

1937 Steelcraft Auburn
by Murray®
(club edition, 1996)
Die-Cast Metal • PALM
1595QXC4174 • **Value $60**

7

Murray® Dump Truck
(4th, 1997)
Die-Cast Metal • PALM
1395QX6195 • **Value $27**

8

1937 Steelcraft Airflow
by Murray®
(club edition, 1997)
Die-Cast Metal • PALM
1595QXC5185 • **Value $51**

9

1955 Murray® Tractor
and Trailer (5th, 1998)
Die-Cast Metal • PALM
1695QX6376 • **Value $30**

10

1935 Steelcraft
by Murray®
(club edition, 1998)
Die-Cast Metal • PALM
1595QXC4496 • **Value $42**

11

1968 Murray® Jolly
Roger Flagship
(6th, 1999)
Die-Cast Metal • PALM
1395QX6279 • **Value $25**

12

1939 Garton® Ford
Station Wagon
(club edition, 1999)
Die-Cast Metal • PALM
1595QXC4509 • **Value $28**

13

1924 Toledo Fire
Engine #6 (7th, 2000)
Die-Cast Metal • PALM
1395QX6691 • **Value $23**

14

1938 Garton®
Lincoln Zephyr
(club edition, 2000)
Handcrafted • PALM
1595QXC4501 • **Value $22**

15

New!
1930 Custom Biplane
(8th , 2001)
Die-Cast Metal • PALM
1395QX6975 • **Value $13.95**

16

New!
Kris And The Kringles
(1st , 2001)
Handcrafted • CROW
2400QX8112 • **Value $24**

17

Pansy (1st, 1996)
Handcrafted • TAGU
1595QK1171 • **Value $58**

18
Snowdrop Angel
(2nd, 1997)
Handcrafted • TAGU
1595QX1095 • **Value $31**

19

Iris Angel (3rd, 1998)
Handcrafted • TAGU
1595QX6156 • **Value $30**

20

Rose Angel
(4th & final, 1999)
Handcrafted • TAGU
1595QX6289 • **Value $26**

	Price Paid	Value
Joyful Santa		
1.		
2.		
Kiddie Car Classics		
3.		
4.		
5.		
6.		
7.		
8.		
9.		
10.		
11.		
12.		
13.		
14.		
15.		
Kris And The Kringles		
16.		
The Language Of Flowers		
17.		
18.		
19.		
20.		
Totals		

1

700E Hudson Steam Locomotive (1st, 1996)
Die-Cast Metal • N/A
1895QX5531 • **Value $70**

2

1950 Santa Fe F3 Diesel Locomotive (2nd, 1997)
Die-Cast Metal • N/A
1895QX6145 • **Value $42**

3

Pennsylvania GG-1 Locomotive (3rd, 1998)
Die-Cast Metal • N/A
1895QX6346 • **Value $33**

4

746 Norfolk and Western Steam Locomotive (4th, 1999)
Die-Cast Metal • N/A
1895QX6377 • **Value $30**

5

Lionel® General Steam Locomotive (5th, 2000)
Die-Cast Metal • N/A
1895QX6684 • **Value $27**

6

New!

LIONEL® Chessie Steam Special Locomotive (6th, 2001)
Die-Cast Metal • N/A
1895QX6092 • **Value $18.95**

7

New!

Tender-LIONEL® Chessie Steam Special (complements the series, 2001)
Die-Cast Metal • N/A
1395QX6285 • **Value $13.95**

8

Cinderella – 1995 (1st, 1996)
Handcrafted • FRAN
1495QX6311 • **Value $44**

9

Little Red Riding Hood – 1991 (2nd, 1997)
Handcrafted • FRAN
1495QX6155 • **Value $33**

10

Mop Top Wendy (3rd, 1998)
Handcrafted • FRAN
1495QX6353 • **Value $28**

11

Red Queen – Alice in Wonderland (4th, 1999)
Handcrafted • FRAN
1495QX6379 • **Value $27**

12

Christmas Holly (5th, 2000)
Handcrafted • FRAN
1495QX6611 • **Value $25**

13

New!

Victorian Christmas (6th, 2001)
Handcrafted • FRAN
1495QX6855 • **Value $14.95**

14

Glorious Angel (1st, 1998)
Handcrafted • FRAN
1495QX6493 • **Value $29**

15

Angel of The Nativity (2nd, 1999)
Handcrafted • FRAN
1495QX6419 • **Value $33**

16

Twilight Angel (3rd & final, 2000)
Handcrafted • FRAN
1495QX6614 • **Value $28**

17

New!

Margaret "Meg" March (1st, 2001)
Porcelain • FORS
1595QX6315 • **Value $15.95**

18

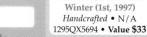

Snowshoe Rabbits in Winter (1st, 1997)
Handcrafted • N/A
1295QX5694 • **Value $33**

19

Timber Wolves at Play (2nd, 1998)
Handcrafted • N/A
1295QX6273 • **Value $27**

20

Curious Raccoons (3rd, 1999)
Handcrafted • N/A
1295QX6287 • **Value $25**

	Price Paid	Value
LIONEL® Train		
1.		
2.		
3.		
4.		
5.		
6.		
7.		
Madame Alexander®		
8.		
9.		
10.		
11.		
12.		
13.		
Madame Alexander® Holiday Angels		
14.		
15.		
16.		
Madame Alexander® Little Women		
17.		
Majestic Wilderness		
18.		
19.		
20.		
Totals		

1

Foxes in the Forest
(4th & final, 2000)
Handcrafted • N/A
1295QX6794 • **Value $23**

2

Marilyn Monroe
(1st, 1997)
Handcrafted • ANDR
1495QX5704 • **Value $31**

3

Marilyn Monroe
(2nd, 1998)
Handcrafted • ANDR
1495QX6333 • **Value $28**

4

Marilyn Monroe
(3rd & final, 1999)
Handcrafted • ANDR
1495QX6389 • **Value $26**

5

Buttercup (1st, 1988)
Handcrafted • CHAD
500QX4074 • **Value $58**

6

Bluebell (2nd, 1989)
Handcrafted • CHAD
575QX4545 • **Value $96**

7

Rosebud (3rd, 1990)
Handcrafted • CHAD
575QX4423 • **Value $50**

8
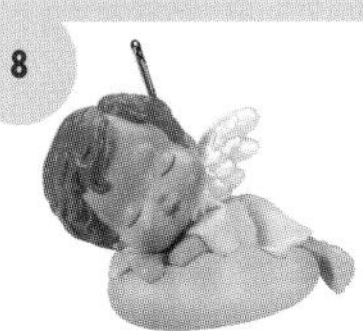
Iris (4th, 1991)
Handcrafted • CHAD
675QX4279 • **Value $50**

9
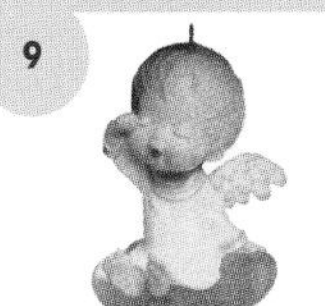
Lily (5th, 1992)
Handcrafted • CHAD
675QX4274 • **Value $57**

10
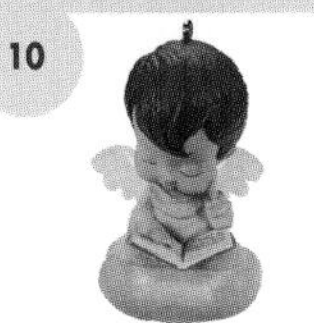
Ivy (6th, 1993)
Handcrafted • CHAD
675QX4282 • **Value $29**

11

Jasmine (7th, 1994)
Handcrafted • CHAD
695QX5276 • **Value $25**

12

Camellia (8th, 1995)
Handcrafted • CHAD
695QX5149 • **Value $22**

13
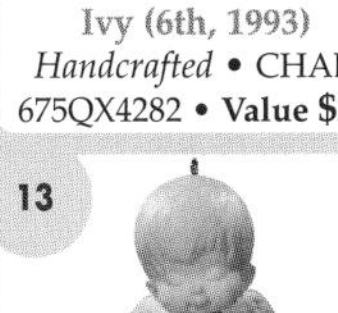
Violet (9th, 1996)
Handcrafted • CHAD
695QX5664 • **Value $21**

14

Daisy (10th, 1997)
Handcrafted • CHAD
795QX6242 • **Value $20**

15

Daphne (11th, 1998)
Handcrafted • CHAD
795QX6153 • **Value $20**

16

Heather (12th, 1999)
Handcrafted • CHAD
795QX6329 • **Value $21**

17
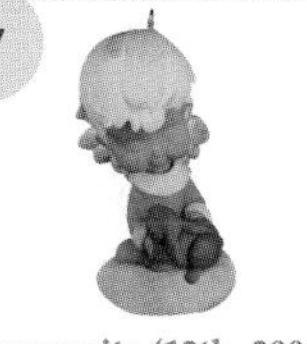
Marguerite (13th, 2000)
Handcrafted • CHAD
795QX6571 • **Value $17**

18

New!
Chrysantha (14th, 2001)
Handcrafted • CHAD
795QX6985 • **Value $7.95**

19

Merry Olde Santa
(1st, 1990)
Handcrafted • SEAL
1475QX4736 • **Value $86**

20

Merry Olde Santa
(2nd, 1991)
Handcrafted • JLEE
1475QX4359 • **Value $89**

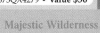

	Price Paid	Value
Majestic Wilderness		
1.		
Marilyn Monroe		
2.		
3.		
4.		
Mary's Angels		
5.		
6.		
7.		
8.		
9.		
10.		
11.		
12.		
13.		
14.		
15.		
16.		
17.		
18.		
Merry Olde Santa		
19.		
20.		
Totals		

1

Merry Olde Santa
(3rd, 1992)
Handcrafted • UNRU
1475QX4414 • **Value $39**

2

Merry Olde Santa
(4th, 1993)
Handcrafted • RGRS
1475QX4842 • **Value $39**

3

Merry Olde Santa
(5th, 1994)
Handcrafted • CHAD
1495QX5256 • **Value $35**

4

Merry Olde Santa
(6th, 1995)
Handcrafted • ANDR
1495QX5139 • **Value $29**

5

Merry Olde Santa
(7th, 1996)
Handcrafted • CROW
1495QX5654 • **Value $29**

6

Merry Olde Santa
(8th, 1997)
Handcrafted • LYLE
1495QX6225 • **Value $30**

7

Merry Olde Santa
(9th, 1998)
Handcrafted • UNRU
1595QX6386 • **Value $30**

8

Merry Olde Santa
(10th & final, 1999)
Handcrafted • RHOD
1595QX6359 • **Value $29**

9

Bandleader Mickey
(1st, 1997)
Handcrafted • SIED
1395QXD4022 • **Value $26**

10

Minnie Plays the Flute
(2nd, 1998)
Handcrafted • N/A
1395QXD4106 • **Value $24**

11
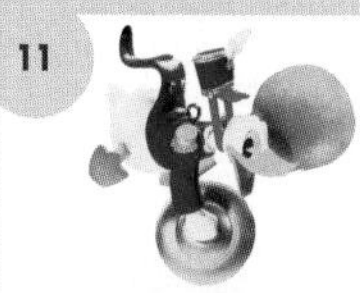
Donald Plays the
Cymbals (3rd, 1999)
Handcrafted • N/A
1395QXD4057 • **Value $23**

12

Baton Twirler Daisy
(4th, 2000)
Handcrafted • N/A
1395QXD4034 • **Value $20**

13

Pluto Plays Triangle
(5th, 2001)
Handcrafted • N/A
1395QXD4112 • **Value $13.95**

14

Miniature Crèche
(1st, 1985)
Wood/Straw • SEAL
875QX4825 • **Value $36**

15
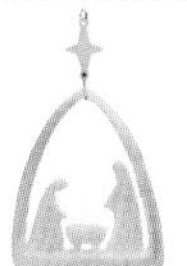
Miniature Crèche
(2nd, 1986)
Porcelain • SEAL
900QX4076 • **Value $60**

16

Miniature Crèche
(3rd, 1987)
Brass • SEAL
900QX4819 • **Value $39**

17

Miniature Crèche
(4th, 1988)
Acrylic • UNRU
850QX4034 • **Value $35**

18

Miniature Crèche
(5th & final, 1989)
Handcrafted • RGRS
925QX4592 • **Value $23**

19

Mischievous Kittens
(1st, 1999)
Handcrafted • AUBE
995QX6427 • **Value $28**

20

Mischievous Kittens
(Premiere, gray, complements the series, 1999)
Handcrafted • AUBE
(N/C) QX6427 • **Value $20**

Merry Olde Santa

	Price Paid	Value
1.		
2.		
3.		
4.		
5.		
6.		
7.		
8.		

Mickey's Holiday Parade

	Price Paid	Value
9.		
10.		
11.		
12.		
13.		

Miniature Creche

	Price Paid	Value
14.		
15.		
16.		
17.		
18.		

Mischievous Kittens

	Price Paid	Value
19.		
20.		

Price Paid	Value

Totals

1

Mischievous Kittens
(2nd, 2000)
Handcrafted • AUBE
995QX6641 • **Value $20**

2

New!
Mischievous Kittens
(3rd, 2001)
Handcrafted • AUBE
995QX8025 • **Value $9.95**

3

New!
Mistletoe Miss
(1st, 2001)
Porcelain • AUBE
1495QX8092 • **Value $14.95**

4

Humpty Dumpty
(1st, 1993)
Handcrafted • SEAL/VOTR
1375QX5282 • **Value $43**

5

Hey Diddle, Diddle
(2nd, 1994)
Handcrafted • SEAL
1395QX5213 • **Value $46**

6

Jack and Jill (3rd, 1995)
Handcrafted • SEAL/VOTR
1395QX5099 • **Value $29**

7

Mary Had a Little Lamb (4th, 1996)
Handcrafted • SEAL/VOTR
1395QX5644 • **Value $29**

8

Little Boy Blue
(5th & final, 1997)
Handcrafted • SEAL/VOTR
1395QX6215 • **Value $29**

9

Merry Mistletoe Time
(1st, 1986)
Handcrafted • UNRU
1300QX4026 • **Value $110**

10

Home Cooking
(2nd, 1987)
Handcrafted • UNRU
1325QX4837 • **Value $68**

11

Shall We Dance
(3rd, 1988)
Handcrafted • UNRU
1300QX4011 • **Value $56**

12

Holiday Duet (4th, 1989)
Handcrafted • UNRU
1325QX4575 • **Value $55**

13

Popcorn Party (5th, 1990)
Handcrafted • UNRU
1375QX4393 • **Value $75**

14

Checking His List
(6th, 1991)
Handcrafted • UNRU
1375QX4339 • **Value $48**

15

Gift Exchange
(7th, 1992)
Handcrafted • UNRU
1475QX4294 • **Value $43**

16

A Fitting Moment
(8th, 1993)
Handcrafted • FRAN
1475QX4202 • **Value $43**

17

A Handwarming Present (9th, 1994)
Handcrafted • UNRU
1495QX5283 • **Value $38**

18

Christmas Eve Kiss
(10th & final, 1995)
Handcrafted • UNRU
1495QX5157 • **Value $31**

19
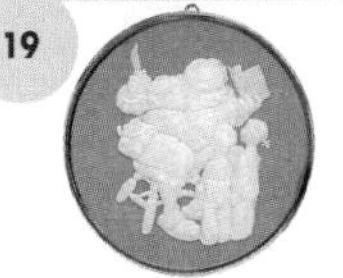
Santa's Visitors
(1st, 1980)
Cameo • N/A
650QX3061 • **Value $250**

	Price Paid	Value
Mischievous Kittens		
1.		
2.		
Mistletoe Miss		
3.		
Mother Goose		
4.		
5.		
6.		
7.		
8.		
Mr. And Mrs. Claus		
9.		
10.		
11.		
12.		
13.		
14.		
15.		
16.		
17.		
18.		
Norman Rockwell		
19.		
Totals		

1

The Carolers (2nd, 1981)
Cameo • N/A
850QX5115 • **Value $50**

2

Filling the Stockings (3rd, 1982)
Cameo • N/A
850QX3053 • **Value $33**

3

Dress Rehearsal (4th, 1983)
Cameo • N/A
750QX3007 • **Value $39**

4

Caught Napping (5th, 1984)
Cameo • MCGE
750QX3411 • **Value $37**

5

Jolly Postman (6th, 1985)
Cameo • MCGE
750QX3745 • **Value $35**

6
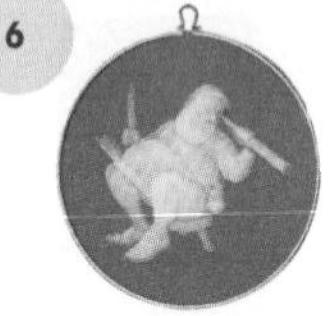
Checking Up (7th, 1986)
Cameo • PIKE
775QX3213 • **Value $30**

7

The Christmas Dance (8th, 1987)
Cameo • PALM
775QX3707 • **Value $25**

8

And to All a Good Night (9th & final, 1988)
Cameo • N/A
775QX3704 • **Value $25**

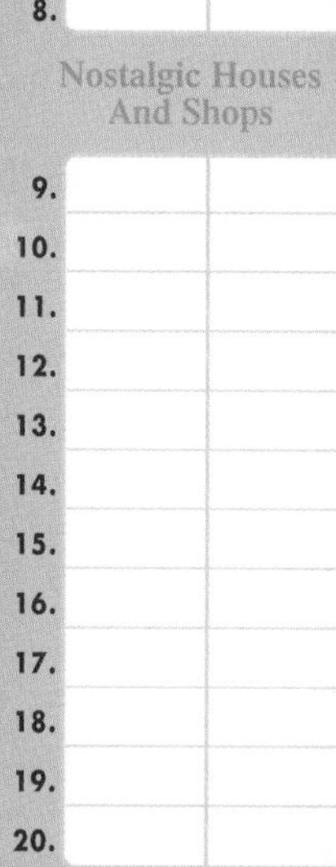

Norman Rockwell

	Price Paid	Value
1.		
2.		
3.		
4.		
5.		
6.		
7.		
8.		

Nostalgic Houses And Shops

	Price Paid	Value
9.		
10.		
11.		
12.		
13.		
14.		
15.		
16.		
17.		
18.		
19.		
20.		
Totals		

9

Victorian Dollhouse (1st, 1984)
Handcrafted • DLEE
1300QX4481 • **Value $220**

10

Old-Fashioned Toy Shop (2nd, 1985)
Handcrafted • DLEE
1375QX4975 • **Value $155**

11

Christmas Candy Shoppe (3rd, 1986)
Handcrafted • DLEE
1375QX4033 • **Value $315**

12

House on Main St. (4th, 1987)
Handcrafted • DLEE
1400QX4839 • **Value $83**

13

Hall Bro's Card Shop (5th, 1988)
Handcrafted • DLEE
1450QX4014 • **Value $66**

14

U.S. Post Office (6th, 1989)
Handcrafted • DLEE
1425QX4582 • **Value $72**

15

Holiday Home (7th, 1990)
Handcrafted • DLEE
1475QX4696 • **Value $78**

16

Fire Station (8th, 1991)
Handcrafted • DLEE
1475QX4139 • **Value $70**

17

Five and Ten Cent Store (9th, 1992)
Handcrafted • DLEE
1475QX4254 • **Value $44**

18
Cozy Home (10th, 1993)
Handcrafted • DLEE
1475QX4175 • **Value $47**

19

Tannenbaum's Dept. Store (complements the series, 1993)
Handcrafted • DLEE
2600QX5612 • **Value $55**

20

Neighborhood Drugstore (11th, 1994)
Handcrafted • DLEE
1495QX5286 • **Value $38**

1

Town Church
(12th, 1995)
Handcrafted • PALM
1495QX5159 • **Value $33**

2

Accessories for Nostalgic Houses and Shops (1995, set/3)
Handcrafted • JLEE
895QX5089 • **Value $19**

3

Victorian Painted Lady
(13th, 1996)
Handcrafted • PALM
1495QX5671 • **Value $29**

4

Cafe (14th, 1997)
Handcrafted • PALM
1695QX6245 • **Value $30**

5

Grocery Store
(15th, 1998)
Handcrafted • PALM
1695QX6266 • **Value $29**

6

Halls Station (complements the series, 1998)
Handcrafted • PALM
2500QX6833 • **Value $45**

7

House on Holly Lane
(16th, 1999)
Handcrafted • PALM
1695QX6349 • **Value $29**

8

Schoolhouse
(17th, 2000)
Handcrafted • PALM
1495QX6591 • **Value $25**

9
New!

Service Station
(18th, 2001)
Handcrafted • PALM
1495QX8045 • **Value $14.95**

10

Pony Express Rider
(1st, 1998)
Handcrafted • UNRU
1395QX6323 • **Value $28**

11

Prospector (2nd, 1999)
Handcrafted • UNRU
1395QX6317 • **Value $25**

12

Mountain Man
(3rd & final, 2000)
Handcrafted • UNRU
1595QX6594 • **Value $23**

13

Owliver (1st, 1992)
Handcrafted • SIED
775QX4544 • **Value $21**

14

Owliver (2nd, 1993)
Handcrafted • SIED
775QX5425 • **Value $19**

15
Owliver
(3rd & final, 1994)
Handcrafted • SIED
795QX5226 • **Value $20**

16
Italy (1st, 1991)
Handcrafted • SICK
1175QX5129 • **Value $26**

17
Spain (2nd, 1992)
Handcrafted • SICK
1175QX5174 • **Value $23**

18

Poland (3rd & final, 1993)
Handcrafted • SICK
1175QX5242 • **Value $25**

19

The PEANUTS® Gang
(1st, 1993)
Handcrafted • RHOD
975QX5315 • **Value $59**

20

The PEANUTS® Gang
(2nd, 1994)
Handcrafted • BISH
995QX5203 • **Value $27**

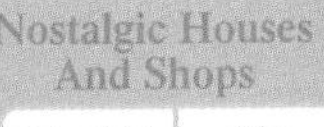

	Price Paid	Value
1.		
2.		
3.		
4.		
5.		
6.		
7.		
8.		
9.		
The Old West		
10.		
11.		
12.		
Owliver		
13.		
14.		
15.		
Peace On Earth		
16.		
17.		
18.		
The PEANUTS® Gang		
19.		
20.		
Totals		

1

The PEANUTS® Gang
(3rd, 1995)
Handcrafted • SIED
995QX5059 • **Value $25**

2

The PEANUTS® Gang
(4th & final, 1996)
Handcrafted • FRAN
995QX5381 • **Value $20**

3

A Pony for Christmas
(1st, 1998)
Handcrafted • SICK
1095QX6316 • **Value $30**

4

A Pony for Christmas
(2nd, 1999)
Handcrafted • SICK
1095QX6299 • **Value $24**

5

A Pony for Christmas
(3rd, 2000)
Handcrafted • SICK
1295QX6624 • **Value $20**

6

New!
A Pony for Christmas
(4th, 2001)
Handcrafted • SICK
1295QX6995 • **Value $12.95**

7

Cinnamon Teddy
(1st, 1983)
Porcelain • DUTK
700QX4289 • **Value $82**

8

Cinnamon Bear
(2nd, 1984)
Porcelain • N/A
700QX4541 • **Value $55**

9

Porcelain Bear
(3rd, 1985)
Porcelain • DUTK
750QX4792 • **Value $62**

10

Porcelain Bear
(4th, 1986)
Porcelain • N/A
775QX4056 • **Value $45**

11

Porcelain Bear
(5th, 1987)
Porcelain • N/A
775QX4427 • **Value $42**

12

Porcelain Bear
(6th, 1988)
Porcelain • PIKE
800QX4044 • **Value $40**

13

Porcelain Bear
(7th, 1989)
Porcelain • PIKE
875QX4615 • **Value $39**

14

Porcelain Bear
(8th & final, 1990)
Porcelain • N/A
875QX4426 • **Value $35**

15

Puppy Love (1st, 1991)
Handcrafted/Brass • RGRS
775QX5379 • **Value $66**

16

Puppy Love (2nd, 1992)
Handcrafted/Brass • RGRS
775QX4484 • **Value $43**

17

Puppy Love (3rd, 1993)
Handcrafted/Brass • RGRS
775QX5045 • **Value $30**

18

Puppy Love (4th, 1994)
Handcrafted/Brass • RGRS
795QX5253 • **Value $25**

19

Puppy Love (5th, 1995)
Handcrafted/Brass • RGRS
795QX5137 • **Value $25**

20

Puppy Love (6th, 1996)
Handcrafted/Brass • RGRS
795QX5651 • **Value $21**

	Price Paid	Value
The PEANUTS® Gang		
1.		
2.		
A Pony for Christmas		
3.		
4.		
5.		
6.		
Porcelain Bear		
7.		
8.		
9.		
10.		
11.		
12.		
13.		
14.		
Puppy Love		
15.		
16.		
17.		
18.		
19.		
20.		
Totals		

1

Puppy Love (7th, 1997)
Handcrafted/Brass • RGRS
795QX6222 • **Value $22**

2

Puppy Love (8th, 1998)
Handcrafted/Brass • RGRS
795QX6163 • **Value $18**

3

Puppy Love (9th, 1999)
Handcrafted • RGRS
795QX6327 • **Value $19**

4

Puppy Love (10th, 2000)
Handcrafted/Brass • RGRS
795QX6554 • **Value $18**

5
New!

Puppy Love (11th, 2001)
Handcrafted/Brass • RGRS
795QX6982 • **Value $7.95**

6

Dasher (1st, 1986)
Handcrafted • SIED
750QX4223 • **Value $150**

7

Dancer (2nd, 1987)
Handcrafted • SIED
750QX4809 • **Value $53**

8

Prancer (3rd, 1988)
Handcrafted • SIED
750QX4051 • **Value $39**

9

Vixen (4th, 1989)
Handcrafted • SIED
775QX4562 • **Value $22**

10

Comet (5th, 1990)
Handcrafted • SIED
775QX4433 • **Value $30**

11

Cupid (6th, 1991)
Handcrafted • SIED
775QX4347 • **Value $29**

12

Donder (7th, 1992)
Handcrafted • SIED
875QX5284 • **Value $34**

13

Blitzen
(8th & final, 1993)
Handcrafted • SIED
875QX4331 • **Value $27**

14

Robot Parade (1st, 2000)
Handcrafted/Pressed Tin • WILL
1495QX6771 • **Value $22**

15
New!

Robot Parade (2nd, 2001)
Handcrafted/Pressed Tin • WILL
1495QX8162 • **Value $14.95**

16

Rocking Horse (1st, 1981)
Handcrafted • SICK
900QX4222 • **Value $640**

17
Rocking Horse (2nd, 1982)
Handcrafted • SICK
1000QX5023 • **Value $440**

18

Rocking Horse (3rd, 1983)
Handcrafted • SICK
1000QX4177 • **Value $310**

19

Rocking Horse (4th, 1984)
Handcrafted • SICK
1000QX4354 • **Value $93**

20

Rocking Horse (5th, 1985)
Handcrafted • SICK
1075QX4932 • **Value $83**

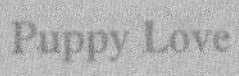

	Price Paid	Value
Puppy Love		
1.		
2.		
3.		
4.		
5.		
Reindeer Champs		
6.		
7.		
8.		
9.		
10.		
11.		
12.		
13.		
Robot Parade		
14.		
15.		
Rocking Horse		
16.		
17.		
18.		
19.		
20.		
Totals		

1

Rocking Horse (6th, 1986)
Handcrafted • SICK
1075QX4016 • **Value $82**

2

Rocking Horse (7th, 1987)
Handcrafted • SICK
1075QX4829 • **Value $80**

3

Rocking Horse (8th, 1988)
Handcrafted • SICK
1075QX4024 • **Value $68**

4

Rocking Horse (9th, 1989)
Handcrafted • SICK
1075QX4622 • **Value $60**

5

Rocking Horse
(10th, 1990)
Handcrafted • SICK
1075QX4646 • **Value $100**

6

Rocking Horse
(11th, 1991)
Handcrafted • SICK
1075QX4147 • **Value $49**

7

Rocking Horse
(12th, 1992)
Handcrafted • SICK
1075QX4261 • **Value $46**

8

Rocking Horse
(13th, 1993)
Handcrafted • SICK
1075QX4162 • **Value $39**

9

Rocking Horse
(14th, 1994)
Handcrafted • SICK
1095QX5016 • **Value $30**

10

Rocking Horse
(15th, 1995)
Handcrafted • SICK
1095QX5167 • **Value $29**

11

Pewter Rocking Horse
(15th Anniversary
Edition, 1995)
Pewter • SICK
2000QX6167 • **Value $41**

12

Rocking Horse
(16th & final, 1996)
Handcrafted • SICK
1095QX5674 • **Value $30**

13

Donald and Daisy in
Venice (1st, 1998)
Handcrafted • LARS
1495QXD4103 • **Value $26**

14

Mickey and Minnie in
Paradise (2nd, 1999)
Handcrafted • N/A
1495QXD4049 • **Value $24**

15
Donald and Daisy at
Lovers' Lodge
(3rd & final, 2000)
Handcrafted • N/A
1495QXD4031 • **Value $21**

16
New!

Safe and Snug
(1st, 2001)
Porcelain • FORS
1295QX8342 • **Value $12.95**

17

Scarlett O'Hara™
(1st, 1997)
Handcrafted • ANDR
1495QX6125 • **Value $32**

18
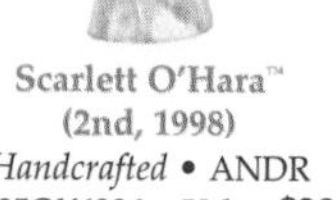
Scarlett O'Hara™
(2nd, 1998)
Handcrafted • ANDR
1495QX6336 • **Value $30**

19

Scarlett O'Hara™
(3rd, 1999)
Handcrafted • ANDR
1495QX6397 • **Value $26**

20

Scarlett O'Hara™
(4th & final, 2000)
Handcrafted • ANDR
1495QX6671 • **Value $22**

	Price Paid	Value
Rocking Horse		
1.		
2.		
3.		
4.		
5.		
6.		
7.		
8.		
9.		
10.		
11.		
12.		
Romantic Vacations		
13.		
14.		
15.		
Safe and Snug		
16.		
Scarlett O'Hara™		
17.		
18.		
19.		
20.		
Totals		

1

The Flight at Kitty Hawk (1st, 1997)
Handcrafted • NORT
1495QX5574 • **Value $33**

2

1917 Curtiss JN-4D "Jenny" (2nd, 1998)
Handcrafted • NORT
1495QX6286 • **Value $30**

3

Curtiss R3C-2 Seaplane (3rd, 1999)
Handcrafted • NORT
1495QX6387 • **Value $27**

4

Spirit of St. Louis (4th, 2000)
Handcrafted • NORT
1495QX6634 • **Value $22**

5

New!
Gee Bee R-1 Super Sportster (5th, 2001)
Handcrafted • NORT
1495QX8005 • **Value $14.95**

6

Ice Hockey Holiday (1st, 1979)
Handcrafted • N/A
800QX1419 • **Value $162**

7

Ski Holiday (2nd, 1980)
Handcrafted • FRAN
900QX1541 • **Value $170**

8

SNOOPY® and Friends (3rd, 1981)
Handcrafted • FRAN
1200QX4362 • **Value $130**

9

SNOOPY® and Friends (4th, 1982)
Handcrafted • SEAL
1300QX4803 • **Value $125**

10

Santa SNOOPY® (5th & final, 1983)
Handcrafted • SICK
1300QX4169 • **Value $97**

11

New!
A Little Nap (1st, 2001)
Handcrafted • ESCH
795QX8072 • **Value $7.95**

12

Snow Buddies (1st, 1998)
Handcrafted • HADD
795QX6853 • **Value $28**

13

Snow Buddies (2nd, 1999)
Handcrafted • HADD
795QX6319 • **Value $22**

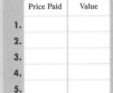

14

Snow Buddies (3rd, 2000)
Handcrafted • HADD
795QX6654 • **Value $18**

15
New!
Snow Buddies (4th, 2001)
Handcrafted • HADD
795QX6972 • **Value $7.95**

16
Joe Cool (1st, 1998)
Handcrafted • SIED
995QX6453 • **Value $24**

17

Famous Flying Ace (2nd, 1999)
Handcrafted • SIED
995QX6409 • **Value $24**

18

The Detective (3rd, 2000)
Handcrafted • SIED
995QX6564 • **Value $20**

19

New!
Beaglescout (4th, 2001)
Handcrafted • SIED
995QX6085 • **Value $9.95**

20

Luke Skywalker™ (1st, 1997)
Handcrafted • RHOD
1395QXI5484 • **Value $33**

	Price Paid	Value
Sky's The Limit		
1.		
2.		
3.		
4.		
5.		
SNOOPY® and Friends		
6.		
7.		
8.		
9.		
10.		
Snowball and Tuxedo		
11.		
Snow Buddies		
12.		
13.		
14.		
15.		
Spotlight on SNOOPY®		
16.		
17.		
18.		
19.		
STAR WARS™		
20.		
Totals		

1

Princess Leia™
(2nd, 1998)
Handcrafted • RHOD
1395QXI4026 • **Value $28**

2

Han Solo™ (3rd, 1999)
Handcrafted • ANDR
1395QXI4007 • **Value $26**

3

Obi-Wan Kenobi™
(4th, 2000)
Handcrafted • RHOD
1495QXI6704 • **Value $22**

4

New!
R2-D2™ (5th, 2001)
Handcrafted • KLIN
1495QX6875 • **Value $14.95**

5

Jeff Gordon (1st, 1997)
Handcrafted • SEAL
1595QXI6165 • **Value $42**

6

Richard Petty (2nd, 1998)
Handcrafted • SEAL
1595QXI4143 • **Value $30**

7

Bill Elliott
(3rd & final, 1999)
Handcrafted • SEAL
1595QXI4039 • **Value $30**

8
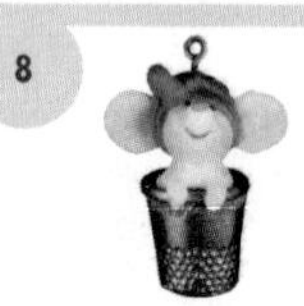
Mouse in a Thimble (1st, 1978, re-issued in 1979)
Handcrafted • N/A
250QX1336 • **Value $300**

9

A Christmas Salute (2nd, 1979, re-issued in 1980)
Handcrafted • N/A
300QX1319 • **Value $180**

10

Mouse in a Thimble
(1979, re-issued from 1978)
Handcrafted • N/A
300QX1336 • **Value $295**

11

Thimble Elf (3rd, 1980)
Handcrafted • N/A
400QX1321 • **Value $185**

12

A Christmas Salute
(1980, re-issued from 1979)
Handcrafted • N/A
400QX1319 • **Value $180**

13

Thimble Angel (4th, 1981)
Handcrafted • N/A
450QX4135 • **Value $158**

14

Thimble Mouse
(5th, 1982)
Handcrafted • N/A
500QX4513 • **Value $78**

15

Thimble Elf (6th, 1983)
Handcrafted • N/A
500QX4017 • **Value $40**

16

Thimble Angel (7th, 1984)
Handcrafted • N/A
500QX4304 • **Value $62**

17

Thimble Santa (8th, 1985)
Handcrafted • SIED
550QX4725 • **Value $38**

18

Thimble Partridge
(9th, 1986)
Handcrafted • N/A
575QX4066 • **Value $27**

19

Thimble Drummer
(10th, 1987)
Handcrafted • SIED
575QX4419 • **Value $30**

20

Thimble Snowman
(11th, 1988)
Handcrafted • SIED
575QX4054 • **Value $26**

	Price Paid	Value
STAR WARS™		
1.		
2.		
3.		
4.		
Stock Car Champions		
5.		
6.		
7.		
Thimble Series		
8.		
9.		
10.		
11.		
12.		
13.		
14.		
15.		
16.		
17.		
18.		
19.		
20.		
Totals		

1

Thimble Puppy
(12th & final, 1989)
Handcrafted • RGRS
575QX4552 • **Value $28**

2

Victorian Christmas
Thomas Kinkade, Painter of Light™ (1st, 1997)
Porcelain • SEAL
1095QXI6135 • **Value $29**

3

Victorian Christmas II,
Thomas Kinkade, Painter of Light™ (2nd, 1998)
Ceramic • N/A
1095QX61343 • **Value $30**

4

Victorian Christmas III
Thomas Kinkade,
Painter of Light™
(3rd & final, 1999)
Ceramic • N/A
1095QX6407 • **Value $23**

5

Tin Locomotive (1st, 1982)
Pressed Tin • SICK
1300QX4603 • **Value $660**

6

Tin Locomotive (2nd, 1983)
Pressed Tin • SICK
1300QX4049 • **Value $295**

7

Tin Locomotive (3rd, 1984)
Pressed Tin • SICK
1400QX4404 • **Value $89**

8

Tin Locomotive (4th, 1985)
Pressed Tin • SICK
1475QX4972 • **Value $84**

9

Tin Locomotive (5th, 1986)
Pressed Tin • SICK
1475QX4036 • **Value $80**

10

Tin Locomotive (6th, 1987)
Pressed Tin • SICK
1475QX4849 • **Value $66**

11

Tin Locomotive (7th, 1988)
Pressed Tin • SICK
1475QX4004 • **Value $55**

12

Tin Locomotive
(8th & final, 1989)
Pressed Tin • SICK
1475QX4602 • **Value $60**

13

Tobin Fraley Carousel
(1st, 1992)
Porcelain/Brass • FRAL
2800QX4891 • **Value $58**

14

Tobin Fraley Carousel
(2nd, 1993)
Porcelain/Brass • FRAL
2800QX5502 • **Value $48**

15
Tobin Fraley Carousel
(3rd, 1994)
Porcelain/Brass • FRAL
2800QX5223 • **Value $59**

16
Tobin Fraley Carousel
(4th & final, 1995)
Porcelain • FRAL
2800QX5069 • **Value $52**

17

Farm House (1st, 1999)
Pressed Tin • SICK
1595QX6439 • **Value $33**

18

Red Barn (complements the series, 1999)
Pressed Tin • SICK
1595QX6947 • **Value $30**

19

Bait Shop With Boat
(2nd, 2000)
Pressed Tin • SICK
1595QX6631 • **Value $23**

20
New!

Fire Station No. 1
(3rd, 2001)
Pressed Tin • SICK
1595QX8052 • **Value $15.95**

	Price Paid	Value
Thimble Series		
1.		
Thomas Kinkade		
2.		
3.		
4.		
Tin Locomotive		
5.		
6.		
7.		
8.		
9.		
10.		
11.		
12.		
Tobin Fraley Carousel		
13.		
14.		
15.		
16.		
Town and Country		
17.		
18.		
19.		
20.		
Totals		

1

Toymaker Santa
(1st, 2000)
Handcrafted • CROW
1495QX6751 • **Value $23**

2
New!

Toymaker Santa
(2nd, 2001)
Handcrafted • CROW
1495QX8032 • **Value $14.95**

3

The Fireman (1st, 1995)
Die-Cast Metal • CROW
1695QK1027 • **Value $42**

4

Uncle Sam (2nd, 1996)
Die-Cast Metal • CROW
1695QK1084 • **Value $33**

5

Santa Claus
(3rd & final, 1997)
Die-Cast Metal • CROW
1695QX1215 • **Value $26**

6

Partridge in a Pear Tree
(1st, 1984)
Acrylic • N/A
600QX3484 • **Value $285**

7

Two Turtle Doves
(2nd, 1985)
Acrylic • PIKE
650QX3712 • **Value $73**

8

Three French Hens
(3rd, 1986)
Acrylic • VOTR
650QX3786 • **Value $49**

9

Four Colly Birds
(4th, 1987)
Acrylic • PIKE
650QX3709 • **Value $39**

10

Five Golden Rings
(5th, 1988)
Acrylic • PIKE
650QX3714 • **Value $29**

11

Six Geese A-Laying
(6th, 1989)
Acrylic • N/A
675QX3812 • **Value $26**

12
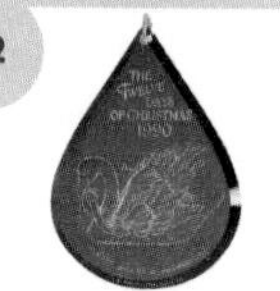
Seven Swans A-Swimming (7th, 1990)
Acrylic • N/A
675QX3033 • **Value $30**

13

Eight Maids A-Milking
(8th, 1991)
Acrylic • N/A
675QX3089 • **Value $30**

14

Nine Ladies Dancing
(9th, 1992)
Acrylic • PYDA
675QX3031 • **Value $25**

15

Ten Lords A-Leaping
(10th, 1993)
Acrylic • CHAD
675QX3012 • **Value $25**

16

Eleven Pipers Piping
(11th, 1994)
Acrylic • N/A
695QX3183 • **Value $19**

17

Twelve Drummers Drumming
(12th & final, 1995)
Acrylic • N/A
695QX3009 • **Value $19**

18

U.S. Christmas Stamps
(1st, 1993)
Enamel/Copper • SICK
1075QX5292 • **Value $30**

19
U.S. Christmas Stamps
(2nd, 1994)
Enamel/Copper • N/A
1095QX5206 • **Value $26**

20

U.S. Christmas Stamps
(3rd & final, 1995)
Enamel/Copper • N/A
1095QX5067 • **Value $23**

	Price Paid	Value
Toymaker Santa		
1.		
2.		
Turn-of-the-Century Parade		
3.		
4.		
5.		
The Twelve Days Of Christmas		
6.		
7.		
8.		
9.		
10.		
11.		
12.		
13.		
14.		
15.		
16.		
17.		
U.S. Christmas Stamps		
18.		
19.		
20.		
Totals		

1

Cruella de Vil
Walt Disney's *101 Dalmatians* (1st, 1998)
Handcrafted • ESCH
1495QXD4063 • **Value $26**

2

Snow White's Jealous Queen (2nd, 1999)
Handcrafted • N/A
1495QXD4089 • **Value $23**

3

Sleeping Beauty's Maleficent
(3rd & final, 2000)
Handcrafted • N/A
1495QXD4001 • **Value $19**

4

Feliz Navidad (1st, 1985)
Handcrafted • DLEE
975QX4902 • **Value $100**

5

Vrolyk Kerstfeest
(2nd, 1986)
Handcrafted • SIED
1000QX4083 • **Value $66**

6

Mele Kalikimaka
(3rd, 1987)
Handcrafted • DLEE
1000QX4827 • **Value $33**

7

Joyeux Noël (4th, 1988)
Handcrafted • DLEE
1000QX4021 • **Value $33**

8

Fröhliche Weihnachten
(5th, 1989)
Handcrafted • DLEE
1075QX4625 • **Value $31**

9

Nollaig Shona
(6th & final, 1990)
Handcrafted • DLEE
1075QX4636 • **Value $28**

10

A Visit From Piglet
(1st, 1998)
Handcrafted • N/A
1395QXD4086 • **Value $27**

11

Honey Time (2nd, 1999)
Handcrafted • N/A
1395QXD4129 • **Value $23**

12
A Blustery Day
(3rd, 2000)
Handcrafted • N/A
1395QXD4021• **Value $20**

13

New!

Tracking The Jaguar
(4th, 2001)
Handcrafted • N/A
1395QXD4132 • **Value $13.95**

14

Playing With Pooh
(1st, 1999)
Handcrafted • N/A
1395QXD4197 • **Value $24**

15

Story Time With Pooh
(2nd, 2000)
Handcrafted • N/A
1395QXD4024 • **Value $24**

16

New!
A Story For Pooh
(3rd & final, 2001)
Handcrafted • N/A
1395QXD4135 • **Value $13.95**

17

Winter Surprise
(1st, 1989)
Handcrafted • FRAN
1075QX4272 • **Value $26**

18

Winter Surprise
(2nd, 1990)
Handcrafted • FRAN
1075QX4443 • **Value $24**

19

Winter Surprise
(3rd, 1991)
Handcrafted • LYLE
1075QX4277 • **Value $29**

20
Winter Surprise
(4th & final, 1992)
Handcrafted • FRAN
1175QX4271 • **Value $28**

	Price Paid	Value
Unforgettable Villains		
1.		
2.		
3.		
Windows of the World		
4.		
5.		
6.		
7.		
8.		
9.		
Winnie the Pooh		
10.		
11.		
12.		
13.		
Winnie the Pooh and Christopher Robin, Too		
14.		
15.		
16.		
Winter Surprise		
17.		
18.		
19.		
20.		
Totals		

1

Wooden Lamb (1st, 1984)
Wood • N/A
650QX4394 • **Value $45**

2

Wooden Train (2nd, 1985)
Wood • DUTK
700QX4722 • **Value $48**

3

Wooden Reindeer (3rd, 1986)
Wood • CROW
750QX4073 • **Value $30**

4

Wooden Horse (4th, 1987)
Wood • SIED
750QX4417 • **Value $27**

5

Wooden Airplane (5th, 1988)
Wood • DUTK
750QX4041 • **Value $24**

6

Wooden Truck (6th & final, 1989)
Wood • N/A
775QX4595 • **Value $20**

7

Yuletide Central (1st, 1994)
Pressed Tin • SICK
1895QX5316 • **Value $55**

8

Yuletide Central (2nd, 1995)
Pressed Tin • SICK
1895QX5079 • **Value $33**

9

Yuletide Central (3rd, 1996)
Pressed Tin • SICK
1895QX5011 • **Value $40**

10

Yuletide Central (4th, 1997)
Pressed Tin • SICK
1895QX5812 • **Value $37**

11

Yuletide Central (5th & final, 1998)
Pressed Tin • SICK
1895QX6373 • **Value $45**

Magic Series

Since 1985, a total of 9 Magic Series have made their way into the Hallmark Keepsake collection. The ornaments in these series, which feature light, sound and motion, continue to delight collectors today. Two series celebrate new editions in 2001, including "Candlelight Services" and "Lighthouse Greetings."

12

The Stone Church (1st, 1998)
Handcrafted • SEAL
1895QLX7636 • **Value $52**

13

Colonial Church (2nd, 1999)
Handcrafted • SEAL
1895QLX7387 • **Value $36**

14

Adobe Church (3rd, 2000)
Handcrafted • SEAL
1895QLX7334 • **Value $28**

15
New!

Candlelight Services (4th, 2001)
Handcrafted • SEAL
1895QLX7552 • **Value $18.95**

Wood Childhood Ornaments

	Price Paid	Value
1.		
2.		
3.		
4.		
5.		
6.		

Yuletide Central

	Price Paid	Value
7.		
8.		
9.		
10.		
11.		

Candlelight Services

	Price Paid	Value
12.		
13.		
14.		
15.		
Totals		

1

Chris Mouse (1st, 1985)
Handcrafted • SIED
1250QLX7032 • **Value $93**

2

Chris Mouse Dreams
(2nd, 1986)
Handcrafted • DUTK
1300QLX7056 • **Value $82**

3

Chris Mouse Glow
(3rd, 1987)
Handcrafted • SIED
1100QLX7057 • **Value $64**

4

Chris Mouse Star
(4th, 1988)
Handcrafted • SIED
875QLX7154 • **Value $63**

5

Chris Mouse Cookout
(5th, 1989)
Handcrafted • RGRS
950QLX7225 • **Value $63**

6

Chris Mouse Wreath
(6th, 1990)
Handcrafted • RGRS
1000QLX7296 • **Value $43**

7
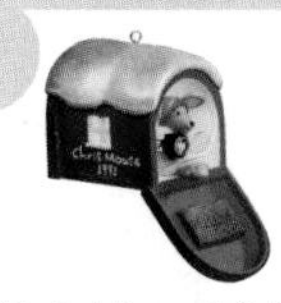
Chris Mouse Mail
(7th, 1991)
Handcrafted • SIED
1000QLX7207 • **Value $41**

8

Chris Mouse Tales
(8th, 1992)
Handcrafted • RGRS
1200QLX7074 • **Value $29**

9

Chris Mouse Flight
(9th, 1993)
Handcrafted • RGRS
1200QLX7152 • **Value $34**

10

Chris Mouse Jelly
(10th, 1994)
Handcrafted • RGRS
1200QLX7393 • **Value $30**

11

Chris Mouse Tree
(11th, 1995)
Handcrafted • RGRS
1250QLX7307 • **Value $29**

12

Chris Mouse Inn
(12th, 1996)
Handcrafted • SIED
1450QLX7371 • **Value $29**

13

Chris Mouse Luminaria
(13th & final, 1997)
Handcrafted • SIED
1495QLX7525 • **Value $29**

14

The Nutcracker Ballet – Sugarplum Fairy
(1st, 1986)
Handcrafted • N/A
1750QLX7043 • **Value $85**

15

A Christmas Carol
(2nd, 1987)
Handcrafted • N/A
1600QLX7029 • **Value $75**

16

Night Before Christmas
(3rd, 1988)
Handcrafted • DLEE
1500QLX7161 • **Value $45**

17
Little Drummer Boy
(4th, 1989)
Handcrafted • DLEE
1350QLX7242 • **Value $44**

18

The Littlest Angel
(5th & final, 1990)
Handcrafted • FRAN
1400QLX7303 • **Value $51**

19

Forest Frolics (1st, 1989)
Handcrafted • PIKE
2450QLX7282 • **Value $92**

20

Forest Frolics (2nd, 1990)
Handcrafted • PIKE
2500QLX7236 • **Value $72**

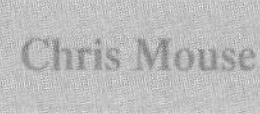

	Price Paid	Value
Chris Mouse		
1.		
2.		
3.		
4.		
5.		
6.		
7.		
8.		
9.		
10.		
11.		
12.		
13.		
Christmas Classics		
14.		
15.		
16.		
17.		
18.		
Forest Frolics		
19.		
20.		
Totals		

1
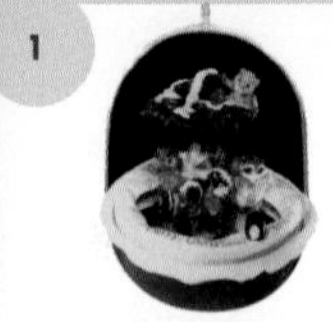
Forest Frolics (3rd, 1991)
Handcrafted • PIKE
2500QLX7219 • **Value $70**

2

Forest Frolics (4th, 1992)
Handcrafted • PIKE
2800QLX7254 • **Value $65**

3

Forest Frolics (5th, 1993)
Handcrafted • PIKE
2500QLX7165 • **Value $55**

4

Forest Frolics (6th, 1994)
Handcrafted • PIKE
2800QLX7436 • **Value $60**

5

Forest Frolics (7th & final, 1995)
Handcrafted • PIKE
2800QLX7299 • **Value $50**

6

Freedom 7 (1st, 1996)
Handcrafted • SEAL
2400QLX7524 • **Value $70**

7

Friendship 7 (2nd, 1997)
Handcrafted • SEAL
2400QLX7532 • **Value $52**

8
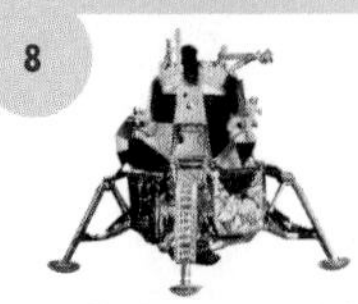
Apollo Lunar Module (3rd, 1998)
Handcrafted • N/A
2400QLX7543 • **Value $48**

9

Lunar Rover Vehicle (4th & final, 1999)
Handcrafted • SEAL
2400QLX7377 • **Value $44**

10

Lighthouse Greetings (1st, 1997)
Handcrafted • FRAN
2400QLX7442 • **Value $76**

11

Lighthouse Greetings (2nd, 1998)
Handcrafted • FRAN
2400QLX7536 • **Value $50**

12

Lighthouse Greetings (3rd, 1999)
Handcrafted • FRAN
2400QLX7379 • **Value $45**

13

Lighthouse Greetings (4th, 2000)
Handcrafted • FRAN
2400QLX7344 • **Value $38**

14

New!
Lighthouse Greetings (5th, 2001)
Handcrafted • FRAN
2400QLX7572 • **Value $24**

15

PEANUTS® (1st, 1991)
Handcrafted • RHOD
1800QLX7229 • **Value $82**

16
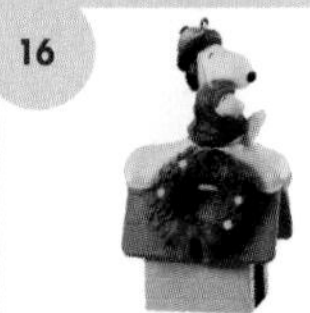
PEANUTS® (2nd, 1992)
Handcrafted • RHOD
1800QLX7214 • **Value $58**

17

PEANUTS® (3rd, 1993)
Handcrafted • RHOD
1800QLX7155 • **Value $50**

18

PEANUTS® (4th, 1994)
Handcrafted • RHOD
2000QLX7406 • **Value $46**

19

PEANUTS® (5th & final, 1995)
Handcrafted • RHOD
2450QLX7277 • **Value $50**

	Price Paid	Value
Forest Frolics		
1.		
2.		
3.		
4.		
5.		
Journeys Into Space		
6.		
7.		
8.		
9.		
Lighthouse Greetings		
10.		
11.		
12.		
13.		
14.		
PEANUTS®		
15.		
16.		
17.		
18.		
19.		
Totals		

1

Lighting the Tree
(1st, 1986)
Handcrafted • N/A
2200QLX7033 • **Value $102**

2

Perfect Portrait
(2nd, 1987)
Handcrafted • N/A
1950QLX7019 • **Value $72**

3

On With the Show
(3rd & final, 1988)
Handcrafted • DLEE
1950QLX7191 • **Value $45**

4

Tobin Fraley Holiday Carousel (1st, 1994)
Handcrafted • UNRU
3200QLX7496 • **Value $70**

5

Tobin Fraley Holiday Carousel (2nd, 1995)
Handcrafted • FRAL
3200QLX7269 • **Value $60**

6

Tobin Fraley Holiday Carousel
(3rd & final, 1996)
Handcrafted • FRAN
3200QLX7461 • **Value $52**

Crown Reflections

Introduced by Hallmark in 1998, the Crown Reflections series was formed to recreate the beauty of traditional, blown glass ornaments of yesteryear. The "Holiday Traditions" series ran from 1998 through 2000, giving collectors a total of 5 beautiful blown glass ornaments.

7

Red Poinsettias
(1st, 1998)
Blown Glass • N/A
3500QBG6906 • **Value $47**

8

Pink Poinsettias (complements the series, 1998)
Blown Glass • N/A
2500QBG6926 • **Value $38**

9

White Poinsettias (complements the series, 1998)
Blown Glass • N/A
2500QBG6923 • **Value $38**

10

Festival of Fruit
(2nd, 1999)
Handcrafted • N/A
3500QBG6069 • **Value $37**

11

Christmas Rose
(3rd & final, 2000)
Blown Glass • N/A
3500QBG4054 • **Value $36**

Santa and Sparky

	Price Paid	Value
1.		
2.		
3.		

Tobin Fraley Holiday Carousel

	Price Paid	Value
4.		
5.		
6.		

Holiday Traditions

	Price Paid	Value
7.		
8.		
9.		
10.		
11.		
Totals		

Miniature Series

2001 saw the debut of one miniature series ("Sky's The Limit") as well as the retirement of six well-loved favorites as "Holiday Flurries," "LIONEL® Norfolk and Western," "Miniature Kiddie Car Luxury Edition," "The Nativity," "Seaside Scenes" and "The Wonders of Oz™" all saw their final editions.

1

Alice in Wonderland
(1st, 1995)
Handcrafted • ANDR
675QXM4777 • **Value $17**

2

Mad Hatter (2nd, 1996)
Handcrafted • ANDR
675QXM4074 • **Value $16**

3

White Rabbit (3rd, 1997)
Handcrafted • ANDR
695QXM4142 • **Value $15**

4

Cheshire Cat
(4th & final, 1998)
Handcrafted • ANDR
695QXM4186 • **Value $14**

5

Antique Tractors
(1st, 1997)
Die-Cast Metal • SICK
695QXM4185 • **Value $22**

6

Antique Tractors
(2nd, 1998)
Die-Cast Metal • SICK
695QXM4166 • **Value $17**

7

Antique Tractors
(3rd, 1999)
Die-Cast Metal • SICK
695QXM4567 • **Value $15**

8

Antique Tractors
(4th, 2000)
Die-Cast Metal • SICK
695QXM5994 • **Value $13**

9

Antique Tractors
(5th, 2001)
Die-Cast Metal • SICK
695QXM5252 • **Value $6.95**

10

The Bearymores
(1st, 1992)
Handcrafted • RGRS
575QXM5544 • **Value $20**

11

The Bearymores
(2nd, 1993)
Handcrafted • RGRS
575QXM5125 • **Value $18**

12

The Bearymores
(3rd & final, 1994)
Handcrafted • RGRS
575QXM5133 • **Value $16**

13

Centuries of Santa
(1st, 1994)
Handcrafted • SICK
600QXM5153 • **Value $28**

14

Centuries of Santa
(2nd, 1995)
Handcrafted • SICK
575QXM4789 • **Value $20**

15

Centuries of Santa
(3rd, 1996)
Handcrafted • SICK
575QXM4091 • **Value $16**

16

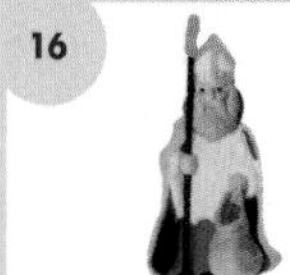

Centuries of Santa
(4th, 1997)
Handcrafted • SICK
595QXM4295 • **Value $13**

	Price Paid	Value
Alice In Wonderland		
1.		
2.		
3.		
4.		
Antique Tractors		
5.		
6.		
7.		
8.		
9.		
The Bearymores		
10.		
11.		
12.		
Centuries Of Santa		
13.		
14.		
15.		
16.		
Totals		

1

Centuries of Santa
(5th, 1998)
Handcrafted • SICK
595QXM4206 • **Value $13**

2

Centuries of Santa
(6th & final, 1999)
Handcrafted • SICK
595QXM4589 • **Value $13**

3

Christmas Bells
(1st, 1995)
Handcrafted/Metal • SEAL
475QXM4007 • **Value $24**

4

Christmas Bells
(2nd, 1996)
Handcrafted/Metal • SEAL
475QXM4071 • **Value $17**

5

Christmas Bells
(3rd, 1997)
Handcrafted/Metal • SEAL
495QXM4162 • **Value $16**

6

Christmas Bells
(4th, 1998)
Handcrafted/Metal • SEAL
495QXM4196 • **Value $13**

7

Christmas Bells
(5th, 1999)
Handcrafted/Metal • SEAL
495QXM4489 • **Value $12**

8

Christmas Bells
(6th, 2000)
Handcrafted/Metal • SEAL
495QXM5964 • **Value $10**

9
New!

Christmas Bells
(7th, 2001)
Handcrafted/Metal • SEAL
495QXM5245 • **Value $4.95**

10

Holiday Flurries
(1st, 1999)
Handcrafted • SICK
695QXM4547 • **Value $16**

11

Holiday Flurries
(2nd, 2000)
Handcrafted • SICK
695QXM5311 • **Value $13**

12
New!

Holiday Flurries
(3rd & final, 2001)
Handcrafted • SICK
695QXM5272 • **Value $6.95**

13

Ice Block Buddies
(1st, 2000)
Handcrafted • SICK
595QXM6011 • **Value $11**

14
New!

Ice Block Buddies
(2nd, 2001)
Handcrafted • SICK
595QXM5295 • **Value $5.95**

15

Kittens in Toyland
(1st, 1988)
Handcrafted • CROW
500QXM5621 • **Value $25**

16

Kittens in Toyland
(2nd, 1989)
Handcrafted • CROW
450QXM5612 • **Value $20**

17
Kittens in Toyland
(3rd, 1990)
Handcrafted • CROW
450QXM5736 • **Value $19**

18
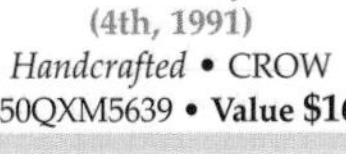
Kittens in Toyland
(4th, 1991)
Handcrafted • CROW
450QXM5639 • **Value $16**

19

Kittens in Toyland
(5th & final, 1992)
Handcrafted • CROW
450QXM5391 • **Value $17**

	Price Paid	Value
Centuries Of Santa		
1.		
2.		
Christmas Bells		
3.		
4.		
5.		
6.		
7.		
8.		
9.		
Holiday Flurries		
10.		
11.		
12.		
Ice Block Buddies		
13.		
14.		
Kittens In Toyland		
15.		
16.		
17.		
18.		
19.		
Totals		

1

The Kringles (1st, 1989)
Handcrafted • RGRS
600QXM5625 • **Value $28**

2

The Kringles (2nd, 1990)
Handcrafted • RGRS
600QXM5753 • **Value $24**

3

The Kringles (3rd, 1991)
Handcrafted • RGRS
600QXM5647 • **Value $26**

4

The Kringles (4th, 1992)
Handcrafted • RGRS
600QXM5381 • **Value $20**

5

The Kringles
(5th & final, 1993)
Handcrafted • RGRS
575QXM5135 • **Value $17**

6

Locomotive and Tender
(1st, 1999, set/2)
Die-Cast Metal • SEAL
1095QXM4549 • **Value $23**

7

Horse Car and Milk Car
(2nd, 2000, set/2,)
Die-Cast Metal • SEAL
1295QXM5971 • **Value $19**

8
New!

Car Carrier and Caboose
(3rd & final, 2001, set/2)
Die-Cast Metal • N/A
1295QXM5265 • **Value $12.95**

9

March of the Teddy Bears (1st, 1993)
Handcrafted • UNRU
450QXM4005 • **Value $20**

10

March of the Teddy Bears (2nd, 1994)
Handcrafted • UNRU
450QXM5106 • **Value $18**

11

March of the Teddy Bears (3rd, 1995)
Handcrafted • UNRU
475QXM4799 • **Value $15**

12

March of the Teddy Bears (4th & final, 1996)
Handcrafted • UNRU
475QXM4094 • **Value $13**

13

Miniature Clothespin Soldier (1st, 1995)
Handcrafted • SICK
375QXM4097 • **Value $18**

14

Miniature Clothespin Soldier (2nd, 1996)
Handcrafted • SICK
475QXM4144 • **Value $14**

15

Miniature Clothespin Soldier (3rd, 1997)
Handcrafted • SICK
495QXM4155 • **Value $12**

16

Miniature Clothespin Soldier (4th, 1998)
Handcrafted • SICK
495QXM4193 • **Value $11**

17

Miniature Clothespin Soldier (5th, 1999)
Handcrafted • SICK
495QXM4579 • **Value $11**

18

Sailor (6th & final, 2000)
Handcrafted • SICK
495QXM5334 • **Value $10**

19

Electra-Glide®
(1st, 1999)
Die-Cast Metal • PALM
795QXI6137 • **Value $20**

20

1962 Duo-Glide™
(2nd, 2000)
Die-Cast Metal • PALM
795QXI6001 • **Value $15**

The Kringles

	Price Paid	Value
1.		
2.		
3.		
4.		
5.		

LIONEL® Norfolk and Western

	Price Paid	Value
6.		
7.		
8.		

March of the Teddy Bears

	Price Paid	Value
9.		
10.		
11.		
12.		

Miniature Clothespin Soldier

	Price Paid	Value
13.		
14.		
15.		
16.		
17.		
18.		

Miniature Harley-Davidson® Motorcycle

	Price Paid	Value
19.		
20.		
Totals		

1

1947 Servi-Car™
(3rd, 2001)
Die-Cast Metal • PALM
795QXI5282 • **Value $7.95**

2

Murray® "Champion"
(1st, 1995)
Die-Cast Metal • PALM
575QXM4079 • **Value $20**

3

Murray® "Fire Truck"
(2nd, 1996)
Die-Cast Metal • PALM
675QXM4031 • **Value $18**

4

Murray Inc.® "Pursuit"
Airplane (3rd, 1997)
Die-Cast Metal • PALM
695QXM4132 • **Value $15**

5

Murray Inc.® Dump
Truck (4th, 1998)
Die-Cast Metal • PALM
695QXM4183 • **Value $15**

6

1955 Murray® Tractor
and Trailer (5th, 1999)
Die-Cast Metal • PALM
695QXM4479 • **Value $14**

7

1968 Murray® Jolly
Roger Flagship
(6th, 2000)
Die-Cast Metal • WEBB
695QXM5944 • **Value $12**

8

1924 Toledo Fire
Engine #6 (7th, 2001)
Die-Cast Metal • WEBB
695QXM5192 • **Value $6.95**

9

1937 Steelcraft Auburn
(1st, 1998)
Die-Cast Metal • PALM
695QXM4143 • **Value $17**

10

1937 Steelcraft Airflow
by Murray® (2nd, 1999)
Die-Cast Metal • PALM
695QXM4477 • **Value $15**

11

1935 Steelcraft by
Murray® (3rd, 2000)
Die-Cast Metal • WEBB
695QXM5951 • **Value $13**

12

New!

1937 Garton® Ford
(4th & final, 2001)
Die-Cast Metal • WEBB
695QXM5195 • **Value $6.95**

13

Sack of Money
(1st, 2000)
Pewter • PIKE
895QXM5341 • **Value $16**

14

Race Car (2nd, 2001)
Pewter • PIKE
895QXM5292 • **Value $8.95**

15

The Nativity (1st, 1998)
Pewter • UNRU
995QXM4156 • **Value $28**

16

The Nativity (2nd, 1999)
Pewter • UNRU
995QXM4497 • **Value $23**

17

The Nativity (3rd, 2000)
Pewter • UNRU
995QXM5961 • **Value $18**

18

The Nativity
(4th & final, 2001)
Pewter • UNRU
995QXM5255 • **Value $9.95**

19

Nature's Angels
(1st, 1990)
Handcrafted/Brass • SEAL
450QXM5733 • **Value $26**

20

Nature's Angels
(2nd, 1991)
Handcrafted/Brass • PIKE
450QXM5657 • **Value $23**

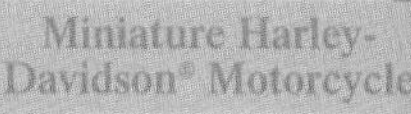

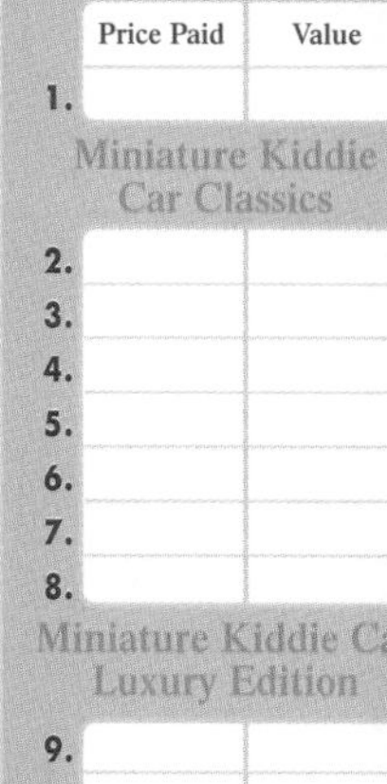

Miniature Harley-Davidson® Motorcycle

	Price Paid	Value
1.		

Miniature Kiddie Car Classics

	Price Paid	Value
2.		
3.		
4.		
5.		
6.		
7.		
8.		

Miniature Kiddie Car Luxury Edition

	Price Paid	Value
9.		
10.		
11.		
12.		

MONOPOLY® Game: Advance to Go!

	Price Paid	Value
13.		
14.		

The Nativity

	Price Paid	Value
15.		
16.		
17.		
18.		

Nature's Angels

	Price Paid	Value
19.		
20.		

Price Paid	Value

Totals

1

Nature's Angels
(3rd, 1992)
Handcrafted/Brass • PIKE
450QXM5451 • **Value $21**

2

Nature's Angels
(4th, 1993)
Handcrafted/Brass • ANDR
450QXM5122 • **Value $19**

3

Nature's Angels
(5th, 1994)
Handcrafted/Brass • VOTR
450QXM5126 • **Value $14**

4

Nature's Angels
(6th, 1995)
Handcrafted/Brass • ANDR
475QXM4809 • **Value $17**

5

Nature's Angels
(7th & final, 1996)
Handcrafted/Brass • PIKE
475QXM4111 • **Value $13**

6

The Night Before
Christmas (1st, 1992,
w/display house)
Handcrafted • UNRU
1375QXM5541 • **Value $32**

7

The Night Before
Christmas (2nd, 1993)
Handcrafted • UNRU
450QXM5115 • **Value $20**

8

The Night Before
Christmas (3rd, 1994)
Handcrafted • UNRU
450QXM5123 • **Value $15**

9

The Night Before
Christmas (4th, 1995)
Handcrafted • UNRU
475QXM4807 • **Value $19**

10

The Night Before
Christmas
(5th & final, 1996)
Handcrafted • UNRU
575QXM4104 • **Value $14**

11

Locomotive (1st, 1989)
Handcrafted • SICK
850QXM5762 • **Value $46**

12

Coal Car (2nd, 1990)
Handcrafted • SICK
850QXM5756 • **Value $35**

13

Passenger Car
(3rd, 1991)
Handcrafted • SICK
850QXM5649 • **Value $52**

14

Box Car (4th, 1992)
Handcrafted • SICK
700QXM5441 • **Value $30**

15

Flatbed Car (5th, 1993)
Handcrafted • SICK
700QXM5105 • **Value $28**

16

Stock Car (6th, 1994)
Handcrafted • SICK
700QXM5113 • **Value $23**

17

Milk Tank Car
(7th, 1995)
Handcrafted • SICK
675QXM4817 • **Value $19**

18

Cookie Car (8th, 1996)
Handcrafted • SICK
675QXM4114 • **Value $18**

19

Candy Car (9th, 1997)
Handcrafted • SICK
695QXM4175 • **Value $15**

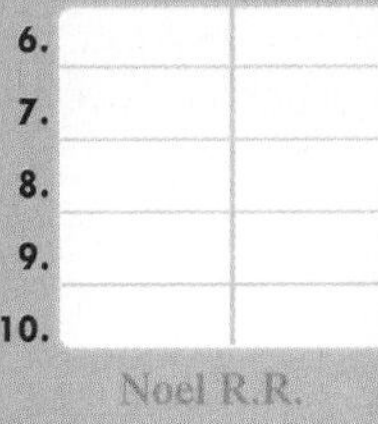

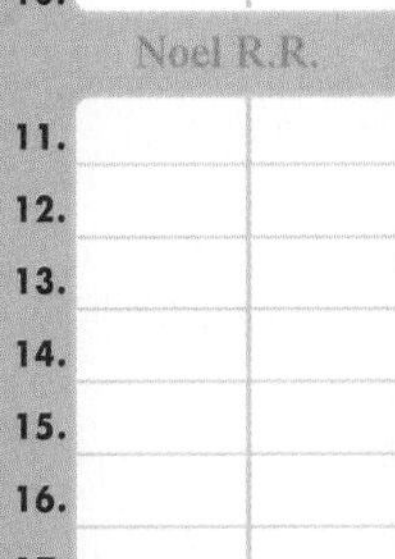

	Price Paid	Value
Nature's Angels		
1.		
2.		
3.		
4.		
5.		
The Night Before Christmas		
6.		
7.		
8.		
9.		
10.		
Noel R.R.		
11.		
12.		
13.		
14.		
15.		
16.		
17.		
18.		
19.		
Totals		

1

Caboose
(10th & final, 1998)
Handcrafted • SICK
695QXM4216 • **Value $15**

2

Noel R.R. Locomotive 1989-1998 (Anniversary Edition, 1998)
Pewter • SICK
1095QXM4286 • **Value $21**

3

The Nutcracker Ballet
(1st, 1996, w/display stage)
Handcrafted • VOTR
1475QXM4064 • **Value $29**

4

Herr Drosselmeyer
(2nd, 1997)
Handcrafted • VOTR
595QXM4135 • **Value $14**

5

Nutcracker (3rd, 1998)
Handcrafted • VOTR
595QXM4146 • **Value $17**

6

Mouse King (4th, 1999)
Handcrafted • VOTR
595QXM4487 • **Value $16**

7

Sugarplum Fairy
(5th & final, 2000)
Handcrafted • VOTR
595QXM5984 • **Value $12**

8

Nutcracker Guild
(1st, 1994)
Handcrafted • SICK
575QXM5146 • **Value $23**

9

Nutcracker Guild
(2nd, 1995)
Handcrafted • SICK
575QXM4787 • **Value $18**

10

Nutcracker Guild
(3rd, 1996)
Handcrafted • SICK
575QXM4084 • **Value $16**

11

Nutcracker Guild
(4th, 1997)
Handcrafted • SICK
695QXM4165 • **Value $15**

12

Nutcracker Guild
(5th, 1998)
Handcrafted • SICK
695QXM4203 • **Value $15**

13

Nutcracker Guild
(6th, 1999)
Handcrafted • SICK
695QXM4587 • **Value $14**

14

Nutcracker Guild
(7th & final, 2000)
Handcrafted • SICK
695QXM5991 • **Value $13**

15

Family Home (1st, 1988)
Handcrafted • DLEE
850QXM5634 • **Value $45**

16

Sweet Shop (2nd, 1989)
Handcrafted • JLEE
850QXM5615 • **Value $29**

17

School (3rd, 1990)
Handcrafted • JLEE
850QXM5763 • **Value $25**

18

Inn (4th, 1991)
Handcrafted • JLEE
850QXM5627 • **Value $30**

19

Church (5th, 1992)
Handcrafted • JLEE
700QXM5384 • **Value $36**

20

Toy Shop (6th, 1993)
Handcrafted • JLEE
700QXM5132 • **Value $21**

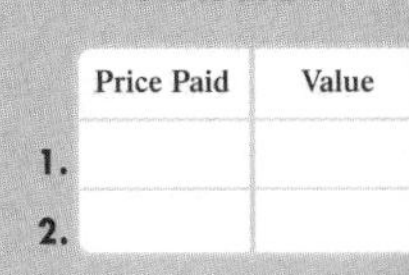

	Price Paid	Value
Noel R.R.		
1.		
2.		
The Nutcracker Ballet		
3.		
4.		
5.		
6.		
7.		
Nutcracker Guild		
8.		
9.		
10.		
11.		
12.		
13.		
14.		
Old English Village		
15.		
16.		
17.		
18.		
19.		
20.		
Totals		

1

Hat Shop (7th, 1994)
Handcrafted • ANDR
700QXM5143 • **Value $20**

2

Tudor House (8th, 1995)
Handcrafted • JLEE
675QXM4819 • **Value $18**

3

Village Mill (9th, 1996)
Handcrafted • RHOD
675QXM4124 • **Value $16**

4

Village Depot
(10th & final, 1996)
Handcrafted • LARS
695QXM4182 • **Value $15**

5

On the Road (1st, 1993)
Pressed Tin • SICK
575QXM4002 • **Value $21**

6

On the Road (2nd, 1994)
Pressed Tin • SICK
575QXM5103 • **Value $18**

7

On the Road (3rd, 1995)
Pressed Tin • SICK
575QXM4797 • **Value $17**

8

On the Road (4th, 1996)
Pressed Tin • SICK
575QXM4101 • **Value $14**

9

On the Road (5th, 1997)
Pressed Tin • SICK
595QXM4172 • **Value $13**

10

On the Road
(6th & final, 1998)
Pressed Tin • SICK
595QXM4213 • **Value $12**

11

Penguin Pal (1st, 1988)
Handcrafted • SIED
375QXM5631 • **Value $27**

12

Penguin Pal (2nd, 1989)
Handcrafted • N/A
450QXM5602 • **Value $21**

13

Penguin Pal (3rd, 1990)
Handcrafted • N/A
450QXM5746 • **Value $19**

14

Penguin Pal
(4th & final, 1991)
Handcrafted • SIED
450QXM5629 • **Value $17**

15

Rocking Horse
(1st, 1988)
Handcrafted • SICK
450QXM5624 • **Value $47**

16

Rocking Horse
(2nd, 1989)
Handcrafted • SICK
450QXM5605 • **Value $33**

17

Rocking Horse
(3rd, 1990)
Handcrafted • SICK
450QXM5743 • **Value $29**

18

Rocking Horse
(4th, 1991)
Handcrafted • SICK
450QXM5637 • **Value $29**

19

Rocking Horse
(5th, 1992)
Handcrafted • SICK
450QXM5454 • **Value $24**

	Price Paid	Value
Old English Village		
1.		
2.		
3.		
4.		
On the Road		
5.		
6.		
7.		
8.		
9.		
10.		
Penguin Pal		
11.		
12.		
13.		
14.		
Rocking Horse		
15.		
16.		
17.		
18.		
19.		
Totals		

1

Rocking Horse
(6th, 1993)
Handcrafted • SICK
450QXM5112 • **Value $20**

2

Rocking Horse
(7th, 1994)
Handcrafted • SICK
450QXM5116 • **Value $19**

3

Rocking Horse
(8th, 1995)
Handcrafted • SICK
450QXM4827 • **Value $16**

4

Rocking Horse
(9th, 1996)
Handcrafted • SICK
475QXM4121 • **Value $15**

5

Rocking Horse
(10th & final, 1997)
Handcrafted • SICK
495QXM4302 • **Value $13**

6

Santa's Little Big Top
(1st, 1995)
Handcrafted • CROW
675QXM4779 • **Value $20**

7

Santa's Little Big Top
(2nd, 1996)
Handcrafted • CROW
675QXM4081 • **Value $15**

8

Santa's Little Big Top
(3rd & final, 1997)
Handcrafted • CROW
695QXM4152 • **Value $15**

9

Seaside Scenes
(1st, 1999)
Handcrafted • SEAL
795QXM4649 • **Value $19**

10

Seaside Scenes
(2nd, 2000)
Handcrafted • SEAL
795QXM5974 • **Value $16**

11
New!

Seaside Scenes
(3rd & final, 2001)
Handcrafted • SEAL
795QXM5275 • **Value $7.95**

12
New!

The Flight at Kitty Hawk (1st, 2001)
Handcrafted • NORT
695QXM5215 • **Value $6.95**

13

Snowflake Ballet
(1st, 1997)
Handcrafted • ANDR
595QXM4192 • **Value $19**

14

Snowflake Ballet
(2nd, 1998)
Handcrafted • ANDR
595QXM4173 • **Value $15**

15
Snowflake Ballet
(3rd & final, 1999)
Handcrafted • ANDR
595QXM4569 • **Value $13**

16

Teddy-Bear Style
(1st, 1997)
Handcrafted • UNRU
595QXM4215 • **Value $15**

17
Teddy-Bear Style
(2nd, 1998)
Handcrafted • UNRU
595QXM4176 • **Value $13**

18

Teddy-Bear Style
(3rd, 1999)
Handcrafted • UNRU
595QXM4499 • **Value $13**

19
Teddy-Bear Style
(4th & final, 2000)
Handcrafted • UNRU
595QXM5954 • **Value $11**

	Price Paid	Value
Rocking Horse		
1.		
2.		
3.		
4.		
5.		
Santa's Little Big Top		
6.		
7.		
8.		
Seaside Scenes		
9.		
10.		
11.		
Sky's the Limit		
12.		
Snowflake Ballet		
13.		
14.		
15.		
Teddy-Bear Style		
16.		
17.		
18.		
19.		
Totals		

1
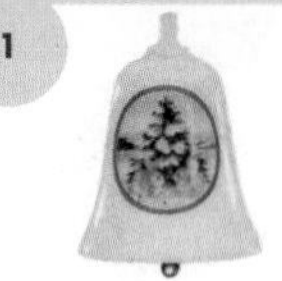
Thimble Bells
(1st, 1990)
Porcelain • PYDA
600QXM5543 • **Value $21**

2

Thimble Bells
(2nd, 1991)
Porcelain • PYDA
600QXM5659 • **Value $21**

3
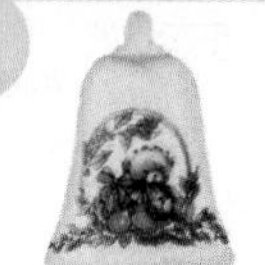
Thimble Bells
(3rd, 1992)
Porcelain • LYLE
600QXM5461 • **Value $21**

4

Thimble Bells
(4th & final, 1993)
Porcelain • VOTR
575QXM5142 • **Value $15**

5

Welcome Friends
(1st, 1997)
Handcrafted • PIKE
695QXM4205 • **Value $17**

6

Welcome Friends
(2nd, 1998)
Handcrafted • PIKE
695QXM4153 • **Value $15**

7

Welcome Friends
(3rd & final, 1999)
Handcrafted • PIKE
695QXM4577 • **Value $14**

8

Winter Fun With
SNOOPY® (1st, 1998)
Handcrafted • LARS
695QXM4243 • **Value $16**

9

Winter Fun With
SNOOPY® (2nd, 1999)
Handcrafted • LARS
695QXM4559 • **Value $17**

10

Winter Fun With
SNOOPY® (3rd, 2000)
Handcrafted • LARS
695QXM5324 • **Value $13**

11

Winter Fun with
SNOOPY® (4th, 2001)
Handcrafted • LARS
695QXM5262 • **Value $6.95**

12

Dorothy's Ruby Slippers
(1st, 1999)
Handcrafted • KLIN
595QXM4599 • **Value $39**

13

The Tin Man's Heart
(2nd, 2000)
Handcrafted • RGRS
595QXM5981 • **Value $20**

14

Toto
(3rd & final, 2001)
Handcrafted • LYLE
595QXM5285 • **Value $5.95**

15

Woodland Babies
(1st, 1991)
Handcrafted • CROW
600QXM5667 • **Value $24**

16

Woodland Babies
(2nd, 1992)
Handcrafted • PALM
600QXM5444 • **Value $16**

17

Woodland Babies
(3rd & final, 1993)
Handcrafted • FRAN
575QXM5102 • **Value $15**

	Price Paid	Value
Thimble Bells		
1.		
2.		
3.		
4.		
Welcome Friends		
5.		
6.		
7.		
Winter Fun With SNOOPY®		
8.		
9.		
10.		
11.		
The Wonders of Oz™		
12.		
13.		
14.		
Woodland Babies		
15.		
16.		
17.		
Totals		

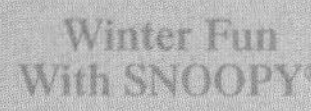

2001

The ornament releases for 2001 are a delightful mix of old and new, with ornament replicas of everything from antique toys and brand new automobiles. Collectors will be thrilled with even more additions to the pop culture ornament lines such as Star Trek™ and The Wizard of Oz™. See the collectible series section for more 2001 ornaments.

1

1950s BARBIE™ Ornament
Handcrafted • ANDR
1495QXI8882 • **Value $14.95**

2

1961 BARBIE™ Hatbox Case
Vinyl • N/A
995QX6922 • **Value $9.95**

3

1968 Silhouette™ and Case (set/2)
Handcrafted • WEBB
1495QX6605 • **Value $14.95**

4

2001 Jeep™ Sport Wrangler
Die-Cast Metal • WEBB
1495QXI6362 • **Value $14.95**

5

2001 Time Capsule
Handcrafted • VISK
995QX2802 • **Value $9.95**

6

2001 Vacation
Handcrafted • WEBB
995QX2822• **Value $9.95**

7

All-Sport Santa
Handcrafted • RHOD
995QX8332 • **Value $9.95**

8

All-Star Kid Memory Keeper Ornament
Handcrafted • VOTR
995QX2805 • **Value $9.95**

9

America for Me!
Handcrafted • FORS
995QX2882 • **Value $9.95**

10

Anakin Skywalker™
Handcrafted • ANDR
1495QX6942 • **Value $14.95**

11

Angel of Faith
Porcelain • LYLE
1495QXI5375 • **Value $14.95**

12

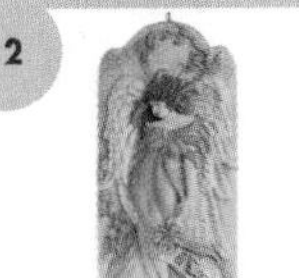

Angel's Whisper
Porcelain • LYLE
995QX8852 • **Value $9.95**

13

Baby Boy's First Christmas
Handcrafted • HADD
895QX8365 • **Value $8.95**

14

Baby Girl's First Christmas
Handcrafted • HADD
895QX8372 • **Value $8.95**

15

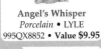

Baby's First Christmas
Handcrafted • FRAN
795QX8375 • **Value $7.95**

16

Baby's First Christmas
Handcrafted • AUBE
895QX8355 • **Value $8.95**

General Keepsake

	Price Paid	Value
1.		
2.		
3.		
4.		
5.		
6.		
7.		
8.		
9.		
10.		
11.		
12.		
13.		
14.		
15.		
16.		
Totals		

1

Baby's First Christmas
Porcelain • HADD
895QX8362 • **Value $8.95**

2

Baby's First Christmas BABY LOONEY TUNES
Porcelain • RGRS
995QX8482 • **Value $9.95**

3

Baby's Second Christmas
Handcrafted • FRAN
795QX8382 • **Value $7.95**

4

BARBIE™ and KELLY™ on the Ice Ornament
Handcrafted • BRIC
1595QXI6915 • **Value $15.95**

5

BARBIE™ Angel Ornament (set/2)
Handcrafted • RGRS
1595QXI6925 • **Value $15.95**

6

BARBIE™ as the Sugar Plum Princess Ornament (set/2)
Handcrafted/Fabric • ANDR
1595QXI6132 • **Value $15.95**

7

Beautiful Cross
Pewter • UNRU
995QX8825 • **Value $9.95**

8

Beginning Ballet
Handcrafted • AUBE
1295QX2875 • **Value $12.95**

9

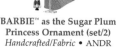

Bell-Ringing Santa-Mickey Mouse
Handcrafted • N/A
995QXD4125 • **Value $9.95**

10

Blue and Periwinkle Blue's Clues™
Handcrafted • KLIN
995QXI6142 • **Value $9.95**

11

Captain Benjamin Sisko™ STAR TREK: Deep Space Nine
Handcrafted • NORT
1495QX6865 • **Value $14.95**

12

Carving Santa
Handcrafted • LARS
1295QX8265 • **Value $12.95**

13

Child's Fifth Christmas
Handcrafted • CROW
795QX8582 • **Value $7.95**

14

Child's Fourth Christmas
Handcrafted • FRAN
795QX8392 • **Value $7.95**

15

Child's Third Christmas
Handcrafted • FRAN
795QX8385 • **Value $7.95**

16

Christmas Brings Us Together
Ceramic • LARS
995QX8285 • **Value $9.95**

General Keepsake

	Price Paid	Value
1.		
2.		
3.		
4.		
5.		
6.		
7.		
8.		
9.		
10.		
11.		
12.		
13.		
14.		
15.		
16.		
Totals		

1
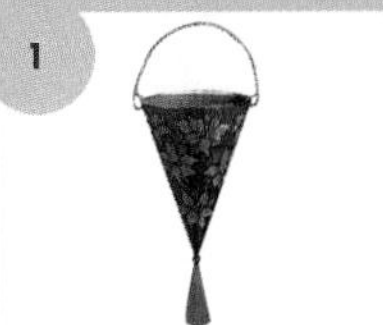
The Christmas Cone
Pressed Tin • SICK
895QX8875 • **Value $8.95**

2

Christmas Parrot
Handcrafted • VISK
895QX8175 • **Value $8.95**

3

Cinderella's Castle
Handcrafted • N/A
1800QXD4172 • **Value $18**

4

Color Crew Chief CRAYOLA® Crayon
Handcrafted • TAGU
1095QX6185 • **Value $10.95**

5

Cozy Home
Porcelain • VOTR
995QX8965 • **Value $9.95**

6

Creative Cutter – Cooking for Christmas
Handcrafted • ESCH
995QX8865 • **Value $9.95**

7

A Cup of Friendship
Handcrafted • CHAD
895QX8472 • **Value $8.95**

8

Dad
Handcrafted • SICK
895QX8422 • **Value $8.95**

9

Photo Unavailable
Dale Jarrett
Handcrafted • WEBB
1495QXI5205 • **Value $14.95**

10

Daughter
Handcrafted • SICK
895QX8425 • **Value $8.95**

11

Disney's School Bus (set/2)
Pressed Tin/Handcrafted • N/A
1495QXD4115 • **Value $14.95**

12

Donald Goes Motoring
Handcrafted/Metal • N/A
1295QXD4122 • **Value $12.95**

13

Eeyore Helps Out
Handcrafted • N/A
1295QXD4145 • **Value $12.95**

14

Eye of God – Feliz Navidad
Handcrafted • FORS
995QX8185 • **Value $9.95**

15

A Familiar Face
Handcrafted • N/A
1295QXD4152 • **Value $12.95**

16

Fluffy™ on Guard
Handcrafted • BRIC
1295QXE4415 • **Value $12.95**

17

Flying School Airplane Hangar
Pressed Tin • SICK
1595QX8172 • **Value $15.95**

18

Four-Alarm Friends
Handcrafted/Metal • HADD
995QX8325 • **Value $9.95**

19

Friendly Elves (set/2)
Handcrafted • FORS
1495QX8805 • **Value $14.95**

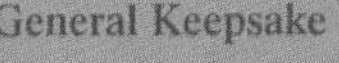

General Keepsake

	Price Paid	Value
1.		
2.		
3.		
4.		
5.		
6.		
7.		
8.		
9.		
10.		
11.		
12.		
13.		
14.		
15.		
16.		
17.		
18.		
19.		
Totals		

1

G.I. Joe® Fighter Pilot
Handcrafted • CROW
1395QX6045 • **Value $13.95**

2

Godchild
Porcelain • TAGU
795QX8452 • **Value $7.95**

3

Gouda Reading
Handcrafted • KLIN
995QX2855 • **Value $9.95**

4

Graceful Angel Bell
Porcelain • VOTR
995QX8182 • **Value $9.95**

5
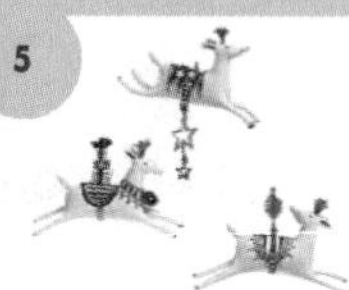
Graceful Reindeer (set/3)
Porcelain • KLIN
1595QX8912 • **Value $15.95**

6
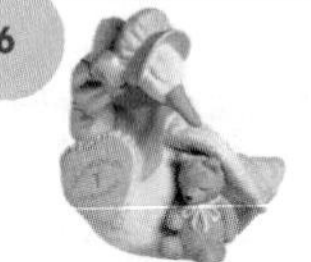
Grandchild's First Christmas
Porcelain • VOTR
895QX8485 • **Value $8.95**

7

Granddaughter
Handcrafted • PIKE
895QX8435 • **Value $8.95**

8

Grandmother
Porcelain • PIKE
995QX8445 • **Value $9.95**

9

Grandson
Handcrafted • PIKE
895QX8442 • **Value $8.95**

10

Guiding Star
Pewter • VISK
995QX8962 • **Value $9.95**

11

Hagrid™ and Norbert™ the Dragon
Handcrafted • FORS
1595QXE4412 • **Value $15.95**

12

Happy Snowmen
Paper • N/A
895QX8942 • **Value $8.95**

13
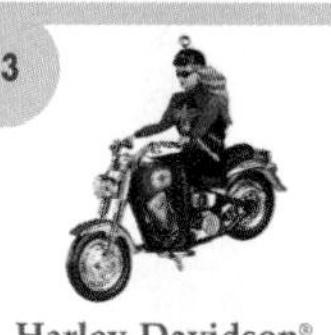
Harley-Davidson® BARBIE™ Ornament
Handcrafted/Metal • RGRS
1595QXI8885 • **Value $15.95**

14

Harry Potter™
Pewter • N/A
1295QXE4402 • **Value $12.95**

15

Hello, Dumbo!
Handcrafted • N/A
1295QXD4162 • **Value $12.95**

16

Hermione Granger's™ Trunk (set/6)
Handcrafted/Pewter • PIKE
1495QXE4422 • **Value $14.95**

17

Hogwarts™ School Crests (set/5)
Handcrafted • N/A
1295QXE4452 • **Value $12.95**

18
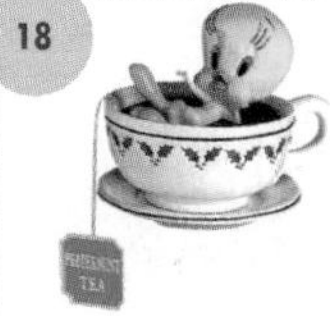
Holiday Spa Tweety
Porcelain • CHAD
995QX6945 • **Value $9.95**

General Keepsake

	Price Paid	Value
1.		
2.		
3.		
4.		
5.		
6.		
7.		
8.		
9.		
10.		
11.		
12.		
13.		
14.		
15.		
16.		
17.		
18.		
Totals		

1

I ♥ My Dog
Handcrafted • RGRS
1695QX8802 • **Value $16.95**

2

It Had To Be You
Handcrafted • UNRU
995QX2815 • **Value $9.95**

3

Jar Jar Binks™
Handcrafted • RHOD
1495QX6882 • **Value $14.95**

4

The Jetsons™ (set/2)
Handcrafted/Pressed Tin • N/A
1495QX6312 • **Value $14.95**

5

Jolly Santa Bells (set/3)
Porcelain • AUBE
1995QX8915 • **Value $19.95**

6

Jolly Visitor
Glass • LARS
695QX2235 • **Value $6.95**

7

Journey to Bethlehem Bell
Porcelain • BRIC
1495QX8386 • **Value $14.95**

8

Just What They Wanted!
Handcrafted • N/A
1295QXD4142 • **Value $12.95**

9

Kiss the Cook
Handcrafted • SIED
995QX2852 • **Value $9.95**

10

The Land of Christmastime
Handcrafted/Paper • SICK
1295QX8282 • **Value $12.95**

11

Laptop Santa
Handcrafted • RHOD
795QX8972 • **Value $7.95**

12
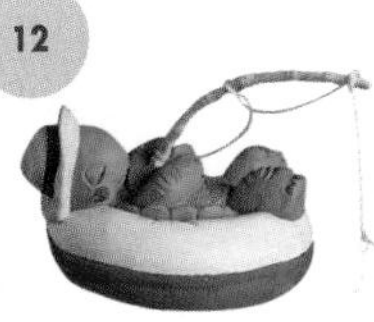
Lazy Afternoon
Handcrafted • FRAN
995QX8335 • **Value $9.95**

13

LIONEL® I-400E Blue Comet Locomotive
Blown Glass • N/A
3500QBG4355 • **Value $35**

14

Lionel™ Plays With Words
Handcrafted • CROW
1495QXI6902 • **Value $14.95**

15
"Lucy Does A TV Commercial" I Love Lucy®
Handcrafted • VOTR
1595QX6862 • **Value $15.95**

16

A Magical Dress for Briar Rose
Handcrafted • N/A
1495QXD4202 • **Value $14.95**

17

Mary and Joseph
Porcelain • UNRU
1895QX8195 • **Value $18.95**

18

Mary Hamilton Angel Chorus
Glass • N/A
695QX2232 • **Value $6.95**

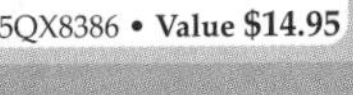
General Keepsake

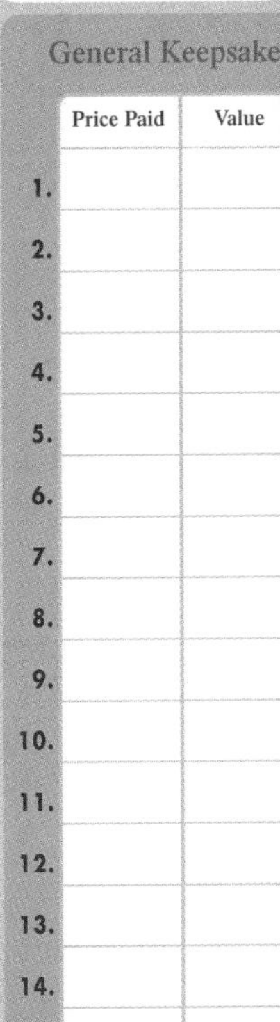

	Price Paid	Value
1.		
2.		
3.		
4.		
5.		
6.		
7.		
8.		
9.		
10.		
11.		
12.		
13.		
14.		
15.		
16.		
17.		
18.		
Totals		

Value Guide — Hallmark Keepsake Ornaments

1

Mickey Mantle – New York Yankees™
Handcrafted • RHOD
1495QXI6804 • **Value $14.95**

2

Mickey's Sweetheart – Minnie Mouse
Handcrafted/Fabric • N/A
995QXD4192 • **Value $9.95**

3

Minnie's Sweetheart – Mickey Mouse
Handcrafted/Fabric • N/A
995QXD4195 • **Value $9.95**

4

The Mirror of Erised™
Handcrafted • WILL
1595QXI8645 • **Value $15.95**

5

Mitford Snowman Jubilee (set/4)
Handcrafted • TAGU
1995QX2825 • **Value $19.95**

6

Mom
Handcrafted • SICK
895QX8415 • **Value $8.95**

7

Mom and Dad
Handcrafted • PIKE
995QX8462 • **Value $9.95**

8

Monsters, Inc.
Handcrafted • N/A
1495QXI6145 • **Value $14.95**

9

Mother and Daughter
Enameled cloisonné • VOTR
995QX6962 • **Value $9.95**

10

Moose's Merry Christmas
Handcrafted • LARS
1295QX8835 • **Value $12.95**

11

Mrs. Claus's Chair
Handcrafted • CHAD
1295QX6955 • **Value $12.95**

12

Mrs. Potts and Chip (set/2)
Porcelain • N/A
1295QXD4165 • **Value $12.95**

13

My First Snowman
Handcrafted • LYLE
995QX4442 • **Value $9.95**

14

The Mystery Machine™ SCOOBY-DOO™
Handcrafted • CHAD
1395QX6295 • **Value $13.95**

15

Naboo Royal Starship
Handcrafted • WEBB
1895QX8475 • **Value $18.95**

16

No. 1 Teacher
Handcrafted/Glass • FRAN
995QX2865 • **Value $9.95**

General Keepsake

	Price Paid	Value
1.		
2.		
3.		
4.		
5.		
6.		
7.		
8.		
9.		
10.		
11.		
12.		
13.		
14.		
15.		
16.		
Totals		

1

Noah's Ark
Handcrafted/Metal • ESCH
1295QX2835 • **Value $12.95**

2

Noche de Paz
Handcrafted/Brass • SICK
1295QX8192 • **Value $12.95**

3

Old-World Santa
Chalkware • SICK
995QX8975 • **Value $9.95**

4

One Little Angel
Paper/Metal • N/A
895QX8935 • **Value $8.95**

5

Our Christmas Together (set/4)
Porcelain • VISK
1995QX8412 • **Value $19.95**

6

Our Family
Handcrafted • LYLE
895QX8995 • **Value $8.95**

7

Our First Christmas Together
Acrylic • VOTR
795QX3162 • **Value $7.95**

8

Our First Christmas Together
Handcrafted/Brass • CHAD
895QX6012 • **Value $8.95**

9

Our First Christmas Together
Handcrafted • KLIN
995QX8405 • **Value $9.95**

10

A Partridge in a Pear Tree
Porcelain • VOTR
1295QX8215 • **Value $12.95**

11

Pat the Bunny
Handcrafted • KLIN
995QX8582 • **Value $9.95**

12

PEANUTS® Pageant (set/2)
Porcelain • HADD
1495QX2832 • **Value $14.95**

13

Peek-a-Boo Present
Handcrafted • WILL
995QX8302 • **Value $9.95**

14

Peggy Fleming
Handcrafted • ANDR
1495QXI6845 • **Value $14.95**

15

Penguins at Play
Handcrafted • KLIN
995QX8982 • **Value $9.95**

16

A Perfect Blend
Porcelain • KLIN
995QX8985 • **Value $9.95**

17

A Perfect Christmas!
Handcrafted • KLIN
1295QXI6895 • **Value $12.95**

18

Portrait of Scarlett™
Porcelain • ANDR
1595QX2885 • **Value $15.95**

General Keepsake

	Price Paid	Value
1.		
2.		
3.		
4.		
5.		
6.		
7.		
8.		
9.		
10.		
11.		
12.		
13.		
14.		
15.		
16.		
17.		
18.		
Totals		

1

The Potions Master™
Handcrafted • LARS
1495QXI8652 • **Value $14.95**

2

Q™ Star Trek: The Next Generation™ CROWN REFLECTIONS
Blown Glass • RGRS
2400QBG4345 • **Value $24**

3

Raggedy Andy
Handcrafted • RGRS
1095QX8574 • **Value $10.95**

4

Raggedy Ann
Handcrafted • RGRS
1095QX8571 • **Value $10.95**

5

Ready Reindeer (complements the 2001 club ornaments and "Santa's Sleigh")
Handcrafted • UNRU
1395QX8295 • **Value $13.95**

6

Ready Teddy
Fabric • TAGU
995QX8842 • **Value $9.95**

7

Rocking Reindeer
Handcrafted • VISK
1295QX8261 • **Value $12.95**

8

Ron Weasley™ and Scabbers™
Pewter • BRIC
1295QXE4405 • **Value $12.95**

9

Samantha "Sam" Stephens
Handcrafted • CHAD
1495QXI6892 • **Value $14.95**

10

Santa Sneaks A Sweet – Cooking For Christmas
Handcrafted • UNRU
1595QX8862 • **Value $15.95**

11

Santa's Day Off
Handcrafted • RGRS
995QX2872 • **Value $9.95**

12

Santa's Sweet Surprise
Porcelain • VOTR
1495QX8275 • **Value $14.95**

13

Santa's Workshop
Handcrafted • PIKE
995QX2812 • **Value $9.95**

14

Sew Sweet Angel
Handcrafted • TAGU
995QX2862 • **Value $9.95**

15

Sharing Santa's Snacks
Handcrafted • AUBE
895QX8212 • **Value $8.95**

16

Sisters
Handcrafted • VISK
895QX8455 • **Value $8.95**

17

Skating Sugar Bear Bell
Porcelain • TAGU
995QX6005 • **Value $9.95**

18

Snow Blossom
Handcrafted • ANDR
995QX8494 • **Value $9.95**

19

Snuggly Sugar Bear Bell
Porcelain • TAGU
995QX8922 • **Value $9.95**

General Keepsake

	Price Paid	Value
1.		
2.		
3.		
4.		
5.		
6.		
7.		
8.		
9.		
10.		
11.		
12.		
13.		
14.		
15.		
16.		
17.		
18.		
19.		
Totals		

1

Son
Handcrafted • SICK
895QX8432 • **Value $8.95**

2

Springing Santa
Handcrafted • HADD
795QX8085 • **Value $7.95**

3

Steve Young – San Francisco 49ers
Handcrafted • UNRU
1495QXI6305 • **Value $14.95**

4

Sylvester's Bang-Up Gift
Handcrafted • CHAD
1295QX6912 • **Value $12.95**

5

Thomas O'Malley and Duchess
Handcrafted • N/A
1495QXD4175 • **Value $14.95**

6

TONKA® 1955 Steam Shovel
Die-Cast Metal • N/A
1395QX6292 • **Value $13.95**

7

Tootle the Train (w/book)
Handcrafted • VOTR
1195QX6052 • **Value $11.95**

8

Victorian BARBIE™ with Cedric Bear™ Ornament
Porcelain • ANDR
1595QXI6952 • **Value $15.95**

9

Victorian Christmas Memories, Thomas Kinkade, Painter of Light™ (set/3)
Handcrafted • BRIC
1495QX8292 • **Value $14.95**

10

Victorian Sleigh
Die-Cast Metal • CROW
1295QX8855 • **Value $12.95**

11

Waddles
Wood • VISK
895QX8952 • **Value $8.95**

12

Waggles
Wood • VISK
895QX8945 • **Value $8.95**

13

Waiting for Santa Larry the Cucumber™ and Bob the Tomato™ Veggietales®
Handcrafted • KLIN
1295QXI6932 • **Value $12.95**

14

What A Grinchy Trick!
Handcrafted • WILL
1495QXI6405 • **Value $14.95**

15

Wiggles
Wood • VISK
895QX8955 • **Value $8.95**

16

Winter Friends
Glass • HADD
695QX2242 • **Value $6.95**

17

A Wise Follower
Handcrafted • KLIN
895QX8202 • **Value $8.95**

18

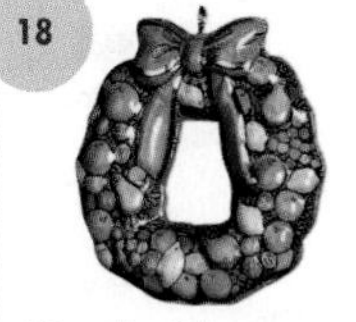

Wreath of Evergreens
Pressed Tin • SICK
895QX8832 • **Value $8.95**

19

2000 OSCAR MAYER Wienermobile™
Handcrafted • WEBB
1295QX6935 • **Value $12.95**

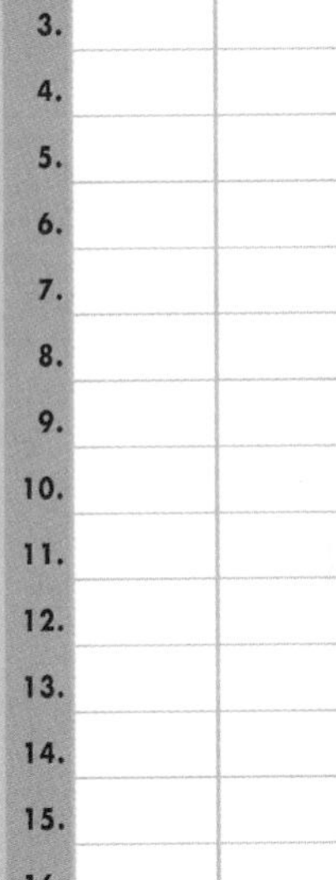

General Keepsake

	Price Paid	Value
1.		
2.		
3.		
4.		
5.		
6.		
7.		
8.		
9.		
10.		
11.		
12.		
13.		
14.		
15.		
16.		
17.		
18.		

General Magic

19.		

Totals

1

Bambi Discovers Winter
Handcrafted • N/A
2400QXD7541 • **Value $24**

2

Farewell Scene
Handcrafted • ANDR
2400QLX7562 • **Value $24**

3

Merry Carolers
Handcrafted • N/A
2400QXD7585 • **Value $24**

4

Poppy Field
Handcrafted • CROW
2400QLX7565 • **Value $24**

5

Snoozing Santa
Handcrafted • CROW
1895QX8165 • **Value $18.95**

6
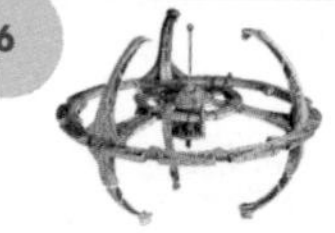
Space Station Deep Space 9 – STAR TREK: Deep Space Nine™
Handcrafted • NORT
3200QX6065 • **Value $32**

7

Up on the Housetop
Handcrafted • CROW
4200QLX7575 • **Value $42**

8
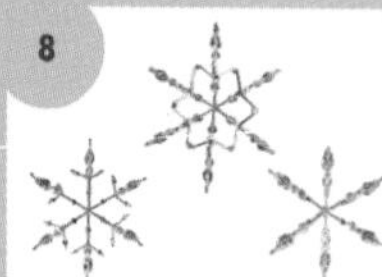
Beaded Snowflakes (blue, set/3)
Handcrafted • N/A
995QP1712 • **Value $9.95**

9
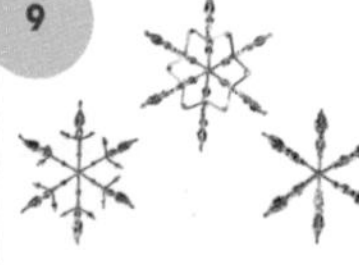
Beaded Snowflakes (periwinkle, set/3)
Handcrafted • N/A
995QP1725 • **Value $9.95**

10
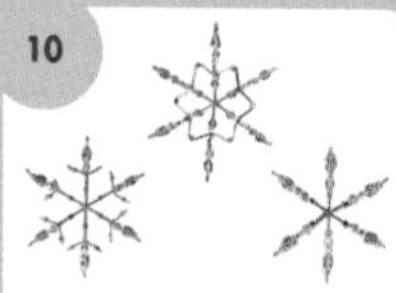
Beaded Snowflakes (violet, set/3)
Handcrafted • N/A
995QP1732 • **Value $9.95**

11

Faerie Brilliana
Handcrafted • ESCH
1495QP1672 • **Value $14.95**

12

Faerie Candessa
Handcrafted • ESCH
1495QP1665 • **Value $14.95**

13

Faerie Delandra
Handcrafted • ESCH
1495QP1685 • **Value $14.95**

14

Faerie Estrella
Handcrafted • ESCH
1495QP1695 • **Value $14.95**

15

Faerie Floriella
Handcrafted • ESCH
1495QP1692 • **Value $14.95**

16

Frostlight Flowers (set/3)
Fabric • N/A
1595QP1705 • **Value $15.95**

17
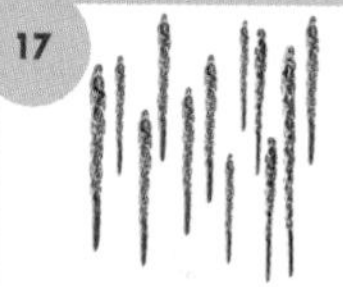
Glistening Icicles (set/12)
Handcrafted/Glass • N/A
1295QP1742 • **Value $12.95**

18

Battle of Naboo (set/3)
Handcrafted • RHOD
1495QXM5212 • **Value $14.95**

19

Bouncy Kangaroos (complements Noah's Ark Special Edition)
Handcrafted • SICK
595QXM5332 • **Value $5.95**

General Magic

	Price Paid	Value
1.		
2.		
3.		
4.		
5.		
6.		
7.		

Frostlight Faeries

	Price Paid	Value
8.		
9.		
10.		
11.		
12.		
13.		
14.		
15.		
16.		
17.		

General Miniature

	Price Paid	Value
18.		
19.		
Totals		

1

Dashing Through the Snow
Handcrafted • CROW
695QXM5335 • **Value $6.95**

2

Gearing up for Christmas
Handcrafted/Metal • CROW
695QXM5352 • **Value $6.95**

3

The Glass Slipper
Handcrafted • N/A
795QXD4182 • **Value $7.95**

4

Holiday Shoe
Handcrafted • ESCH
495QXM5365 • **Value $4.95**

5

Jiminy Cricket
Handcrafted • N/A
795QXD4185 • **Value $7.95**

6

Radiant Christmas
Crystal/Pewter • VOTR
795QXM5342 • **Value $7.95**

7

Ready for a Ride
Handcrafted/Metal • AUBE
695QXM5302 • **Value $6.95**

8

Santa-in-a-Box
Handcrafted • FRAN
695QXM5355 • **Value $6.95**

9

Scooby-Doo™
Handcrafted • CHAD
695QXM5322 • **Value $6.95**

10

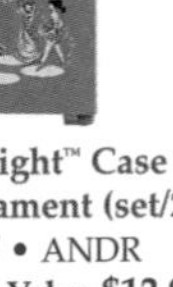

Solo in the Spotlight™ Case and BARBIE™ Ornament (set/2)
Handcrafted • ANDR
1295QXM5312 • **Value $12.95**

11

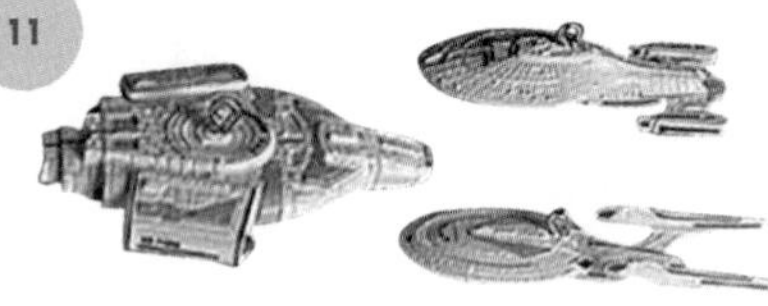

Starfleet Legends – STAR TREK™ (set/3)
Handcrafted • NORT
1495QXM5325 • **Value $14.95**

12

Sweet Contribution – Cooking for Christmas
Handcrafted • LARS
495QXM4492 • **Value $4.95**

13

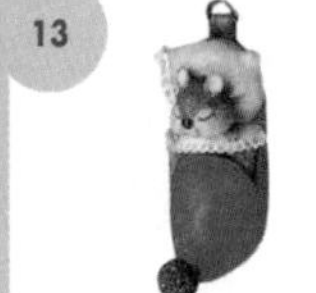

Sweet Slipper Dream
Handcrafted • AUBE
495QXM5345 • **Value $4.95**

14

Thing One and Thing Two™! (set/3)
Handcrafted • WILL
1495QXM5315 • **Value $14.95**

15

Tweety
Handcrafted • CHAD
695QXM5305 • **Value $6.95**

16

1958 Custom Corvette®
Handcrafted • N/A
N/A • **Value N/E**

17

Gift for a Friend
Handcrafted • RGRS
N/A • **Value N/E**

General Miniature

	Price Paid	Value
1.		
2.		
3.		
4.		
5.		
6.		
7.		
8.		
9.		
10.		
11.		
12.		
13.		
14.		
15.		

Collector's Club

	Price Paid	Value
16.		
17.		
Totals		

1

Globus, Lettera & Mrs. Claus
(set/3, keepsake of membership)
Handcrafted • VARI
N/A • **Value N/E**

2

Nesting Nativity
Handcrafted • SICK
N/A • **Value N/E**

3

Ready for Delivery
(early renewal piece)
Handcrafted • RGRS
N/A • **Value N/E**

4

Santa Marionette
Handcrafted • CROW
N/A • **Value N/E**

5

Santa's Desk – 2001 Studio Limited
Edition (set/4, mail order exclusive)
Handcrafted • VARI
N/A • **Value N/E**

6

Santa's Sleigh with
Sack and Miniature
Ornament
Handcrafted • UNRU
1895QX8872 • **Value $18.95**

7

Collegiate Collection
(10 assorted)
Handcrafted • RHOD

1. Alabama® Crimson Tide®
995QSR2132 • **Value $9.95**
2. Florida Gators®
995QSR2165 • **Value $9.95**
3. Florida State® Seminoles®
995QSR2162 • **Value $9.95**
4. Michigan Wolverines™
995QSR2142 • **Value $9.95**
5. Nebraska Cornhuskers™
995QSR2135 • **Value $9.95**
6. North Carolina® Tar Heels®
995QSR2155 • **Value $9.95**
7. Notre Dame® Fighting Irish™
995QSR2145 • **Value $9.95**
8. Penn State® Nittany Lions®
995QSR2122 • **Value $9.95**
9. Tennessee Volunteers®
995QSR2125 • **Value $9.95**
10. The University of
Kentucky® Wildcats™
995QSR2152 • **Value $9.95**

8

Alphabet Seuss
Porcelain • WILL
2000QSU2057 • **Value $20**

9

Horton the Elephant
Porcelain • LYLE
1200QSU2040 • **Value $12**

10

Pup in Cup
Porcelain • PIKE
1500QSU2048 • **Value $15**

11

Rainy Day Games
Porcelain • WILL
2000QSU2044 • **Value $20**

12

The Sneetches
Porcelain • CHAD
1800QSU2058 • **Value $18**

13

Santa Claus with
Miniature Panda Bear
Handcrafted • ANDR
1295QXI5395 • **Value $12.95**

14

Santa's Toy Box with 3 Miniature Ornaments (set/4)
Handcrafted • VARI
1295QXI5392 • **Value $12.95**

	Price Paid	Value
Collector's Club		
1.		
2.		
3.		
4.		
5.		
Premiere Ornaments		
6.		
Collegiate Collection		
7.		
Dr. Seuss™ Collection		
8.		
9.		
10.		
11.		
12.		
13.		
Event Pieces		
14.		
Totals		

1

With Help From Pup
(set/2, exclusive to collector's club events)
Handcrafted • TAGU
N/A • **Value N/E**

2

3

4

5

6

7

8

9

10

11

12

F-14A Tomcat (LE-12,500)
Handcrafted • N/A
4000QHA1006 • **Value $40**

13

P-51 Mustang "Big Beautiful Doll" (LE-12,500)
Handcrafted • N/A
3000QHA1016 • **Value $30**

14

SPAD XIII Escadrille SPA 3 (LE-12,500)
Handcrafted • N/A
2800QHA1014 • **Value $28**

15

VX-9 F-14 Blackcat (LE-12,500)
Handcrafted • N/A
3200QHA1020 • **Value $32**

16

Wright Flyer (LE-12,500)
Handcrafted • N/A
3500QHA1001 • **Value $35**

17

NFL Collection
(10 assorted)
Handcrafted • GOSL

1. Cleveland Browns
995QSR5572 • **Value $9.95**
2. Dallas Cowboys
995QSR5622 • **Value $9.95**
3. Denver Broncos
995QSR5545 • **Value $9.95**
4. Green Bay Packers
995QSR5625 • **Value $9.95**
5. Kansas City Chiefs
995QSR5542 • **Value $9.95**
6. Miami Dolphins
995QSR5555 • **Value $9.95**
7. Minnesota Vikings
995QSR5575 • **Value $9.95**
8. Pittsburgh Steelers
995QSR5565 • **Value $9.95**
9. San Francisco 49ers
995QSR5562 • **Value $9.95**
10. Washington Redskins
995QSR5552 • **Value $9.95**

	Price Paid	Value
Event Pieces		
1.		
Jubilee Pieces		
2.		
3.		
4.		
5.		
6.		
7.		
8.		
9.		
10.		
11.		
Legends in Flight™		
12.		
13.		
14.		
15.		
16.		
NFL Collection		
17.		
Totals		

1

Ornament Charms
(24 assorted,
re-issued from 2000)
N/A • N/A

1. Believe
QX2831 • **Value $.95**
2. Brass Cross
QX2734 • **Value $.95**
3. Brass Heart
QX2821 • **Value $.95**
4. Brother
QX2641 • **Value $.95**
5. Congrats!
QX2824 • **Value $.95**
6. Dad
QX2621 • **Value $.95**
7. Daughter
QX2644 • **Value $.95**
8. Friends Forever
QX2701 • **Value $.95**
9. Granddaughter
QX2654 • **Value $.95**
10. Grandma
QX2624 • **Value $.95**
11. Grandpa
QX2631 • **Value $.95**
12. Grandson
QX2661 • **Value $.95**
13. Great Teacher!
QX2674 • **Value $.95**
14. Happy Birthday
QX2704 • **Value $.95**
15. Happy Holidays
QX2684 • **Value $.95**
16. I Love You
QX2694 • **Value $.95**
17. Mom
QX2601 • **Value $.95**
18. Nephew
QX2671 • **Value $.95**
19. Niece
QX2664 • **Value $.95**
20. Peace on Earth
QX2711 • **Value $.95**
21. Sister
QX2634 • **Value $.95**
22. Son
QX2651 • **Value $.95**
23. Thank You
QX2681 • **Value $.95**
24. Thinking of You
QX2691 • **Value $.95**

Ornament Charms	Price Paid	Value
1.		
Peanuts® Gallery		
2.		
3.		
4.		
5.		
6.		
7.		
8.		
9.		
10.		
11.		
12.		
13.		
Totals		

2

An Ace in Action
Handcrafted • N/A
1500QPC4032 • **Value $15**

3

Campfire Friends
(2nd in the *Snoopy and Friends Series*)
Porcelain/Fabric • N/A
2000QPC4030 • **Value $20**

4

Cyber Chuck
Porcelain • RGRS
1800QPC4062 • **Value $18**

5

Franklin
Porcelain • N/A
2500QPC4037 • **Value $25**

6

Great Times
Porcelain • KLIN
2000QPC4042 • **Value $20**

7

A Happy Dance
Handcrafted • N/A
995QPC4029 • **Value $9.95**

8

Joe Cool
Porcelain • N/A
2500QPC4034 • **Value $25**

9

King of the Sandbox
Porcelain • KLIN
1500QPC4027 • **Value $15**

10

Linus, M.D.
Porcelain • KLIN
1500QPC4046 • **Value $15**

11

Lovebirds
Porcelain • VOTR
1500QPC4038 • **Value $15**

12

Mood Booth
Porcelain • SIED
2000QPC4031 • **Value $20**

13

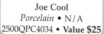

Ms. Van Pelt
Porcelain • RGRS
1800QPC4028 • **Value $18**

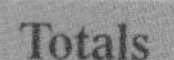

1

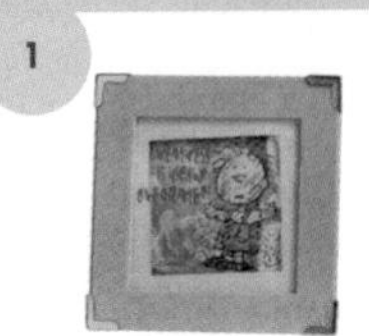

A Neat Philosophy
Porcelain • N/A
995QPC4033 • **Value $9.95**

2

Nurse Sally
Porcelain • RGRS
1500QPC4060 • **Value $15**

3

Special Blessings
Porcelain • KLIN
1500QPC4047 • **Value $15**

4

The Suit
Porcelain • RGRS
1500QPC4026 • **Value $15**

5

Woodstock and Friends (set/3)
Porcelain • N/A
2500QPC4035 • **Value $25**

6

Bewitched™
Pressed Tin • N/A
1095QHM8824 • **Value $10.95**

7

Bozo (LE-24,500)
Pressed Tin • N/A
1195QHM8906 • **Value $11.95**

8

Disney's School Bus (LE-24,500)
Pressed Tin • N/A
1195QHM8907 • **Value $11.95**

9

G.I. Joe® (LE-19,500)
Pressed Tin • N/A
1395QHM8827 • **Value $13.95**

10

Porky's Lunch Wagon (LE-24,500)
Pressed Tin • N/A
1195QHM8903 • **Value $11.95**

11

Star Wars: Return of the Jedi
Pressed Tin • N/A
1095QHM8825 • **Value $10.95**

12

Walt Disney's *Cinderella* (LE-24,500)
Pressed Tin • N/A
1395QHM8826 • **Value $13.95**

Peanuts® Gallery

	Price Paid	Value
1.		
2.		
3.		
4.		
5.		

School Days Lunch Boxes

	Price Paid	Value
6.		
7.		
8.		
9.		
10.		
11.		
12.		
Totals		

2000 Collection

2000

In 2000, 350 new ornaments were introduced, including 25 in the new Li'l Blown Glass series of miniature blown glass ornaments. The American Spirit™ Collection, Peanuts® Gallery and the Dr. Seuss™ Collection also made their heartwarming debut. See the collectibles series section for more 2000 ornaments.

1
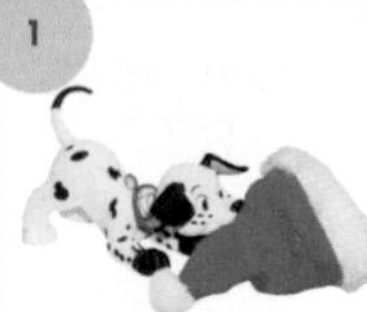
102 Dalmatians
Handcrafted • N/A
1295QXI5231 • **Value $22**

2

1955 Murray® Dump Truck
Blown Glass • N/A
3500QBG4081 • **Value $55**

3

1962 BARBIE™ Hatbox Doll Case
Handcrafted • N/A
995QX6791 • **Value $16**

4

Alice Meets the Cheshire Cat
Handcrafted • N/A
1495QXD4011 • **Value $25**

5

All Things Beautiful
Handcrafted/Paper • ESCH
1395QX8351 • **Value $22**

6

Angel-Blessed Tree
Handcrafted • RGRS
895QX8241 • **Value $15**

7
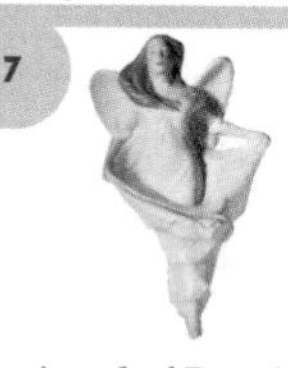
Angel of Promise
Porcelain • ANDR
1495QXI4144 • **Value $24**

8

Angelic Trio
Handcrafted • HADD
1095QX8234 • **Value $22**

9

Arnold Palmer
Handcrafted • UNRU
1495QXI4324 • **Value $25**

10

Baby's First Christmas
Handcrafted • FRAN
795QX6914 • **Value $17**

11

Baby's First Christmas
Handcrafted • HADD
895QX8031 • **Value $16**

12

Baby's First Christmas
Handcrafted • SEAL
1095QX8034 • **Value $21**

13

Baby's First Christmas
Handcrafted • AUBE
1895QX8041 • **Value $32**

14

Baby's Second Christmas
Handcrafted • FRAN
795QX6921 • **Value $15**

15

Backpack Bear
Blown Glass • TAGU
3000QBG4071 • **Value $42**

16

Balthasar – The Magi (re-issued from 1999)
Porcelain • N/A
1295QX8037 • **Value $20**

17

BARBIE™ Angel of Joy™ Ornament
Handcrafted • RGRS
1495QXI6861 • **Value $25**

General Keepsake

	Price Paid	Value
1.		
2.		
3.		
4.		
5.		
6.		
7.		
8.		
9.		
10.		
11.		
12.		
13.		
14.		
15.		
16.		
17.		
Totals		

1

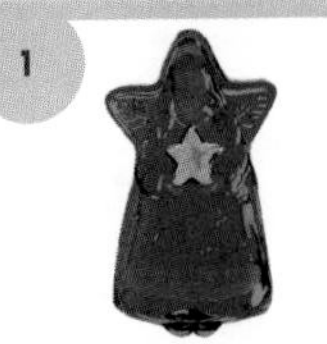

Blue Glass Angel
Glass • TAGU
795QX8381 • **Value $15**

2

Bob the Tomato™ and Larry the Cucumber™
Handcrafted • LYLE
995QXI4334 • **Value $16**

3

Bringing Her Gift
Handcrafted • KLIN
1095QX8334 • **Value $19**

4

Bugs Bunny and Gossamer
Handcrafted • CHAD
1295QX6574 • **Value $22**

5

Busy Bee Shopper
Handcrafted • CHAD
795QX6964 • **Value $15**

6

Buzz Lightyear
Handcrafted • N/A
1495QXI5234 • **Value $25**

7

Caroler's Best Friend
Handcrafted • ESCH
1295QX8354 • **Value $22**

8

Caspar – The Magi (re-issued from 1999)
Porcelain • N/A
1295QX8039 • **Value $20**

9

Celebrate His Birth!
Glass • HADD
695QX2464 • **Value $13**

10

Child's Fifth Christmas
Handcrafted • CROW
795QX6934 • **Value $15**

11

Child's Fourth Christmas
Handcrafted • CROW
795QX6931 • **Value $15**

12

Child's Third Christmas
Handcrafted • FRAN
795QX6924 • **Value $15**

13

The Christmas Belle
Porcelain • AUBE
1095QX8311 • **Value $20**

14

Christmas Tree Surprise
Porcelain • TAGU
1695QX8321 • **Value $28**

15

A Class Act
Handcrafted • HADD
795QX8074 • **Value $13**

16

Close-Knit Friends (set/2)
Handcrafted • SEAL
1495QX8204 • **Value $25**

17

Cool Character
Pressed Tin • SICK
1295QX8271 • **Value $22**

18

Dad
Handcrafted • CHAD
895QX8071 • **Value $15**

19

Dale Earnhardt
Handcrafted • SEAL
1495QXI6754 • **Value $60**

20

Dancin' In Christmas
Handcrafted • TAGU
795QX6971 • **Value $14**

General Keepsake

	Price Paid	Value
1.		
2.		
3.		
4.		
5.		
6.		
7.		
8.		
9.		
10.		
11.		
12.		
13.		
14.		
15.		
16.		
17.		
18.		
19.		
20.		
Totals		

1

Darth Maul™
Handcrafted • ANDR
1495QXI6885 • **Value $25**

2

Daughter
Porcelain • ESCH
895QX8081 • **Value $15**

3

Dog Dish Dilemma
Handcrafted • N/A
1295QXD4044 • **Value $22**

4

Dousin' Dalmatian
Handcrafted • SEAL
995QX8024 • **Value $17**

5

Dressing Cinderella
Handcrafted • N/A
1295QXD4109 • **Value $22**

6

Feliz Navidad
Handcrafted • RGRS
895QX8214 • **Value $17**

7

The Fishing Hole
Handcrafted • VISK
1295QX6984 • **Value $22**

8

Friendly Greeting
Handcrafted /Pressed Tin • ESCH
995QX8174 • **Value $16**

9

Friends in Harmony
Handcrafted • FRAN
995QX8001 • **Value $16**

10

Frosty Friends (set/2)
Blown Glass • SEAL
4000QBG4094 • **Value $68**

11

G.I. Joe® Action Pilot
Handcrafted • CROW
1395QX6734 • **Value $22**

12

Gifts for the Grinch
Handcrafted • KLIN
1295QXI5344 • **Value $30**

13

Gingerbread Church
Handcrafted • LAPR
995QX8244 • **Value $16**

14

Godchild
Handcrafted • TAGU
795QX8161 • **Value $14**

15

Gold-Star Teacher
Handcrafted • PIKE
795QX6951 • **Value $14**

16

Golfer Supreme
Handcrafted • SEAL
1095QX6991 • **Value $19**

17

The Good Book
Handcrafted • UNRU
1395QX8254 • **Value $22**

18

Graceful Glory
Handcrafted • VOTR
1895QX8304 • **Value $29**

19

Granddaughter
Porcelain • FORS
895QX8091 • **Value $16**

20

Grandma's House
Porcelain • LARS
1095QX8141 • **Value $18**

General Keepsake

	Price Paid	Value
1.		
2.		
3.		
4.		
5.		
6.		
7.		
8.		
9.		
10.		
11.		
12.		
13.		
14.		
15.		
16.		
17.		
18.		
19.		
20.		
Totals		

1

Grandson
Porcelain • FORS
895QX8094 • **Value $15**

2

Harley-Davidson® BARBIE™ Ornament
Handcrafted • RGRS
1495QXI8554 • **Value $22**

3

A Holiday Gathering
Porcelain • N/A
1095QX8561 • **Value $18**

4

Holly Berry Bell
Porcelain • FORS
1495QX8291 • **Value $25**

5

The Holy Family (set/3, re-issued from 1999)
Porcelain • N/A
2500QX6523 • **Value $48**

6

Hooray for the U.S.A.
Handcrafted • CHAD
995QX8281 • **Value $18**

7

Hopalong Cassidy (set/2)
Pressed Tin/Handcrafted • N/A
1495QX6714 • **Value $25**

8

Hot Wheels™ 1968 Deora™ (green)
Handcrafted • UNRU
1495QXI6891 • **Value $26**

9

Hot Wheels™ 1968 Deora™ (red)
Handcrafted • UNRU
1495QXI6891 • **Value $26**

10

Imperial Stormtrooper™
Handcrafted • KLIN
1495QXI6711 • **Value $25**

11

Jeannie I Dream of Jeannie (set/2)
Handcrafted • ANDR
1495QXI8564 • **Value $25**

12
King of the Ring
Handcrafted • TAGU
1095QX6864 • **Value $24**

13

Kris "Cross-Country" Kringle
Handcrafted • VISK
1295QX6954 • **Value $21**

14

Kristi Yamaguchi
Handcrafted • BRIC
1395QXI6854 • **Value $23**

15

Larry, Moe, and Curly (set/3)
Handcrafted • LARS
3000QX6851 • **Value $44**

16

Lieutenant Commander Worf™ STAR TREK: Deep Space Nine™
Blown Glass • RGRS
3000QBG4064 • **Value $44**

17

LIONEL® 4501 Southern Mikado Steam Locomotive
Blown Glass • N/A
3500QBG4074 • **Value $52**

18

Loggin' On to Santa
Handcrafted • PIKE
895QX8224 • **Value $15**

19

The Lone Ranger™
Handcrafted • UNRU
1595QX6941 • **Value $25**

20

"Lucy Is Enciente"
Handcrafted • VOTR
1595QX6884 • **Value $25**

General Keepsake

	Price Paid	Value
1.		
2.		
3.		
4.		
5.		
6.		
7.		
8.		
9.		
10.		
11.		
12.		
13.		
14.		
15.		
16.		
17.		
18.		
19.		
20.		
Totals		

1

The Lullabye League (set/3)
Handcrafted • LYLE
1995QX6604 • **Value $28**

2

Max (complements the "The Snowmen of Mitford" from 1999)
Handcrafted • N/A
795QX8584 • **Value $16**

3

Melchior – The Magi (re-issued from 1999)
Porcelain • N/A
1295QX6819 • **Value $20**

4

Memories of Christmas
Pressed Tin • SICK
1295QX8264 • **Value $22**

5

Merry Ballooning
Pressed Tin • BRIC
1695QX8384 • **Value $29**

6

Mickey's Bedtime Reading
Handcrafted • N/A
1095QXD4077 • **Value $18**

7

Mickey's Sky Rider
Handcrafted • N/A
1895QXD4159 • **Value $30**

8

Millennium Time Capsule
Handcrafted • UNRU
1095QX8044 • **Value $15**

9

Mom
Handcrafted • CHAD
895QX8064 • **Value $16**

10

Mom and Dad
Porcelain • BRIC
995QX8061 • **Value $16**

11

Mother and Daughter
Porcelain • RGRS
995QX8154 • **Value $17**

12

Mr. Monopoly™
Handcrafted • SIED
1095QX8101 • **Value $19**

13

Mrs. Claus's Holiday
Handcrafted • KLIN
995QX8011 • **Value $16**

14

New Home
Handcrafted • SEAL
895QX8171 • **Value $15**

15
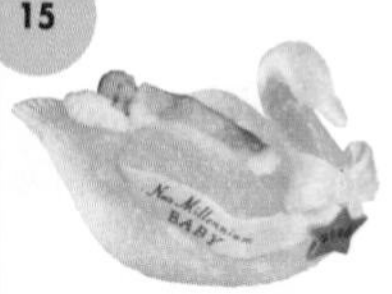
New Millennium Baby
Handcrafted • VOTR
1095QX8581 • **Value $22**

16

The Newborn Prince
Handcrafted • N/A
1395QXD4194 • **Value $22**

17

North Pole Network
Handcrafted • SEAL
1095QX6994 • **Value $18**

18

Northern Art Bear
Handcrafted • LAPR
895QX8294 • **Value $15**

19

Off to Neverland!
Handcrafted • N/A
1295QXD4004 • **Value $22**

20

Our Christmas Together
Porcelain • KLIN
995QX8054 • **Value $14**

General Keepsake

	Price Paid	Value
1.		
2.		
3.		
4.		
5.		
6.		
7.		
8.		
9.		
10.		
11.		
12.		
13.		
14.		
15.		
16.		
17.		
18.		
19.		
20.		
Totals		

1
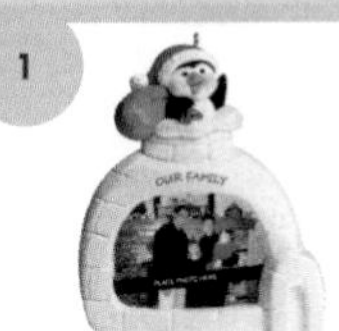
Our Family
Handcrafted • AUBE
795QX8211 • **Value $14**

2

Our First Christmas Together
Acrylic • VOTR
795QX3104 • **Value $14**

3

Our First Christmas Together
Handcrafted • SIED
895QX8051 • **Value $15**

4
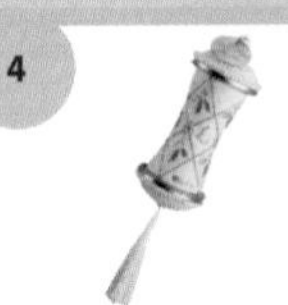
Our First Christmas Together
Handcrafted • UNRU
1095QX8701 • **Value $17**

5

Our Lady of Guadalupe
Handcrafted • VISK
1295QX8231 • **Value $22**

6

Piglet's Jack-in-the-Box
Handcrafted • N/A
1495QXD4187 • **Value $25**

7

Pooh Chooses the Tree
Handcrafted • N/A
1295QXD4157 • **Value $22**

8

Qui-Gon Jinn™
Handcrafted • ANDR
1495QXI6741 • **Value $25**

9

A Reader to the Core
Handcrafted • AUBE
995QX6974 • **Value $15**

10

Rhett Butler™
Handcrafted • ANDR
1295QX6674 • **Value $21**

11

Safe In Noah's Ark
Handcrafted • HADD
1095QX8514 • **Value $18**

12
Santa's Chair
Handcrafted • CHAD
1295QX8314 • **Value $22**

13

Scooby-Doo™
Handcrafted • RGRS
1295QXI8394 • **Value $22**

14

Scuffy the Tugboat™ (w/book)
Handcrafted • VOTR
1195QX6871 • **Value $20**

15

Self-Portrait
Handcrafted • PIKE
1095QX6644 • **Value $18**

16
Seven of Nine™ STAR TREK: Voyager
Handcrafted • RGRS
1495QX6844 • **Value $24**

17

The Shepherds (set/2)
Porcelain • N/A
2500QX8361 • **Value $38**

18

Sister to Sister
Porcelain • VOTR
1295QX8144 • **Value $22**

19

Snow Girl
Handcrafted • ESCH
995QX8274 • **Value $16**

20

Snowy Garden
Handcrafted • LYLE
1395QX8284 • **Value $22**

General Keepsake

	Price Paid	Value
1.		
2.		
3.		
4.		
5.		
6.		
7.		
8.		
9.		
10.		
11.		
12.		
13.		
14.		
15.		
16.		
17.		
18.		
19.		
20.		
Totals		

1

Son
Porcelain • ESCH
895QX8084 • **Value $15**

2

Stroll Round the Pole
Handcrafted • AUBE
1095QX8164 • **Value $18**

3

Super Friends™ (set/2)
Handcrafted/Pressed Tin • N/A
1495QX6724 • **Value $25**

4

Surprise Package
Handcrafted • BRIC
1095QXI8391 • **Value $19**

5

The Tender
Die-Cast Metal • N/A
1395QX6834 • **Value $25**

6

Tending Her Topiary
Handcrafted • KLIN
995QX8004 • **Value $17**

7

Thimble Soldier
Blown Glass • N/A
2200QBG4061 • **Value $33**

8

Time for Joy
Handcrafted • CROW
2400QX6904 • **Value $46**

9

Together We Serve
Handcrafted • WILL
995QX8021 • **Value $18**

10

Tonka® Dump Truck
Die-Cast Metal • N/A
1395QX6681 • **Value $22**

11

Toy Shop Serenade
Handcrafted • HADD
1695QX8301 • **Value $27**

12

Tree Guy
Handcrafted • CHAD
895QX6961 • **Value $15**

13

A Visit from St. Nicholas
Porcelain • LARS
1095QX8344 • **Value $18**

14

Warm Kindness
Porcelain • HADD
895QX8014 • **Value $15**

15

Warmed by Candleglow
Glass • LARS
695QX2471 • **Value $13**

16

Winter Fun with BARBIE™ and KELLY™ Ornament
Handcrafted • ESCH
1595QXI6561 • **Value $24**

17

Winterberry Santa
Handcrafted • CHAD
1495QXI4331 • **Value $24**

18

The Yellow Submarine
Handcrafted • WILL
1395QXI6841 • **Value $23**

19

Yule Tide Runner
Handcrafted • KLIN
995QX6981 • **Value $16**

General Keepsake

	Price Paid	Value
1.		
2.		
3.		
4.		
5.		
6.		
7.		
8.		
9.		
10.		
11.		
12.		
13.		
14.		
15.		
16.		
17.		
18.		
19.		
Totals		

1

Angels Over Bethlehem
Handcrafted • RHOD
1895QLX7563 • **Value $28**

2

Big Twin Evolution® Engine
Handcrafted • PALM
2400QXI7571 • **Value $35**

3

The Blessed Family
Porcelain • LARS
1895QLX7564 • **Value $28**

4

Borg™ Cube STAR TREK: Voyager
Handcrafted • NORT
2400QLX7354 • **Value $36**

5

The Great Oz
Handcrafted • CROW
3200QLX7361 • **Value $50**

6

Gungan™ Submarine
Handcrafted • RHOD
2400QXI7351 • **Value $40**

7

Mary's Angels
Handcrafted • CHAD
1895QLX7561 • **Value $27**

8

Millennium Express
Handcrafted • CROW
4200QLX7364 • **Value $65**

9

Angel Light
Archival Paper • N/A
795QLZ4311 • **Value N/E**

10

Fun-Stuffed Stocking
Archival Paper • N/A
595QLZ4291 • **Value N/E**

11

Heavenly Peace
Archival Paper • N/A
695QLZ4314 • **Value N/E**

12

Jack-in-the-Box
Archival Paper • N/A
895QLZ4321 • **Value N/E**

13

Lovely Dove
Archival Paper • N/A
795QLZ4294 • **Value N/E**

14

The Nativity
Archival Paper • N/A
895QLZ4301 • **Value N/E**

15

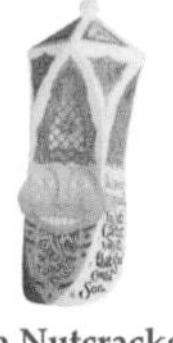
The Nutcracker
Archival Paper • N/A
595QLZ4284 • **Value N/E**

16

A Visit From Santa
Archival Paper • N/A
895QLZ4281 • **Value N/E**

17

Li'l Apple
Blown Glass • N/A
795QBG4261 • **Value N/E**

18

Li'l Cascade – Red
Blown Glass • N/A
795QBG4241 • **Value N/E**

19

Li'l Cascade – White
Blown Glass • N/A
795QBG4244 • **Value N/E**

20

Li'l Christmas Tree
Blown Glass • N/A
795QBG4361 • **Value N/E**

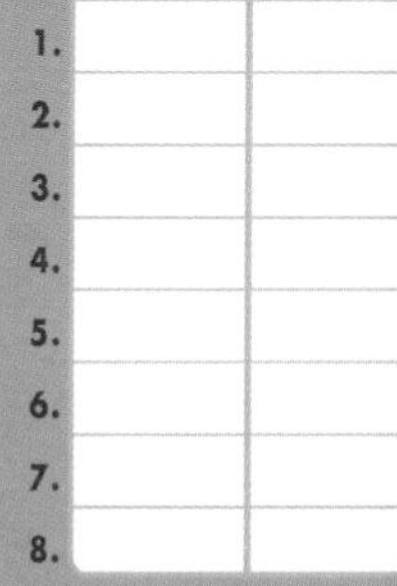

	Price Paid	Value
General Magic		
1.		
2.		
3.		
4.		
5.		
6.		
7.		
8.		
Laser Gallery		
9.		
10.		
11.		
12.		
13.		
14.		
15.		
16.		
Li'l Blown Glass		
17.		
18.		
19.		
20.		
Totals		

1

Li'l Gift – Green Bow
Blown Glass • N/A
795QBG4344 • **Value N/E**

2

Li'l Gift – Red Bow
Blown Glass • N/A
795QBG4341 • **Value N/E**

3

Li'l Grapes
Blown Glass • N/A
795QBG4141 • **Value N/E**

4

Li'l Jack-in-the-Box
Blown Glass • N/A
795QBG4274 • **Value N/E**

5
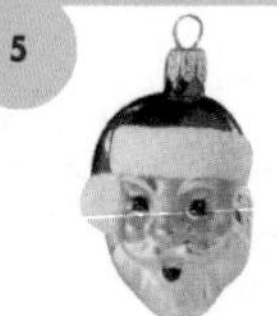
Li'l Mr. Claus
Blown Glass • N/A
795QBG4364 • **Value N/E**

6

Li'l Mrs. Claus
Blown Glass • N/A
795QBG4371 • **Value N/E**

7
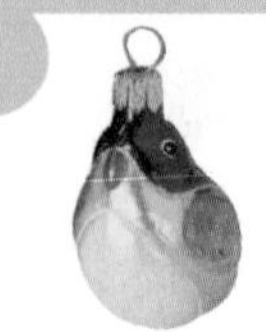
Li'l Partridge
Blown Glass • N/A
795QBG4374 • **Value N/E**

8

Li'l Pear
Blown Glass • N/A
795QBG4254 • **Value N/E**

9

Li'l Pineapple
Blown Glass • N/A
795QBG4251 • **Value N/E**

10

Li'l Robot
Blown Glass • N/A
795QBG4271 • **Value N/E**

11

Li'l Roly-Poly Penguin
Blown Glass • N/A
795QBG4281 • **Value N/E**

12

Li'l Roly-Poly Santa
Blown Glass • N/A
795QBG4161 • **Value N/E**

13

Li'l Roly-Poly Snowman
Blown Glass • N/A
795QBG4284 • **Value N/E**

14

Li'l Santa – Traditional
Blown Glass • N/A
795QBG4354 • **Value N/E**

15

Li'l Snowman – Traditional
Blown Glass • N/A
795QBG4351 • **Value N/E**

16

Li'l Stars – Metallic Look (set/3)
Blown Glass • N/A
995QBG4221 • **Value N/E**

17

Li'l Stars – Patriotic (set/3)
Blown Glass • N/A
995QBG4214 • **Value N/E**

18

Li'l Stars – Traditional (set/3)
Blown Glass • N/A
995QBG4224 • **Value N/E**

19

Li'l Swirl – Green
Blown Glass • N/A
795QBG4234 • **Value N/E**

20

Li'l Swirl – Red
Blown Glass • N/A
795QBG4231 • **Value N/E**

Li'l Blown Glass

	Price Paid	Value
1.		
2.		
3.		
4.		
5.		
6.		
7.		
8.		
9.		
10.		
11.		
12.		
13.		
14.		
15.		
16.		
17.		
18.		
19.		
20.		
Totals		

1
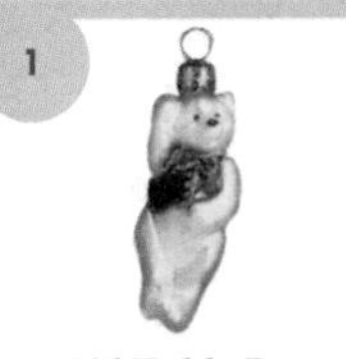
Li'l Teddy Bear
Blown Glass • N/A
795QBG4264 • **Value N/E**

2

Bugs Bunny and Elmer Fudd
Handcrafted • CHAD
995QXM5934 • **Value $16**

3

Catwoman™
Handcrafted • RGRS
995QXM6021 • **Value $16**

4

Celestial Bunny
Porcelain • AUBE
695QXM6641 • **Value $12**

5

Devoted Donkey
Handcrafted • SICK
695QXM6044 • **Value $30**

6

Green Eggs and Ham™ (set/3)
Handcrafted • WILL
1995QXM6034 • **Value $12**

7

Jedi Council Members: Saesee Tiin™, Yoda™ and Ki-Adi-Mundi™ (set/3)
Handcrafted • BRIC
1995QXI6744 • **Value $29**

8

Kindly Lions
Handcrafted • SICK
595QXM5314 • **Value $11**

9

Loyal Elephant
Handcrafted • SICK
695QXM6041 • **Value $12**

10

Mickey and Minnie Mouse (set/2)
Handcrafted • N/A
1295QXD4041 • **Value $22**

11

Mr. Potato Head™
Handcrafted • SIED
595QXM6014 • **Value $11**

12

Precious Penguin
Crystal/Pewter • VOTR
995QXM6104 • **Value $18**

13

Santa's Journey Begins
Handcrafted • CROW
995QXM6004 • **Value $18**

14

Silken Flame™ BARBIE™ Ornament and Travel Case (set/2)
Handcrafted • ANDR
1295QXM6031 • **Value $21**

15

Star Fairy
Handcrafted • ESCH
495QXM6101 • **Value $10**

16

Tigger-ific Tidings to Pooh
Handcrafted • N/A
895QXD4014 • **Value $18**

17

Welcoming Angel
Handcrafted • ESCH
595QXM5321 • **Value $11**

18

Angelic Bell
Handcrafted • BRIC
1695QXC4504 • **Value $19**

19

Bell-Bearing Elf (early renewal gift)
Handcrafted • CROW
QXC4514 • **Value N/E**

20

A Friend Chimes In (keepsake of membership)
Handcrafted • TAGU
QXC4491 • **Value N/E**

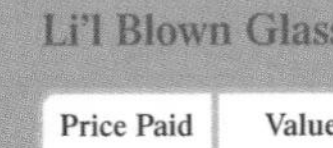
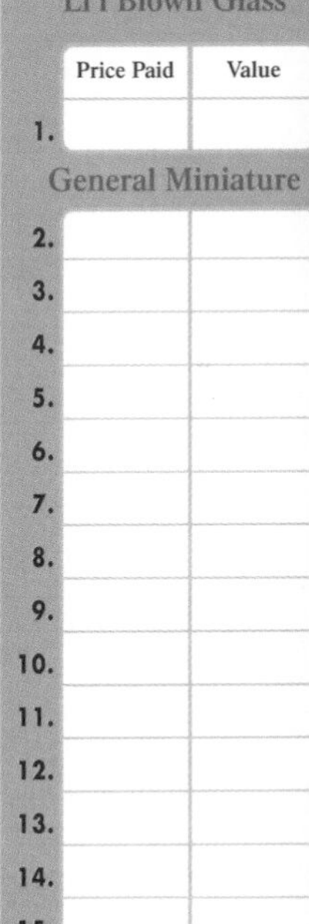

	Price Paid	Value
Li'l Blown Glass		
1.		
General Miniature		
2.		
3.		
4.		
5.		
6.		
7.		
8.		
9.		
10.		
11.		
12.		
13.		
14.		
15.		
16.		
17.		
Collector's Club		
18.		
19.		
20.		
Totals		

1

Jingle Bell Kringle (keepsake of membership)
Handcrafted • CROW
QXC4481 • **Value N/E**

2

The Proud Collector (exclusive to local clubs)
Hancrafted • SEAL
QXC4511 • **Value N/E**

3

Ringing Reindeer (keepsake of membership)
Handcrafted • ESCH
QXC4484 • **Value N/E**

4

Treasure Tree (LE-25,000, mail order exclusive)
Handcrafted • VARI
N/A • **Value N/E**

5

Charlie Brown Ornament
Handcrafted • SIED
495QRP4191• **Value $11**

6

Linus Ornament
Handcrafted • SIED
495QRP4204 • **Value $11**

7

Lucy Ornament
Handcrafted • SIED
495QRP4174 • **Value $11**

8

Snoopy Ornament
Handcrafted • SIED
495QRP4184 • **Value $11**

9
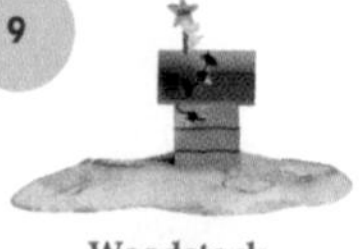
Woodstock On Doghouse – Display Piece
Handcrafted • SIED
495QRP4211 • **Value $11**

10

Busy Bee Shopper (green bag)
Handcrafted • CHAD
QX6964 • **Value N/E**

11

Connecticut
Double-Stamped Metal • N/A
1295QMP9404 • **Value N/E**

12

Delaware
Double-Stamped Metal • N/A
1295QMP9400 • **Value N/E**

13

Georgia
Double-Stamped Metal • N/A
1295QMP9403 • **Value N/E**

14

Maryland
Double-Stamped Metal • N/A
1295QMP9426 • **Value N/E**

15

Massachusetts
Double-Stamped Metal • N/A
1295QMP9423 • **Value N/E**

16

New Hampshire
Double-Stamped Metal • N/A
1495QMP9432 • **Value N/E**

17

New Jersey
Double-Stamped Metal • N/A
1295QMP9402 • **Value N/E**

18

Pennsylvania
Double-Stamped Metal • N/A
1295QMP9401 • **Value N/E**

19

South Carolina
Double-Stamped Metal • N/A
1495QMP9429 • **Value N/E**

20

Virginia
Double-Stamped Metal • N/A
1495QMP9440 • **Value N/E**

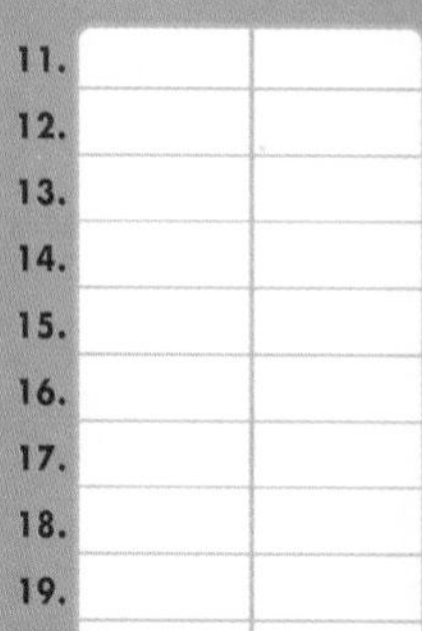

Collector's Club

	Price Paid	Value
1.		
2.		
3.		
4.		
Open House Ornaments		
5.		
6.		
7.		
8.		
9.		
Premiere Ornaments		
10.		
American Spirit Collection™		
11.		
12.		
13.		
14.		
15.		
16.		
17.		
18.		
19.		
20.		
Totals		

1

American Spirit Collection Coin and Figurine Sets (10 assorted)
Gift Set/Pewter • N/A

1. Connecticut
   1695QMP9410 • Value N/E
2. Delaware
   1695QMP9406 • Value N/E
3. Georgia
   1695QMP9409 • Value N/E
4. Maryland
   1695QMP9427 • Value N/E
5. Massachusetts
   1695QMP9424 • Value N/E
6. New Hampshire
   1895QMP9433 • Value N/E
7. New Jersey
   1695QMP9408 • Value N/E
8. Pennsylvania
   1695QMP9407 • Value N/E
9. South Carolina
   1895QMP9430 • Value N/E
10. Virginia
    1895QMP9441 • Value N/E

2

5-piece Citizen Set
Double-Stamped Metal • N/A
595QMP9448 • Value N/E

3

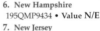

American Spirit Collection Citizen Sets (10 assorted)
Gift Set • N/A

1. Connecticut
   195QMP9421 • Value N/E
2. Delaware
   195QMP9417 • Value N/E
3. Georgia
   195QMP9420 • Value N/E
4. Maryland
   195QMP9428 • Value N/E
5. Massachusetts
   195QMP9425 • Value N/E
6. New Hampshire
   195QMP9434 • Value N/E
7. New Jersey
   195QMP9419 • Value N/E
8. Pennsylvania
   195QMP9418 • Value N/E
9. South Carolina
   195QMP9431 • Value N/E
10. Virginia
    195QMP9442 • Value N/E

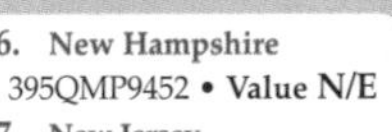

4

American Spirit Collection D/P Citizen Sets (10 assorted)
Gift Set • N/A

1. Connecticut
   295QMP9447 • Value N/E
2. Delaware
   295QMP9443 • Value N/E
3. Georgia
   295QMP9446 • Value N/E
4. Maryland
   295QMP9450 • Value N/E
5. Massachusetts
   295QMP9449 • Value N/E
6. New Hampshire
   395QMP9452 • Value N/E
7. New Jersey
   295QMP9445 • Value N/E
8. Pennsylvania
   295QMP9444 • Value N/E
9. South Carolina
   395QMP9451 • Value N/E
10. Virginia
    395QMP9453 • Value N/E

5

50 State Quarters™ Collector's Kit
Embossed Metal • N/A
1495QMP9416 • Value N/E

6

Signature Snowman
Handcrafted • HADD
QXC4524 • Value N/E

7

Gold-Star Teacher (silver star)
Handcrafted • PIKE
QX6951 • Value N/E

8

A Pony for Christmas (brown)
Handcrafted • SICK
QX6624 • Value N/E

9

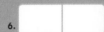

Collegiate Collection (10 assorted)
Acrylic/Brass • N/A

1. Alabama® Crimson Tide®
   995QSR2344 • Value N/E
2. Florida Gators®
   995QSR2324 • Value N/E
3. Florida State® Seminoles®
   995QSR2341 • Value N/E
4. Michigan Wolverines™
   995QSR2271 • Value N/E
5. Nebraska Cornhuskers™
   995QSR2321 • Value N/E
6. North Carolina® Tar Heels®
   995QSR2304 • Value N/E
7. Notre Dame® Fighting Irish™
   995QSR2284 • Value N/E
8. Penn State® Nittany Lions®
   995QSR2311 • Value N/E
9. Tennessee Volunteers®
   995QSR2334 • Value N/E
10. The University of Kentucky® Wildcats™
    995QSR2291 • Value N/E

American Spirit Collection™

	Price Paid	Value
1.		
2.		
3.		
4.		
5.		

Artists On Tour Pieces

	Price Paid	Value
6.		

Club Tour Pieces

	Price Paid	Value
7.		
8.		

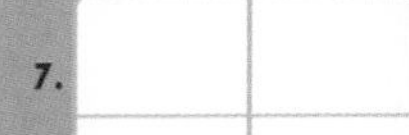

Collegiate Collection

	Price Paid	Value
9.		

Totals

1

The Cat in the Hat™
Porcelain • CROW
1200QSU2026 • **Value N/E**

2

The Ends
N/A • CHAD
4500QSU2038 • **Value N/E**

3

A Faithful Friend
Porcelain • ESCH
1200QSU2029 • **Value N/E**

4

Funny Fish
Porcelain • WILL
2000QSU2033 • **Value N/E**

5

The Great Birthday Bird
Porcelain • BRIC
1200QSU2028 • **Value N/E**

6

The Grinch™
Porcelain • PIKE
1200QSU2055 • **Value N/E**

7

Hat Tricks!
Porcelain • CHAD
1500QSU2027 • **Value N/E**

8

Hop on Pop™
Porcelain • KLIN
2000QSU2031 • **Value N/E**

9

Max the Reindeer
N/A • HADD
1800QSU2056 • **Value N/E**

10

Merry Grinchmas!
N/A • PIKE
2000QSU2030 • **Value N/E**

11

On a Train?
Porcelain • RHOD
1800QSU2036 • **Value N/E**

12

On Top of the World
Porcelain • WILL
2000QSU2034 • **Value N/E**

13

Sam and Ham
Porcelain • WILL
2000QSU2032 • **Value N/E**

14

A Seuss Safe
Porcelain • CROW
1500QSU2037 • **Value N/E**

15

Socks and Blocks
Porcelain • WILL
2000QSU2035 • **Value N/E**

16

Harry Potter™
Pewter • BRIC
1295QXE4381 • **Value N/E**

17

Hermione Granger™
Pewter • BRIC
1295QXE4391 • **Value N/E**

18

Hedwig The Owl™
Pewter • BRIC
795QXE4394 • **Value N/E**

19

Professor Dumbledore™
Pewter • BRIC
1295QXE4384 • **Value N/E**

20

Photo Unavailable
Hogwarts™ Charms (set/6)
Pewter • BRIC
1295QXE4404 • **Value N/E**

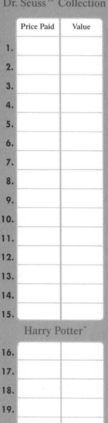

Dr. Seuss™ Collection

	Price Paid	Value
1.		
2.		
3.		
4.		
5.		
6.		
7.		
8.		
9.		
10.		
11.		
12.		
13.		
14.		
15.		

Harry Potter™

	Price Paid	Value
16.		
17.		
18.		
19.		
20.		
Totals		

1

Blériot XI
Handcrafted • N/A
2500QHA1009 • **Value N/E**

2

Curtiss R3C-2 Seaplane
Handcrafted • N/A
3200QHA1002 • **Value N/E**

3

F-86F Sabre
Handcrafted • N/A
2700QHA1010 • **Value N/E**

4

F4U-ID Corsair
Handcrafted • N/A
3200QHA1008 • **Value N/E**

5

Ryan NYP "Spirit of St. Louis"
Handcrafted • N/A
3000QHA1004 • **Value N/E**

6

SPAD XIII "Smith IV"
Handcrafted • N/A
3200QHA1003 • **Value N/E**

7

Vega 5B
Handcrafted • N/A
3000QHA1007 • **Value N/E**

8

NFL Collection (10 assorted)
Handcrafted/Brass • SIED

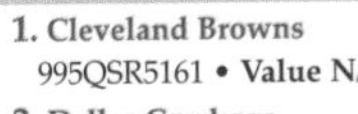

1. **Cleveland Browns** 995QSR5161 • **Value N/E**
2. **Dallas Cowboys** 995QSR5121 • **Value N/E**
3. **Denver Broncos** 995QSR5111 • **Value N/E**
4. **Green Bay Packers** 995QSR5114 • **Value N/E**
5. **Kansas City Chiefs** 995QSR5131 • **Value N/E**
6. **Miami Dolphins** 995QSR5144 • **Value N/E**
7. **Minnesota Vikings** 995QSR5164 • **Value N/E**
8. **Pittsburgh Steelers** 995QSR5124 • **Value N/E**
9. **San Francisco 49ers** 995QSR5134 • **Value N/E**
10. **Washington Redskins** 995QSR5151 • **Value N/E**

9

Ornament Charms (24 assorted, re-issued in 2001)
N/A • N/A

1. **Believe** QX2831 • **Value $.95**
2. **Brass Cross** QX2734 • **Value $.95**
3. **Brass Heart** QX2821 • **Value $.95**
4. **Brother** QX2641 • **Value $.95**
5. **Congrats!** QX2824 • **Value $.95**
6. **Dad** QX2621 • **Value $.95**
7. **Daughter** QX2644 • **Value $.95**
8. **Friends Forever** QX2701 • **Value $.95**
9. **Granddaughter** QX2654 • **Value $.95**
10. **Grandma** QX2624 • **Value $.95**
11. **Grandpa** QX2631 • **Value $.95**
12. **Grandson** QX2661 • **Value $.95**
13. **Great Teacher!** QX2674 • **Value $.95**
14. **Happy Birthday** QX2704 • **Value $.95**
15. **Happy Holidays** QX2684 • **Value $.95**
16. **I Love You** QX2694 • **Value $.95**
17. **Mom** QX2601 • **Value $.95**
18. **Nephew** QX2671 • **Value $.95**
19. **Niece** QX2664 • **Value $.95**
20. **Peace on Earth** QX2711 • **Value $.95**
21. **Sister** QX2634 • **Value $.95**
22. **Son** QX2651 • **Value $.95**
23. **Thank You** QX2681 • **Value $.95**
24. **Thinking of You** QX2691 • **Value $.95**

Legends in Flight™

	Price Paid	Value
1.		
2.		
3.		
4.		
5.		
6.		
7.		
NFL Collection		
8.		
Ornament Charms		
9.		
Totals		

1

Being There
Pewter • BRIC
1500QPC4005 • **Value N/E**

2

Celebrate!
N/A • N/A
1295QPC4015 • **Value N/E**

3

Charlie Brown (LE-24,500)
Porcelain • N/A
2500QPC4025 • **Value N/E**

4

Don't Give Up!
N/A • N/A
1295QPC4016 • **Value N/E**

5

Fall Ball
Porcelain • WILL
2000QPC4010 • **Value N/E**

6

Five Decades of Charlie Brown
Pewter • SIED
1300QPC4002 • **Value N/E**

7

Five Decades of Lucy
Pewter • SIED
1300QPC4003 • **Value N/E**

8

Five Decades of Snoopy
Pewter • SIED
1300QPC4001 • **Value N/E**

9

Flying High
Pewter • CHAD
1500QPC4004 • **Value N/E**

10

Golf is Life!
N/A • N/A
1295QPC4012 • **Value N/E**

11

The Great Pumpkin
Porcelain • RGRS
2000QPC4022 • **Value N/E**

12

Hanging On!
N/A • N/A
1295QPC4014 • **Value N/E**

13

Hugs
Porcelain • PIKE
1500QPC4007 • **Value N/E**

14
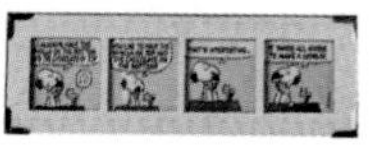
It Takes All Kinds!
N/A • N/A
1295QPC4013 • **Value N/E**

15
Joe Cool and Friend
Porcelain • FRAN
1500QPC4011 • **Value N/E**

16

Jolly Holidays
Porcelain/Metal • LAPR
2000QPC4023 • **Value N/E**

17

A Joyful Song (LE-24,500)
Porcelain • SIED
2500QPC4024 • **Value N/E**

18

Linus (LE-24,500)
Porcelain • N/A
2500QPC4019 • **Value N/E**

19

Lucy (LE-24,500)
Porcelain • N/A
2500QPC4018 • **Value N/E**

20

On the Course (1st in *Snoopy and Friends Series*)
Porcelain • AUBE
2000QPC4008 • **Value N/E**

Peanuts® Gallery

	Price Paid	Value
1.		
2.		
3.		
4.		
5.		
6.		
7.		
8.		
9.		
10.		
11.		
12.		
13.		
14.		
15.		
16.		
17.		
18.		
19.		
20.		
Totals		

1

Sally
Porcelain • N/A
2500QPC4020 • **Value N/E**

2

Seventh Inning Stretch
Porcelain • SIED
1500QPC4009 • **Value N/E**

3

Snoopy (LE-24,500)
Porcelain • N/A
2500QPC4021 • **Value N/E**

4

The Winning Team (LE-24,500)
Porcelain/Acrylic • RGRS
3000QPC4006 • **Value N/E**

5

1950s Hopalong Cassidy
Pressed Tin • N/A
1095QHM8809 • **Value N/E**

6

1950s Mickey Mouse Circus
Pressed Tin • N/A
1095QHM8816 • **Value N/E**

7

1960s Yellow Submarine™ (LE-24,500)
Pressed Tin • N/A
1195QHM8901 • **Value N/E**

8

1963 The Jetsons™ (LE-24,500)
Pressed Tin • N/A
1195QHM8900 • **Value N/E**

9

1969 Disney Fire Fighters (LE-24,500)
Pressed Tin • N/A
1195QHM8904 • **Value N/E**

10

1980 The Empire Strikes Back
Pressed Tin • N/A
1095QHM8820 • **Value N/E**

11

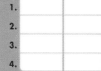

Batman™ and Robin™ Lunch Box with Drink Container (LE-19,500)
Pressed Tin • N/A
1395QHM8808 • **Value N/E**

12

Snoopy Doghouse (LE-24,500)
Pressed Tin • N/A
1195QHM8905 • **Value N/E**

13

Winnie the Pooh
Pressed Tin • N/A
1095QHM8821 • **Value N/E**

14

The Wizard of Oz™ (LE-19,500)
Pressed Tin • N/A
1395QHM8822 • **Value N/E**

15

700 E J Hudson Steam Locomotive (100th Anniversary Piece)
Die-Cast Metal • N/A
2200QXI5261 • **Value N/E**

16

Millennium Snowma'am
Handcrafted • N/A
895QXI5241 • **Value N/E**

17

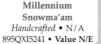

Millennium Snowman (color change, exclusive to KOCC retailers)
Handcrafted • N/A
N/A • **Value N/E**

18

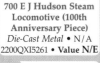

Mitford Snowmen (set/4)
Handcrafted • N/A
1995QXI5244 • **Value N/E**

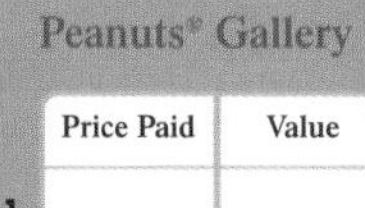

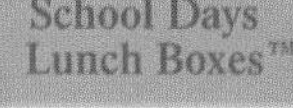

	Price Paid	Value
Peanuts® Gallery		
1.		
2.		
3.		
4.		
School Days Lunch Boxes™		
5.		
6.		
7.		
8.		
9.		
10.		
11.		
12.		
13.		
14.		
Special Edition Pieces		
15.		
16.		
17.		
18.		
Totals		

1999

The Keepsake Collection grew by 212 pieces in 1999. And collectors were thrilled with the two new lines that joined the Hallmark Ornament family: Laser Creations, a series of ornaments cut by laser light; and Legends of Flight, a group of die-cast model airplanes. See the collectible series section for more 1999 ornaments.

1

1949 Cadillac® Coupe deVille
Die-Cast Metal • WILL
1495QX6429 • **Value $29**

2

40th Anniversary BARBIE® Ornament
Handcrafted • ANDR
1595QXI8049 • **Value $28**

3

Adding the Best Part
Handcrafted • CROW
795QX6569 • **Value $15**

4

African-American Millennium Princess BARBIE® Ornament
Handcrafted • RGRS
1595QXI6449 • **Value $30**

5

All Sooted Up
Handcrafted • KLIN
995QX6837 • **Value $16**

6

Angel in Disguise
Handcrafted • AUBE
895QX6629 • **Value $16**

7
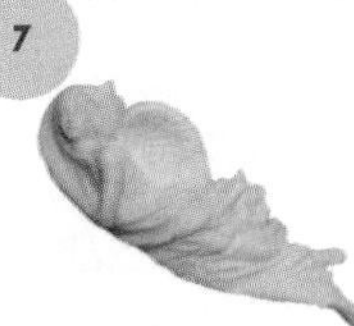
Angel of Hope
Porcelain • ANDR
1495QXI6339 • **Value $26**

8

Angel Song
Handcrafted • VOTR
1895QX6939 • **Value $30**

9

Baby Mickey's Sweet Dreams
Handcrafted • N/A
1095QXD4087 • **Value $18**

10

Baby's First Christmas
Handcrafted • HADD
795QX6649 • **Value $20**

11

Baby's First Christmas
Handcrafted • FRAN
795QX6667 • **Value $20**

12
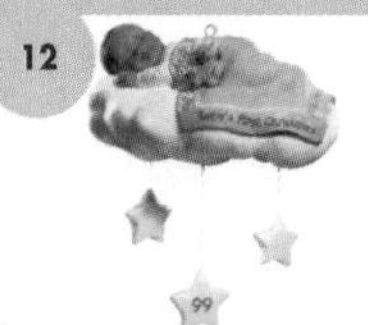
Baby's First Christmas
Handcrafted • VOTR
895QX6657 • **Value $16**

13

Baby's First Christmas
Porcelain • TAGU
995QX6659 • **Value $23**

14

Baby's First Christmas
Handcrafted • ANDR
1895QX6647 • **Value $33**

15

Baby's Second Christmas
Handcrafted • FRAN
795QX6669 • **Value $18**

16

Balthasar – The Magi (re-issued in 2000)
Porcelain • LYLE
1295QX6819 • **Value $20**

17

BARBIE® Doll Dreamhouse™ Playhouse Ornament
Handcrafted • ANDR
1495QXI8047 • **Value $28**

General Keepsake

	Price Paid	Value
1.		
2.		
3.		
4.		
5.		
6.		
7.		
8.		
9.		
10.		
11.		
12.		
13.		
14.		
15.		
16.		
17.		
Totals		

1

Best Pals
Handcrafted • AUBE
1895QX6879 • **Value $48**

2

Bowling's a Ball
Handcrafted • KLIN
795QX6577 • **Value $15**

3

Caspar – The Magi (re-issued in 2000)
Porcelain • LYLE
1295QX8039 • **Value $20**

4

Chewbacca™
Handcrafted • RHOD
1495QXI4009 • **Value $30**

5

Child of Wonder
Handcrafted • UNRU
1495QX6817 • **Value $30**

6

Child's Fifth Christmas
Handcrafted • CROW
795QX6679 • **Value $17**

7

Child's Fourth Christmas
Handcrafted • CROW
795QX6687 • **Value $18**

8

Child's Third Christmas
Handcrafted • CROW
795QX6677 • **Value $18**

9

The Christmas Story
Handcrafted • UNRU
2200QX6897 • **Value $38**

10

Clownin' Around CRAYOLA® Crayon
Handcrafted • TAGU
1095QX6487 • **Value $22**

11

Cocoa Break HERSHEY's™
Handcrafted • KLIN
1095QX8009 • **Value $23**

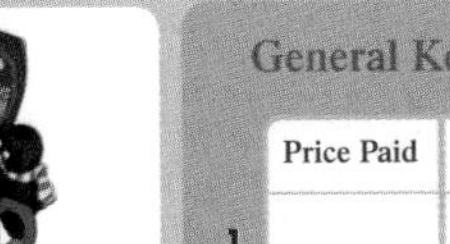

12

Counting On Success
Handcrafted • PIKE
795QX6707 • **Value $15**

13

Cross of Hope
Pewter/Lead Crystal • UNRU
995QX6557 • **Value $25**

14

Dad
Pressed Tin • BRIC
895QX6719 • **Value $16**

15

Dance for the Season
Handcrafted • ESCH
995QX6587 • **Value $17**

16

Daughter
Handcrafted • ESCH
895QX6729 • **Value $17**

17

Dorothy and Glinda, the Good Witch™
Handcrafted • LYLE
2400QX6509 • **Value $40**

18

Dumbo's First Flight
Handcrafted • N/A
1395QXD4117 • **Value $23**

19

The Family Portrait
Handcrafted • N/A
1495QXD4149 • **Value $26**

20

Feliz Navidad Santa
Handcrafted • TAGU
895QX6999 • **Value $19**

General Keepsake

	Price Paid	Value
1.		
2.		
3.		
4.		
5.		
6.		
7.		
8.		
9.		
10.		
11.		
12.		
13.		
14.		
15.		
16.		
17.		
18.		
19.		
20.		
Totals		

1

Flame-Fighting Friends
Handcrafted • TAGU
1495QX6619 • **Value $23**

2

The Flash™
Handcrafted • RGRS
1295QX6469 • **Value $22**

3

For My Grandma
Handcrafted • LYLE
795QX6747 • **Value $15**

4

Forecast for Fun
Handcrafted/Glass • TAGU
1495QX6869 • **Value $24**

5

G.I. Joe®, Action Soldier™
Handcrafted • CROW
1395QX6537 • **Value $23**

6

Godchild
Handcrafted • TAGU
795QX6759 • **Value $15**

7

Goofy As Santa's Helper
Handcrafted • N/A
1295QXD4079 • **Value $21**

8

Granddaughter
Handcrafted • SEAL
895QX6739 • **Value $16**

9

Grandson
Handcrafted • SEAL
895QX6737 • **Value $16**

10

Handled With Care
Handcrafted • RHOD
895QX6769 • **Value $16**

11

Hello, Hello (set/2)
Handcrafted • SEAL
1495QX6777 • **Value $22**

12

The Holy Family (set/3, re-issued from 1998)
Porcelain • LYLE
2500QX6523 • **Value $48**

13

Howdy Doody™ (set/2)
Pressed Tin/Handcrafted • N/A
1495QX6519 • **Value $23**

14

In The Workshop
Handcrafted • AUBE
995QX6979 • **Value $15**

15

Jazzy Jalopy
Handcrafted • CROW
2400QX6549 • **Value $45**

16

Jet Threat™ Car With Case (set/2)
Handcrafted • UNRU
1295QX6527 • **Value $21**

17

Jolly Locomotive
Die-Cast Metal • CROW
1495QX6859 • **Value $30**

18

Joyous Angel
Handcrafted • VOTR
895QX6787 • **Value $18**

19

A Joyous Christmas
Glass • N/A
595QX6827 • **Value $14**

20

King Malh – Third King
Handcrafted • ANDR
1395QX6797 • **Value $26**

General Keepsake

	Price Paid	Value
1.		
2.		
3.		
4.		
5.		
6.		
7.		
8.		
9.		
10.		
11.		
12.		
13.		
14.		
15.		
16.		
17.		
18.		
19.		
20.		
Totals		

1

Kringle's Whirligig
Handcrafted • CROW
1295QX6847 • **Value $20**

2

Larry, Moe, and Curly (set/3)
Handcrafted • LARS
3000QX6499 • **Value $46**

3

Lieutenant Commander Worf™
Handcrafted • RGRS
1495QXI4139 • **Value $22**

4

Little Cloud Keeper
Porcelain • HADD
1695QX6877 • **Value $28**

5

The Lollipop Guild™ (set/3)
Handcrafted • LYLE
1995QX8029 • **Value $35**

6

"Lucy Gets In Pictures"
Handcrafted • VOTR
1395QX6547 • **Value $26**

7

Mary's Bears
Handcrafted • TAGU
1295QX5569 • **Value $19**

8

Melchoir – The Magi (re-issued in 2000)
Porcelain • LYLE
1295QX6819 • **Value $20**

9

Merry Motorcycle
Pressed Tin • SICK
895QX6637 • **Value $16**

10

Military on Parade
Handcrafted • CROW
1095QX6639 • **Value $21**

11

Milk 'n' Cookies Express
Handcrafted • CHAD
895QX6839 • **Value $16**

12

Millennium Princess BARBIE® Ornament
Handcrafted • RGRS
1595QXI4019 • **Value $48**

13

Millennium Snowman
Handcrafted • SEAL
895QX8059 • **Value $50**

14

Mom
Pressed Tin • BRIC
895QX6717 • **Value $15**

15

Mom and Dad
Handcrafted • SEAL
995QX6709 • **Value $19**

16

Mother and Daughter
Precious Metal • VOTR
895QX6757 • **Value $23**

17

Muhammad Ali
Handcrafted • UNRU
1495QXI4147 • **Value $23**

18

A Musician of Note
Handcrafted • HADD
795QX6567 • **Value $14**

19

My Sister, My Friend
Handcrafted • TAGU
995QX6749 • **Value $15**

20

Naboo Starfighter™
Handcrafted • WEBB
1895QXI7613 • **Value $40**

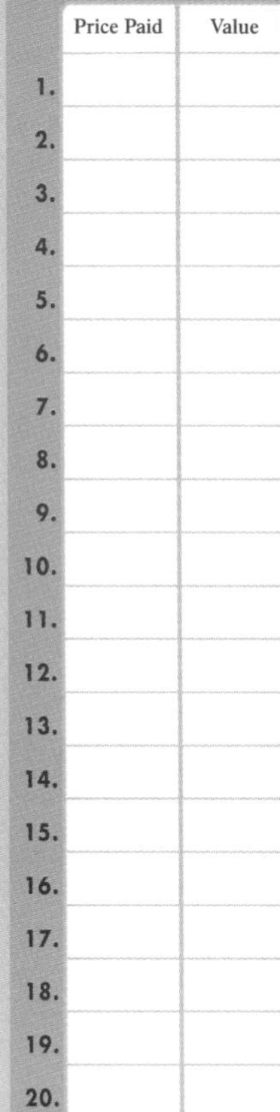

General Keepsake

	Price Paid	Value
1.		
2.		
3.		
4.		
5.		
6.		
7.		
8.		
9.		
10.		
11.		
12.		
13.		
14.		
15.		
16.		
17.		
18.		
19.		
20.		
Totals		

1

New Home
Handcrafted • SEAL
995QX6347 • **Value $17**

2

Noah's Ark
Handcrafted • ESCH
1295QX6809 • **Value $23**

3

North Pole Mr. Potato Head™
Handcrafted • N/A
1095QX8027 • **Value $21**

4

North Pole Star
Handcrafted • CHAD
895QX6589 • **Value $18**

5

On Thin Ice
Handcrafted • PIKE
1095QX6489 • **Value $20**

6

Our Christmas Together
Handcrafted • KLIN
995QX6689 • **Value $17**

7

Our First Christmas Together
Acrylic • VOTR
795QX3207 • **Value $14**

8

Our First Christmas Together
Handcrafted • TAGU
895QX6697 • **Value $16**

9

Our First Christmas Together
Handcrafted • UNRU
2200QX6699 • **Value $36**

10

Outstanding Teacher
Handcrafted • KLIN
895QX6627 • **Value $15**

11

Pepé LePew and Penelope
Handcrafted • CHAD
1295QX6507 • **Value $23**

12

Piano Player Mickey
Handcrafted • N/A
2400QXD7389 • **Value $48**

13

Pinocchio and Geppetto
Handcrafted • N/A
1695QXD4107 • **Value $24**

14

Playful Snowman
Handcrafted • SICK
1295QX6867 • **Value $24**

15

The Poky Little Puppy™ (w/book)
Handcrafted • VOTR
1195QX6479 • **Value $21**

16

Praise the Day
Handcrafted • TAGU
1495QX6799 • **Value $23**

17

Presents From Pooh
Handcrafted • N/A
1495QXD4093 • **Value $25**

18

Queen Amidala™
Handcrafted • RHOD
1495QXI4187 • **Value $28**

19

Reel Fun
Handcrafted • TAGU
1095QX6609 • **Value $19**

20

Rhett Butler™
Handcrafted • ANDR
1295QX6467 • **Value $24**

General Keepsake

	Price Paid	Value
1.		
2.		
3.		
4.		
5.		
6.		
7.		
8.		
9.		
10.		
11.		
12.		
13.		
14.		
15.		
16.		
17.		
18.		
19.		
20.		
Totals		

1

Scooby-Doo™ (set/2)
Handcrafted/Pressed Tin • N/A
1495QX6997 • **Value $26**

2

Sew Handy
Handcrafted • TAGU
895QX6597 • **Value $26**

3

Sleddin' Buddies
Handcrafted • CROW
995QX6849 • **Value $18**

4

The Snowmen of Mitford (set/3)
Handcrafted • N/A
1595QXI8587 • **Value $48**

5

Son
Handcrafted • ESCH
895QX6727 • **Value $16**

6

Special Dog
Handcrafted • KLIN
795QX6767 • **Value $15**

7

Spellin' Santa
Handcrafted • WILL
995QX6857 • **Value $17**

8

Sprinkling Stars
Handcrafted • AUBE
995QX6599 • **Value $18**

9

Sundae Golfer
Handcrafted • TAGU
1295QX6617 • **Value $20**

10

Surfin' the Net
Handcrafted • SEAL
995QX6607 • **Value $19**

11

Sweet Friendship
Handcrafted • HADD
995QX6779 • **Value $18**

12

Sweet Skater
Handcrafted • TAGU
795QX6579 • **Value $15**

13

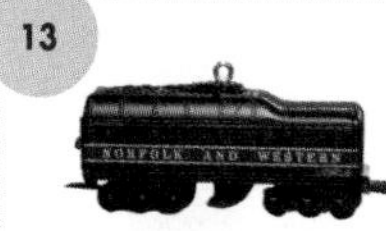

The Tender LIONEL® 746 Norfolk and Western
Die-Cast Metal • N/A
1495QX6497 • **Value $30**

14

Tigger Plays Soccer
Handcrafted • N/A
1095QXD4119 • **Value $20**

15

A Time of Peace
Handcrafted • LARS
895QX6807 • **Value $20**

16

Tonka® 1956 Suburban Pumper No. 5
Die-Cast Metal • N/A
1395QX6459 • **Value $27**

17

Welcome to 2000
Handcrafted • LARS
1095QX6829 • **Value $50**

18

Wintertime Treat
Handcrafted • UNRU
1295QX6989 • **Value $24**

19

Woody's Roundup
Handcrafted • N/A
1395QXI4207 • **Value $23**

20

Darth Vader's TIE Fighter
Handcrafted • RHOD
2400QXI7399 • **Value $45**

General Keepsake	Price Paid	Value
1.		
2.		
3.		
4.		
5.		
6.		
7.		
8.		
9.		
10.		
11.		
12.		
13.		
14.		
15.		
16.		
17.		
18.		
19.		
General Magic		
20.		
Totals		

1

Let It Snow!
Porcelain • LARS
1895QLX7427 • **Value $35**

2

Runabout – U.S.S. Rio Grande
Handcrafted • NORT
2400QXI7593 • **Value $48**

3

Warm Welcome
Handcrafted • HADD
1695QLX7417 • **Value $30**

4

1950 LIONEL® Santa Fe F3 Diesel Locomotive
Blown Glass • N/A
3500QBG6119 • **Value $50**

5

1955 Murray® Ranch Wagon
Blown Glass • N/A
3500QBG6077 • **Value $50**

6

Childhood Treasures (set/3)
Blown Glass • N/A
3000QBG4237 • **Value $42**

7
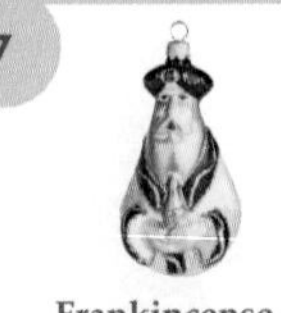
Frankincense (re-issued from 1998)
Blown Glass • N/A
2200QBG6896 • **Value $33**

8

Frosty Friends
Blown Glass • N/A
3500QBG6067 • **Value $50**

9

Gold (re-issued from 1998)
Blown Glass • N/A
2200QBG6836 • **Value $33**

10

Harvest of Grapes
Blown Glass • N/A
2500QBG6047 • **Value $35**

11

The Holy Family
Blown Glass • N/A
3000QBG6127 • **Value $40**

12

Jolly Snowman
Blown Glass • N/A
2000QBG6059 • **Value $35**

13

Myrrh (re-issued from 1998)
Blown Glass • N/A
2200QBG6893 • **Value $35**

14

U.S.S. Enterprise™ NCC-1701
Blown Glass • N/A
2500QBG6117 • **Value $75**

15

Village Church
Blown Glass • N/A
3000QBG6057 • **Value $45**

16

Yummy Memories (set/8)
Blown Glass • N/A
4500QBG6049 • **Value $60**

17

Angelic Messenger
Archival Paper • N/A
795QLZ4287 • **Value $13**

18

Christmas In Bloom
Archival Paper • N/A
895QLZ4257 • **Value $15**

19

Don't Open Till 2000
Archival Paper • N/A
895QLZ4289 • **Value $22**

20

Inside Santa's Workshop
Archival Paper • N/A
895QLZ4239 • **Value $15**

	Price Paid	Value
General Magic		
1.		
2.		
3.		
General Crown Reflections		
4.		
5.		
6.		
7.		
8.		
9.		
10.		
11.		
12.		
13.		
14.		
15.		
16.		
General Laser Creations		
17.		
18.		
19.		
20.		
Totals		

1

Ringing In Christmas
Archival Paper • N/A
695QLZ4277 • **Value $13**

2
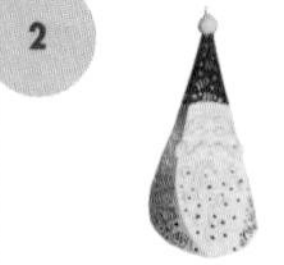
A Visit From St. Nicholas
Archival Paper • N/A
595QLZ4229 • **Value $13**

3

A Wish For Peace
Archival Paper • N/A
695QLZ4249 • **Value $13**

4

Yuletide Charm
Archival Paper • N/A
595QLZ4269 • **Value $13**

5

Betsey's Perfect 10
Handcrafted • KLIN
495QXM4609 • **Value $10**

6

Celestial Kitty
Porcelain • AUBE
695QXM4639 • **Value $12**

7

Classic Batman™ and Robin™ (set/2)
Handcrafted • CHAD
1295QXM4659 • **Value $20**

8

Crystal Claus
Silver Plated/Crystal • VOTR
995QXM4637 • **Value $19**

9

Girl Talk (set/2)
Handcrafted • N/A
1295QXD4069 • **Value $19**

10

Love to Share
Handcrafted • SICK
695QXM4557 • **Value $11**

11

Marvin The Martian
Handcrafted • CHAD
895QXM4657 • **Value $14**

12

Max Rebo Band™ (set/3)
Handcrafted • BRIC
1995QXI4597 • **Value $30**

13

Merry Grinch-mas! (set/3)
Handcrafted • WILL
1995QXI4627 • **Value $27**

14

Roll-a-Bear
Handcrafted • SICK
695QXM4629 • **Value $11**

15

Santa Time
Handcrafted • UNRU
795QXM4647 • **Value $15**

16

Skating with Pooh
Handcrafted • N/A
695QXD4127 • **Value $11**

17

Taz and the She-Devil
Handcrafted • CHAD
895QXM4619 • **Value $13**

18

Travel Case and BARBIE™ Ornament (set/2)
Handcrafted • ANDR
1295QXI6129 • **Value $20**

19

Trusty Reindeer
Handcrafted • SICK
595QXM4617 • **Value $13**

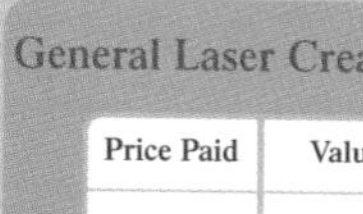
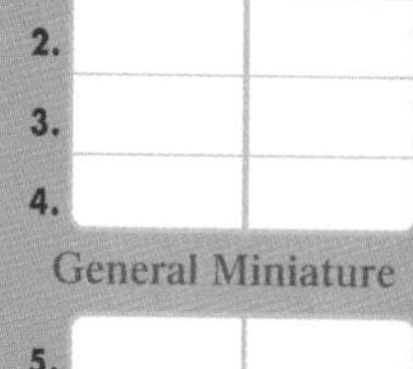

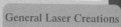

	Price Paid	Value
General Laser Creations		
1.		
2.		
3.		
4.		
General Miniature		
5.		
6.		
7.		
8.		
9.		
10.		
11.		
12.		
13.		
14.		
15.		
16.		
17.		
18.		
19.		
Totals		

1

Arctic Artist
(keepsake of membership)
Handcrafted • HADD
QXC4527 • **Value $16**

2

Collecting Friends
(exclusive to local clubs)
Handcrafted • SIED
QXC4679 • **Value N/E**

3

Snow Day–PEANUTS®
(set/2, club edition)
Handcrafted • RHOD
1895QXC4517 • **Value $42**

4

Snowy Surprise
(keepsake of membership)
Handcrafted • HADD
QXC4529 • **Value $16**

5

The Toymaker's Gift
(keepsake of membership)
Handcrafted • CHAD
QXC4519 • **Value $16**

6

Waiting for a Hug
(early renewal gift)
Handcrafted • CHAD
QXC4537 • **Value $14**

7

Jolly Locomotive
(green)
Handcrafted • CROW
(N/C) QX6859 • **Value N/E**

8

Zebra Fantasy
Handcrafted • SICK
1495QX6559 • **Value $30**

9

1968 Murray® Jolly Roger Flagship
Die-Cast Metal • PALM
(N/C) QX6279 • **Value N/E**

10

Gold Locomotive
(miniature)
N/A • N/A
(N/C) No stock # • **Value N/E**

11

Hollow Log Café
Handcrafted • VARI
(N/C) QXC4667 • **Value N/E**

12
North Pole Pond
Handcrafted • VARI
(N/C) QXC4677 • **Value N/E**

13

A Pony for Christmas
Handcrafted • SICK
(N/C) QX6299 • **Value N/E**

14
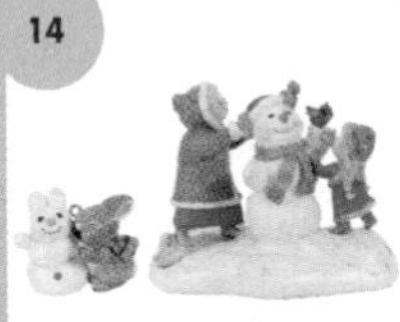
Snowy Plaza
Handcrafted • VARI
(N/C) QXC4669 • **Value N/E**

15

Yummy Memories
Blown Glass • KLIN
(N/C) QBG6049 • **Value N/E**

16

Holiday Sensation™ BARBIE® Doll
(3rd & final, *Holiday Homecoming Collector Series*)
Handcrafted • N/A
5000QHB3403 • **Value N/E**

17

The Cat in the Hat Dr. Seuss™ Books
Ceramic/Brass • N/A
995QXI8579 • **Value $22**

18
I Love Lucy®
Ceramic/Brass • N/A
995QXI8567 • **Value $22**

	Price Paid	Value
Collector's Club		
1.		
2.		
3.		
4.		
5.		
6.		
Premiere Ornaments		
7.		
8.		
Artists On Tour Pieces		
9.		
10.		
11.		
12.		
13.		
14.		
15.		
BARBIE™ Collectibles		
16.		
Century Stamp Ornaments		
17.		
18.		
Totals		

1

Silken Flame™
BARBIE Ornament
Ceramic/Brass • N/A
995QXI8559 • **Value $18**

2

Superman™
Ceramic/Brass • N/A
995QXI8569 • **Value $18**

3

U.S.S. Enterprise™
NCC-1701 STAR TREK™
Ceramic/Brass • N/A
995QXI8557 • **Value $18**

4

Yellow Submarine
THE BEATLES
Ceramic/Brass • N/A
995QXI8577 • **Value $18**

5

Collegiate Collection
Handcrafted • AUBE

1. **Arizona® Wildcats™**
   995QSR2429 • **Value N/E**
2. **Duke™ Blue Devils®**
   995QSR2437 • **Value N/E**
3. **Florida State® Seminoles®**
   995QSR2439 • **Value N/E**
4. **Georgetown Hoyas**
   995QSR2447 • **Value N/E**
5. **Kentucky Wildcats®**
   995QSR2449 • **Value N/E**
6. **Michigan Wolverines™**
   995QSR2457 • **Value N/E**
7. **Nebraska Cornhuskers™**
   995QSR2459 • **Value N/E**
8. **North Carolina Tar Heels™**
   995QSR2467 • **Value N/E**
9. **Notre Dame Fighting Irish™**
   995QSR2427 • **Value N/E**
10. **Penn State Nittany Lions™**
    995QSR2469 • **Value N/E**

6

Kenny Rogers
Christmas From The
Heart (concert piece)
Pewter • N/A
(N/C) No stock # • **Value N/E**

7

1954 Lionel® Catalog
Cover Tin Sign
Pressed Tin • N/A
1800QHT3707 • **Value N/E**

8

Lionel® 671 Turbine
Steam Locomotive
(LE-29,500, 4th in *20th Century Series*)
Handcrafted • N/A
11500QHT7806 • **Value N/E**

9

Lionel® 726 Berkshire
Steam Locomotive
(Artists On Tour)
Die-Cast Metal • N/A
(N/C) No stock # • **Value N/E**

10

Lionel® 773 Hudson
Steam Locomotive
(LE-29,500, 5th & final in *20th Century Series*)
Handcrafted • N/A
12500QHT7807 • **Value N/E**

11

Lionel® 2333 New York
Central F3A-A Diesel
Locomotives (LE-29,500, 3rd in *20th Century Series*)
Die-Cast Metal • N/A
10000QHT7802 • **Value N/E**

12

Oceanside Depot
(LE-29,500)
Handcrafted • N/A
6500QHT3501 • **Value N/E**

13

Curtiss P-40 Warhawk
Handcrafted • N/A
3000QHA1000 • **Value N/E**

14

F-14A Tomcat (LE-24,500)
Handcrafted • N/A
4800QHA1006 • **Value N/E**

15

Fokker Dr.I "Red Baron"
Handcrafted • N/A
3800QHA1005 • **Value N/E**

16

Wright Flyer
Handcrafted • N/A
3500QHA1001 • **Value N/E**

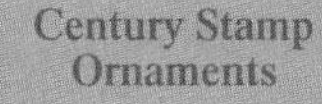

	Price Paid	Value
Century Stamp Ornaments		
1.		
2.		
3.		
4.		
Collegiate Collection		
5.		
Event Pieces		
6.		
Great American Railways™		
7.		
8.		
9.		
10.		
11.		
12.		
Legends in Flight™		
13.		
14.		
15.		
16.		
Totals		

1

NBA Collection
(10 assorted)
Handcrafted • KLIN

1. **Charlotte Hornets™** 1095QSR1057 • **Value N/E**
2. **Chicago Bulls™** 1095QSR1019 • **Value N/E**
3. **Detroit Pistons™** 1095QSR1027 • **Value N/E**
4. **Houston Rockets™** 1095QSR1029 • **Value N/E**
5. **Indiana Pacers™** 1095QSR1037 • **Value N/E**
6. **Los Angeles Lakers™** 1095QSR1039 • **Value N/E**
7. **New York Knicks™** 1095QSR1047 • **Value N/E**
8. **Orlando Magic™** 1095QSR1059 • **Value N/E**
9. **Seattle SuperSonics™** 1095QSR1067 • **Value N/E**
10. **Utah Jazz™** 1095QSR1069 • **Value N/E**

2

NFL Collection
(15 assorted)
Handcrafted • HADD

1. **Carolina Panthers™** 1095QSR5217 • **Value N/E**
2. **Chicago Bears™** 1095QSR5219 • **Value N/E**
3. **Dallas Cowboys™** 1095QSR5227 • **Value N/E**
4. **Denver Broncos™** 1095QSR5229 • **Value N/E**
5. **Green Bay Packers™** 1095QSR5237 • **Value N/E**
6. **Kansas City Chiefs™** 1095QSR5197 • **Value N/E**
7. **Miami Dolphins™** 1095QSR5239 • **Value N/E**
8. **Minnesota Vikings™** 1095QSR5247 • **Value N/E**
9. **New England Patriots™** 1095QSR5279 • **Value N/E**
10. **New York Giants™** 1095QSR5249 • **Value N/E**
11. **Oakland Raiders™** 1095QSR5257 • **Value N/E**
12. **Philadelphia Eagles™** 1095QSR5259 • **Value N/E**
13. **Pittsburgh Steelers™** 1095QSR5267 • **Value N/E**
14. **San Francisco 49ers™** 1095QSR5269 • **Value N/E**
15. **Washington Redskins™** 1095QSR5277 • **Value N/E**

3

1950s Donald Duck
Pressed Tin • N/A
1095QHM8806 • **Value N/E**

4

1960s Mickey's School Days
Pressed Tin • N/A
1095QHM8804 • **Value N/E**

5

1960s Star Trek™
Pressed Tin • N/A
1095QHM8810 • **Value N/E**

6

1962 Barbie™
Pressed Tin • N/A
1095QHM8807 • **Value N/E**

7

1970s Snow White
Pressed Tin • N/A
1095QHM8814 • **Value N/E**

8

1973 Super Friends™
Pressed Tin • N/A
1095QHM8815 • **Value N/E**

9

1977 Star Wars™
Pressed Tin • N/A
1095QHM8817 • **Value N/E**

10

1980 Peanuts®
Pressed Tin • N/A
1095QHM8812 • **Value N/E**

11

A Charlie Brown Christmas
Pressed Tin • N/A
N/A • **Value N/E**

12

Looney Tunes Rodeo
Pressed Tin • N/A
1095QHM8805 • **Value N/E**

13

Scooby-Doo™
Pressed Tin • N/A
1095QHM8818 • **Value N/E**

	Price Paid	Value
NBA Collection		
1.		
NFL Collection		
2.		
School Days Lunch Boxes		
3.		
4.		
5.		
6.		
7.		
8.		
9.		
10.		
11.		
12.		
13.		
Totals		

1

Between Friends
Resin • N/A
1800QHC8219 • **Value N/E**

2

Bundle of Joy
Resin • N/A
1500QHC8220 • **Value N/E**

3

Congratulations!
Resin • N/A
2200QHC8233 • **Value N/E**

4

For You!
Resin • VOTR
1800QHC8226 • **Value N/E**

5

Gift of Love
Resin • N/A
1800QHC8221 • **Value N/E**

6

Happily Ever After
Resin • TAGU
1800QHC8223 • **Value N/E**

7

Happy Cake-and-Friends Day
Resin • PIKE
1800QHC8222 • **Value N/E**

8

Hello, Friend!
Resin • N/A
1500QHC8218 • **Value N/E**

9

Love Like No Other
Resin • RGRS
2200QHC8224 • **Value N/E**

10

Sweet Memories
Resin • HADD
2200QHC8231 • **Value N/E**

1998

The 25th year of Hallmark Keepsake Ornaments brought much celebration, including a number of commemorative Anniversary Edition pieces. The 165 new ornaments in the Keepsake line, were joined by 12 new Magic and 25 new Miniature ornaments. See the collectible series section for more 1998 ornaments.

11

#1 Student
Handcrafted • N/A
795QX6646 • **Value $15**

12

1998 Corvette® Convertible
Handcrafted • PALM
1395QX6416 • **Value $28**

13

Angelic Flight (LE-25,000)
Crystal/Silver-Plated • ANDR
8500QXI4146 • **Value $135**

14

Baby's First Christmas
Handcrafted • FRAN
795QX6603 • **Value $22**

15

Baby's First Christmas
Handcrafted • KLIN
895QX6596 • **Value $21**

16

Baby's First Christmas
Handcrafted • TAGU
995QX6233 • **Value $16**

Spoonful of Stars™

	Price Paid	Value
1.		
2.		
3.		
4.		
5.		
6.		
7.		
8.		
9.		
10.		

General Keepsake

	Price Paid	Value
11.		
12.		
13.		
14.		
15.		
16.		
Totals		

1

Baby's First Christmas
Handcrafted • ESCH
995QX6586 • **Value $18**

2

Baby's Second Christmas
Handcrafted • CROW
795QX6606 • **Value $17**

3

Boba Fett™
Handcrafted • RHOD
1495QXI4053 • **Value $28**

4

Bouncy Baby-sitter
Handcrafted • SIED
1295QXD4096 • **Value $22**

5

Bugs Bunny
Handcrafted • CHAD
1395QX6443 • **Value $23**

6

Building a Snowman
Handcrafted • SIED
1495QXD4133 • **Value $27**

7

Buzz Lightyear
Handcrafted • CROW
1495QXD4066 • **Value $32**

8
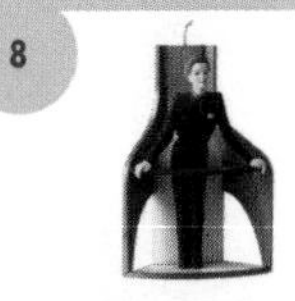
Captain Kathryn Janeway™
Handcrafted • RGRS
1495QXI4046 • **Value $28**

9

Catch of the Season
Handcrafted • SEAL
1495QX6786 • **Value $24**

10

Chatty Chipmunk
Handcrafted • CROW
995QX6716 • **Value $17**

11

Checking Santa's Files
Handcrafted • TAGU
895QX6806 • **Value $16**

12

A Child Is Born
Handcrafted • VOTR
1295QX6176 • **Value $20**

13

Child's Fifth Christmas
Handcrafted • CROW
795QX6623 • **Value $17**

14

Child's Fourth Christmas
Handcrafted • CROW
795QX6616 • **Value $17**

15

Child's Third Christmas
Handcrafted • CROW
795QX6613 • **Value $17**

16

A Christmas Eve Story Becky Kelly
Handcrafted • TAGU
1395QXD6873 • **Value $23**

17

Christmas Request
Handcrafted • FRAN
1495QX6193 • **Value $23**

18

Christmas Sleigh Ride
Die-Cast Metal • CROW
1295QX6556 • **Value $24**

19

Cinderella's Coach
Handcrafted • WILL
1495QXD4083 • **Value $24**

20

Compact Skater
Handcrafted • TAGU
995QX6766 • **Value $17**

General Keepsake

	Price Paid	Value
1.		
2.		
3.		
4.		
5.		
6.		
7.		
8.		
9.		
10.		
11.		
12.		
13.		
14.		
15.		
16.		
17.		
18.		
19.		
20.		
Totals		

1

Country Home
Marjolein Bastin
Handcrafted • FRAN
1095QX5172 • **Value $20**

2

Cross of Peace
Metal • KLIN
995QX6856 • **Value $17**

3

Cruising into Christmas
Handcrafted/Tin • CROW
1695QX6196 • **Value $28**

4

Dad
Handcrafted • KLIN
895QX6663 • **Value $17**

5

Daughter
Handcrafted • AUBE
895QX6673 • **Value $17**

6

Daydreams
Handcrafted • BRIC
1395QXD4136 • **Value $25**

7

Decorating
Maxine-Style
Handcrafted • N/A
1095QXE6883 • **Value $20**

8

Downhill Dash
Handcrafted • CROW
1395QX6776 • **Value $27**

9

Fancy Footwork
Handcrafted • VOTR
895QX6536 • **Value $17**

10

Feliz Navidad
Handcrafted • CHAD
895QX6173 • **Value $18**

11

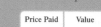

Flik
Handcrafted • N/A
1295QXD4153 • **Value $27**

12

Forever Friends Bear
Handcrafted • PIKE
895QX6303 • **Value $17**

13

Friend of My Heart
(set/2)
Handcrafted • SEAL
1495QX6723 • **Value $22**

14

Future Ballerina
Handcrafted • TAGU
795QX6756 • **Value $16**

15

Gifted Gardener
Handcrafted • CHAD
795QX6736 • **Value $15**

16

Godchild
Handcrafted • CHAD
795QX6703 • **Value $16**

17

Good Luck Dice
Handcrafted • HADD
995QX6813 • **Value $15**

18

Goofy Soccer Star
Handcrafted • CHAD
1095QXD4123 • **Value $18**

19

Granddaughter
Handcrafted • FRAN
795QX6683 • **Value $15**

20

Grandma's Memories
Handcrafted • KLIN
895QX6686 • **Value $16**

General Keepsake

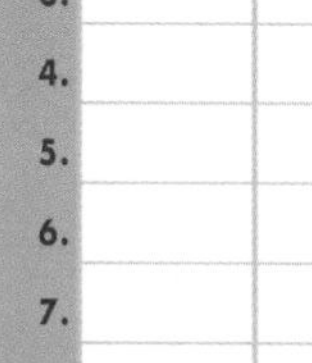

	Price Paid	Value
1.		
2.		
3.		
4.		
5.		
6.		
7.		
8.		
9.		
10.		
11.		
12.		
13.		
14.		
15.		
16.		
17.		
18.		
19.		
20.		
Totals		

1

Grandson
Handcrafted • FRAN
795QX6676 • **Value $15**

2

The Grinch
Handcrafted • CHAD
1395QXI6466 • **Value $58**

3

Guardian Friend
Handcrafted • LYLE
895QX6543 • **Value $18**

4

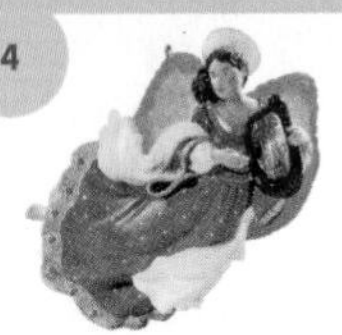

Heavenly Melody
Handcrafted • VOTR
1895QX6576 • **Value $32**

5

Holiday Camper
Handcrafted • SEAL
1295QX6783 • **Value $21**

6

Holiday Decorator
Handcrafted • WILL
1395QX6566 • **Value $20**

7

The Holy Family (re-issued in 1999 and 2000, set/3)
Porcelain • LYLE
2500QX6523 • **Value $48**

8

Hot Wheels™
Handcrafted • CROW
1395QX6436 • **Value $22**

9

Iago, Abu and the Genie
Handcrafted • WILL
1295QXD4076 • **Value $22**

10

Joe Montana Notre Dame
Handcrafted • UNRU
1495QXI6843 • **Value $22**

11

Journey To Bethlehem
Handcrafted • UNRU
1695QX6223 • **Value $30**

12

Joyful Messenger
Handcrafted/Silver-Plated • LYLE
1895QXI6733 • **Value $30**

13

King Kharoof– Second King
Handcrafted • ANDR
1295QX6186 • **Value $27**

14

Larry, Moe, and Curly The Three Stooges™ (set/3)
Handcrafted • LARS
2700QX6503 • **Value $52**

15

Madonna and Child
Handcrafted • RGRS
1295QX6516 • **Value $24**

16

Make-Believe Boat
Handcrafted • ESCH
1295QXD4113 • **Value $23**

17

Maxine
Handcrafted • PIKE
995QX6446 • **Value $17**

18

Memories of Christmas
Glass • LARS
595QX2406 • **Value $13**

19

Merry Chime
Handcrafted/Brass • CROW
995QX6692 • **Value $19**

20

The Mickey and Minnie Handcar
Handcrafted • WILL
1495QXD4116 • **Value $23**

General Keepsake

	Price Paid	Value
1.		
2.		
3.		
4.		
5.		
6.		
7.		
8.		
9.		
10.		
11.		
12.		
13.		
14.		
15.		
16.		
17.		
18.		
19.		
20.		
Totals		

1

Mickey's Favorite Reindeer
Handcrafted • LARS
1395QXD4013 • **Value $22**

2

Miracle in Bethlehem
Handcrafted • SEAL
1295QX6513 • **Value $26**

3

Mistletoe Fairy
Handcrafted • ESCH
1295QX6216 • **Value $28**

4

Mom
Handcrafted • KLIN
895QX6656 • **Value $16**

5

Mom and Dad
Handcrafted • KLIN
995QX6653 • **Value $17**

6

Mother and Daughter
Porcelain • VOTR
895QX6696 • **Value $17**

7

Mrs. Potato Head®
Handcrafted • N/A
1095QX6886 • **Value $22**

8

Mulan, Mushu and Cri-Kee (set/2)
Handcrafted • N/A
1495QXD4156 • **Value $25**

9

Munchkinland™ Mayor and Coroner (set/2)
Handcrafted • LYLE
1395QX6463 • **Value $27**

10
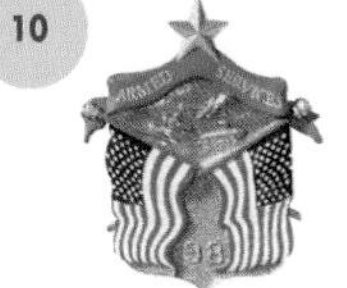
National Salute
Handcrafted • RHOD
895QX6293 • **Value $18**

11

New Arrival
Porcelain • VOTR
1895QX6306 • **Value $30**

12

New Home
Handcrafted • SEAL
995QX6713 • **Value $22**

13

Nick's Wish List
Handcrafted • ANDR
895QX6863 • **Value $17**

14

Night Watch
Handcrafted • SIED
995QX6725 • **Value $20**

15

North Pole Reserve
Handcrafted • SEAL
1095QX6803 • **Value $20**

16

Our First Christmas Together
Acrylic • VOTR
795QX3193 • **Value $15**

17

Our First Christmas Together
Brass/Porcelain • VOTR
1895QX6643 • **Value $30**

18

Our First Christmas Together
Handcrafted • TAGU
895QX6636 • **Value $18**

19

OUR SONG
Ceramic • N/A
995QX6183 • **Value $17**

20

Peekaboo Bears
Handcrafted • CROW
1295QX6563 • **Value $28**

General Keepsake

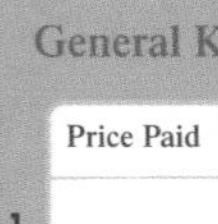
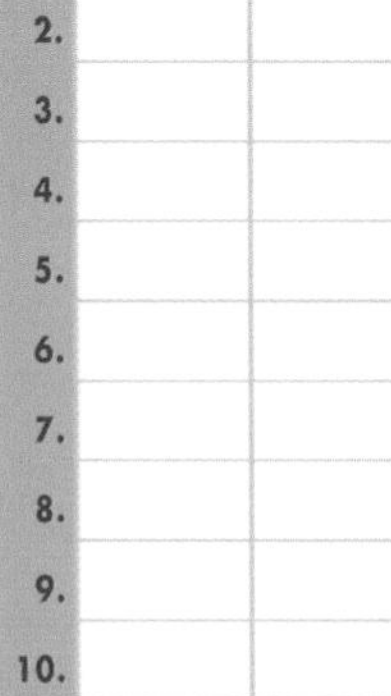
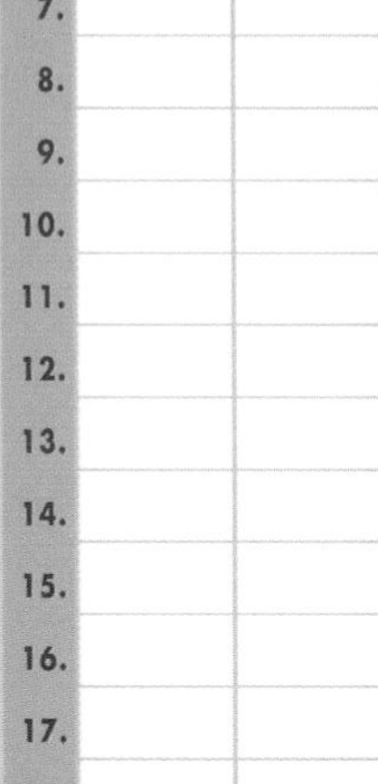

	Price Paid	Value
1.		
2.		
3.		
4.		
5.		
6.		
7.		
8.		
9.		
10.		
11.		
12.		
13.		
14.		
15.		
16.		
17.		
18.		
19.		
20.		
Totals		

1

A Perfect Match
Handcrafted • RHOD
1095QX6633 • **Value $17**

2

Polar Bowler
Handcrafted • ESCH
795QX6746 • **Value $16**

3

Princess Aurora (set/2)
Handcrafted • BRIC
1295QXD4126 • **Value $28**

4

Purr-fect Little Deer
Handcrafted • PIKE
795QX6526 • **Value $24**

5

Puttin' Around
Handcrafted • RHOD
895QX6763 • **Value $15**

6

Rocket to Success
Handcrafted • PIKE
895QX6793 • **Value $14**

7

Runaway Toboggan (set/2)
Handcrafted • N/A
1695QXD4003 • **Value $27**

8

Santa's Deer Friend
Handcrafted • CHAD
2400QX6583 • **Value $43**

9

Santa's Flying Machine
Handcrafted/Tin • SEAL
1695QX6573 • **Value $29**

10

Santa's Hidden Surprise
Ceramic • N/A
1495QX6913 • **Value $26**

11

"Sew" Gifted
Handcrafted • TAGU
795QX6743 • **Value $15**

12

Simba & Nala
Handcrafted • N/A
1395QXD4073 • **Value $25**

13

Sister to Sister
Handcrafted • PIKE
895QX6693 • **Value $17**

14

Soaring With Angels
Handcrafted • SICK
1695QX6213 • **Value $33**

15

Son
Handcrafted • AUBE
895QX6666 • **Value $16**

16
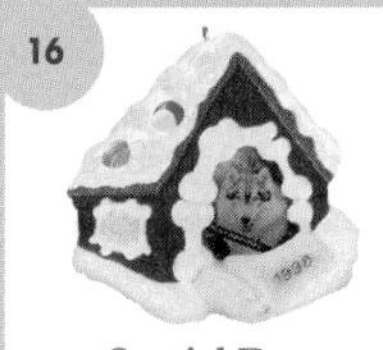
Special Dog
Handcrafted • N/A
795QX6706 • **Value $14**

17

Spoonful of Love
Handcrafted • TAGU
895QX6796 • **Value $15**

18

Superman™
Pressed Tin • N/A
1295QX6423 • **Value $21**

19

Surprise Catch
Handcrafted • FRAN
795QX6753 • **Value $15**

20

Sweet Rememberings
Handcrafted • TAGU
895QX6876 • **Value $17**

General Keepsake

	Price Paid	Value
1.		
2.		
3.		
4.		
5.		
6.		
7.		
8.		
9.		
10.		
11.		
12.		
13.		
14.		
15.		
16.		
17.		
18.		
19.		
20.		
Totals		

1

Sweet Treat
Handcrafted • KLIN
1095QX6433 • **Value $24**

2

Tin Locomotive
Pressed Tin • SICK
2500QX6826 • **Value $49**

3

Tonka® Road Grader
Die-Cast Metal • N/A
1395QX6483 • **Value $28**

4

Treetop Choir
Handcrafted • FRAN
995QX6506 • **Value $20**

5

Warm and Cozy
Handcrafted • SICK
895QX6866 • **Value $20**

6

Watchful Shepherd
Handcrafted • KLIN
895QX6496 • **Value $19**

7

Woody the Sheriff
Handcrafted • N/A
1495QXD4163 • **Value $33**

8

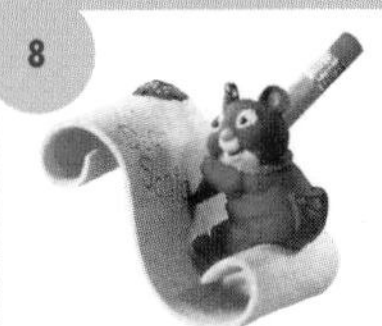

Writing to Santa
Handcrafted • AUBE
795QX6533 • **Value $16**

9

1998 Corvette®
Handcrafted • PALM
2400QLX7605 • **Value $38**

10

Cinderella at the Ball
Handcrafted • N/A
2400QXD7576 • **Value $60**

11

Mickey's Comet
Handcrafted • WILL
2400QXD7586 • **Value $38**

12

St. Nicholas Circle Thomas Kinkade, Painter of Light™
Handcrafted • UNRU
1895QXI7556 • **Value $36**

13

Santa's Show'n' Tell
Handcrafted • CROW
1895QLX7566 • **Value $35**

14

Santa's Spin Top
Handcrafted • TAGU
2200QLX7573 • **Value $40**

15

U.S.S. Enterprise™ NCC-1701-E
Handcrafted • NORT
2400QXI7633 • **Value $52**

16

The Washington Monument
Handcrafted • SEAL
2400QLX7553 • **Value $46**

17

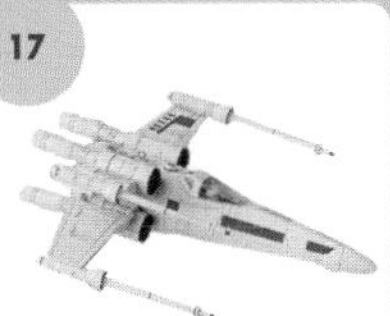

X-wing Starfighter™
Handcrafted • RHOD
2400QXI7596 • **Value $40**

18

1955 Murray® Fire Truck
Blown Glass • HADD
3500QBG6909 • **Value $50**

19

Festive Locomotive
Blown Glass • TAGU
3500QBG6903 • **Value $50**

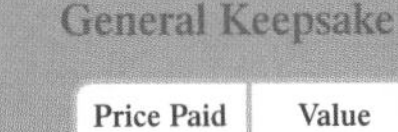

General Keepsake

	Price Paid	Value
1.		
2.		
3.		
4.		
5.		
6.		
7.		
8.		

General Magic

	Price Paid	Value
9.		
10.		
11.		
12.		
13.		
14.		
15.		
16.		
17.		

General Crown Reflections

	Price Paid	Value
18.		
19.		

	Price Paid	Value
Totals		

1

Frankincense
(re-issued in 1999)
Blown Glass • LARS
2200QBG6896 • **Value $33**

2

Frosty Friends (set/2)
Blown Glass • SEAL
4800QBG6907 • **Value $68**

3
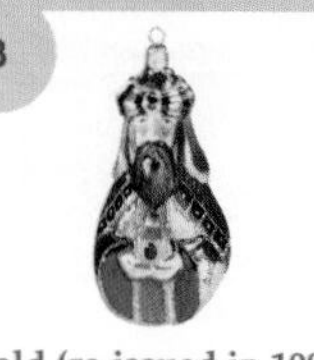
Gold (re-issued in 1999)
Blown Glass • LARS
2200QBG6836 • **Value $33**

4

Myrrh
(re-issued in 1999)
Blown Glass • LARS
2200QBG6893 • **Value $35**

5

Sugarplum Cottage
Blown Glass • HADD
3500QBG6917 • **Value $60**

6

Sweet Memories (set/8)
Blown Glass • KLIN
4500QBG6933 • **Value $72**

7

Angel Chime
Die-Cast Metal • TAGU
895QXM4283 • **Value $16**

8

Betsey's Prayer
Handcrafted • KLIN
495QXM4263 • **Value $11**

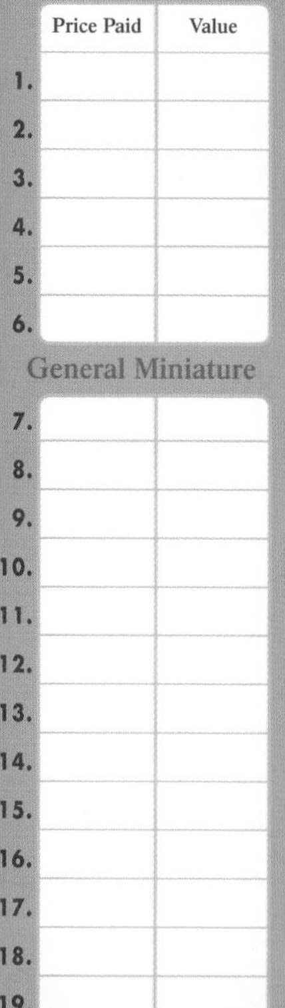

General Crown Reflections	Price Paid	Value
1.		
2.		
3.		
4.		
5.		
6.		
General Miniature		
7.		
8.		
9.		
10.		
11.		
12.		
13.		
14.		
15.		
16.		
17.		
18.		
19.		
Collector's Club		
20.		
Totals		

9

"Coca-Cola" Time
Handcrafted • UNRU
695QXM4296 • **Value $13**

10

Ewoks™ (set/3)
Handcrafted • BRIC
1695QXI4223 • **Value $28**

11

Fishy Surprise
Handcrafted • ESCH
695QXM4276 • **Value $13**

12

Glinda, The Good Witch™
Wicked Witch of the
West™ (set/2)
Handcrafted • LYLE
1495QXM4233 • **Value $28**

13

Holly-Jolly Jig
Handcrafted • TAGU
695QXM4266 • **Value $13**

14

Peaceful Pandas
Handcrafted • SICK
595QXM4253 • **Value $14**

15

Pixie Parachute
Handcrafted • ESCH
495QXM4256 • **Value $13**

16

Sharing Joy
Handcrafted • N/A
495QXM4273 • **Value $12**

17

Singin' in the Rain™
(set/2)
Handcrafted • ANDR
1095QXM4303 • **Value $22**

18

Superman™ (set/2)
Handcrafted • CHAD
1095QXM4313 • **Value $20**

19

Tree Trimmin' Time
(set/3)
Handcrafted • N/A
1995QXD4236 • **Value $40**

20

Follow the Leader
(club edition, set/2)
Handcrafted • SIED
1695QXC4503 • **Value $40**

1

Kringle Bells (keepsake of membership, miniature)
Handcrafted • BRIC
QXC4486 • **Value $17**

2

Making His Way (keepsake of membership)
Handcrafted • SICK
QXC4523 • **Value $26**

3

New Christmas Friend (keepsake of membership)
Handcrafted • ESCH
QXC4516 • **Value $25**

4

Our 25th Anniversary
Silver-Plated • N/A
(N/C) No stock # • **Value N/E**

5

Santa's Merry Workshop Musical Figurine
Handcrafted • SEAL
3200QX6816 • **Value $52**

6

Holiday Memories™ BARBIE™ Ornament
Handcrafted • N/A
1495QHB6020 • **Value $27**

7

Holiday Memories™ BARBIE™ Porcelain Plate (LE-24,500)
Porcelain • N/A
3000QHB6021 • **Value N/E**

8

Holiday Voyage™ BARBIE™ Card-Display Figurine
Handcrafted • N/A
4000QHB6019 • **Value N/E**

9

Holiday Voyage™ BARBIE® Doll (2nd in *Holiday Homecoming Collector Series™*)
Vinyl • N/A
5000QHB6022 • **Value N/E**

10

Holiday Voyage™ BARBIE™ Ornament
Handcrafted • N/A
1495QHB6016 • **Value N/E**

11

Holiday Voyage™ BARBIE™ Porcelain Figurine (LE-24,500)
Porcelain • N/A
4500QHB6017 • **Value N/E**

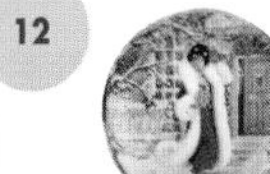
12

Holiday Voyage™ BARBIE™ Porcelain Plate (LE-24,500)
Porcelain • N/A
3000QHB6018 • **Value N/E**

13

Collegiate Collection (5 assorted)
Handcrafted • HADD

1. **Florida State Seminoles™** 995QSR2316 • **Value N/E**
2. **Michigan Wolverines™** 995QSR2323 • **Value N/E**
3. **North Carolina Tar Heels™** 995QSR2333 • **Value N/E**
4. **Notre Dame Fighting Irish™** 995QSR2313 • **Value N/E**
5. **Penn State Nittany Lions™** 995QSR2326 • **Value N/E**

14

1955 Murray® Tractor and Trailer (white)
Die-Cast Metal • PALM
(N/C) No stock # • **Value N/E**

15

Snow Buddies (gray rabbit)
Handcrafted • HADD
(N/C) No stock # • **Value N/E**

16
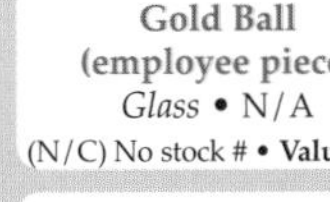
25th Anniversary Gold Ball (employee piece)
Glass • N/A
(N/C) No stock # • **Value N/E**

17

Elf
Handcrafted • CHAD
(N/C) No stock # • **Value N/E**

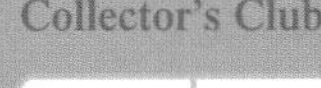

	Price Paid	Value
Collector's Club		
1.		
2.		
3.		
4.		
Premiere Figurines		
5.		
BARBIE™ Collectibles		
6.		
7.		
8.		
9.		
10.		
11.		
12.		
Collegiate Collection		
13.		
Convention Pieces		
14.		
15.		
16.		
17.		
Totals		

1

Iris Angel (white)
Handcrafted • TAGU
(N/C) No stock # • **Value N/E**

2

Joe Cool (green coat)
Handcrafted • SIED
(N/C) No stock # • **Value N/E**

3

K.C. Drummer Boy
Silver-Plated • N/A
(N/C) No stock # • **Value N/E**

4

K.C. Snowflake
Silver-Plated • UNRU
(N/C) No stock # • **Value N/E**

5

Kansas City Angel (precious edition)
Lead Crystal/Silver-Plated • VOTR
QXC4526 • **Value N/E**

6

A Late Night Snack (complements the "Studio Edition Sleigh")
Handcrafted • CHAD/HADD
(N/C) No stock # • **Value N/E**

7

Mouse
Handcrafted • SIED
(N/C) No stock # • **Value N/E**

8

A Pony for Christmas (black)
Handcrafted • SICK
(N/C) No stock # • **Value N/E**

9

Santa's Deer Friend
Handcrafted • CHAD
(N/C) No stock # • **Value N/E**

10

Snow Man (local club piece)
Handcrafted • N/A
(N/C) No stock # • **Value N/E**

11

Studio Edition Sleigh (artist signing piece)
Handcrafted • VARI
(N/C) No stock # • **Value N/E**

12

1926 Lionel® Catalog Cover Tin Sign
Pressed Tin • N/A
1800QHT3701 • **Value N/E**

13

1929 Lionel® Catalog Cover Tin Sign
Pressed Tin • N/A
1800QHT3703 • **Value N/E**

14

1952 Lionel® Catalog Cover Tin Sign
Pressed Tin • N/A
1800QHT3702 • **Value N/E**

15
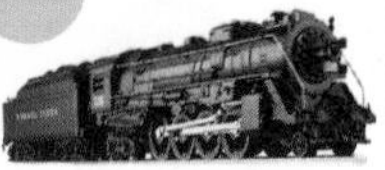

Lionel® 726 Berkshire Steam Locomotive (1st in *20th Century Series*)
Die-Cast Metal • N/A
($120)1QHT7801 • **Value N/E**

16

Lionel® 746 Norfolk and Western Steam Locomotive (1st in *Norfolk and Western Train Series*)
Die-Cast Metal • N/A
9000QHT7803 • **Value N/E**

17

Lionel® 2332 Pennsylvania GG1 Electric Locomotive (2nd in *20th Century Series*)
Die-Cast Metal • N/A
9500QHT7804 • **Value N/E**

18

NBA Collection (10 assorted)
Handcrafted • SIED

1. **Charlotte Hornets** 995QSR1033 • **Value N/E**
2. **Chicago Bulls** 995QSR1036 • **Value N/E**
3. **Detroit Pistons** 995QSR1043 • **Value N/E**
4. **Houston Rockets** 995QSR1046 • **Value N/E**
5. **Indiana Pacers** 995QSR1053 • **Value N/E**
6. **Los Angeles Lakers** 995QSR1056 • **Value N/E**
7. **New York Knickerbockers** 995QSR1063 • **Value N/E**
8. **Orlando Magic** 995QSR1066 • **Value N/E**
9. **Seattle Supersonics** 995QSR1076 • **Value N/E**
10. **Utah Jazz** 995QSR1083 • **Value N/E**

	Price Paid	Value
Convention Pieces		
1.		
2.		
3.		
4.		
5.		
6.		
7.		
8.		
9.		
10.		
11.		
Great American Railways™		
12.		
13.		
14.		
15.		
16.		
17.		
NBA Collection		
18.		
Totals		

1

NFL Collection
(15 assorted)
Handcrafted • FRAN

1. **Carolina Panthers™** 995QSR5026 • **Value N/E**
2. **Chicago Bears™** 995QSR5033 • **Value N/E**
3. **Dallas Cowboys™** 995QSR5046 • **Value N/E**
4. **Denver Broncos™** 995QSR5053 • **Value N/E**
5. **Green Bay Packers™** 995QSR5063 • **Value N/E**
6. **Kansas City Chiefs™** 995QSR5013 • **Value N/E**
7. **Miami Dolphins™** 995QSR5096 • **Value N/E**
8. **Minnesota Vikings™** 995QSR5126 • **Value N/E**
9. **New York Giants™** 995QSR5143 • **Value N/E**
10. **Oakland Raiders™** 995QSR5086 • **Value N/E**
11. **Philadelphia Eagles™** 995QSR5153 • **Value N/E**
12. **Pittsburgh Steelers™** 995QSR5163 • **Value N/E**
13. **St. Louis Rams™** 995QSR5093 • **Value N/E**
14. **San Francisco 49ers™** 995QSR5173 • **Value N/E**
15. **Washington Redskins™** 995QSR5186 • **Value N/E**

2

1950s HOWDY DOODY™
Pressed Tin • N/A
1950QHM8801 • **Value N/E**

3

1950s Lone Ranger™
Pressed Tin • N/A
1950QHM8802 • **Value N/E**

4

1950s SUPERMAN™
Pressed Tin • N/A
1950QHM8803 • **Value N/E**

5

1970s Hot Wheels™
Pressed Tin • N/A
1950QHM8813 • **Value N/E**

6

Christmas Caring
Resin • BRIC
1800QHC8251 • **Value N/E**

7

Dreams and Wishes
Resin • VOTR
2500QHC8250 • **Value N/E**

8

Splendid Days
Resin • TAGU
1800QHC8216 • **Value N/E**

9

Thoughtful Ways
Resin • HADD/TAGU
1800QHC8215 • **Value N/E**

10

Together Days
Resin • BRIC
1800QHC8217 • **Value N/E**

Highlights for 1997 included a brand new collection of Disney ornaments, as well as several ornaments based on popular television shows and the STAR WARS™ movies. The 1997 collection featured 144 Keepsake ornaments, 17 Magic ornaments and 36 Miniature ornaments. See the collectible series section for more 1997 ornaments.

11

1997 Corvette
Handcrafted • PALM
1395QXI6455 • **Value $28**

12

All-Round Sports Fan
Handcrafted • WILL
895QX6392 • **Value $29**

13

All-Weather Walker
Handcrafted • WILL
895QX6415 • **Value $18**

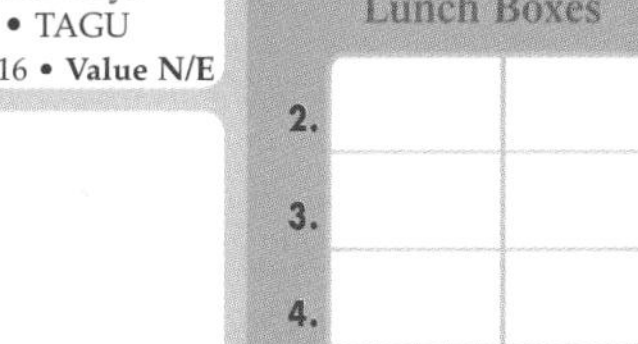

	Price Paid	Value
NFL Collection		
1.		
School Days Lunch Boxes		
2.		
3.		
4.		
5.		
Spoonful of Stars		
6.		
7.		
8.		
9.		
10.		
General Keepsake		
11.		
12.		
13.		
Totals		

1

Angel Friend
Handcrafted • FRAN
1495QX6762 • **Value $27**

2

Ariel, The Little Mermaid
Handcrafted • BRIC
1295QXI4072 • **Value $23**

3

Baby's First Christmas
Handcrafted • N/A
795QX6482 • **Value $28**

4

Baby's First Christmas
Handcrafted • CROW
795QX6495 • **Value $26**

5

Baby's First Christmas
Handcrafted • VOTR
995QX6485 • **Value $25**

6

Baby's First Christmas
Handcrafted • ANDR
995QX6492 • **Value $20**

7

Baby's First Christmas
Porcelain • VOTR
1495QX6535 • **Value $25**

8

Baby's Second Christmas
Handcrafted • CROW
795QX6502 • **Value $21**

9

Biking Buddies
Handcrafted • PALM
1295QX6682 • **Value $22**

10

Book of the Year
Handcrafted • BRIC
795QX6645 • **Value $17**

11

Breezin' Along
Handcrafted • SEAL
895QX6722 • **Value $18**

12

Bucket Brigade
Handcrafted • FRAN
895QX6382 • **Value $17**

13

Catch of the Day
Handcrafted • TAGU
995QX6712 • **Value $19**

14

Child's Fifth Christmas
Handcrafted • CROW
795QX6515 • **Value $16**

15

Child's Fourth Christmas
Handcrafted • CROW
795QX6512 • **Value $16**

16

Child's Third Christmas
Handcrafted • CROW
795QX6505 • **Value $18**

17

Christmas Checkup
Handcrafted • SIED
795QX6385 • **Value $16**

18

Classic Cross
Precious Metal • VOTR
1395QX6805 • **Value $20**

19

Clever Camper
Handcrafted • CHAD
795QX6445 • **Value $19**

20

Commander Data™
Handcrafted • RGRS
1495QXI6345 • **Value $27**

General Keepsake

	Price Paid	Value
1.		
2.		
3.		
4.		
5.		
6.		
7.		
8.		
9.		
10.		
11.		
12.		
13.		
14.		
15.		
16.		
17.		
18.		
19.		
20.		
Totals		

1

Cycling Santa
Handcrafted • WILL
1495QX6425 • **Value $25**

2

Dad
Handcrafted • SIED
895QX6532 • **Value $18**

3

Daughter
Pressed Tin • BRIC
795QX6612 • **Value $18**

4

Downhill Run
Handcrafted • CROW
995QX6705 • **Value $20**

5

Dr. Leonard H. McCoy™
Handcrafted • RGRS
1495QXI6352 • **Value $27**

6

Elegance on Ice
Handcrafted • LYLE
995QX6432 • **Value $20**

7

Expressly for Teacher
Handcrafted • TAGU
795QX6375 • **Value $16**

8

Feliz Navidad
Handcrafted • SEAL
895QX6665 • **Value $30**

9

Friendship Blend
Handcrafted • SEAL
995QX6655 • **Value $22**

10

Garden Bouquet
Handcrafted • LYLE
1495QX6752 • **Value $30**

11

Gift of Friendship
Porcelain • N/A
1295QXE6835 • **Value $21**

12

Godchild
Handcrafted • BRIC
795QX6662 • **Value $16**

13

God's Gift of Love
Porcelain • LYLE
1695QX6792 • **Value $35**

14

Goofy's Ski Adventure
Handcrafted • CHAD
1295QXD4042 • **Value $23**

15

Granddaughter
Handcrafted • TAGU
795QX6622 • **Value $18**

16

Grandma
Handcrafted • PIKE
895QX6625 • **Value $16**

17

Grandson
Handcrafted • TAGU
795QX6615 • **Value $18**

18

Gus & Jaq, Cinderella
Handcrafted • CROW
1295QXD4052 • **Value $29**

19

Heavenly Song
Acrylic • VOTR
1295QX6795 • **Value $24**

20

Hercules
Handcrafted • WILL
1295QXI4005 • **Value $20**

General Keepsake

	Price Paid	Value
1.		
2.		
3.		
4.		
5.		
6.		
7.		
8.		
9.		
10.		
11.		
12.		
13.		
14.		
15.		
16.		
17.		
18.		
19.		
20.		
Totals		

1

Honored Guests
Handcrafted • FRAN
1495QX6745 • **Value $31**

2

Howdy Doody™
Handcrafted • LARS
1295QX6272 • **Value $29**

3

The Incredible Hulk®
Handcrafted • N/A
1295QX5471 • **Value $24**

4

Jasmine & Aladdin, Aladdin & the King of Thieves
Handcrafted • RGRS
1495QXD4062 • **Value $25**

5

Jingle Bell Jester
Handcrafted • PIKE
995QX6695 • **Value $23**

6

Juggling Stars
Handcrafted • TAGU
995QX6595 • **Value $19**

7

King Noor–First King
Handcrafted • ANDR
1295QX6552 • **Value $31**

8

Leading The Way
Handcrafted • SICK
1695QX6782 • **Value $30**

9

Lion and Lamb
Handcrafted • WILL
795QX6602 • **Value $20**

10

The Lone Ranger™
Pressed Tin • N/A
1295QX6265 • **Value $34**

11

Love to Sew
Handcrafted • TAGU
795QX6435 • **Value $18**

12

Madonna del Rosario
Handcrafted • SICK
1295QX6545 • **Value $25**

13

Marbles Champion
Handcrafted • UNRU
1095QX6342 • **Value $22**

14

Meadow Snowman
Pressed Tin • SICK
1295QX6715 • **Value $32**

15

Megara and Pegasus
Handcrafted • CROW
1695QXI4012 • **Value $30**

16

Michigan J. Frog
Handcrafted • CHAD
995QX6332 • **Value $23**

17

Mickey's Long Shot
Handcrafted • SIED
1095QXD6412 • **Value $22**

18

Mickey's Snow Angel
Handcrafted • SIED
995QXD4035 • **Value $20**

19

Miss Gulch
Handcrafted • LYLE
1395QX6372 • **Value $30**

20

Mom
Handcrafted • SIED
895QX6525 • **Value $18**

General Keepsake

	Price Paid	Value
1.		
2.		
3.		
4.		
5.		
6.		
7.		
8.		
9.		
10.		
11.		
12.		
13.		
14.		
15.		
16.		
17.		
18.		
19.		
20.		
Totals		

1

Mom and Dad
Handcrafted • SIED
995QX6522 • **Value $19**

2

Mr. Potato Head®
Handcrafted • SIED
1095QX6335 • **Value $26**

3

Nativity Tree
Handcrafted • UNRU
1495QX6575 • **Value $33**

4

New Home
Handcrafted • PIKE
895QX6652 • **Value $19**

5

New Pair of Skates
Handcrafted • LARS
1395QXD4032 • **Value $25**

6

The Night Before Christmas
Handcrafted • CROW
2400QX5721 • **Value $44**

7

Our Christmas Together
Pewter • N/A
1695QX6475 • **Value $26**

8

Our First Christmas Together
Acrylic • N/A
795QX3182 • **Value $17**

9

Our First Christmas Together
Handcrafted • PIKE
895QX6472 • **Value $20**

10

Our First Christmas Together
Handcrafted • SEAL
1095QX6465 • **Value $21**

11

Phoebus & Esmeralda, The Hunchback of Notre Dame
Handcrafted • CROW
1495QXD6344 • **Value $23**

12

Playful Shepherd
Handcrafted • TAGU
995QX6592 • **Value $21**

13

Porcelain Hinged Box
Porcelain • VOTR
1495QX6772 • **Value $32**

14

Praise Him
Handcrafted • SICK
895QX6542 • **Value $20**

15

Prize Topiary
Handcrafted • SEAL
1495QX6675 • **Value $23**

16

Sailor Bear
Handcrafted • UNRU
1495QX6765 • **Value $23**

17

Santa Mail
Handcrafted • WILL
1095QX6702 • **Value $25**

18

Santa's Friend
Handcrafted • UNRU
1295QX6685 • **Value $26**

19

Santa's Magical Sleigh
Handcrafted • UNRU
2400QX6672 • **Value $42**

20

Santa's Merry Path
Handcrafted • SICK
1695QX6785 • **Value $34**

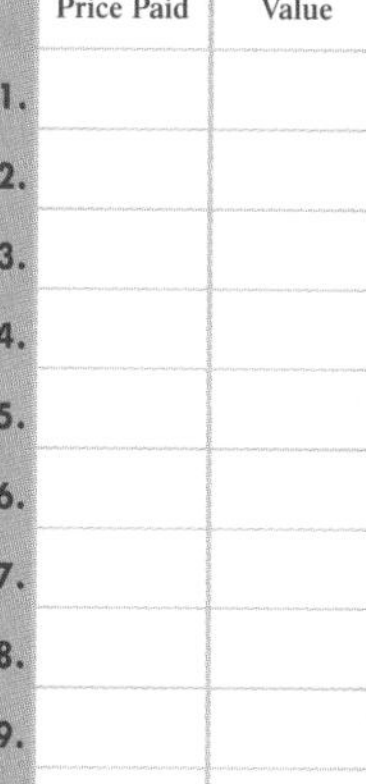

General Keepsake

	Price Paid	Value
1.		
2.		
3.		
4.		
5.		
6.		
7.		
8.		
9.		
10.		
11.		
12.		
13.		
14.		
15.		
16.		
17.		
18.		
19.		
20.		
Totals		

1

Santa's Polar Friend
Handcrafted • CHAD
1695QX6755 • **Value $35**

2

Santa's Ski Adventure
Handcrafted • CHAD
1295QX6422 • **Value $25**

3

Sister to Sister
Handcrafted • PIKE
995QX6635 • **Value $20**

4

Snow Bowling
Handcrafted • WILL
695QX6395 • **Value $16**

5

Snow White, Anniversary Edition (set/2)
Handcrafted • ESCH
1695QXD4055 • **Value $33**

6

Snowgirl
Handcrafted • TAGU
795QX6562 • **Value $18**

7

Son
Pressed Tin • BRIC
795QX6605 • **Value $16**

8

Special Dog
Handcrafted • BRIC
795QX6632 • **Value $17**

9

The Spirit of Christmas
Handcrafted • LARS
995QX6585 • **Value $26**

10

Stealing a Kiss
Handcrafted • TAGU
1495QX6555 • **Value $29**

11

Sweet Discovery
Handcrafted • SICK
1195QX6325 • **Value $25**

12
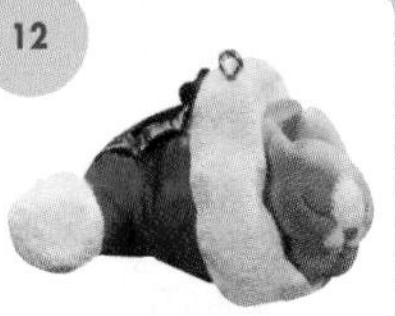
Sweet Dreamer
Handcrafted • BRIC
695QX6732 • **Value $17**

13

Swinging in the Snow
Handcrafted/Glass • TAGU
1295QX6775 • **Value $22**

14

Taking A Break
Handcrafted • UNRU
1495QX6305 • **Value $30**

15

Timon & Pumbaa, The Lion King
Handcrafted • WILL
1295QXD4065 • **Value $24**

16

Tomorrow's Leader
Ceramic • N/A
995QX6452 • **Value $16**

17

Tonka® Mighty Front Loader
Die-Cast Metal • N/A
1395QX6362 • **Value $29**

18

Two-Tone, 101 Dalmatians
Handcrafted • CHAD
995QXD4015 • **Value $19**

19

Waitin' on Santa – Winnie the Pooh
Handcrafted • SIED
1295QXD6365 • **Value $26**

20

What a Deal!
Handcrafted • PIKE
895QX6442 • **Value $17**

General Keepsake

	Price Paid	Value
1.		
2.		
3.		
4.		
5.		
6.		
7.		
8.		
9.		
10.		
11.		
12.		
13.		
14.		
15.		
16.		
17.		
18.		
19.		
20.		
Totals		

1

Yoda™
Handcrafted • BRIC
995QXI6355 • **Value $40**

2

Darth Vader™
Handcrafted • RHOD
2400QXI7531 • **Value $43**

3

Decorator Taz
Handcrafted • CHAD
3000QLX7502 • **Value $48**

4

Glowing Angel
Handcrafted • VOTR
1895QLX7435 • **Value $35**

5

Holiday Serenade
Handcrafted • FRAN
2400QLX7485 • **Value $39**

6

Joy to the World
Handcrafted • TAGU
1495QLX7512 • **Value $30**

7

The Lincoln Memorial
Handcrafted • SEAL
2400QLX7522 • **Value $46**

8
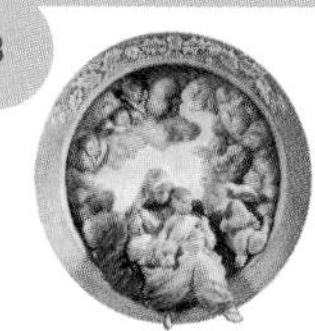

Madonna and Child
Handcrafted • LYLE
1995QLX7425 • **Value $38**

9

Motorcycle Chums
Handcrafted • SEAL
2400QLX7495 • **Value $44**

10

Santa's Secret Gift
Handcrafted • CHAD
2400QLX7455 • **Value $40**

11

Santa's Showboat
Handcrafted • CROW
4200QLX7465 • **Value $75**

12
SNOOPY Plays Santa
Handcrafted • RGRS
2200QLX7475 • **Value $42**

13

Teapot Party
Handcrafted • TAGU
1895QLX7482 • **Value $36**

14

U.S.S. Defiant™
Handcrafted • NORT
2400QXI7481 • **Value $42**

15

The Warmth of Home
Handcrafted • LARS
1895QXI7545 • **Value $35**

16

C-3PO™ and R2-D2™ (set/2)
Handcrafted • RHOD
1295QXI4265 • **Value $30**

17

Casablanca™ (set/3)
Handcrafted • ANDR
1995QXM4272 • **Value $34**

18

Future Star
Handcrafted • PIKE
595QXM4232 • **Value $14**

19

Gentle Giraffes
Handcrafted • SICK
595QXM4221 • **Value $15**

20

He Is Born
Handcrafted • VOTR
795QXM4235 • **Value $17**

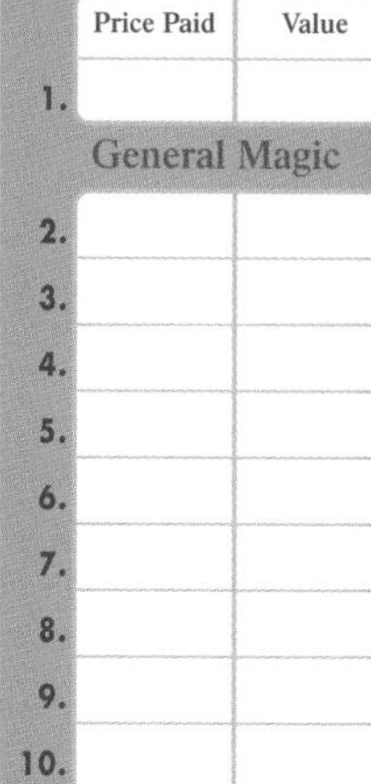

	Price Paid	Value
General Keepsake		
1.		
General Magic		
2.		
3.		
4.		
5.		
6.		
7.		
8.		
9.		
10.		
11.		
12.		
13.		
14.		
15.		
General Miniature		
16.		
17.		
18.		
19.		
20.		
Totals		

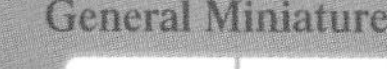

1

Heavenly Music
Handcrafted • TAGU
595QXM4292 • **Value $12**

2

Home Sweet Home
Handcrafted • SEAL
595QXM4222 • **Value $13**

3

Honey of a Gift – Winnie the Pooh
Handcrafted • LARS
695QXD4255 • **Value $15**

4

Ice Cold Coca-Cola®
Handcrafted • CHAD
695QXM4252 • **Value $15**

5

King of the Forest (set/4)
Handcrafted • RGRS
2400QXM4262 • **Value $44**

6

Miniature 1997 Corvette
Handcrafted • PALM
695QXI4322 • **Value $15**

7

Our Lady of Guadalupe
Pewter • CHAD
895QXM4275 • **Value $17**

8

Peppermint Painter
Handcrafted • TAGU
495QXM4312 • **Value $13**

9

Polar Buddies
Handcrafted • FRAN
495QXM4332 • **Value $13**

10

Seeds of Joy
Handcrafted • TAGU
695QXM4242 • **Value $13**

11

Sew Talented
Handcrafted • SEAL
595QXM4195 • **Value $13**

12

Shutterbug
Handcrafted • TAGU
595QXM4212 • **Value $14**

13

Snowboard Bunny
Handcrafted • TAGU
495QXM4315 • **Value $13**

14

Tiny Home Improvers (set/6)
Handcrafted • SEAL
2900QXM4282 • **Value $45**

15

Victorian Skater
Handcrafted • UNRU
595QXM4305 • **Value $13**

16

Away to the Window (keepsake of membership)
Handcrafted • WILL
QXC5135 • **Value $20**

17

Farmer's Market, Tender Touches (club edition)
Handcrafted • SEAL
1500QXC5182 • **Value $32**

18

Happy Christmas to All! (keepsake of membership)
Handcrafted • WILL
QXC5132 • **Value $21**

19

Jolly Old Santa (keepsake of membership, miniature)
Handcrafted • WILL
QXC5145 • **Value $17**

20

Ready for Santa (keepsake of membership, miniature)
Handcrafted • WILL
QXC5142 • **Value $14**

General Miniature

	Price Paid	Value
1.		
2.		
3.		
4.		
5.		
6.		
7.		
8.		
9.		
10.		
11.		
12.		
13.		
14.		
15.		

Collector's Club

16.		
17.		
18.		
19.		
20.		

Totals

1

The Perfect Tree, Tender Touches
Handcrafted • SEAL
1500QX6572 • **Value $26**

2

1953 GMC (green)
Handcrafted • PALM
(N/C) No stock # • **Value N/E**

3

First Class Thank You
Handcrafted • RGRS
(N/C) No stock # • **Value N/E**

4

Mrs. Claus's Story
Handcrafted • ESCH/KLIN
($14.95) No stock # • **Value N/E**

5

Murray® Dump Truck (orange)
Die-Cast Metal • PALM
(N/C) No stock # • **Value N/E**

6

Murray Inc.® "Pursuit" Airplane (miniature, tan)
Die-Cast Metal • PALM
(N/C) No stock # • **Value N/E**

7

Santa's Magical Sleigh (silver runners)
Handcrafted • UNRU
(N/C) No stock # • **Value N/E**

8

Trimming Santa's Tree (set/2)
Handcrafted • VARI
6000QXC5175 • **Value N/E**

9

BARBIE™ Lapel Pin (re-issued from 1996)
Handcrafted • N/A
495XLP3544 • **Value N/E**

10

Holiday BARBIE™ Stocking Hanger (re-issued from 1996)
Handcrafted • N/A
1995XSH3101 • **Value N/E**

11

Holiday Traditions™ BARBIE® Doll (1st in *Holiday Homecoming Collector Series™*)
Vinyl • N/A
5000QHB3402 • **Value N/E**

12

Holiday Traditions™ BARBIE™ Ornament
Handcrafted • N/A
1495QHB6002 • **Value $24**

13

Holiday Traditions™ BARBIE™ Porcelain Figurine
Porcelain • N/A
4500QHB6001 • **Value N/E**

14

Holiday Traditions™ BARBIE™ Porcelain Plate
Porcelain • N/A
3000QHB6003 • **Value N/E**

15

Victorian Elegance™ BARBIE™ Ornament
Handcrafted • N/A
1495QHB6004 • **Value $22**

16

Victorian Elegance™ BARBIE™ Porcelain Plate
Porcelain • N/A
3000QHB6005 • **Value N/E**

17

NBA COLLECTION (10 assorted)
Ceramic • N/A

1. **Charlotte Hornets™** 995QSR1222 • **Value N/E**
2. **Chicago Bulls™** 995QSR1232 • **Value N/E**
3. **Detroit Pistons™** 995QSR1242 • **Value N/E**
4. **Houston Rockets™** 995QSR1245 • **Value N/E**
5. **Indiana Pacers™** 995QSR1252 • **Value N/E**
6. **Los Angeles Lakers™** 995QSR1262 • **Value N/E**
7. **New York Knickerbockers™** 995QSR1272 • **Value N/E**
8. **Orlando Magic™** 995QSR1282 • **Value N/E**
9. **Phoenix Suns™** 995QSR1292 • **Value N/E**
10. **Seattle Supersonics™** 995QSR1295 • **Value N/E**

	Price Paid	Value
Premiere Ornaments		
1.		
Artists On Tour Pieces		
2.		
3.		
4.		
5.		
6.		
7.		
8.		
BARBIE™ Collectibles		
9.		
10.		
11.		
12.		
13.		
14.		
15.		
16.		
NBA Collection		
17.		
Totals		

1

NFL COLLECTION
(30 assorted)
Handcrafted • SIED

1. **Arizona Cardinals™** 995QSR5505 • **Value N/E**
2. **Atlanta Falcons™** 995QSR5305 • **Value N/E**
3. **Baltimore Ravens™** 995QSR5352 • **Value N/E**
4. **Buffalo Bills™** 995QSR5312 • **Value N/E**
5. **Carolina Panthers™** 995QSR5315 • **Value N/E**
6. **Chicago Bears™** 995QSR5322 • **Value N/E**
7. **Cincinnati Bengals™** 995QSR5325 • **Value N/E**
8. **Dallas Cowboys™** 995QSR5355 • **Value N/E**
9. **Denver Broncos™** 995QSR5362 • **Value N/E**
10. **Detroit Lions™** 995QSR5365 • **Value N/E**
11. **Green Bay Packers™** 995QSR5372 • **Value N/E**
12. **Houston Oilers™** 995QSR5375 • **Value N/E**
13. **Indianapolis Colts™** 995QSR5411 • **Value N/E**
14. **Jacksonville Jaguars™** 995QSR5415 • **Value N/E**
15. **Kansas City Chiefs™** 995QSR5302 • **Value N/E**
16. **Miami Dolphins™** 995QSR5472 • **Value N/E**
17. **Minnesota Vikings™** 995QSR5475 • **Value N/E**
18. **New England Patriots™** 995QSR5482 • **Value N/E**
19. **New Orleans Saints™** 995QSR5485 • **Value N/E**
20. **New York Giants™** 995QSR5492 • **Value N/E**
21. **New York Jets™** 995QSR5495 • **Value N/E**
22. **Oakland Raiders™** 995QSR5422 • **Value N/E**
23. **Philadelphia Eagles™** 995QSR5502 • **Value N/E**
24. **Pittsburgh Steelers™** 995QSR5512 • **Value N/E**
25. **St. Louis Rams™** 995QSR5425 • **Value N/E**
26. **San Diego Chargers™** 995QSR5515 • **Value N/E**
27. **San Francisco 49ers™** 995QSR5522 • **Value N/E**
28. **Seattle Seahawks™** 995QSR5525 • **Value N/E**
29. **Tampa Bay Buccaneers™** 995QSR5532 • **Value N/E**
30. **Washington Redskins™** 995QSR5535 • **Value N/E**

NFL Collection

	Price Paid	Value
1.		

General Keepsake

	Price Paid	Value
2.		
3.		
4.		
5.		
6.		
7.		
8.		
9.		
10.		
Totals		

1996

Hallmark introduced several new ornaments and collectibles commemorating the Centennial Olympic Games in Atlanta, Georgia in 1996. Overall, there were 135 Keepsake ornaments in the collection, as well as 23 Magic, 13 Showcase and 34 Miniature ornaments. See the collectible series section for more 1996 ornaments.

2

101 Dalmatians
Handcrafted • N/A
1295QXI6544 • **Value $22**

3

Antlers Aweigh!
Handcrafted • CHAD
995QX5901 • **Value $21**

4

Apple for Teacher
Handcrafted • AUBE
795QX6121 • **Value $13**

5

Baby's First Christmas
Handcrafted • SEAL
795QX5761 • **Value $22**

6

Baby's First Christmas
Handcrafted • CROW
795QX5764 • **Value $25**

7

Baby's First Christmas
Handcrafted • ANDR
995QX5754 • **Value $23**

8

Baby's First Christmas
Porcelain • N/A
1095QX5751 • **Value $25**

9

Baby's First Christmas
Porcelain • VOTR
1895QX5744 • **Value $30**

10

Baby's Second Christmas
Handcrafted • CROW
795QX5771 • **Value $22**

1

Bounce Pass
Handcrafted • SIED
795QX6031 • **Value $15**

2

Bowl 'em Over
Handcrafted • SIED
795QX6014 • **Value $15**

3

Child Care Giver
Handcrafted • SIED
895QX6071 • **Value $16**

4

Child's Fifth Christmas
Handcrafted • RHOD
695QX5784 • **Value $17**

5

Child's Fourth Christmas
Handcrafted • CROW
795QX5781 • **Value $18**

6

Child's Third Christmas
Handcrafted • CROW
795QX5774 • **Value $20**

7

Christmas Joy
Handcrafted • UNRU
1495QX6241 • **Value $26**

8

Christmas Snowman
Handcrafted • UNRU
995QX6214 • **Value $21**

9

Close-Knit Friends
Handcrafted • BRIC
995QX5874 • **Value $18**

10

Come All Ye Faithful
Handcrafted • CROW
1295QX6244 • **Value $25**

11

Commander William T. Riker™
Handcrafted • RGRS
1495QXI5551 • **Value $30**

12

Dad
Handcrafted • SIED
795QX5831 • **Value $17**

13

Daughter
Handcrafted • PALM
895QX6077 • **Value $20**

14

Esmeralda and Djali
Handcrafted • CROW
1495QXI6351 • **Value $24**

15

Evergreen Santa
Handcrafted • LYLE
2200QX5714 • **Value $42**

16

Fan-tastic Season
Handcrafted • CHAD
995QX5924 • **Value $21**

17

Feliz Navidad
Handcrafted • SICK
995QX6304 • **Value $22**

18

Foghorn Leghorn and Henery Hawk (set/2)
Handcrafted • CHAD
1395QX5444 • **Value $23**

19

Glad Tidings
Handcrafted • LYLE
1495QX6231 • **Value $26**

20

Goal Line Glory (set/2)
Handcrafted • SEAL
1295QX6001 • **Value $25**

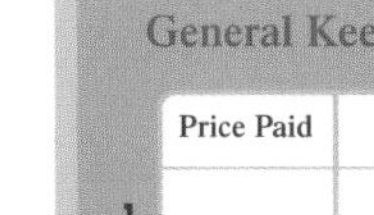
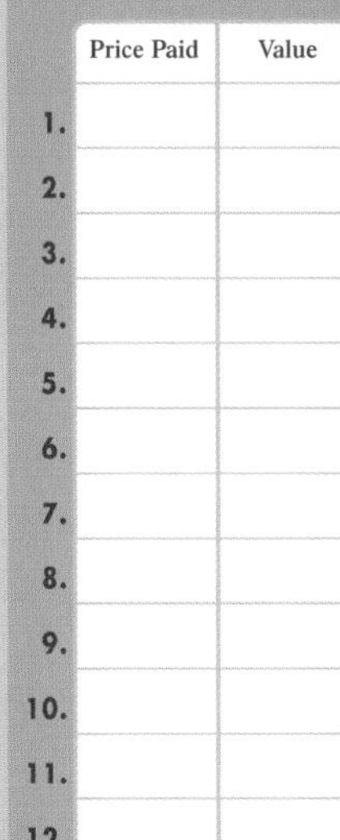

General Keepsake

	Price Paid	Value
1.		
2.		
3.		
4.		
5.		
6.		
7.		
8.		
9.		
10.		
11.		
12.		
13.		
14.		
15.		
16.		
17.		
18.		
19.		
20.		
Totals		

1

Godchild
Handcrafted • RGRS
895QX5841 • **Value $16**

2

Granddaughter
Handcrafted • RGRS
795QX5697 • **Value $16**

3

Grandma
Handcrafted • VOTR
895QX5844 • **Value $17**

4

Grandpa
Handcrafted • VOTR
895QX5851 • **Value $17**

5

Grandson
Handcrafted • RGRS
795QX5699 • **Value $16**

6

Growth of a Leader
Ceramic • N/A
995QX5541 • **Value $17**

7

Happy Holi-doze
Handcrafted • RHOD
995QX5904 • **Value $19**

8

Hearts Full of Love
Handcrafted • RHOD
995QX5814 • **Value $20**

9

High Style
Handcrafted • CHAD
895QX6064 • **Value $19**

10

Hillside Express
Handcrafted • AUBE
1295QX6134 • **Value $23**

11

Holiday Haul
Handcrafted • SICK
1495QX6201 • **Value $32**

12

Hurrying Downstairs
Handcrafted • FRAN
895QX6074 • **Value $18**

13

I Dig Golf
Handcrafted • RHOD
1095QX5891 • **Value $20**

14

Invitation to the Games (set/2)
Ceramic • MCGE
1495QXE5511 • **Value $26**

15

It's A Wonderful Life™
Handcrafted • CROW
1495QXI6531 • **Value $36**

16

IZZY™ – The Mascot
Handcrafted • PALM
995QXE5724 • **Value $17**

17

Jackpot Jingle
Handcrafted • SIED
995QX5911 • **Value $19**

18

Jolly Wolly Ark
Handcrafted • CROW
1295QX6221 • **Value $25**

19

Kindly Shepherd
Handcrafted • ANDR
1295QX6274 • **Value $26**

20

Laverne, Victor and Hugo
Handcrafted • CROW
1295QXI6354 • **Value $21**

General Keepsake

	Price Paid	Value
1.		
2.		
3.		
4.		
5.		
6.		
7.		
8.		
9.		
10.		
11.		
12.		
13.		
14.		
15.		
16.		
17.		
18.		
19.		
20.		
Totals		

1

Lighting the Way
Handcrafted • CHAD
1295QX6124 • **Value $22**

2

A Little Song and Dance
Handcrafted • CROW
995QX6211 • **Value $19**

3

Little Spooners
Handcrafted • UNRU
1295QX5504 • **Value $24**

4

Madonna and Child
Tin • SICK
1295QX6324 • **Value $21**

5

Making His Rounds
Handcrafted • FRAN
1495QX6271 • **Value $25**

6

Marvin the Martian
Handcrafted • CHAD
1095QX5451 • **Value $24**

7

Matchless Memories
Handcrafted • CROW
995QX6061 • **Value $18**

8

Maxine
Handcrafted • PIKE
995QX6224 • **Value $26**

9
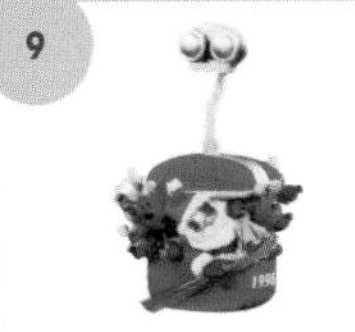
Merry Carpoolers
Handcrafted • CROW
1495QX5884 • **Value $26**

10

Mom
Handcrafted • LYLE
795QX5824 • **Value $18**

11

Mom and Dad
Handcrafted • RHOD
995QX5821 • **Value $18**

12

Mom-to-Be
Handcrafted • UNRU
795QX5791 • **Value $16**

13

Mr. Spock
Handcrafted • RGRS
1495QXI5544 • **Value $35**

14

New Home
Handcrafted • SEAL
895QX5881 • **Value $20**

15

Olive Oyl and Swee' Pea
Handcrafted • CHAD
1095QX5481 • **Value $23**

16

Olympic Triumph
Handcrafted • SEAL
1095QXE5731 • **Value $19**

17

On My Way
Handcrafted • TAGU
795QX5861 • **Value $16**

18

Our Christmas Together
Handcrafted • PALM
1895QX5794 • **Value $35**

19

Our Christmas Together Photo Holder
Handcrafted • CROW
895QX5804 • **Value $18**

20

Our First Christmas Together
Acrylic • VOTR
695QX3051 • **Value $17**

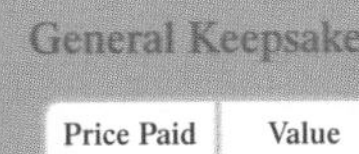
General Keepsake

	Price Paid	Value
1.		
2.		
3.		
4.		
5.		
6.		
7.		
8.		
9.		
10.		
11.		
12.		
13.		
14.		
15.		
16.		
17.		
18.		
19.		
20.		
Totals		

1

Our First Christmas Together
Handcrafted • PALM
995QX5811 • **Value $22**

2

Our First Christmas Together Collector's Plate
Porcelain • N/A
1095QX5801 • **Value $22**

3

Parade of Nations
Porcelain • N/A
1095QXE5741 • **Value $18**

4

Peppermint Surprise
Handcrafted • PIKE
795QX6234 • **Value $18**

5

Percy the Small Engine – No. 6
Handcrafted • RHOD
995QX6314 • **Value $21**

6
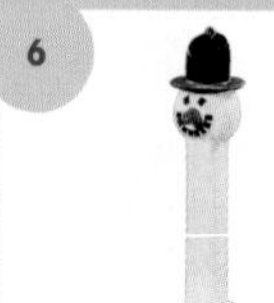
PEZ® Snowman
Handcrafted • N/A
795QX6534 • **Value $17**

7

Polar Cycle
Handcrafted • UNRU
1295QX6034 • **Value $24**

8

Prayer for Peace
Handcrafted • LYLE
795QX6261 • **Value $17**

9

Precious Child
Handcrafted • VOTR
895QX6251 • **Value $18**

10

Pup-Tenting
Handcrafted • PALM
795QX6011 • **Value $16**

11

Quasimodo
Handcrafted • CROW
995QXI6341 • **Value $18**

12

Regal Cardinal
Handcrafted • FRAN
995QX6204 • **Value $21**

13

Sew Sweet
Handcrafted • AUBE
895QX5921 • **Value $17**

14

Sister to Sister
Handcrafted • LYLE
995QX5834 • **Value $18**

15

Son
Handcrafted • PALM
895QX6079 • **Value $18**

16
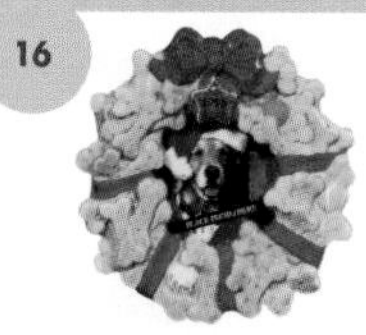
Special Dog
Handcrafted • TAGU
795QX5864 • **Value $16**

17

SPIDER-MAN™
Handcrafted • CHAD
1295QX5757 • **Value $30**

18

Star of the Show
Handcrafted • AUBE
895QX6004 • **Value $18**

19

Tamika
Handcrafted • BRIC
795QX6301 • **Value $17**

General Keepsake

	Price Paid	Value
1.		
2.		
3.		
4.		
5.		
6.		
7.		
8.		
9.		
10.		
11.		
12.		
13.		
14.		
15.		
16.		
17.		
18.		
19.		
Totals		

1

Tender Lovin' Care
Handcrafted • SEAL
795QX6114 • **Value $17**

2

Thank You, Santa
Handcrafted • BRIC
795QX5854 • **Value $17**

3

This Big!
Handcrafted • SEAL
995QX5914 • **Value $18**

4

Time for a Treat
Handcrafted • SICK
1195QX5464 • **Value $22**

5

Tonka® Mighty Dump Truck
Die-Cast Metal • N/A
1395QX6321 • **Value $34**

6

A Tree for SNOOPY
Handcrafted • SIED
895QX5507 • **Value $18**

7

Welcome Guest
Handcrafted • UNRU
1495QX5394 • **Value $27**

8

Welcome Him
Handcrafted • TAGU
895QX6264 • **Value $18**

9

Winnie the Pooh and Piglet
Handcrafted • SIED
1295QX5454 • **Value $33**

10

Witch of the West
Handcrafted • LYLE
1395QX5554 • **Value $32**

11

WONDER WOMAN™
Handcrafted • RGRS
1295QX5941 • **Value $25**

12

Woodland Santa
Pressed Tin • SICK
1295QX6131 • **Value $23**

13

Yogi Bear™ and Boo Boo™
Handcrafted • RGRS
1295QX5521 • **Value $23**

14

Yuletide Cheer
Handcrafted • VOTR
795QX6054 • **Value $16**

15

Ziggy®
Handcrafted • CHAD
995QX6524 • **Value $22**

16

Baby's First Christmas
Handcrafted • FRAN
2200QLX7404 • **Value $40**

17

Chicken Coop Chorus
Handcrafted • CROW
2450QLX7491 • **Value $43**

18

Emerald City
Handcrafted • CROW
3200QLX7454 • **Value $65**

19

Father Time
Handcrafted • CHAD
2450QLX7391 • **Value $45**

20

THE JETSONS™
Handcrafted • CROW
2800QLX7411 • **Value $50**

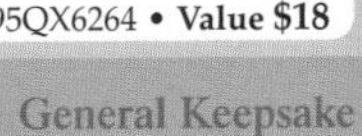
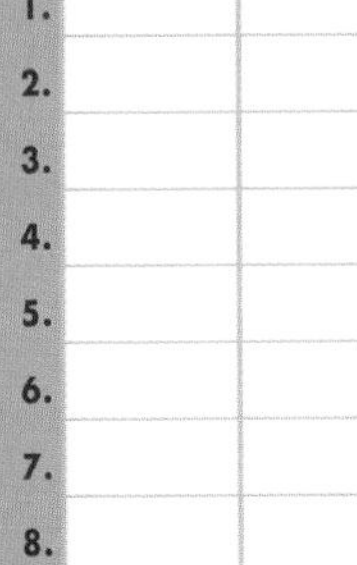

General Keepsake

	Price Paid	Value
1.		
2.		
3.		
4.		
5.		
6.		
7.		
8.		
9.		
10.		
11.		
12.		
13.		
14.		
15.		
General Magic		
16.		
17.		
18.		
19.		
20.		
Totals		

1

Jukebox Party
Handcrafted • PALM
2450QLX7339 • **Value $52**

2

Let Us Adore Him
Handcrafted • LYLE
1650QLX7381 • **Value $35**

3

Lighting the Flame
Handcrafted • UNRU
2800QXE7444 • **Value $44**

4

Millennium Falcon™
Handcrafted • N/A
2400QLX7474 • **Value $50**

5

North Pole Volunteers
Handcrafted • SEAL
4200QLX7471 • **Value $84**

6

Over the Rooftops
Handcrafted • SEAL
1450QLX7374 • **Value $30**

7

PEANUTS®
Handcrafted • CHAD
1850QLX7394 • **Value $43**

8

Pinball Wonder
Handcrafted • CROW
2800QLX7451 • **Value $52**

9

Sharing a Soda
Handcrafted • CROW
2450QLX7424 • **Value $43**

10

Slippery Day
Handcrafted • SIED
2450QLX7414 • **Value $50**

11

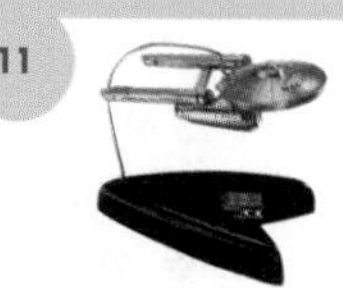

STAR TREK®, 30 Years (set/2, w/display base)
Handcrafted • NORT/RHOD
4500QXI7534 • **Value $82**

12

The Statue of Liberty
Handcrafted • SEAL
2450QLX7421 • **Value $46**

13

Treasured Memories
Handcrafted • SICK
1850QLX7384 • **Value $37**

14

U.S.S. Voyager™
Handcrafted • NORT
2400QXI7544 • **Value $52**

15

Video Party
Handcrafted • SIED
2800QLX7431 • **Value $48**

16

Carmen
Cookie Jar Friends
Porcelain • RGRS
1595QK1164 • **Value $26**

17

Clyde
Cookie Jar Friends
Porcelain • AUBE
1595QK1161 • **Value $23**

18

Caroling Angel
Folk Art Americana
Handcrafted/Copper • SICK
1695QK1134 • **Value $30**

19

Mrs. Claus
Folk Art Americana
Handcrafted/Copper • SICK
1895QK1204 • **Value $30**

20

Santa's Gifts
Folk Art Americana
Handcrafted/Copper • SICK
1895QK1124 • **Value $37**

General Magic

	Price Paid	Value
1.		
2.		
3.		
4.		
5.		
6.		
7.		
8.		
9.		
10.		
11.		
12.		
13.		
14.		
15.		

General Showcase

	Price Paid	Value
16.		
17.		
18.		
19.		
20.		
Totals		

1

Balthasar (Frankincense)
Magi Bells
Porcelain • VOTR
1395QK1174 • **Value $26**

2

Caspar (Myrrh)
Magi Bells
Porcelain • VOTR
1395QK1184 • **Value $26**

3

Melchoir (Gold)
Magi Bells
Porcelain • VOTR
1395QK1181 • **Value $26**

4

The Birds' Christmas Tree
Nature's Sketchbook
Handcrafted • UNRU
1895QK1114 • **Value $30**

5

Christmas Bunny
Nature's Sketchbook
Handcrafted • FRAN
1895QK1104 • **Value $42**

6

The Holly Basket
Nature's Sketchbook
Handcrafted • LYLE
1895QK1094 • **Value $34**

7

Madonna and Child
Sacred Masterworks
Handcrafted • SICK
1595QK1144 • **Value $25**

8

Praying Madonna
Sacred Masterworks
Handcrafted • SICK
1595QK1154 • **Value $28**

9

African Elephants
Handcrafted • SICK
575QXM4224 • **Value $19**

10

Baby Sylvester
Handcrafted • PALM
575QXM4154 • **Value $16**

11

Baby Tweety
Handcrafted • PALM
575QXM4014 • **Value $26**

12

A Child's Gifts
Handcrafted • ANDR
675QXM4234 • **Value $13**

13

Christmas Bear
Handcrafted • SEAL
475QXM4241 • **Value $14**

14

Cloisonné Medallion
Cloisonné • MCGE
975QXE4041 • **Value $19**

15

Cool Delivery
Coca-Cola®
Handcrafted • PIKE
575QXM4021 • **Value $15**

16

GONE WITH THE WIND™ (set/3)
Handcrafted • ANDR
1995QXM4211 • **Value $38**

17

Hattie Chapeau
Handcrafted • RHOD
475QXM4251 • **Value $12**

18

Joyous Angel
Handcrafted • ANDR
475QXM4231 • **Value $12**

19
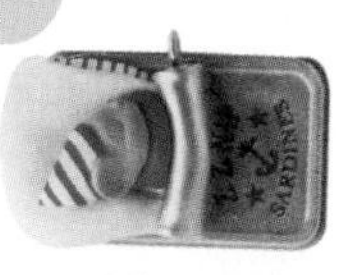
Long Winter's Nap
Handcrafted • ANDR
575QXM4244 • **Value $13**

20

Message for Santa
Handcrafted • SEAL
675QXM4254 • **Value $14**

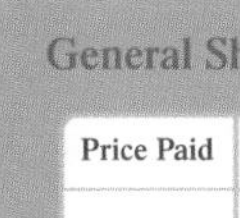

	Price Paid	Value
General Showcase		
1.		
2.		
3.		
4.		
5.		
6.		
7.		
8.		
General Miniature		
9.		
10.		
11.		
12.		
13.		
14.		
15.		
16.		
17.		
18.		
19.		
20.		
Totals		

Value Guide — Hallmark Keepsake Ornaments

1

O Holy Night (set/4)
Handcrafted • RHOD
2450QXM4204 • **Value $34**

2

Peaceful Christmas
Handcrafted • UNRU
475QXM4214 • **Value $13**

3

Sparkling Crystal Angel
Lead Crystal/Silver • VOTR
975QXM4264 • **Value $22**

4

Tiny Christmas Helpers (set/6)
Handcrafted • SEAL
2900QXM4261 • **Value $50**

5

A Tree for WOODSTOCK
Handcrafted • SIED
575QXM4767 • **Value $18**

6

The Vehicles of STAR WARS™ (set/3)
Handcrafted • RHOD
1995QXM4024 • **Value $42**

7

Winnie the Pooh and Tigger
Handcrafted • SIED
975QXM4044 • **Value $24**

8

Airmail for Santa (gift membership bonus)
Handcrafted • RGRS
QXC4194 • **Value $22**

9

Holiday Bunny (early renewal piece, miniature)
Handcrafted • FRAN
QXC4191 • **Value $15**

10

Rudolph the Red-Nosed Reindeer® (keepsake of membership, magic)
Handcrafted • SIED
QXC7341 • **Value $24**

11

Rudolph®'s Helper (keepsake of membership, miniature)
Handcrafted • SIED
QXC4171 • **Value $16**

12

Santa (keepsake of membership)
Handcrafted • SIED
QXC4164 • **Value $20**

13

The Wizard of OZ™ (club edition)
Handcrafted • RGRS
1295QXC4161 • **Value $65**

14

"Get Hooked On Collecting" Starter Set (book with "Filled With Memories" ornament)
Handcrafted • N/A
799XPR837 • **Value N/E**

15

Welcome Sign, Tender Touches
Handcrafted • SEAL
1500QX6331 • **Value $25**

16

1955 Chevrolet Cameo (red)
Handcrafted • PALM
(N/C) No stock # • **Value N/E**

17

Gold Rocking Horse (miniature)
Handcrafted • SICK
($12.95) No stock # • **Value $48**

18

Murray® Airplane (tan)
Die-Cast Metal • PALM
(N/C) No stock # • **Value N/E**

19

Murray® Fire Truck (miniature, white)
Die-Cast Metal • PALM
(N/C) No stock # • **Value $15**

20

Santa's Toy Shop (set/2, artist signing piece)
Handcrafted • VARI
6000QXC4201 • **Value $124**

	Price Paid	Value
General Miniature		
1.		
2.		
3.		
4.		
5.		
6.		
7.		
Collector's Club		
8.		
9.		
10.		
11.		
12.		
13.		
Premiere Ornaments		
14.		
15.		
Artists On Tour Pieces		
16.		
17.		
18.		
19.		
20.		
Totals		

1

Toy Shop Santa
Handcrafted • UNRU
($14.95) No stock # • **Value $38**

2

BARBIE™ Lapel Pin
(re-issued in 1997)
Handcrafted • N/A
495XLP3544 • **Value N/E**

3

Holiday BARBIE™
Stocking Hanger
(re-issued in 1997)
Handcrafted • N/A
1995XSH3101 • **Value N/E**

4

Yuletide Romance™
BARBIE® Doll
(3rd & final in series)
Vinyl • N/A
5000QHX3401 • **Value $100**

5

Reindeer Rooters
Handcrafted • CROW
(N/C) No stock # • **Value N/E**

6

Golden Age
Batman and Robin™
"The Dynamic Duo™"
Handcrafted • UNRU
7000QHF3103 • **Value N/E**

7

Golden Age
Superman™ "Man of
Steel™" (LE-14,500)
Handcrafted • N/A
8000QHF3101 • **Value N/E**

8

Golden Age Wonder
Woman™ "Champion
of Freedom"
Handcrafted • RGRS
3500QHF3107 • **Value N/E**

9

Modern Era Batman™
"Guardian of
Gotham City™"
Handcrafted • CHAD
5500QHF3104 • **Value N/E**

10

Modern Era Robin™
"World's Bravest
Teenager"
Handcrafted • CHAD
4000QHF3105 • **Value N/E**

11

Modern Era
Superman™ "In A
Single Bound"
Handcrafted • N/A
6000QHF3102 • **Value N/E**

12

Modern Era Wonder
Woman™ "Warrior of
Strength and Wisdom"
Handcrafted • RGRS
3500QHF3106 • **Value N/E**

13

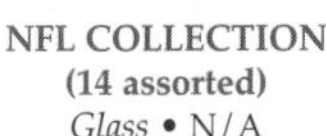

NFL COLLECTION
(14 assorted)
Glass • N/A

1. **Buffalo Bills™**
595BIL2035 • **Value $10**
2. **Carolina Panthers™**
(re-issued from 1995)
595PNA2035 • **Value $10**
3. **Chicago Bears™**
(re-issued from 1995)
595BRS2035 • **Value $10**
4. **Dallas Cowboys™**
(re-issued from 1995)
595COW2035 • **Value $10**
5. **Green Bay Packers™**
595PKR2035 • **Value $10**
6. **Kansas City Chiefs™**
(re-issued from 1995)
595CHF2035 • **Value $10**
7. **Los Angeles Raiders™**
(re-issued from 1995)
595RDR2035 • **Value $10**
8. **Minnesota Vikings™**
(re-issued from 1995)
595VIK2035 • **Value $10**
9. **New England Patriots™**
(re-issued from 1995)
595NEP2035 • **Value $10**
10. **Philadelphia Eagles™**
(re-issued from 1995)
595EAG2035 • **Value $10**
11. **Pittsburgh Steelers™**
595PIT2035 • **Value $10**
12. **St. Louis Rams™**
595RAM2035 • **Value $10**
13. **San Francisco 49ers™**
(re-issued from 1995)
595FOR2035 • **Value $10**
14. **Washington Redskins™**
(re-issued from 1995)
595RSK2035 • **Value $10**

14

NFL COLLECTION
(30 assorted)
Handcrafted • UNRU

1. **Arizona Cardinals™**
995QSR6484 • **Value $15**
2. **Atlanta Falcons™**
995QSR6364 • **Value $15**
3. **Browns™**
995QSR6391 • **Value $15**
4. **Buffalo Bills™**
995QSR6371 • **Value $15**
5. **Carolina Panthers™**
995QSR6374 • **Value $15**
6. **Chicago Bears™**
995QSR6381 • **Value $15**
7. **Cincinnati Bengals™**
995QSR6384 • **Value $15**
8. **Dallas Cowboys™**
995QSR6394 • **Value $16**
9. **Denver Broncos™**
995QSR6411 • **Value $15**
10. **Detroit Lions™**
995QSR6414 • **Value $15**
11. **Green Bay Packers™**
995QSR6421 • **Value $20**
12. **Indianapolis Colts™**
995QSR6431 • **Value $15**

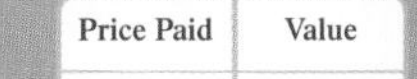

	Price Paid	Value
Artists On Tour Pieces		
1.		
BARBIE™ Collectibles		
2.		
3.		
4.		
Club Tour Ornaments		
5.		
D.C. Super Heroes Figurines		
6.		
7.		
8.		
9.		
10.		
11.		
12.		
NFL Collection		
13.		
14.		
Totals		

13. Jacksonville Jaguars™ 995QSR6434 • **Value $15**
14. Kansas City Chiefs™ 995QSR6361 • **Value $15**
15. Miami Dolphins™ 995QSR6451 • **Value $15**
16. Minnesota Vikings™ 995QSR6454 • **Value $15**
17. New England Patriots™ 995QSR6461 • **Value $15**
18. New Orleans Saints™ 995QSR6464 • **Value $15**
19. New York Giants™ 995QSR6471 • **Value $15**
20. New York Jets™ 995QSR6474 • **Value $15**
21. Oakland Raiders™ 995QSR6441 • **Value $15**
22. Oilers™ 995QSR6424 • **Value $15**
23. Philadelphia Eagles™ 995QSR6481 • **Value $15**
24. Pittsburgh Steelers™ 995QSR6491 • **Value $15**
25. St. Louis Rams™ 995QSR6444 • **Value $15**
26. San Diego Chargers™ 995QSR6494 • **Value $15**
27. San Francisco 49ers™ 995QSR6501 • **Value $15**
28. Seattle Seahawks™ 995QSR6504 • **Value $15**
29. Tampa Bay Buccaneers™ 995QSR6511 • **Value $15**
30. Washington Redskins™ 995QSR6514 • **Value $15**

1

Gymnastics Figurine
Handcrafted • LYLE
1750QHC8204 • **Value N/E**

2

Olympic Triumph Figurine (LE-24,500)
Handcrafted • UNRU
5000QHC8191 • **Value N/E**

3

Parade of Nations Plate
Porcelain • N/A
3000QHC8194 • **Value N/E**

4

Swimming Figurine
Handcrafted • CHAD
1750QHC8211 • **Value N/E**

5

Track and Field Figurine
Handcrafted • N/A
1750QHC8201 • **Value N/E**

1995

More great BARBIE™, STAR TREK™ and sports ornaments were released in 1995, as well as a record number of Showcase ornaments. In the 1995 line, there were 146 Keepsake, 20 Magic, 20 Showcase and 36 Miniature ornaments. See the collectible series section for more 1995 ornaments.

6

Acorn 500
Handcrafted • SIED
1095QX5929 • **Value $21**

7

Across the Miles
Handcrafted • FRAN
895QX5847 • **Value $20**

8

Air Express
Handcrafted • SEAL
795QX5977 • **Value $18**

9

Anniversary Year
Handcrafted • UNRU
895QX5819 • **Value $17**

10

Baby's First Christmas
Handcrafted • VOTR
795QX5549 • **Value $19**

11

Baby's First Christmas
Handcrafted • CROW
795QX5559 • **Value $25**

12

Baby's First Christmas
Handcrafted • ANDR
995QX5557 • **Value $18**

13

Baby's First Christmas
Handcrafted • ANDR
1895QX5547 • **Value $43**

14

Baby's First Christmas – Baby Boy
Glass • N/A
500QX2319 • **Value $17**

Olympic Collectibles

	Price Paid	Value
1.		
2.		
3.		
4.		
5.		

General Keepsake

	Price Paid	Value
6.		
7.		
8.		
9.		
10.		
11.		
12.		
13.		
14.		
Totals		

1

Baby's First Christmas – Baby Girl
Glass • N/A
500QX2317 • **Value $17**

2

Baby's Second Christmas
Handcrafted • CROW
795QX5567 • **Value $25**

3

Barrel-Back Rider
Handcrafted • FRAN
995QX5189 • **Value $25**

4

Batmobile
Handcrafted • PALM
1495QX5739 • **Value $26**

5

Betty and Wilma
Handcrafted • RHOD
1495QX5417 • **Value $23**

6

Beverly and Teddy
Handcrafted • UNRU
2175QX5259 • **Value $34**

7

Bingo Bear
Handcrafted • VOTR
795QX5919 • **Value $18**

8

Bobbin' Along
Handcrafted • CROW
895QX5879 • **Value $30**

9

Brother
Handcrafted • LYLE
695QX5679 • **Value $16**

10

Bugs Bunny
Handcrafted • CHAD
895QX5019 • **Value $22**

11

Captain James T. Kirk
Handcrafted • RGRS
1395QXI5539 • **Value $27**

12

Captain Jean-Luc Picard
Handcrafted • RGRS
1395QXI5737 • **Value $28**

13

Captain John Smith and Meeko
Handcrafted • CROW
1295QXI6169 • **Value $21**

14

Catch the Spirit
Handcrafted • SIED
795QX5899 • **Value $19**

15

Child's Fifth Christmas
Handcrafted • RHOD
695QX5637 • **Value $18**

16

Child's Fourth Christmas
Handcrafted • FRAN
695QX5629 • **Value $19**

17

Child's Third Christmas
Handcrafted • CROW
795QX5627 • **Value $19**

18

Christmas Fever
Handcrafted • AUBE
795QX5967 • **Value $18**

19

Christmas Morning
Handcrafted • FRAN
1095QX5997 • **Value $19**

20

Christmas Patrol
Handcrafted • ANDR
795QX5959 • **Value $19**

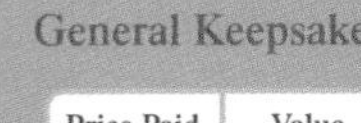

General Keepsake

	Price Paid	Value
1.		
2.		
3.		
4.		
5.		
6.		
7.		
8.		
9.		
10.		
11.		
12.		
13.		
14.		
15.		
16.		
17.		
18.		
19.		
20.		
Totals		

1

Colorful World
Handcrafted • CROW
1095QX5519 • **Value $26**

2

Cows of Bali
Handcrafted • ANDR
895QX5999 • **Value $18**

3

Dad
Handcrafted • SIED
795QX5649 • **Value $16**

4

Dad-to-Be
Handcrafted • RHOD
795QX5667 • **Value $15**

5

Daughter
Handcrafted • PALM
695QX5677 • **Value $19**

6

Delivering Kisses
Handcrafted • SICK
1095QX4107 • **Value $24**

7

Dream On
Handcrafted • FRAN
1095QX6007 • **Value $21**

8

Dudley the Dragon
Handcrafted • PIKE
1095QX6209 • **Value $21**

9

Faithful Fan
Handcrafted • SIED
895QX5897 • **Value $18**

10

Feliz Navidad
Handcrafted • RHOD
795QX5869 • **Value $20**

11

For My Grandma
Handcrafted • PALM
695QX5729 • **Value $16**

12

Forever Friends Bear
Handcrafted • BRWN
895QX5258 • **Value $22**

13

Friendly Boost
Handcrafted • PALM
895QX5827 • **Value $21**

14

GARFIELD®
Handcrafted • N/A
1095QX5007 • **Value $26**

15

Glinda, Witch of the North
Handcrafted • LYLE
1395QX5749 • **Value $40**

16

Godchild
Handcrafted/Brass • PALM
795QX5707 • **Value $20**

17

Godparent
Glass • VOTR
500QX2417 • **Value $15**

18

Gopher Fun
Handcrafted • SIED
995QX5887 • **Value $19**

19

Grandchild's First Christmas
Handcrafted • FRAN
795QX5777 • **Value $16**

20

Granddaughter
Handcrafted • RGRS
695QX5779 • **Value $18**

General Keepsake

	Price Paid	Value
1.		
2.		
3.		
4.		
5.		
6.		
7.		
8.		
9.		
10.		
11.		
12.		
13.		
14.		
15.		
16.		
17.		
18.		
19.		
20.		
Totals		

1

Grandmother
Handcrafted • ANDR
795QX5767 • **Value $21**

2

Grandpa
Handcrafted • CROW
895QX5769 • **Value $17**

3

Grandparents
Glass • LYLE
500QX2419 • **Value $14**

4

Grandson
Handcrafted • RGRS
695QX5787 • **Value $18**

5

Happy Wrappers (set/2)
Handcrafted • CROW
1095QX6037 • **Value $21**

6

Heaven's Gift (set/2)
Handcrafted • ANDR
2000QX6057 • **Value $47**

7

Hockey Pup
Handcrafted • CROW
995QX5917 • **Value $23**

8

Important Memo
Handcrafted • SICK
895QX5947 • **Value $17**

9

In a Heartbeat
Handcrafted • ANDR
895QX5817 • **Value $20**

10

In Time With Christmas
Handcrafted • CROW
1295QX6049 • **Value $27**

11

Joy to the World
Handcrafted • ANDR
895QX5867 • **Value $21**

12

LEGO® Fireplace With Santa
Handcrafted • CROW
1095QX4769 • **Value $26**

13

Lou Rankin Bear
Handcrafted • SIED
995QX4069 • **Value $22**

14

The Magic School Bus™
Handcrafted • RHOD
1095QX5849 • **Value $22**

15

Mary Engelbreit
Glass • N/A
500QX2409 • **Value $16**

16

Merry RV
Handcrafted • PALM
1295QX6027 • **Value $25**

17

Mom
Handcrafted • SIED
795QX5647 • **Value $18**

18

Mom and Dad
Handcrafted • RGRS
995QX5657 • **Value $26**

19

Mom-to-Be
Handcrafted • RHOD
795QX5659 • **Value $16**

20

Muletide Greetings
Handcrafted • CHAD
795QX6009 • **Value $16**

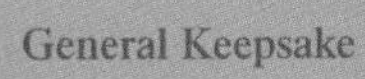

General Keepsake

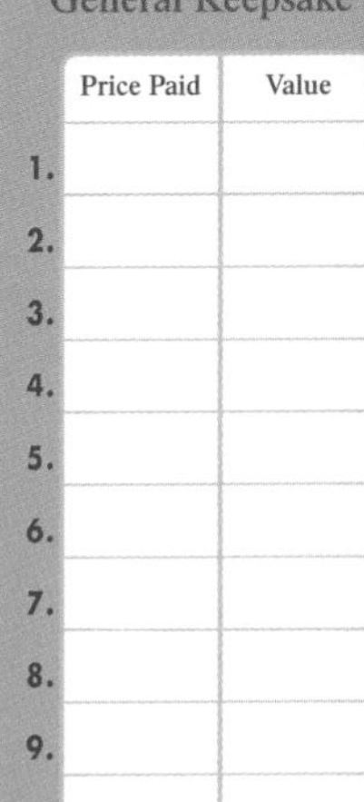

	Price Paid	Value
1.		
2.		
3.		
4.		
5.		
6.		
7.		
8.		
9.		
10.		
11.		
12.		
13.		
14.		
15.		
16.		
17.		
18.		
19.		
20.		
Totals		

1

New Home
Handcrafted • ANDR
895QX5839 • **Value $18**

2

North Pole 911
Handcrafted • SEAL
1095QX5957 • **Value $23**

3

Number One Teacher
Handcrafted • SEAL
795QX5949 • **Value $17**

4

The Olympic Spirit Centennial Games Atlanta 1996
Acrylic • N/A
795QX3169 • **Value $20**

5

On the Ice
Handcrafted • CROW
795QX6047 • **Value $21**

6

Our Christmas Together
Handcrafted • LYLE
995QX5809 • **Value $19**

7

Our Family
Handcrafted • CHAD
795QX5709 • **Value $17**

8

Our First Christmas
Handcrafted • LYLE
1695QX5797 • **Value $30**

9
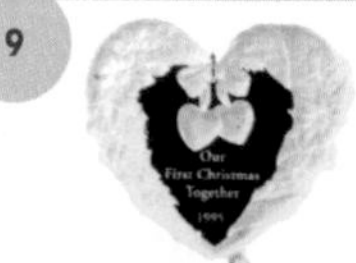

Our First Christmas Together
Acrylic • LYLE
695QX3177 • **Value $17**

10

Our First Christmas Together
Handcrafted • SIED
895QX5799 • **Value $22**

11

Our First Christmas Together
Handcrafted • SEAL
895QX5807 • **Value $20**

12

Our Little Blessings
Handcrafted • CROW
1295QX5209 • **Value $27**

13

Packed With Memories
Handcrafted • SEAL
795QX5639 • **Value $20**

14

Percy, Flit and Meeko
Handcrafted • CROW
995QXI6179 • **Value $22**

15

Perfect Balance
Handcrafted • SIED
795QX5927 • **Value $18**

16

PEZ® Santa
Handcrafted • FRAN
795QX5267 • **Value $20**

17

Pocahontas
Handcrafted • CROW
1295QXI6177 • **Value $23**

18

Pocahontas and Captain John Smith
Handcrafted • CROW
1495QXI6197 • **Value $25**

19

Polar Coaster
Handcrafted • CROW
895QX6117 • **Value $24**

20

Popeye®
Handcrafted • CHAD
1095QX5257 • **Value $26**

General Keepsake

	Price Paid	Value
1.		
2.		
3.		
4.		
5.		
6.		
7.		
8.		
9.		
10.		
11.		
12.		
13.		
14.		
15.		
16.		
17.		
18.		
19.		
20.		
Totals		

1

Refreshing Gift
Handcrafted • UNRU
1495QX4067 • **Value $31**

2
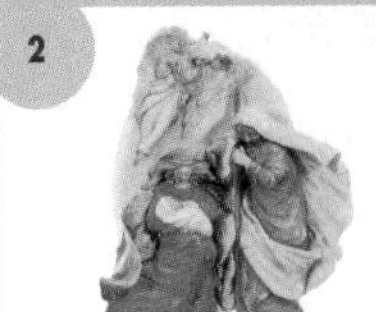
Rejoice!
Handcrafted • LYLE
1095QX5987 • **Value $24**

3

Roller Whiz
Handcrafted • SEAL
795QX5937 • **Value $19**

4

Santa In Paris
Handcrafted • SICK
895QX5877 • **Value $26**

5

Santa's Serenade
Handcrafted • CROW
895QX6017 • **Value $19**

6

Santa's Visitors
Glass • N/A
500QX2407 • **Value $18**

7

Simba, Pumbaa and Timon
Handcrafted • CROW
1295QX6159 • **Value $21**

8

Sister
Handcrafted • LYLE
695QX5687 • **Value $16**

9

Sister to Sister
Handcrafted • VOTR
895QX5689 • **Value $18**

10

Ski Hound
Handcrafted • RHOD
895QX5909 • **Value $20**

11

Son
Handcrafted • PALM
695QX5669 • **Value $18**

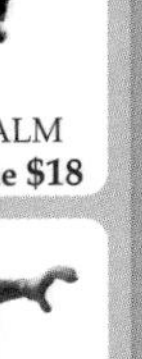

12

Special Cat
Handcrafted • CHAD
795QX5717 • **Value $17**

13

Special Dog
Handcrafted • CHAD
795QX5719 • **Value $17**

14

Surfin' Santa
Handcrafted • CROW
995QX6019 • **Value $26**

15

Sylvester and Tweety (set/2)
Handcrafted • CHAD
1395QX5017 • **Value $25**

16

Takin' a Hike
Handcrafted • FRAN
795QX6029 • **Value $19**

17

Tennis, Anyone?
Handcrafted • AUBE
795QX5907 • **Value $19**

18

Thomas the Tank Engine – No. 1
Handcrafted • RHOD
995QX5857 • **Value $33**

19

Three Wishes
Handcrafted • ANDR
795QX5979 • **Value $21**

20

Two for Tea
Handcrafted • JLEE
995QX5829 • **Value $29**

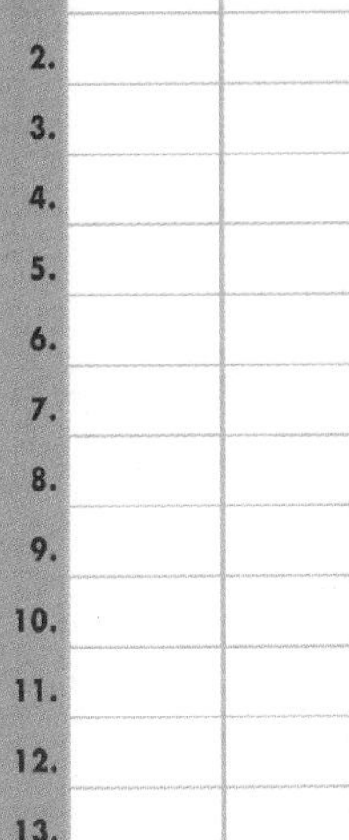

General Keepsake

	Price Paid	Value
1.		
2.		
3.		
4.		
5.		
6.		
7.		
8.		
9.		
10.		
11.		
12.		
13.		
14.		
15.		
16.		
17.		
18.		
19.		
20.		
Totals		

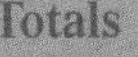

1

Vera the Mouse
Porcelain • N/A
895QX5537 • **Value $18**

2

Waiting Up for Santa
Handcrafted • PALM
895QX6106 • **Value $17**

3

Water Sports (set/2)
Handcrafted • SIED
1495QX6039 • **Value $37**

4

Wheel of Fortune®
Handcrafted • SICK
1295QX6187 • **Value $25**

5

Winnie the Pooh and Tigger
Handcrafted • SIED
1295QX5009 • **Value $33**

6

The Winning Play
Handcrafted • SIED
795QX5889 • **Value $22**

7

Baby's First Christmas
Handcrafted • CROW
2200QLX7317 • **Value $40**

8

Coming to See Santa
Handcrafted • PALM
3200QLX7369 • **Value $64**

9

Fred and Dino
Handcrafted • RHOD
2800QLX7289 • **Value $53**

10

Friends Share Fun
Handcrafted • RGRS
1650QLX7349 • **Value $35**

11

Goody Gumballs!
Handcrafted • SIED
1250QLX7367 • **Value $32**

12

Headin' Home
Handcrafted • JLEE
2200QLX7327 • **Value $46**

13

Holiday Swim
Handcrafted • RGRS
1850QLX7319 • **Value $37**

14

Jumping for Joy
Handcrafted • FRAN
2800QLX7347 • **Value $53**

15

My First HOT WHEELS™
Handcrafted • CROW
2800QLX7279 • **Value $50**

16

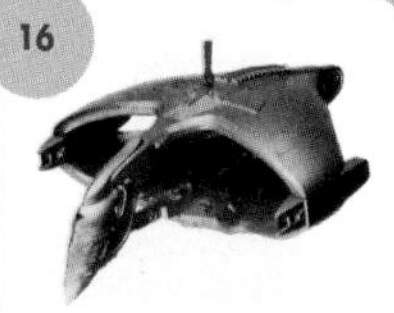

Romulan Warbird™
Handcrafted • NORT
2400QXI7267 • **Value $43**

17

Santa's Diner
Handcrafted • VOTR
2450QLX7337 • **Value $37**

18

Space Shuttle
Handcrafted • CROW
2450QLX7396 • **Value $46**

19

Superman™
Handcrafted • CHAD
2800QLX7309 • **Value $50**

20

Victorian Toy Box
Handcrafted • LYLE
4200QLX7357 • **Value $64**

	Price Paid	Value
General Keepsake		
1.		
2.		
3.		
4.		
5.		
6.		
General Magic		
7.		
8.		
9.		
10.		
11.		
12.		
13.		
14.		
15.		
16.		
17.		
18.		
19.		
20.		
Totals		

1

Wee Little Christmas
Handcrafted • CROW
2200QLX7329 • **Value $44**

2

Winnie the Pooh Too Much Hunny
Handcrafted • SIED
2450QLX7297 • **Value $53**

3

Angel of Light
All Is Bright
Handcrafted • ANDR
1195QK1159 • **Value $23**

4

Gentle Lullaby
All Is Bright
Handcrafted • ANDR
1195QK1157 • **Value $23**

5

Carole
Angel Bells
Porcelain • VOTR
1295QK1147 • **Value $28**

6

Joy
Angel Bells
Porcelain • VOTR
1295QK1137 • **Value $31**

7

Noelle
Angel Bells
Porcelain • VOTR
1295QK1139 • **Value $25**

8

Fetching the Firewood
Folk Art Americana
Handcrafted • SICK
1595QK1057 • **Value $35**

9

Fishing Party
Folk Art Americana
Handcrafted • SICK
1595QK1039 • **Value $35**

10

Guiding Santa
Folk Art Americana
Handcrafted • SICK
1895QK1037 • **Value $46**

11

Learning to Skate
Folk Art Americana
Handcrafted • SICK
1495QK1047 • **Value $38**

12

Away in a Manger
Holiday Enchantment
Porcelain • N/A
1395QK1097 • **Value $27**

13

Following the Star
Holiday Enchantment
Porcelain • VOTR
1395QK1099 • **Value $27**

14

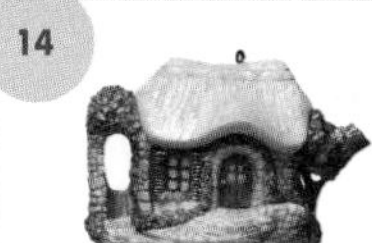

Cozy Cottage Teapot
Invitation To Tea
Handcrafted • ANDR
1595QK1127 • **Value $29**

15

European Castle Teapot
Invitation To Tea
Handcrafted • ANDR
1595QK1129 • **Value $29**

16

Victorian Home Teapot
Invitation To Tea
Handcrafted • ANDR
1595QK1119 • **Value $33**

17

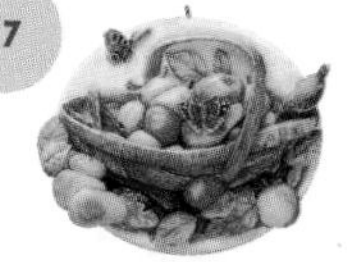

Backyard Orchard
Nature's Sketchbook
Handcrafted • FRAN
1895QK1069 • **Value $32**

18

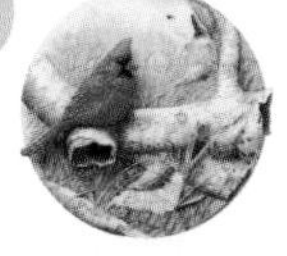

Christmas Cardinal
Nature's Sketchbook
Handcrafted • LYLE
1895QK1077 • **Value $35**

19

Raising a Family
Nature's Sketchbook
Handcrafted • LYLE
1895QK1067 • **Value $32**

20

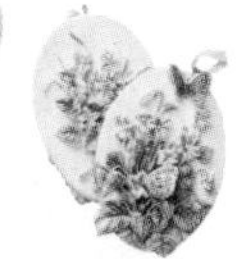

Violets and Butterflies
Nature's Sketchbook
Handcrafted • LYLE
1695QK1079 • **Value $32**

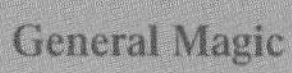

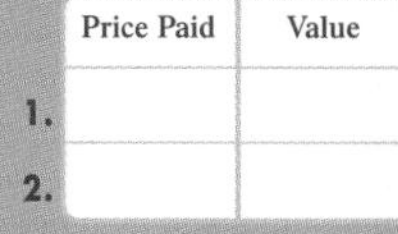

	Price Paid	Value
General Magic		
1.		
2.		
General Showcase		
3.		
4.		
5.		
6.		
7.		
8.		
9.		
10.		
11.		
12.		
13.		
14.		
15.		
16.		
17.		
18.		
19.		
20.		
Totals		

1
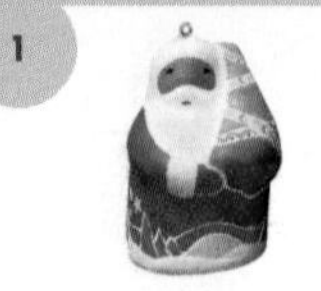
Jolly Santa
Symbols Of Christmas
Handcrafted • ANDR
1595QK1087 • **Value $27**

2

Sweet Song
Symbols Of Christmas
Handcrafted • ANDR
1595QK1089 • **Value $27**

3

Baby's First Christmas
Handcrafted • SEAL
475QXM4027 • **Value $14**

4

Calamity Coyote
Handcrafted • RGRS
675QXM4467 • **Value $16**

5

Christmas Wishes
Handcrafted • SEAL
375QXM4087 • **Value $16**

6

Cloisonné Partridge
Cloisonné • VOTR
975QXM4017 • **Value $19**

7

Downhill Double
Handcrafted • PALM
475QXM4837 • **Value $12**

8

Friendship Duet
Handcrafted • UNRU
475QXM4019 • **Value $13**

9

Furrball
Handcrafted • RGRS
575QXM4459 • **Value $16**

10

Grandpa's Gift
Handcrafted • RGRS
575QXM4829 • **Value $14**

11

Heavenly Praises
Handcrafted • ANDR
575QXM4037 • **Value $14**

12

Joyful Santa
Handcrafted • UNRU
475QXM4089 • **Value $13**

13

Little Beeper
Handcrafted • RGRS
575QXM4469 • **Value $16**

14

Merry Walruses
Handcrafted • SICK
575QXM4057 • **Value $22**

15
A Moustershire Christmas (set/4)
Handcrafted • RHOD
2450QXM4839 • **Value $43**

16

Pebbles and Bamm-Bamm
Handcrafted • RHOD
975QXM4757 • **Value $18**

17

Playful Penguins
Handcrafted • SICK
575QXM4059 • **Value $24**

18

Precious Creations
Handcrafted • SICK
975QXM4077 • **Value $19**

19

Santa's Visit
Handcrafted • CROW
775QXM4047 • **Value $18**

20
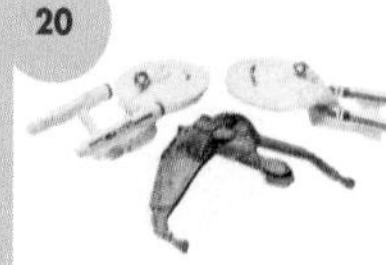
The Ships of STAR TREK® (set/3)
Handcrafted • N/A
1995QXI4109 • **Value $29**

	Price Paid	Value
General Showcase		
1.		
2.		
General Miniature		
3.		
4.		
5.		
6.		
7.		
8.		
9.		
10.		
11.		
12.		
13.		
14.		
15.		
16.		
17.		
18.		
19.		
20.		
Totals		

1

Starlit Nativity
Handcrafted • UNRU
775QXM4039 • **Value $19**

2

Sugarplum Dreams
Handcrafted • CROW
475QXM4099 • **Value $13**

3

Tiny Treasures (set/6)
Handcrafted • SEAL
2900QXM4009 • **Value $47**

4

Tunnel of Love
Handcrafted • CROW
475QXM4029 • **Value $13**

5

Cinderella's Stepsisters (gift membership bonus, Merry Miniature)
Handcrafted • PIKE
375QXC4159 • **Value $60**

6

Collecting Memories (keepsake of membership)
Handcrafted • SIED
QXC4117 • **Value $22**

7

Cool Santa (keepsake of membership, miniature)
Handcrafted • FRAN
QXC4457 • **Value $16**

8

Cozy Christmas (early renewal gift, miniature)
Handcrafted • FRAN
QXC4119 • **Value $19**

9

Fishing For Fun (keepsake of membership)
Handcrafted • SEAL
QXC5207 • **Value $22**

10

A Gift From Rodney (keepsake of membership, miniature)
Handcrafted • SICK
QXC4129 • **Value $16**

11

Home From The Woods (club edition)
Handcrafted • SICK
1595QXC1059 • **Value $55**

12

May Flower (club edition, Easter sidekick)
Handcrafted • SIED
495QXC8246 • **Value $48**

13

Happy Holidays
Handcrafted • VOTR
295QX6307 • **Value $14**

14

Hooked On Collecting – 1995 – Ornament Premiere
Handcrafted • PALM
(N/C) No stock # • **Value $10**

15
Wish List
Handcrafted • SEAL
1500QX5859 • **Value $24**

16

Charlie Brown
A Charlie Brown Christmas
Handcrafted • SIED
395QRP4207 • **Value $25**

17
Linus
A Charlie Brown Christmas
Handcrafted • RGRS
395QRP4217 • **Value $20**

18
Lucy
A Charlie Brown Christmas
Handcrafted • SIED
395QRP4209 • **Value $20**

19
SNOOPY
A Charlie Brown Christmas
Handcrafted • RGRS
395QRP4219 • **Value $27**

20

WOODSTOCK w/tree and snowbase
A Charlie Brown Christmas
Handcrafted • RGRS
395QRP4227 • **Value $18**

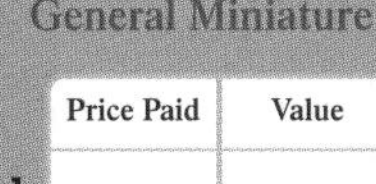

	Price Paid	Value
General Miniature		
1.		
2.		
3.		
4.		
Collector's Club		
5.		
6.		
7.		
8.		
9.		
10.		
11.		
12.		
Premiere Ornaments		
13.		
14.		
15.		
Reach Ornaments		
16.		
17.		
18.		
19.		
20.		
Totals		

1

Happy Holidays® BARBIE™ Stocking Hanger
Handcrafted • N/A
1995XSH3119 • **Value $16**

2

Holiday BARBIE™ Lapel Pin
Handcrafted • N/A
495XLP3547 • **Value N/E**

3

Holiday Memories™ BARBIE® Doll (2nd in series)
Vinyl • N/A
4500XPF3407 • **Value $115**

4

1956 Ford Truck (black)
Handcrafted • PALM
(N/C) No stock # • **Value N/E**

5

Artists' Caricature Ball Ornament
Glass • N/A
($7.95) No stock # • **Value $25**

6

Christmas Eve Bake-Off
Handcrafted • VARI
6000QXC4049 • **Value $115**

7

Cookie Time
Handcrafted • VOTR
($12.95) No stock # • **Value $24**

8

Murray® Champion (red)
Die-Cast Metal • PALM
(N/C) No stock # • **Value N/E**

9

Murray® Fire Truck (white)
Die-Cast Metal • PALM
(N/C) No stock # • **Value N/E**

10

Pewter Rocking Horse (miniature)
Pewter • N/A
($7.95) No stock # • **Value $55**

11

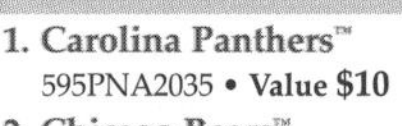

NFL COLLECTION (10 assorted, re-issued in 1996)
Glass • N/A

1. **Carolina Panthers™** 595PNA2035 • **Value $10**
2. **Chicago Bears™** 595BRS2035 • **Value $10**
3. **Dallas Cowboys™** 595COW2035 • **Value $10**
4. **Kansas City Chiefs™** 595CHF2035 • **Value $10**
5. **Los Angeles Raiders™** 595RDR2035 • **Value $10**
6. **Minnesota Vikings™** 595VIK2035 • **Value $10**
7. **New England Patriots™** 595NEP2035 • **Value $10**
8. **Philadelphia Eagles™** 595EAG2035 • **Value $10**
9. **San Francisco 49ers™** 595FOR2035 • **Value $10**
10. **Washington Redskins™** 595RSK2035 • **Value $10**

12

NFL COLLECTION (10 assorted)
Handcrafted • SIED

1. **Carolina Panthers™** 995QSR6227 • **Value $30**
2. **Chicago Bears™** 995QSR6237 • **Value $30**
3. **Dallas Cowboys™** 995QSR6217 • **Value $30**
4. **Kansas City Chiefs™** 995QSR6257 • **Value $30**
5. **Los Angeles Raiders™** 995QSR6249 • **Value $30**
6. **Minnesota Vikings™** 995QSR6267 • **Value $30**
7. **New England Patriots™** 995QSR6228 • **Value $30**
8. **Philadelphia Eagles™** 995QSR6259 • **Value $30**
9. **San Francisco 49ers™** 995QSR6239 • **Value $30**
10. **Washington Redskins™** 995QSR6247 • **Value $30**

13

Baby Bear
Handcrafted • ANDR
1295QP6157 • **Value N/E**

14

The Champ
Handcrafted • VOTR
1295QP6127 • **Value N/E**

15

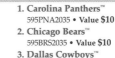

Computer Cat 'n' Mouse (re-issued from 1994)
Handcrafted • SEAL
1295QP6046 • **Value N/E**

	Price Paid	Value
BARBIE™ Collectibles		
1.		
2.		
3.		
Expo Ornaments		
4.		
5.		
6.		
7.		
8.		
9.		
10.		
NFL Collection		
11.		
12.		
Personalized Ornaments		
13.		
14.		
15.		
Totals		

1

Cookie Time
(re-issued from 1994)
Handcrafted • VOTR
1295QP6073 • **Value N/E**

2

Etch-A-Sketch®
(re-issued from 1994)
Handcrafted • CROW
1295QP6015 • **Value N/E**

3

From The Heart
(re-issued from 1994)
Handcrafted • RHOD
1495QP6036 • **Value N/E**

4

Key Note
Handcrafted • SEAL
1295QP6149 • **Value N/E**

5

Mailbox Delivery
(re-issued from 1993)
Handcrafted • CROW
1495QP6015 • **Value N/E**

6

Novel Idea
(re-issued from 1994)
Handcrafted • VOTR
1295QP6066 • **Value N/E**

7

On the Billboard
(re-issued from 1993)
Handcrafted • CROW
1295QP6022 • **Value N/E**

8

Playing Ball
(re-issued from 1993)
Handcrafted • FRAN
1295QP6032 • **Value N/E**

9

Reindeer Rooters
(re-issued from 1994)
Handcrafted • CROW
1295QP6056 • **Value N/E**

1994

Hallmark created a sensation in 1994 with the release of "The Beatles Gift Set," as well as several new ornaments featuring LOONEY TUNES™ and Wizard of OZ™ characters. The 1994 collection featured 149 Keepsake, 24 Magic, 18 Showcase and 38 Miniature ornaments. See the collectible series section for more 1994 ornaments.

10

Across the Miles
Handcrafted • ANDR
895QX5656 • **Value $20**

11

All Pumped Up
Handcrafted • RHOD
895QX5923 • **Value $20**

12

Angel Hare
Handcrafted/Brass • SICK
895QX5896 • **Value $22**

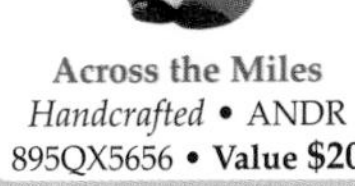

13

Anniversary Year
Brass/Chrome • BISH
1095QX5683 • **Value $23**

14

Baby's First Christmas
Handcrafted • VOTR
795QX5636 • **Value $25**

15

Baby's First Christmas
Handcrafted • N/A
795QX5713 • **Value $31**

Personalized Ornaments

	Price Paid	Value
1.		
2.		
3.		
4.		
5.		
6.		
7.		
8.		
9.		

General Keepsake

	Price Paid	Value
10.		
11.		
12.		
13.		
14.		
15.		
Totals		

1

Baby's First Christmas
Handcrafted • SEAL
1295QX5743 • **Value $28**

2

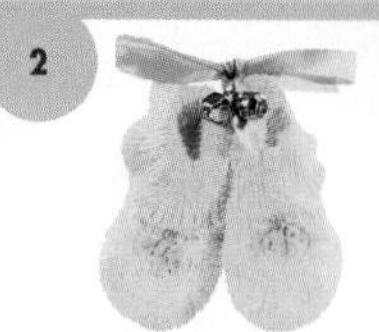

Baby's First Christmas
Porcelain/Brass • UNRU
1895QX5633 • **Value $30**

3

Baby's First Christmas – Baby Boy
Glass • N/A
500QX2436 • **Value $18**

4

Baby's First Christmas – Baby Girl
Glass • N/A
500QX2433 • **Value $18**

5

Baby's Second Christmas
Handcrafted • CROW
795QX5716 • **Value $23**

6

Barney™
Handcrafted • RHOD
995QX5966 • **Value $25**

7

Batman
Handcrafted • CHAD
1295QX5853 • **Value $28**

8

The Beatles Gift Set
Handcrafted • RGRS
4800QX5373 • **Value $102**

9

Big Shot
Handcrafted • SIED
795QX5873 • **Value $19**

10

Brother
Handcrafted • PIKE
695QX5516 • **Value $17**

11

Busy Batter
Handcrafted • SIED
795QX5876 • **Value $20**

12

Candy Caper
Handcrafted • ANDR
895QX5776 • **Value $22**

13

Caring Doctor
Handcrafted • RGRS
895QX5823 • **Value $18**

14

Champion Teacher
Handcrafted • SIED
695QX5836 • **Value $17**

15

Cheers To You!
Handcrafted/Brass • CROW
1095QX5796 • **Value $27**

16

Cheery Cyclists
Handcrafted • CROW
1295QX5786 • **Value $27**

17

Child Care Giver
Handcrafted • VOTR
795QX5906 • **Value $16**

18

Child's Fifth Christmas
Handcrafted • RHOD
695QX5733 • **Value $19**

19

Child's Fourth Christmas
Handcrafted • FRAN
695QX5726 • **Value $20**

20

Child's Third Christmas
Handcrafted • FRAN
695QX5723 • **Value $21**

General Keepsake

	Price Paid	Value
1.		
2.		
3.		
4.		
5.		
6.		
7.		
8.		
9.		
10.		
11.		
12.		
13.		
14.		
15.		
16.		
17.		
18.		
19.		
20.		
Totals		

1

Coach
Handcrafted • UNRU
795QX5933 • **Value $18**

2

Cock-a-Doodle Christmas
Handcrafted • VOTR
895QX5396 • **Value $27**

3

Colors of Joy
Handcrafted • SEAL
795QX5893 • **Value $20**

4

The Cowardly Lion
Handcrafted • ANDR
995QX5446 • **Value $47**

5

Dad
Handcrafted • RGRS
795QX5463 • **Value $17**

6

Dad-to-Be
Handcrafted • PIKE
795QX5473 • **Value $18**

7

Daffy Duck
Handcrafted • PALM
895QX5415 • **Value $23**

8

Daisy Days
Handcrafted • CHAD
995QX5986 • **Value $21**

9

Daughter
Handcrafted • ANDR
695QX5623 • **Value $19**

10

Dear Santa Mouse (set/2)
Handcrafted • CROW
1495QX5806 • **Value $30**

11

Dorothy and Toto
Handcrafted • LYLE
1095QX5433 • **Value $83**

12

Extra-Special Delivery
Handcrafted • CROW
795QX5833 • **Value $19**

13

Feelin' Groovy
Handcrafted • N/A
795QX5953 • **Value $25**

14

A Feline of Christmas
Handcrafted • ANDR
895QX5816 • **Value $30**

15
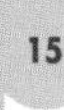

Feliz Navidad
Handcrafted • RGRS
895QX5793 • **Value $24**

16

Follow the Sun
Handcrafted • CROW
895QX5846 • **Value $19**

17

For My Grandma
Handcrafted • DLEE
695QX5613 • **Value $17**

18

Fred and Barney
Handcrafted • RHOD
1495QX5003 • **Value $33**

19

Friendly Push
Handcrafted • SIED
895QX5686 • **Value $20**

20

Friendship Sundae
Handcrafted • SICK
1095QX4766 • **Value $26**

General Keepsake

	Price Paid	Value
1.		
2.		
3.		
4.		
5.		
6.		
7.		
8.		
9.		
10.		
11.		
12.		
13.		
14.		
15.		
16.		
17.		
18.		
19.		
20.		
Totals		

1

GARFIELD
Handcrafted • N/A
1295QX5753 • **Value $31**

2

Gentle Nurse
Handcrafted • LYLE
695QX5973 • **Value $21**

3

Godchild
Handcrafted • RGRS
895QX4453 • **Value $25**

4

Godparent
Glass • N/A
500QX2423 • **Value $21**

5

Grandchild's First Christmas
Handcrafted • UNRU
795QX5676 • **Value $19**

6

Granddaughter
Handcrafted • PIKE
695QX5523 • **Value $17**

7

Grandmother
Handcrafted • ANDR
795QX5673 • **Value $18**

8

Grandpa
Handcrafted • UNRU
795QX5616 • **Value $20**

9

Grandparents
Glass • N/A
500QX2426 • **Value $17**

10

Grandson
Handcrafted • PIKE
695QX5526 • **Value $18**

11

Happy Birthday, Jesus
Handcrafted • LYLE
1295QX5423 • **Value $30**

12

Harvest Joy
Handcrafted • CHAD
995QX5993 • **Value $19**

13
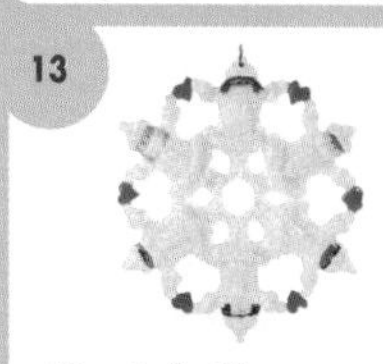
Hearts in Harmony
Porcelain • ANDR
1095QX4406 • **Value $25**

14

Helpful Shepherd
Handcrafted • CHAD
895QX5536 • **Value $21**

15

Holiday Patrol
Handcrafted • RHOD
895QX5826 • **Value $18**

16

Ice Show
Handcrafted • ANDR
795QX5946 • **Value $19**

17

In the Pink
Handcrafted • ANDR
995QX5763 • **Value $23**

18

It's a Strike
Handcrafted • SIED
895QX5856 • **Value $21**

19

Jingle Bell Band
Handcrafted • CROW
1095QX5783 • **Value $30**

20

Joyous Song
Handcrafted • ANDR
895QX4473 • **Value $19**

General Keepsake

	Price Paid	Value
1.		
2.		
3.		
4.		
5.		
6.		
7.		
8.		
9.		
10.		
11.		
12.		
13.		
14.		
15.		
16.		
17.		
18.		
19.		
20.		
Totals		

1

Jump-along Jackalope
Handcrafted • FRAN
895QX5756 • **Value $18**

2

Keep on Mowin'
Handcrafted • SIED
895QX5413 • **Value $17**

3

Kickin' Roo
Handcrafted • SIED
795QX5916 • **Value $18**

4

Kitty's Catamaran
Handcrafted • SEAL
1095QX5416 • **Value $24**

5

Kringle's Kayak
Handcrafted • SEAL
795QX5886 • **Value $22**

6

Lou Rankin Seal
Handcrafted • BISH
995QX5456 • **Value $22**

7

Lucinda and Teddy
Handcrafted/Fabric • UNRU
2175QX4813 • **Value $42**

8

Magic Carpet Ride
Handcrafted • SEAL
795QX5883 • **Value $24**

9

Making It Bright
Handcrafted • RHOD
895QX5403 • **Value $20**

10

Mary Engelbreit
Glass • N/A
500QX2416 • **Value $20**

11

Merry Fishmas
Handcrafted • PALM
895QX5913 • **Value $22**

12

Mistletoe Surprise (set/2)
Handcrafted • SEAL
1295QX5996 • **Value $32**

13

Mom
Handcrafted • RGRS
795QX5466 • **Value $18**

14

Mom and Dad
Handcrafted • SIED
995QX5666 • **Value $24**

15

Mom-to-Be
Handcrafted • PIKE
795QX5506 • **Value $18**

16
Mufasa and Simba
Handcrafted • CROW
1495QX5406 • **Value $30**

17

Nephew
Handcrafted • FRAN
795QX5546 • **Value $17**

18

New Home
Handcrafted • ANDR
895QX5663 • **Value $22**

19
Niece
Handcrafted • FRAN
795QX5543 • **Value $17**

20

Norman Rockwell Art
Glass • LYLE
500QX2413 • **Value $17**

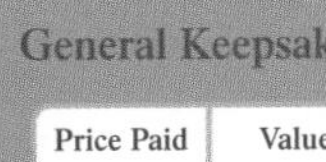

General Keepsake

	Price Paid	Value
1.		
2.		
3.		
4.		
5.		
6.		
7.		
8.		
9.		
10.		
11.		
12.		
13.		
14.		
15.		
16.		
17.		
18.		
19.		
20.		
Totals		

1

Open-and-Shut Holiday
Handcrafted • SIED
995QX5696 • **Value $23**

2

Our Christmas Together
Handcrafted • RGRS
995QX4816 • **Value $22**

3

Our Family
Handcrafted • ANDR
795QX5576 • **Value $19**

4

Our First Christmas Together
Acrylic • VOTR
695QX3186 • **Value $17**

5

Our First Christmas Together
Brass/Fabric • ANDR
1895QX5706 • **Value $33**

6

Our First Christmas Together
Handcrafted • PALM
895QX5653 • **Value $23**

7

Our First Christmas Together
Handcrafted • BISH
995QX5643 • **Value $24**

8

Out of This World Teacher
Handcrafted • UNRU
795QX5766 • **Value $20**

9

Practice Makes Perfect
Handcrafted • PALM
895QX5863 • **Value $19**

10

Red Hot Holiday
Handcrafted • RGRS
795QX5843 • **Value $17**

11

Reindeer Pro
Handcrafted • RHOD
795QX5926 • **Value $20**

12

Relaxing Moment
Handcrafted • FRAN
1495QX5356 • **Value $32**

13

Road Runner and Wile E. Coyote
Handcrafted • CHAD
1295QX5602 • **Value $30**

14

Santa's LEGO® Sleigh
Handcrafted • CROW
1095QX5453 • **Value $32**

15

The Scarecrow
Handcrafted • UNRU
995QX5436 • **Value $52**

16

Secret Santa
Handcrafted • UNRU
795QX5736 • **Value $19**

17

A Sharp Flat
Handcrafted • CROW
1095QX5773 • **Value $24**

18

Simba and Nala (set/2)
Handcrafted • CROW
1295QX5303 • **Value $33**

19

Sister
Handcrafted • PIKE
695QX5513 • **Value $19**

20

Sister to Sister
Handcrafted • RHOD
995QX5533 • **Value $26**

General Keepsake

	Price Paid	Value
1.		
2.		
3.		
4.		
5.		
6.		
7.		
8.		
9.		
10.		
11.		
12.		
13.		
14.		
15.		
16.		
17.		
18.		
19.		
20.		
Totals		

1

Son
Handcrafted • ANDR
695QX5626 • **Value $17**

2

Special Cat
Acrylic • RHOD
795QX5606 • **Value $17**

3

Special Dog
Handcrafted • RHOD
795QX5603 • **Value $17**

4

Speedy Gonzales
Handcrafted • PALM
895QX5343 • **Value $21**

5

Stamp of Approval
Handcrafted • SICK
795QX5703 • **Value $18**

6

Sweet Greeting (set/2)
Handcrafted • PALM
1095QX5803 • **Value $25**

7

The Tale of Peter Rabbit
BEATRIX POTTER
Glass • N/A
500QX2443 • **Value $22**

8

Tasmanian Devil
Handcrafted • PALM
895QX5605 • **Value $57**

9

Thick 'n' Thin
Handcrafted • RGRS
1095QX5693 • **Value $22**

10

Thrill a Minute
Handcrafted • SIED
895QX5866 • **Value $21**

11

Time of Peace
Handcrafted • ANDR
795QX5813 • **Value $18**

12

Timon and Pumbaa
Handcrafted • CROW
895QX5366 • **Value $24**

13

The Tin Man
Handcrafted • UNRU
995QX5443 • **Value $55**

14

Tou Can Love
Handcrafted • RGRS
895QX5646 • **Value $21**

15

Tulip Time
Handcrafted • CHAD
995QX5983 • **Value $20**

16

Winnie the Pooh and Tigger
Handcrafted • SIED
1295QX5746 • **Value $37**

17

Yosemite Sam
Handcrafted • PALM
895QX5346 • **Value $20**

18

Yuletide Cheer
Handcrafted • CHAD
995QX5976 • **Value $20**

19

Away in a Manger
Handcrafted • LYLE
1600QLX7383 • **Value $38**

20
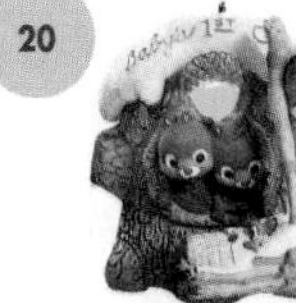

Baby's First Christmas
Handcrafted • FRAN
2000QLX7466 • **Value $44**

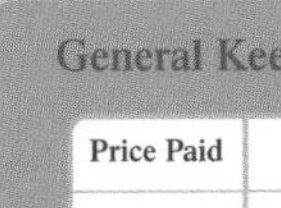
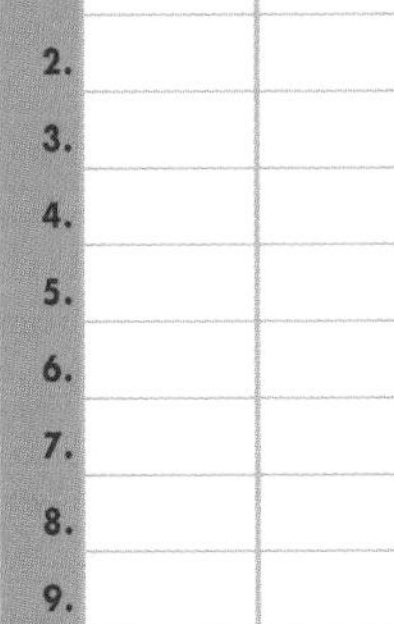

General Keepsake	Price Paid	Value
1.		
2.		
3.		
4.		
5.		
6.		
7.		
8.		
9.		
10.		
11.		
12.		
13.		
14.		
15.		
16.		
17.		
18.		
General Magic		
19.		
20.		
Totals		

1

Barney™
Handcrafted • N/A
2400QLX7506 • **Value $48**

2

Candy Cane Lookout
Handcrafted • FRAN
1800QLX7376 • **Value $77**

3

Conversations With Santa
Handcrafted • SEAL
2800QLX7426 • **Value $60**

4

Country Showtime
Handcrafted • SICK
2200QLX7416 • **Value $49**

5

The Eagle Has Landed
Handcrafted • SEAL
2400QLX7486 • **Value $53**

6

Feliz Navidad
Handcrafted • CROW
2800QLX7433 • **Value $62**

7

Gingerbread Fantasy
Handcrafted • PALM
4400QLX7382 • **Value $95**

8

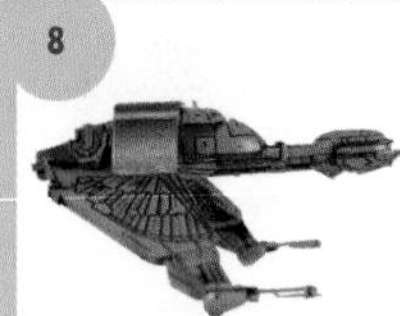

Klingon Bird of Prey™
Handcrafted • NORT
2400QLX7386 • **Value $50**

9

Kringle Trolley
Handcrafted • CROW
2000QLX7413 • **Value $46**

10

Maxine
Handcrafted • SICK
2000QLX7503 • **Value $51**

11

Peekaboo Pup
Handcrafted • RGRS
2000QLX7423 • **Value $45**

12

Rock Candy Miner
Handcrafted • SIED
2000QLX7403 • **Value $38**

13

Santa's Sing-Along
Handcrafted • CROW
2400QLX7473 • **Value $56**

14

Simba, Sarabi and Mufasa
Handcrafted • CROW
2000QLX7516 • **Value $40**

15

Simba, Sarabi and Mufasa (recalled due to defective sound)
Handcrafted • CROW
3200QLX7513 • **Value $78**

16

Very Merry Minutes
Handcrafted • VOTR
2400QLX7443 • **Value $49**

17

White Christmas
Handcrafted • DLEE
2800QLX7463 • **Value $65**

18

Winnie the Pooh Parade
Handcrafted • CROW
3200QLX7493 • **Value $72**

19

Home for the Holidays
Christmas Lights
Porcelain • PALM
1575QK1123 • **Value $22**

20

Moonbeams
Christmas Lights
Porcelain • ANDR
1575QK1116 • **Value $20**

General Magic	Price Paid	Value
1.		
2.		
3.		
4.		
5.		
6.		
7.		
8.		
9.		
10.		
11.		
12.		
13.		
14.		
15.		
16.		
17.		
18.		
General Showcase		
19.		
20.		
Totals		

1

Mother and Child
Christmas Lights
Porcelain • RGRS
1575QK1126 • **Value $20**

2

Peaceful Village
Christmas Lights
Porcelain • CHAD
1575QK1106 • **Value $20**

3

Catching 40 Winks
Folk Art Americana
Handcrafted • SICK
1675QK1183 • **Value $36**

4

Going to Town
Folk Art Americana
Handcrafted • SICK
1575QK1166 • **Value $35**

5

Racing Through the Snow
Folk Art Americana
Handcrafted • SICK
1575QK1173 • **Value $48**

6

Rarin' to Go
Folk Art Americana
Handcrafted • SICK
1575QK1193 • **Value $38**

7

Roundup Time
Folk Art Americana
Handcrafted • SICK
1675QK1176 • **Value $35**

8

Dapper Snowman
Holiday Favorites
Porcelain • VOTR
1375QK1053 • **Value $20**

9

Graceful Fawn
Holiday Favorites
Porcelain • VOTR
1175QK1033 • **Value $20**

10

Jolly Santa
Holiday Favorites
Porcelain • VOTR
1375QK1046 • **Value $26**

11

Joyful Lamb
Holiday Favorites
Porcelain • VOTR
1175QK1036 • **Value $20**

12

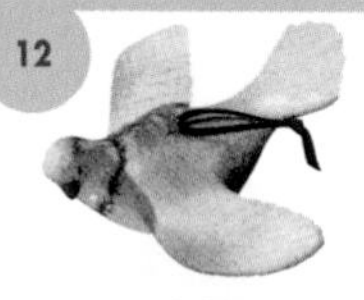

Peaceful Dove
Holiday Favorites
Porcelain • VOTR
1175QK1043 • **Value $20**

13

Silver Bells
Old-World Silver
Silver-Plated • UNRU
2475QK1026 • **Value $32**

14

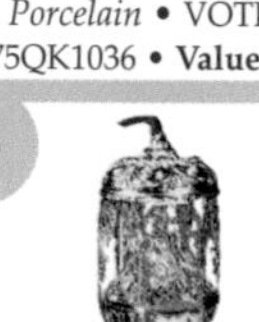

Silver Bows
Old-World Silver
Silver-Plated • PALM
2475QK1023 • **Value $32**

15

Silver Poinsettia
Old-World Silver
Silver-Plated • UNRU
2475QK1006 • **Value $33**

16

Silver Snowflakes
Old-World Silver
Silver-Plated • UNRU
2475QK1016 • **Value $32**

17

Babs Bunny
Handcrafted • PALM
575QXM4116 • **Value $16**

18

Baby's First Christmas
Handcrafted • LYLE
575QXM4003 • **Value $16**

19

Baking Tiny Treats (set/6)
Handcrafted • SEAL
2900QXM4033 • **Value $65**

20

Beary Perfect Tree
Handcrafted • BISH
475QXM4076 • **Value $14**

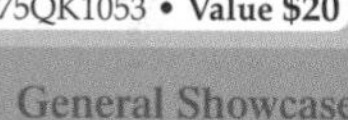

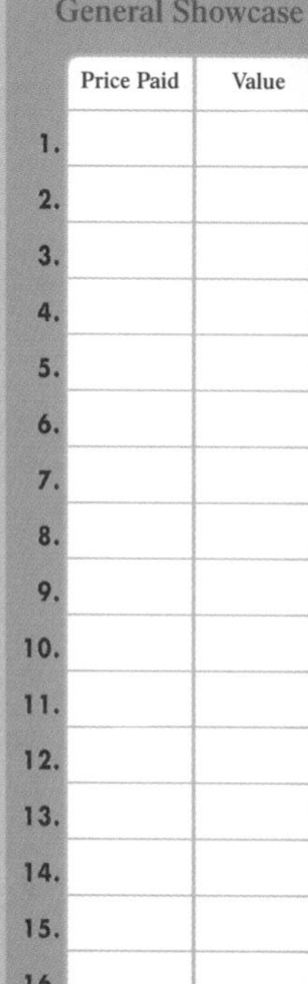

General Showcase	Price Paid	Value
1.		
2.		
3.		
4.		
5.		
6.		
7.		
8.		
9.		
10.		
11.		
12.		
13.		
14.		
15.		
16.		
General Miniature		
17.		
18.		
19.		
20.		
Totals		

1

Buster Bunny
Handcrafted • PALM
575QXM5163 • **Value $15**

2

Corny Elf
Handcrafted • RHOD
450QXM4063 • **Value $13**

3

Cute as a Button
Handcrafted • CROW
375QXM4103 • **Value $15**

4

Dazzling Reindeer
Handcrafted • VOTR
975QXM4026 • **Value $23**

5

Dizzy Devil
Handcrafted • PALM
575QXM4133 • **Value $16**

6

Friends Need Hugs
Handcrafted • LYLE
450QXM4016 • **Value $15**

7

Graceful Carousel Horse
Pewter • BISH
775QXM4056 • **Value $19**

8

Hamton
Handcrafted • PALM
575QXM4126 • **Value $15**

9

Have a Cookie
Handcrafted • DLEE
575QXM5166 • **Value $15**

10

Hearts A-Sail
Handcrafted • BISH
575QXM4006 • **Value $14**

11

Jolly Visitor
Handcrafted • SICK
575QXM4053 • **Value $16**

12

Jolly Wolly Snowman
Handcrafted • VOTR
375QXM4093 • **Value $14**

13

Journey to Bethlehem
Handcrafted • LYLE
575QXM4036 • **Value $19**

14

Just My Size
Handcrafted • BISH
375QXM4086 • **Value $13**

15

Love Was Born
Handcrafted • SICK
450QXM4043 • **Value $15**

16

Melodic Cherub
Handcrafted • RGRS
375QXM4066 • **Value $12**

17

A Merry Flight
Handcrafted • CROW
575QXM4073 • **Value $14**

18

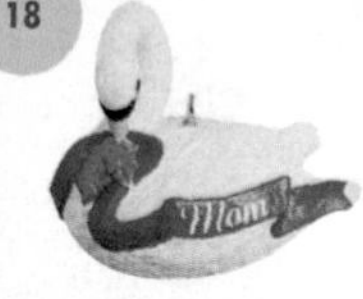

Mom
Handcrafted • RGRS
450QXM4013 • **Value $14**

19

Noah's Ark (set/3)
Handcrafted • SICK
2450QXM4106 • **Value $63**

20

Plucky Duck
Handcrafted • PALM
575QXM4123 • **Value $15**

General Miniature

	Price Paid	Value
1.		
2.		
3.		
4.		
5.		
6.		
7.		
8.		
9.		
10.		
11.		
12.		
13.		
14.		
15.		
16.		
17.		
18.		
19.		
20.		
Totals		

1
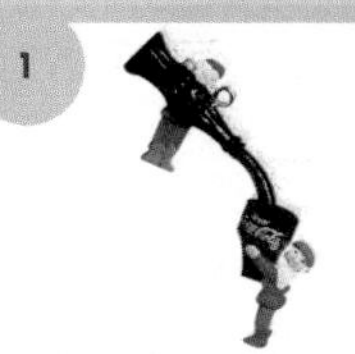
Pour Some More
Handcrafted • CHAD
575QXM5156 • **Value $14**

2

Scooting Along
Handcrafted • FRAN
675QXM5173 • **Value $17**

3

Sweet Dreams
Handcrafted • CROW
300QXM4096 • **Value $13**

4

Tea With Teddy
Handcrafted • RGRS
725QXM4046 • **Value $18**

5

First Hello
(gift membership bonus)
Handcrafted • RGRS
QXC4846 • **Value $34**

6

Happy Collecting
(early renewal piece,
Merry Miniature)
Handcrafted • N/A
QXC4803 • **Value $36**

7

Holiday Pursuit
(keepsake of membership)
Handcrafted • FRAN
QXC4823 • **Value $30**

8

Jolly Holly Santa
(club edition)
Handcrafted • LYLE
2200QXC4833 • **Value $52**

9

Majestic Deer
(club edition)
Porcelain/Pewter • UNRU
2500QXC4836 • **Value $55**

10

On Cloud Nine
(club edition)
Handcrafted • DLEE
1200QXC4853 • **Value $38**

11

Sweet Bouquet
(keepsake of
membership, miniature)
Handcrafted • N/A
QXC4806 • **Value $33**

12

Tilling Time
(Easter sidekick gift)
Handcrafted • SEAL
QXC8256 • **Value $58**

13

Collector's Survival Kit
Premiere '94
Handcrafted • RGRS
(N/C) No stock # • **Value $24**

14

Eager for Christmas
Handcrafted • SEAL
1500QX5336 • **Value $30**

15
The Country Church
Sarah, Plain and Tall
Handcrafted • BAUR
795XPR9450 • **Value $22**

16

The Hays Train Station
Sarah, Plain and Tall
Handcrafted • BAUR
795XPR9452 • **Value $22**

17

Mrs. Parkley's
General Store
Sarah, Plain and Tall
Handcrafted • BAUR
795XPR9451 • **Value $22**

18
Sarah's Maine Home
Sarah, Plain and Tall
Handcrafted • BAUR
795XPR9454 • **Value $24**

19

Sarah's Prairie Home
Sarah, Plain and Tall
Handcrafted • BAUR
795XPR9453 • **Value $24**

20

Victorian Elegance™
BARBIE® Doll
(1st in series)
Vinyl • N/A
4000XPF3546 • **Value $95**

	Price Paid	Value
General Miniature		
1.		
2.		
3.		
4.		
Collector's Club		
5.		
6.		
7.		
8.		
9.		
10.		
11.		
12.		
Premiere Ornaments		
13.		
14.		
Reach Figurines		
15.		
16.		
17.		
18.		
19.		
BARBIE™ Collectibles		
20.		
Totals		

Value Guide — Hallmark Keepsake Ornaments

1

Golden Bows
Gold-Plated • PALM
($10.00) No stock # • **Value $20**

2

Golden Dove of Peace
Gold-Plated • PALM
($10.00) No stock # • **Value $20**

3

Golden Poinsettia
Gold-Plated • UNRU
($10.00) No stock # • **Value $20**

4

Golden Santa
Gold-Plated • UNRU
($10.00) No stock # • **Value $20**

5

Golden Sleigh
Gold-Plated • PALM
($10.00) No stock # • **Value $20**

6

Golden Stars and Holly
Gold-Plated • PALM
($10.00) No stock # • **Value $20**

7

Mrs. Claus' Cupboard
(w/ miniature ornaments)
Handcrafted • N/A
5500QXC4843 • **Value N/E**

8

Baby Block Photoholder
(re-issued from 1993)
Handcrafted • FRAN
1495QP6035 • **Value N/E**

9

Computer Cat 'n' Mouse
(re-issued in 1995)
Handcrafted • SEAL
1295QP6046 • **Value N/E**

10

Cookie Time
(re-issued in 1995)
Handcrafted • VOTR
1295QP6073 • **Value N/E**

11

Etch-A-Sketch®
(re-issued in 1995)
Handcrafted • CROW
1295QP6006 • **Value N/E**

12

Festive Album Photoholder
(re-issued from 1993)
Handcrafted • VOTR
1295QP6025 • **Value N/E**

13

From The Heart
(re-issued in 1995)
Handcrafted • RHOD
1495QP6036 • **Value N/E**

14

Goin' Fishin'
Handcrafted • PALM
1495QP6023 • **Value N/E**

15

Going Golfin'
(re-issued from 1993)
Handcrafted • PALM
1295QP6012 • **Value N/E**

16

Holiday Hello
Handcrafted • SIED
2495QXR6116 • **Value $42**

17

Mailbox Delivery
(re-issued from 1993)
Handcrafted • CROW
1495QP6015 • **Value N/E**

18

Novel Idea
(re-issued in 1995)
Handcrafted • VOTR
1295QP6066 • **Value N/E**

19

On the Billboard
(re-issued from 1993)
Handcrafted • CROW
1295QP6022 • **Value N/E**

20

Playing Ball
(re-issued from 1993)
Handcrafted • FRAN
1295QP6032 • **Value N/E**

Expo Ornaments

	Price Paid	Value
1.		
2.		
3.		
4.		
5.		
6.		
7.		

Personalized Ornaments

	Price Paid	Value
8.		
9.		
10.		
11.		
12.		
13.		
14.		
15.		
16.		
17.		
18.		
19.		
20.		
Totals		

1

Reindeer Rooters
(re-issued in 1995)
Handcrafted • CROW
1295QP6056 • **Value N/E**

2

Santa Says
(re-issued from 1993)
Handcrafted • SEAL
1495QP6005 • **Value N/E**

1993

The 20th anniversary of Keepsake Ornaments was celebrated in 1993 with four special ornaments, including "Glowing Pewter Wreath" and pieces to complement three popular collectible series. Overall, there were 141 Keepsake, 21 Magic, 19 Showcase and 36 Miniature ornaments. See the collectible series section for more 1993 ornaments.

3

Across the Miles
Handcrafted • FRAN
875QX5912 • **Value $21**

4

Anniversary Year Photoholder
Brass/Chrome • LYLE
975QX5972 • **Value $21**

5

Apple for Teacher
Handcrafted • SEAL
775QX5902 • **Value $16**

6

Baby's First Christmas
Handcrafted • CROW
775QX5525 • **Value $32**

7

Baby's First Christmas
Handcrafted • ANDR
1075QX5515 • **Value $23**

8

Baby's First Christmas
Silver-Plated • PALM
1875QX5512 • **Value $42**

9

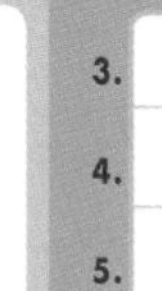
Baby's First Christmas – Baby Boy
Glass • VOTR
475QX2105 • **Value $17**

10
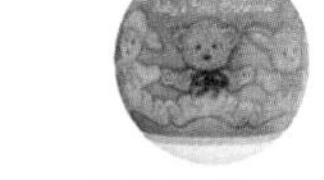
Baby's First Christmas – Baby Girl
Glass • VOTR
475QX2092 • **Value $17**

11

Baby's First Christmas Photoholder
Handcrafted/Lace • RGRS
775QX5522 • **Value $24**

12
Baby's Second Christmas
Handcrafted • FRAN
675QX5992 • **Value $26**

13

Beary Gifted
Handcrafted • CROW
775QX5762 • **Value $19**

14

Big on Gardening
Handcrafted • VOTR
975QX5842 • **Value $17**

15

Big Roller
Handcrafted • SIED
875QX5352 • **Value $19**

Personalized Ornaments

	Price Paid	Value
1.		
2.		

General Keepsake

	Price Paid	Value
3.		
4.		
5.		
6.		
7.		
8.		
9.		
10.		
11.		
12.		
13.		
14.		
15.		
Totals		

1

Bird-Watcher
Handcrafted • JLEE
975QX5252 • **Value $17**

2
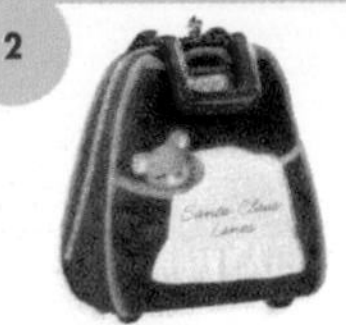
Bowling for ZZZs
Handcrafted • FRAN
775QX5565 • **Value $15**

3

Brother
Handcrafted • RGRS
675QX5542 • **Value $13**

4

Bugs Bunny
Handcrafted • SICK
875QX5412 • **Value $28**

5

Caring Nurse
Handcrafted • FRAN
675QX5785 • **Value $19**

6

A Child's Christmas
Handcrafted • FRAN
975QX5882 • **Value $23**

7

Child's Fifth Christmas
Handcrafted • RHOD
675QX5222 • **Value $16**

8

Child's Fourth Christmas
Handcrafted • FRAN
675QX5215 • **Value $17**

9

Child's Third Christmas
Handcrafted • FRAN
675QX5995 • **Value $18**

10

Christmas Break
Handcrafted • SEAL
775QX5825 • **Value $23**

11

Clever Cookie
Handcrafted/Tin • SICK
775QX5662 • **Value $26**

12

Coach
Handcrafted • PALM
675QX5935 • **Value $16**

13

Curly 'n' Kingly
Handcrafted/Brass • CROW
1075QX5285 • **Value $22**

14

Dad
Handcrafted • JLEE
775QX5855 • **Value $19**

15

Dad-to-Be
Handcrafted • JLEE
675QX5532 • **Value $15**

16

Daughter
Handcrafted • VOTR
675QX5872 • **Value $22**

17

Dickens Caroler Bell – Lady Daphne
Porcelain • CHAD
2175QX5505 • **Value $42**

18

Dunkin' Roo
Handcrafted • SIED
775QX5575 • **Value $17**

19
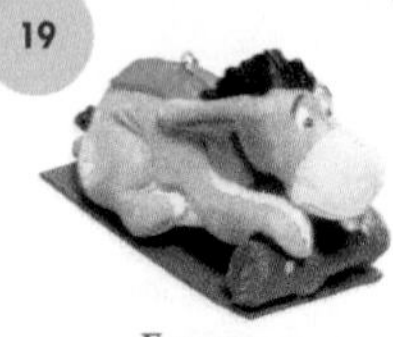
Eeyore
Handcrafted • SIED
975QX5712 • **Value $24**

20

Elmer Fudd
Handcrafted • LYLE
875QX5495 • **Value $20**

General Keepsake

	Price Paid	Value
1.		
2.		
3.		
4.		
5.		
6.		
7.		
8.		
9.		
10.		
11.		
12.		
13.		
14.		
15.		
16.		
17.		
18.		
19.		
20.		
Totals		

1

Faithful Fire Fighter
Handcrafted • VOTR
775QX5782 • **Value $18**

2

Feliz Navidad
Handcrafted/Brass • DLEE
875QX5365 • **Value $21**

3

Fills the Bill
Handcrafted • SIED
875QX5572 • **Value $19**

4

Glowing Pewter Wreath
Pewter • UNRU
1875QX5302 • **Value $38**

5

Godchild
Handcrafted • CHAD
875QX5875 • **Value $19**

6

Grandchild's First Christmas
Handcrafted • FRAN
675QX5552 • **Value $16**

7

Granddaughter
Handcrafted • CHAD
675QX5635 • **Value $16**

8
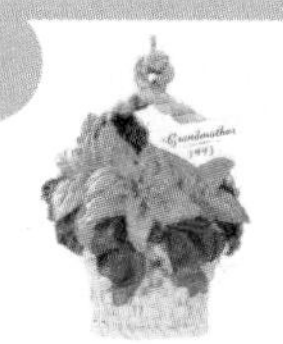
Grandmother
Handcrafted • ANDR
675QX5665 • **Value $15**

9

Grandparents
Glass • VOTR
475QX2085 • **Value $16**

10

Grandson
Handcrafted • CHAD
675QX5632 • **Value $16**

11

Great Connections (set/2)
Handcrafted • RGRS
1075QX5402 • **Value $27**

12

He Is Born
Handcrafted • LYLE
975QX5362 • **Value $40**

13

High Top-Purr
Handcrafted • SEAL
875QX5332 • **Value $27**

14

Home for Christmas
Handcrafted • SIED
775QX5562 • **Value $17**

15

Howling Good Time
Handcrafted • RGRS
975QX5255 • **Value $20**

16

Icicle Bicycle
Handcrafted • JLEE
975QX5835 • **Value $21**

17

Julianne and Teddy
Handcrafted • UNRU
2175QX5295 • **Value $46**

18

Kanga and Roo
Handcrafted • SIED
975QX5672 • **Value $22**

19

Little Drummer Boy
Handcrafted • PALM
875QX5372 • **Value $20**

20
Look for the Wonder
Handcrafted • DLEE
1275QX5685 • **Value $25**

General Keepsake

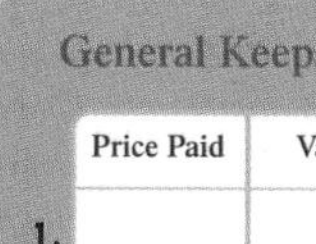

	Price Paid	Value
1.		
2.		
3.		
4.		
5.		
6.		
7.		
8.		
9.		
10.		
11.		
12.		
13.		
14.		
15.		
16.		
17.		
18.		
19.		
20.		
Totals		

1

Lou Rankin Polar Bear
Handcrafted • RHOD
975QX5745 • **Value $28**

2

Makin' Music
Handcrafted/Brass • SEAL
975QX5325 • **Value $19**

3

Making Waves
Handcrafted • PALM
975QX5775 • **Value $28**

4

Mary Engelbreit
Glass • N/A
500QX2075 • **Value $19**

5

Maxine
Handcrafted • SICK
875QX5385 • **Value $25**

6

Mom
Handcrafted • JLEE
775QX5852 • **Value $18**

7

Mom and Dad
Handcrafted • PALM
975QX5845 • **Value $19**

8

Mom-to-Be
Handcrafted • JLEE
675QX5535 • **Value $17**

9

Nephew
Handcrafted • RGRS
675QX5735 • **Value $13**

10

New Home
Enamel/Metal • PALM
775QX5905 • **Value $35**

11

Niece
Handcrafted • RGRS
675QX5732 • **Value $13**

12

On Her Toes
Handcrafted • ANDR
875QX5265 • **Value $22**

13

One-Elf Marching Band
Handcrafted/Brass • CHAD
1275QX5342 • **Value $28**

14

Our Christmas Together
Handcrafted • DLEE
1075QX5942 • **Value $24**

15

Our Family Photoholder
Handcrafted • UNRU
775QX5892 • **Value $19**

16
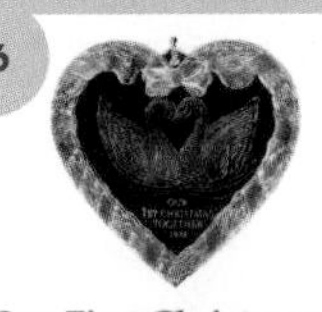
Our First Christmas Together
Acrylic • ANDR
675QX3015 • **Value $18**

17

Our First Christmas Together
Brass/Silver-Plated • RGRS
1875QX5955 • **Value $40**

18
Our First Christmas Together
Handcrafted • LYLE
975QX5642 • **Value $18**

19

Our First Christmas Together Photoholder
Handcrafted • UNRU
875QX5952 • **Value $19**

20

Owl
Handcrafted • SIED
975QX5695 • **Value $20**

General Keepsake

	Price Paid	Value
1.		
2.		
3.		
4.		
5.		
6.		
7.		
8.		
9.		
10.		
11.		
12.		
13.		
14.		
15.		
16.		
17.		
18.		
19.		
20.		
Totals		

1

PEANUTS®
Glass • N/A
500QX2072 • **Value $25**

2

Peek-a-Boo Tree
Handcrafted • CROW
1075QX5245 • **Value $25**

3
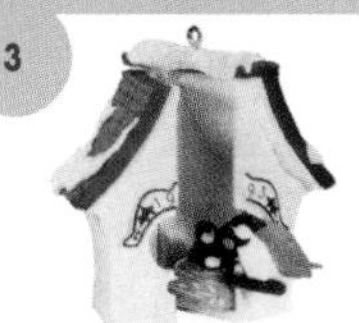

Peep Inside
Handcrafted • DLEE
1375QX5322 • **Value $27**

4

People Friendly
Handcrafted • SEAL
875QX5932 • **Value $19**

5
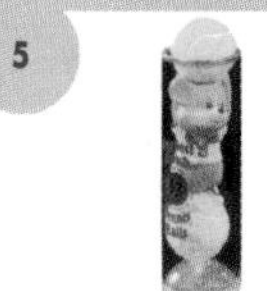

Perfect Match
Handcrafted • SIED
875QX5772 • **Value $19**

6

The Pink Panther
Handcrafted • PALM
1275QX5755 • **Value $24**

7

Playful Pals
Handcrafted • RGRS
1475QX5742 • **Value $30**

8

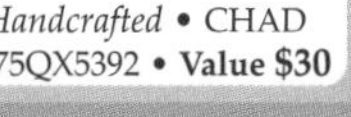

Popping Good Times (set/2)
Handcrafted • CHAD
1475QX5392 • **Value $30**

9

Porky Pig
Handcrafted • ANDR
875QX5652 • **Value $20**

10

Putt-Putt Penguin
Handcrafted • JLEE
975QX5795 • **Value $20**

11

Quick as a Fox
Handcrafted • CROW
875QX5792 • **Value $19**

12

Rabbit
Handcrafted • SIED
975QX5702 • **Value $22**

13

Ready for Fun
Handcrafted/Tin • LYLE
775QX5124 • **Value $18**

14
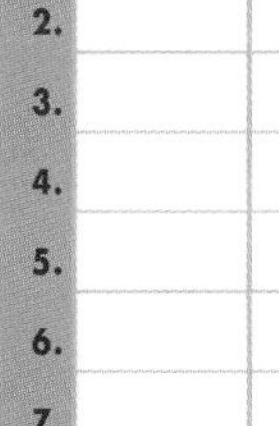

Room for One More
Handcrafted • CROW
875QX5382 • **Value $48**

15

Silvery Noel
Silver-Plated • LYLE
1275QX5305 • **Value $35**

16

Sister
Handcrafted • RGRS
675QX5545 • **Value $19**

17

Sister to Sister
Handcrafted • SEAL
975QX5885 • **Value $54**

18

Smile! It's Christmas Photoholder
Handcrafted • SEAL
975QX5335 • **Value $21**

19

Snow Bear Angel
Handcrafted • JLEE
775QX5355 • **Value $19**

20

Snowbird
Handcrafted • JLEE
775QX5765 • **Value $19**

General Keepsake

	Price Paid	Value
1.		
2.		
3.		
4.		
5.		
6.		
7.		
8.		
9.		
10.		
11.		
12.		
13.		
14.		
15.		
16.		
17.		
18.		
19.		
20.		
Totals		

1
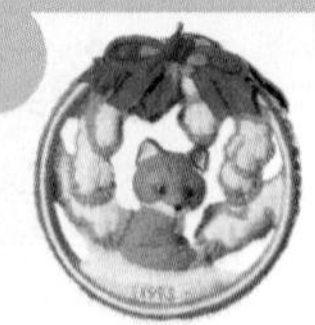
Snowy Hideaway
Handcrafted • FRAN
975QX5312 • **Value $22**

2

Son
Handcrafted • VOTR
675QX5865 • **Value $19**

3

Special Cat Photoholder
Handcrafted/Brass • VOTR
775QX5235 • **Value $14**

4

Special Dog Photoholder
Handcrafted/Brass • VOTR
775QX5962 • **Value $15**

5

Star of Wonder
Handcrafted • LYLE
675QX5982 • **Value $40**

6

Star Teacher Photoholder
Handcrafted • ANDR
575QX5645 • **Value $13**

7

Strange and Wonderful Love
Handcrafted • SICK
875QX5965 • **Value $18**

8

Superman™
Handcrafted • CHAD
1275QX5752 • **Value $48**

9

The Swat Team (set/2)
Handcrafted/Yarn • ANDR
1275QX5395 • **Value $31**

10

Sylvester and Tweety
Handcrafted • PALM
975QX5405 • **Value $34**

11

That's Entertainment
Handcrafted • SIED
875QX5345 • **Value $20**

12

Tigger and Piglet
Handcrafted • SIED
975QX5705 • **Value $47**

13

Tin Airplane
Pressed Tin • SICK
775QX5622 • **Value $28**

14

Tin Blimp
Pressed Tin • SICK
775QX5625 • **Value $18**

15

Tin Hot Air Balloon
Pressed Tin • SICK
775QX5615 • **Value $21**

16

To My Grandma Photoholder
Handcrafted • DLEE
775QX5555 • **Value $17**

17
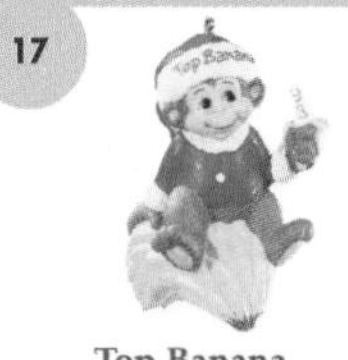
Top Banana
Handcrafted • RGRS
775QX5925 • **Value $18**

18

Wake-Up Call
Handcrafted • UNRU
875QX5262 • **Value $20**

19

Warm and Special Friends
Handcrafted/Metal • VOTR
1075QX5895 • **Value $26**

20

Water Bed Snooze
Handcrafted • JLEE
975QX5375 • **Value $22**

General Keepsake

	Price Paid	Value
1.		
2.		
3.		
4.		
5.		
6.		
7.		
8.		
9.		
10.		
11.		
12.		
13.		
14.		
15.		
16.		
17.		
18.		
19.		
20.		
Totals		

1

Winnie the Pooh
Handcrafted • SIED
975QX5715 • **Value $36**

2

Baby's First Christmas
Handcrafted • FRAN
2200QLX7365 • **Value $46**

3

Bells Are Ringing
Handcrafted • CROW
2800QLX7402 • **Value $64**

4

Dog's Best Friend
Handcrafted • JLEE
1200QLX7172 • **Value $25**

5

Dollhouse Dreams
Handcrafted • CROW
2200QLX7372 • **Value $48**

6

Home on the Range
Handcrafted • SICK
3200QLX7395 • **Value $68**

7

The Lamplighter
Handcrafted • PALM
1800QLX7192 • **Value $43**

8

Last Minute Shopping
Handcrafted • VOTR
2800QLX7385 • **Value $64**

9

Messages of Christmas
Handcrafted • SIED
3500QLX7476 • **Value $49**

10

North Pole Merrython
Handcrafted • SEAL
2500QLX7392 • **Value $57**

11

Our First Christmas Together
Handcrafted • CHAD
2000QLX7355 • **Value $45**

12

Radio News Flash
Handcrafted • DLEE
2200QLX7362 • **Value $48**

13

Raiding the Fridge
Handcrafted • RGRS
1600QLX7185 • **Value $38**

14

Road Runner and Wile E. Coyote™
Handcrafted • CHAD
3000QLX7415 • **Value $75**

15

Santa's Snow-Getter
Handcrafted • CROW
1800QLX7352 • **Value $42**

16

Santa's Workshop
Handcrafted • SIED
2800QLX7375 • **Value $62**

17

Song of the Chimes
Handcrafted/Brass • ANDR
2500QLX7405 • **Value $58**

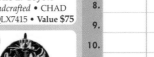

18

U.S.S. Enterprise™ THE NEXT GENERATION™
Handcrafted • NORT
2400QLX7412 • **Value $55**

19

Winnie the Pooh
Handcrafted • SIED
2400QLX7422 • **Value $50**

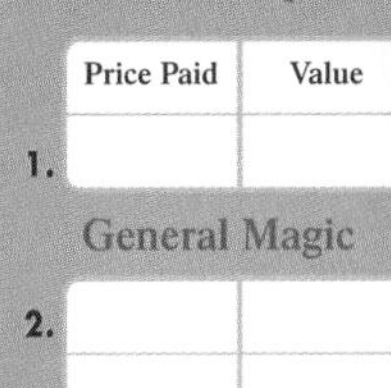

General Keepsake

	Price Paid	Value
1.		

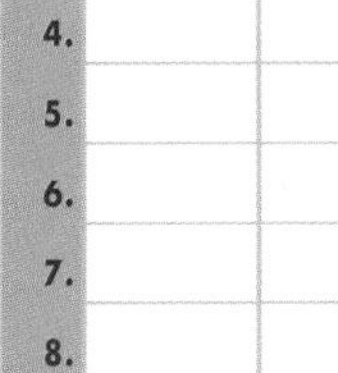

General Magic

	Price Paid	Value
2.		
3.		
4.		
5.		
6.		
7.		
8.		
9.		
10.		
11.		
12.		
13.		
14.		
15.		
16.		
17.		
18.		
19.		

Totals		

1

Angel in Flight
Folk Art Americana
Handcrafted • SICK
1575QK1052 • **Value $52**

2

Polar Bear Adventure
Folk Art Americana
Handcrafted • SICK
1500QK1055 • **Value $66**

3

Riding in the Woods
Folk Art Americana
Handcrafted • SICK
1575QK1065 • **Value $70**

4

Riding the Wind
Folk Art Americana
Handcrafted • SICK
1575QK1045 • **Value $60**

5

Santa Claus
Folk Art Americana
Handcrafted • SICK
1675QK1072 • **Value $220**

6

Angelic Messengers
Holiday Enchantment
Porcelain • VOTR
1375QK1032 • **Value $35**

7

Bringing Home the Tree
Holiday Enchantment
Porcelain • CHAD
1375QK1042 • **Value $32**

8

Journey to the Forest
Holiday Enchantment
Porcelain • N/A
1375QK1012 • **Value $30**

9
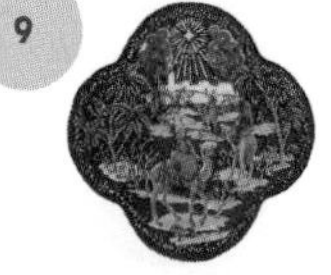
The Magi
Holiday Enchantment
Porcelain • N/A
1375QK1025 • **Value $32**

10

Visions of Sugarplums
Holiday Enchantment
Porcelain • N/A
1375QK1005 • **Value $32**

11

Silver Dove of Peace
Old-World Silver
Silver-Plated • PALM
2475QK1075 • **Value $37**

12

Silver Santa
Old-World Silver
Silver-Plated • UNRU
2475QK1092 • **Value $52**

13

Silver Sleigh
Old-World Silver
Silver-Plated • PALM
2475QK1082 • **Value $40**

14

Silver Stars and Holly
Old-World Silver
Silver-Plated • PALM
2475QK1085 • **Value $36**

15

Christmas Feast
Portraits in Bisque
Porcelain • PIKE
1575QK1152 • **Value $33**

16

Joy of Sharing
Portraits in Bisque
Porcelain • LYLE
1575QK1142 • **Value $33**

17

Mistletoe Kiss
Portraits in Bisque
Porcelain • PIKE
1575QK1145 • **Value $31**

18

Norman Rockwell – Filling the Stockings
Portraits in Bisque
Porcelain • DUTK
1575QK1155 • **Value $35**

19

Norman Rockwell – Jolly Postman
Portraits in Bisque
Porcelain • DUTK
1575QK1162 • **Value $35**

General Showcase

	Price Paid	Value
1.		
2.		
3.		
4.		
5.		
6.		
7.		
8.		
9.		
10.		
11.		
12.		
13.		
14.		
15.		
16.		
17.		
18.		
19.		
Totals		

1

Baby's First Christmas
Handcrafted • VOTR
575QXM5145 • **Value $13**

2

Cheese Please
Handcrafted • SIED
375QXM4072 • **Value $10**

3

Christmas Castle
Handcrafted • SEAL
575QXM4085 • **Value $14**

4

Cloisonné Snowflake
Cloisonné/Brass • VOTR
975QXM4012 • **Value $21**

5

Country Fiddling
Handcrafted • FRAN
375QXM4062 • **Value $12**

6

Crystal Angel
Crystal/Gold-Plated • PALM
975QXM4015 • **Value $56**

7

Ears to Pals
Handcrafted • ANDR
375QXM4075 • **Value $9**

8

Grandma
Handcrafted • SEAL
450QXM5162 • **Value $13**

9

I Dream of Santa
Handcrafted • SICK
375QXM4055 • **Value $12**

10

Into the Woods
Handcrafted • SEAL
375QXM4045 • **Value $10**

11

Learning to Skate
Handcrafted • CHAD
300QXM4122 • **Value $10**

12

Lighting a Path
Handcrafted • CHAD
300QXM4115 • **Value $10**

13

Merry Mascot
Handcrafted • SIED
375QXM4042 • **Value $12**

14

Mom
Handcrafted • ANDR
450QXM5155 • **Value $14**

15

Monkey Melody
Handcrafted • SICK
575QXM4092 • **Value $15**

16

North Pole Fire Truck
Handcrafted • PALM
475QXM4105 • **Value $14**

17

Pear-Shaped Tones
Handcrafted • LYLE
375QXM4052 • **Value $10**

18

Pull Out a Plum
Handcrafted • FRAN
575QXM4095 • **Value $15**

19

Refreshing Flight
Handcrafted • CHAD
575QXM4112 • **Value $15**

20

'Round the Mountain
Handcrafted • CROW
725QXM4025 • **Value $19**

General Miniature

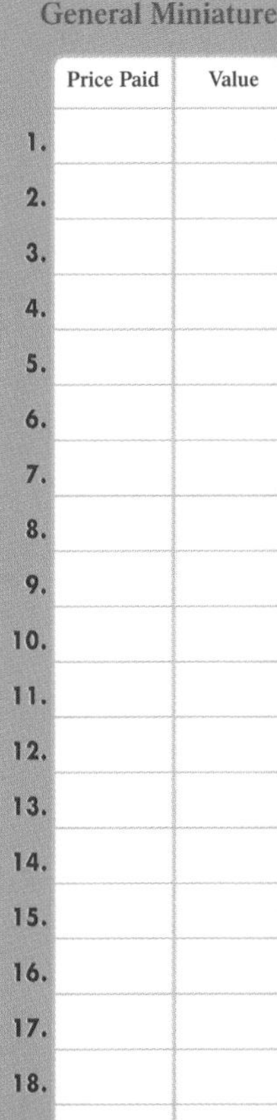

	Price Paid	Value
1.		
2.		
3.		
4.		
5.		
6.		
7.		
8.		
9.		
10.		
11.		
12.		
13.		
14.		
15.		
16.		
17.		
18.		
19.		
20.		
Totals		

1

Secret Pal
Handcrafted • RGRS
375QXM5172 • **Value $11**

2

Snuggle Birds
Handcrafted • ANDR
575QXM5182 • **Value $16**

3

Special Friends
Handcrafted • FRAN
450QXM5165 • **Value $11**

4

Tiny Green Thumbs (set/6)
Handcrafted • SEAL
2900QXM4032 • **Value $50**

5

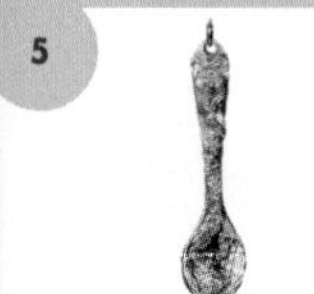

Visions of Sugarplums
Pewter • PALM
725QXM4022 • **Value $18**

6

Circle of Friendship (gift membership bonus)
Glass • N/A
QXC2112 • **Value $280**

7

Forty Winks (keepsake of membership, miniature)
Handcrafted • FRAN
QXC5294 • **Value $34**

8

Gentle Tidings (club edition, LE-17,500)
Porcelain • ANDR
2500QXC5442 • **Value $53**

9

It's in the Mail (keepsake of membership)
Handcrafted • SEAL
QXC5272 • **Value $26**

10

Sharing Christmas (club edition, LE-16,500)
Handcrafted • LYLE
2000QXC5435 • **Value $50**

11

Trimmed With Memories (club edition)
Handcrafted • SICK
1200QXC5432 • **Value $46**

12

You're Always Welcome
Handcrafted • SEAL
975QX5692 • **Value $62**

13

Abearnathy
The Bearingers of Victoria Circle
Handcrafted • N/A
495XPR9747 • **Value $11**

14

Bearnadette
The Bearingers of Victoria Circle
Handcrafted • N/A
495XPR9748 • **Value $11**

15

Fireplace Base
The Bearingers of Victoria Circle
Handcrafted • N/A
495XPR9749 • **Value $13**

16

Mama Bearinger
The Bearingers of Victoria Circle
Handcrafted • N/A
495XPR9745 • **Value $11**

17

Papa Bearinger
The Bearingers of Victoria Circle
Handcrafted • N/A
495XPR9746 • **Value $11**

18

25 Years Together
Porcelain • N/A
800AGA7687 • **Value $20**

19

50 Years Together
Porcelain • N/A
800AGA7788 • **Value $20**

	Price Paid	Value
General Miniature		
1.		
2.		
3.		
4.		
5.		
Collector's Club		
6.		
7.		
8.		
9.		
10.		
11.		
Premiere Ornaments		
12.		
Reach Ornaments		
13.		
14.		
15.		
16.		
17.		
Anniversary Bells		
18.		
19.		
Totals		

1

Our First Anniversary
Porcelain • N/A
1000AGA7865 • **Value $20**

2

Our Fifth Anniversary
Porcelain • N/A
1000AGA7866 • **Value $20**

3

Our Tenth Anniversary
Porcelain • N/A
1000AGA7867 • **Value $20**

4

25 Years Together
Porcelain • N/A
1000AGA7686 • **Value $20**

5

40 Years Together
Porcelain • N/A
1000AGA7868 • **Value $20**

6

50 Years Together
Porcelain • N/A
1000AGA7787 • **Value $20**

7

Santa's Favorite Stop
Handcrafted • VARI
5500QXC4125 • **Value $350**

8

Baby's Christening
Handcrafted • N/A
1200BBY2917 • **Value $18**

9

Baby's Christening Photoholder
Silver-Plated • N/A
1000BBY1335 • **Value $15**

10

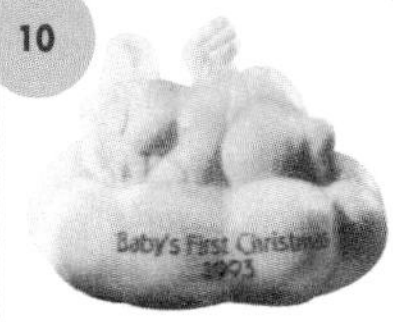

Baby's First Christmas
Handcrafted • N/A
1200BBY2918 • **Value $17**

11

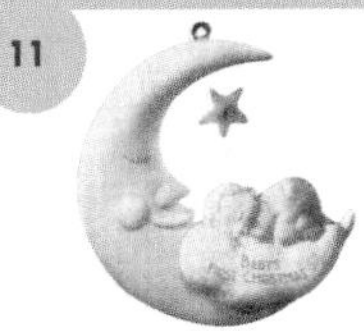

Baby's First Christmas
Handcrafted • N/A
1400BBY2919 • **Value $20**

12

Baby's First Christmas Photoholder
Silver-Plated • N/A
1000BBY1470 • **Value $15**

13

Granddaughter's First Christmas
Handcrafted • N/A
1400BBY2802 • **Value $18**

14

Grandson's First Christmas
Handcrafted • N/A
1400BBY2801 • **Value $18**

15

K.C. Angel
Silver-Plated • N/A
(N/C) No stock # • **Value $575**

16

Baby Block Photoholder (re-issued in 1994)
Handcrafted • FRAN
1475QP6035 • **Value N/E**

17

Cool Snowman
Glass • N/A
875QP6052 • **Value N/E**

18

Festive Album Photoholder (re-issued in 1994)
Handcrafted • VOTR
1275QP6025 • **Value N/E**

19

Filled With Cookies
Handcrafted • RGRS
1275QP6042 • **Value N/E**

20

Going Golfin' (re-issued in 1994)
Handcrafted • PALM
1275QP6012 • **Value N/E**

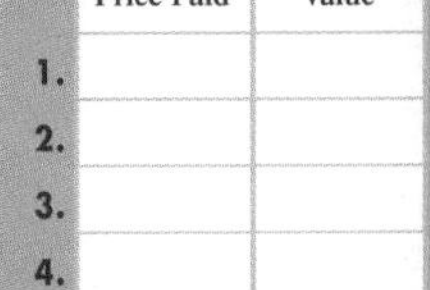

	Price Paid	Value
Anniversary Ornaments		
1.		
2.		
3.		
4.		
5.		
6.		
Artists On Tour Pieces		
7.		
Baby Ornaments		
8.		
9.		
10.		
11.		
12.		
13.		
14.		
Convention Ornaments		
15.		
Personalized Ornaments		
16.		
17.		
18.		
19.		
20.		
Totals		

1

Here's Your Fortune
Handcrafted • SEAL
1075QP6002 • **Value N/E**

2

Mailbox Delivery
(re-issued in 1994 and 1995)
Handcrafted • CROW
1475QP6015 • **Value N/E**

3

On the Billboard
(re-issued in 1994 and 1995)
Handcrafted • CROW
1275QP6022 • **Value N/E**

4

PEANUTS®
Glass • N/A
900QP6045 • **Value N/E**

5

Playing Ball
(re-issued in 1994 and 1995)
Handcrafted • FRAN
1275QP6032 • **Value N/E**

6

Reindeer in the Sky
Glass • N/A
875QP6055 • **Value N/E**

7

Santa Says
(re-issued in 1994)
Handcrafted • SEAL
1475QP6005 • **Value N/E**

Personalized Ornaments

	Price Paid	Value
1.		
2.		
3.		
4.		
5.		
6.		
7.		

General Keepsake

	Price Paid	Value
8.		
9.		
10.		
11.		
12.		
13.		
14.		
15.		
16.		
Totals		

1992

Of note in the 1992 collection was the debut of the "unofficial series" of handcrafted Coca-Cola® Santa ornaments in the Keepsake and Miniature lines. For 1992, there were 126 Keepsake ornaments, 21 Magic ornaments and 48 Miniature ornaments. See the collectible series section for more 1992 ornaments.

8

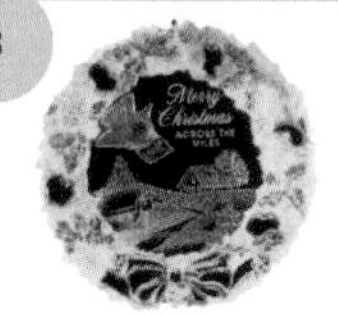

Across The Miles
Acrylic • RHOD
675QX3044 • **Value $16**

9

Anniversary Year Photoholder
Chrome/Brass • UNRU
975QX4851 • **Value $27**

10

Baby's First Christmas
Handcrafted • FRAN
775QX4644 • **Value $38**

11

Baby's First Christmas
Porcelain • ANDR
1875QX4581 • **Value $38**

12

Baby's First Christmas – Baby Boy
Satin • VOTR
475QX2191 • **Value $18**

13

Baby's First Christmas – Baby Girl
Satin • VOTR
475QX2204 • **Value $18**

14

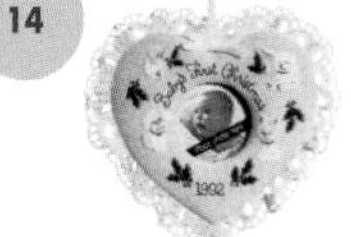

Baby's First Christmas Photoholder
Fabric • VOTR
775QX4641 • **Value $26**

15

Baby's Second Christmas
Handcrafted • FRAN
675QX4651 • **Value $24**

16

Bear Bell Champ
Handcrafted/Brass • SEAL
775QX5071 • **Value $27**

1

Brother
Handcrafted • CROW
675QX4684 • **Value $16**

2

Cheerful Santa
Handcrafted • UNRU
975QX5154 • **Value $31**

3

A Child's Christmas
Handcrafted • FRAN
975QX4574 • **Value $19**

4

Child's Fifth Christmas
Handcrafted • RHOD
675QX4664 • **Value $20**

5

Child's Fourth Christmas
Handcrafted • FRAN
675QX4661 • **Value $23**

6

Child's Third Christmas
Handcrafted • FRAN
675QX4654 • **Value $22**

7

Cool Fliers (set/2)
Handcrafted • JLEE
1075QX5474 • **Value $26**

8

Dad
Handcrafted • SIED
775QX4674 • **Value $21**

9

Dad-to-Be
Handcrafted • JLEE
675QX4611 • **Value $19**

10

Daughter
Handcrafted • FRAN
675QX5031 • **Value $28**

11

Deck the Hogs
Handcrafted • FRAN
875QX5204 • **Value $27**

12

Dickens Caroler Bell – Lord Chadwick
Porcelain • CHAD
2175QX4554 • **Value $45**

13

Down-Under Holiday
Handcrafted • CROW
775QX5144 • **Value $22**

14

Egg Nog Nest
Handcrafted • N/A
775QX5121 • **Value $18**

15

Elfin Marionette
Handcrafted • CHAD
1175QX5931 • **Value $25**

16

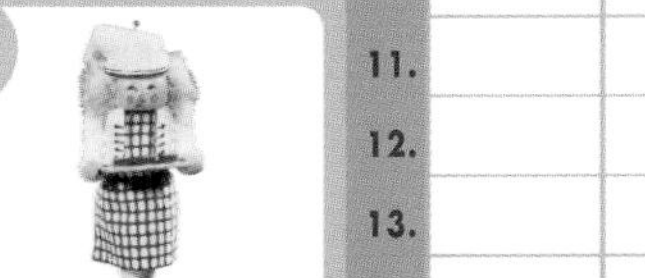

Elvis
Brass-Plated • RHOD/LYLE
1475QX5624 • **Value $26**

17

Eric the Baker
Handcrafted • SICK
875QX5244 • **Value $22**

18

Feliz Navidad
Handcrafted • ANDR
675QX5181 • **Value $24**

19

For My Grandma Photoholder
Fabric • N/A
775QX5184 • **Value $20**

20

For The One I Love
Porcelain • LYLE
975QX4844 • **Value $24**

General Keepsake

	Price Paid	Value
1.		
2.		
3.		
4.		
5.		
6.		
7.		
8.		
9.		
10.		
11.		
12.		
13.		
14.		
15.		
16.		
17.		
18.		
19.		
20.		
Totals		

1
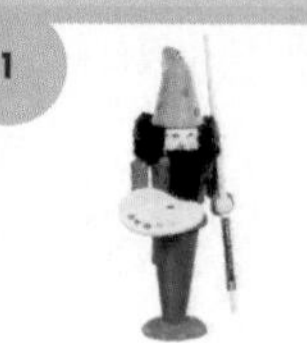
Franz the Artist
Handcrafted • SICK
875QX5261 • **Value $26**

2

Frieda the Animals' Friend
Handcrafted • SICK
875QX5264 • **Value $24**

3

Friendly Greetings
Handcrafted • CHAD
775QX5041 • **Value $17**

4

Friendship Line
Handcrafted • SEAL
975QX5034 • **Value $32**

5

From Our Home to Yours
Glass • VOTR
475QX2131 • **Value $18**

6

Fun on a Big Scale
Handcrafted • CROW
1075QX5134 • **Value $25**

7

GARFIELD
Handcrafted • PALM
775QX5374 • **Value $23**

8

Genius at Work
Handcrafted • CROW
1075QX5371 • **Value $24**

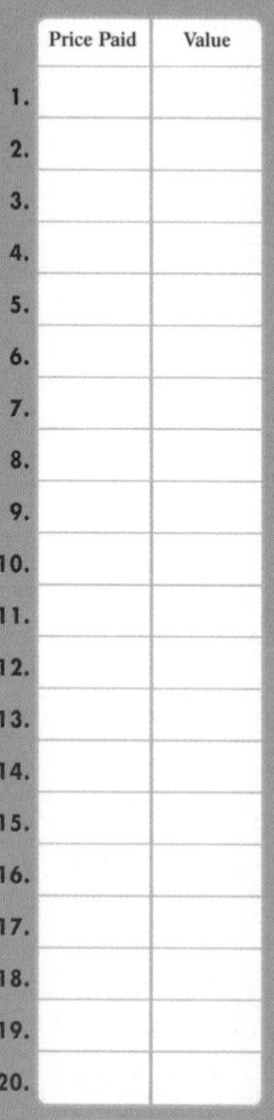

General Keepsake

	Price Paid	Value
1.		
2.		
3.		
4.		
5.		
6.		
7.		
8.		
9.		
10.		
11.		
12.		
13.		
14.		
15.		
16.		
17.		
18.		
19.		
20.		
Totals		

9
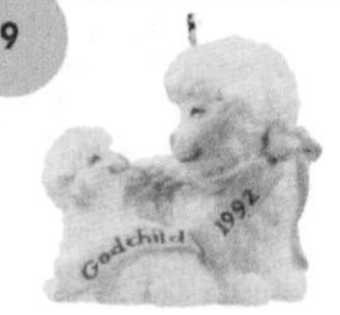

Godchild
Handcrafted • UNRU
675QX5941 • **Value $23**

10

Golf's a Ball
Handcrafted • SCHU
675QX5984 • **Value $30**

11

Gone Wishin'
Handcrafted • DLEE
875QX5171 • **Value $18**

12

Granddaughter
Handcrafted • SEAL
675QX5604 • **Value $21**

13

Granddaughter's First Christmas
Handcrafted • SIED
675QX4634 • **Value $19**

14

Grandmother
Glass • N/A
475QX2011 • **Value $19**

15

Grandparents
Glass • N/A
475QX2004 • **Value $17**

16

Grandson
Handcrafted • SEAL
675QX5611 • **Value $18**

17

Grandson's First Christmas
Handcrafted • SIED
675QX4621 • **Value $19**

18

Green Thumb Santa
Handcrafted • PALM
775QX5101 • **Value $19**

19

Hello-Ho-Ho
Handcrafted • CROW
975QX5141 • **Value $25**

20

Holiday Memo
Handcrafted • RGRS
775QX5044 • **Value $18**

1

Holiday Teatime (set/2)
Handcrafted • RGRS
1475QX5431 • **Value $30**

2

Holiday Wishes
Handcrafted • PIKE
775QX5131 • **Value $18**

3

Honest George
Handcrafted • JLEE
775QX5064 • **Value $16**

4

Jesus Loves Me
Cameo • ANDR
775QX3024 • **Value $18**

5

Love to Skate
Handcrafted • RGRS
875QX4841 • **Value $22**

6

Loving Shepherd
Handcrafted/Brass • ANDR
775QX5151 • **Value $19**

7

Ludwig the Musician
Handcrafted • SICK
875QX5281 • **Value $21**

8

Max the Tailor
Handcrafted • SICK
875QX5251 • **Value $24**

9

Memories to Cherish Photoholder
Porcelain • ANDR
1075QX5161 • **Value $24**

10

Merry "Swiss" Mouse
Handcrafted • SEAL
775QX5114 • **Value $16**

11

Mom
Handcrafted • RGRS
775QX5164 • **Value $20**

12

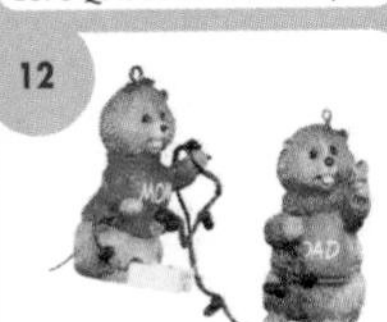

Mom and Dad
Handcrafted • SIED
975QX4671 • **Value $39**

13

Mom-to-Be
Handcrafted • JLEE
675QX4614 • **Value $18**

14

Mother Goose
Handcrafted • CROW
1375QX4984 • **Value $30**

15

New Home
Handcrafted • PIKE
875QX5191 • **Value $18**

16

Norman Rockwell Art
Glass • LYLE
500QX2224 • **Value $24**

17

North Pole Fire Fighter
Handcrafted/Brass • SEAL
975QX5104 • **Value $22**

18

Otto the Carpenter
Handcrafted • SICK
875QX5254 • **Value $23**

19

Our First Christmas Together
Acrylic • VOTR
675QX3011 • **Value $20**

20

Our First Christmas Together
Handcrafted • JLEE
975QX5061 • **Value $21**

General Keepsake

	Price Paid	Value
1.		
2.		
3.		
4.		
5.		
6.		
7.		
8.		
9.		
10.		
11.		
12.		
13.		
14.		
15.		
16.		
17.		
18.		
19.		
20.		
Totals		

1

Our First Christmas Together Photoholder
Handcrafted • SEAL
875QX4694 • **Value $27**

2

Owl
Handcrafted • SIED
975QX5614 • **Value $28**

3

Partridge IN a Pear Tree
Handcrafted • SIED
875QX5234 • **Value $22**

4

PEANUTS®
Glass • N/A
500QX2244 • **Value $28**

5

Please Pause Here
Handcrafted • DLEE
1475QX5291 • **Value $35**

6

Polar Post
Handcrafted • SEAL
875QX4914 • **Value $21**

7

Rapid Delivery
Handcrafted • PALM
875QX5094 • **Value $22**

8

A Santa-Full!
Handcrafted • FRAN
975QX5991 • **Value $44**

9

Santa Maria
Handcrafted • CROW
1275QX5074 • **Value $23**

10

Santa's Hook Shot (set/2)
Handcrafted • SEAL
1275QX5434 • **Value $30**

11

Santa's Roundup
Handcrafted • JLEE
875QX5084 • **Value $25**

12

Secret Pal
Handcrafted • RGRS
775QX5424 • **Value $16**

13

Silver Star Train Set (set/3)
Die-Cast Metal • SICK
2800QX5324 • **Value $58**

14

Sister
Handcrafted • CROW
675QX4681 • **Value $17**

15

Skiing 'Round
Handcrafted • JLEE
875QX5214 • **Value $19**

16

Sky Line Caboose
Die-Cast Metal • SICK
975QX5321 • **Value $25**

17

Sky Line Coal Car
Die-Cast Metal • SICK
975QX5401 • **Value $22**

18

Sky Line Locomotive
Die-Cast Metal • SICK
975QX5311 • **Value $47**

19

Sky Line Stock Car
Die-Cast Metal • SICK
975QX5314 • **Value $21**

20

SNOOPY® and WOODSTOCK
Handcrafted • RGRS
875QX5954 • **Value $40**

General Keepsake

	Price Paid	Value
1.		
2.		
3.		
4.		
5.		
6.		
7.		
8.		
9.		
10.		
11.		
12.		
13.		
14.		
15.		
16.		
17.		
18.		
19.		
20.		
Totals		

1

Son
Handcrafted • FRAN
675QX5024 • **Value $24**

2

Special Cat Photoholder
Handcrafted • CHAD
775QX5414 • **Value $19**

3

Special Dog Photoholder
Handcrafted • CHAD
775QX5421 • **Value $30**

4

Spirit of Christmas Stress
Handcrafted • CHAD
875QX5231 • **Value $21**

5

Stocked With Joy
Pressed Tin • SICK
775QX5934 • **Value $20**

6

Tasty Christmas
Handcrafted • FRAN
975QX5994 • **Value $25**

7

Teacher
Glass • N/A
475QX2264 • **Value $19**

8

Toboggan Tail
Handcrafted • ANDR
775QX5459 • **Value $17**

9

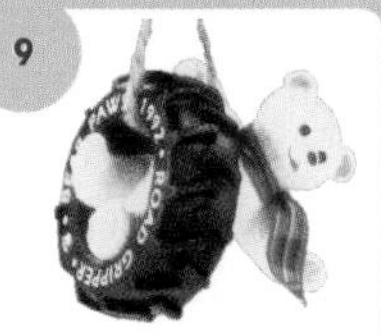

Tread Bear
Handcrafted • SEAL
875QX5091 • **Value $25**

10

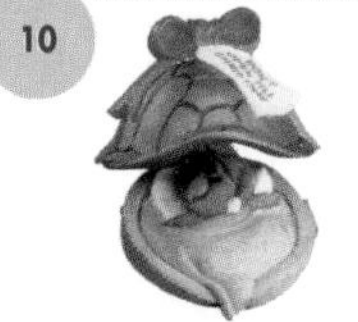

Turtle Dreams
Handcrafted • JLEE
875QX4991 • **Value $24**

11

Uncle Art's Ice Cream
Handcrafted • SIED
875QX5001 • **Value $24**

12

V.P. of Important Stuff
Handcrafted • SIED
675QX5051 • **Value $16**

13

World-Class Teacher
Handcrafted • SIED
775QX5054 • **Value $18**

14

Baby's First Christmas
Handcrafted • CROW
2200QLX7281 • **Value $100**

15

Christmas Parade
Handcrafted • SICK
3000QLX7271 • **Value $65**

16

Continental Express
Handcrafted • SICK
3200QLX7264 • **Value $78**

17

The Dancing Nutcracker
Handcrafted • VOTR
3000QLX7261 • **Value $60**

18

Enchanted Clock
Handcrafted • CROW
3000QLX7274 • **Value $64**

19

Feathered Friends
Handcrafted • SICK
1400QLX7091 • **Value $33**

20

Good Sledding Ahead
Handcrafted • PALM
2800QLX7244 • **Value $58**

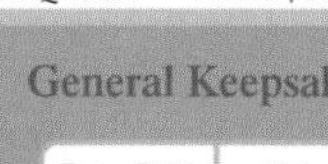
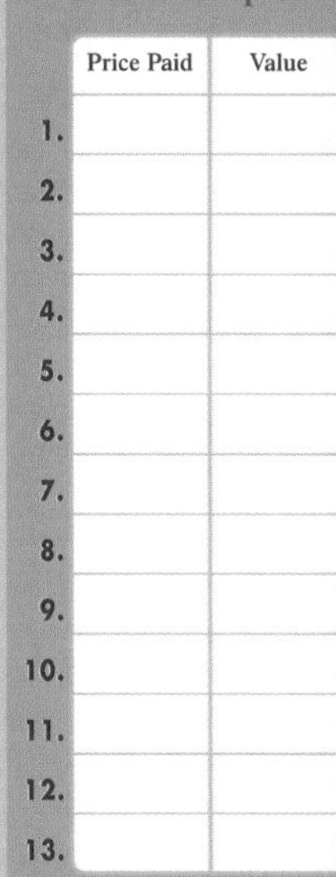

General Keepsake

	Price Paid	Value
1.		
2.		
3.		
4.		
5.		
6.		
7.		
8.		
9.		
10.		
11.		
12.		
13.		

General Magic

	Price Paid	Value
14.		
15.		
16.		
17.		
18.		
19.		
20.		
Totals		

1
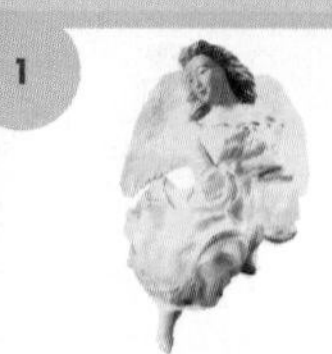
Lighting the Way
Handcrafted • ANDR
1800QLX7231 • **Value $48**

2

Look! It's Santa
Handcrafted • DLEE
1400QLX7094 • **Value $46**

3

Nut Sweet Nut
Handcrafted • CROW
1000QLX7081 • **Value $24**

4

Our First Christmas Together
Panorama Ball • CHAD
2000QLX7221 • **Value $45**

5

Santa Special (re-issued from 1991)
Handcrafted • SEAL
4000QLX7167 • **Value $80**

6

Santa Sub
Handcrafted • CROW
1800QLX7321 • **Value $38**

7

Santa's Answering Machine
Handcrafted • JLEE
2200QLX7241 • **Value $41**

8

Shuttlecraft Galileo™ From the Starship Enterprise™
Handcrafted • RHOD
2400QLX7331 • **Value $48**

9

Under Construction
Handcrafted • PALM
1800QLX7324 • **Value $42**

10

Watch Owls
Porcelain • FRAN
1200QLX7084 • **Value $30**

11

Yuletide Rider
Handcrafted • SEAL
2800QLX7314 • **Value $60**

12

A+ Teacher
Handcrafted • UNRU
375QXM5511 • **Value $11**

13

Angelic Harpist
Handcrafted • LYLE
450QXM5524 • **Value $17**

14

Baby's First Christmas
Handcrafted/Brass • LYLE
450QXM5494 • **Value $21**

15

Black-Capped Chickadee
Handcrafted • FRAN
300QXM5484 • **Value $18**

16
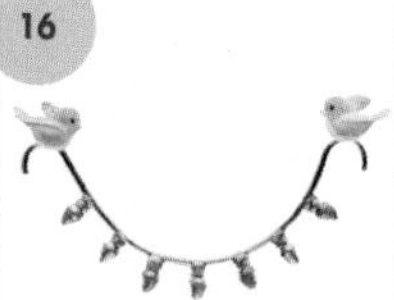
Bright Stringers
Handcrafted • SEAL
375QXM5841 • **Value $18**

17

Buck-A-Roo
Handcrafted • CROW
450QXM5814 • **Value $15**

18

Christmas Bonus
Handcrafted • PALM
300QXM5811 • **Value $9**

19

Christmas Copter
Handcrafted • FRAN
575QXM5844 • **Value $15**

20

Coca-Cola® Santa
Handcrafted • UNRU
575QXM5884 • **Value $17**

General Magic

	Price Paid	Value
1.		
2.		
3.		
4.		
5.		
6.		
7.		
8.		
9.		
10.		
11.		

General Miniature

	Price Paid	Value
12.		
13.		
14.		
15.		
16.		
17.		
18.		
19.		
20.		
Totals		

1

Cool Uncle Sam
Handcrafted • JLEE
300QXM5561 • **Value $15**

2

Cozy Kayak
Handcrafted • JLEE
375QXM5551 • **Value $14**

3

Fast Finish
Handcrafted • RHOD
375QXM5301 • **Value $12**

4

Feeding Time
Handcrafted • CROW
575QXM5481 • **Value $16**

5

Friendly Tin Soldier
Pressed Tin • SICK
450QXM5874 • **Value $17**

6

Friends Are Tops
Handcrafted • CROW
450QXM5521 • **Value $11**

7

Gerbil Inc.
Handcrafted • SIED
375QXM5924 • **Value $11**

8

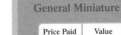

Going Places
Handcrafted • ANDR
375QXM5871 • **Value $11**

9

Grandchild's First Christmas
Handcrafted • FRAN
575QXM5501 • **Value $14**

10

Grandma
Handcrafted • UNRU
450QXM5514 • **Value $15**

11

Harmony Trio (set/3)
Handcrafted • VOTR
1175QXM5471 • **Value $21**

12

Hickory, Dickory, Dock
Handcrafted • CHAD
375QXM5861 • **Value $13**

13

Holiday Holly
Gold-Plated • N/A
975QXM5364 • **Value $17**

14

Holiday Splash
Handcrafted • FRAN
575QXM5834 • **Value $14**

15

Hoop It Up
Handcrafted • CROW
450QXM5831 • **Value $13**

16

Inside Story
Handcrafted • SEAL
725QXM5881 • **Value $20**

17

Little Town of Bethlehem
Handcrafted • SICK
300QXM5864 • **Value $24**

18

Minted for Santa
Copper • UNRU
375QXM5854 • **Value $15**

19

Mom
Handcrafted • ANDR
450QXM5504 • **Value $15**

20

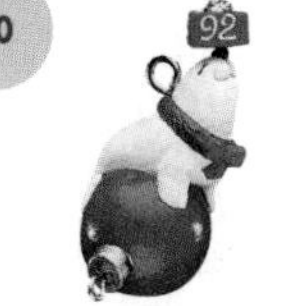

Perfect Balance
Handcrafted • RGRS
300QXM5571 • **Value $13**

General Miniature

	Price Paid	Value
1.		
2.		
3.		
4.		
5.		
6.		
7.		
8.		
9.		
10.		
11.		
12.		
13.		
14.		
15.		
16.		
17.		
18.		
19.		
20.		
Totals		

1

Polar Polka
Handcrafted • SEAL
450QXM5534 • **Value $15**

2

Puppet Show
Handcrafted • SIED
300QXM5574 • **Value $13**

3

Sew, Sew Tiny (set/6)
Handcrafted • SEAL
2900QXM5794 • **Value $58**

4

Ski for Two
Handcrafted • ANDR
450QXM5821 • **Value $15**

5

Snowshoe Bunny
Handcrafted • VOTR
375QXM5564 • **Value $13**

6

Snug Kitty
Handcrafted • PIKE
375QXM5554 • **Value $13**

7

Spunky Monkey
Handcrafted • CHAD
300QXM5921 • **Value $15**

8

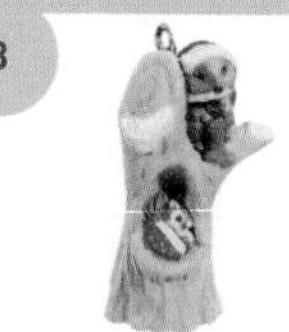

Visions of Acorns
Handcrafted • ANDR
450QXM5851 • **Value $16**

9

Wee Three Kings
Handcrafted • PALM
575QXM5531 • **Value $19**

10

Chipmunk Parcel Service (early renewal piece, miniature)
Handcrafted • SEAL
QXC5194 • **Value $26**

11

Christmas Treasures (set/4, club edition, LE-15,500, miniature)
Handcrafted • CHAD
2200QXC5464 • **Value $160**

12

Rodney Takes Flight (keepsake of membership)
Handcrafted • DLEE
QXC5081 • **Value $30**

13

Santa's Club List (club edition, magic)
Handcrafted • SEAL
1500QXC7291 • **Value $44**

14

Victorian Skater (club edition, LE-14,700)
Porcelain • UNRU
2500QXC4067 • **Value $69**

15

O Christmas Tree
Porcelain • VOTR
1075QX5411 • **Value $30**

16

Comet and Cupid
Santa and His Reindeer
Handcrafted/Brass • CROW
495XPR9737 • **Value $23**

17

Dasher and Dancer
Santa and His Reindeer
Handcrafted/Brass • CROW
495XPR9735 • **Value $45**

18

Donder and Blitzen
Santa and His Reindeer
Handcrafted/Brass • CROW
495XPR9738 • **Value $38**

19

Prancer and Vixen
Santa and His Reindeer
Handcrafted/Brass • CROW
495XPR9736 • **Value $23**

20

Santa Claus
Santa and His Reindeer
Handcrafted/Brass • CROW
495XPR9739 • **Value $30**

	Price Paid	Value
General Miniature		
1.		
2.		
3.		
4.		
5.		
6.		
7.		
8.		
9.		
Collector's Club		
10.		
11.		
12.		
13.		
14.		
Premiere Ornaments		
15.		
Reach Ornaments		
16.		
17.		
18.		
19.		
20.		
Totals		

1

25 Years Together
Porcelain • N/A
800AGA7134 • **Value $17**

2

50 Years Together
Porcelain • N/A
800AGA7235 • **Value $17**

3

Our First Anniversary
Porcelain • N/A
1000AGA7318 • **Value $19**

4

Our Fifth Anniversary
Porcelain • N/A
1000AGA7319 • **Value $19**

5

Our Tenth Anniversary
Porcelain • N/A
1000AGA7317 • **Value $19**

6

25 Years Together
Porcelain • N/A
1000AGA7113 • **Value $19**

7

40 Years Together
Porcelain • N/A
1000AGA7316 • **Value $20**

8

50 Years Together
Porcelain • N/A
1000AGA7214 • **Value $20**

9

Baby's Christening
Fabric • N/A
850BBY1331 • **Value $15**

10

Baby's First Christmas
Fabric • N/A
850BBY1456 • **Value $15**

11
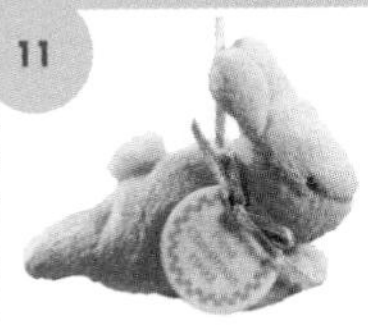

Baby's First Christmas
Plush • N/A
850BBY1557 • **Value $15**

1991

In 1991, an exciting Magic ornament depicting the "Starship Enterprise™" (the first of many STAR TREK® ornaments) was issued and quickly became a collectors' favorite. This year's collection featured 128 Keepsake, 23 Magic and 47 Miniature ornaments. See the collectible series section for more 1991 ornaments.

12

Across the Miles
Acrylic • LYLE
675QX3157 • **Value $17**

13

All-Star
Handcrafted • SIED
675QX5329 • **Value $22**

14

Baby's First Christmas
Handcrafted • FRAN
775QX4889 • **Value $42**

15

Baby's First Christmas
Silver-Plated • FRAN
1775QX5107 • **Value $46**

16

Baby's First Christmas – Baby Boy
Satin • HAMI
475QX2217 • **Value $21**

17
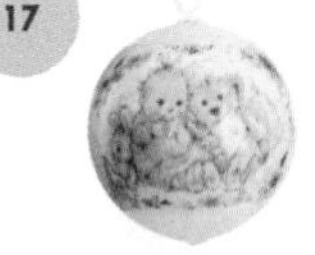

Baby's First Christmas – Baby Girl
Satin • HAMI
475QX2227 • **Value $21**

	Price Paid	Value
Anniversary Bells		
1.		
2.		
Anniversary Ornaments		
3.		
4.		
5.		
6.		
7.		
8.		
Baby Ornaments		
9.		
10.		
11.		
General Keepsake		
12.		
13.		
14.		
15.		
16.		
17.		
Totals		

1

Baby's First Christmas Photoholder
Fabric • VOTR
775QX4869 • **Value $30**

2

Baby's Second Christmas
Handcrafted • FRAN
675QX4897 • **Value $32**

3

Basket Bell Players
Handcrafted/Wicker • SEAL
775QX5377 • **Value $28**

4

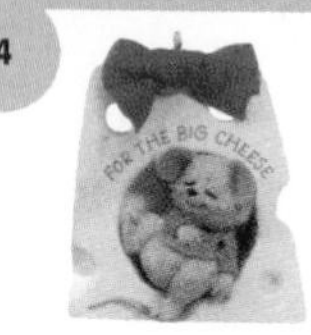

The Big Cheese
Handcrafted • SIED
675QX5327 • **Value $19**

5

Bob Cratchit
Porcelain • UNRU
1375QX4997 • **Value $37**

6

Brother
Handcrafted • SIED
675QX5479 • **Value $21**

7

A Child's Christmas
Handcrafted • FRAN
975QX4887 • **Value $17**

8

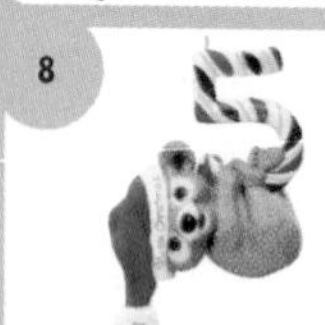

Child's Fifth Christmas
Handcrafted • RHOD
675QX4909 • **Value $19**

9

Child's Fourth Christmas
Handcrafted • FRAN
675QX4907 • **Value $20**

10

Child's Third Christmas
Handcrafted • FRAN
675QX4899 • **Value $29**

11

Chilly Chap
Handcrafted • DLEE
675QX5339 • **Value $18**

12

Christmas Welcome
Handcrafted • SICK
975QX5299 • **Value $24**

13

Christopher Robin
Handcrafted • SIED
975QX5579 • **Value $40**

14

Cuddly Lamb
Handcrafted • RGRS
675QX5199 • **Value $22**

15

Dad
Handcrafted • JLEE
775QX5127 • **Value $20**

16

Dad-to-Be
Handcrafted • JLEE
575QX4879 • **Value $17**

17

Daughter
Handcrafted • SIED
575QX5477 • **Value $42**

18

Dickens Caroler Bell – Mrs. Beaumont
Porcelain • CHAD
2175QX5039 • **Value $43**

19

Dinoclaus
Handcrafted • CHAD
775QX5277 • **Value $23**

20

Ebenezer Scrooge
Porcelain • UNRU
1375QX4989 • **Value $48**

General Keepsake

	Price Paid	Value
1.		
2.		
3.		
4.		
5.		
6.		
7.		
8.		
9.		
10.		
11.		
12.		
13.		
14.		
15.		
16.		
17.		
18.		
19.		
20.		
Totals		

1

Evergreen Inn
Handcrafted • SEAL
875QX5389 • **Value $18**

2

Extra-Special Friends
Glass • N/A
475QX2279 • **Value $16**

3

Fanfare Bear
Handcrafted • SEAL
875QX5337 • **Value $20**

4

Feliz Navidad
Handcrafted • JLEE
675QX5279 • **Value $27**

5

Fiddlin' Around
Handcrafted • VOTR
775QX4387 • **Value $18**

6

Fifty Years Together Photoholder
Handcrafted/Brass • VOTR
875QX4947 • **Value $19**

7

First Christmas Together
Acrylic • PIKE
675QX3139 • **Value $26**

8

First Christmas Together
Glass • N/A
475QX2229 • **Value $22**

9

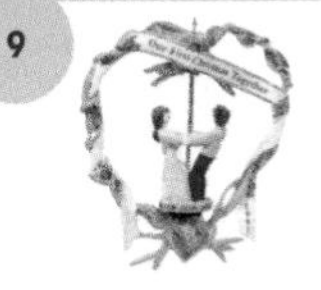

First Christmas Together
Handcrafted • SICK
875QX4919 • **Value $29**

10

First Christmas Together Photoholder
Handcrafted/Brass • VOTR
875QX4917 • **Value $29**

11

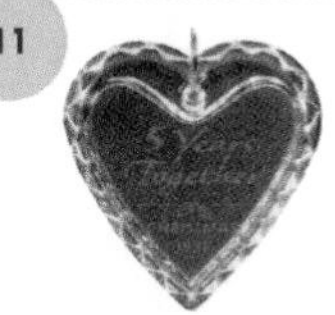

Five Years Together
Faceted Glass • N/A
775QX4927 • **Value $18**

12

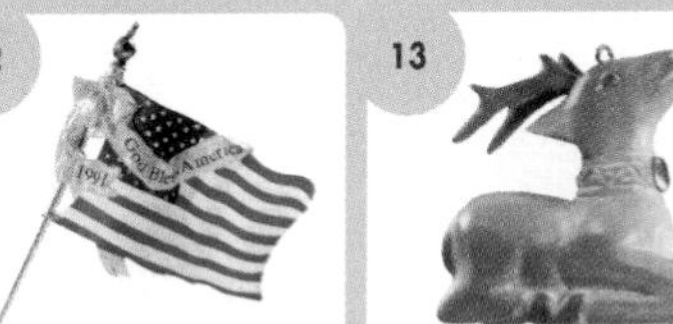

Flag of Liberty
Handcrafted • DLEE
675QX5249 • **Value $16**

13

Folk Art Reindeer
Wood/Brass • VOTR
875QX5359 • **Value $20**

14

Forty Years Together
Faceted Glass • N/A
775QX4939 • **Value $18**

15

Friends Are Fun
Handcrafted • CROW
975QX5289 • **Value $23**

16

From Our Home to Yours
Glass • VOTR
475QX2287 • **Value $22**

17

GARFIELD®
Handcrafted • RHOD
775QX5177 • **Value $34**

18

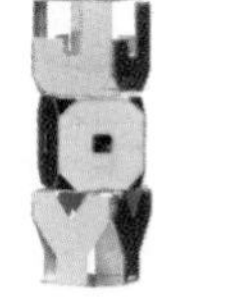

Gift of Joy
Brass/Chrome/Copper • MCGE
875QX5319 • **Value $26**

19

Glee Club Bears
Handcrafted • SEAL
875QX4969 • **Value $22**

20

Godchild
Handcrafted • BISH
675QX5489 • **Value $23**

General Keepsake

	Price Paid	Value
1.		
2.		
3.		
4.		
5.		
6.		
7.		
8.		
9.		
10.		
11.		
12.		
13.		
14.		
15.		
16.		
17.		
18.		
19.		
20.		
Totals		

1

Granddaughter
Glass • PYDA
475QX2299 • **Value $26**

2

Granddaughter's First Christmas
Handcrafted • CHAD
675QX5119 • **Value $22**

3

Grandmother
Glass • N/A
475QX2307 • **Value $20**

4

Grandparents
Glass • PYDA
475QX2309 • **Value $15**

5

Grandson
Glass • PYDA
475QX2297 • **Value $24**

6

Grandson's First Christmas
Handcrafted • CHAD
675QX5117 • **Value $23**

7

Holiday Cafe
Handcrafted • SEAL
875QX5399 • **Value $17**

8

Hooked on Santa
Handcrafted • JLEE
775QX4109 • **Value $28**

9

Jesus Loves Me
Cameo • RHOD
775QX3147 • **Value $18**

10

Jolly Wolly Santa
Pressed Tin • SICK
775QX5419 • **Value $28**

11

Jolly Wolly Snowman
Pressed Tin • SICK
775QX5427 • **Value $28**

12

Jolly Wolly Soldier
Pressed Tin • SICK
775QX5429 • **Value $22**

13

Joyous Memories Photoholder
Handcrafted • VOTR
675QX5369 • **Value $27**

14

Kanga and Roo
Handcrafted • SIED
975QX5617 • **Value $50**

15

Look Out Below
Handcrafted • SEAL
875QX4959 • **Value $22**

16

Loving Stitches
Handcrafted • SEAL
875QX4987 • **Value $33**

17

Mary Engelbreit
Glass • N/A
475QX2237 • **Value $30**

18

Merry Carolers
Porcelain • UNRU
2975QX4799 • **Value $96**

19

Mom and Dad
Handcrafted • N/A
975QX5467 • **Value $26**

20

Mom-to-Be
Handcrafted • JLEE
575QX4877 • **Value $22**

General Keepsake

	Price Paid	Value
1.		
2.		
3.		
4.		
5.		
6.		
7.		
8.		
9.		
10.		
11.		
12.		
13.		
14.		
15.		
16.		
17.		
18.		
19.		
20.		
Totals		

1

Mother
Porcelain/Tin • N/A
975QX5457 • **Value $35**

2

Mrs. Cratchit
Porcelain • UNRU
1375QX4999 • **Value $35**

3

New Home
Handcrafted • BISH
675QX5449 • **Value $32**

4

Night Before Christmas
Handcrafted • SICK
975QX5307 • **Value $23**

5

Noah's Ark
Handcrafted • CROW
1375QX4867 • **Value $50**

6

Norman Rockwell Art
Glass • LYLE
500QX2259 • **Value $28**

7

Notes of Cheer
Handcrafted • SIED
575QX5357 • **Value $14**

8
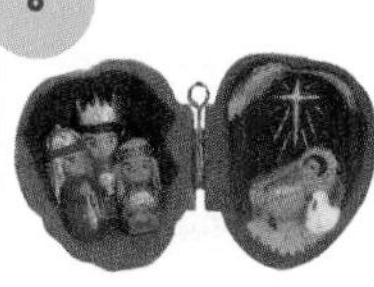
Nutshell Nativity
Handcrafted • RGRS
675QX5176 • **Value $28**

9

Nutty Squirrel
Handcrafted • PIKE
575QX4833 • **Value $16**

10

Old-Fashioned Sled
Handcrafted • SICK
875QX4317 • **Value $21**

11
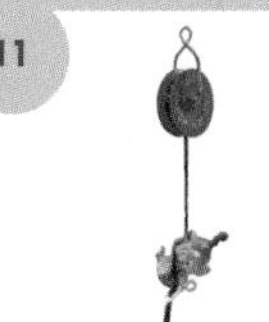

On a Roll
Handcrafted • CROW
675QX5347 • **Value $20**

12

Partridge in a Pear Tree
Handcrafted • SICK
975QX5297 • **Value $19**

13

PEANUTS®
Glass • N/A
500QX2257 • **Value $28**

14

Piglet and Eeyore
Handcrafted • SIED
975QX5577 • **Value $60**

15

Plum Delightful
Handcrafted • SEAL
875QX4977 • **Value $20**

16

Polar Circus Wagon
Handcrafted • SICK
1375QX4399 • **Value $27**

17

Polar Classic
Handcrafted • SIED
675QX5287 • **Value $21**

18

Rabbit
Handcrafted • SIED
975QX5607 • **Value $38**

19

Santa Sailor
Handcrafted/Metal • SEAL
975QX4389 • **Value $27**

20

Santa's Studio
Handcrafted • SEAL
875QX5397 • **Value $19**

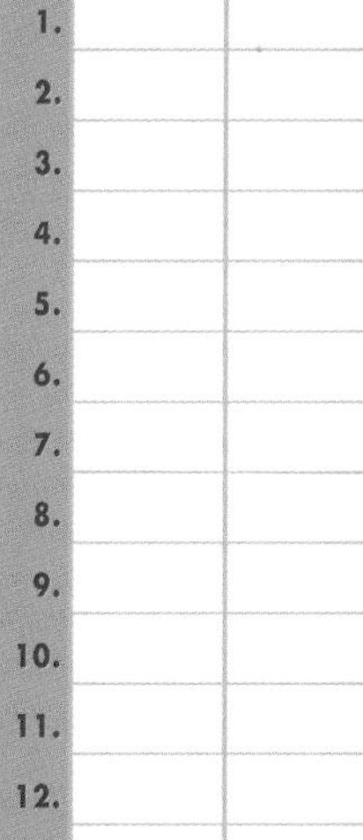

General Keepsake

	Price Paid	Value
1.		
2.		
3.		
4.		
5.		
6.		
7.		
8.		
9.		
10.		
11.		
12.		
13.		
14.		
15.		
16.		
17.		
18.		
19.		
20.		
Totals		

1

Sister
Handcrafted • LYLE
675QX5487 • **Value $20**

2

Ski Lift Bunny
Handcrafted • JLEE
675QX5447 • **Value $20**

3

SNOOPY® and WOODSTOCK
Handcrafted • RHOD
675QX5197 • **Value $37**

4

Snow Twins
Handcrafted • SEAL
875QX4979 • **Value $22**

5

Snowy Owl
Handcrafted • SICK
775QX5269 • **Value $20**

6

Son
Handcrafted • SIED
575QX5469 • **Value $20**

7

Sweet Talk
Handcrafted • UNRU
875QX5367 • **Value $28**

8

Sweetheart
Porcelain • N/A
975QX4957 • **Value $27**

9

Teacher
Glass • RGRS
475QX2289 • **Value $13**

10

Ten Years Together
Faceted Glass • N/A
775QX4929 • **Value $19**

11

Terrific Teacher
Handcrafted • SICK
675QX5309 • **Value $18**

12

Tigger
Handcrafted • SIED
975QX5609 • **Value $130**

13

Tiny Tim
Porcelain • UNRU
1075QX5037 • **Value $42**

14

Tramp and Laddie
Handcrafted • FRAN
775QX4397 • **Value $47**

15

Twenty-Five Years Together Photoholder
Handcrafted/Chrome • VOTR
875QX4937 • **Value $16**

16

Under the Mistletoe
Handcrafted • PIKE
875QX4949 • **Value $22**

17

Up 'N' Down Journey
Handcrafted • CROW
975QX5047 • **Value $30**

18

Winnie-the-Pooh
Handcrafted • SIED
975QX5569 • **Value $59**

19

Yule Logger
Handcrafted • SEAL
875QX4967 • **Value $24**

20

Arctic Dome
Handcrafted • CROW
2500QLX7117 • **Value $58**

General Keepsake

	Price Paid	Value
1.		
2.		
3.		
4.		
5.		
6.		
7.		
8.		
9.		
10.		
11.		
12.		
13.		
14.		
15.		
16.		
17.		
18.		
19.		

General Magic

	Price Paid	Value
20.		
Totals		

1991 Collection

1

Baby's First Christmas
Handcrafted • SEAL
3000QLX7247 • **Value $100**

2

Bringing Home the Tree
Handcrafted • UNRU
2800QLX7249 • **Value $65**

3

Elfin Engineer
Handcrafted • CHAD
1000QLX7209 • **Value $27**

4

Father Christmas
Handcrafted • UNRU
1400QLX7147 • **Value $40**

5

Festive Brass Church
Brass • MCGE
1400QLX7179 • **Value $35**

6

First Christmas Together
Handcrafted • SICK
2500QLX7137 • **Value $57**

7

Friendship Tree
Handcrafted • DUTK
1000QLX7169 • **Value $27**

8

Holiday Glow
Panorama Ball • PIKE
1400QLX7177 • **Value $32**

9

It's a Wonderful Life
Handcrafted • DLEE
2000QLX7237 • **Value $75**

10

Jingle Bears
Handcrafted • JLEE
2500QLX7323 • **Value $56**

11
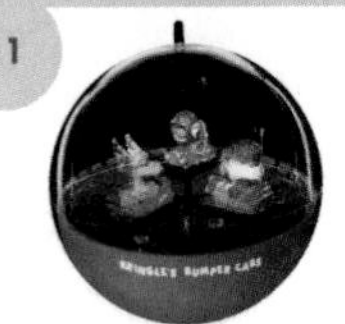
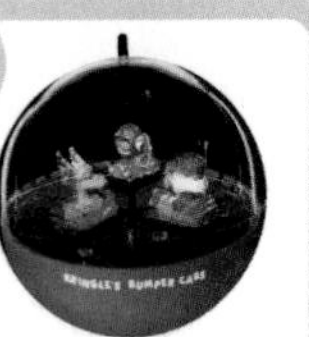
Kringle's Bumper Cars
Handcrafted • SICK
2500QLX7119 • **Value $58**

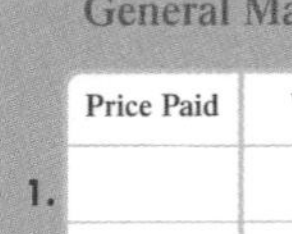

12

Mole Family Home
Handcrafted • JLEE
2000QLX7149 • **Value $48**

13

Salvation Army Band
Handcrafted • UNRU
3000QLX7273 • **Value $77**

14

Santa Special (re-issued in 1992)
Handcrafted • SEAL
4000QLX7167 • **Value $80**

15

Santa's Hot Line
Handcrafted • CROW
1800QLX7159 • **Value $42**

16
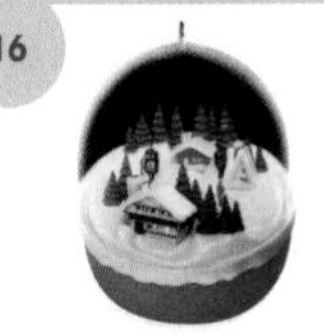
Ski Trip
Handcrafted • SEAL
2800QLX7266 • **Value $63**

17

Sparkling Angel
Handcrafted • CHAD
1800QLX7157 • **Value $40**

18

Starship Enterprise™
Handcrafted • NORT
2000QLX7199 • **Value $395**

19

Toyland Tower
Handcrafted • CROW
2000QLX7129 • **Value $47**

20

All Aboard
Handcrafted • CHAD
450QXM5869 • **Value $18**

General Magic

	Price Paid	Value
1.		
2.		
3.		
4.		
5.		
6.		
7.		
8.		
9.		
10.		
11.		
12.		
13.		
14.		
15.		
16.		
17.		
18.		
19.		
General Miniature		
20.		
Totals		

1

Baby's First Christmas
Handcrafted • FRAN
600QXM5799 • **Value $22**

2

Brass Bells
Brass • ANDR
300QXM5977 • **Value $11**

3

Brass Church
Brass • N/A
300QXM5979 • **Value $11**

4

Brass Soldier
Brass • N/A
300QXM5987 • **Value $11**

5

Bright Boxers
Handcrafted • RHOD
450QXM5877 • **Value $16**

6

Busy Bear
Wood • RHOD
450QXM5939 • **Value $12**

7

Cardinal Cameo
Handcrafted • LYLE
600QXM5957 • **Value $19**

8
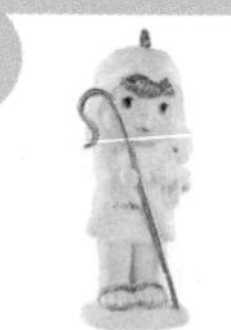

Caring Shepherd
Porcelain • FRAN
600QXM5949 • **Value $18**

9

Cool 'n Sweet
Porcelain • PIKE
450QXM5867 • **Value $24**

10

Country Sleigh
Enamel • VOTR
450QXM5999 • **Value $16**

11

Courier Turtle
Handcrafted • PIKE
450QXM5857 • **Value $15**

12

Fancy Wreath
Handcrafted • LYLE
450QXM5917 • **Value $13**

13

Feliz Navidad
Handcrafted/Straw • RGRS
600QXM5887 • **Value $17**

14

First Christmas Together
Handcrafted/Brass • UNRU
600QXM5819 • **Value $17**

15

Fly By
Handcrafted • CROW
450QXM5859 • **Value $17**

16

Friendly Fawn
Handcrafted • JLEE
600QXM5947 • **Value $17**

17

Grandchild's First Christmas
Porcelain • RGRS
450QXM5697 • **Value $14**

18

Heavenly Minstrel
Handcrafted • DLEE
975QXM5687 • **Value $26**

19

Holiday Snowflake
Acrylic • RHOD
300QXM5997 • **Value $14**

20

Key to Love
Handcrafted • CROW
450QXM5689 • **Value $17**

General Miniature

	Price Paid	Value
1.		
2.		
3.		
4.		
5.		
6.		
7.		
8.		
9.		
10.		
11.		
12.		
13.		
14.		
15.		
16.		
17.		
18.		
19.		
20.		
Totals		

1
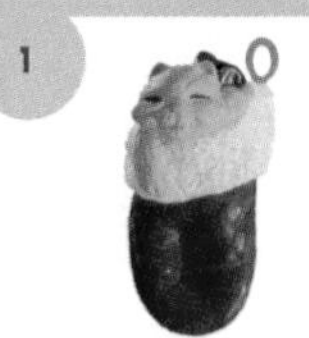
Kitty in a Mitty
Handcrafted • ANDR
450QXM5879 • **Value $13**

2

Li'l Popper
Handcrafted • SICK
450QXM5897 • **Value $22**

3

Love Is Born
Porcelain • VOTR
600QXM5959 • **Value $21**

4

Lulu & Family
Handcrafted • RGRS
600QXM5677 • **Value $23**

5

Mom
Handcrafted • SIED
600QXM5699 • **Value $19**

6

N. Pole Buddy
Handcrafted • PALM
450QXM5927 • **Value $18**

7

Noel
Acrylic • N/A
300QXM5989 • **Value $14**

8

Ring-A-Ding Elf
Handcrafted/Brass • CHAD
850QXM5669 • **Value $21**

9

Seaside Otter
Handcrafted • SIED
450QXM5909 • **Value $14**

10

Silvery Santa
Silver-Plated • JLEE
975QXM5679 • **Value $23**

11

Special Friends
Handcrafted/Wicker • JLEE
850QXM5797 • **Value $20**

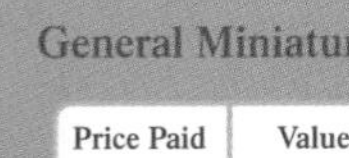

12

Tiny Tea Party Set (set/6)
Handcrafted/Porcelain • SEAL
2900QXM5827 • **Value $165**

13

Top Hatter
Handcrafted • SEAL
600QXM5889 • **Value $18**

14

Treeland Trio
Handcrafted • CHAD
850QXM5899 • **Value $18**

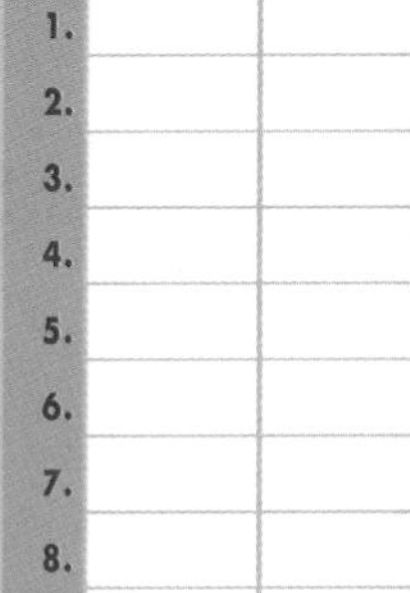

15
Upbeat Bear
Handcrafted/Metal • FRAN
600QXM5907 • **Value $17**

16

Vision of Santa
Handcrafted • CHAD
450QXM5937 • **Value $14**

17
Wee Toymaker
Handcrafted • BISH
850QXM5967 • **Value $17**

18

Beary Artistic
(club edition, magic)
Handcrafted/Acrylic • SIED
1000QXC7259 • **Value $38**

19

Five Years Together
(charter member gift)
Acrylic • N/A
QXC3159 • **Value $58**

20

Galloping Into Christmas
(club edition, LE-28,400)
Pressed Tin • SICK
1975QXC4779 • **Value $115**

General Miniature

	Price Paid	Value
1.		
2.		
3.		
4.		
5.		
6.		
7.		
8.		
9.		
10.		
11.		
12.		
13.		
14.		
15.		
16.		
17.		

Collector's Club

18.		
19.		
20.		

Totals

1

Hidden Treasure & Li'l Keeper (set/2, keepsake of membership)
Handcrafted • CROW
QXC4769 • **Value $45**

2

Secrets for Santa (club edition, LE-28,700)
Handcrafted • RGRS
2375QXC4797 • **Value $60**

3

Santa's Premiere
Porcelain • N/A
1075QX5237 • **Value $35**

4

Caboose
Claus & Co. R.R.
Handcrafted • PALM
($3.95)411XPR9733 • **Value $20**

5
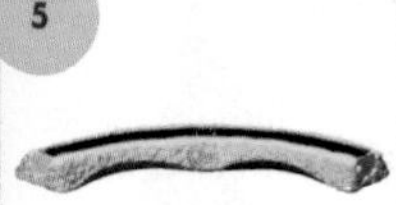
Claus & Co. R.R. Trestle Display Stand
Claus & Co. R.R.
Handcrafted • PALM
($2.95)411XPR9734 • **Value $12**

6

Gift Car
Claus & Co. R.R.
Handcrafted • PALM
($3.95)411XPR9731 • **Value $15**

7

Locomotive
Claus & Co. R.R.
Handcrafted • PALM
($3.95)411XPR9730 • **Value $34**

8

Passenger Car
Claus & Co. R.R.
Handcrafted • PALM
($3.95)411XPR9732 • **Value $15**

9

Baby's Christening 1991
Porcelain • JLEE
1000BBY1317 • **Value $18**

10

Baby's First Christmas 1991
Porcelain • JLEE
1000BBY1416 • **Value $18**

11
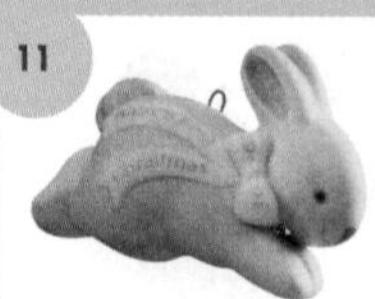
Baby's First Christmas 1991
Porcelain • RGRS
1000BBY1514 • **Value $18**

12

Kansas City Santa
Silver-Plated • N/A
(N/C) No stock # • **Value $1000**

1990

The 1990 collection included an adorable group of six "polar penguins" as well as the first of four porcelain ornaments in the "Dickens Caroler Bell" collection. In all, there were 128 Keepsake ornaments, 21 Magic ornaments and a whopping 54 Miniature ornaments in the 1990 line. See the collectible series section for more 1990 ornaments.

13

Across the Miles
Acrylic • VOTR
675QX3173 • **Value $17**

14

Angel Kitty
Handcrafted • PYDA
875QX4746 • **Value $25**

15

Baby Unicorn
Porcelain • RGRS
975QX5486 • **Value $23**

	Price Paid	Value
Collector's Club		
1.		
2.		
Premiere Ornaments		
3.		
Reach Ornaments		
4.		
5.		
6.		
7.		
8.		
Baby Celebrations		
9.		
10.		
11.		
Convention Ornaments		
12.		
General Keepsake		
13.		
14.		
15.		
Totals		

1

Baby's First Christmas
Acrylic • RGRS
675QX3036 • **Value $23**

2

Baby's First Christmas
Handcrafted • FRAN
775QX4856 • **Value $40**

3

Baby's First Christmas
Handcrafted • FRAN
975QX4853 • **Value $23**

4

Baby's First Christmas – Baby Boy
Satin • N/A
475QX2063 • **Value $24**

5
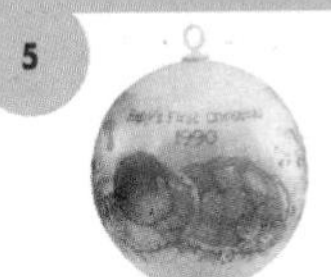
Baby's First Christmas – Baby Girl
Satin • N/A
475QX2066 • **Value $24**

6

Baby's First Christmas Photoholder
Fabric • N/A
775QX4843 • **Value $30**

7

Baby's Second Christmas
Handcrafted • FRAN
675QX4863 • **Value $38**

8

Bearback Rider
Handcrafted • CROW
975QX5483 • **Value $31**

9

Beary Good Deal
Handcrafted • SIED
675QX4733 • **Value $16**

10

Billboard Bunny
Handcrafted • JLEE
775QX5196 • **Value $21**

11

Born to Dance
Handcrafted • PIKE
775QX5043 • **Value $23**

12

Brother
Handcrafted • SIED
575QX4493 • **Value $14**

13
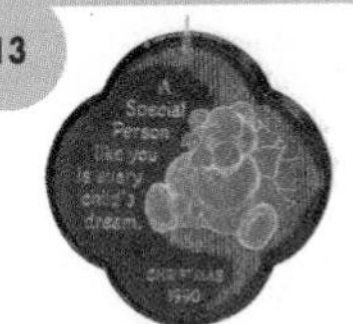
Child Care Giver
Acrylic • N/A
675QX3166 • **Value $13**

14

Child's Fifth Christmas
Handcrafted • RHOD
675QX4876 • **Value $21**

15

Child's Fourth Christmas
Handcrafted • FRAN
675QX4873 • **Value $21**

16

Child's Third Christmas
Handcrafted • FRAN
675QX4866 • **Value $25**

17
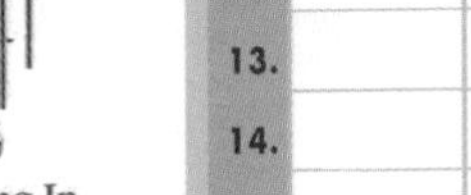
Chiming In
Handcrafted/Brass • PIKE
975QX4366 • **Value $23**

18

Christmas Croc
Handcrafted • PYDA
775QX4373 • **Value $25**

19
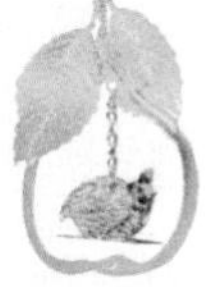
Christmas Partridge
Dimensional Brass • SICK
775QX5246 • **Value $23**

20

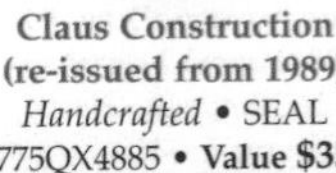
Claus Construction (re-issued from 1989)
Handcrafted • SEAL
775QX4885 • **Value $35**

General Keepsake

	Price Paid	Value
1.		
2.		
3.		
4.		
5.		
6.		
7.		
8.		
9.		
10.		
11.		
12.		
13.		
14.		
15.		
16.		
17.		
18.		
19.		
20.		

Totals

1

Copy of Cheer
Handcrafted • SIED
775QX4486 • **Value $18**

2

Country Angel (cancelled after limited production)
Handcrafted • N/A
675QX5046 • **Value $195**

3

Coyote Carols
Handcrafted • JLEE
875QX4993 • **Value $27**

4

Cozy Goose
Handcrafted • PIKE
575QX4966 • **Value $15**

5

Dad
Handcrafted • JLEE
675QX4533 • **Value $17**

6

Dad-to-Be
Handcrafted • SIED
575QX4913 • **Value $22**

7

Daughter
Handcrafted • SIED
575QX4496 • **Value $22**

8

Dickens Caroler Bell – Mr. Ashbourne
Porcelain • CHAD
2175QX5056 • **Value $49**

9

Donder's Diner
Handcrafted • DLEE
1375QX4823 • **Value $22**

10

Feliz Navidad
Handcrafted • N/A
675QX5173 • **Value $28**

11

Fifty Years Together
Faceted Glass • PATT
975QX4906 • **Value $20**

12
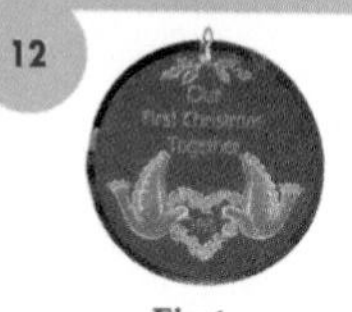
First Christmas Together
Acrylic • VOTR
675QX3146 • **Value $27**

13

First Christmas Together
Glass • VOTR
475QX2136 • **Value $27**

14
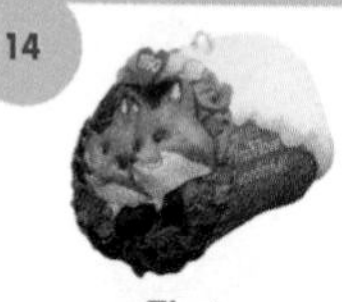
First Christmas Together
Handcrafted • PYDA
975QX4883 • **Value $26**

15

First Christmas Together – Photoholder
Fabric • VOTR
775QX4886 • **Value $20**

16
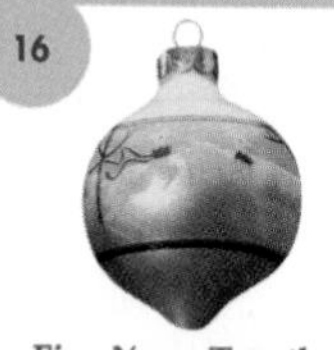
Five Years Together
Glass • VOTR
475QX2103 • **Value $17**

17

Forty Years Together
Faceted Glass • PATT
975QX4903 • **Value $19**

18
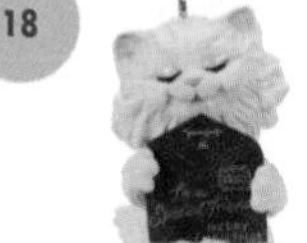
Friendship Kitten
Handcrafted • RHOD
675QX4143 • **Value $25**

19
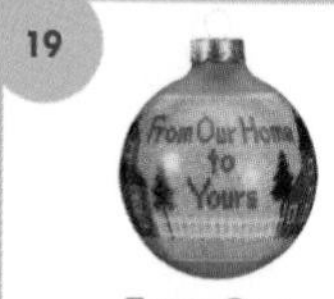

From Our Home to Yours
Glass • N/A
475QX2166 • **Value $23**

20

GARFIELD®
Glass • N/A
475QX2303 • **Value $25**

General Keepsake

	Price Paid	Value
1.		
2.		
3.		
4.		
5.		
6.		
7.		
8.		
9.		
10.		
11.		
12.		
13.		
14.		
15.		
16.		
17.		
18.		
19.		
20.		
Totals		

1

Gentle Dreamers
Handcrafted • FRAN
875QX4756 • **Value $32**

2

Gingerbread Elf
Handcrafted • N/A
575QX5033 • **Value $20**

3

Godchild
Acrylic • FRAN
675QX3176 • **Value $20**

4

Golf's My Bag
Handcrafted • JLEE
775QX4963 • **Value $30**

5

Goose Cart
Handcrafted • N/A
775QX5236 • **Value $16**

6

Granddaughter
Glass • LYLE
475QX2286 • **Value $27**

7

Granddaughter's First Christmas
Acrylic • FRAN
675QX3106 • **Value $21**

8

Grandmother
Glass • VOTR
475QX2236 • **Value $19**

9

Grandparents
Glass • N/A
475QX2253 • **Value $19**

10

Grandson
Glass • VOTR
475QX2293 • **Value $20**

11

Grandson's First Christmas
Acrylic • FRAN
675QX3063 • **Value $21**

12

Hang in There
Handcrafted • SEAL
675QX4713 • **Value $23**

13

Happy Voices
Wood • VOTR
675QX4645 • **Value $16**

14
Happy Woodcutter
Handcrafted • JLEE
975QX4763 • **Value $23**

15

Holiday Cardinals
Dimensional Brass • LYLE
775QX5243 • **Value $24**

16

Home for the Owlidays
Handcrafted • N/A
675QX5183 • **Value $17**

17

Hot Dogger
Handcrafted • CROW
775QX4976 • **Value $19**

18

Jesus Loves Me
Acrylic • PATT
675QX3156 • **Value $16**

19
Jolly Dolphin
Handcrafted • RGRS
675QX4683 • **Value $36**

20

Joy is in the Air
Handcrafted • CROW
775QX5503 • **Value $27**

General Keepsake

	Price Paid	Value
1.		
2.		
3.		
4.		
5.		
6.		
7.		
8.		
9.		
10.		
11.		
12.		
13.		
14.		
15.		
16.		
17.		
18.		
19.		
20.		
Totals		

1

King Klaus
Handcrafted • SEAL
775QX4106 • **Value $20**

2

Kitty's Best Pal
Handcrafted • FRAN
675QX4716 • **Value $23**

3

Little Drummer Boy
Handcrafted • UNRU
775QX5233 • **Value $22**

4

Long Winter's Nap
Handcrafted • RGRS
675QX4703 • **Value $29**

5

Loveable Dears
Handcrafted • UNRU
875QX5476 • **Value $21**

6

Meow Mart
Handcrafted • PIKE
775QX4446 • **Value $28**

7

Mom and Dad
Handcrafted • CHAD
875QX4593 • **Value $27**

8

Mom-to-Be
Handcrafted • SIED
575QX4916 • **Value $33**

9

Mooy Christmas
Handcrafted • N/A
675QX4933 • **Value $32**

10

Mother
Ceramic/Bisque • VOTR
875QX4536 • **Value $24**

11

Mouseboat
Handcrafted • SEAL
775QX4753 • **Value $17**

12

New Home
Handcrafted • PYDA
675QX4343 • **Value $29**

13

Norman Rockwell Art
Glass • LYLE
475QX2296 • **Value $26**

14
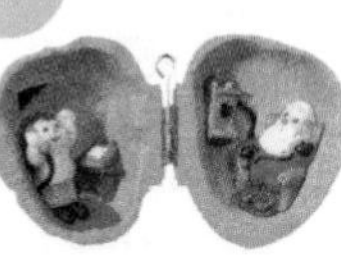
Nutshell Chat
Handcrafted • N/A
675QX5193 • **Value $27**

15
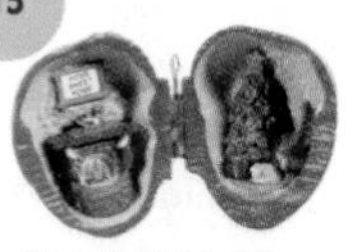
Nutshell Holiday
(re-issued from 1989)
Handcrafted • RGRS
575QX4652 • **Value $27**

16

Peaceful Kingdom
Glass • N/A
475QX2106 • **Value $24**

17

PEANUTS®
Glass • N/A
475QX2233 • **Value $27**

18

Pepperoni Mouse
Handcrafted • SIED
675QX4973 • **Value $19**

19

Perfect Catch
Handcrafted • SIED
775QX4693 • **Value $20**

20

Polar Jogger
Handcrafted • SIED
575QX4666 • **Value $19**

General Keepsake

	Price Paid	Value
1.		
2.		
3.		
4.		
5.		
6.		
7.		
8.		
9.		
10.		
11.		
12.		
13.		
14.		
15.		
16.		
17.		
18.		
19.		
20.		
Totals		

1
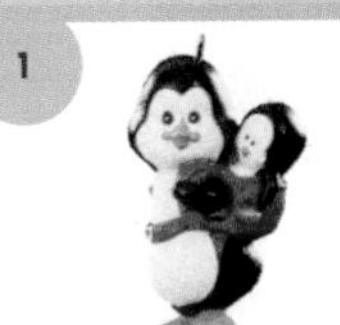
Polar Pair
Handcrafted • SIED
575QX4626 • **Value $26**

2

Polar Sport
Handcrafted • SIED
775QX5156 • **Value $24**

3

Polar TV
Handcrafted • SIED
775QX5166 • **Value $19**

4

Polar V.I.P.
Handcrafted • SIED
575QX4663 • **Value $18**

5

Polar Video
Handcrafted • SIED
575QX4633 • **Value $18**

6

Poolside Walrus
Handcrafted • JLEE
775QX4986 • **Value $24**

7

S. Claus Taxi
Handcrafted • DUTK
1175QX4686 • **Value $28**

8

Santa Schnoz
Handcrafted • CROW
675QX4983 • **Value $32**

9

Sister
Glass • N/A
475QX2273 • **Value $23**

10

SNOOPY and WOODSTOCK
Handcrafted • RHOD
675QX4723 • **Value $38**

11

Son
Handcrafted • SIED
575QX4516 • **Value $27**

12

Spencer® Sparrow, Esq. (re-issued from 1989)
Handcrafted • PIKE
675QX4312 • **Value $25**

13

Spoon Rider
Handcrafted • ANDR
975QX5496 • **Value $20**

14

Stitches of Joy
Handcrafted • JLEE
775QX5186 • **Value $25**

15

Stocking Kitten (re-issued from 1989)
Handcrafted • PIKE
675QX4565 • **Value $21**

16

Stocking Pals
Handcrafted • SEAL
1075QX5493 • **Value $26**

17

Sweetheart
Handcrafted • RHOD
1175QX4893 • **Value $29**

18

Teacher
Handcrafted • SEAL
775QX4483 • **Value $15**

19

Ten Years Together
Glass • LYLE
475QX2153 • **Value $22**

20

Three Little Piggies
Handcrafted • CROW
775QX4996 • **Value $26**

General Keepsake

	Price Paid	Value
1.		
2.		
3.		
4.		
5.		
6.		
7.		
8.		
9.		
10.		
11.		
12.		
13.		
14.		
15.		
16.		
17.		
18.		
19.		
20.		
Totals		

1

Time for Love
Glass • LYLE
475QX2133 • **Value $26**

2

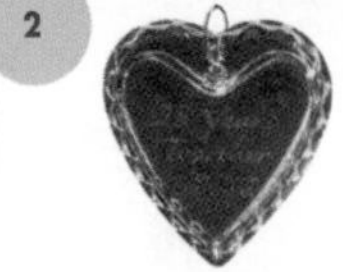

Twenty-Five Years Together
Faceted Glass • PATT
975QX4896 • **Value $21**

3

Two Peas in a Pod
Handcrafted • ANDR
475QX4926 • **Value $35**

4

Welcome, Santa
Handcrafted • CROW
1175QX4773 • **Value $26**

5

Baby's First Christmas
Handcrafted • PALM
2800QLX7246 • **Value $62**

6

Beary Short Nap
Handcrafted • SIED
1000QLX7326 • **Value $31**

7

Blessings of Love
Panorama Ball • N/A
1400QLX7363 • **Value $52**

8

Children's Express
Handcrafted • SICK
2800QLX7243 • **Value $77**

9

Christmas Memories
Handcrafted • UNRU
2500QLX7276 • **Value $56**

10

Deer Crossing
Handcrafted • SIED
1800QLX7213 • **Value $48**

11

Elf of the Year
Handcrafted • ANDR
1000QLX7356 • **Value $25**

12

Elfin Whittler
Handcrafted • CROW
2000QLX7265 • **Value $52**

13

First Christmas Together
Handcrafted • DLEE
1800QLX7255 • **Value $46**

14

Holiday Flash
Handcrafted • CHAD
1800QLX7333 • **Value $39**

15

Hop 'N Pop Popper
Handcrafted • SIED
2000QLX7353 • **Value $95**

16

Letter to Santa
Handcrafted • RGRS
1400QLX7226 • **Value $37**

17

Mrs. Santa's Kitchen
Handcrafted • RHOD
2500QLX7263 • **Value $70**

18

Partridges in a Pear
Dimensional Brass • LYLE
1400QLX7212 • **Value $35**

19

Santa's Ho-Ho-Hoedown
Handcrafted • CROW
2500QLX7256 • **Value $90**

20

Song and Dance
Handcrafted • RGRS
2000QLX7253 • **Value $93**

General Keepsake

	Price Paid	Value
1.		
2.		
3.		
4.		

General Magic

	Price Paid	Value
5.		
6.		
7.		
8.		
9.		
10.		
11.		
12.		
13.		
14.		
15.		
16.		
17.		
18.		
19.		
20.		
Totals		

1

Starlight Angel
Handcrafted • RGRS
1400QLX7306 • **Value $38**

2

Starship Christmas
Handcrafted • SIED
1800QLX7336 • **Value $50**

3

Acorn Squirrel
(re-issued from 1989)
Handcrafted • PIKE
450QXM5682 • **Value $13**

4

Acorn Wreath
Handcrafted • CROW
600QXM5686 • **Value $13**

5

Air Santa
Handcrafted • N/A
450QXM5656 • **Value $15**

6

Baby's First Christmas
Handcrafted • FRAN
850QXM5703 • **Value $17**

7

Basket Buddy
Handcrafted/Wicker • RGRS
600QXM5696 • **Value $13**

8

Bear Hug
Handcrafted • PALM
600QXM5633 • **Value $14**

9

Brass Bouquet
Brass • LYLE
600QXM5776 • **Value $7**

10
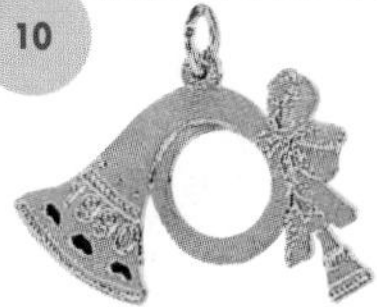
Brass Horn
Brass • N/A
300QXM5793 • **Value $10**

11

Brass Peace
Brass • N/A
300QXM5796 • **Value $10**

12

Brass Santa
Brass • PATT
300QXM5786 • **Value $8**

13

Brass Year
Brass • N/A
300QXM5833 • **Value $8**

14

Busy Carver
Handcrafted • CROW
450QXM5673 • **Value $10**

15

Christmas Dove
Handcrafted • SIED
450QXM5636 • **Value $16**

16

Cloisonné Poinsettia
Cloisonné • VOTR
1050QXM5533 • **Value $24**

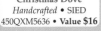

17
Country Heart
Handcrafted • RGRS
450QXM5693 • **Value $10**

18

Cozy Skater
(re-issued from 1989)
Handcrafted • LYLE
450QXM5735 • **Value $14**

19

First Christmas Together
Porcelain • ANDR
600QXM5536 • **Value $13**

20

Going Sledding
Handcrafted • JLEE
450QXM5683 • **Value $17**

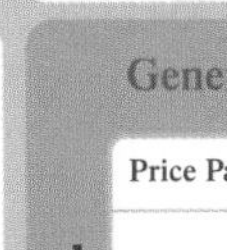
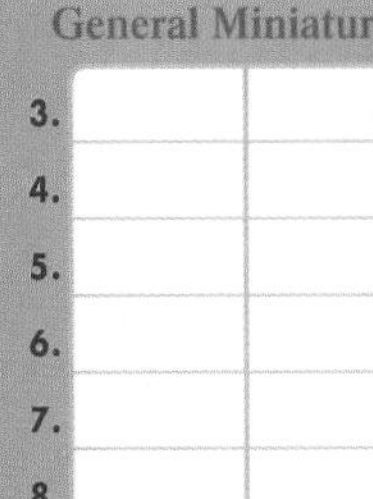

General Magic

	Price Paid	Value
1.		
2.		

General Miniature

	Price Paid	Value
3.		
4.		
5.		
6.		
7.		
8.		
9.		
10.		
11.		
12.		
13.		
14.		
15.		
16.		
17.		
18.		
19.		
20.		
Totals		

1

Grandchild's First Christmas
Handcrafted • SIED
600QXM5723 • **Value $12**

2

Happy Bluebird (re-issued from 1989)
Handcrafted • RGRS
450QXM5662 • **Value $15**

3

Holiday Cardinal
Acrylic • FRAN
300QXM5526 • **Value $13**

4

Lion and Lamb
Wood • SICK
450QXM5676 • **Value $11**

5

Little Soldier (re-issued from 1989)
Handcrafted • SICK
450QXM5675 • **Value $12**

6

Loving Hearts
Acrylic • N/A
300QXM5523 • **Value $13**

7

Madonna and Child
Handcrafted • RGRS
600QXM5643 • **Value $13**

8

Mother
Cameo • LYLE
450QXM5716 • **Value $17**

9

Nativity
Handcrafted • UNRU
450QXM5706 • **Value $21**

10

Old-World Santa (re-issued from 1989)
Handcrafted • SIED
300QXM5695 • **Value $11**

11

Panda's Surprise
Handcrafted • FRAN
450QXM5616 • **Value $13**

12

Perfect Fit
Handcrafted • CHAD
450QXM5516 • **Value $15**

13

Puppy Love
Handcrafted • PALM
600QXM5666 • **Value $14**

14

Roly-Poly Pig (re-issued from 1989)
Handcrafted • PIKE
300QXM5712 • **Value $19**

15

Ruby Reindeer
Glass • PATT
600QXM5816 • **Value $13**

16

Santa's Journey
Handcrafted • SICK
850QXM5826 • **Value $21**

17

Santa's Streetcar
Handcrafted • DLEE
850QXM5766 • **Value $19**

18
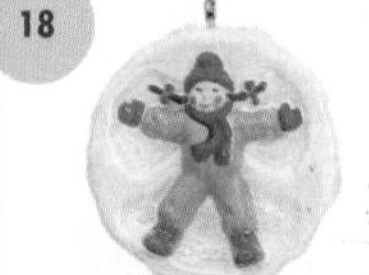
Snow Angel
Handcrafted • JLEE
600QXM5773 • **Value $14**

19

Special Friends
Handcrafted • PIKE
600QXM5726 • **Value $15**

20

Stamp Collector
Handcrafted • CROW
450QXM5623 • **Value $11**

General Miniature

	Price Paid	Value
1.		
2.		
3.		
4.		
5.		
6.		
7.		
8.		
9.		
10.		
11.		
12.		
13.		
14.		
15.		
16.		
17.		
18.		
19.		
20.		
Totals		

1

Stocking Pal
(re-issued from 1989)
Handcrafted • JLEE
450QXM5672 • **Value $12**

2

Stringing Along
Handcrafted • SEAL
850QXM5606 • **Value $17**

3

Sweet Slumber
Handcrafted • SIED
450QXM5663 • **Value $12**

4

Teacher
Handcrafted • PIKE
450QXM5653 • **Value $10**

5

Type of Joy
Handcrafted • CHAD
450QXM5646 • **Value $11**

6

Warm Memories
Handcrafted • SEAL
450QXM5713 • **Value $10**

7

Wee Nutcracker
Handcrafted • SIED
850QXM5843 • **Value $16**

8

Armful of Joy
(members only ornament)
Handcrafted • FRAN
975QXC4453 • **Value $46**

9

Christmas Limited
(club edition, LE-38,700)
Die-Cast Metal • SICK
1975QXC4766 • **Value $108**

10

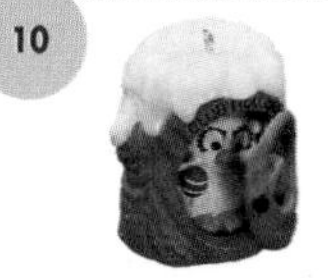

Club Hollow
(keepsake of membership)
Handcrafted • CROW
QXC4456 • **Value $38**

11

Crown Prince
(keepsake of
membership, miniature)
Handcrafted • RGRS
QXC5603 • **Value $37**

12

Dove of Peace
(club edition, LE-25,400)
Porcelain/Brass • SICK
2475QXC4476 • **Value $77**

13

Sugar Plum Fairy
(club edition, LE-25,400)
Porcelain • ANDR
2775QXC4473 • **Value $60**

14

Little Bear (miniature)
Handcrafted • SIED
($2.95)620XPR9723 • **Value $10**

15

Little Frosty (miniature)
Handcrafted • SIED
($2.95)620XPR9720 • **Value $11**

16

Little Husky (miniature)
Handcrafted • SEAL
($2.95)620XPR9722 • **Value $12**

17

Little Seal (miniature)
Handcrafted • JLEE
($2.95)620XPR9721 • **Value $10**

18

Memory Wreath
(miniature)
Handcrafted • DLEE
($2.95)620XPR9724 • **Value $10**

19

Baby's Christening 1990
Porcelain • JLEE
1000BBY1326 • **Value $27**

20

Baby's First
Christmas 1990
Handcrafted • JLEE
1000BBY1454 • **Value $27**

	Price Paid	Value
General Miniature		
1.		
2.		
3.		
4.		
5.		
6.		
7.		
Collector's Club		
8.		
9.		
10.		
11.		
12.		
13.		
Reach Ornaments		
14.		
15.		
16.		
17.		
18.		
Baby Celebrations		
19.		
20.		
Totals		

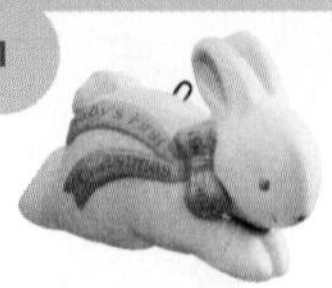

Baby's First Christmas 1990
Porcelain • RGRS
1000BBY1554 • **Value $27**

In 1989, Hallmark debuted a popular collection of dated teddy bear ornaments to help celebrate a child's first five Christmases. In the 1989 collection, there were a total of 123 Keepsake ornaments, 19 Magic ornaments and 41 Miniature ornaments. See the collectibles series section for more 1989 ornaments.

2

Baby Partridge
Handcrafted • FRAN
675QX4525 • **Value $15**

3

Baby's First Christmas
Acrylic • FRAN
675QX3815 • **Value $19**

4

Baby's First Christmas
Handcrafted • CHAD
725QX4492 • **Value $88**

5

Baby's First Christmas – Baby Boy
Satin • VOTR
475QX2725 • **Value $20**

6

Baby's First Christmas – Baby Girl
Satin • VOTR
475QX2722 • **Value $20**

7

Baby's First Christmas Photoholder
Handcrafted • VOTR
625QX4682 • **Value $52**

8

Baby's Second Christmas
Handcrafted • FRAN
675QX4495 • **Value $32**

9

Balancing Elf
Handcrafted • CHAD
675QX4895 • **Value $24**

10

Bear-i-Tone
Handcrafted • SIED
475QX4542 • **Value $20**

11

Brother
Handcrafted • LYLE
725QX4452 • **Value $20**

12

Cactus Cowboy
Handcrafted • DUTK
675QX4112 • **Value $44**

13

Camera Claus
Handcrafted • SIED
575QX5465 • **Value $22**

14

Carousel Zebra
Handcrafted • SICK
925QX4515 • **Value $24**

15

Cherry Jubilee
Handcrafted • SICK
500QX4532 • **Value $27**

16

Child's Fifth Christmas
Handcrafted • RHOD
675QX5435 • **Value $20**

17

Child's Fourth Christmas
Handcrafted • FRAN
675QX5432 • **Value $20**

Baby Celebrations

	Price Paid	Value
1.		

General Keepsake

	Price Paid	Value
2.		
3.		
4.		
5.		
6.		
7.		
8.		
9.		
10.		
11.		
12.		
13.		
14.		
15.		
16.		
17.		
Totals		

1

Child's Third Christmas
Handcrafted • FRAN
675QX4695 • **Value $23**

2

Claus Construction
(re-issued in 1990)
Handcrafted • SEAL
775QX4885 • **Value $35**

3

Cool Swing
Handcrafted • CROW
625QX4875 • **Value $35**

4

Country Cat
Handcrafted • PYDA
625QX4672 • **Value $21**

5

Cranberry Bunny
Handcrafted • RGRS
575QX4262 • **Value $18**

6

Dad
Handcrafted • N/A
725QX4412 • **Value $16**

7

Daughter
Handcrafted • SICK
625QX4432 • **Value $21**

8

Deer Disguise
Handcrafted • SIED
575QX4265 • **Value $25**

9

Feliz Navidad
Handcrafted • PYDA
675QX4392 • **Value $30**

10

Festive Angel
Dimensional Brass • N/A
675QX4635 • **Value $27**

11

Festive Year
Acrylic • VOTR
775QX3842 • **Value $23**

12

Fifty Years
Together Photoholder
Porcelain • RGRS
875QX4862 • **Value $17**

13

The First Christmas
Cameo • N/A
775QX5475 • **Value $20**

14

First Christmas Together
Acrylic • RHOD
675QX3832 • **Value $24**

15

First Christmas Together
Glass • N/A
475QX2732 • **Value $28**

16

First Christmas Together
Handcrafted • RGRS
975QX4852 • **Value $26**

17

Five Years Together
Glass • N/A
475QX2735 • **Value $20**

18
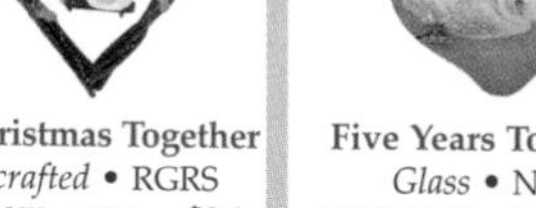
Forty Years
Together Photoholder
Porcelain • RGRS
875QX5452 • **Value $17**

19

Friendship Time
Handcrafted • N/A
975QX4132 • **Value $35**

20

From Our
Home to Yours
Acrylic • N/A
625QX3845 • **Value $22**

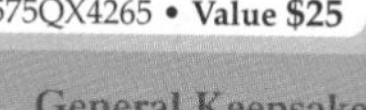

General Keepsake

	Price Paid	Value
1.		
2.		
3.		
4.		
5.		
6.		
7.		
8.		
9.		
10.		
11.		
12.		
13.		
14.		
15.		
16.		
17.		
18.		
19.		
20.		
Totals		

1

Gentle Fawn
Handcrafted • RGRS
775QX5485 • **Value $22**

2

George Washington Bicentennial
Acrylic • N/A
625QX3862 • **Value $19**

3

Godchild
Acrylic • FRAN
625QX3112 • **Value $18**

4

Goin' South
Handcrafted • CROW
425QX4105 • **Value $23**

5

Gone Fishing (re-issued from 1988)
Handcrafted • SIED
575QX4794 • **Value $24**

6

Graceful Swan
Dimensional Brass • N/A
675QX4642 • **Value $21**

7

Granddaughter
Glass • N/A
475QX2782 • **Value $26**

8
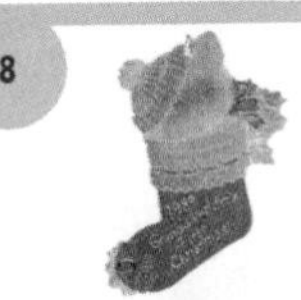
Granddaughter's First Christmas
Acrylic • FRAN
675QX3822 • **Value $22**

General Keepsake

	Price Paid	Value
1.		
2.		
3.		
4.		
5.		
6.		
7.		
8.		
9.		
10.		
11.		
12.		
13.		
14.		
15.		
16.		
17.		
18.		
19.		
20.		

Totals

9

Grandmother
Glass • LYLE
475QX2775 • **Value $18**

10
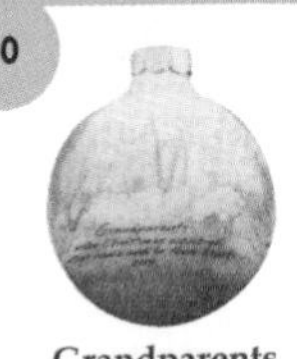
Grandparents
Glass • LYLE
475QX2772 • **Value $18**

11

Grandson
Glass • N/A
475QX2785 • **Value $22**

12

Grandson's First Christmas
Acrylic • FRAN
675QX3825 • **Value $18**

13

Gratitude
Acrylic • VOTR
675QX3852 • **Value $15**

14

Gym Dandy
Handcrafted • SIED
575QX4185 • **Value $20**

15

Hang in There
Handcrafted • CROW
525QX4305 • **Value $33**

16

Here's the Pitch
Handcrafted • SIED
575QX5455 • **Value $22**

17

Hoppy Holidays
Handcrafted • SIED
775QX4692 • **Value $24**

18
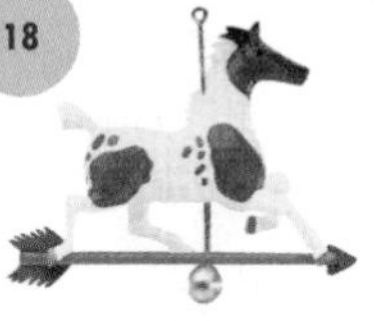
Horse Weathervane
Handcrafted • SICK
575QX4632 • **Value $18**

19

Joyful Trio
Handcrafted • FRAN
975QX4372 • **Value $17**

20

A KISS™ From Santa (re-issued from 1988)
Handcrafted • UNRU
450QX4821 • **Value $30**

1

Kristy Claus
Handcrafted • SIED
575QX4245 • **Value $15**

2

Language of Love
Acrylic • N/A
625QX3835 • **Value $25**

3

Let's Play
Handcrafted • CROW
725QX4882 • **Value $29**

4

Mail Call
Handcrafted • SEAL
875QX4522 • **Value $21**

5

Merry-Go-Round Unicorn
Porcelain • RGRS
1075QX4472 • **Value $24**

6

Mom and Dad
Handcrafted • PIKE
975QX4425 • **Value $22**

7

Mother
Porcelain • N/A
975QX4405 • **Value $30**

8

New Home
Glass • VOTR
475QX2755 • **Value $24**

9

Norman Rockwell
Glass • LYLE
475QX2762 • **Value $22**

10

North Pole Jogger
Handcrafted • SIED
575QX5462 • **Value $23**

11

Nostalgic Lamb
Handcrafted • PYDA
675QX4665 • **Value $16**

12

Nutshell Dreams
Handcrafted • CHAD
575QX4655 • **Value $24**

13

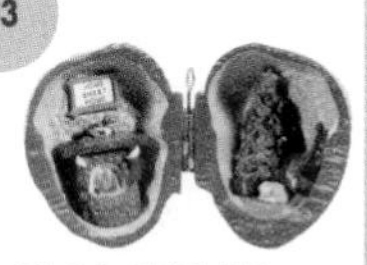

Nutshell Holiday (re-issued in 1990)
Handcrafted • RGRS
575QX4652 • **Value $27**

14

Nutshell Workshop
Handcrafted • CHAD
575QX4872 • **Value $24**

15

Old-World Gnome
Handcrafted • N/A
775QX4345 • **Value $24**

16

On the Links
Handcrafted • SIED
575QX4192 • **Value $23**

17

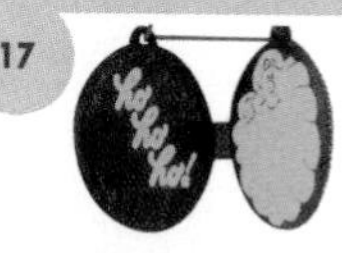

OREO® Chocolate Sandwich Cookies (re-issued from 1988)
Handcrafted • UNRU
400QX4814 • **Value $22**

18

The Ornament Express (set/3)
Handcrafted • SICK
2200QX5805 • **Value $45**

19

Owliday Greetings
Handcrafted • PIKE
400QX4365 • **Value $21**

20

Paddington™ Bear
Handcrafted • FRAN
575QX4292 • **Value $23**

General Keepsake

	Price Paid	Value
1.		
2.		
3.		
4.		
5.		
6.		
7.		
8.		
9.		
10.		
11.		
12.		
13.		
14.		
15.		
16.		
17.		
18.		
19.		
20.		
Totals		

1

Party Line
(re-issued from 1988)
Handcrafted • PIKE
875QX4761 • **Value $31**

2

PEANUTS® – A Charlie Brown Christmas
Glass • N/A
475QX2765 • **Value $47**

3

Peek-a-Boo Kitties
(re-issued from 1988)
Handcrafted • CROW
750QX4871 • **Value $25**

4

Peppermint Clown
Porcelain • DUTK
2475QX4505 • **Value $44**

5
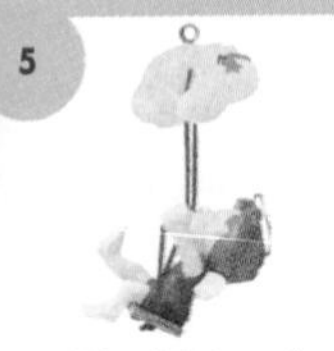
Playful Angel
Handcrafted • DLEE
675QX4535 • **Value $24**

6

Polar Bowler
(re-issued from 1988)
Handcrafted • SIED
575QX4784 • **Value $18**

7

Rodney Reindeer
Handcrafted • SIED
675QX4072 • **Value $16**

8

Rooster Weathervane
Handcrafted • SICK
575QX4675 • **Value $18**

9

Sea Santa
Handcrafted • SIED
575QX4152 • **Value $29**

10

Sister
Glass • N/A
475QX2792 • **Value $21**

11

SNOOPY and WOODSTOCK
Handcrafted • RHOD
675QX4332 • **Value $40**

12

Snowplow Santa
Handcrafted • SIED
575QX4205 • **Value $23**

13

Son
Handcrafted • SICK
625QX4445 • **Value $21**

14

Sparkling Snowflake
Brass • LYLE
775QX5472 • **Value $24**

15

Special Delivery
Handcrafted • RGRS
525QX4325 • **Value $24**

16

Spencer® Sparrow, Esq.
(re-issued in 1990)
Handcrafted • PIKE
675QX4312 • **Value $25**

17

Stocking Kitten
(re-issued in 1990)
Handcrafted • PIKE
675QX4565 • **Value $21**

18

Sweet Memories Photoholder
Handcrafted • N/A
675QX4385 • **Value $25**

19

Sweetheart
Handcrafted • SICK
975QX4865 • **Value $35**

20

Teacher
Handcrafted • SIED
575QX4125 • **Value $24**

General Keepsake

	Price Paid	Value
1.		
2.		
3.		
4.		
5.		
6.		
7.		
8.		
9.		
10.		
11.		
12.		
13.		
14.		
15.		
16.		
17.		
18.		
19.		
20.		
Totals		

1

Teeny Taster
(re-issued from 1988)
Handcrafted • SEAL
475QX4181 • **Value $31**

2

Ten Years Together
Glass • LYLE
475QX2742 • **Value $28**

3

TV Break
Handcrafted • DLEE
625QX4092 • **Value $20**

4

Twenty-Five Years Together Photoholder
Porcelain • RGRS
875QX4855 • **Value $17**

5

Wiggly Snowman
Handcrafted • RHOD
675QX4892 • **Value $29**

6

World of Love
Glass • N/A
475QX2745 • **Value $37**

7

Angel Melody
Acrylic • VOTR
950QLX7202 • **Value $24**

8

The Animals Speak
Panorama Ball • FRAN
1350QLX7232 • **Value $122**

9

Baby's First Christmas
Handcrafted • SEAL
3000QLX7272 • **Value $60**

10

Backstage Bear
Handcrafted • SIED
1350QLX7215 • **Value $37**

11

Busy Beaver
Handcrafted • DLEE
1750QLX7245 • **Value $50**

12

First Christmas Together
Handcrafted • DLEE
1750QLX7342 • **Value $45**

13

Holiday Bell
Lead Crystal • N/A
1750QLX7222 • **Value $36**

14

Joyous Carolers
Handcrafted • UNRU
3000QLX7295 • **Value $72**

15

Kringle's Toy Shop
(re-issued from 1988)
Handcrafted • SEAL
2450QLX7017 • **Value $54**

16
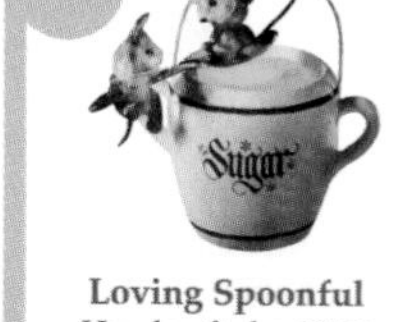
Loving Spoonful
Handcrafted • SIED
1950QLX7262 • **Value $40**

17

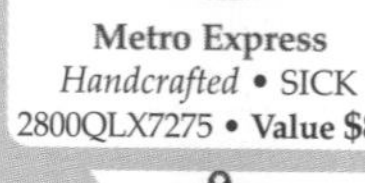
Metro Express
Handcrafted • SICK
2800QLX7275 • **Value $84**

18

Moonlit Nap
(re-issued from 1988)
Handcrafted • CHAD
875QLX7134 • **Value $29**

19
Rudolph the Red-Nosed Reindeer®
Handcrafted • CHAD
1950QLX7252 • **Value $62**

20

Spirit of St. Nick
Handcrafted • SEAL
2450QLX7285 • **Value $72**

General Keepsake

	Price Paid	Value
1.		
2.		
3.		
4.		
5.		
6.		

General Magic

	Price Paid	Value
7.		
8.		
9.		
10.		
11.		
12.		
13.		
14.		
15.		
16.		
17.		
18.		
19.		
20.		
Totals		

1

Tiny Tinker
Handcrafted • CROW
1950QLX7174 • **Value $58**

2

Unicorn Fantasy
Handcrafted • RHOD
950QLX7235 • **Value $23**

3

Acorn Squirrel
(re-issued in 1990)
Handcrafted • PIKE
450QXM5682 • **Value $13**

4

Baby's First Christmas
Handcrafted • PIKE
600QXM5732 • **Value $14**

5

Brass Partridge
Brass • LYLE
300QXM5725 • **Value $13**

6

Brass Snowflake
Dimensional Brass • LYLE
450QXM5702 • **Value $14**

7

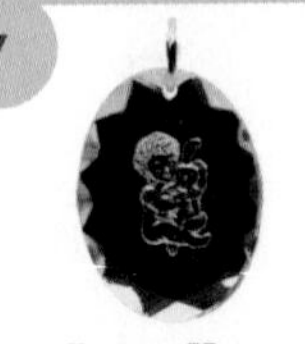

Bunny Hug
Acrylic • VOTR
300QXM5775 • **Value $11**

8

Country Wreath
(re-issued from 1988)
Handcrafted • RGRS
450QXM5731 • **Value $12**

9

Cozy Skater
(re-issued in 1990)
Handcrafted • LYLE
450QXM5735 • **Value $14**

10

First
Christmas Together
Ceramic • VOTR
850QXM5642 • **Value $12**

11

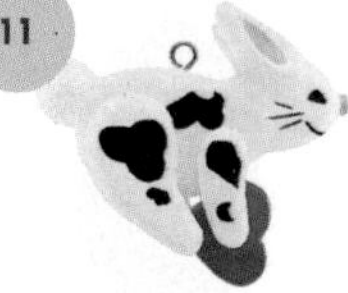

Folk Art Bunny
Handcrafted • PATT
450QXM5692 • **Value $12**

12

Happy Bluebird
(re-issued in 1990)
Handcrafted • RGRS
450QXM5662 • **Value $15**

13

Holiday Deer
Acrylic • VOTR
300QXM5772 • **Value $12**

14

Holy Family
(re-issued from 1988)
Handcrafted • UNRU
850QXM5611 • **Value $16**

15

Kitty Cart
Wood • PATT
300QXM5722 • **Value $11**

16

Little Soldier
(re-issued in 1990)
Handcrafted • SICK
450QXM5675 • **Value $12**

17

Little Star Bringer
Handcrafted • LYLE
600QXM5622 • **Value $21**

18

Load of Cheer
Handcrafted • RHOD
600QXM5745 • **Value $19**

19

Lovebirds
Handcrafted/Brass • PIKE
600QXM5635 • **Value $14**

20

Merry Seal
Porcelain • FRAN
600QXM5755 • **Value $16**

	Price Paid	Value
General Magic		
1.		
2.		
General Miniature		
3.		
4.		
5.		
6.		
7.		
8.		
9.		
10.		
11.		
12.		
13.		
14.		
15.		
16.		
17.		
18.		
19.		
20.		
Totals		

1

Mother
Cameo • N/A
600QXM5645 • **Value $13**

2

Old-World Santa
(re-issued in 1990)
Handcrafted • SIED
300QXM5695 • **Value $11**

3

Pinecone Basket
Handcrafted • RHOD
450QXM5734 • **Value $10**

4

Puppy Cart
Wood • SICK
300QXM5715 • **Value $10**

5

Rejoice
Acrylic • VOTR
300QXM5782 • **Value $10**

6

Roly-Poly Pig
(re-issued in 1990)
Handcrafted • PIKE
300QXM5712 • **Value $19**

7

Roly-Poly Ram
Handcrafted • N/A
300QXM5705 • **Value $16**

8

Santa's Magic Ride
Handcrafted • RGRS
850QXM5632 • **Value $21**

9

Santa's Roadster
Handcrafted • CROW
600QXM5665 • **Value $20**

10

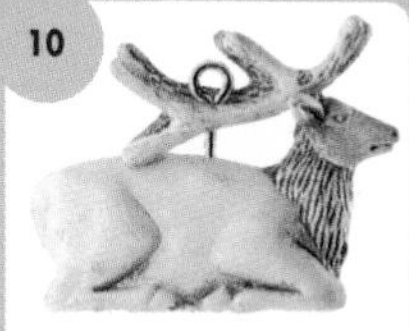

Scrimshaw Reindeer
Handcrafted • VOTR
450QXM5685 • **Value $12**

11

Sharing a Ride
Handcrafted • DUTK
850QXM5765 • **Value $18**

12

Slow Motion
Handcrafted • SIED
600QXM5752 • **Value $17**

13

Special Friend
Handcrafted/Willow • N/A
450QXM5652 • **Value $14**

14

Starlit Mouse
Handcrafted • RHOD
450QXM5655 • **Value $18**

15

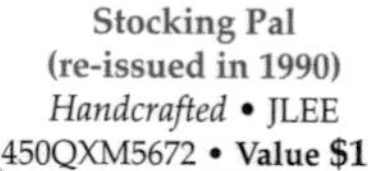

Stocking Pal
(re-issued in 1990)
Handcrafted • JLEE
450QXM5672 • **Value $12**

16

Strollin' Snowman
Porcelain • SIED
450QXM5742 • **Value $17**

17

Three Little Kitties
(re-issued from 1988)
Handcrafted/Willow • PIKE
600QXM5694 • **Value $18**

18

Christmas is Peaceful
(club edition, LE-49,900)
Bone China • SEAL
1850QXC4512 • **Value $47**

19

Collect a Dream
(club edition)
Handcrafted • PIKE
900QXC4285 • **Value $68**

20

Noelle
(club edition, LE-49,900)
Porcelain • UNRU
1975QXC4483 • **Value $58**

General Miniature

	Price Paid	Value
1.		
2.		
3.		
4.		
5.		
6.		
7.		
8.		
9.		
10.		
11.		
12.		
13.		
14.		
15.		
16.		
17.		

Collector's Club

	Price Paid	Value
18.		
19.		
20.		

Totals

1

Sitting Purrty (keepsake of membership, miniature)
Handcrafted • DUTK
QXC5812 • **Value $50**

2

Visit From Santa (keepsake of membership)
Handcrafted • CROW
QXC5802 • **Value $55**

3
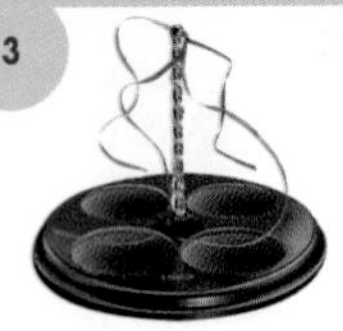
Carousel Display Stand
Handcrafted/Brass • N/A
($1.00)629XPR9723 • **Value $10**

4

Ginger
Handcrafted/Brass • JLEE
($3.95)629XPR9721 • **Value $20**

5

Holly
Handcrafted/Brass • JLEE
($3.95)629XPR9722 • **Value $20**

6

Snow
Handcrafted/Brass • JLEE
($3.95)629XPR9719 • **Value $33**

7

Star
Handcrafted/Brass • JLEE
($3.95)629XPR9720 • **Value $20**

8

Baby's Christening Keepsake
Acrylic • N/A
700BBY1325 • **Value $30**

9

Baby's First Birthday
Acrylic • N/A
550BBY1729 • **Value $30**

10

Baby's First Christmas – Baby Boy (same as #475QX2725)
Satin • VOTR
475BBY1453 • **Value $16**

11

Baby's First Christmas – Baby Girl (same as #475QX2722)
Satin • VOTR
475BBY1553 • **Value $16**

1988

1988 was the year that Hallmark introduced its famous collection of adorable Miniature ornaments to the Keepsake family. In its debut year, the Miniature line featured 27 ornaments, while the Keepsake line included 118 and the Magic line included 20 new designs. See the collectible series section for more 1988 ornaments.

12

Americana Drum
Tin • SICK
775QX4881 • **Value $34**

13

Arctic Tenor
Handcrafted • SIED
400QX4721 • **Value $17**

14

Baby Redbird
Handcrafted • CHAD
500QX4101 • **Value $22**

15

Baby's First Christmas
Acrylic • PIKE
600QX3721 • **Value $23**

16

Baby's First Christmas
Handcrafted • CROW
975QX4701 • **Value $40**

17

Baby's First Christmas – Baby Boy
Satin • N/A
475QX2721 • **Value $25**

	Price Paid	Value
Collector's Club		
1.		
2.		
Reach Ornaments		
3.		
4.		
5.		
6.		
7.		
Baby Celebrations		
8.		
9.		
10.		
11.		
General Keepsake		
12.		
13.		
14.		
15.		
16.		
17.		
Totals		

1

Baby's First Christmas – Baby Girl
Satin • N/A
475QX2724 • **Value $25**

2

Baby's First Christmas Photoholder
Fabric • N/A
750QX4704 • **Value $32**

3

Baby's Second Christmas
Handcrafted • PIKE
600QX4711 • **Value $35**

4

Babysitter
Glass • SICK
475QX2791 • **Value $13**

5

Child's Third Christmas
Handcrafted • CHAD
600QX4714 • **Value $29**

6

Christmas Cardinal
Handcrafted • RGRS
475QX4941 • **Value $21**

7

Christmas Cuckoo
Handcrafted • CROW
800QX4801 • **Value $33**

8

Christmas Memories Photoholder
Acrylic • PATT
650QX3724 • **Value $27**

9

Cool Juggler
Handcrafted • CROW
650QX4874 • **Value $23**

10

Cymbals of Christmas
Handcrafted/Acrylic • DLEE
550QX4111 • **Value $30**

11

Dad
Handcrafted • SIED
700QX4141 • **Value $26**

12

Daughter
Handcrafted • PATT
575QX4151 • **Value $60**

13

Feliz Navidad
Handcrafted • UNRU
675QX4161 • **Value $36**

14

Fifty Years Together
Acrylic • N/A
675QX3741 • **Value $19**

15

Filled With Fudge
Handcrafted • SEAL
475QX4191 • **Value $34**

16

First Christmas Together
Acrylic • VOTR
675QX3731 • **Value $28**

17

First Christmas Together
Glass • N/A
475QX2741 • **Value $25**

18
First Christmas Together
Handcrafted • PIKE
900QX4894 • **Value $34**

19
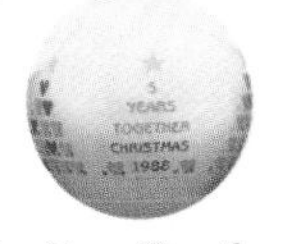
Five Years Together
Glass • MCGE
475QX2744 • **Value $19**

20

From Our Home to Yours
Glass • PATT
475QX2794 • **Value $19**

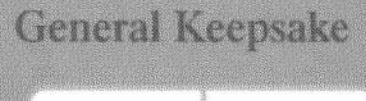
General Keepsake

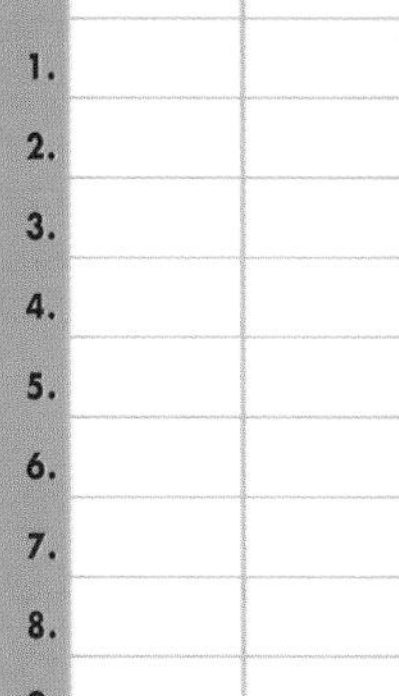

	Price Paid	Value
1.		
2.		
3.		
4.		
5.		
6.		
7.		
8.		
9.		
10.		
11.		
12.		
13.		
14.		
15.		
16.		
17.		
18.		
19.		
20.		
Totals		

1

Glowing Wreath
Dimensional Brass • PATT
600QX4921 • **Value $15**

2

Go for the Gold
Handcrafted • SIED
800QX4174 • **Value $29**

3

Godchild
Glass • N/A
475QX2784 • **Value $21**

4

Goin' Cross Country
Handcrafted • SICK
850QX4764 • **Value $26**

5

Gone Fishing
(re-issued in 1989)
Handcrafted • SIED
500QX4794 • **Value $24**

6

Granddaughter
Glass • VOTR
475QX2774 • **Value $37**

7

Grandmother
Glass • N/A
475QX2764 • **Value $21**

8

Grandparents
Glass • PATT
475QX2771 • **Value $22**

9

Grandson
Glass • VOTR
475QX2781 • **Value $33**

10

Gratitude
Acrylic • PATT
600QX3754 • **Value $14**

11

Happy Holidata
(re-issued from 1987)
Handcrafted • SIED
650QX4717 • **Value $32**

12

Hoe-Hoe-Hoe!
Handcrafted • SIED
500QX4221 • **Value $18**

13

Holiday Hero
Handcrafted • SIED
500QX4231 • **Value $22**

14

In a Nutshell
(re-issued from 1987)
Handcrafted • UNRU
550QX4697 • **Value $33**

15

Jingle Bell Clown
Handcrafted • N/A
1500QX4774 • **Value $34**

16

Jolly Walrus
Handcrafted • RGRS
450QX4731 • **Value $27**

17

A KISS™ From Santa
(re-issued in 1989)
Handcrafted • UNRU
450QX4821 • **Value $30**

18

Kiss the Claus
Handcrafted • SIED
500QX4861 • **Value $17**

19

Kringle Moon
Handcrafted • RGRS
550QX4951 • **Value $36**

20

Kringle Portrait
Handcrafted • N/A
750QX4961 • **Value $35**

General Keepsake

	Price Paid	Value
1.		
2.		
3.		
4.		
5.		
6.		
7.		
8.		
9.		
10.		
11.		
12.		
13.		
14.		
15.		
16.		
17.		
18.		
19.		
20.		
Totals		

1

Kringle Tree
Handcrafted • N/A
650QX4954 • **Value $42**

2

Little Jack Horner
Handcrafted • SIED
800QX4081 • **Value $27**

3

Love Fills the Heart
Acrylic • VOTR
600QX3744 • **Value $26**

4

Love Grows
Glass • VOTR
475QX2754 • **Value $36**

5

Love Santa
Handcrafted • SIED
500QX4864 • **Value $19**

6

Loving Bear
Handcrafted • RGRS
475QX4934 • **Value $21**

7

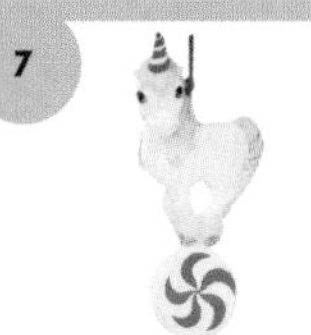

Merry-Mint Unicorn
Porcelain • RGRS
850QX4234 • **Value $24**

8

Midnight Snack
Handcrafted • SIED
600QX4104 • **Value $24**

9

Mistletoad
(re-issued from 1987)
Handcrafted • CROW
700QX4687 • **Value $32**

10

Mother
Acrylic • N/A
650QX3751 • **Value $20**

11

Mother and Dad
Porcelain • LYLE
800QX4144 • **Value $21**

12

New Home
Acrylic • VOTR
600QX3761 • **Value $24**

13

Nick the Kick
Handcrafted • SIED
500QX4224 • **Value $26**

14

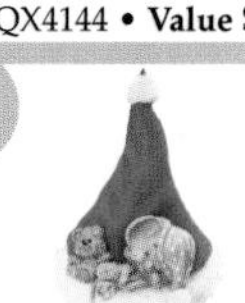

Night Before Christmas
(re-issued from 1987)
Handcrafted • CROW
650QX4517 • **Value $36**

15

Noah's Ark
Pressed Tin • SICK
850QX4904 • **Value $45**

16

Norman Rockwell: Christmas Scenes
Glass • LYLE
475QX2731 • **Value $27**

17

Old-Fashioned Church
Wood • SICK
400QX4981 • **Value $25**

18

Old-Fashioned Schoolhouse
Wood • SICK
400QX4971 • **Value $25**

19

OREO® Chocolate Sandwich Cookies
(re-issued in 1989)
Handcrafted • UNRU
400QX4814 • **Value $22**

20

"Owliday" Wish
(re-issued from 1987)
Handcrafted • PIKE
650QX4559 • **Value $21**

General Keepsake

	Price Paid	Value
1.		
2.		
3.		
4.		
5.		
6.		
7.		
8.		
9.		
10.		
11.		
12.		
13.		
14.		
15.		
16.		
17.		
18.		
19.		
20.		
Totals		

1

Par for Santa
Handcrafted • SIED
500QX4791 • **Value $23**

2

Party Line
(re-issued in 1989)
Handcrafted • PIKE
875QX4761 • **Value $31**

3

PEANUTS®
Glass • N/A
475QX2801 • **Value $53**

4

Peek-a-Boo Kitties
(re-issued in 1989)
Handcrafted • CROW
750QX4871 • **Value $25**

5

Polar Bowler
(re-issued in 1989)
Handcrafted • SIED
500QX4784 • **Value $18**

6

Purrfect Snuggle
Handcrafted • RGRS
625QX4744 • **Value $30**

7

Reindoggy
(re-issued from 1987)
Handcrafted • SIED
575QX4527 • **Value $39**

8

Sailing! Sailing!
Pressed Tin • SICK
850QX4911 • **Value $27**

9

St. Louie Nick
(re-issued from 1987)
Handcrafted • DUTK
775QX4539 • **Value $33**

10

Santa Flamingo
Handcrafted • PYDA
475QX4834 • **Value $37**

11

Shiny Sleigh
Dimensional Brass • PATT
575QX4924 • **Value $19**

12
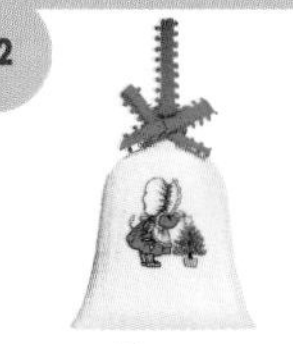
Sister
Porcelain • VOTR
800QX4994 • **Value $33**

13

Slipper Spaniel
Handcrafted • CROW
425QX4724 • **Value $19**

14

SNOOPY® and WOODSTOCK
Handcrafted • UNRU
600QX4741 • **Value $48**

15

Soft Landing
Handcrafted • CHAD
700QX4751 • **Value $26**

16

Son
Handcrafted • PATT
575QX4154 • **Value $41**

17

Sparkling Tree
Dimensional Brass • PATT
600QX4931 • **Value $20**

18

Spirit of Christmas
Glass • LYLE
475QX2761 • **Value $25**

19

Squeaky Clean
Handcrafted • PIKE
675QX4754 • **Value $23**

20
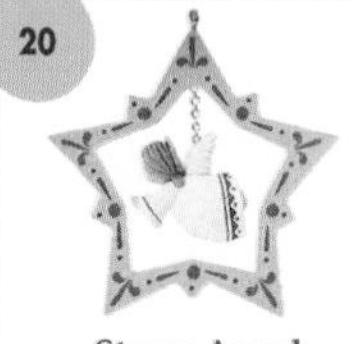
Starry Angel
Handcrafted • RGRS
475QX4944 • **Value $21**

General Keepsake

	Price Paid	Value
1.		
2.		
3.		
4.		
5.		
6.		
7.		
8.		
9.		
10.		
11.		
12.		
13.		
14.		
15.		
16.		
17.		
18.		
19.		
20.		
Totals		

1988 Collection

1

Sweet Star
Handcrafted • SEAL
500QX4184 • **Value $33**

2

Sweetheart
Handcrafted • UNRU
975QX4901 • **Value $25**

3

Teacher
Handcrafted • PIKE
625QX4171 • **Value $21**

4

Teeny Taster
(re-issued in 1989)
Handcrafted • SEAL
475QX4181 • **Value $31**

5

Ten Years Together
Glass • N/A
475QX2751 • **Value $22**

6

The Town Crier
Handcrafted • SEAL
550QX4734 • **Value $22**

7

Travels with Santa
Handcrafted • DLEE
1000QX4771 • **Value $40**

8

Treetop Dreams
(re-issued from 1987)
Handcrafted • SEAL
675QX4597 • **Value $32**

9

Twenty-Five Years Together
Acrylic • PATT
675QX3734 • **Value $18**

10

Uncle Sam Nutcracker
Handcrafted • DLEE
700QX4884 • **Value $36**

11

Very Strawbeary
Handcrafted • DUTK
475QX4091 • **Value $23**

12

Winter Fun
Handcrafted • CHAD
850QX4781 • **Value $22**

13

The Wonderful Santacycle
Handcrafted • SEAL
2250QX4114 • **Value $47**

14
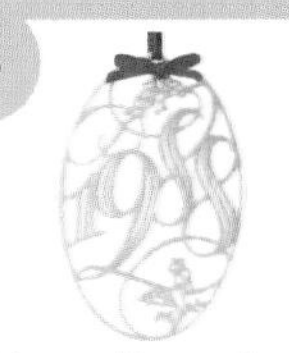
Year to Remember
Ceramic • N/A
700QX4164 • **Value $25**

15

Baby's First Christmas
Handcrafted • SEAL
2400QLX7184 • **Value $60**

16

Bearly Reaching
Handcrafted • SICK
950QLX7151 • **Value $37**

17

Christmas Is Magic
Handcrafted • CROW
1200QLX7171 • **Value $58**

18

Christmas Morning
(re-issued from 1987)
Handcrafted • CROW
2450QLX7013 • **Value $48**

19

Circling the Globe
Handcrafted • CROW
1050QLX7124 • **Value $44**

20

Country Express
Handcrafted • SICK
2450QLX7211 • **Value $72**

General Keepsake

	Price Paid	Value
1.		
2.		
3.		
4.		
5.		
6.		
7.		
8.		
9.		
10.		
11.		
12.		
13.		
14.		

General Magic

	Price Paid	Value
15.		
16.		
17.		
18.		
19.		
20.		
Totals		

1

Festive Feeder
Handcrafted • SICK
1150QLX7204 • **Value $50**

2
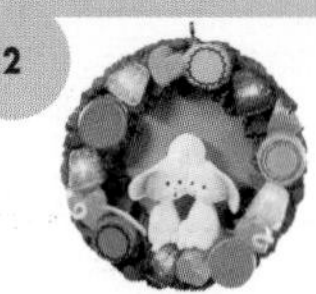
First Christmas Together
Handcrafted • SICK
1200QLX7027 • **Value $40**

3

Heavenly Glow
Brass • PYDA
1175QLX7114 • **Value $29**

4

Kitty Capers
Handcrafted • PIKE
1300QLX7164 • **Value $45**

5

Last-Minute Hug
Handcrafted • UNRU
2200QLX7181 • **Value $48**

6

Moonlit Nap (re-issued in 1989)
Handcrafted • CHAD
875QLX7134 • **Value $29**

7

Parade of the Toys
Handcrafted • SICK
2450QLX7194 • **Value $53**

8
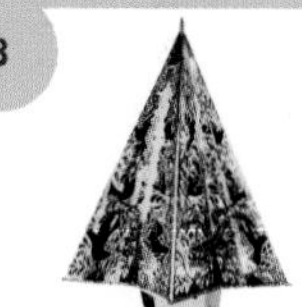
Radiant Tree
Brass • LYLE
1175QLX7121 • **Value $27**

9

Skater's Waltz
Handcrafted • UNRU
2450QLX7201 • **Value $53**

10

Song of Christmas
Acrylic • N/A
850QLX7111 • **Value $28**

11

Tree of Friendship
Acrylic • N/A
850QLX7104 • **Value $27**

12

Baby's First Christmas
Handcrafted • DLEE
600QXM5744 • **Value $12**

13
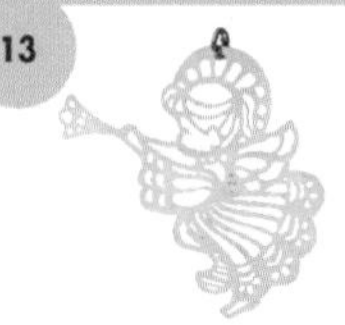
Brass Angel
Brass • LYLE
150QXM5671 • **Value $21**

14

Brass Star
Brass • LYLE
150QXM5664 • **Value $21**

15

Brass Tree
Brass • LYLE
150QXM5674 • **Value $21**

16

Candy Cane Elf
Handcrafted • SIED
300QXM5701 • **Value $20**

17

Country Wreath (re-issued in 1989)
Handcrafted • RGRS
400QXM5731 • **Value $12**

18

First Christmas Together
Wood/Straw • MCGE
400QXM5741 • **Value $13**

19

Folk Art Lamb
Wood • PATT
275QXM5681 • **Value $24**

20

Folk Art Reindeer
Wood • PATT
300QXM5684 • **Value $20**

General Magic	Price Paid	Value
1.		
2.		
3.		
4.		
5.		
6.		
7.		
8.		
9.		
10.		
11.		
General Miniature		
12.		
13.		
14.		
15.		
16.		
17.		
18.		
19.		
20.		
Totals		

1

Friends Share Joy
Acrylic • PATT
200QXM5764 • **Value $15**

2

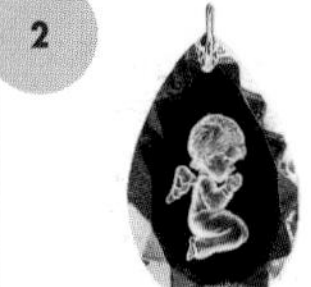

Gentle Angel
Acrylic • VOTR
200QXM5771 • **Value $20**

3

Happy Santa
Glass • PATT
450QXM5614 • **Value $22**

4

Holy Family
(re-issued in 1989)
Handcrafted • UNRU
850QXM5611 • **Value $16**

5

Jolly St. Nick
Handcrafted • UNRU
800QXM5721 • **Value $32**

6

Joyous Heart
Wood • MCGE
350QXM5691 • **Value $30**

7

Little Drummer Boy
Handcrafted • SIED
450QXM5784 • **Value $28**

8

Love Is Forever
Acrylic • PATT
200QXM5774 • **Value $16**

9

Mother
Handcrafted • PIKE
300QXM5724 • **Value $13**

10

Skater's Waltz
Handcrafted • UNRU
700QXM5601 • **Value $20**

11

Sneaker Mouse
Handcrafted • N/A
400QXM5711 • **Value $21**

12

Snuggly Skater
Handcrafted • SIED
450QXM5714 • **Value $27**

13

Sweet Dreams
Handcrafted • N/A
700QXM5604 • **Value $22**

14

Three Little Kitties
(re-issued in 1989)
Handcrafted/Willow • PIKE
600QXM5694 • **Value $18**

15

Angelic Minstrel
(club edition, LE-49,900)
Porcelain • DLEE
2950QX4084 • **Value $50**

16

Christmas is Sharing
(club edition, LE-49,900)
Bone China • SEAL
1750QX4071 • **Value $48**

17

Hold on Tight
(early renewal
piece, miniature)
Handcrafted • SIED
QXC5704 • **Value $78**

18

Our Clubhouse
(keepsake of membership)
Handcrafted • SIED
QXC5804 • **Value $48**

19

Seal of Friendship
(gift membership bonus,
Merry Miniature)
Handcrafted • VOTR
QXC5104 • **Value $60**

20

Sleighful of Dreams
(club edition)
Handcrafted • SICK
800QXC5801 • **Value $70**

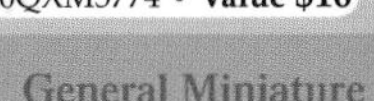

General Miniature

	Price Paid	Value
1.		
2.		
3.		
4.		
5.		
6.		
7.		
8.		
9.		
10.		
11.		
12.		
13.		
14.		

Collector's Club

	Price Paid	Value
15.		
16.		
17.		
18.		
19.		
20.		
Totals		

1

Kringle's Toy Shop
(re-issued in 1989, magic)
Handcrafted • SEAL
2450QLX7017 • **Value $54**

1987

Among the most sought-after ornaments from 1987 is "Bright Christmas Dreams," which is coveted by collectors of the "CRAYOLA® Crayon" collectible series, although it is not officially a part of that series. Overall, there were 122 Keepsake ornaments and 18 Magic ornaments. See the collectible series section for more 1987 ornaments.

2

Baby Locket
Textured Metal • N/A
1500QX4617 • **Value $30**

3

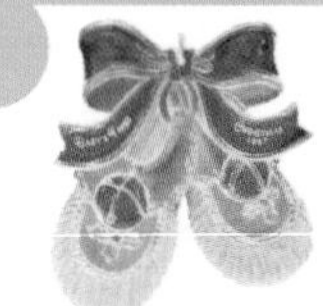

Baby's First Christmas
Acrylic • N/A
600QX3729 • **Value $26**

4

Baby's First Christmas
Handcrafted • DLEE
975QX4113 • **Value $28**

5

Baby's First Christmas – Baby Boy
Satin • PATT
475QX2749 • **Value $30**

6

Baby's First Christmas – Baby Girl
Satin • PATT
475QX2747 • **Value $27**

7

Baby's First Christmas Photoholder
Fabric • N/A
750QX4619 • **Value $31**

8

Baby's Second Christmas
Handcrafted • DLEE
575QX4607 • **Value $33**

9

Babysitter
Glass • PIKE
475QX2797 • **Value $22**

10

Beary Special
Handcrafted • SIED
475QX4557 • **Value $28**

11

Bright Christmas Dreams
Handcrafted • SIED
725QX4737 • **Value $90**

12

Child's Third Christmas
Handcrafted • CROW
575QX4599 • **Value $28**

13

Chocolate Chipmunk
Handcrafted • SEAL
600QX4567 • **Value $55**

14

Christmas Cuddle
Handcrafted • N/A
575QX4537 • **Value $35**

15

Christmas Fun Puzzle
Handcrafted • DLEE
800QX4679 • **Value $30**

16

Christmas is Gentle
(LE-24,700)
Bone China • SEAL
1750QX4449 • **Value $82**

17

Christmas Keys
Handcrafted • UNRU
575QX4739 • **Value $33**

Open House Ornaments

	Price Paid	Value
1.		

General Keepsake

	Price Paid	Value
2.		
3.		
4.		
5.		
6.		
7.		
8.		
9.		
10.		
11.		
12.		
13.		
14.		
15.		
16.		
17.		
Totals		

1

Christmas Time Mime (LE-24,700)
Porcelain • UNRU
2750QX4429 • **Value $60**

2

The Constitution
Acrylic • PATT
650QX3777 • **Value $28**

3

Country Wreath
Wood/Straw • PYDA
575QX4709 • **Value $31**

4

Currier & Ives: American Farm Scene
Glass • LYLE
475QX2829 • **Value $32**

5

Dad
Handcrafted • SIED
600QX4629 • **Value $41**

6

Daughter
Handcrafted • SICK
575QX4637 • **Value $30**

7

December Showers
Handcrafted • DLEE
550QX4487 • **Value $37**

8

Doc Holiday
Handcrafted • SEAL
800QX4677 • **Value $46**

9

Dr. Seuss: The Grinch's Christmas
Glass • N/A
475QX2783 • **Value $105**

10

Favorite Santa
Porcelain • DUTK
2250QX4457 • **Value $50**

11

Fifty Years Together
Porcelain • SEAL
800QX4437 • **Value $28**

12

First Christmas Together
Acrylic • N/A
650QX3719 • **Value $25**

13

First Christmas Together
Glass • LYLE
475QX2729 • **Value $24**

14

First Christmas Together
Handcrafted • N/A
800QX4459 • **Value $38**

15

First Christmas Together
Handcrafted • DLEE
950QX4467 • **Value $30**

16

First Christmas Together
Textured Brass • N/A
1500QX4469 • **Value $30**

17

Folk Art Santa
Handcrafted • SICK
525QX4749 • **Value $36**

18

From Our Home to Yours
Glass • PYDA
475QX2799 • **Value $48**

19

Fudge Forever
Handcrafted • DUTK
500QX4497 • **Value $40**

20

Godchild
Glass • PYDA
475QX2767 • **Value $24**

General Keepsake

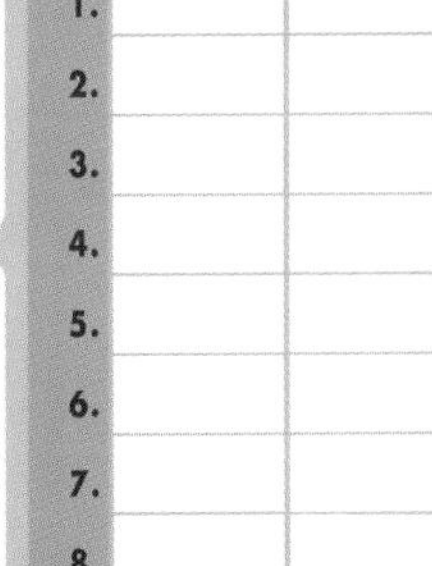

	Price Paid	Value
1.		
2.		
3.		
4.		
5.		
6.		
7.		
8.		
9.		
10.		
11.		
12.		
13.		
14.		
15.		
16.		
17.		
18.		
19.		
20.		
Totals		

1

Goldfinch
Porcelain • SICK
700QX4649 • **Value $85**

2

Grandchild's First Christmas
Handcrafted • SEAL
900QX4609 • **Value $25**

3
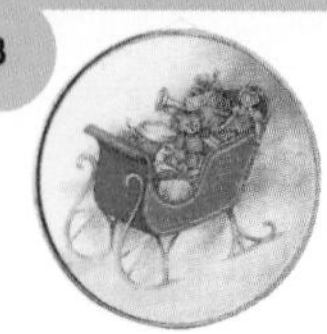
Granddaughter
Bezeled Satin • VOTR
600QX3747 • **Value $26**

4

Grandmother
Glass • N/A
475QX2779 • **Value $18**

5

Grandparents
Glass • PIKE
475QX2777 • **Value $19**

6

Grandson
Glass • VOTR
475QX2769 • **Value $29**

7

Happy Holidata (re-issued in 1988)
Handcrafted • SIED
650QX4717 • **Value $32**

8

Happy Santa
Handcrafted • CROW
475QX4569 • **Value $32**

9

Heart in Blossom
Acrylic • VOTR
600QX3727 • **Value $23**

10

Heavenly Harmony
Handcrafted • CROW
1500QX4659 • **Value $34**

11

Holiday Greetings
Bezeled Foil • N/A
600QX3757 • **Value $13**

12

Holiday Hourglass
Handcrafted • UNRU
800QX4707 • **Value $28**

13

Hot Dogger
Handcrafted • UNRU
650QX4719 • **Value $29**

14

Husband
Cameo • VOTR
700QX3739 • **Value $12**

15

I Remember Santa
Glass • LYLE
475QX278-9 • **Value $37**

16

Icy Treat
Handcrafted • SIED
450QX4509 • **Value $29**

17
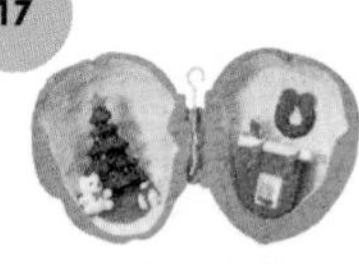
In a Nutshell (re-issued in 1988)
Handcrafted • UNRU
550QX4697 • **Value $33**

18

Jack Frosting
Handcrafted • SEAL
700QX4499 • **Value $54**

19

Jammie Pies™
Glass • N/A
475QX2839 • **Value $21**

20

Jogging Through the Snow
Handcrafted • DUTK
725QX4577 • **Value $40**

General Keepsake

	Price Paid	Value
1.		
2.		
3.		
4.		
5.		
6.		
7.		
8.		
9.		
10.		
11.		
12.		
13.		
14.		
15.		
16.		
17.		
18.		
19.		
20.		
Totals		

1

Jolly Follies
Handcrafted • CROW
850QX4669 • **Value $37**

2

Jolly Hiker
(re-issued from 1986)
Handcrafted • SIED
500QX4832 • **Value $30**

3

Joy Ride
Handcrafted • SEAL
1150QX4407 • **Value $77**

4

Joyous Angels
Handcrafted • SEAL
775QX4657 • **Value $26**

5

Let It Snow
Handcrafted • N/A
650QX4589 • **Value $26**

6

L'il Jingler
(re-issued from 1986)
Handcrafted • SEAL
675QX4193 • **Value $42**

7

Little Whittler
Handcrafted • DUTK
600QX4699 • **Value $36**

8

Love Is Everywhere
Glass • LYLE
475QX2787 • **Value $27**

9

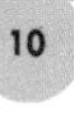

Merry Koala
(re-issued from 1986)
Handcrafted • SICK
500QX4153 • **Value $25**

10

Mistletoad
(re-issued in 1988)
Handcrafted • CROW
700QX4687 • **Value $32**

11

Mother
Acrylic • PIKE
650QX3737 • **Value $18**

12

Mother and Dad
Porcelain • PIKE
700QX4627 • **Value $26**

13
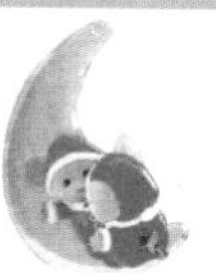

Mouse in the Moon
(re-issued from 1986)
Handcrafted • SEAL
550QX4166 • **Value $24**

14

Nature's Decorations
Glass • VOTR
475QX2739 • **Value $36**

15

New Home
Acrylic • PATT
600QX3767 • **Value $29**

16

Niece
Glass • N/A
475QX2759 • **Value $12**

17

Night Before Christmas
(re-issued in 1988)
Handcrafted • CROW
650QX4517 • **Value $36**

18

Norman Rockwell:
Christmas Scenes
Glass • LYLE
475QX2827 • **Value $27**

19

Nostalgic Rocker
Wood • SICK
650QX4689 • **Value $33**

20

"Owliday" Wish
(re-issued in 1988)
Handcrafted • PIKE
650QX4559 • **Value $21**

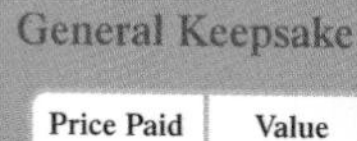
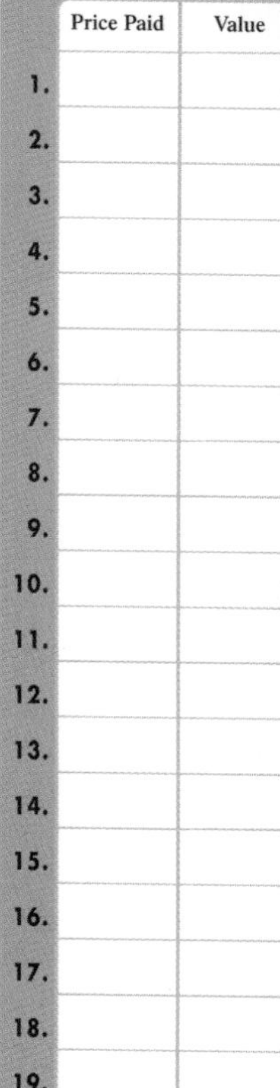

General Keepsake

	Price Paid	Value
1.		
2.		
3.		
4.		
5.		
6.		
7.		
8.		
9.		
10.		
11.		
12.		
13.		
14.		
15.		
16.		
17.		
18.		
19.		
20.		
Totals		

1

Paddington™ Bear
Handcrafted • PIKE
550QX4727 • **Value $34**

2

PEANUTS®
Glass • N/A
475QX2819 • **Value $40**

3

Pretty Kitty
Handcrafted/Glass • CROW
1100QX4489 • **Value $34**

4

Promise of Peace
Acrylic • PIKE
650QX3749 • **Value $27**

5

Raccoon Biker
Handcrafted • SIED
700QX4587 • **Value $32**

6

Reindoggy
(re-issued in 1988)
Handcrafted • SIED
575QX4527 • **Value $39**

7

St. Louie Nick
(re-issued in 1988)
Handcrafted • DUTK
775QX4539 • **Value $33**

8

Santa at the Bat
Handcrafted • SIED
775QX4579 • **Value $29**

9

Seasoned Greetings
Handcrafted • SEAL
625QX4549 • **Value $30**

10

Sister
Wood • SICK
600QX4747 • **Value $16**

11

Sleepy Santa
Handcrafted • CROW
625QX4507 • **Value $40**

12

SNOOPY and WOODSTOCK
Handcrafted • SIED
725QX4729 • **Value $52**

13
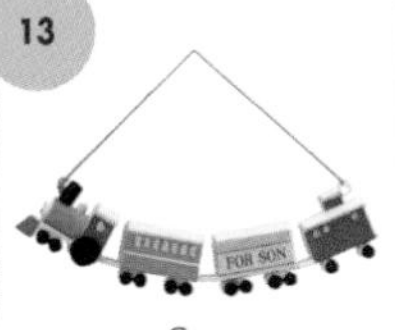
Son
Handcrafted • SICK
575QX4639 • **Value $45**

14

Special Memories Photoholder
Fabric • N/A
675QX4647 • **Value $28**

15

Spots 'n Stripes
Handcrafted • N/A
550QX4529 • **Value $28**

16

Sweetheart
Handcrafted • SICK
1100QX4479 • **Value $30**

17

Teacher
Handcrafted • SIED
575QX4667 • **Value $23**

18
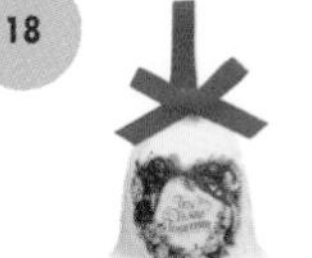
Ten Years Together
Porcelain • VOTR
700QX4447 • **Value $24**

19

Three Men in a Tub
Handcrafted • DLEE
800QX4547 • **Value $27**

20

Time for Friends
Glass • VOTR
475QX2807 • **Value $24**

General Keepsake

	Price Paid	Value
1.		
2.		
3.		
4.		
5.		
6.		
7.		
8.		
9.		
10.		
11.		
12.		
13.		
14.		
15.		
16.		
17.		
18.		
19.		
20.		
Totals		

1

Treetop Dreams
(re-issued in 1988)
Handcrafted • SEAL
675QX4597 • **Value $32**

2

Treetop Trio
(re-issued from 1986)
Handcrafted • DLEE
1100QX4256 • **Value $35**

3

Twenty-Five
Years Together
Porcelain • N/A
750QX4439 • **Value $28**

4

Walnut Shell Rider
(re-issued from 1986)
Handcrafted • SEAL
600QX4196 • **Value $27**

5

Warmth of Friendship
Acrylic • N/A
600QX3759 • **Value $12**

6

Wee Chimney Sweep
Handcrafted • SEAL
625QX4519 • **Value $27**

7

Word of Love
Porcelain • N/A
800QX4477 • **Value $25**

8

Angelic Messengers
Panorama Ball • UNRU
1875QLX7113 • **Value $58**

9

Baby's First Christmas
Handcrafted • N/A
1350QLX7049 • **Value $37**

10

Bright Noel
Acrylic • VOTR
700QLX7059 • **Value $33**

11

Christmas Morning
(re-issued in 1988)
Handcrafted • CROW
2450QLX7013 • **Value $48**

12

First
Christmas Together
Handcrafted • N/A
1150QLX7087 • **Value $50**

13

Good Cheer Blimp
Handcrafted • SICK
1600QLX7046 • **Value $58**

14

Keep on Glowin'!
(re-issued from 1986)
Handcrafted • CROW
1000QLX7076 • **Value $48**

15

Keeping Cozy
Handcrafted • CROW
1175QLX7047 • **Value $37**

16

Lacy Brass Snowflake
Brass • N/A
1150QLX7097 • **Value $26**

17

Loving Holiday
Handcrafted • SEAL
2200QLX7016 • **Value $55**

18

Memories Are
Forever Photoholder
Handcrafted • SEAL
850QLX7067 • **Value $38**

19

Meowy Christmas!
Handcrafted • PIKE
1000QLX7089 • **Value $62**

20

Season for Friendship
Acrylic • N/A
850QLX7069 • **Value $23**

	Price Paid	Value
General Keepsake		
1.		
2.		
3.		
4.		
5.		
6.		
7.		
General Magic		
8.		
9.		
10.		
11.		
12.		
13.		
14.		
15.		
16.		
17.		
18.		
19.		
20.		
Totals		

1

Train Station
Handcrafted • DLEE
1275QLX7039 • **Value $52**

2

Village Express
(re-issued from 1986)
Handcrafted • SICK
2450QLX7072 • **Value $118**

3

Carousel Reindeer
(club edition)
Handcrafted • SICK
800QXC5817 • **Value $68**

4

Wreath of Memories
(keepsake of membership)
Handcrafted • UNRU
QXC5809 • **Value $55**

5

North Pole
Power & Light
Handcrafted • CROW
($2.95)627XPR9333 • **Value $27**

1986

One of the biggest stories among Hallmark collectors in 1986 was the hard-to-find porcelain "Magical Unicorn" ornament which was limited to 24,700 pieces. The 1986 collection featured 120 Keepsake ornaments and 16 Magic ornaments. See the collectible series section for more 1986 ornaments.

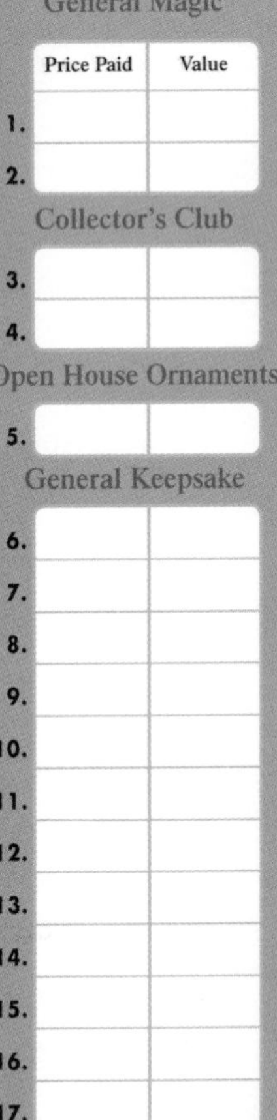

	Price Paid	Value
General Magic		
1.		
2.		
Collector's Club		
3.		
4.		
Open House Ornaments		
5.		
General Keepsake		
6.		
7.		
8.		
9.		
10.		
11.		
12.		
13.		
14.		
15.		
16.		
17.		
Totals		

6

Acorn Inn
Handcrafted • UNRU
850QX4243 • **Value $32**

7

Baby Locket
Textured Brass • MCGE
1600QX4123 • **Value $29**

8

Baby's First Christmas
Acrylic • PALM
600QX3803 • **Value $25**

9

Baby's First Christmas
Handcrafted • SICK
900QX4126 • **Value $42**

10

Baby's First Christmas
Satin • PATT
550QX2713 • **Value $27**

11

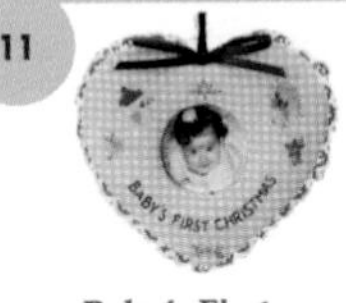

Baby's First
Christmas Photoholder
Fabric • PATT
800QX3792 • **Value $26**

12

Baby's
Second Christmas
Handcrafted • SIED
650QX4133 • **Value $29**

13

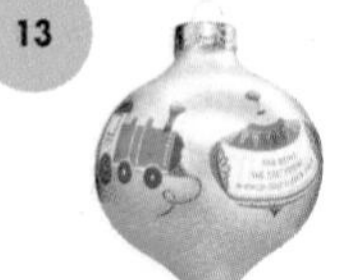

Baby-Sitter
Glass • N/A
475QX2756 • **Value $14**

14

Beary Smooth Ride
(re-issued from 1985)
Handcrafted • SICK
650QX4805 • **Value $24**

15

Bluebird
Porcelain • SICK
725QX4283 • **Value $57**

16

Chatty Penguin
Plush • CROW
575QX4176 • **Value $27**

17

Child's Third Christmas
Fabric • VOTR
650QX4136 • **Value $25**

1

Christmas Beauty
Lacquer • PATT
600QX3223 • **Value $13**

2
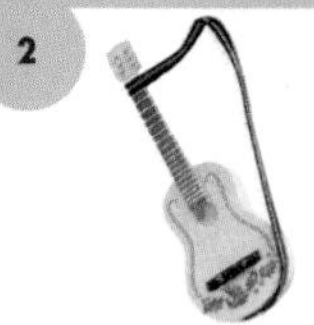
Christmas Guitar
Handcrafted • UNRU
700QX5126 • **Value $23**

3

Cookies for Santa
Handcrafted • MCGE
450QX4146 • **Value $31**

4

Country Sleigh
Handcrafted • SICK
1000QX5113 • **Value $28**

5

Daughter
Handcrafted • SEAL
575QX4306 • **Value $50**

6

Do Not Disturb Bear (re-issued from 1985)
Handcrafted • SEAL
775QX4812 • **Value $34**

7

Father
Wood • VOTR
650QX4313 • **Value $14**

8

Favorite Tin Drum
Tin • SICK
850QX5143 • **Value $32**

9
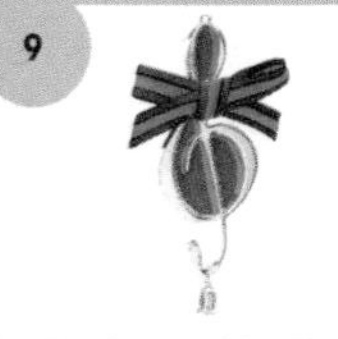

Festive Treble Clef
Handcrafted • SIED
875QX5133 • **Value $25**

10

Fifty Years Together
Porcelain • PIKE
1000QX4006 • **Value $20**

11

First Christmas Together
Acrylic • MCGE
700QX3793 • **Value $20**

12

First Christmas Together
Glass • N/A
475QX2703 • **Value $20**

13
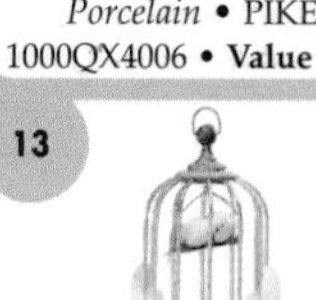
First Christmas Together
Handcrafted • SICK
1200QX4096 • **Value $30**

14

First Christmas Together
Textured Brass • N/A
1600QX4003 • **Value $25**

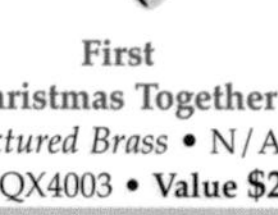

15

Friends Are Fun
Glass • CROW
475QX2723 • **Value $45**

16

Friendship Greeting
Fabric • N/A
800QX4273 • **Value $16**

17

Friendship's Gift
Acrylic • N/A
600QX3816 • **Value $18**

18

From Our Home to Yours
Acrylic • N/A
600QX3833 • **Value $17**

19
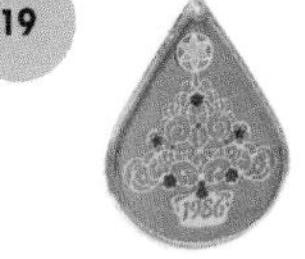

Glowing Christmas Tree
Acrylic • PATT
700QX4286 • **Value $16**

20
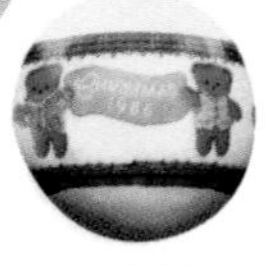
Godchild
Satin • N/A
475QX2716 • **Value $19**

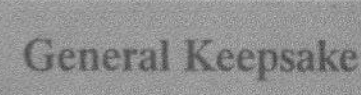

General Keepsake

	Price Paid	Value
1.		
2.		
3.		
4.		
5.		
6.		
7.		
8.		
9.		
10.		
11.		
12.		
13.		
14.		
15.		
16.		
17.		
18.		
19.		
20.		
Totals		

1

Grandchild's First Christmas
Handcrafted • N/A
1000QX4116 • **Value $17**

2

Granddaughter
Glass • LYLE
475QX2736 • **Value $25**

3

Grandmother
Satin • PATT
475QX2743 • **Value $16**

4

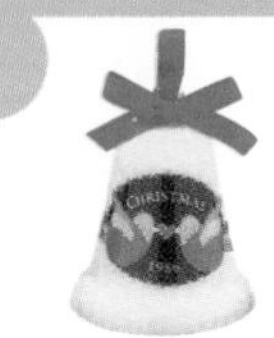

Grandparents
Porcelain • PATT
750QX4323 • **Value $23**

5

Grandson
Glass • VOTR
475QX2733 • **Value $32**

6

Gratitude
Satin/Wood • PIKE
600QX4326 • **Value $14**

7

Happy Christmas to Owl
Handcrafted • UNRU
600QX4183 • **Value $26**

8

Heathcliff
Handcrafted • SEAL
750QX4363 • **Value $27**

9

Heavenly Dreamer
Handcrafted • DLEE
575QX4173 • **Value $35**

10

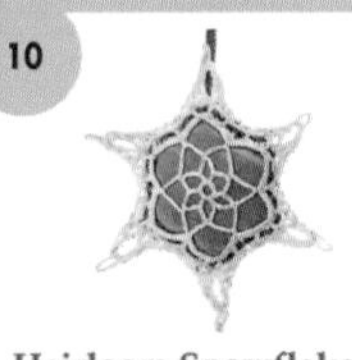

Heirloom Snowflake
Fabric • PATT
675QX5153 • **Value $21**

11

Holiday Horn
Porcelain • UNRU
800QX5146 • **Value $35**

12

Holiday Jingle Bell
Handcrafted • N/A
1600QX4046 • **Value $56**

13

Husband
Cameo • PIKE
800QX3836 • **Value $13**

14

Jolly Hiker (re-issued in 1987)
Handcrafted • SIED
500QX4832 • **Value $30**

15

Jolly St. Nick
Porcelain • UNRU
2250QX4296 • **Value $72**

16

Joy of Friends
Bezeled Satin • PATT
675QX3823 • **Value $16**

17

Joyful Carolers
Handcrafted • SICK
975QX5136 • **Value $38**

18

Katybeth
Porcelain • N/A
700QX4353 • **Value $28**

19

Kitty Mischief (re-issued from 1985)
Handcrafted • DUTK
500QX4745 • **Value $25**

20

Li'l Jingler (re-issued in 1987)
Handcrafted • SEAL
675QX4193 • **Value $42**

General Keepsake

	Price Paid	Value
1.		
2.		
3.		
4.		
5.		
6.		
7.		
8.		
9.		
10.		
11.		
12.		
13.		
14.		
15.		
16.		
17.		
18.		
19.		
20.		
Totals		

1

Little Drummers
Handcrafted • CROW
1250QX5116 • **Value $35**

2

Loving Memories
Handcrafted • SEAL
900QX4093 • **Value $36**

3

The Magi
Glass • PIKE
475QX2726 • **Value $23**

4

Magical Unicorn (LE-24,700)
Porcelain • UNRU
2750QX4293 • **Value $120**

5

Marionette Angel (cancelled after limited production)
Handcrafted • N/A
850QX4023 • **Value $400**

6

Mary Emmerling: American Country Collection
Glass • N/A
795QX2752 • **Value $27**

7

Memories to Cherish
Ceramic • VOTR
750QX4276 • **Value $32**

8

Merry Koala (re-issued in 1987)
Handcrafted • SICK
500QX4153 • **Value $25**

9

Merry Mouse (re-issued from 1985)
Handcrafted • DUTK
450QX4032 • **Value $33**

10

Mother
Acrylic • N/A
700QX3826 • **Value $20**

11

Mother and Dad
Porcelain • PYDA
750QX4316 • **Value $22**

12
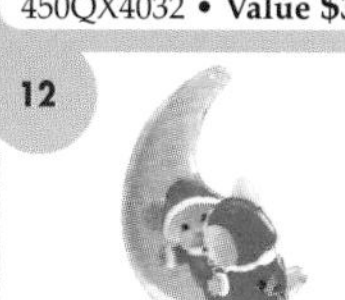
Mouse in the Moon (re-issued in 1987)
Handcrafted • SEAL
550QX4166 • **Value $24**

13

Nephew
Bezeled Lacquer • N/A
625QX3813 • **Value $15**

14

New Home
Glass • CROW
475QX2746 • **Value $67**

15

Niece
Fabric/Wood • N/A
600QX4266 • **Value $13**

16

Norman Rockwell
Glass • PIKE
475QX2763 • **Value $30**

17

Nutcracker Santa
Handcrafted • UNRU
1000QX5123 • **Value $50**

18

Open Me First
Handcrafted • N/A
725QX4226 • **Value $34**

19
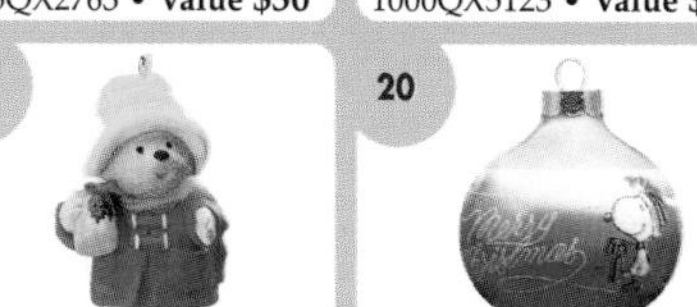
Paddington™ Bear
Handcrafted • SIED
600QX4356 • **Value $42**

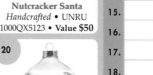

20

PEANUTS®
Glass • N/A
475QX2766 • **Value $47**

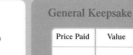

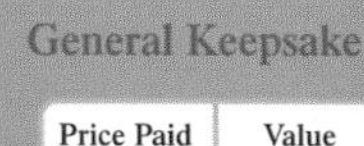
General Keepsake

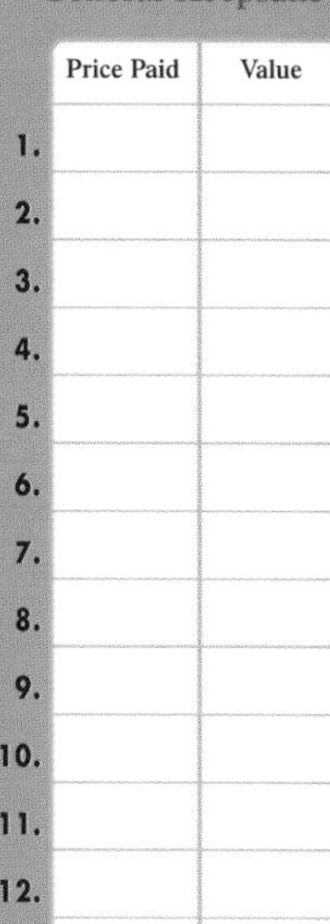

	Price Paid	Value
1.		
2.		
3.		
4.		
5.		
6.		
7.		
8.		
9.		
10.		
11.		
12.		
13.		
14.		
15.		
16.		
17.		
18.		
19.		
20.		
Totals		

1

Playful Possum
Handcrafted/Glass • CROW
1100QX4253 • **Value $31**

2

Popcorn Mouse
Handcrafted • SICK
675QX4213 • **Value $52**

3

Puppy's Best Friend
Handcrafted • UNRU
650QX4203 • **Value $28**

4

Rah Rah Rabbit
Handcrafted • CROW
700QX4216 • **Value $36**

5

Remembering Christmas
Porcelain • N/A
875QX5106 • **Value $29**

6

Santa's Hot Tub
Handcrafted • SEAL
1200QX4263 • **Value $60**

7

Season of the Heart
Glass • PATT
475QX2706 • **Value $17**

8

Shirt Tales™ Parade
Glass • N/A
475QX2773 • **Value $17**

9

Sister
Bezeled Satin • VOTR
675QX3806 • **Value $15**

10

Skateboard Raccoon (re-issued from 1985)
Handcrafted • DUTK
650QX4732 • **Value $42**

11

Ski Tripper
Handcrafted • SIED
675QX4206 • **Value $23**

12

SNOOPY® and WOODSTOCK
Handcrafted • SIED
800QX4346 • **Value $59**

13

Snow Buddies
Handcrafted • DUTK
800QX4236 • **Value $42**

14

Snow-Pitching Snowman (re-issued from 1985)
Handcrafted • DLEE
450QX4702 • **Value $23**

15

Soccer Beaver (re-issued from 1985)
Handcrafted • DUTK
650QX4775 • **Value $27**

16

Son
Handcrafted • SEAL
575QX4303 • **Value $38**

17

Special Delivery
Handcrafted • SIED
500QX4156 • **Value $28**

18

Star Brighteners
Acrylic • VOTR
600QX3226 • **Value $19**

19

The Statue of Liberty
Acrylic • PYDA
600QX3843 • **Value $27**

20

Sweetheart
Handcrafted • SEAL
1100QX4086 • **Value $72**

General Keepsake

	Price Paid	Value
1.		
2.		
3.		
4.		
5.		
6.		
7.		
8.		
9.		
10.		
11.		
12.		
13.		
14.		
15.		
16.		
17.		
18.		
19.		
20.		
Totals		

1
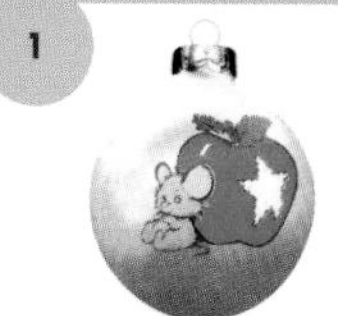
Teacher
Glass • N/A
475QX2753 • **Value $12**

2

Ten Years Together
Porcelain • N/A
750QX4013 • **Value $23**

3

Timeless Love
Acrylic • VOTR
600QX3796 • **Value $30**

4

Tipping the Scales
Handcrafted • DUTK
675QX4186 • **Value $26**

5

Touchdown Santa
Handcrafted • DUTK
800QX4233 • **Value $45**

6

Treetop Trio
(re-issued in 1987)
Handcrafted • DLEE
1100QX4256 • **Value $35**

7

Twenty-Five Years Together
Porcelain • VOTR
800QX4103 • **Value $23**

8

Walnut Shell Rider
(re-issued in 1987)
Handcrafted • SEAL
600QX4196 • **Value $27**

9

Welcome, Christmas
Handcrafted • CROW
825QX5103 • **Value $34**

10

Wynken, Blynken and Nod
Handcrafted • DLEE
975QX4246 • **Value $45**

11

Baby's First Christmas
Panorama Ball • CROW
1950QLX7103 • **Value $52**

12

Christmas Sleigh Ride
Handcrafted • SEAL
2450QLX7012 • **Value $145**

13

First Christmas Together
Handcrafted • SEAL
1400QLX7073 • **Value $48**

14

General Store
Handcrafted • DLEE
1575QLX7053 • **Value $60**

15

Gentle Blessings
Panorama Ball • SICK
1500QLX7083 • **Value $170**

16

Keep on Glowin'!
(re-issued in 1987)
Handcrafted • CROW
1000QLX7076 • **Value $48**

17

Merry Christmas Bell
Acrylic • VOTR
850QLX7093 • **Value $24**

18

Mr. and Mrs. Santa
(re-issued from 1985)
Handcrafted • N/A
1450QLX7052 • **Value $88**

19

Santa's On His Way
Panorama Ball • UNRU
1500QLX7115 • **Value $74**

20

Santa's Snack
Handcrafted • CROW
1000QLX7066 • **Value $60**

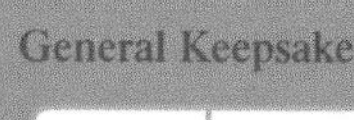

	Price Paid	Value
General Keepsake		
1.		
2.		
3.		
4.		
5.		
6.		
7.		
8.		
9.		
10.		
General Magic		
11.		
12.		
13.		
14.		
15.		
16.		
17.		
18.		
19.		
20.		
Totals		

1

Sharing Friendship
Acrylic • VOTR
850QLX7063 • **Value $25**

2

Sugarplum Cottage (re-issued from 1984)
Handcrafted • N/A
1100QLX7011 • **Value $50**

3

Village Express (re-issued in 1987)
Handcrafted • SICK
2450QLX7072 • **Value $118**

4

On the Right Track
Porcelain • DUTK
1500QSP4201 • **Value $48**

5

Coca-Cola® Santa
Glass • N/A
475QXO2796 • **Value $24**

6

Old-Fashioned Santa
Handcrafted • SICK
1275QXO4403 • **Value $60**

7

Santa and His Reindeer
Handcrafted • N/A
975QXO4406 • **Value $38**

8

Santa's Panda Pal
Handcrafted • N/A
500QXO4413 • **Value $29**

1985

Some of the most popular pieces in 1985 were based on favorite characters and themes such as Santa Claus, SNOOPY® and the nostalgic artwork of Norman Rockwell. For 1985, there were a total of 114 Keepsake ornament designs and 14 Magic ornaments. See the collectible series section for more 1985 ornaments.

9

Baby Locket
Textured Brass • MCGE
1600QX4012 • **Value $34**

10

Baby's First Christmas
Acrylic • N/A
575QX3702 • **Value $19**

11

Baby's First Christmas
Embroidered Fabric • N/A
700QX4782 • **Value $17**

12

Baby's First Christmas
Fabric • N/A
1600QX4995 • **Value $43**

13

Baby's First Christmas
Handcrafted • DLEE
1500QX4992 • **Value $57**

14

Baby's First Christmas
Satin • VOTR
500QX2602 • **Value $25**

15

Baby's Second Christmas
Handcrafted • N/A
600QX4785 • **Value $38**

16

Babysitter
Glass • PYDA
475QX2642 • **Value $14**

17

Baker Elf
Handcrafted • SEAL
575QX4912 • **Value $33**

	Price Paid	Value
General Magic		
1.		
2.		
3.		
Gold Crown Ornaments		
4.		
Open House Ornaments		
5.		
6.		
7.		
8.		
General Keepsake		
9.		
10.		
11.		
12.		
13.		
14.		
15.		
16.		
17.		
Totals		

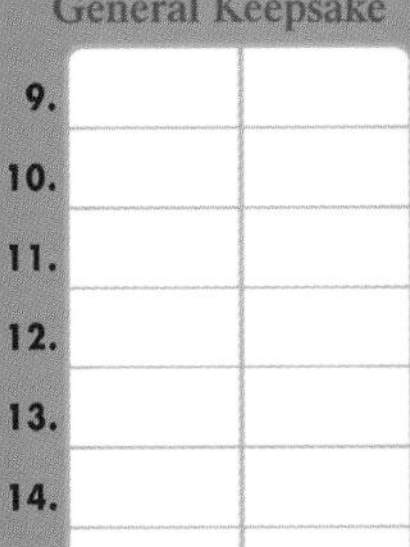

1

Beary Smooth Ride
(re-issued in 1986)
Handcrafted • SICK
650QX4805 • **Value $24**

2

Betsey Clark
Porcelain • N/A
850QX5085 • **Value $34**

3

Bottlecap Fun Bunnies
Handcrafted • SIED
775QX4815 • **Value $37**

4

Candle Cameo
Bezeled Cameo • PIKE
675QX3742 • **Value $15**

5

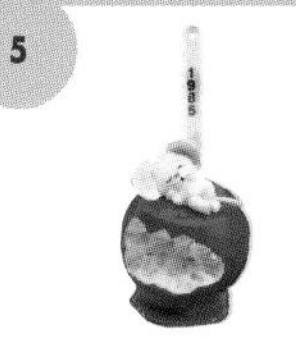

Candy Apple Mouse
Handcrafted • SICK
650QX4705 • **Value $66**

6

Charming Angel
Fabric • PYDA
975QX5125 • **Value $26**

7

Children in the Shoe
Handcrafted • SEAL
950QX4905 • **Value $52**

8

Child's Third Christmas
Handcrafted • SEAL
600QX4755 • **Value $30**

9

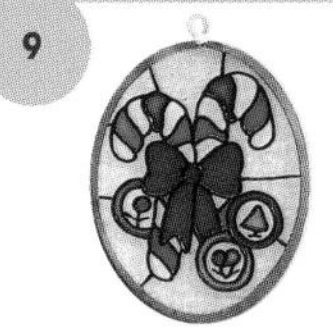

Christmas Treats
Bezeled Glass • N/A
550QX5075 • **Value $18**

10

Country Goose
Wood • PYDA
775QX5185 • **Value $16**

11

Dapper Penguin
Handcrafted • SEAL
500QX4772 • **Value $33**

12

Daughter
Wood • N/A
550QX5032 • **Value $21**

13

A DISNEY Christmas
Glass • N/A
475QX2712 • **Value $36**

14

Do Not Disturb Bear
(re-issued in 1986)
Handcrafted • SEAL
775QX4812 • **Value $34**

15

Doggy in a Stocking
Handcrafted • N/A
550QX4742 • **Value $43**

16

Engineering Mouse
Handcrafted • SIED
550QX4735 • **Value $28**

17

Father
Wood • VOTR
650QX3762 • **Value $13**

18

First Christmas Together
Acrylic • N/A
675QX3705 • **Value $20**

19

First Christmas Together
Brass • SEAL
1675QX4005 • **Value $27**

20

First Christmas Together
Fabric/Wood • N/A
800QX5072 • **Value $15**

General Keepsake

	Price Paid	Value
1.		
2.		
3.		
4.		
5.		
6.		
7.		
8.		
9.		
10.		
11.		
12.		
13.		
14.		
15.		
16.		
17.		
18.		
19.		
20.		
Totals		

1

First Christmas Together
Glass • N/A
475QX2612 • **Value $20**

2

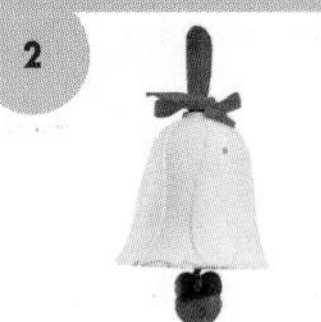

First Christmas Together
Porcelain • SICK
1300QX4935 • **Value $25**

3

FRAGGLE ROCK™ Holiday
Glass • N/A
475QX2655 • **Value $30**

4

Friendship
Bezeled Satin • PYDA
675QX3785 • **Value $19**

5

Friendship
Embroidered Satin • PATT
775QX5062 • **Value $16**

6

From Our House to Yours
Needlepoint Fabric • PATT
775QX5202 • **Value $15**

7

Godchild
Bezeled Satin • MCGE
675QX3802 • **Value $15**

8

Good Friends
Glass • N/A
475QX2652 • **Value $31**

9

Grandchild's First Christmas
Handcrafted • N/A
1100QX4955 • **Value $23**

10

Grandchild's First Christmas
Satin • VOTR
500QX2605 • **Value $15**

11

Granddaughter
Glass • N/A
475QX2635 • **Value $29**

12

Grandmother
Glass • PATT
475QX2625 • **Value $18**

13

Grandparents
Bezeled Lacquer • PIKE
700QX3805 • **Value $14**

14

Grandson
Glass • VOTR
475QX2622 • **Value $29**

15

Heart Full of Love
Bezeled Satin • N/A
675QX3782 • **Value $21**

16

Heavenly Trumpeter (LE-24,700)
Porcelain • DLEE
2750QX4052 • **Value $105**

17

Holiday Heart
Porcelain • N/A
800QX4982 • **Value $26**

18

Hugga Bunch™
Glass • N/A
500QX2715 • **Value $30**

19

Ice Skating Owl
Handcrafted • SIED
500QX4765 • **Value $25**

20

Keepsake Basket
Fabric • PIKE
1500QX5145 • **Value $23**

General Keepsake

	Price Paid	Value
1.		
2.		
3.		
4.		
5.		
6.		
7.		
8.		
9.		
10.		
11.		
12.		
13.		
14.		
15.		
16.		
17.		
18.		
19.		
20.		
Totals		

1

Kit the Shepherd
Handcrafted • SIED
575QX4845 • **Value $26**

2

Kitty Mischief
(re-issued in 1986)
Handcrafted • DUTK
500QX4745 • **Value $25**

3

Lacy Heart
Fabric • N/A
875QX5112 • **Value $27**

4

Lamb in Legwarmers
Handcrafted • N/A
700QX4802 • **Value $25**

5

Love at Christmas
Acrylic • MCGE
575QX3715 • **Value $40**

6

Merry Mouse
(re-issued in 1986)
Handcrafted • DUTK
450QX4032 • **Value $33**

7

Merry Shirt Tales™
Glass • N/A
475QX2672 • **Value $23**

8

Mother
Acrylic • PIKE
675QX3722 • **Value $14**

9

Mother and Dad
Porcelain • VOTR
775QX5092 • **Value $23**

10

Mouse Wagon
Handcrafted • N/A
575QX4762 • **Value $63**

11

Muffin the Angel
Handcrafted • SIED
575QX4835 • **Value $27**

12

Nativity Scene
Glass • N/A
475QX2645 • **Value $35**

13

New Home
Glass • PYDA
475QX2695 • **Value $32**

14

Niece
Acrylic • N/A
575QX5205 • **Value $13**

15

Night Before Christmas
Panorama Ball • SEAL
1300QX4494 • **Value $45**

16

Norman Rockwell
Glass • MCGE
475QX2662 • **Value $43**

17

Nostalgic Sled
(re-issued from 1984)
Handcrafted • SICK
600QX4424 • **Value $28**

18

Old-Fashioned Doll
Fabric/Porcelain • N/A
1450QX5195 • **Value $42**

19

Old-Fashioned Wreath
Brass/Acrylic • N/A
750QX3735 • **Value $26**

20

Peaceful Kingdom
Acrylic • PIKE
575QX3732 • **Value $32**

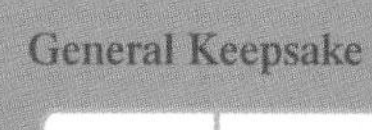
General Keepsake

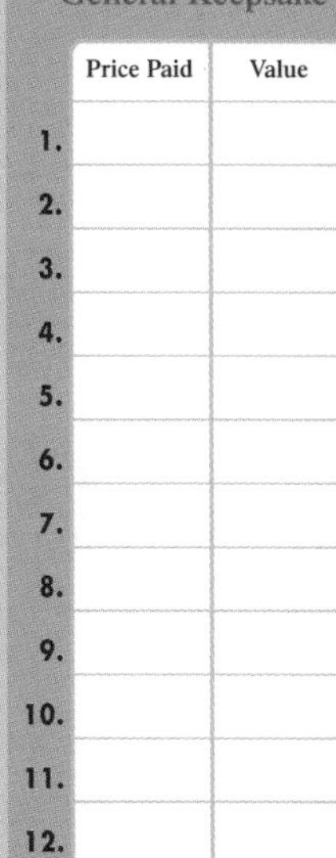

	Price Paid	Value
1.		
2.		
3.		
4.		
5.		
6.		
7.		
8.		
9.		
10.		
11.		
12.		
13.		
14.		
15.		
16.		
17.		
18.		
19.		
20.		
Totals		

1

PEANUTS®
Glass • N/A
475QX2665 • **Value $38**

2

Porcelain Bird
Porcelain • SICK
650QX4795 • **Value $35**

3

Rainbow Brite™ and Friends
Glass • N/A
475QX2682 • **Value $26**

4

Rocking Horse Memories
Fabric/Wood • VOTR
1000QX5182 • **Value $18**

5

Roller Skating Rabbit (re-issued from 1984)
Handcrafted • SEAL
500QX4571 • **Value $32**

6

Santa Pipe
Handcrafted • DUTK
950QX4942 • **Value $26**

7

Santa's Ski Trip
Handcrafted • SEAL
1200QX4962 • **Value $62**

8

Sewn Photoholder
Embroidered Fabric • PIKE
700QX3795 • **Value $37**

9

Sheep at Christmas
Handcrafted • SICK
825QX5175 • **Value $29**

10

Sister
Porcelain • PATT
725QX5065 • **Value $24**

11

Skateboard Raccoon (re-issued in 1986)
Handcrafted • DUTK
650QX4732 • **Value $42**

12

SNOOPY® and WOODSTOCK
Handcrafted • SIED
750QX4915 • **Value $85**

13
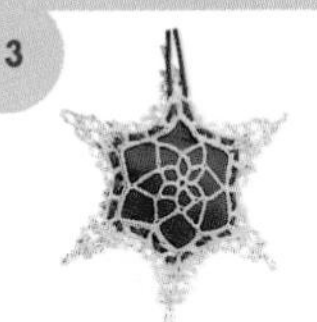
Snowflake
Fabric • PATT
650QX5105 • **Value $22**

14

Snow-Pitching Snowman (re-issued in 1986)
Handcrafted • DLEE
450QX4702 • **Value $23**

15

Snowy Seal (re-issued from 1984)
Handcrafted • SEAL
400QX4501 • **Value $22**

16

Soccer Beaver (re-issued in 1986)
Handcrafted • DUTK
650QX4775 • **Value $27**

17

Son
Handcrafted • SIED
550QX5025 • **Value $50**

18

Special Friends
Arylic • PALM
575QX3725 • **Value $12**

19

The Spirit of Santa Claus
Handcrafted • DLEE
2250QX4985 • **Value $107**

20

Stardust Angel
Handcrafted • DLEE
575QX4752 • **Value $38**

General Keepsake

	Price Paid	Value
1.		
2.		
3.		
4.		
5.		
6.		
7.		
8.		
9.		
10.		
11.		
12.		
13.		
14.		
15.		
16.		
17.		
18.		
19.		
20.		
Totals		

1

Sun and Fun Santa
Handcrafted • SIED
775QX4922 • **Value $42**

2

Swinging Angel Bell
Handcrafted/Glass • SIED
1100QX4925 • **Value $37**

3

Teacher
Handcrafted • N/A
600QX5052 • **Value $20**

4

Three Kittens in a Mitten (re-issued from 1984)
Handcrafted • DLEE
800QX4311 • **Value $56**

5

Trumpet Panda
Handcrafted • SEAL
450QX4712 • **Value $26**

6

Twenty-Five Years Together
Porcelain • N/A
800QX5005 • **Value $17**

7

Victorian Lady
Porcelain/Fabric • N/A
950QX5132 • **Value $26**

8

Whirligig Santa
Wood • N/A
1250QX5192 • **Value $28**

9

With Appreciation
Acrylic • N/A
675QX3752 • **Value $14**

10

All Are Precious (re-issued from 1984)
Acrylic • N/A
800QLX7044 • **Value $30**

11

Baby's First Christmas
Handcrafted • SEAL
1650QLX7005 • **Value $42**

12

Christmas Eve Visit
Etched Brass • N/A
1200QLX7105 • **Value $34**

13

Katybeth
Acrylic • N/A
1075QLX7102 • **Value $44**

14

Little Red Schoolhouse
Handcrafted • DLEE
1575QLX7112 • **Value $93**

15

Love Wreath
Acrylic • VOTR
850QLX7025 • **Value $30**

16

Mr. and Mrs. Santa (re-issued in 1986)
Handcrafted • N/A
1450QLX7052 • **Value $88**

17

Nativity (re-issued from 1984)
Panorama Ball • SEAL
1200QLX7001 • **Value $33**

18

Santa's Workshop (re-issued from 1984)
Panorama Ball • N/A
1300QLX7004 • **Value $66**

19

Season of Beauty
Classic Shape • LYLE
800QLX7122 • **Value $27**

20

Sugarplum Cottage (re-issued from 1984)
Handcrafted • N/A
1100QLX7011 • **Value $50**

General Keepsake

	Price Paid	Value
1.		
2.		
3.		
4.		
5.		
6.		
7.		
8.		
9.		

General Magic

	Price Paid	Value
10.		
11.		
12.		
13.		
14.		
15.		
16.		
17.		
18.		
19.		
20.		
Totals		

1

Swiss Cheese Lane
Handcrafted • N/A
1300QLX7065 • **Value $49**

2

Village Church (re-issued from 1984)
Handcrafted • DLEE
1500QLX7021 • **Value $52**

3

Santa Claus
Lacquer • N/A
675QX3005 • **Value $12**

4

Santa's Village
Lacquer • N/A
675QX3002 • **Value $12**

1984

1984 was a landmark year for Hallmark ornaments with the debut of lighted Magic ornaments (then called "Lighted Ornaments"). In later years, these ornaments would also incorporate motion and sound. There were 10 Magic ornaments issued in 1984, as well as 110 Keepsake designs. See the collectible series section for more 1984 ornaments.

5

Alpine Elf
Handcrafted • SEAL
600QX4521 • **Value $40**

General Magic

	Price Paid	Value
1.		
2.		

Santa Claus – The Movie

	Price Paid	Value
3.		
4.		

General Keepsake

	Price Paid	Value
5.		
6.		
7.		
8.		
9.		
10.		
11.		
12.		
13.		
14.		
15.		
16.		
17.		
Totals		

6

Amanda
Fabric/Porcelain • N/A
900QX4321 • **Value $33**

7

Baby's First Christmas
Acrylic • N/A
600QX3401 • **Value $42**

8

Baby's First Christmas
Classic Shape • DLEE
1600QX9041 • **Value $48**

9

Baby's First Christmas
Handcrafted • N/A
1400QX4381 • **Value $48**

10

Baby's First Christmas – Boy
Satin • N/A
450QX2404 • **Value $30**

11

Baby's First Christmas – Girl
Satin • N/A
450QX2401 • **Value $29**

12

Baby's First Christmas – Photoholder
Fabric • N/A
700QX3001 • **Value $20**

13

Baby's Second Christmas
Satin • N/A
450QX2411 • **Value $42**

14

Baby-sitter
Glass • N/A
450QX2531 • **Value $16**

15

Bell Ringer Squirrel
Handcrafted/Glass • SEAL
1000QX4431 • **Value $40**

16

Betsey Clark Angel
Porcelain • N/A
900QX4624 • **Value $36**

17

Chickadee
Porcelain • SICK
600QX4514 • **Value $42**

1

Child's Third Christmas
Satin • N/A
450QX2611 • **Value $25**

2

Christmas Memories Photoholder
Fabric • N/A
650QX3004 • **Value $28**

3

Christmas Owl
Handcrafted/Acrylic • SEAL
600QX4441 • **Value $33**

4

A Christmas Prayer
Satin • N/A
450QX2461 • **Value $24**

5

Classical Angel (LE-24,700)
Porcelain • DLEE
2750QX4591 • **Value $105**

6

Cuckoo Clock
Handcrafted • DLEE
1000QX4551 • **Value $57**

7

Currier & Ives
Glass • N/A
450QX2501 • **Value $26**

8

Daughter
Glass • N/A
450QX2444 • **Value $37**

9

DISNEY
Glass • N/A
450QX2504 • **Value $43**

10

Embroidered Heart (re-issued from 1983)
Fabric • N/A
650QX4217 • **Value $27**

11

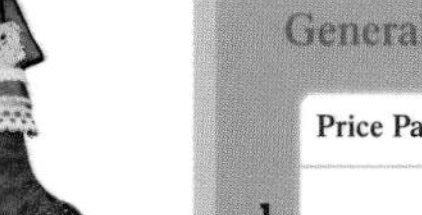
Embroidered Stocking (re-issued from 1983)
Fabric • SICK
650QX4796 • **Value $23**

12

Father
Acrylic • N/A
600QX2571 • **Value $20**

13

First Christmas Together
Acrylic • N/A
600QX3421 • **Value $22**

14

First Christmas Together
Brushed Brass • SEAL
1500QX4364 • **Value $37**

15

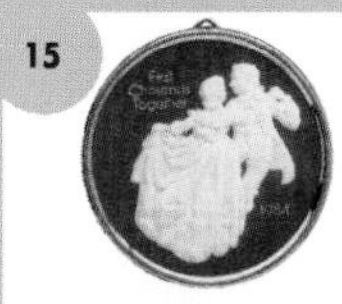
First Christmas Together
Cameo • MCGE
750QX3404 • **Value $25**

16

First Christmas Together
Classic Shape • MCGE
1600QX9044 • **Value $43**

17

First Christmas Together
Glass • N/A
450QX2451 • **Value $30**

18

Flights of Fantasy
Glass • N/A
450QX2564 • **Value $24**

19

Fortune Cookie Elf
Handcrafted • SICK
450QX4524 • **Value $42**

20
Friendship
Glass • N/A
450QX2481 • **Value $22**

General Keepsake

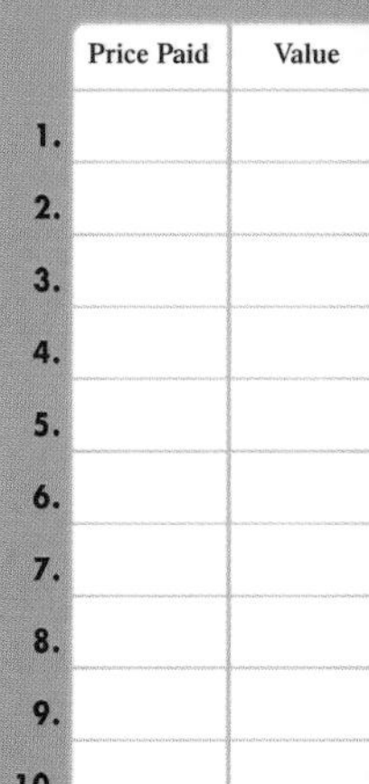
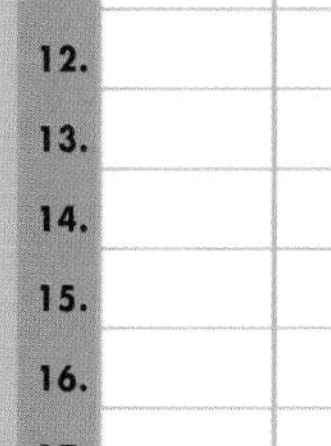

	Price Paid	Value
1.		
2.		
3.		
4.		
5.		
6.		
7.		
8.		
9.		
10.		
11.		
12.		
13.		
14.		
15.		
16.		
17.		
18.		
19.		
20.		
Totals		

1

Frisbee® Puppy
Handcrafted • N/A
500QX4444 • **Value $55**

2

From Our Home to Yours
Glass • N/A
450QX2484 • **Value $54**

3

The Fun of Friendship
Acrylic • N/A
600QX3431 • **Value $36**

4

A Gift of Friendship
Glass • N/A
450QX2604 • **Value $26**

5

Gift of Music
Handcrafted • SEAL
1500QX4511 • **Value $100**

6

Godchild
Glass • N/A
450QX2421 • **Value $19**

7

Grandchild's First Christmas
Handcrafted • N/A
1100QX4601 • **Value $27**

8

Grandchild's First Christmas
Satin • N/A
450QX2574 • **Value $18**

9

Granddaughter
Glass • N/A
450QX2431 • **Value $27**

10

Grandmother
Glass • N/A
450QX2441 • **Value $19**

11

Grandparents
Glass • N/A
450QX2561 • **Value $19**

12

Grandson
Glass • N/A
450QX2424 • **Value $28**

13

Gratitude
Acrylic • N/A
600QX3444 • **Value $15**

14

Heartful of Love
Bone China • N/A
1000QX4434 • **Value $49**

15

Holiday Friendship
Panorama Ball • N/A
1300QX4451 • **Value $32**

16

Holiday Jester
Handcrafted • SICK
1100QX4374 • **Value $35**

17

Holiday Starburst
Glass • N/A
500QX2534 • **Value $23**

18

Katybeth
Porcelain • N/A
900QX4631 • **Value $30**

19

Kit
Handcrafted • N/A
550QX4534 • **Value $31**

20

Love
Glass • N/A
450QX2554 • **Value $28**

General Keepsake

	Price Paid	Value
1.		
2.		
3.		
4.		
5.		
6.		
7.		
8.		
9.		
10.		
11.		
12.		
13.		
14.		
15.		
16.		
17.		
18.		
19.		
20.		
Totals		

1

Love . . . the Spirit of Christmas
Glass • N/A
450QX2474 • **Value $44**

2

Madonna and Child
Acrylic • PALM
600QX3441 • **Value $50**

3

Marathon Santa
Handcrafted • SEAL
800QX4564 • **Value $43**

4

The Miracle of Love
Acrylic • N/A
600QX3424 • **Value $35**

5

Mother
Acrylic • N/A
600QX3434 • **Value $18**

6
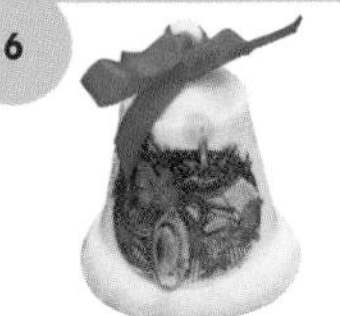
Mother and Dad
Bone China • N/A
650QX2581 • **Value $29**

7

Mountain Climbing Santa (re-issued from 1983)
Handcrafted • SEAL
650QX4077 • **Value $38**

8

Muffin
Handcrafted • DLEE
550QX4421 • **Value $32**

9

The MUPPETS™
Glass • N/A
450QX2514 • **Value $35**

10

Musical Angel
Handcrafted • DLEE
550QX4344 • **Value $73**

11

Napping Mouse
Handcrafted • N/A
550QX4351 • **Value $52**

12

Needlepoint Wreath
Fabric • PIKE
650QX4594 • **Value $18**

13

New Home
Glass • N/A
450QX2454 • **Value $85**

14

Norman Rockwell
Glass • MCGE
450QX2511 • **Value $32**

15

Nostalgic Sled (re-issued in 1985)
Handcrafted • SICK
600QX4424 • **Value $28**

16

Old Fashioned Rocking Horse
Acrylic/Brass • N/A
750QX3464 • **Value $23**

17
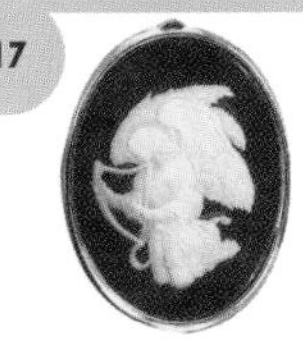
Peace on Earth
Cameo • N/A
750QX3414 • **Value $32**

18

PEANUTS®
Satin • N/A
450QX2521 • **Value $40**

19

Peppermint 1984
Handcrafted • DLEE
450QX4561 • **Value $54**

20

Polar Bear Drummer
Handcrafted • SEAL
450QX4301 • **Value $32**

General Keepsake

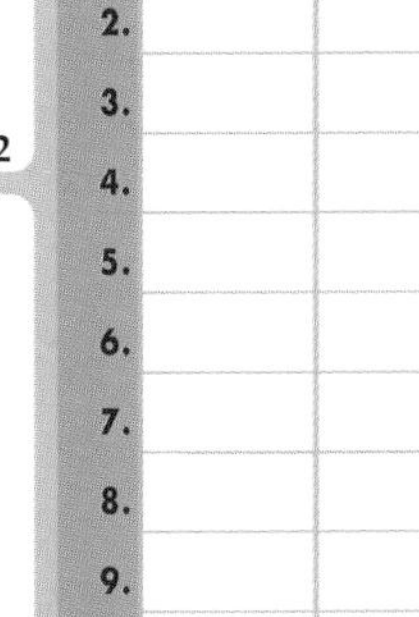

	Price Paid	Value
1.		
2.		
3.		
4.		
5.		
6.		
7.		
8.		
9.		
10.		
11.		
12.		
13.		
14.		
15.		
16.		
17.		
18.		
19.		
20.		
Totals		

1

Raccoon's Christmas
Handcrafted • SEAL
900QX4474 • **Value $55**

2

Reindeer Racetrack
Glass • N/A
450QX2544 • **Value $26**

3

Roller Skating Rabbit (re-issued in 1985)
Handcrafted • SEAL
500QX4571 • **Value $32**

4

Santa
Fabric • N/A
750QX4584 • **Value $22**

5

Santa Mouse
Handcrafted • SIED
450QX4334 • **Value $52**

6

Santa Star
Handcrafted • N/A
550QX4504 • **Value $39**

7

Santa Sulky Driver
Etched Brass • N/A
900QX4361 • **Value $35**

8

A Savior is Born
Glass • N/A
450QX2541 • **Value $34**

9

Shirt Tales™
Satin • N/A
450QX2524 • **Value $21**

10
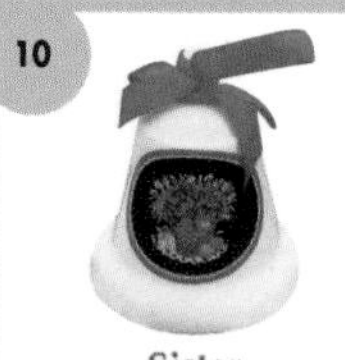
Sister
Bone China • N/A
650QX2594 • **Value $30**

11

SNOOPY® and WOODSTOCK
Handcrafted • SEAL
750QX4391 • **Value $98**

12

Snowmobile Santa
Handcrafted • N/A
650QX4314 • **Value $37**

13

Snowshoe Penguin
Handcrafted • SICK
650QX4531 • **Value $48**

14

Snowy Seal (re-issued in 1985)
Handcrafted • SEAL
400QX4501 • **Value $22**

15

Son
Glass • N/A
450QX2434 • **Value $32**

16

Teacher
Glass • N/A
450QX2491 • **Value $15**

17

Ten Years Together
Bone China • N/A
650QX2584 • **Value $17**

18

Three Kittens in a Mitten (re-issued in 1985)
Handcrafted • DLEE
800QX4311 • **Value $56**

19

Twelve Days of Christmas
Handcrafted • SEAL
1500QX4159 • **Value $110**

20

Twenty-Five Years Together
Bone China • N/A
650QX2591 • **Value $20**

General Keepsake

	Price Paid	Value
1.		
2.		
3.		
4.		
5.		
6.		
7.		
8.		
9.		
10.		
11.		
12.		
13.		
14.		
15.		
16.		
17.		
18.		
19.		
20.		
Totals		

1

Uncle Sam
Pressed Tin • SICK
600QX4491 • **Value $52**

2

White Christmas
Classic Shape • N/A
1600QX9051 • **Value $95**

3
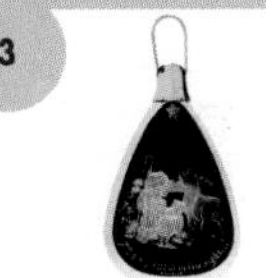
All Are Precious (re-issued in 1985)
Acrylic • N/A
800QLX7044 • **Value $30**

4

Brass Carousel
Etched Brass • N/A
900QLX7071 • **Value $88**

5

Christmas in the Forest
Classic Shape • N/A
800QLX7034 • **Value $22**

6

City Lights
Handcrafted • SIED
1000QLX7014 • **Value $55**

7

Nativity (re-issued in 1985)
Panorama Ball • SEAL
1200QLX7001 • **Value $33**

8

Santa's Arrival
Panorama Ball • DLEE
1300QLX7024 • **Value $65**

9

Santa's Workshop (re-issued in 1985)
Panorama Ball • N/A
1300QLX7004 • **Value $66**

10

Stained Glass
Classic Shape • N/A
800QLX7031 • **Value $23**

11

Sugarplum Cottage (re-issued in 1985 and 1986)
Handcrafted • N/A
1100QLX7011 • **Value $50**

12

Village Church (re-issued in 1985)
Handcrafted • DLEE
1500QLX7021 • **Value $52**

1983

1983 marked the 10th anniversary of Keepsake ornaments. Among the popular pieces from 1983 were a pair of angel ornaments, "Baroque Angels" and "Rainbow Angel," as well as three ornaments featuring Muppets™ characters. The 1983 line featured 111 Keepsake ornaments. See the collectible series section for more 1983 ornaments.

13

25th Christmas Together
Glass • N/A
450QX2247 • **Value $23**

14

1983
Glass • N/A
450QX2209 • **Value $30**

15

Angel Messenger
Handcrafted • SEAL
650QX4087 • **Value $99**

	Price Paid	Value
General Keepsake		
1.		
2.		
General Magic		
3.		
4.		
5.		
6.		
7.		
8.		
9.		
10.		
11.		
12.		
General Keepsake		
13.		
14.		
15.		
Totals		

1

Angels
Glass • N/A
500QX2197 • **Value $26**

2

The Annunciation
Glass • N/A
450QX2167 • **Value $33**

3

Baby's First Christmas
Acrylic • N/A
700QX3029 • **Value $24**

4

Baby's First Christmas
Cameo • SICK
750QX3019 • **Value $18**

5

Baby's First Christmas
Handcrafted • DLEE
1400QX4027 • **Value $38**

6

Baby's First Christmas – Boy
Satin • N/A
450QX2009 • **Value $30**

7

Baby's First Christmas – Girl
Satin • N/A
450QX2007 • **Value $30**

8

Baby's Second Christmas
Satin • N/A
450QX2267 • **Value $36**

9

Baroque Angels
Handcrafted • DLEE
1300QX4229 • **Value $130**

10

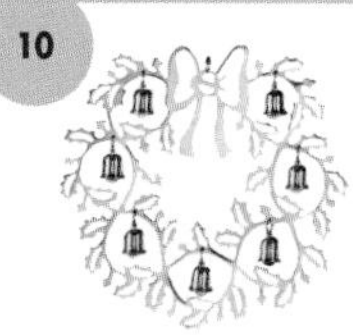

Bell Wreath
Brass • SICK
650QX4209 • **Value $35**

11

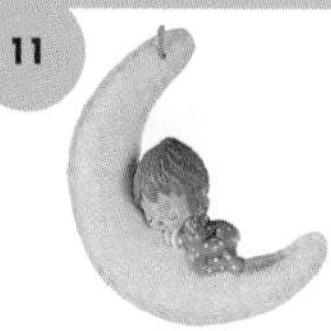

Betsey Clark
Handcrafted • SEAL
650QX4047 • **Value $34**

12

Betsey Clark
Porcelain • N/A
900QX4401 • **Value $35**

13

Brass Santa
Brass • SEAL
900QX4239 • **Value $25**

14

Caroling Owl
Handcrafted • SEAL
450QX4117 • **Value $41**

15

Child's Third Christmas
Satin Piqué • N/A
450QX2269 • **Value $27**

16

Christmas Joy
Satin • N/A
450QX2169 • **Value $33**

17

Christmas Kitten (re-issued from 1982)
Handcrafted • N/A
400QX4543 • **Value $40**

18

Christmas Koala
Handcrafted • SEAL
400QX4199 • **Value $34**

19

Christmas Stocking
Acrylic • N/A
600QX3039 • **Value $42**

20

Christmas Wonderland
Glass • N/A
450QX2219 • **Value $130**

General Keepsake

	Price Paid	Value
1.		
2.		
3.		
4.		
5.		
6.		
7.		
8.		
9.		
10.		
11.		
12.		
13.		
14.		
15.		
16.		
17.		
18.		
19.		
20.		
Totals		

1

Currier & Ives
Glass • N/A
450QX2159 • **Value $25**

2

Cycling Santa
(re-issued from 1982)
Handcrafted • N/A
2000QX4355 • **Value $160**

3

Daughter
Glass • N/A
450QX2037 • **Value $46**

4

DISNEY
Glass • N/A
450QX2129 • **Value $56**

5

Embroidered Heart
(re-issued in 1984)
Fabric • N/A
650QX4217 • **Value $27**

6

Embroidered Stocking
(re-issued in 1984)
Fabric • SICK
650QX4796 • **Value $23**

7

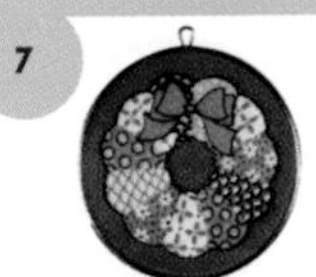

Enameled Christmas Wreath
Enameled • N/A
900QX3119 • **Value $15**

8

First Christmas Together
Acrylic • N/A
600QX3069 • **Value $25**

9

First Christmas Together
Cameo • N/A
750QX3017 • **Value $23**

10

First Christmas Together
Classic Shape • N/A
600QX3107 • **Value $38**

11

First Christmas Together
Glass • SICK
450QX2089 • **Value $32**

12

First Christmas Together – Brass Locket
Brass • SEAL
1500QX4329 • **Value $38**

13

Friendship
Acrylic • N/A
600QX3059 • **Value $21**

14

Friendship
Glass • N/A
450QX2077 • **Value $22**

15

Godchild
Glass • N/A
450QX2017 • **Value $19**

16

Grandchild's First Christmas
Classic Shape • N/A
600QX3129 • **Value $24**

17

Grandchild's First Christmas
Handcrafted • N/A
1400QX4309 • **Value $37**

18

Granddaughter
Glass • N/A
450QX2027 • **Value $30**

19

Grandmother
Glass • N/A
450QX2057 • **Value $23**

20

Grandparents
Ceramic • N/A
650QX4299 • **Value $23**

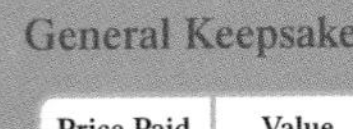

General Keepsake

	Price Paid	Value
1.		
2.		
3.		
4.		
5.		
6.		
7.		
8.		
9.		
10.		
11.		
12.		
13.		
14.		
15.		
16.		
17.		
18.		
19.		
20.		
Totals		

1

Grandson
Satin • N/A
450QX2019 • **Value $30**

2

Heart
Acrylic • SICK
400QX3079 • **Value $52**

3

Here Comes Santa
Glass • N/A
450QX2177 • **Value $42**

4

Hitchhiking Santa
Handcrafted • SEAL
800QX4247 • **Value $42**

5

Holiday Puppy
Handcrafted • N/A
350QX4127 • **Value $30**

6

Jack Frost
Handcrafted • N/A
900QX4079 • **Value $62**

7

Jolly Santa
Handcrafted • N/A
350QX4259 • **Value $36**

8

KERMIT the FROG™
(re-issued from 1982)
Handcrafted • DLEE
1100QX4956 • **Value $110**

9

Love
Acrylic • N/A
600QX3057 • **Value $20**

10

Love
Classic Shape • N/A
600QX3109 • **Value $40**

11

Love
Glass • N/A
450QX2079 • **Value $56**

12

Love
Porcelain • SICK
1300QX4227 • **Value $38**

13

Love Is a Song
Glass • N/A
450QX2239 • **Value $32**

14

Madonna and Child
Porcelain • N/A
1200QX4287 • **Value $45**

15

Mailbox Kitten
Handcrafted • N/A
650QX4157 • **Value $61**

16

Mary Hamilton
Glass • N/A
450QX2137 • **Value $46**

17

Memories to Treasure
Acrylic • N/A
700QX3037 • **Value $36**

18

MISS PIGGY™
Handcrafted • N/A
1300QX4057 • **Value $225**

19

Mom and Dad
Ceramic • PIKE
650QX4297 • **Value $26**

20

Mother
Acrylic • N/A
600QX3067 • **Value $21**

General Keepsake

	Price Paid	Value
1.		
2.		
3.		
4.		
5.		
6.		
7.		
8.		
9.		
10.		
11.		
12.		
13.		
14.		
15.		
16.		
17.		
18.		
19.		
20.		
Totals		

1
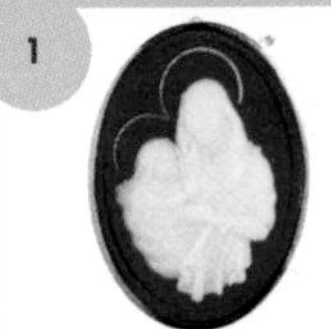
Mother and Child
Cameo • N/A
750QX3027 • **Value $40**

2

Mountain Climbing Santa (re-issued in 1984)
Handcrafted • SEAL
650QX4077 • **Value $38**

3

Mouse in Bell
Handcrafted/Glass • N/A
1000QX4197 • **Value $70**

4

Mouse on Cheese
Handcrafted • SICK
650QX4137 • **Value $50**

5

The MUPPETS™
Satin • N/A
450QX2147 • **Value $52**

6

New Home
Satin • N/A
450QX2107 • **Value $36**

7

Norman Rockwell
Glass • N/A
450QX2157 • **Value $35**

8

An Old Fashioned Christmas
Glass • N/A
450QX2179 • **Value $32**

9

Old-Fashioned Santa
Handcrafted • SICK
1100QX4099 • **Value $69**

10

Oriental Butterflies
Glass • N/A
450QX2187 • **Value $32**

11

PEANUTS®
Satin • N/A
450QX2127 • **Value $40**

12

Peppermint Penguin
Handcrafted • N/A
650QX4089 • **Value $45**

13

Porcelain Doll, Diana
Porcelain/Fabric • DLEE
900QX4237 • **Value $33**

14

Rainbow Angel
Handcrafted • DLEE
550QX4167 • **Value $115**

15
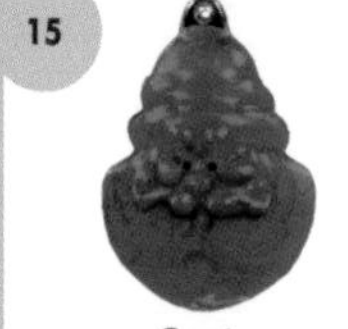
Santa
Acrylic • N/A
400QX3087 • **Value $35**

16
Santa's Many Faces
Classic Shape • N/A
600QX3117 • **Value $35**

17
Santa's on His Way
Handcrafted • N/A
1000QX4269 • **Value $38**

18

Santa's Workshop (re-issued from 1982)
Handcrafted • DLEE
1000QX4503 • **Value $85**

19

Scrimshaw Reindeer
Handcrafted • SEAL
800QX4249 • **Value $35**

20
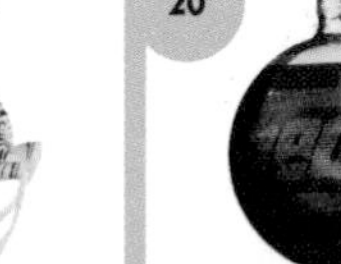
Season's Greetings
Glass • N/A
450QX2199 • **Value $26**

General Keepsake

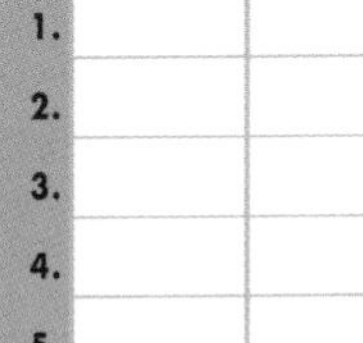

	Price Paid	Value
1.		
2.		
3.		
4.		
5.		
6.		
7.		
8.		
9.		
10.		
11.		
12.		
13.		
14.		
15.		
16.		
17.		
18.		
19.		
20.		
Totals		

1

SHIRT TALES™
Glass • N/A
450QX2149 • **Value $28**

2

Sister
Glass • N/A
450QX2069 • **Value $25**

3

Skating Rabbit
Handcrafted • N/A
800QX4097 • **Value $55**

4

Ski Lift Santa
Handcrafted/Brass • N/A
800QX4187 • **Value $73**

5

Skiing Fox
Handcrafted • DLEE
800QX4207 • **Value $40**

6

Sneaker Mouse
Handcrafted • SEAL
450QX4009 • **Value $42**

7

Son
Satin • N/A
450QX2029 • **Value $40**

8

Star of Peace
Acrylic • SEAL
600QX3047 • **Value $20**

9

Teacher
Acrylic • N/A
600QX3049 • **Value $15**

10

Teacher
Glass • N/A
450QX2249 • **Value $16**

11
Tenth Christmas Together
Ceramic • N/A
650QX4307 • **Value $25**

12
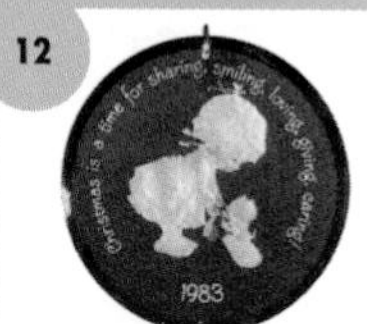

Time for Sharing
Acrylic • N/A
600QX3077 • **Value $38**

13

Tin Rocking Horse
Pressed Tin • SICK
650QX4149 • **Value $53**

14

Unicorn
Porcelain • N/A
1000QX4267 • **Value $66**

15
The Wise Men
Glass • N/A
450QX2207 • **Value $55**

16

Baby's First Christmas
Classic Shape • N/A
1600QMB9039 • **Value $90**

17

Friendship
Classic Shape • N/A
1600QMB9047 • **Value $115**

18

Nativity
Classic Shape • N/A
1600QMB9049 • **Value $125**

19

Twelve Days of Christmas
Handcrafted • SEAL
1500QMB4159 • **Value $100**

General Keepsake

	Price Paid	Value
1.		
2.		
3.		
4.		
5.		
6.		
7.		
8.		
9.		
10.		
11.		
12.		
13.		
14.		
15.		

Musical Ornaments

	Price Paid	Value
16.		
17.		
18.		
19.		

Price Paid	Value

Totals

1982

The 1982 collection was highlighted by the always-popular creations of Hallmark artist, Donna Lee. Among her sought-after 1982 designs were "Baroque Angel," "Pinecone Home" and "Raccoon Surprises." Overall, there were 104 Keepsake ornaments issued in 1982. See the collectible series section for more 1982 ornaments.

1
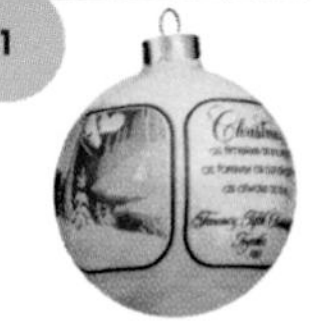

25th Christmas Together
Glass • N/A
450QX2116 • **Value $21**

2

50th Christmas Together
Glass • N/A
450QX2123 • **Value $21**

3
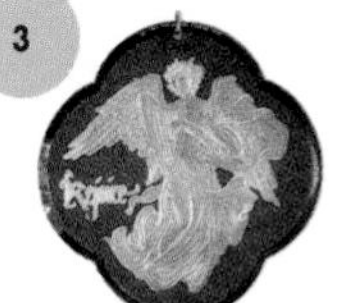

Angel
Acrylic • N/A
550QX3096 • **Value $34**

4

Angel Chimes
Chrome-Plated Brass • N/A
550QX5026 • **Value $37**

5

Arctic Penguin
Acrylic • N/A
400QX3003 • **Value $22**

6

Baby's First Christmas
Acrylic • SEAL
550QX3023 • **Value $38**

7

Baby's First Christmas
Handcrafted • SEAL
1300QX4553 • **Value $50**

8

Baby's First Christmas – Boy
Satin • N/A
450QX2163 • **Value $28**

9

Baby's First Christmas – Girl
Satin • N/A
450QX2073 • **Value $28**

10

Baby's First Christmas – Photoholder
Acrylic • N/A
650QX3126 • **Value $30**

11

Baroque Angel
Handcrafted/Brass • DLEE
1500QX4566 • **Value $177**

12

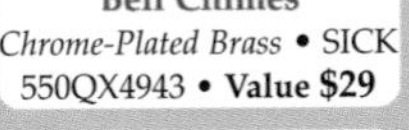

Bell Chimes
Chrome-Plated Brass • SICK
550QX4943 • **Value $29**

13

Betsey Clark
Cameo • N/A
850QX3056 • **Value $28**

14

Brass Bell
Brass • DLEE
1200QX4606 • **Value $29**

15

Christmas Angel
Glass • N/A
450QX2206 • **Value $27**

16

Christmas Fantasy (re-issued from 1981)
Handcrafted/Brass • N/A
1300QX1554 • **Value $90**

17

Christmas Kitten (re-issued in 1983)
Handcrafted • N/A
400QX4543 • **Value $40**

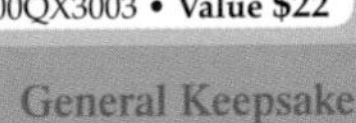

General Keepsake

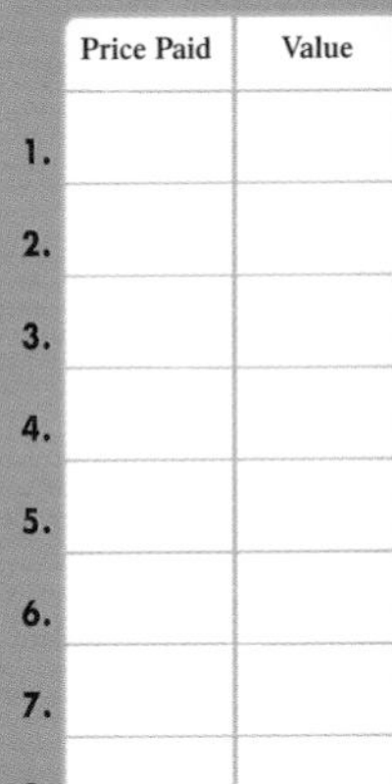

	Price Paid	Value
1.		
2.		
3.		
4.		
5.		
6.		
7.		
8.		
9.		
10.		
11.		
12.		
13.		
14.		
15.		
16.		
17.		
Totals		

1

Christmas Magic
Acrylic • N/A
550QX3113 • **Value $30**

2

Christmas Memories – Photoholder
Acrylic • SICK
650QX3116 • **Value $25**

3

Christmas Owl (re-issued from 1980)
Handcrafted • N/A
400QX1314 • **Value $49**

4

Christmas Sleigh
Acrylic • N/A
550QX3093 • **Value $72**

5

Cloisonné Angel
Cloisonné • N/A
1200QX1454 • **Value $98**

6

Cookie Mouse
Handcrafted • SICK
450QX4546 • **Value $61**

7

Cowboy Snowman
Handcrafted • N/A
800QX4806 • **Value $57**

8

Currier & Ives
Glass • N/A
450QX2013 • **Value $25**

9

Cycling Santa (re-issued in 1983)
Handcrafted • N/A
2000QX4355 • **Value $160**

10

Daughter
Satin • N/A
450QX2046 • **Value $35**

11

DISNEY
Satin • N/A
450QX2173 • **Value $37**

12

THE DIVINE MISS PIGGY™ (re-issued from 1981)
Handcrafted • FRAN
1200QX4255 • **Value $94**

13

Dove Love
Acrylic • SICK
450QX4623 • **Value $52**

14
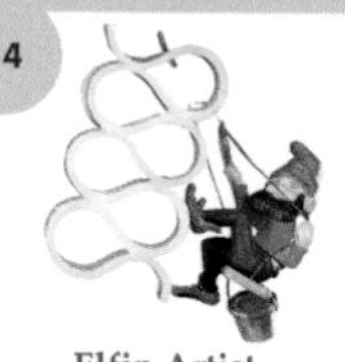
Elfin Artist
Handcrafted • SICK
900QX4573 • **Value $50**

15

Embroidered Tree
Fabric • N/A
650QX4946 • **Value $40**

16

Father
Satin • SICK
450QX2056 • **Value $22**

17

First Christmas Together
Acrylic • SEAL
550QX3026 • **Value $20**

18

First Christmas Together
Cameo • N/A
850QX3066 • **Value $46**

19

First Christmas Together
Glass • N/A
450QX2113 • **Value $37**

20

First Christmas Together – Locket
Brass • SEAL
1500QX4563 • **Value $26**

General Keepsake

	Price Paid	Value
1.		
2.		
3.		
4.		
5.		
6.		
7.		
8.		
9.		
10.		
11.		
12.		
13.		
14.		
15.		
16.		
17.		
18.		
19.		
20.		
Totals		

1

Friendship
Acrylic • N/A
550QX3046 • **Value $24**

2

Friendship
Satin • N/A
450QX2086 • **Value $21**

3

Godchild
Glass • N/A
450QX2226 • **Value $23**

4

Granddaughter
Glass • N/A
450QX2243 • **Value $26**

5

Grandfather
Satin • N/A
450QX2076 • **Value $20**

6

Grandmother
Satin • N/A
450QX2003 • **Value $19**

7

Grandparents
Glass • N/A
450QX2146 • **Value $18**

8

Grandson
Satin • N/A
450QX2246 • **Value $27**

9

Ice Sculptor
(re-issued from 1981)
Handcrafted • DLEE
800QX4322 • **Value $97**

10

Jingling Teddy
Brass • SEAL
400QX4776 • **Value $40**

11

Joan Walsh Anglund
Satin • N/A
450QX2193 • **Value $23**

12

Jogging Santa
Handcrafted • N/A
800QX4576 • **Value $50**

13

Jolly Christmas Tree
Handcrafted • N/A
650QX4653 • **Value $83**

14

KERMIT the FROG™
(re-issued in 1983)
Handcrafted • DLEE
1100QX4956 • **Value $110**

15
Love
Acrylic • N/A
550QX3043 • **Value $30**

16

Love
Satin • N/A
450QX2096 • **Value $18**

17

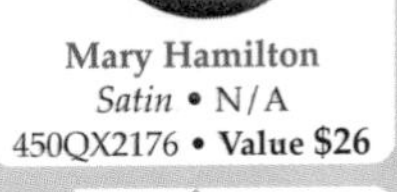
Mary Hamilton
Satin • N/A
450QX2176 • **Value $26**

18

Merry Christmas
Glass • N/A
450QX2256 • **Value $24**

19

Merry Moose
Handcrafted • N/A
550QX4155 • **Value $60**

20

MISS PIGGY™
and KERMIT™
Satin • N/A
450QX2183 • **Value $42**

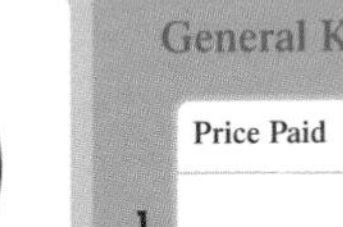

General Keepsake

	Price Paid	Value
1.		
2.		
3.		
4.		
5.		
6.		
7.		
8.		
9.		
10.		
11.		
12.		
13.		
14.		
15.		
16.		
17.		
18.		
19.		
20.		
Totals		

1

Moments of Love
Satin • N/A
450QX2093 • **Value $20**

2

Mother
Glass • N/A
450QX2053 • **Value $20**

3

Mother and Dad
Glass • N/A
450QX2223 • **Value $17**

4

MUPPETS™ Party
Satin • N/A
450QX2186 • **Value $42**

5

Musical Angel
Handcrafted • DLEE
550QX4596 • **Value $130**

6

Nativity
Acrylic • N/A
450QX3083 • **Value $50**

7

New Home
Satin • N/A
450QX2126 • **Value $23**

8

Norman Rockwell
Satin • N/A
450QX2023 • **Value $28**

9

Old Fashioned Christmas
Glass • N/A
450QX2276 • **Value $50**

10

Old World Angels
Glass • N/A
450QX2263 • **Value $27**

11

Patterns of Christmas
Glass • N/A
450QX2266 • **Value $23**

12

PEANUTS®
Satin • N/A
450QX2006 • **Value $40**

13

Peeking Elf
Handcrafted • N/A
650QX4195 • **Value $40**

14

Perky Penguin (re-issued from 1981)
Handcrafted • N/A
400QX4095 • **Value $60**

15

Pinecone Home
Handcrafted • DLEE
800QX4613 • **Value $175**

16

Raccoon Surprises
Handcrafted • DLEE
900QX4793 • **Value $166**

17

Santa
Glass • BLAC
450QX2216 • **Value $23**

18

Santa and Reindeer
Handcrafted/Brass • SICK
900QX4676 • **Value $52**

19

Santa Bell
Porcelain • N/A
1500QX1487 • **Value $60**

20

Santa's Flight
Acrylic • N/A
450QX3086 • **Value $47**

General Keepsake

	Price Paid	Value
1.		
2.		
3.		
4.		
5.		
6.		
7.		
8.		
9.		
10.		
11.		
12.		
13.		
14.		
15.		
16.		
17.		
18.		
19.		
20.		
Totals		

1

Santa's Sleigh
Brass • SEAL
900QX4786 • **Value $35**

2

Santa's Workshop (re-issued in 1983)
Handcrafted • DLEE
1000QX4503 • **Value $85**

3

Season for Caring
Satin • N/A
450QX2213 • **Value $26**

4

Sister
Glass • N/A
450QX2083 • **Value $33**

5

Snowy Seal
Acrylic • N/A
400QX3006 • **Value $22**

6

Son
Satin • N/A
450QX2043 • **Value $32**

7

The Spirit of Christmas
Handcrafted • SICK
1000QX4526 • **Value $130**

8

Stained Glass
Glass • N/A
450QX2283 • **Value $27**

9

Teacher
Acrylic • SICK
650QX3123 • **Value $19**

10

Teacher
Glass • N/A
450QX2143 • **Value $14**

11

Teacher – Apple
Acrylic • SEAL
550QX3016 • **Value $16**

12

Three Kings
Cameo • BLAC
850QX3073 • **Value $27**

13

Tin Soldier
Pressed Tin • SICK
650QX4836 • **Value $48**

14

Tree Chimes
Stamped Brass • SEAL
550QX4846 • **Value $43**

15

Twelve Days of Christmas
Glass • N/A
450QX2036 • **Value $33**

16

Dimensional Ornament
Dimensional Brass • N/A
($3.50) No stock # • **Value $42**

17

Baby's First Christmas
Classic Shape • N/A
1600QMB9007 • **Value $89**

18
First Christmas Together
Classic Shape • N/A
1600QMB9019 • **Value $86**

19

Love
Classic Shape • N/A
1600QMB9009 • **Value $89**

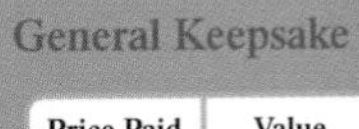
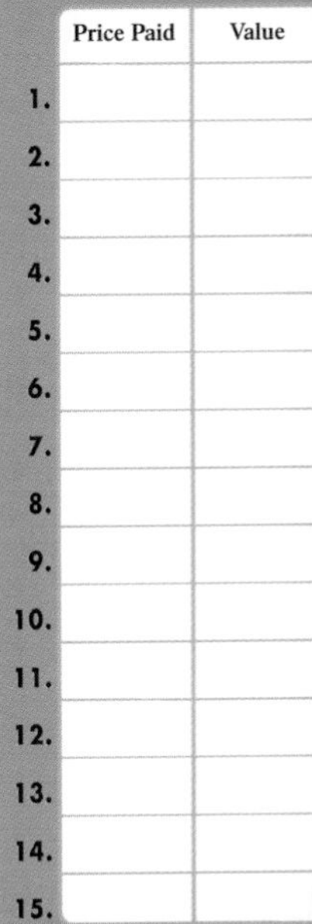
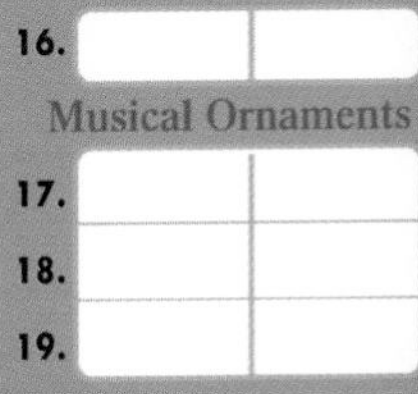

General Keepsake

	Price Paid	Value
1.		
2.		
3.		
4.		
5.		
6.		
7.		
8.		
9.		
10.		
11.		
12.		
13.		
14.		
15.		
Early Promotional Ornaments		
16.		
Musical Ornaments		
17.		
18.		
19.		
Totals		

1981

Santa Claus was well-represented in Hallmark's collection for 1981 with several coveted designs, including the handcrafted ornaments "Sailing Santa" and "Space Santa," as well as the ball ornament "Traditional (Black Santa)." The 1981 line featured 99 Keepsake ornaments. See the collectible series section for more 1981 ornaments.

1

25th Christmas Together
Acrylic • N/A
550QX5042 • **Value $23**

2

25th Christmas Together
Glass • N/A
450QX7075 • **Value $23**

3

50th Christmas
Glass • N/A
450QX7082 • **Value $18**

4

Angel
Acrylic • N/A
400QX5095 • **Value $68**

5

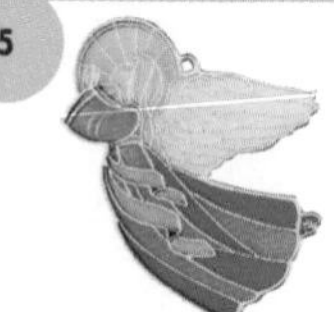

Angel
Acrylic • N/A
450QX5075 • **Value $27**

6

Angel (re-issued from 1980)
Yarn • N/A
300QX1621 • **Value $12**

7

Baby's First Christmas
Acrylic • N/A
550QX5162 • **Value $34**

8

Baby's First Christmas
Cameo • N/A
850QX5135 • **Value $20**

9

Baby's First Christmas
Handcrafted • N/A
1300QX4402 • **Value $53**

10

Baby's First Christmas – Black
Satin • N/A
450QX6022 • **Value $29**

11

Baby's First Christmas – Boy
Satin • N/A
450QX6015 • **Value $25**

12

Baby's First Christmas – Girl
Satin • N/A
450QX6002 • **Value $26**

13

Betsey Clark
Cameo • N/A
850QX5122 • **Value $32**

14

Betsey Clark
Handcrafted • FRAN
900QX4235 • **Value $78**

15

Calico Kitty
Fabric • N/A
300QX4035 • **Value $20**

16

Candyville Express
Handcrafted • N/A
750QX4182 • **Value $110**

17

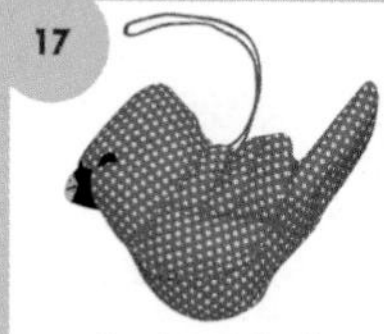

Cardinal Cutie
Fabric • N/A
300QX4002 • **Value $23**

General Keepsake

	Price Paid	Value
1.		
2.		
3.		
4.		
5.		
6.		
7.		
8.		
9.		
10.		
11.		
12.		
13.		
14.		
15.		
16.		
17.		
Totals		

1

Checking It Twice
(re-issued from 1980)
Handcrafted • BLAC
2250QX1584 • **Value $200**

2

Christmas 1981 – Schneeberg
Satin • N/A
450QX8095 • **Value $27**

3

Christmas Dreams
Handcrafted • DLEE
1200QX4375 • **Value $225**

4

Christmas Fantasy
(re-issued in 1982)
Handcrafted • N/A
1300QX1554 • **Value $90**

5

Christmas in the Forest
Glass • N/A
450QX8135 • **Value $145**

6

Christmas Magic
Satin • N/A
450QX8102 • **Value $27**

7

Christmas Star
Acrylic • N/A
550QX5015 • **Value $30**

8

Christmas Teddy
Plush • N/A
550QX4042 • **Value $23**

9

Clothespin Drummer Boy
Handcrafted • N/A
450QX4082 • **Value $47**

10

Daughter
Satin • N/A
450QX6075 • **Value $41**

11
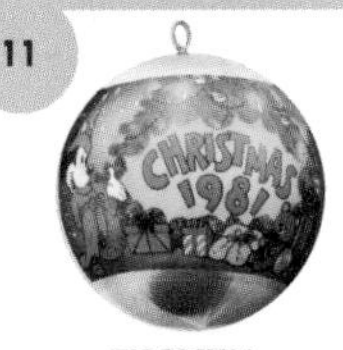
DISNEY
Satin • N/A
450QX8055 • **Value $33**

12

THE DIVINE MISS PIGGY™
(re-issued in 1982)
Handcrafted • FRAN
1200QX4255 • **Value $94**

13

Dough Angel
(re-issued from 1978)
Handcrafted • DLEE
550QX1396 • **Value $90**

14

Drummer Boy
Wood • N/A
250QX1481 • **Value $47**

15

Father
Satin • N/A
450QX6095 • **Value $20**

16

First Christmas Together
Acrylic • N/A
550QX5055 • **Value $24**

17
First Christmas Together
Glass • N/A
450QX7062 • **Value $26**

18
The Friendly Fiddler
Handcrafted • DLEE
800QX4342 • **Value $82**

19

Friendship
Acrylic • N/A
550QX5035 • **Value $35**

20

Friendship
Satin • N/A
450QX7042 • **Value $28**

General Keepsake

	Price Paid	Value
1.		
2.		
3.		
4.		
5.		
6.		
7.		
8.		
9.		
10.		
11.		
12.		
13.		
14.		
15.		
16.		
17.		
18.		
19.		
20.		
Totals		

1

The Gift of Love
Glass • N/A
450QX7055 • **Value $27**

2

Gingham Dog
Fabric • N/A
300QX4022 • **Value $23**

3

Godchild
Satin • N/A
450QX6035 • **Value $24**

4

Granddaughter
Satin • N/A
450QX6055 • **Value $25**

5

Grandfather
Glass • N/A
450QX7015 • **Value $23**

6

Grandmother
Satin • N/A
450QX7022 • **Value $22**

7

Grandparents
Glass • N/A
450QX7035 • **Value $21**

8

Grandson
Satin • N/A
450QX6042 • **Value $25**

9
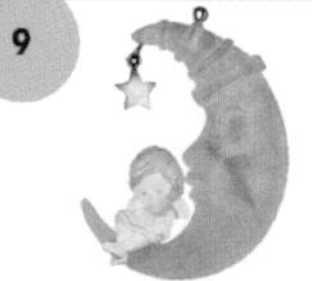
A Heavenly Nap (re-issued from 1980)
Handcrafted • DLEE
650QX1394 • **Value $50**

10

Home
Satin • N/A
450QX7095 • **Value $22**

11

Ice Fairy
Handcrafted • DLEE
650QX4315 • **Value $110**

12

The Ice Sculptor (re-issued in 1982)
Handcrafted • DLEE
800QX4322 • **Value $97**

13

Joan Walsh Anglund
Satin • N/A
450QX8042 • **Value $27**

14

Jolly Snowman
Handcrafted • N/A
350QX4075 • **Value $57**

15

KERMIT the FROG™
Handcrafted • FRAN
900QX4242 • **Value $100**

16

Let Us Adore Him
Glass • N/A
450QX8115 • **Value $65**

17

Love
Acrylic • N/A
550QX5022 • **Value $50**

18

Love and Joy (Porcelain Chimes)
Porcelain • N/A
900QX4252 • **Value $98**

19

Marty Links™
Satin • N/A
450QX8082 • **Value $28**

20

Mary Hamilton
Glass • N/A
450QX8062 • **Value $21**

General Keepsake

	Price Paid	Value
1.		
2.		
3.		
4.		
5.		
6.		
7.		
8.		
9.		
10.		
11.		
12.		
13.		
14.		
15.		
16.		
17.		
18.		
19.		
20.		
Totals		

1

Merry Christmas
Glass • N/A
450QX8142 • **Value $27**

2

Mother
Satin • N/A
450QX6082 • **Value $22**

3

Mother and Dad
Satin • N/A
450QX7002 • **Value $17**

4

Mouse
Acrylic • N/A
400QX5082 • **Value $30**

5

Mr. & Mrs. Claus (set/2, re-issued from 1975)
Handcrafted • N/A
1200QX4485 • **Value $130**

6

MUPPETS™
Satin • N/A
450QX8075 • **Value $36**

7

PEANUTS®
Satin • N/A
450QX8035 • **Value $37**

8

Peppermint Mouse
Fabric • N/A
300QX4015 • **Value $42**

9

Perky Penguin (re-issued in 1982)
Handcrafted • N/A
350QX4095 • **Value $60**

10

Puppy Love
Handcrafted • N/A
350QX4062 • **Value $38**

11

Raccoon Tunes
Plush • N/A
550QX4055 • **Value $27**

12

Sailing Santa
Handcrafted • N/A
1300QX4395 • **Value $295**

13

St. Nicholas
Pressed Tin • SICK
550QX4462 • **Value $58**

14

Santa (re-issued from 1980)
Yarn • N/A
300QX1614 • **Value $11**

15

Santa Mobile (re-issued from 1980)
Chrome Plate • N/A
550QX1361 • **Value $48**

16

Santa's Coming
Satin • N/A
450QX8122 • **Value $30**

17

Santa's Surprise
Satin • N/A
450QX8155 • **Value $27**

18
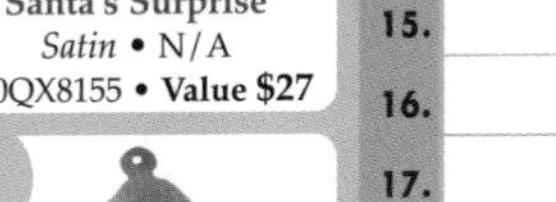

Shepherd Scene
Acrylic • N/A
550QX5002 • **Value $31**

19

Snowflake Chimes (re-issued from 1980)
Chrome Plate • SICK
550QX1654 • **Value $32**

20

Snowman
Acrylic • N/A
400QX5102 • **Value $29**

General Keepsake

	Price Paid	Value
1.		
2.		
3.		
4.		
5.		
6.		
7.		
8.		
9.		
10.		
11.		
12.		
13.		
14.		
15.		
16.		
17.		
18.		
19.		
20.		
Totals		

1

Snowman
(re-issued from 1980)
Yarn • N/A
300QX1634 • **Value $10**

2

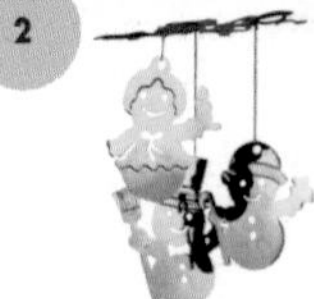

Snowman Chimes
Chrome Plate • N/A
550QX4455 • **Value $32**

3

Soldier
(re-issued from 1980)
Yarn • N/A
300QX1641 • **Value $11**

4

Son
Satin • N/A
450QX6062 • **Value $31**

5

Space Santa
Handcrafted • N/A
650QX4302 • **Value $118**

6

Star Swing
Handcrafted/Brass • SICK
550QX4215 • **Value $45**

7

The Stocking Mouse
Handcrafted • N/A
450QX4122 • **Value $92**

8

Teacher
Satin • N/A
450QX8002 • **Value $16**

9

Topsy-Turvy Tunes
Handcrafted • DLEE
750QX4295 • **Value $75**

10

Traditional (Black Santa)
Satin • N/A
450QX8015 • **Value $100**

11

Tree Photoholder
Acrylic • N/A
550QX5155 • **Value $32**

12

Unicorn
Cameo • N/A
850QX5165 • **Value $25**

13

A Well-Stocked Stocking
Handcrafted • N/A
900QX1547 • **Value $79**

1980

Teddy bear lovers have always been able to find great Hallmark bear ornaments and in 1980 Hallmark offered up two special treats in "Caroling Bear" and "Christmas Teddy." In the collection for 1980 there were a total of 85 Keepsake ornaments. See the collectible series section for more 1980 ornaments.

14

25th Christmas Together
Glass • N/A
400QX2061 • **Value $22**

15

Angel
(re-issued in 1981)
Yarn • N/A
300QX1621 • **Value $12**

16

Angel Music
(re-issued from 1979)
Fabric • N/A
200QX3439 • **Value $25**

General Keepsake

	Price Paid	Value
1.		
2.		
3.		
4.		
5.		
6.		
7.		
8.		
9.		
10.		
11.		
12.		
13.		

General Keepsake

	Price Paid	Value
14.		
15.		
16.		

Totals

1

The Animals' Christmas
Handcrafted • DLEE
800QX1501 • **Value $63**

2

Baby's First Christmas
Handcrafted • SICK
12QX1561 • **Value $48**

3

Baby's First Christmas
Satin • N/A
400QX2001 • **Value $28**

4

Beauty of Friendship
Acrylic • N/A
400QX3034 • **Value $67**

5

Betsey Clark
Cameo • N/A
650QX3074 • **Value $55**

6

Betsey Clark's Christmas
Handcrafted • N/A
750X1494 • **Value $38**

7

Black Baby's First Christmas
Satin • N/A
400QX2294 • **Value $31**

8

Caroling Bear
Handcrafted • DLEE
750QX1401 • **Value $150**

9

Checking It Twice (re-issued in 1981)
Handcrafted • BLAC
2000QX1584 • **Value $200**

10

Christmas at Home
Glass • N/A
400QX2101 • **Value $40**

11

Christmas Cardinals
Glass • N/A
400QX2241 • **Value $32**

12

Christmas Choir
Glass • N/A
400QX2281 • **Value $83**

13

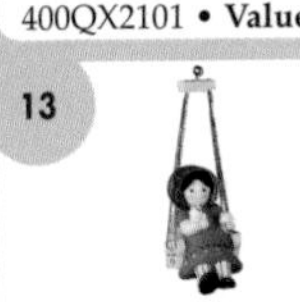

Christmas is for Children (re-issued from 1979)
Handcrafted • N/A
550QX1359 • **Value $90**

14

Christmas Love
Glass • N/A
400QX2074 • **Value $52**

15

Christmas Owl (re-issued in 1982)
Handcrafted • N/A
400QX1314 • **Value $49**

16

Christmas Teddy
Handcrafted • N/A
250QX1354 • **Value $135**

17

Christmas Time
Satin • N/A
400QX2261 • **Value $35**

18

A Christmas Treat (re-issued from 1979)
Handcrafted • N/A
550QX1347 • **Value $84**

19

A Christmas Vigil
Handcrafted • DLEE
900QX1441 • **Value $135**

20

Clothespin Soldier
Handcrafted • N/A
350QX1341 • **Value $42**

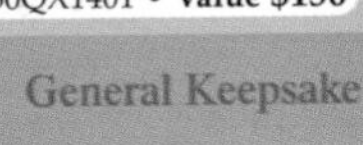

General Keepsake

	Price Paid	Value
1.		
2.		
3.		
4.		
5.		
6.		
7.		
8.		
9.		
10.		
11.		
12.		
13.		
14.		
15.		
16.		
17.		
18.		
19.		
20.		
Totals		

1

Dad
Glass • N/A
400QX2141 • **Value $18**

2

Daughter
Glass • N/A
400QX2121 • **Value $45**

3

DISNEY
Satin • N/A
400QX2181 • **Value $36**

4
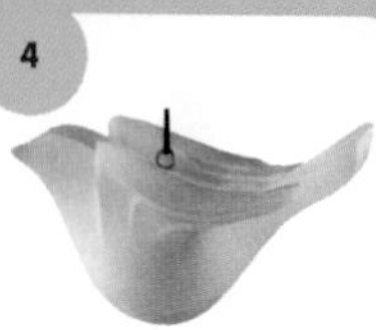
Dove
Acrylic • N/A
400QX3081 • **Value $42**

5
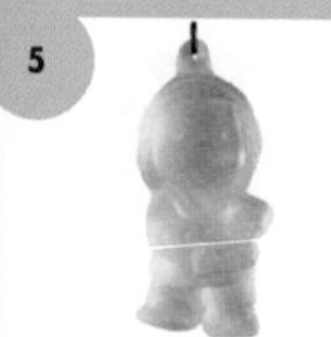
Drummer Boy
Acrylic • N/A
400QX3094 • **Value $32**

6

Drummer Boy
Handcrafted • DLEE
550QX1474 • **Value $95**

7

Elfin Antics
Handcrafted • N/A
900QX1421 • **Value $220**

8

First Christmas Together
Acrylic • N/A
400QX3054 • **Value $48**

9

First Christmas Together
Glass • N/A
400QX2054 • **Value $42**

10

Friendship
Glass • N/A
400QX2081 • **Value $24**

11

Granddaughter
Satin • N/A
400QX2021 • **Value $35**

12

Grandfather
Glass • N/A
400QX2314 • **Value $20**

13

Grandmother
Glass • N/A
400QX2041 • **Value $20**

14

Grandparents
Glass • N/A
400QX2134 • **Value $43**

15

Grandson
Satin • N/A
400QX2014 • **Value $36**

16

Happy Christmas
Satin • N/A
400QX2221 • **Value $27**

17

Heavenly Minstrel
Handcrafted • DLEE
1500QX1567 • **Value $340**

18
A Heavenly Nap (re-issued in 1981)
Handcrafted • DLEE
650QX1394 • **Value $50**

19
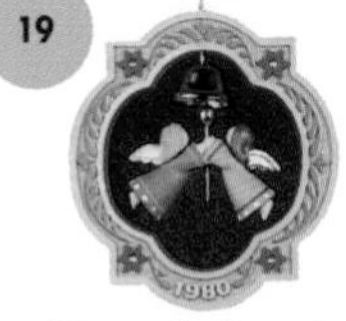
Heavenly Sounds
Handcrafted • N/A
750QX1521 • **Value $99**

20

Joan Walsh Anglund
Satin • N/A
400QX2174 • **Value $24**

General Keepsake

	Price Paid	Value
1.		
2.		
3.		
4.		
5.		
6.		
7.		
8.		
9.		
10.		
11.		
12.		
13.		
14.		
15.		
16.		
17.		
18.		
19.		
20.		
Totals		

1

Jolly Santa
Glass • N/A
400QX2274 • **Value $29**

2

Joy
Acrylic • N/A
400QX3501 • **Value $31**

3

Love
Acrylic • N/A
400QX3021 • **Value $66**

4

Marty Links™
Satin • N/A
400QX2214 • **Value $21**

5

Mary Hamilton
Glass • N/A
400QX2194 • **Value $23**

6

Merry Redbird
Handcrafted • N/A
350QX1601 • **Value $70**

7

Merry Santa
(re-issued from 1979)
Fabric • N/A
200QX3427 • **Value $19**

8

Mother
Acrylic • N/A
400QX3041 • **Value $38**

9

Mother
Satin • N/A
400QX2034 • **Value $22**

10

Mother and Dad
Glass • N/A
400QX2301 • **Value $24**

11

MUPPETS™
Satin • N/A
400QX2201 • **Value $39**

12

Nativity
Glass • N/A
400QX2254 • **Value $90**

13

PEANUTS®
Satin • N/A
400QX2161 • **Value $42**

14

Reindeer Chimes
(re-issued from 1978)
Chrome Plate • SICK
550QX3203 • **Value $52**

15

Rocking Horse
(re-issued from 1979)
Fabric • N/A
200QX3407 • **Value $22**

16

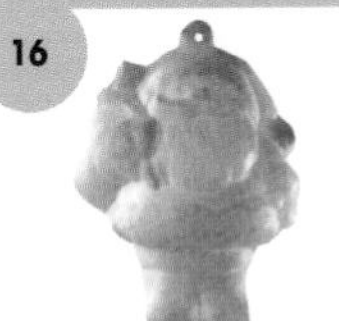

Santa
Acrylic • N/A
400QX3101 • **Value $26**

17

Santa
(re-issued in 1981)
Yarn • N/A
300QX1614 • **Value $11**

18

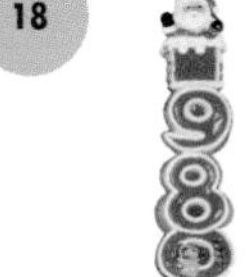

Santa 1980
Handcrafted • N/A
550QX1461 • **Value $98**

19

Santa Mobile
(re-issued in 1981)
Chrome Plate • N/A
550QX1361 • **Value $48**

20

Santa's Flight
Pressed Tin • SICK
550QX1381 • **Value $118**

General Keepsake

	Price Paid	Value
1.		
2.		
3.		
4.		
5.		
6.		
7.		
8.		
9.		
10.		
11.		
12.		
13.		
14.		
15.		
16.		
17.		
18.		
19.		
20.		
Totals		

1

Santa's Workshop
Satin • N/A
400QX2234 • **Value $32**

2

Skating Snowman
(re-issued from 1979)
Handcrafted • DLEE
550QX1399 • **Value $85**

3

Snowflake Chimes
(re-issued in 1981)
Chrome Plate • SICK
550QX1654 • **Value $32**

4

The Snowflake Swing
Handcrafted • N/A
400QX1334 • **Value $45**

5

Snowman
(re-issued in 1981)
Yarn • N/A
300QX1634 • **Value $10**

6

Soldier
(re-issued in 1981)
Yarn • N/A
300QX1641 • **Value $11**

7

Son
Glass • N/A
400QX2114 • **Value $35**

8

A Spot of Christmas Cheer
Handcrafted • DLEE
800QX1534 • **Value $152**

9

Stuffed Full Stocking
(re-issued from 1979)
Fabric • N/A
200QX3419 • **Value $26**

10

Swingin' on a Star
Handcrafted • N/A
400QX1301 • **Value $80**

11

Teacher
Satin • N/A
400QX2094 • **Value $18**

12

Three Wise Men
Acrylic • N/A
400QX3001 • **Value $34**

13

Wreath
Acrylic • N/A
400QX3014 • **Value $82**

1979 *Among the most popular Hallmark ornaments in the early years were the ball ornaments commemorating "Baby's First Christmas." In 1979, Hallmark released its first handcrafted ornament with this theme. Overall, there were 65 Keepsake ornaments in 1979. See the collectible series section for more 1979 ornaments.*

14

Angel Delight
Handcrafted • N/A
300QX1307 • **Value $98**

15

Angel Music
(re-issued in 1980)
Fabric • N/A
200QX3439 • **Value $25**

16

Baby's First Christmas
Handcrafted • N/A
800QX1547 • **Value $130**

General Keepsake

	Price Paid	Value
1.		
2.		
3.		
4.		
5.		
6.		
7.		
8.		
9.		
10.		
11.		
12.		
13.		

General Keepsake

	Price Paid	Value
14.		
15.		
16.		

Totals		

1

Baby's First Christmas
Satin • N/A
350QX2087 • **Value $33**

2

Behold the Star
Satin • N/A
350QX2559 • **Value $39**

3

Black Angel
Glass • BLAC
350QX2079 • **Value $27**

4

Christmas Angel
Acrylic • N/A
350QX3007 • **Value $138**

5

Christmas Cheer
Acrylic • N/A
350QX3039 • **Value $83**

6

Christmas Chickadees
Glass • N/A
350QX2047 • **Value $35**

7

Christmas Collage
Glass • N/A
350QX2579 • **Value $37**

8

Christmas Eve Surprise
Handcrafted • N/A
650QX1579 • **Value $69**

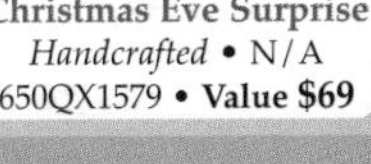

9

Christmas Heart
Handcrafted • SICK
650QX1407 • **Value $105**

10

Christmas is for Children (re-issued in 1980)
Handcrafted • N/A
500QX1359 • **Value $90**

11

Christmas Traditions
Glass • SICK
350QX2539 • **Value $39**

12

A Christmas Treat (re-issued in 1980)
Handcrafted • N/A
500QX1347 • **Value $84**

13
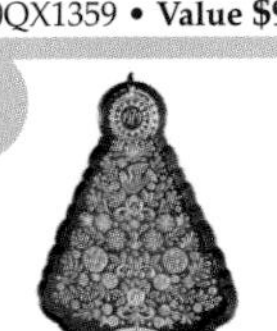
Christmas Tree
Acrylic • N/A
350QX3027 • **Value $73**

14

The Downhill Run
Handcrafted • DLEE
650QX1459 • **Value $170**

15

The Drummer Boy
Handcrafted • N/A
800QX1439 • **Value $130**

16

Friendship
Glass • N/A
350QX2039 • **Value $25**

17
Granddaughter
Satin • N/A
350QX2119 • **Value $36**

18

Grandmother
Glass • N/A
350QX2527 • **Value $28**

19

Grandson
Satin • N/A
350QX2107 • **Value $38**

20

Green Boy (re-issued from 1978)
Yarn • N/A
200QX1231 • **Value $28**

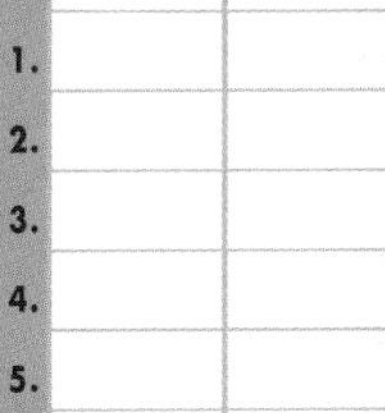

General Keepsake

	Price Paid	Value
1.		
2.		
3.		
4.		
5.		
6.		
7.		
8.		
9.		
10.		
11.		
12.		
13.		
14.		
15.		
16.		
17.		
18.		
19.		
20.		
Totals		

1

Green Girl
(re-issued from 1978)
Yarn • N/A
200QX1261 • **Value $24**

2

Holiday Scrimshaw
Handcrafted • N/A
400QX1527 • **Value $230**

3

Holiday Wreath
Acrylic • N/A
350QX3539 • **Value $44**

4

Joan Walsh Anglund
Satin • N/A
350QX2059 • **Value $37**

5

The Light of Christmas
Glass • N/A
350QX2567 • **Value $33**

6

Love
Acrylic • N/A
350QX3047 • **Value $95**

7

Love
Glass • N/A
350QX2587 • **Value $80**

8

Mary Hamilton
Satin • N/A
350QX2547 • **Value $28**

9

A Matchless Christmas
Handcrafted • N/A
400QX1327 • **Value $86**

10

Merry Santa
(re-issued in 1980)
Fabric • N/A
200QX3427 • **Value $19**

11

Mother
Glass • N/A
350QX2519 • **Value $27**

12

Mr. Claus
(re-issued from 1978)
Yarn • N/A
200QX3403 • **Value $24**

13

Mrs. Claus
(re-issued from 1978)
Yarn • N/A
200QX1251 • **Value $23**

14

New Home
Satin • N/A
350QX2127 • **Value $46**

15

Night Before Christmas
Satin • N/A
350QX2147 • **Value $40**

16

Our First
Christmas Together
Glass • N/A
350QX2099 • **Value $72**

17

Our Twenty-Fifth
Anniversary
Glass • N/A
350QX2507 • **Value $27**

18

Outdoor Fun
Handcrafted • SICK
800QX1507 • **Value $140**

19

Partridge in a Pear Tree
Acrylic • N/A
350QX3519 • **Value $43**

20

PEANUTS®
(Time to Trim)
Satin • N/A
350QX2027 • **Value $46**

General Keepsake

	Price Paid	Value
1.		
2.		
3.		
4.		
5.		
6.		
7.		
8.		
9.		
10.		
11.		
12.		
13.		
14.		
15.		
16.		
17.		
18.		
19.		
20.		
Totals		

1

Raccoon
(re-issued from 1978)
Handcrafted • DLEE
650QX1423 • **Value $96**

2

Ready for Christmas
Handcrafted • DLEE
650QX1339 • **Value $152**

3

Reindeer Chimes
(re-issued from 1978)
Chrome Plate • SICK
450QX3203 • **Value $52**

4

Rocking Horse
(re-issued in 1980)
Fabric • N/A
200QX3407 • **Value $22**

5

Santa
(re-issued from 1978)
Handcrafted • N/A
300QX1356 • **Value $70**

6

Santa's Here
Handcrafted • SICK
500QX1387 • **Value $70**

7

The Skating Snowman
(re-issued in 1980)
Handcrafted • DLEE
500QX1399 • **Value $85**

8

Snowflake
Acrylic • N/A
350QX3019 • **Value $43**

9

Spencer® Sparrow, Esq.
Satin • N/A
350QX2007 • **Value $46**

10

Star Chimes
Chrome Plate • SICK
450QX1379 • **Value $73**

11

Star Over Bethlehem
Acrylic • SICK
350QX3527 • **Value $72**

12

Stuffed Full Stocking
(re-issued in 1980)
Fabric • N/A
200QX3419 • **Value $26**

13

Teacher
Satin • N/A
350QX2139 • **Value $17**

14

Winnie-the-Pooh
Satin • N/A
350QX2067 • **Value $47**

15
Words of Christmas
Acrylic • N/A
350QX3507 • **Value $78**

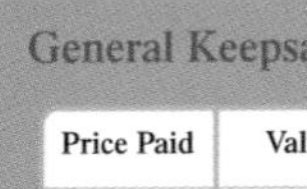

General Keepsake

	Price Paid	Value
1.		
2.		
3.		
4.		
5.		
6.		
7.		
8.		
9.		
10.		
11.		
12.		
13.		
14.		
15.		
Totals		

1978

In the 6th year of Hallmark ornaments several unique handcrafted ornaments proved to be the most popular, including "Angels," "Animal Home," "Calico Mouse," "Red Cardinal" and "Schneeberg Bell." The 1978 collection featured 54 Keepsake ornaments. See the collectible series section for more 1978 ornaments.

1

25th Christmas Together
Glass • N/A
350QX2696 • **Value $35**

2

Angel
Acrylic • N/A
350QX3543 • **Value $47**

3

Angel (re-issued in 1981)
Handcrafted • DLEE
450QX1396 • **Value $92**

4

Angels
Handcrafted • N/A
800QX1503 • **Value $385**

5

Animal Home
Handcrafted • DLEE
600QX1496 • **Value $190**

6

Baby's First Christmas
Satin • N/A
350QX2003 • **Value $96**

7

Calico Mouse
Handcrafted • N/A
450QX1376 • **Value $182**

8

Candle
Acrylic • N/A
350QX3576 • **Value $85**

9

DISNEY
Satin • N/A
350QX2076 • **Value $120**

10

Dove
Acrylic • PALM
350QX3103 • **Value $110**

11

Dove
Handcrafted • SICK
450QX1903 • **Value $88**

12

Drummer Boy
Glass • N/A
350QX2523 • **Value $47**

13

Drummer Boy
Handcrafted • N/A
250QX1363 • **Value $77**

14

First Christmas Together
Satin • N/A
350QX2183 • **Value $52**

15

For Your New Home
Satin • N/A
350QX2176 • **Value $30**

16

Granddaughter
Satin • N/A
350QX2163 • **Value $45**

17

Grandmother
Satin • N/A
350QX2676 • **Value $44**

General Keepsake

	Price Paid	Value
1.		
2.		
3.		
4.		
5.		
6.		
7.		
8.		
9.		
10.		
11.		
12.		
13.		
14.		
15.		
16.		
17.		
Totals		

1

Grandson
Satin • N/A
350QX2156 • **Value $48**

2

Green Boy
(re-issued in 1979)
Yarn • N/A
200QX1231 • **Value $28**

3

Green Girl
(re-issued in 1979)
Yarn • N/A
200QX1261 • **Value $24**

4

Hallmark's Antique Card Collection Design
Satin • N/A
350QX2203 • **Value $45**

5

Holly and Poinsettia Ball
Handcrafted • SICK
600QX1476 • **Value $90**

6

Joan Walsh Anglund
Satin • N/A
350QX2216 • **Value $65**

7

Joy
Glass • N/A
350QX2543 • **Value $50**

8

Joy
Handcrafted • N/A
450QX1383 • **Value $92**

9

Locomotive
Acrylic • N/A
350QX3563 • **Value $60**

10

Love
Glass • N/A
350QX2683 • **Value $60**

11

Merry Christmas
Acrylic • PALM
350QX3556 • **Value $62**

12

Merry Christmas (Santa)
Satin • N/A
350QX2023 • **Value $53**

13

Mother
Glass • N/A
350QX2663 • **Value $42**

14

Mr. Claus
(re-issued in 1979)
Yarn • N/A
200QX3403 • **Value $24**

15

Mrs. Claus
(re-issued in 1979)
Yarn • N/A
200QX1251 • **Value $23**

16

Nativity
Acrylic • PALM
350QX3096 • **Value N/E**

17

Nativity
Glass • N/A
350QX2536 • **Value $110**

18

Panorama Ball
Handcrafted • N/A
600QX1456 • **Value $145**

19

PEANUTS®
Satin • N/A
250QX2036 • **Value $63**

General Keepsake

	Price Paid	Value
1.		
2.		
3.		
4.		
5.		
6.		
7.		
8.		
9.		
10.		
11.		
12.		
13.		
14.		
15.		
16.		
17.		
18.		
19.		
Totals		

1

PEANUTS®
Satin • N/A
250QX2043 • **Value $72**

2

PEANUTS®
Satin • N/A
350QX2056 • **Value $73**

3

PEANUTS®
Satin • N/A
350QX2063 • **Value $63**

4

Praying Angel
Handcrafted • DLEE
250QX1343 • **Value $85**

5

The Quail
Glass • N/A
350QX2516 • **Value $42**

6

Red Cardinal
Handcrafted • UNRU
450QX1443 • **Value $176**

7

Reindeer Chimes
(re-issued in 1979 and 1980)
Chrome Plate • SICK
450QX3203 • **Value $52**

8

Rocking Horse
Handcrafted • N/A
600QX1483 • **Value $95**

9

Santa
Acrylic • PALM
350QX3076 • **Value $86**

10

Santa
(re-issued in 1979)
Handcrafted • N/A
250QX1356 • **Value $70**

11

Schneeberg Bell
Handcrafted • N/A
800QX1523 • **Value $195**

12

Skating Raccoon
(re-issued in 1979)
Handcrafted • DLEE
600QX1423 • **Value $99**

13
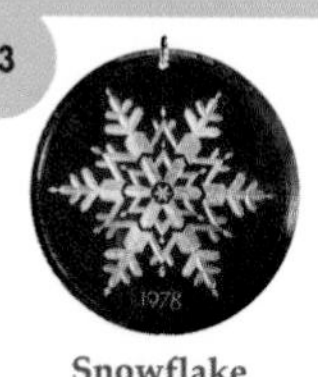
Snowflake
Acrylic • PALM
350QX3083 • **Value $68**

14

Spencer® Sparrow, Esq.
Satin • N/A
350QX2196 • **Value $49**

15

Yesterday's Toys
Glass • N/A
350QX2503 • **Value $42**

General Keepsake

	Price Paid	Value
1.		
2.		
3.		
4.		
5.		
6.		
7.		
8.		
9.		
10.		
11.		
12.		
13.		
14.		
15.		
Totals		

1977

The 1977 collection was highlighted by a group of handcrafted ornaments designed to have an antique wooden appearance. Called the "Nostalgia Collection," these ornaments were "Angel," "Antique Car," "Nativity," and "Toys." In 1977, there were 53 Keepsake ornaments. See the collectible series section for more 1977 ornaments.

1

Angel
Cloth • N/A
175QX2202 • **Value $48**

2

Angel
Handcrafted • DLEE
500QX1822 • **Value $133**

3

Angel
Handcrafted • N/A
600QX1722 • **Value $135**

4

Antique Car
Handcrafted • SICK
500QX1802 • **Value $72**

5

Baby's First Christmas
Satin • N/A
350QX1315 • **Value $86**

6

Bell
Acrylic • SICK
350QX2002 • **Value $50**

7

Bell
Glass • N/A
350QX1542 • **Value $39**

8

Bellringer
Handcrafted • N/A
600QX1922 • **Value $63**

9

Candle
Acrylic • N/A
350QX2035 • **Value $58**

10

Charmers
Glass • N/A
350QX1535 • **Value $63**

11

Christmas Mouse
Satin • N/A
350QX1342 • **Value $60**

12

Currier & Ives
Satin • N/A
350QX1302 • **Value $57**

13

Della Robia Wreath
Handcrafted • DLEE
450QX1935 • **Value $115**

14

Desert
Glass • N/A
250QX1595 • **Value $42**

15
DISNEY
Satin • N/A
350QX1335 • **Value $72**

16

DISNEY (set/2)
Satin • N/A
400QX1375 • **Value $58**

17

Drummer Boy
Acrylic • N/A
350QX3122 • **Value $64**

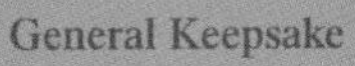
General Keepsake

	Price Paid	Value
1.		
2.		
3.		
4.		
5.		
6.		
7.		
8.		
9.		
10.		
11.		
12.		
13.		
14.		
15.		
16.		
17.		
Totals		

1
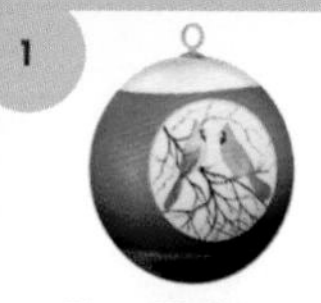
First Christmas Together
Satin • N/A
350QX1322 • **Value $78**

2

For Your New Home
Glass • N/A
350QX2635 • **Value $40**

3

Granddaughter
Satin • N/A
350QX2082 • **Value $110**

4

Grandma Moses
Glass • N/A
350QX1502 • **Value $75**

5

Grandmother
Glass • N/A
350QX2602 • **Value $50**

6

Grandson
Satin • N/A
350QX2095 • **Value $36**

7

House
Handcrafted • N/A
600QX1702 • **Value $140**

8

Jack-in-the-Box
Handcrafted • N/A
600QX1715 • **Value $132**

General Keepsake

	Price Paid	Value
1.		
2.		
3.		
4.		
5.		
6.		
7.		
8.		
9.		
10.		
11.		
12.		
13.		
14.		
15.		
16.		
17.		
18.		
19.		
20.		
Totals		

9

Joy
Acrylic • N/A
350QX2015 • **Value $50**

10

Joy
Acrylic • N/A
350QX3102 • **Value $48**

11

Love
Glass • N/A
350QX2622 • **Value $34**

12

Mandolin
Glass • N/A
350QX1575 • **Value $50**

13

Mother
Glass • N/A
350QX2615 • **Value $38**

14

Mountains
Glass • N/A
250QX1582 • **Value $33**

15

Nativity
Handcrafted • N/A
500QX1815 • **Value $165**

16

Norman Rockwell
Glass • N/A
350QX1515 • **Value $68**

17

Ornaments
Glass • N/A
350QX1555 • **Value $52**

18
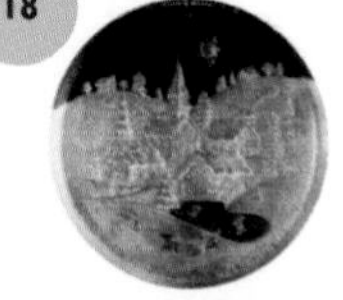
Peace on Earth
Acrylic • N/A
350QX3115 • **Value $62**

19

PEANUTS®
Glass • N/A
250QX1622 • **Value $79**

20

PEANUTS® (set/2)
Glass • N/A
400QX1635 • **Value $94**

1

PEANUTS®
Satin • N/A
350QX1355 • **Value $82**

2

Rabbit
Satin • N/A
250QX1395 • **Value $95**

3

Reindeer
Handcrafted • N/A
600QX1735 • **Value $130**

4

Santa
Cloth • N/A
175QX2215 • **Value $72**

5

Seashore
Glass • N/A
250QX1602 • **Value $48**

6

Snowflake Collection (set/4)
Chrome-Plated Zinc • SICK
500QX2102 • **Value $90**

7

Snowman
Handcrafted • SICK
450QX1902 • **Value $79**

8

Squirrel
Satin • N/A
250QX1382 • **Value $98**

9

Stained Glass
Glass • N/A
350QX1522 • **Value $63**

10

Star
Acrylic • N/A
350QX3135 • **Value $54**

11

Toys
Handcrafted • SICK
500QX1835 • **Value $156**

12

Weather House
Handcrafted • N/A
600QX1915 • **Value $102**

13

Wharf
Glass • N/A
250QX1615 • **Value $40**

14

Wreath
Acrylic • N/A
350QX2022 • **Value $62**

15

Wreath
Glass • N/A
350QX1562 • **Value $50**

General Keepsake

	Price Paid	Value
1.		
2.		
3.		
4.		
5.		
6.		
7.		
8.		
9.		
10.		
11.		
12.		
13.		
14.		
15.		
Totals		

1976

The 1976 collection of ornaments featured popular themes such as Santa Claus, locomotives, partridges, angels and drummer boys, all in a variety of different handcrafted styles. For the Bicentennial year, Hallmark issued a total of 39 Keepsake ornaments. See the collectible series section for more 1976 ornaments.

1

Angel
Handcrafted • N/A
300QX1761 • **Value $170**

2

Angel
Handcrafted • SICK
450QX1711 • **Value $165**

3

Baby's First Christmas
Satin • N/A
250QX2111 • **Value $150**

4

Betsey Clark
Satin • N/A
250QX2101 • **Value $63**

5

Betsey Clark (set/3)
Satin • N/A
450QX2181 • **Value $62**

6

Bicentennial '76 Commemorative
Satin • N/A
250QX2031 • **Value $58**

7

Bicentennial Charmers
Glass • N/A
300QX1981 • **Value $75**

8

Cardinals
Glass • N/A
225QX2051 • **Value $62**

9

Caroler (re-issued from 1975)
Yarn • N/A
175QX1261 • **Value $23**

10

Charmers (set/2)
Satin • N/A
350QX2151 • **Value $76**

11

Chickadees
Glass • N/A
225QX2041 • **Value $62**

12

Colonial Children (set/2)
Glass • N/A
400QX2081 • **Value $80**

13

Currier & Ives
Glass • N/A
300QX1971 • **Value $49**

14

Currier & Ives
Satin • N/A
250QX2091 • **Value $49**

15

Drummer Boy (re-issued from 1975)
Handcrafted • SICK
400QX1301 • **Value $160**

16

Drummer Boy
Handcrafted • N/A
500QX1841 • **Value $150**

17

Drummer Boy (re-issued from 1975)
Yarn • N/A
175QX1231 • **Value $24**

General Keepsake

	Price Paid	Value
1.		
2.		
3.		
4.		
5.		
6.		
7.		
8.		
9.		
10.		
11.		
12.		
13.		
14.		
15.		
16.		
17.		
Totals		

1

Happy the Snowman (set/2)
Satin • N/A
350QX2161 • **Value $53**

2

Locomotive (re-issued from 1975)
Handcrafted • SICK
400QX2221 • **Value $190**

3

Marty Links™ (set/2)
Glass • N/A
400QX2071 • **Value $55**

4

Mrs. Santa (re-issued from 1975)
Yarn • N/A
175QX1251 • **Value $22**

5

Norman Rockwell
Glass • N/A
300QX1961 • **Value $82**

6

Partridge
Handcrafted • SICK
450QX1741 • **Value $195**

7

Partridge
Handcrafted • N/A
500QX1831 • **Value $118**

8

Peace on Earth (re-issued from 1975)
Handcrafted • SICK
400QX2231 • **Value $160**

9

Raggedy Andy™ (re-issued from 1975)
Yarn • N/A
175QX1221 • **Value $45**

10

Raggedy Ann™
Satin • N/A
250X2121 • **Value $60**

11

Raggedy Ann™ (re-issued from 1975)
Yarn • N/A
175QX1211 • **Value $45**

12

Reindeer
Handcrafted • N/A
300QX1781 • **Value $112**

13

Rocking Horse (re-issued from 1975)
Handcrafted • SICK
400QX1281 • **Value $170**

14

Rudolph and Santa
Satin • N/A
250QX2131 • **Value $94**

15

Santa
Handcrafted • N/A
300QX1771 • **Value $225**

16

Santa
Handcrafted • SICK
450QX1721 • **Value $105**

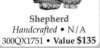

17
Santa
Handcrafted • N/A
500QX1821 • **Value $170**

18

Santa (re-issued from 1975)
Yarn • N/A
175QX1241 • **Value $24**

19

Shepherd
Handcrafted • N/A
300QX1751 • **Value $135**

20

Soldier
Handcrafted • SICK
450QX1731 • **Value $100**

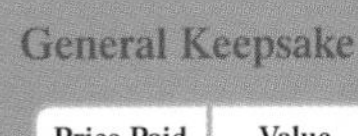
General Keepsake

	Price Paid	Value
1.		
2.		
3.		
4.		
5.		
6.		
7.		
8.		
9.		
10.		
11.		
12.		
13.		
14.		
15.		
16.		
17.		
18.		
19.		
20.		
Totals		

1

Train
Handcrafted • N/A
500QX1811 • **Value $148**

1975

A whole new era of Christmas ornaments began when Hallmark debuted 12 handcrafted ornaments in 1975. These early handcrafted designs are highly sought-after by collectors. Overall, there were 32 Keepsake ornaments issued in 1975, double the total of the previous year. See the collectible series section for more 1975 ornaments.

2

Betsey Clark
Handcrafted • DLEE
250QX1571 • **Value $245**

3

Betsey Clark
Satin • N/A
250QX1631 • **Value $47**

4

Betsey Clark (set/2)
Satin • N/A
350QX1671 • **Value $48**

5

Betsey Clark (set/4)
Satin • N/A
450QX1681 • **Value $55**

6

Buttons & Bo (set/4)
Glass • N/A
500QX1391 • **Value $56**

7

Charmers
Glass • N/A
300QX1351 • **Value $50**

8

Currier & Ives (set/2)
Glass • N/A
400QX1371 • **Value $40**

9

Currier & Ives
Satin • N/A
250QX1641 • **Value $42**

10

Drummer Boy
Handcrafted • DLEE
250QX1611 • **Value $255**

11

Drummer Boy (re-issued in 1976)
Handcrafted • SICK
350QX1301 • **Value $160**

12

Drummer Boy (re-issued in 1976)
Yarn • N/A
175QX1231 • **Value $24**

13

Joy
Handcrafted • SICK
350QX1321 • **Value $210**

14

Little Girl (re-issued in 1976)
Yarn • N/A
175QX1261 • **Value $22**

15

Little Miracles (set/4)
Glass • N/A
500QX1401 • **Value $42**

16

Locomotive (re-issued in 1976)
Handcrafted • SICK
350QX1271 • **Value $190**

17

Marty Links™
Glass • N/A
300QX1361 • **Value $52**

General Keepsake

	Price Paid	Value
1.		

General Keepsake

	Price Paid	Value
2.		
3.		
4.		
5.		
6.		
7.		
8.		
9.		
10.		
11.		
12.		
13.		
14.		
15.		
16.		
17.		
Totals		

1

Mrs. Santa
(re-issued in 1981)
Handcrafted • DLEE
250QX1561 • **Value $230**

2

Mrs. Santa
(re-issued in 1976)
Yarn • N/A
175QX1251 • **Value $22**

3

Norman Rockwell
Glass • N/A
300QX1341 • **Value $65**

4

Norman Rockwell
Satin • N/A
250QX1661 • **Value $63**

5

Peace On Earth
(re-issued in 1976)
Handcrafted • SICK
350QX1311 • **Value $160**

6

Raggedy Andy™
Handcrafted • DLEE
250QX1601 • **Value $360**

7

Raggedy Andy™
(re-issued in 1976)
Yarn • N/A
175QX1221 • **Value $45**

8

Raggedy Ann™
Handcrafted • DLEE
250QX1591 • **Value $300**

9

Raggedy Ann™
Satin • N/A
250QX1651 • **Value $55**

10

Raggedy Ann™
(re-issued in 1976)
Yarn • N/A
175QX1211 • **Value $45**

11

Raggedy Ann™ and Raggedy Andy™ (set/2)
Glass • N/A
400QX1381 • **Value $68**

12

Rocking Horse
(re-issued in 1976)
Handcrafted • SICK
350QX1281 • **Value $170**

13

Santa
(re-issued in 1981)
Handcrafted • DLEE
250QX1551 • **Value $230**

14

Santa
(re-issued in 1976)
Yarn • N/A
175QX1241 • **Value $24**

15

Santa & Sleigh
Handcrafted • SICK
350QX1291 • **Value $230**

General Keepsake

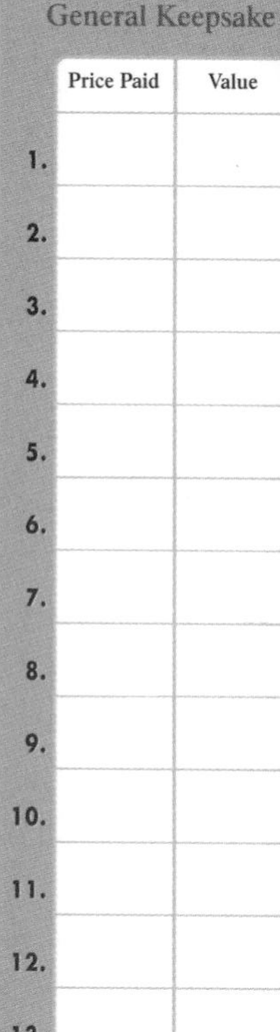

	Price Paid	Value
1.		
2.		
3.		
4.		
5.		
6.		
7.		
8.		
9.		
10.		
11.		
12.		
13.		
14.		
15.		
Totals		

1974

In the second year of Keepsake ornaments, the collection featured popular Christmas scenes from Norman Rockwell, Betsey Clark and Currier & Ives. Of the 16 Keepsake designs or sets offered in 1974, 10 were ball ornaments and 6 were made from yarn. See the collectible series section for more 1974 ornaments.

1

Angel
Glass • N/A
250QX1101 • **Value $77**

2
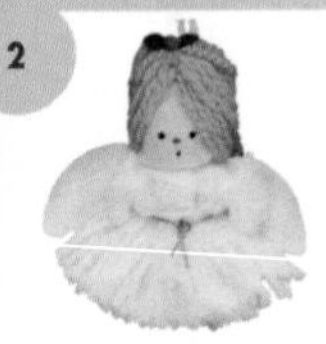
Angel
Yarn • N/A
150QX1031 • **Value $29**

3

Buttons & Bo (set/2)
Glass • N/A
350QX1131 • **Value $50**

4

Charmers
Glass • N/A
250QX1091 • **Value $53**

5

Currier & Ives (set/2)
Glass • N/A
350QX1121 • **Value $60**

6

Elf
Yarn • N/A
150QX1011 • **Value $25**

7

Little Miracles (set/4)
Glass • N/A
450QX1151 • **Value $62**

8

Mrs. Santa
Yarn • N/A
150QX1001 • **Value $24**

9

Norman Rockwell
Glass • N/A
250QX1061 • **Value $98**

10

Norman Rockwell
Glass • N/A
250QX1111 • **Value $88**

11

Raggedy Ann™ and Raggedy Andy™ (set/4)
Glass • N/A
450QX1141 • **Value $90**

12

Santa
Yarn • N/A
150QX1051 • **Value $26**

13

Snowgoose
Glass • N/A
250QX1071 • **Value $72**

14

Snowman
Yarn • N/A
150QX1041 • **Value $24**

15

Soldier
Yarn • N/A
150QX1021 • **Value $24**

General Keepsake

	Price Paid	Value
1.		
2.		
3.		
4.		
5.		
6.		
7.		
8.		
9.		
10.		
11.		
12.		
13.		
14.		
15.		
Totals		

1973

The very first year of Hallmark Keepsake Ornaments was 1973. This year's debut offering consisted of 6 glass ball ornaments and 12 yarn ornaments, making a total of 18 Keepsake designs. The first Keepsake series, "Betsey Clark," also began this year. See the collectible series section for more 1973 ornaments.

1

Angel
Yarn • N/A
125XHD785 • **Value $27**

2
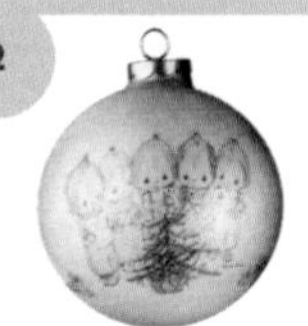
Betsey Clark
Glass • N/A
250XHD1002 • **Value $95**

3

Blue Girl
Yarn • N/A
125XHD852 • **Value $24**

4

Boy Caroler
Yarn • N/A
125XHD832 • **Value $27**

5

Choir Boy
Yarn • N/A
125XHD805 • **Value $27**

6

Christmas Is Love
Glass • N/A
250XHD1062 • **Value $80**

7

Elf
Yarn • N/A
125XHD792 • **Value $26**

8

Elves
Glass • N/A
250XHD1035 • **Value $89**

9

Green Girl
Yarn • N/A
125XHD845 • **Value $25**

10

Little Girl
Yarn • N/A
125XHD825 • **Value $25**

11

Manger Scene
Glass • N/A
250XHD1022 • **Value $96**

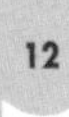
12

Mr. Santa
Yarn • N/A
125XHD745 • **Value $26**

13

Mr. Snowman
Yarn • N/A
125XHD765 • **Value $25**

14

Mrs. Santa
Yarn • N/A
125XHD752 • **Value $26**

15

Mrs. Snowman
Yarn • N/A
125XHD772 • **Value $24**

16

Santa with Elves
Glass • N/A
250XHD1015 • **Value $82**

17

Soldier
Yarn • N/A
100XHD812 • **Value $24**

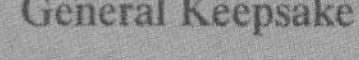
General Keepsake

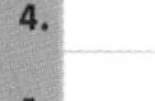

	Price Paid	Value
1.		
2.		
3.		
4.		
5.		
6.		
7.		
8.		
9.		
10.		
11.		
12.		
13.		
14.		
15.		
16.		
17.		
Totals		

Spring Series

Since 1992, select Spring Ornaments that share a common theme have been grouped together in series. 2001 saw the addition of a new series, Birthday Wishes™ BARBIE™ Ornament, as well as new editions to the Easter Egg Surprise, Fairy Berry Bears, Spring Is In The Air, Vintage Roadster and Winner's Circle series.

1

Apple Blossom Lane
(1st, 1995)
Handcrafted • FRAN
895QEO8207 • **Value $22**

2

Apple Blossom Lane
(2nd, 1996)
Handcrafted • FRAN
895QEO8084 • **Value $18**

3

Apple Blossom Lane
(3rd & final, 1997)
Handcrafted • FRAN
895QEO8662 • **Value $19**

4

Peter Rabbit™
(1st, 1996)
Handcrafted • VOTR
895QEO8071 • **Value $82**

5

Jemima Puddle-duck™
(2nd, 1997)
Handcrafted • VOTR
895QEO8645 • **Value $25**

6
Benjamin Bunny™
Beatrix Potter™
(3rd, 1998)
Handcrafted • VOTR
895QEO8383 • **Value $20**

7

Tom Kitten™
(4th, 1999)
Handcrafted • VOTR
895QEO8329 • **Value $18**

8

Mr. Jeremy Fisher™
Beatrix Potter™
(5th & final, 2000)
Handcrafted • VOTR
895QEO8441 • **Value $20**

9
New!

Birthday Wishes™
BARBIE™ Ornament
(1st, 2001)
Handcrafted • RGRS
1495QEO8575 • **Value $14.95**

10

Based on the BARBIE® as
Rapunzel Doll (1st, 1997)
Handcrafted • RGRS
1495QEO8635 • **Value $34**

11

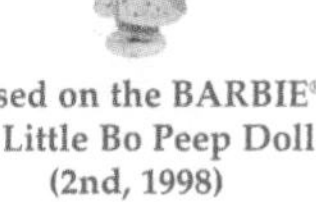
Based on the BARBIE®
as Little Bo Peep Doll
(2nd, 1998)
Handcrafted • RGRS
1495QEO8373 • **Value $25**

12

Based on the BARBIE™
as Cinderella Doll
(3rd & final, 1999)
Handcrafted • RGRS
1495QEO8327 • **Value $26**

13

"Gathering Sunny
Memories" (1st, 1994)
Porcelain • VOTR
775QEO8233 • **Value $33**

14

"Catching the Breeze"
(2nd, 1995)
Porcelain • VOTR
795QEO8219 • **Value $20**

15

"Keeping a Secret"
(3rd, 1996)
Porcelain • VOTR
795QEO8221 • **Value $17**

16
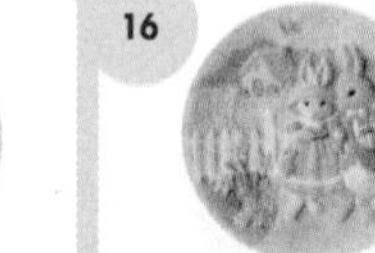
"Sunny Sunday Best"
(4th & final, 1997)
Porcelain • VOTR
795QEO8675 • **Value $16**

	Price Paid	Value
Apple Blossom Lane		
1.		
2.		
3.		
Beatrix Potter™		
4.		
5.		
6.		
7.		
8.		
Birthday Wishes™ BARBIE Ornament™		
9.		
Children's Collector BARBIE™ Ornament		
10.		
11.		
12.		
Collector's Plate		
13.		
14.		
15.		
16.		
Totals		

1

Locomotive (1st, 1996)
Handcrafted • CROW
895QEO8074 • **Value $43**

2

Colorful Coal Car (2nd, 1997)
Handcrafted • CROW
895QEO8652 • **Value $20**

3

Passenger Car (3rd, 1998)
Handcrafted • CROW
995QEO8376 • **Value $20**

4

Flatbed Car (4th, 1999)
Handcrafted • CROW
995QEO8387 • **Value $18**

5

Caboose (5th & final, 2000)
Handcrafted • CROW
995QEO8464 • **Value $15**

6

Easter Egg Surprise (1st, 1999)
Porcelain • VOTR
1495QEO8377 • **Value $26**

7

Rabbit (2nd, 2000)
Porcelain • VOTR
1495QEO8461 • **Value $23**

8

New!

Chick (3rd & final, 2001)
Porcelain • VOTR
1495QEO8532 • **Value $14.95**

9

Easter Parade (1st, 1992)
Handcrafted • CROW
675QEO9301 • **Value $28**

10

Easter Parade (2nd, 1993)
Handcrafted • JLEE
675QEO8325 • **Value $21**

11

Easter Parade (3rd & final, 1994)
Handcrafted • RHOD
675QEO8136 • **Value $20**

12

Eggs in Sports (1st, 1992)
Handcrafted • SIED
675QEO9341 • **Value $33**

13

Eggs in Sports (2nd, 1993)
Handcrafted • SIED
675QEO8332 • **Value $20**

14

Eggs in Sports (3rd & final, 1994)
Handcrafted • SIED
675QEO8133 • **Value $20**

15

Strawberry (1st, 1999)
Handcrafted • TAGU
995QEO8369 • **Value $22**

16

Blueberry (2nd, 2000)
Handcrafted • TAGU
995QEO8454 • **Value $18**

17

New!

Raspberry (3rd & final, 2001)
Handcrafted • TAGU
995QEO8565 • **Value $9.95**

18

Garden Club (1st, 1995)
Handcrafted • SICK
795QEO8209 • **Value $20**

19

Garden Club (2nd, 1996)
Handcrafted • PALM
795QEO8091 • **Value $17**

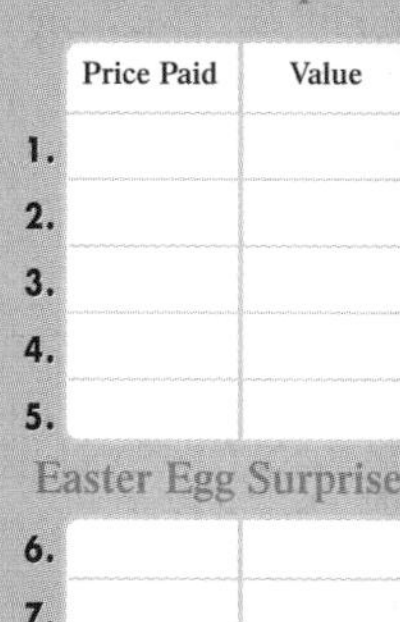

	Price Paid	Value
Cottontail Express		
1.		
2.		
3.		
4.		
5.		
Easter Egg Surprise		
6.		
7.		
8.		
Easter Parade		
9.		
10.		
11.		
Eggs In Sports		
12.		
13.		
14.		
Fairy Berry Bears		
15.		
16.		
17.		
Garden Club		
18.		
19.		
Totals		

1

Garden Club (3rd, 1997)
Handcrafted • BRIC
795QEO8665 • **Value $17**

2

Garden Club
(4th & final, 1998)
Handcrafted • PIKE
795QEO8426 • **Value $17**

3

Here Comes Easter
(1st, 1994)
Handcrafted • CROW
775QEO8093 • **Value $36**

4

Here Comes Easter
(2nd, 1995)
Handcrafted • CROW
795QEO8217 • **Value $20**

5

Here Comes Easter
(3rd, 1996)
Handcrafted • CROW
795QEO8094 • **Value $18**

6

Here Comes Easter
(4th & final, 1997)
Handcrafted • CROW
795QEO8682 • **Value $18**

7

Joyful Angels (1st, 1996)
Handcrafted • LYLE
995QEO8184 • **Value $29**

8

Joyful Angels (2nd, 1997)
Handcrafted • LYLE
1095QEO8655 • **Value $22**

9

Joyful Angels
(3rd & final, 1998)
Handcrafted • LYLE
1095QEO8386 • **Value $19**

10

1935 Steelcraft
Streamline Velocipede
by Murray® (1st, 1997)
Die-Cast Metal • RHOD
1295QEO8632 • **Value $27**

11

1939 Mobo Horse
(2nd, 1998)
Die-Cast Metal • N/A
1295QEO8393 • **Value $26**

12

1950 GARTON®
Delivery Cycle
(3rd, 1999)
Die-Cast Metal • N/A
1295QEO8367 • **Value $24**

13

Hopalong Cassidy™
Velocipede (4th, 2000)
Die-Cast Metal • N/A
1295QEO8411 • **Value $18**

14
New!

1934 Mickey Mouse
Velocipede (5th, 2001)
Die-Cast Metal • N/A
1295QEO8552 • **Value $12.95**

15

Eastern Bluebird
(1st, 2000)
Handcrafted • CROW
995QEO8451 • **Value $15**

16
New!

American Goldfinch
(2nd, 2001)
Handcrafted • CROW
995QEO8535 • **Value $9.95**

17

Springtime BARBIE™
(1st, 1995)
Handcrafted • ANDR
1295QEO8069 • **Value $35**

18

Springtime BARBIE™
(2nd, 1996)
Handcrafted • ANDR
1295QEO8081 • **Value $28**

19

Springtime BARBIE™
(3rd & final, 1997)
Handcrafted • ANDR
1295QEO8642 • **Value $25**

20

Springtime Bonnets
(1st, 1993)
Handcrafted • DLEE
775QEO8322 • **Value $30**

	Price Paid	Value
Garden Club		
1.		
2.		
Here Comes Easter		
3.		
4.		
5.		
6.		
Joyful Angels		
7.		
8.		
9.		
Sidewalk Cruisers		
10.		
11.		
12.		
13.		
14.		
Spring Is In The Air		
15.		
16.		
Springtime BARBIE™		
17.		
18.		
19.		
Springtime Bonnets		
20.		
Totals		

1

Springtime Bonnets
(2nd, 1994)
Handcrafted • BISH
775QEO8096 • **Value $26**

2

Springtime Bonnets
(3rd, 1995)
Handcrafted • UNRU
795QEO8227 • **Value $20**

3

Springtime Bonnets
(4th, 1996)
Handcrafted • PIKE
795QEO8134 • **Value $26**

4

Springtime Bonnets
(5th & final, 1997)
Handcrafted • PIKE
795QEO8672 • **Value $17**

5

1931 Ford Model A
Roadster (1st, 1998)
Die-Cast Metal • PALM
1495QEO8416 • **Value $30**

6

1932 Chevrolet® Standard
Sports Roadster
(2nd, 1999)
Die-Cast Metal • PALM
1495QEO8379 • **Value $28**

7

1935 Auburn
Speedster (3rd, 2000)
Die-Cast Metal • PALM
1495QEO8401 • **Value $20**

8

1930 Cadillac®
(4th, 2001)
Die-Cast Metal • PALM
1495QEO8555 • **Value $14.95**

9

1956 GARTON® Hot
Rod Racer (1st, 1999)
Die-Cast Metal • UNRU
1395QEO8479 • **Value $26**

10

1940 GARTON®
"Red Hot" Roadster
(2nd, 2000)
Die-Cast Metal • PALM
1395QEO8404 • **Value $22**

11

1960 Eight Ball Racer
(3rd, 2001)
Die-Cast Metal • PALM
1395QEO8562 • **Value $13.95**

2001

Spring has sprung again and with it comes eight new Spring Ornaments for 2001. This year's themes include popular cartoon and movie characters, such as the lovable Peter Rabbit, Winnie the Pooh and Taz as well as The Empire Strikes Back. In addition, there are four designs which feature Easter baskets filled with furry surprises!

12

Bashful Bunny
Handcrafted • FRAN
595QEO8502 • **Value $5.95**

13

Charming Chick
Handcrafted • VOTR
595QEO8515 • **Value $5.95**

14

The Empire Strikes
Back (set/2)
Pressed Tin/Handcrafted • N/A
1495QEO8585 • **Value $14.95**

15

Happy Hopper
Handcrafted • AUBE
595QEO8505 • **Value $5.95**

	Price Paid	Value
Springtime Bonnets		
1.		
2.		
3.		
4.		
Vintage Roadster		
5.		
6.		
7.		
8.		
Winner's Circle		
9.		
10.		
11.		
2001 Collection		
12.		
13.		
14.		
15.		
Totals		

1

Lovely Lamb
Handcrafted • HADD
595QEO8512 • **Value $5.95**

2

Peter Rabbit
Handcrafted • VOTR
895QEO8545 • **Value $8.95**

3

Riding on the Breeze
Handcrafted • N/A
1095QEO8612 • **Value $10.95**

4

Taz Paint Egg!
Handcrafted • CHAD
1095QEO8572 • **Value $10.95**

2000

There was something for everyone in the 2000 collection of Spring Ornaments, from ballerinas and bunnies to graduates and gardeners. Among these 10 ornaments were the popular "Alice In Wonderland, Madame Alexander®" and the "Bar and Shield" Harley-Davidson® piece which gave even the toughest collectors something to smile about.

5

Alice in Wonderland, Madame Alexander®
Handcrafted • FRAN
1495QEO8421 • **Value $28**

6

Ballerina BARBIE™
Handcrafted • ANDR
1295QEO8471 • **Value $23**

7

Bar and Shield Harley-Davidson®
Die-Cast Metal • RHOD
1395QEO8544 • **Value $23**

8

Bugs Bunny Looney Tunes™
Pressed Tin • N/A
1095QEO8524 • **Value $18**

9

Frolicking Friends Bambi, Thumper and Flower (set/3)
Handcrafted • N/A
1495QEO8434 • **Value $23**

10

Happy Diploma Day!
Handcrafted • N/A
1095QEO8431 • **Value $20**

11

Peanuts® Lunch Box Set (set/2)
Pressed Tin • N/A
1495QEO8444 • **Value $25**

12

A Snug Hug
Handcrafted • PIKE
995QEO8424 • **Value $20**

13

A Swing With Friends
Handcrafted • N/A
1495QEO8414 • **Value $23**

14

Time in the Garden
Handcrafted/Cast Metal • SEAL
1095QEO8511 • **Value $18**

2001 Collection

	Price Paid	Value
1.		
2.		
3.		
4.		

2000 Collection

	Price Paid	Value
5.		
6.		
7.		
8.		
9.		
10.		
11.		
12.		
13.		
14.		
Totals		

1999

Baseball, golf and bubble blowing were just some of the many spring activities represented in the 17 Spring Ornaments for 1999. For those who just wanted to offer their favorite athlete a little encouragement from the sidelines, there were several pieces available including "Inspirational Angel" and "Friendly Delivery."

1

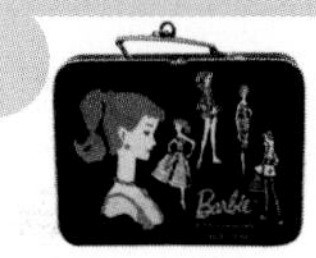

40th Anniversary Edition BARBIE™ Lunch Box
Pressed Tin • N/A
1295QEO8399 • **Value $24**

2

Batter Up! Charlie Brown and Snoopy, PEANUTS® (set/2)
Handcrafted • RHOD
1295QEO8389 • **Value $25**

3

Birthday Celebration
Handcrafted • AUBE
895QEO8409 • **Value $16**

4

Cross of Faith
Precious Metal • VOTR
1395QEO8467 • **Value $25**

5

Easter Egg Nest
Pressed Tin • SICK
795QEO8427 • **Value $18**

6

Final Putt, Minnie Mouse
Handcrafted • N/A
1095QEO8349 • **Value $19**

7

Friendly Delivery, Mary's Bears
Handcrafted • KLIN
1295QEO8419 • **Value $23**

8

Happy Bubble Blower
Handcrafted • TAGU
795QEO8437 • **Value $14**

9

Happy Diploma Day!
Handcrafted • N/A
1095QEO8357 • **Value $20**

10

Inspirational Angel
Handcrafted • LYLE
1295QEO8347 • **Value $23**

11

Mop Top Billy, Madame Alexander® (complements Mop Top Wendy, 1998)
Handcrafted • FRAN
1495QEO8337 • **Value $27**

12

Precious Baby, Commemorative
Handcrafted • LYLE
995QEO8417 • **Value $18**

13

Spring Chick
Handcrafted • AUBE
2200QEO8469 • **Value $37**

14

Springtime Harvest
Handcrafted • SICK
795QEO8429 • **Value $15**

15

The Tale of Peter Rabbit™, Beatrix Potter™ (set/3)
Handcrafted • VOTR
1995QEO8397 • **Value $37**

16

Tiggerific Easter Delivery
Handcrafted • N/A
1095QEO8359 • **Value $20**

17

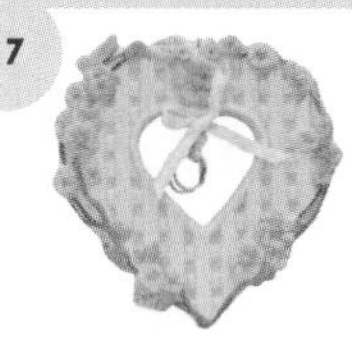

Wedding Memories
Porcelain • UNRU
995QEO8407 • **Value $18**

1999 Collection

	Price Paid	Value
1.		
2.		
3.		
4.		
5.		
6.		
7.		
8.		
9.		
10.		
11.		
12.		
13.		
14.		
15.		
16.		
17.		
Totals		

1998

Friendship was the theme of many of the 17 Spring Ornaments for 1998, including "Special Friends" and "Forever Friends." "Fair Valentine™ BARBIE® Doll" also created quite a stir in 1998, as it was the third and final piece to be released in the tremendously popular Be My Valentine Collector Series™.

1

Bashful Gift (set/2)
Handcrafted • AUBE
1195QEO8446 • **Value $23**

2

Bouquet of Memories
Handcrafted • TAGU
795QEO8456 • **Value $16**

3

Fair Valentine™ BARBIE® Doll
(3rd & final in *Be My Valentine Collector Series™*)
Vinyl • N/A
5000QHV8743 • **Value $52**

4

Forever Friends The Andrew Brownsword Collection
Handcrafted • PIKE
995QEO8423 • **Value $19**

5

The Garden of Piglet and Pooh (set/2)
Handcrafted • N/A
1295QEO8403 • **Value $25**

6

Going Up? Charlie Brown – PEANUTS®
Handcrafted • PIKE
995QEO8433 • **Value $20**

7

Happy Diploma Day!
Handcrafted • HADD
795QEO8476 • **Value $17**

8

Midge™ – 35th Anniversary
Handcrafted • ANDR
1495QEO8413 • **Value $27**

9

Practice Swing – Donald Duck
Handcrafted • N/A
1095QEO8396 • **Value $21**

10

Precious Baby
Handcrafted • TAGU
995QEO8463 • **Value $19**

11

Special Friends
Handcrafted • VOTR
1295QEO8523 • **Value $20**

12

STAR WARS™
Pressed Tin • N/A
1295QEO8406 • **Value $25**

13

Sweet Birthday
Handcrafted • KLIN
795QEO8473 • **Value $16**

14

Tigger in the Garden (Spring Preview)
Handcrafted • N/A
995QEO8436 • **Value $19**

15

Victorian Cross
Pewter • UNRU
895QEO8453 • **Value $18**

16

Wedding Memories
Porcelain • VOTR
995QEO8466 • **Value $19**

17

What's Your Name?
Handcrafted • KLIN
795QEO8443 • **Value $17**

1998 Collection

	Price Paid	Value
1.		
2.		
3.		
4.		
5.		
6.		
7.		
8.		
9.		
10.		
11.		
12.		
13.		
14.		
15.		
16.		
17.		
Totals		

1997

Bunnies were abundant among the 9 Spring Ornaments released in 1997, including "Bumper Crop," a Tender Touches piece, and "Garden Bunnies," created in a Nature's Sketchbook design. "Sentimental Valentine™ BARBIE® Doll," the second piece in the Be My Valentine Collector's Series™ disappeared almost immediately off of store shelves.

1

Bumper Crop, Tender Touches (set/3)
Handcrafted • SEAL
1495QEO8735 • **Value $27**

2

Digging In
Handcrafted • SEAL
795QEO8712 • **Value $17**

3

Eggs-pert Artist, CRAYOLA® Crayon
Handcrafted • TAGU
895QEO8695 • **Value $19**

4

Garden Bunnies, Nature's Sketchbook
Handcrafted • UNRU
1495QEO8702 • **Value $27**

5

Gentle Guardian
Handcrafted • LARS
695QEO8732 • **Value $14**

6

A Purr-fect Princess
Handcrafted • PIKE
795QEO8715 • **Value $16**

7

Sentimental Valentine™ BARBIE® Doll (2nd in *Be My Valentine Collector Series™*)
Vinyl • N/A
5000QHV8742 • **Value $58**

8

Swing-Time
Handcrafted • TAGU
795QEO8705 • **Value $16**

9

Victorian Cross
Pewter • N/A
895QEO8725 • **Value $18**

1996

The 10 Spring Ornaments released in 1996 caused quite a stir as everything from a Tender Touches "Eggstra Special Surprise" to the debut of the Be My Valentine Collector Series™" won the hearts of collectors everywhere. Also popular was "Strike Up The Band," a set of three musical critters that is perfect for nearly any spring season display.

10
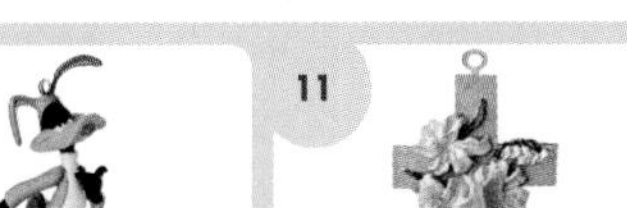
Daffy Duck, LOONEY TUNES
Handcrafted • RGRS
895QEO8154 • **Value $17**

11

Easter Morning
Handcrafted • UNRU
795QEO8164 • **Value $16**

12

Eggstra Special Surprise, Tender Touches
Handcrafted • SEAL
895QEO8161 • **Value $19**

1997 Collection

	Price Paid	Value
1.		
2.		
3.		
4.		
5.		
6.		
7.		
8.		
9.		

1996 Collection

	Price Paid	Value
10.		
11.		
12.		
Totals		

1

Hippity-Hop Delivery, CRAYOLA® Crayon
Handcrafted • CROW
795QEO8144 • **Value $18**

2

Look What I Found!
Handcrafted • FRAN
795QEO8181 • **Value $15**

3

Parade Pals, PEANUTS®
Handcrafted • RHOD
795QEO8151 • **Value $18**

4

Pork 'n Beans
Handcrafted • CHAD
795QEO8174 • **Value $15**

5

Strawberry Patch
Handcrafted • SEAL
695QEO8171 • **Value $17**

6

Strike up the Band! (set/3)
Handcrafted • UNRU
1495QEO8141 • **Value $29**

7

Sweet Valentine™ BARBIE® Doll
(1st in *Be My Valentine Collector Series*™)
Vinyl • N/A
4500QHV8131 • **Value $75**

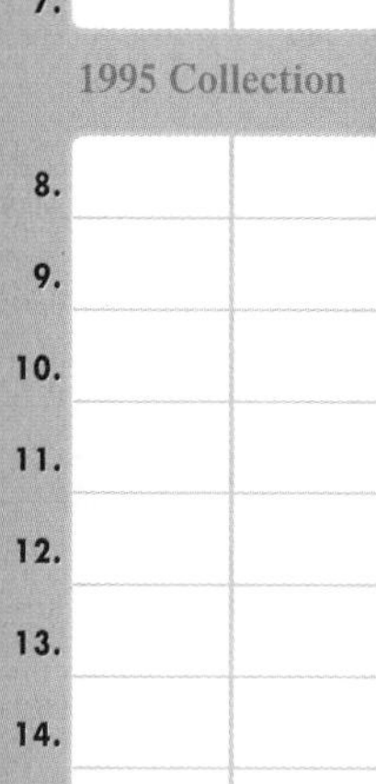

1996 Collection

	Price Paid	Value
1.		
2.		
3.		
4.		
5.		
6.		
7.		

1995 Collection

	Price Paid	Value
8.		
9.		
10.		
11.		
12.		
13.		
14.		
15.		
Totals		

1995

12 Spring Ornaments were released in 1995, including the annual "Baby's First Easter," to help commemorate this important milestone for a child. Also popular were the bunny-eared Snoopy ornament called "PEANUTS®," "Flowerpot Friends" and the adorable "Picture Perfect, Crayola® Crayon."

8

April Shower
Handcrafted • SIED
695QEO8253 • **Value $15**

9

Baby's First Easter
Handcrafted • PALM
795QEO8237 • **Value $17**

10

Bugs Bunny, LOONEY TUNES™
Handcrafted • CHAD
895QEO8279 • **Value $20**

11

Daughter
Handcrafted • RGRS
595QEO8239 • **Value $14**

12
Easter Eggspress
Handcrafted • SIED
495QEO8269 • **Value $15**

13

Elegant Lily
Brass • VOTR
695QEO8267 • **Value $14**

14

Flowerpot Friends (set/3)
Handcrafted • ANDR
1495QEO8229 • **Value $27**

15

Ham 'n Eggs
Handcrafted • CHAD
795QEO8277 • **Value $15**

1

High Hopes, Tender Touches
Handcrafted • SEAL
895QEO8259 • **Value $23**

2

PEANUTS®
Handcrafted • RHOD
795QEO8257 • **Value $26**

3

Picture Perfect, Crayola® Crayon
Handcrafted • CROW
795QEO8249 • **Value $20**

4

Son
Handcrafted • RGRS
595QEO8247 • **Value $17**

1994

Chicks, bunnies and lambs dominated the 1994 Spring Ornaments line. This year's 15 designs featured the lovable characters doing everything from performing to cooking in celebration of the new season. In addition, 1994 saw a few unconventional characters in the collection as well as "PEANUTS®" featured some well-known comic strip favorites

5

Baby's First Easter
Handcrafted • FRAN
675QEO8153 • **Value $21**

6

Colorful Spring
Handcrafted • CROW
775QEO8166 • **Value $32**

7

Daughter
Handcrafted • ANDR
575QEO8156 • **Value $16**

8

Divine Duet
Handcrafted • VOTR
675QEO8183 • **Value $18**

9

Easter Art Show
Handcrafted • VOTR
775QEO8193 • **Value $19**

10

Joyful Lamb
Handcrafted • UNRU
575QEO8206 • **Value $15**

11

PEANUTS®
Handcrafted • UNRU
775QEO8176 • **Value $44**

12

Peeping Out
Handcrafted • UNRU
675QEO8203 • **Value $17**

13

Riding a Breeze
Handcrafted • PALM
575QEO8213 • **Value $18**

14

Son
Handcrafted • ANDR
575QEO8163 • **Value $17**

15

Sunny Bunny Garden (set/3)
Handcrafted • SEAL
1500QEO8146 • **Value $31**

1995 Collection

	Price Paid	Value
1.		
2.		
3.		
4.		

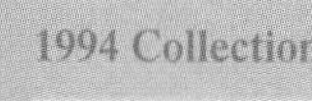

1994 Collection

	Price Paid	Value
5.		
6.		
7.		
8.		
9.		
10.		
11.		
12.		
13.		
14.		
15.		
Totals		

1

Sweet as Sugar
Handcrafted • RGRS
875QEO8086 • **Value $20**

2

Sweet Easter Wishes, Tender Touches
Handcrafted • SEAL
875QEO8196 • **Value $26**

3

Treetop Cottage
Handcrafted • SICK
975QEO8186 • **Value $20**

4

Yummy Recipe
Handcrafted • RGRS
775QEO8143 • **Value $21**

1993

Fun was the name of the game for the 16 Spring Ornaments released in 1993. Among this year's releases, "Barrow of Giggles," and "Li'l Peeper" turned out to be favorites with collectors. The 3-piece set of "Maypole Stroll" also caused quite a stir, with collectors continuing to search the secondary market for this piece even today.

5

Baby's First Easter
Handcrafted • PALM
675QEO8345 • **Value $16**

6

Backyard Bunny
Handcrafted • SICK
675QEO8405 • **Value $17**

7

Barrow of Giggles
Handcrafted • ANDR
875QEO8402 • **Value $21**

8
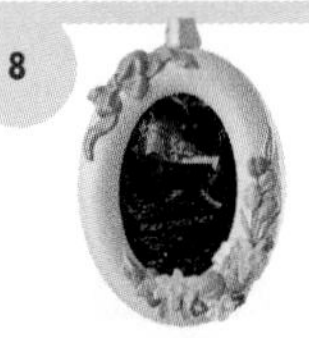
Beautiful Memories
Handcrafted • UNRU
675QEO8362 • **Value $15**

9

Best-dressed Turtle
Handcrafted • JLEE
575QEO8392 • **Value $16**

10
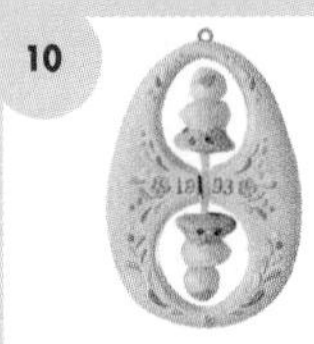
Chicks-on-a-Twirl
Handcrafted • LYLE
775QEO8375 • **Value $17**

11

Daughter
Handcrafted • ANDR
575QEO8342 • **Value $17**

12

Grandchild
Handcrafted • SIED
675QEO8352 • **Value $18**

13

Li'l Peeper
Handcrafted • JLEE
775QEO8312 • **Value $22**

14

Lop-eared Bunny
Handcrafted • SICK
575QEO8315 • **Value $20**

15

Lovely Lamb
Porcelain • VOTR
975QEO8372 • **Value $23**

16

Maypole Stroll (set/3)
Handcrafted/Wood
CHAD/FRAN
2800QEO8395 • **Value $50**

17

Nutty Eggs
Handcrafted • JLEE
675QEO8382 • **Value $16**

	Price Paid	Value
1994 Collection		
1.		
2.		
3.		
4.		
1993 Collection		
5.		
6.		
7.		
8.		
9.		
10.		
11.		
12.		
13.		
14.		
15.		
16.		
17.		
Totals		

1

Radiant Window
Handcrafted • UNRU
775QEO8365 • **Value $18**

2

Son
Handcrafted • ANDR
575QEO8335 • **Value $16**

3

Time for Easter
Handcrafted • CHAD
875QEO8385 • **Value $20**

1992

The second year of Spring Ornaments proved just as popular as the first as the 17 ornaments in the 1992 collection were soon making their way into homes and display cases all around the country. Among the year's most popular offerings were "Somebunny Loves You," the porcelain and nickel-plated "Rocking Bunny" and "CRAYOLA® Bunny."

4

Baby's First Easter
Handcrafted • FRAN
675QEO9271 • **Value $22**

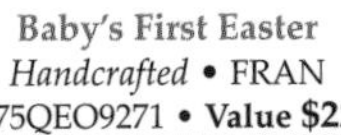

5

Belle Bunny
Porcelain • VOTR
975QEO9354 • **Value $20**

6

Bless You
Handcrafted • FRAN
675QEO9291 • **Value $24**

7

Cosmic Rabbit
Handcrafted • SIED
775QEO9364 • **Value $20**

8

CRAYOLA® Bunny
Handcrafted • RGRS
775QEO9304 • **Value $35**

9

Cultivated Gardener
Handcrafted • SIED
575QEO9351 • **Value $16**

10

Daughter
Handcrafted • RGRS
575QEO9284 • **Value $21**

11

Everything's Ducky
Handcrafted • PIKE
675QEO9331 • **Value $19**

12

Grandchild
Handcrafted • CROW
675QEO9274 • **Value $21**

13

Joy Bearer
Handcrafted • PALM
875QEO9334 • **Value $24**

14

Promise of Easter
Porcelain • LYLE
875QEO9314 • **Value $18**

15

Rocking Bunny
Porcelain/Nickel-Plated • VOTR
975QEO9324 • **Value $23**

16

Somebunny Loves You
Handcrafted • FRAN
675QEO9294 • **Value $32**

1993 Collection

	Price Paid	Value
1.		
2.		
3.		

1992 Collection

	Price Paid	Value
4.		
5.		
6.		
7.		
8.		
9.		
10.		
11.		
12.		
13.		
14.		
15.		
16.		
Totals		

1

Son
Handcrafted • RGRS
575QEO9281 • **Value $19**

2

Springtime Egg
Handcrafted • JLEE
875QEO9321 • **Value $20**

3

Sunny Wisher
Handcrafted • PIKE
575QEO9344 • **Value $17**

4

Warm Memories Photoholder
Fabric • VOTR
775QEO9311 • **Value $17**

1991

There were 11 different Spring Ornament styles to choose from in 1991, the collection's debut year. With these adorable pieces, you could do everything from celebrating your little one's first Easter with a "Baby's First Easter" ornament to welcoming a new arrival into the family with a "Daughter," "Son" or "Grandchild" ornament.

5
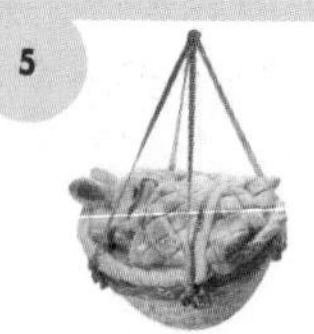
Baby's First Easter
Handcrafted • N/A
875QEO5189 • **Value $25**

6

Daughter
Handcrafted • N/A
575QEO5179 • **Value $32**

7

Easter Memories Photoholder
Fabric • N/A
775QEO5137 • **Value $17**

8

Full of Love
Handcrafted • N/A
775QEO5149 • **Value $50**

9

Gentle Lamb
Handcrafted • N/A
675QEO5159 • **Value $21**

10

Grandchild
Handcrafted • N/A
675QEO5177 • **Value $20**

11

Li'l Dipper
Handcrafted • N/A
675QEO5147 • **Value $24**

12

Lily Egg
Porcelain • UNRU
975QEO5139 • **Value $24**

13

Son
Handcrafted • N/A
575QEO5187 • **Value $27**

14

Spirit of Easter
Handcrafted • N/A
775QEO5169 • **Value $36**

15

Springtime Stroll
Handcrafted • N/A
675QEO5167 • **Value $23**

1992 Collection

	Price Paid	Value
1.		
2.		
3.		
4.		

1991 Collection

	Price Paid	Value
5.		
6.		
7.		
8.		
9.		
10.		
11.		
12.		
13.		
14.		
15.		
Totals		

Merry Miniatures®

A second addition to the popular Madame Alexander® collection arrived in 2001, as well as two new Merry Miniatures® collections. The Kids! Collection celebrates the playfulness and innocence of youngsters, while the Way to Bees Collection features a new buzzworthy piece for each and every month of the year. Happy collecting!

2001

1

Blade
Handcrafted • HADD
495QMM7056 • **Value $4.95**

2

Champ
Handcrafted • HADD
495QMM7043 • **Value $4.95**

3

Cheer
Handcrafted • HADD
495QMM7059 • **Value $4.95**

4

Glitter
Handcrafted • HADD
495QMM7057 • **Value $4.95**

5

Hooper
Handcrafted • HADD
495QMM7055 • **Value $4.95**

6

Hotshot
Handcrafted • HADD
495QMM7054 • **Value $4.95**

7

Lucky
Handcrafted • HADD
495QMM7050 • **Value $4.95**

8

Scout
Handcrafted • HADD
495QMM7049 • **Value $4.95**

9

Slugger
Handcrafted • HADD
495QMM7045 • **Value $4.95**

10

Speedy
Handcrafted • HADD
495QMM7042 • **Value $4.95**

11

Star
Handcrafted • HADD
495QMM7044 • **Value $4.95**

12

Trooper
Handcrafted • HADD
495QMM7058 • **Value $4.95**

13
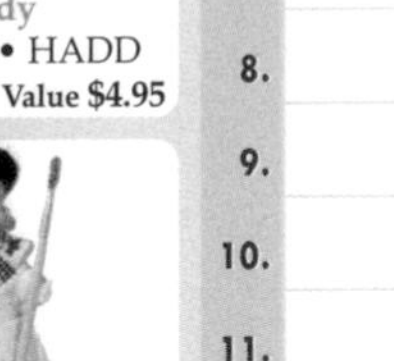
Artiste Wendy – 1997
Handcrafted • FORS
695QMM7028 • **Value $6.95**

14
Christmas Holly – 1998
Handcrafted • FRAN
695QMM7031 • **Value $6.95**

15
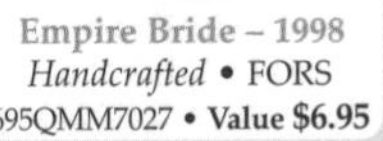
Empire Bride – 1998
Handcrafted • FORS
695QMM7027 • **Value $6.95**

16

Glistening Angel – 1998
Handcrafted • FORS
695QMM7030 • **Value $6.95**

Kids! Collection	Price Paid	Value
1.		
2.		
3.		
4.		
5.		
6.		
7.		
8.		
9.		
10.		
11.		
12.		
Madame Alexander® Collection		
13.		
14.		
15.		
16.		
Totals		

Value Guide — Merry Miniatures®

1

Little Miss Muffet – 1998
Handcrafted • FORS
695QMM7029 • **Value $6.95**

2

Madame Alexander® Display Base
Handcrafted • FORS
895QMM7060 • **Value $8.95**

3

Sleeping Beauty – 1997
Handcrafted • FORS
695QMM7034 • **Value $6.95**

4

Sleeping Beauty's Prince – 1999
Handcrafted • FORS
695QMM7033 • **Value $6.95**

5

Tooth Fairy – 1999
Handcrafted • FORS
695QMM7028 • **Value $6.95**

6

2001 Way to Bees Collection Display Base
Handcrafted • N/A
495QMM7038 • **Value $4.95**

7

Bee Bright (9th)
Handcrafted • TAGU
495QMM7048 • **Value $4.95**

8

Bee Busy (6th)
Handcrafted • TAGU
495QMM7041 • **Value $4.95**

9

Bee Caring (5th)
Handcrafted • TAGU
495QMM7040 • **Value $4.95**

10

Bee Irish (3th)
Handcrafted • TAGU
495QMM7037 • **Value $4.95**

11

Bee Joyful (1st)
Handcrafted • TAGU
495QMM7035 • **Value $4.95**

12

Bee Loving (2nd)
Handcrafted • TAGU
495QMM7036 • **Value $4.95**

13

Bee Merry (12th & final)
Handcrafted • TAGU
495QMM7053 • **Value $4.95**

14

Bee Playful (8th)
Handcrafted • TAGU
495QMM7047 • **Value $4.95**

15

Bee Proud (7th)
Handcrafted • TAGU
495QMM7046 • **Value $4.95**

16

Bee Scary (10th)
Handcrafted • TAGU
495QMM7051 • **Value $4.95**

17

Bee Sweet (4th)
Handcrafted • TAGU
495QMM7039 • **Value $4.95**

18

Bee Thankful (11th)
Handcrafted • TAGU
495QMM7035 • **Value $4.95**

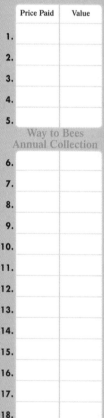

Madame Alexander® Collection

	Price Paid	Value
1.		
2.		
3.		
4.		
5.		

Way to Bees Annual Collection

	Price Paid	Value
6.		
7.		
8.		
9.		
10.		
11.		
12.		
13.		
14.		
15.		
16.		
17.		
18.		
Totals		

2000

1

2000 Happy Hatters Collection Display Base
Handcrafted • N/A
495QMM7003 • **Value $6**

2

B.B. Capps (6th)
Handcrafted • N/A
495QMM7008 • **Value $8**

3

Bonnie Bonnet (4th)
Handcrafted • N/A
495QMM7006 • **Value $8**

4

Booker Beanie (9th)
Handcrafted • TAGU
495QMM7017 • **Value $11**

5

Candy Capper (10th)
Handcrafted • N/A
495QMM7022 • **Value $15**

6

Cora Copia (11th)
Handcrafted • N/A
495QMM7023 • **Value $15**

7

Hattie Boxx (12th & final)
Handcrafted • N/A
495QMM7024 • **Value $8**

8

Libby Crown (7th)
Handcrafted • N/A
495QMM7015 • **Value $8**

9

Missy Milliner (5th)
Handcrafted • N/A
495QMM7007 • **Value $10**

10

Paddy O'Hatty (3rd)
Handcrafted • N/A
495QMM7002 • **Value $8**

11
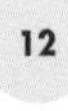
Panama Pete (8th)
Handcrafted • N/A
495QMM7016 • **Value $8**

12

Rosie Chapeauzie (2nd)
Handcrafted • N/A
495QMM7001 • **Value $8**

13

Tiny Topper (1st)
Handcrafted • N/A
495QMM7000 • **Value $9**

14

Fire Fighter Wendy – 1997
Handcrafted • FORS
695QMM7010 • **Value $16**

15

Little Red Riding Hood – 1991 (Premiere)
Handcrafted • FRAN
695QFM7062 • **Value $12**

16

Mary Had a Little Lamb
Handcrafted • FORS
695QMM7014 • **Value $12**

17

Mop Top Billy
Handcrafted • FRAN
695QMM7005 • **Value $18**

18

Mop Top Wendy
Handcrafted • FRAN
695QMM7004 • **Value $20**

Happy Hatters Annual Collection

	Price Paid	Value
1.		
2.		
3.		
4.		
5.		
6.		
7.		
8.		
9.		
10.		
11.		
12.		
13.		

Madame Alexander® Collection

	Price Paid	Value
14.		
15.		
16.		
17.		
18.		
Totals		

1

Mother Goose
Handcrafted • FORS
695QMM7013 • **Value $16**

2

Pink Pristine Angel – 1997
Handcrafted • FORS
695QMM7020 • **Value $16**

3

Santa's Little Helper – 1998
Handcrafted • N/A
695QMM7021 • **Value $12**

1999

4

Anniversary Edition (set/2)
Handcrafted • HADD
1295QFM8529 • **Value $19**

5

Bashful Friends Merry Miniatures® (set/3)
Handcrafted • AUBE
1295QSM8459 • **Value $20**

6
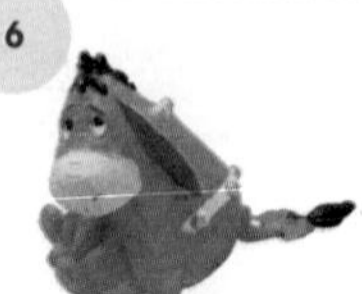
Eeyore
Handcrafted • N/A
495QRP8519 • **Value $15**

7

Favorite Friends (set/2)
Handcrafted • KLIN
895QFM8537 • **Value $18**

8

A Kiss For You–HERSHEY'S™ (set/3, 3rd & final, HERSHEY'S™)
Handcrafted • BRIC
1295QFM8497 • **Value $23**

9

Park Avenue Wendy & Alex the Bellhop Madame Alexander® (Premiere, set/2)
Handcrafted • FRAN
1295QFM8499 • **Value $20**

10

Piglet on Base
Handcrafted • N/A
495QRP8507 • **Value $13**

11
Tigger
Handcrafted • N/A
495QRP8527 • **Value $13**

12

Winnie the Pooh
Handcrafted • N/A
495QRP8509 • **Value $14**

1998

13

Bride and Groom–1996 Madame Alexander® (Premiere)
Handcrafted • FRAN
1295QFM8486 • **Value $23**

14

Donald's Passenger Car
Handcrafted • N/A
595QRP8513 • **Value $15**

15

Goofy's Caboose
Handcrafted • N/A
595QRP8516 • **Value $15**

16
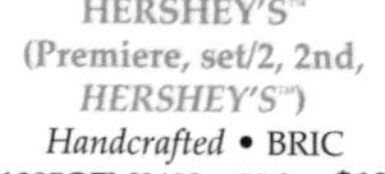

HERSHEY'S™ (Premiere, set/2, 2nd, *HERSHEY'S™*)
Handcrafted • BRIC
1095QFM8493 • **Value $18**

17

Mickey's Locomotive
Handcrafted • N/A
595QRP8496 • **Value $16**

Madame Alexander® Collection

	Price Paid	Value
1.		
2.		
3.		

1999 Collection

	Price Paid	Value
4.		
5.		
6.		
7.		
8.		
9.		
10.		
11.		
12.		

1998 Collection

	Price Paid	Value
13.		
14.		
15.		
16.		
17.		

Totals

1997

1

Minnie's Luggage Car
Handcrafted • N/A
595QRP8506 • **Value $15**

2

Pluto's Coal Car
Handcrafted • N/A
595QRP8503 • **Value $15**

3

Rapunzel
(Spring Preview, set/2)
Handcrafted • TAGU
1295QSM8483 • **Value $21**

4

Apple Harvest – Mary's Bears (set/3)
Handcrafted • HAMI
1295QFM8585 • **Value $25**

5

Bashful Visitors (set/3)
Handcrafted • AUBE
1295QFM8582 • **Value $27**

6

Cupid Cameron
Handcrafted • N/A
495QSM8552 • **Value $14**

7

Easter Parade (set/2)
Handcrafted • TAGU
795QSM8562 • **Value $15**

8

Getting Ready for Spring (set/3)
Handcrafted • TAGU
1295QSM8575 • **Value $19**

9

Happy Birthday Clowns
(3rd & final, *Happy Birthday Clowns*)
Handcrafted • N/A
495QSM8565 • **Value $14**

10

HERSHEY'S™
(set/2, 1st, *HERSHEY'S™*)
Handcrafted • BRIC
1295QFM8625 • **Value $23**

11

Holiday Harmony (set/3)
Handcrafted • TAGU
1295QFM8612 • **Value $23**

12

Making a Wish (set/2)
Handcrafted • TAGU
795QFM8592 • **Value $15**

13

The Nativity (set/2)
Handcrafted • N/A
795QFM8615 • **Value $23**

14

Noah's Friends (set/2)
Handcrafted • ESCH
795QSM8572 • **Value $20**

15

Peter Pan (set/5)
Handcrafted • TAGU
1995QSM8605 • **Value $37**

16

Santa Cameron
Handcrafted • N/A
495QFM8622 • **Value $15**

17

Six Dwarfs (set/3)
Handcrafted • ESCH
1295QFM8685 • **Value $26**

18

Snow White and Dancing Dwarf (set/2)
Handcrafted • ESCH
795QFM8535 • **Value $18**

1998 Collection

	Price Paid	Value
1.		
2.		
3.		

1997 Collection

	Price Paid	Value
4.		
5.		
6.		
7.		
8.		
9.		
10.		
11.		
12.		
13.		
14.		
15.		
16.		
17.		
18.		

Totals

1

Snowbear Season (Premiere, set/3)
Handcrafted • ESCH
1295QFM8602 • **Value $21**

2

Sule and Sara – PendaKids™ (set/2)
Handcrafted • JOHN
795QSM8545 • **Value $14**

3

Tea Time – Mary's Bears (set/3)
Handcrafted • HAMI
1295QSM8542 • **Value $24**

4

Three Wee Kings (set/3)
Handcrafted • N/A
1295QFM8692 • **Value $23**

1996

5

Alice in Wonderland (set/5)
Handcrafted • N/A
1995QSM8014 • **Value $33**

6

Bashful Mistletoe (Premiere, set/3)
Handcrafted • N/A
1295QFM8319 • **Value $25**

7

Blue-Ribbon Bunny
Handcrafted • N/A
495QSM8064 • **Value $15**

8

Busy Bakers (set/2)
Handcrafted • N/A
795QFM8121 • **Value $16**

9

Cowboy Cameron (set/3)
Handcrafted • N/A
1295QFM8041 • **Value $26**

10

Easter Egg Hunt
Handcrafted • N/A
495QSM8024 • **Value $15**

11

Giving Thanks (set/3)
Handcrafted • N/A
1295QFM8134 • **Value $25**

12

Happy Birthday Clowns (set/2, 2nd, *Happy Birthday Clowns*)
Handcrafted • N/A
795QSM8114 • **Value $16**

13

Happy Haunting (set/2)
Handcrafted • N/A
1295QFM8124 • **Value $28**

14

Lucky Cameron (set/2)
Handcrafted • N/A
795QSM8021 • **Value $16**

15

Mr. and Mrs. Claus Bears (set/2)
Handcrafted • N/A
795QFM8044 • **Value $19**

16

Noah and Friends (set/5)
Handcrafted • N/A
1995QSM8111 • **Value $42**

17

PEANUTS® Pumpkin Patch (set/5)
Handcrafted • N/A
1995QFM8131 • **Value $50**

18

Penda Kids (set/2)
Handcrafted • N/A
795QSM8011 • **Value $14**

19

Santa's Helpers (set/3)
Handcrafted • N/A
1295QFM8051 • **Value $25**

1997 Collection

	Price Paid	Value
1.		
2.		
3.		
4.		

1996 Collection

	Price Paid	Value
5.		
6.		
7.		
8.		
9.		
10.		
11.		
12.		
13.		
14.		
15.		
16.		
17.		
18.		
19.		
Totals		

1

The Sewing Club (set/3)
Handcrafted • N/A
1295QFM8061 • **Value $27**

2

Sweetheart Cruise (set/3)
Handcrafted • N/A
1295QSM8004 • **Value $23**

1995

3

Bashful Boy
Handcrafted • N/A
300QSM8107 • **Value $16**

4

Bashful Girl
Handcrafted • N/A
300QSM8109 • **Value $16**

5

Beauregard
Handcrafted • N/A
300QSM8047 • **Value N/E**

6

Birthday Bear (1st, *Happy Birthday Clowns*)
Handcrafted • N/A
375QSM8057 • **Value $15**

7

Bride & Groom
Handcrafted • N/A
375QSM8067 • **Value $15**

8

Cameron
Handcrafted • N/A
375QSM8009 • **Value $19**

9

Cameron/Bunny
Handcrafted • N/A
375QSM8029 • **Value $19**

10

Cameron in Pumpkin Costume
Handcrafted • N/A
375QFM8147 • **Value $18**

11

Cameron on Sled
Handcrafted • N/A
375QFM8199 • **Value $15**

12

Cameron Pilgrim
Handcrafted • N/A
375QFM8169 • **Value $17**

13

Cameron w/Camera
Handcrafted • N/A
375QSM8077 • **Value $18**

14

Caroling Bear
Handcrafted • N/A
325QFM8307 • **Value $14**

15

Caroling Bunny
Handcrafted • N/A
325QFM8309 • **Value $14**

16

Caroling Mouse
Handcrafted • N/A
300QFM8317 • **Value $14**

17

Chipmunk with Corn
Handcrafted • N/A
375QFM8179 • **Value $14**

18

Christmas Tree
Handcrafted • N/A
675QFM8197 • **Value $18**

19

Cinderella
Handcrafted • N/A
400QSM8117 • **Value $35**

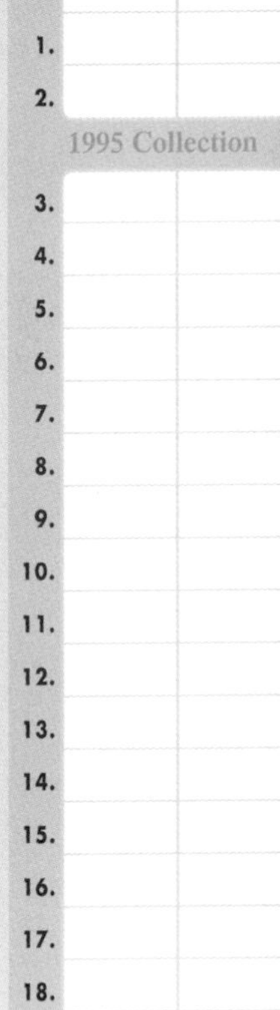

1996 Collection

	Price Paid	Value
1.		
2.		

1995 Collection

	Price Paid	Value
3.		
4.		
5.		
6.		
7.		
8.		
9.		
10.		
11.		
12.		
13.		
14.		
15.		
16.		
17.		
18.		
19.		
Totals		

1

Cottage
Handcrafted • N/A
675QSM8027 • **Value $21**

2

Cute Witch
Handcrafted • N/A
300QFM8157 • **Value $14**

3

Fairy Godmother
Handcrafted • N/A
400QSM8089 • **Value $20**

4

Feast Table
Handcrafted • N/A
475QFM8167 • **Value $14**

5

Friendly Monster
Handcrafted • N/A
300QFM8159 • **Value $14**

6

Groundhog
Handcrafted • N/A
300QSM8079 • **Value $14**

7

Hamster with Cookies
Handcrafted • N/A
325QFM8319 • **Value $16**

8

Haunted House
Handcrafted • N/A
675QFM8139 • **Value $19**

1995 Collection

	Price Paid	Value
1.		
2.		
3.		
4.		
5.		
6.		
7.		
8.		
9.		
10.		
11.		
12.		
13.		
14.		
15.		
16.		
17.		
18.		
19.		
20.		
Totals		

9

Koala Bear
Handcrafted • N/A
375QSM8019 • **Value $15**

10

Leprechaun
Handcrafted • N/A
350QSM8119 • **Value $15**

11

Lion and Lamb
Handcrafted • N/A
400QFM8287 • **Value $16**

12

Mouse with Cranberries
Handcrafted • N/A
300QFM8189 • **Value $12**

13

Mouse with Pumpkin
Handcrafted • N/A
300QFM8187 • **Value $13**

14

Nutcracker
Handcrafted • N/A
375QFM8297 • **Value $14**

15

Prince Charming
Handcrafted • N/A
400QSM8049 • **Value $32**

16

Pumpkin Coach
Handcrafted • N/A
500QFM8127 • **Value $17**

17

Raccoon and Flower
Handcrafted • N/A
300QSM8087 • **Value $12**

18

Rhino Mummy
Handcrafted • N/A
375QFM8149 • **Value $14**

19

St. Bernard
Handcrafted • N/A
375QSM8017 • **Value $15**

20

Santa
Handcrafted • N/A
375QFM8299 • **Value $14**

1

Selby
Handcrafted • N/A
300QSM8039 • **Value $14**

2

Stepmother
Handcrafted • N/A
400QFM8099 • **Value $16**

3

Stylish Rabbit
Handcrafted • N/A
375QSM8037 • **Value $14**

4

Toymaker Beaver
Handcrafted • N/A
375QFM8289 • **Value $14**

5

Tree
Handcrafted • N/A
675QSM8007 • **Value $20**

6

Turkey
Handcrafted • N/A
375QFM8177 • **Value $15**

1994

7

Basket of Apples
Handcrafted • N/A
275QFM8356 • **Value $13**

8

Bear Letter Carrier
Handcrafted • N/A
375QSM8006 • **Value $13**

9

Bear on Skates
Handcrafted • N/A
375QFM8293 • **Value $16**

10

Bear with Flag
Handcrafted • N/A
375QSM8043 • **Value $25**

11

Beaver
Handcrafted • N/A
375QFM8336 • **Value $14**

12

Beaver
Handcrafted • N/A
375QSM8013 • **Value $12**

13
Birds in Nest
Handcrafted • N/A
375QSM8116 • **Value $13**

14

Black Kitten
Handcrafted • N/A
325QFM8273 • **Value $13**

15

Bunny Alien
Handcrafted • N/A
375QFM8266 • **Value $15**

16

Chick in Wagon
Handcrafted • N/A
375QSM8123 • **Value $17**

17

Chipmunk with Kite
Handcrafted • N/A
300QSM8003 • **Value $15**

18

Corn Stalk
Handcrafted • N/A
675QFM8363 • **Value $18**

19

Dock
Handcrafted • N/A
675QSM8076 • **Value $24**

1995 Collection	Price Paid	Value
1.		
2.		
3.		
4.		
5.		
6.		

1994 Collection	Price Paid	Value
7.		
8.		
9.		
10.		
11.		
12.		
13.		
14.		
15.		
16.		
17.		
18.		
19.		
Totals		

1

Document
Handcrafted • N/A
275QSM8053 • **Value $15**

2

Eagle with Hat
Handcrafted • N/A
375QSM8036 • **Value $17**

3

Fence with Lantern
Handcrafted • N/A
675QFM8283 • **Value $19**

4

Flag
Handcrafted • N/A
675QSM8056 • **Value $25**

5

Fox on Skates
Handcrafted • N/A
375QFM8303 • **Value $14**

6

Indian Bunny
Handcrafted • N/A
275QFM8353 • **Value $13**

7

Indian Chickadee
Handcrafted • N/A
325QFM8346 • **Value $16**

8

Lamb
Handcrafted • N/A
325QSM8132 • **Value $12**

9

Mailbox
Handcrafted • N/A
675QSM8023 • **Value $18**

10

Mouse with Flower
Handcrafted • N/A
275QSM8243 • **Value $13**

11

Mrs. Claus
Handcrafted • N/A
375QFM8286 • **Value $16**

12

North Pole Sign
Handcrafted • N/A
675QFM8333 • **Value $22**

13

Owl in Stump
Handcrafted • N/A
275QSM8243 • **Value $13**

14

Pail of Seashells
Handcrafted • N/A
275QSM8052 • **Value $15**

15

Penguin
Handcrafted • N/A
275QFM8313 • **Value $16**

16

Pilgrim Bunny
Handcrafted • N/A
375QFM8343 • **Value $14**

17

Polar Bears
Handcrafted • N/A
325QFM8323 • **Value $15**

18

Pumpkin with Hat
Handcrafted • N/A
275QFM8276 • **Value $13**

19

Rabbit
Handcrafted • N/A
275QSM8066 • **Value $15**

20

Rabbit
Handcrafted • N/A
325QSM8016 • **Value $12**

1994 Collection

	Price Paid	Value
1.		
2.		
3.		
4.		
5.		
6.		
7.		
8.		
9.		
10.		
11.		
12.		
13.		
14.		
15.		
16.		
17.		
18.		
19.		
20.		
Totals		

1

Rabbit with Can
Handcrafted • N/A
325QSM8083 • **Value $13**

2

Rabbit with Croquet
Handcrafted • N/A
375QSM8113 • **Value $11**

3

Raccoon
Handcrafted • N/A
375QSM8063 • **Value $18**

4

Sled Dog
Handcrafted • N/A
325QFM8306 • **Value $15**

5

Snowman
Handcrafted • N/A
275QFM8316 • **Value $11**

6

Squirrel as Clown
Handcrafted • N/A
375QFM8263 • **Value $14**

7

Tree
Handcrafted • N/A
275QFM8326 • **Value $14**

8

Wishing Well
Handcrafted • N/A
675QSM8033 • **Value $22**

1993

9

Animated Cauldron
Handcrafted • N/A
250QFM8425 • **Value $14**

10

Arctic Fox
Handcrafted • N/A
350QFM8242 • **Value $14**

11

Arctic Scene Backdrop
Paper • N/A
175QFM8205 • **Value $7**

12

Baby Walrus
Handcrafted • N/A
300QFM8232 • **Value $12**

13

Baby Whale
Handcrafted • N/A
350QFM8222 • **Value $12**

14

Beach Scene Backdrop
Paper • N/A
175QSM8042 • **Value $7**

15

Bear dressed as Bat
Handcrafted • N/A
300QFM8285 • **Value $13**

16

Bear with Surfboard
Handcrafted • N/A
350QSM8015 • **Value $15**

17

Betsey Ross Lamb
Handcrafted • N/A
350QSM8482 • **Value $18**

18

Bobcat Pilgrim
Handcrafted • N/A
350QFM8172 • **Value $15**

19

Box of Candy
Handcrafted • N/A
250QSM8095 • **Value $18**

1994 Collection

	Price Paid	Value
1.		
2.		
3.		
4.		
5.		
6.		
7.		
8.		

1993 Collection

	Price Paid	Value
9.		
10.		
11.		
12.		
13.		
14.		
15.		
16.		
17.		
18.		
19.		

Totals

Value Guide — Merry Miniatures®

1

Bunny Painting Egg
Handcrafted • N/A
350QSM8115 • **Value $11**

2

Bunny with Basket
Handcrafted • N/A
250QSM8142 • **Value $13**

3

Bunny with Egg
Handcrafted • N/A
300QSM8125 • **Value $12**

4

Bunny with Scarf
Handcrafted • N/A
250QFM8235 • **Value $15**

5

Bunny with Seashell
Handcrafted • N/A
350QSM8005 • **Value $19**

6

Cat & Mouse (3rd & final, *Hugs and Kisses*)
Handcrafted • N/A
350QSM8102 • **Value $15**

7

Chipmunk
Handcrafted • N/A
350QSM8002 • **Value $15**

8

Display Stand
Handcrafted • N/A
675QFM8055 • **Value $9**

9

Dog with Balloon
Handcrafted • N/A
250QSM8092 • **Value $11**

10

Dragon Dog
Handcrafted • N/A
300QFM8295 • **Value $13**

11

Duck with Egg
Handcrafted • N/A
300QSM8135 • **Value $11**

12

Easter Basket
Handcrafted • N/A
250QSM8145 • **Value $14**

13

Easter Garden Backdrop
Paper • N/A
175QSM8152 • **Value $7**

14

Eskimo Child
Handcrafted • N/A
300QFM8215 • **Value $18**

15

Fox with Heart
Handcrafted • N/A
350QSM8065 • **Value $11**

16

Ghost on Tombstone
Handcrafted • N/A
250QFM8282 • **Value $11**

17

Goat Uncle Sam
Handcrafted • N/A
300QSM8472 • **Value $16**

18
Haunted Halloween Backdrop
Paper • N/A
175QFM8275 • **Value $7**

19
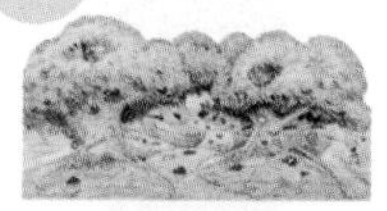
Heartland Forest Backdrop
Paper • N/A
175QSM8082 • **Value $7**

20

Hedgehog
Handcrafted • N/A
300QSM8026 • **Value $13**

1993 Collection

	Price Paid	Value
1.		
2.		
3.		
4.		
5.		
6.		
7.		
8.		
9.		
10.		
11.		
12.		
13.		
14.		
15.		
16.		
17.		
18.		
19.		
20.		
Totals		

1

Hedgehog Patriot
Handcrafted • N/A
350QSM8492 • **Value $13**

2

Hippo
Handcrafted • N/A
300QSM8032 • **Value $13**

3

Husky Puppy
Handcrafted • N/A
350QFM8245 • **Value $15**

4
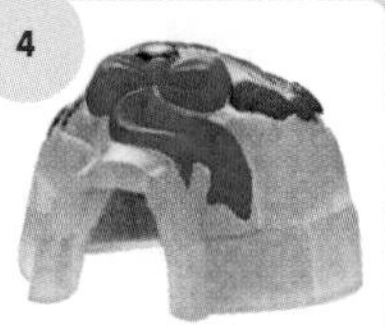
Igloo
Handcrafted • N/A
300QFM8252 • **Value $17**

5

Indian Bear
Handcrafted • N/A
350QFM8162 • **Value $14**

6

Indian Squirrel
Handcrafted • N/A
300QFM8182 • **Value $14**

7

Indian Turkey
Handcrafted • N/A
350QFM8165 • **Value $14**

8

Lamb
Handcrafted • N/A
350QSM8112 • **Value $12**

9

Liberty Bell
Handcrafted • N/A
250QSM8465 • **Value $15**

10

Liberty Mouse
Handcrafted • N/A
300QSM8475 • **Value $17**

11

Mouse in Sunglasses
Handcrafted • N/A
250QSM8035 • **Value $14**

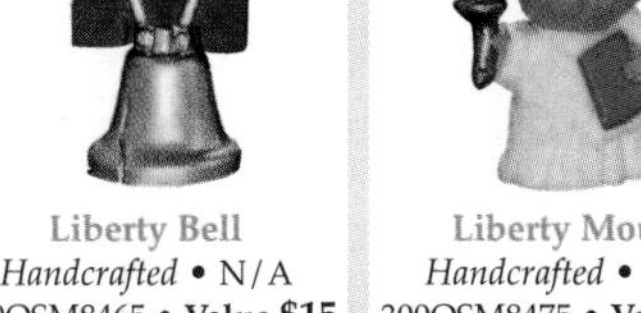

12
Mouse Witch
Handcrafted • N/A
300QFM8292 • **Value $15**

13
Owl and Pumpkin
Handcrafted • N/A
300QFM8302 • **Value $16**

14

Panda (3rd & final, *Sweet Valentines*)
Handcrafted • N/A
350QSM8105 • **Value $15**

15

Patriotic Backdrop
Paper • N/A
175QSM8495 • **Value $8**

16

Penguin in Hat
Handcrafted • N/A
300QFM8212 • **Value $13**

17

Pig in Blanket
Handcrafted • N/A
300QSM8022 • **Value $18**

18
Pilgrim Chipmunk
Handcrafted • N/A
300QFM8185 • **Value $15**

19
Pilgrim Mouse
Handcrafted • N/A
300QFM8175 • **Value $17**

20

Plymouth Rock
Handcrafted • N/A
250QFM8192 • **Value $17**

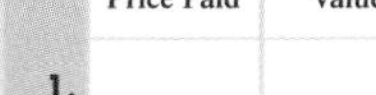

1993 Collection

	Price Paid	Value
1.		
2.		
3.		
4.		
5.		
6.		
7.		
8.		
9.		
10.		
11.		
12.		
13.		
14.		
15.		
16.		
17.		
18.		
19.		
20.		
Totals		

1

Polar Bear (3rd & final, *Music Makers*)
Handcrafted • N/A
350QFM8265 • **Value $17**

2

Prairie Dog
Handcrafted • N/A
350QSM8012 • **Value $18**

3

Princess Cat
Handcrafted • N/A
350QFM8305 • **Value $17**

4

Raccoon with Heart
Handcrafted • N/A
350QSM8062 • **Value $11**

5

Sandcastle
Handcrafted • N/A
300QSM8045 • **Value $16**

6

Santa Eskimo
Handcrafted • N/A
350QFM8262 • **Value $26**

7

Seal with Earmuffs
Handcrafted • N/A
250QFM8272 • **Value $13**

8

Sherlock Duck
Handcrafted • N/A
300QSM8122 • **Value $12**

9

Skunk with Heart
Handcrafted • N/A
300QSM8072 • **Value $11**

10

Stump & Can
Handcrafted • N/A
300QSM8075 • **Value $12**

11

Super Hero Bunny
Handcrafted • N/A
300QFM8422 • **Value $18**

12

Thanksgiving Feast Backdrop
Paper • N/A
175QFM8195 • **Value $7**

1992

13

Baby's 1st Easter
Handcrafted • N/A
350QSM9777 • **Value $13**

14
Ballet Pig
Handcrafted • N/A
250QSM9759 • **Value $15**

15

Bear (2nd, *Sweet Valentines*)
Handcrafted • N/A
350QSM9717 • **Value $21**

16

Bear With Drum (2nd, *Music Makers*)
Handcrafted • N/A
350QFM9134 • **Value $19**

17

Bunny & Carrot
Handcrafted • N/A
250QSM9799 • **Value $14**

18

Cat in P.J.'s
Handcrafted • N/A
350QFM9084 • **Value $14**

19

Chipmunk
Handcrafted • N/A
250QFM9144 • **Value $10**

1993 Collection

	Price Paid	Value
1.		
2.		
3.		
4.		
5.		
6.		
7.		
8.		
9.		
10.		
11.		
12.		

1992 Collection

	Price Paid	Value
13.		
14.		
15.		
16.		
17.		
18.		
19.		
Totals		

1

Clown (3rd & final, *Birthday Clowns*)
Handcrafted • N/A
350QSM9819 • **Value $17**

2

Clown Mouse
Handcrafted • N/A
250QFM9031 • **Value $13**

3

Cow
Handcrafted • N/A
300QFM9034 • **Value $15**

4

Crab
Handcrafted • N/A
300QFM9174 • **Value $11**

5

Dog
Handcrafted • N/A
300QSM9847 • **Value $18**

6

Dog in P.J.'s
Handcrafted • N/A
350QFM9081 • **Value $13**

7

Ghost with Corn Candy
Handcrafted • N/A
300QFM9014 • **Value $15**

8

Giraffe as Tree
Handcrafted • N/A
300QFM9141 • **Value $14**

9

Goldfish
Handcrafted • N/A
300QFM9181 • **Value $12**

10

Goose in Bonnet
Handcrafted • N/A
300QSM9789 • **Value $16**

11

Grad Dog
Handcrafted • N/A
250QSM9817 • **Value $15**

12

Haunted House
Handcrafted • N/A
350QFM9024 • **Value $14**

13

Hedgehog
Handcrafted • N/A
250QSM9859 • **Value $13**

14

Horse
Handcrafted • N/A
300QFM9051 • **Value $18**

15

Indian Bunnies
Handcrafted • N/A
350QFM9004 • **Value $15**

16

Kitten for Dad
Handcrafted • N/A
350QSM9839 • **Value $15**

17

Kitten for Mom
Handcrafted • N/A
350QSM9837 • **Value $15**

18

Kitten in Bib
Handcrafted • N/A
350QSM9829 • **Value $13**

19

Lamb
Handcrafted • N/A
250QFM9044 • **Value $16**

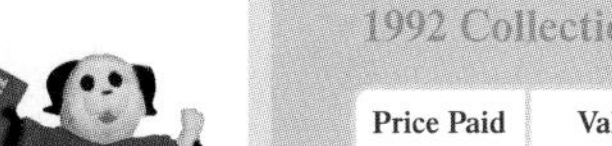

1992 Collection

	Price Paid	Value
1.		
2.		
3.		
4.		
5.		
6.		
7.		
8.		
9.		
10.		
11.		
12.		
13.		
14.		
15.		
16.		
17.		
18.		
19.		
Totals		

Value Guide — Merry Miniatures®

1

Lamb
Handcrafted • N/A
350QSM9787 • **Value $14**

2

Lion
Handcrafted • N/A
350QSM9719 • **Value $14**

3

Mouse
Handcrafted • N/A
300QSM9769 • **Value $11**

4

Mouse in Car
Handcrafted • N/A
300QFM9114 • **Value $13**

5
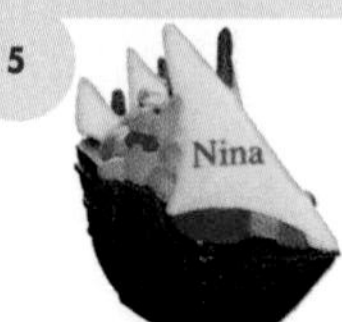

Nina Ship
Handcrafted • N/A
350QFM9154 • **Value $12**

6

Octopus
Handcrafted • N/A
300QFM9171 • **Value $12**

7

Party Dog
Handcrafted • N/A
300QFM9191 • **Value $13**

8

Penguin in Tux
Handcrafted • N/A
300QSM9757 • **Value $16**

9

Penguin Skating
Handcrafted • N/A
350QFM9091 • **Value $15**

10

Pig
Handcrafted • N/A
250QFM9041 • **Value $19**

11

Pilgrim Beaver
Handcrafted • N/A
300QFM9011 • **Value $15**

12

Pinta Ship
Handcrafted • N/A
350QFM9161 • **Value $12**

13

Praying Chipmunk
Handcrafted • N/A
300QSM9797 • **Value $14**

14

Pumpkin
Handcrafted • N/A
300QFM9021 • **Value $14**

15

Puppy
Handcrafted • N/A
250QSM9767 • **Value $16**

16

Rabbit & Squirrel
(2nd, *Hugs and Kisses*)
Handcrafted • N/A
350QSM9827 • **Value $19**

17

Rabbit Holding
Heart Carrot
Handcrafted • N/A
350QFM9201 • **Value $14**

18
Rabbit On Sled
Handcrafted • N/A
300QFM9151 • **Value $12**

19

Santa Bee
Handcrafted • N/A
300QFM9061 • **Value $12**

20

Santa Bell (3rd & final,
Jingle Bell Santa)
Handcrafted • N/A
350QFM9131 • **Value $19**

1992 Collection

	Price Paid	Value
1.		
2.		
3.		
4.		
5.		
6.		
7.		
8.		
9.		
10.		
11.		
12.		
13.		
14.		
15.		
16.		
17.		
18.		
19.		
20.		
Totals		

1

Santa Maria Ship
Handcrafted • N/A
350QFM9164 • **Value $13**

2

Seal
Handcrafted • N/A
300QSM9849 • **Value $13**

3

Skunk with Butterfly
Handcrafted • N/A
350QFM9184 • **Value $13**

4

Snow Bunny
Handcrafted • N/A
400QFM9071 • **Value $12**

5

Squirrel Pal (3rd & final, *Gentle Pals*)
Handcrafted • N/A
350QFM9094 • **Value $20**

6

Squirrels in Nutshell
Handcrafted • N/A
350QFM9064 • **Value $14**

7

Sweatshirt Bunny
Handcrafted • N/A
350QSM9779 • **Value $15**

8

Sweet Angel
Handcrafted • N/A
300QFM9124 • **Value $16**

9

Teacher Cat
Handcrafted • N/A
350QFM9074 • **Value $11**

10

Teddy Bear
Handcrafted • N/A
250QFM9194 • **Value $15**

11
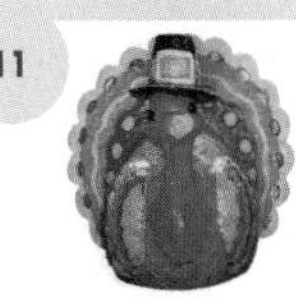
Thankful Turkey (3rd & final, *Thankful Turkey*)
Handcrafted • N/A
350QFM9001 • **Value $22**

12

Turtle & Mouse
Handcrafted • N/A
300QSM9857 • **Value $24**

13

Walrus & Bird
Handcrafted • N/A
350QFM9054 • **Value $15**

14

Waving Reindeer
Handcrafted • N/A
300QFM9121 • **Value $15**

1991

15

1st Christmas Together
Handcrafted • N/A
350QFM1799 • **Value $13**

16

Aerobic Bunny
Handcrafted • N/A
250QFM1817 • **Value $19**

17

Artist Mouse
Handcrafted • N/A
250QSM1519 • **Value $16**

18

Baby Bunny
Handcrafted • N/A
350QSM1619 • **Value $13**

19

Baby's 1st Christmas
Handcrafted • N/A
300QFM1797 • **Value $11**

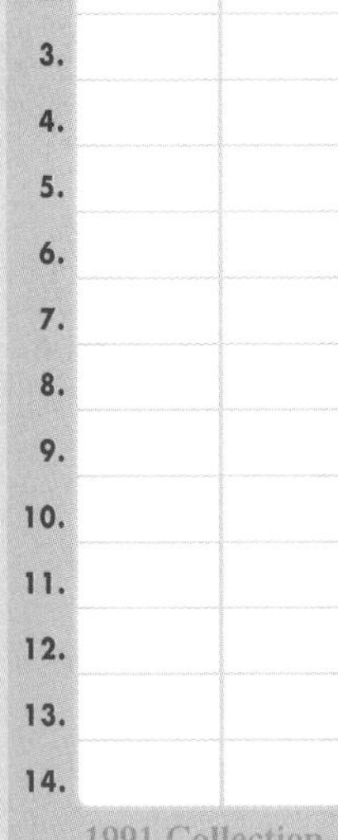

1992 Collection

	Price Paid	Value
1.		
2.		
3.		
4.		
5.		
6.		
7.		
8.		
9.		
10.		
11.		
12.		
13.		
14.		

1991 Collection

15.		
16.		
17.		
18.		
19.		

Totals

Merry Miniatures®

1

Baby's 1st Easter
Handcrafted • N/A
300QSM1557 • **Value $14**

2

Backpack Chipmunk
Handcrafted • N/A
250QFM1809 • **Value $18**

3

Baseball Bear
Handcrafted • N/A
300QFM1827 • **Value $20**

4

Bear
Handcrafted • N/A
250QFM1669 • **Value $22**

5

Bear
(also avail. in Carousel Set, #2000QSM1667)
Handcrafted • N/A
300QSM1637 • **Value $13**

6

Bear
(1st, *Sweet Valentines*)
Handcrafted • N/A
350QSM1509 • **Value $23**

7

Bears Hugging
(1st, *Hugs and Kisses*)
Handcrafted • N/A
350QSM1609 • **Value $25**

8

Birthday Clown
(2nd, *Birthday Clowns*)
Handcrafted • N/A
350QSM1617 • **Value $20**

9

Bunny
Handcrafted • N/A
300QFM1719 • **Value $13**

10

Bunny
Handcrafted • N/A
300QSM1537 • **Value $15**

11

Bunny Praying
Handcrafted • N/A
250QSM1597 • **Value $17**

12

Camel
(also avail. in Carousel Set, #2000QSM1667)
Handcrafted • N/A
300QSM1629 • **Value $13**

13

Carousel Display
(also avail. in Carousel Set, #2000QSM1667)
Handcrafted • N/A
500QSM1627 • **Value $17**

14

Cat Witch
Handcrafted • N/A
300QFM1677 • **Value $16**

15

Cookie Elf
Handcrafted • N/A
300QFM1769 • **Value $13**

16

Cookie Reindeer
Handcrafted • N/A
300QFM1777 • **Value $13**

17

Cookie Santa
Handcrafted • N/A
300QFM1767 • **Value $13**

18

Daughter Bunny
Handcrafted • N/A
250QSM1587 • **Value $15**

19

Dog in Cap & Gown
Handcrafted • N/A
250QSM1607 • **Value $14**

20

Duck
Handcrafted • N/A
300QSM1549 • **Value $19**

1991 Collection

	Price Paid	Value
1.		
2.		
3.		
4.		
5.		
6.		
7.		
8.		
9.		
10.		
11.		
12.		
13.		
14.		
15.		
16.		
17.		
18.		
19.		
20.		
Totals		

1

Elephant
(also avail. in Carousel Set, #2000QSM1667)
Handcrafted • N/A
300QSM1647 • **Value $13**

2

Football Beaver
Handcrafted • N/A
350QFM1829 • **Value $21**

3

Fox
Handcrafted • N/A
350QFM1689 • **Value $13**

4

Frog
Handcrafted • N/A
300QFM1729 • **Value $13**

5

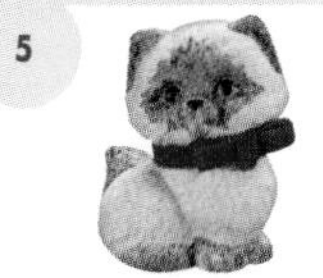

Gentle Pals Kitten
(2nd, *Gentle Pals*)
Handcrafted • N/A
350QFM1709 • **Value $19**

6

Horse
(also avail. in Carousel Set, #2000QSM1667)
Handcrafted • N/A
300QSM1649 • **Value $23**

7

I Love Dad
Handcrafted • N/A
250QSM1657 • **Value $14**

8

I Love Mom
Handcrafted • N/A
250QSM1659 • **Value $14**

9

Indian Maiden
Handcrafted • N/A
250QFM1687 • **Value $14**

10

Irish Frog
Handcrafted • N/A
350QSM1539 • **Value $15**

11

Jingle Bell Santa
(2nd, *Jingle Bell Santa*)
Handcrafted • N/A
350QFM1717 • **Value $23**

12

Kitten
Handcrafted • N/A
300QFM1737 • **Value $13**

13

Lamb & Duck
Handcrafted • N/A
350QSM1569 • **Value $13**

14

Lion
(also avail. in Carousel Set, #2000QSM1667)
Handcrafted • N/A
300QSM1639 • **Value $17**

15

Mother Bunny
Handcrafted • N/A
300QSM1577 • **Value $17**

16

Mouse
Handcrafted • N/A
250QFM1789 • **Value $15**

17

Mummy
Handcrafted • N/A
250QFM1679 • **Value $15**

18

Music Makers Bear
(1st, *Music Makers*)
Handcrafted • N/A
300QFM1779 • **Value $23**

19

Pig
Handcrafted • N/A
300QFM1739 • **Value $15**

20

Puppy
Handcrafted • N/A
300QFM1727 • **Value $15**

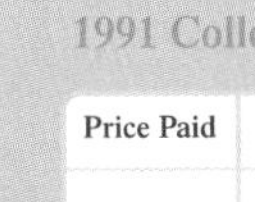

1991 Collection

	Price Paid	Value
1.		
2.		
3.		
4.		
5.		
6.		
7.		
8.		
9.		
10.		
11.		
12.		
13.		
14.		
15.		
16.		
17.		
18.		
19.		
20.		
Totals		

1

Puppy
Handcrafted • N/A
300QFM1787 • **Value $14**

2

Puppy
Handcrafted • N/A
300QSM1529 • **Value $23**

3

Raccoon Thief
Handcrafted • N/A
350QSM1517 • **Value $13**

4

Skating Raccoon
Handcrafted • N/A
350QFM1837 • **Value $21**

5

Snow Bunny
Handcrafted • N/A
250QFM1749 • **Value $13**

6

Snow Lamb
Handcrafted • N/A
250QFM1759 • **Value $13**

7

Snow Mice
Handcrafted • N/A
250QFM1757 • **Value $13**

8

Soccer Skunk
Handcrafted • N/A
300QFM1819 • **Value $20**

9

Teacher Raccoon
Handcrafted • N/A
350QFM1807 • **Value $11**

10

Turkey
(2nd, *Thankful Turkey*)
Handcrafted • N/A
350QFM1697 • **Value $22**

11

Turtle
Handcrafted • N/A
300QFM1747 • **Value $14**

1990

12

1st Christmas Together
Handcrafted • N/A
350QFM1686 • **Value $13**

13

Alligator
Handcrafted • N/A
300QSM1573 • **Value $11**

14

Artist Raccoon
Handcrafted • N/A
350QSM1543 • **Value $16**

15

Baby's 1st Christmas
Handcrafted • N/A
250QFM1683 • **Value $11**

16

Baby's 1st Easter
Handcrafted • N/A
300QSM1536 • **Value $14**

17

Baseball Bunny
Handcrafted • N/A
250QSM1576 • **Value $11**

18

Bear & Balloon
Handcrafted • N/A
300QFM1716 • **Value $11**

19

Birthday Clown
(1st, *Birthday Clowns*)
Handcrafted • N/A
350QFM1706 • **Value $20**

	Price Paid	Value
1991 Collection		
1.		
2.		
3.		
4.		
5.		
6.		
7.		
8.		
9.		
10.		
11.		
1990 Collection		
12.		
13.		
14.		
15.		
16.		
17.		
18.		
19.		
Totals		

1

Boy Bunny
Handcrafted • N/A
350QSM1682 • **Value $12**

2

Bunny
Handcrafted • N/A
300QSM1593 • **Value $12**

3

Bunny in Tux
Handcrafted • N/A
300QFM1713 • **Value $13**

4

Candy Caboose
Handcrafted • N/A
350QFM1693 • **Value $15**

5

E-Bunny
Handcrafted • N/A
300QSM1726 • **Value $14**

6

Elephant
Handcrafted • N/A
350QSM1566 • **Value $13**

7

Gentle Pal – Lamb
(1st, *Gentle Pals*)
Handcrafted • N/A
350QFM1656 • **Value $21**

8

Get Well Puppy
Handcrafted • N/A
300QFM1703 • **Value $11**

9

Girl Bunny
Handcrafted • N/A
350QSM1675 • **Value $13**

10

Green Monster
Handcrafted • N/A
350QFM1613 • **Value $15**

11
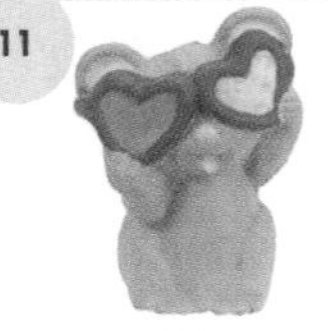
Grey Mouse
Handcrafted • N/A
250QSM1533 • **Value $15**

12

Hippo Cupid
Handcrafted • N/A
350QSM1513 • **Value $20**

13

Indian Chipmunk
Handcrafted • N/A
300QFM1626 • **Value $16**

14

Jingle Bell Santa
(1st, *Jingle Bell Santa*)
Handcrafted • N/A
350QFM1663 • **Value $24**

15
Kangaroo
Handcrafted • N/A
350QFM1653 • **Value $11**

16

Kitten
Handcrafted • N/A
300QSM1516 • **Value $14**

17

Mama Polar Bear
Handcrafted • N/A
300QFM1666 • **Value $13**

18

Mouse
Handcrafted • N/A
250QSM1603 • **Value $14**

19

Mouse & Bunny
Handcrafted • N/A
350QSM1546 • **Value $16**

20

Owl
Handcrafted • N/A
300QSM1563 • **Value $19**

1990 Collection

	Price Paid	Value
1.		
2.		
3.		
4.		
5.		
6.		
7.		
8.		
9.		
10.		
11.		
12.		
13.		
14.		
15.		
16.		
17.		
18.		
19.		
20.		
Totals		

1

Papa Polar Bear & Child
Handcrafted • N/A
350QFM1673 • **Value $14**

2

Pig
Handcrafted • N/A
300QSM1526 • **Value $17**

3

Pilgrim Mouse
Handcrafted • N/A
250QFM1636 • **Value $14**

4

Pilgrim Squirrel
Handcrafted • N/A
300QFM1633 • **Value $15**

5

Puppy
Handcrafted • N/A
250QSM1583 • **Value $13**

6

Raccoon
Handcrafted • N/A
350QSM1586 • **Value $14**

7

Scarecrow
Handcrafted • N/A
350QFM1616 • **Value $15**

8

Snowman
Handcrafted • N/A
250QFM1646 • **Value $13**

9

Squirrel
Handcrafted • N/A
250QSM1553 • **Value $19**

10

Squirrel Caroler
Handcrafted • N/A
300QFM1696 • **Value $19**

11

Squirrel Hobo
Handcrafted • N/A
300QFM1606 • **Value $14**

12

Stitched Teddy
Handcrafted • N/A
350QSM1506 • **Value $28**

13

Teacher Mouse
Handcrafted • N/A
300QFM1676 • **Value $10**

14

Thankful Turkey
(1st, *Thankful Turkey*)
Handcrafted • N/A
350QFM1623 • **Value $24**

15

Walrus
Handcrafted • N/A
250QFM1643 • **Value $14**

1989

16

Baby Boy
Handcrafted • N/A
300QFM1585 • **Value $20**

17

Baby Girl
Handcrafted • N/A
300QFM1592 • **Value $20**

18

Baby's 1st Christmas
Handcrafted • N/A
300QFM1615 • **Value $16**

19

Bear
Handcrafted • N/A
250QSM1525 • **Value $16**

1990 Collection

	Price Paid	Value
1.		
2.		
3.		
4.		
5.		
6.		
7.		
8.		
9.		
10.		
11.		
12.		
13.		
14.		
15.		

1989 Collection

	Price Paid	Value
16.		
17.		
18.		
19.		
Totals		

1

Bear Baker
Handcrafted • N/A
350QSM1522 • **Value $20**

2

Blue King
(also avail. in Nativity Set, #3550QFM1685)
Handcrafted • N/A
300QFM1632 • **Value $25**

3

Bunny
Handcrafted • N/A
250QSM1512 • **Value $19**

4

Bunny
Handcrafted • N/A
300QFM1565 • **Value $14**

5

Bunny
Handcrafted • N/A
350QSM1552 • **Value $16**

6

Bunny & Skateboard
Handcrafted • N/A
350EBO3092 • **Value $25**

7

Bunny Caroler
Handcrafted • N/A
300QFM1662 • **Value $21**

8

Dog & Kitten
Handcrafted • N/A
350QSM1515 • **Value $30**

9

Elf
Handcrafted • N/A
300QFM1622 • **Value $16**

10

Grey Mouse
Handcrafted • N/A
250QSM1502 • **Value $22**

11

Joy Elf
Handcrafted • N/A
300QFM1605 • **Value $14**

12

Kitten
Handcrafted • N/A
250QSM1505 • **Value $24**

13

Lamb
Handcrafted • N/A
350QSM1545 • **Value $20**

14

Momma Bear
Handcrafted • N/A
350QFM1582 • **Value $17**

15

Mouse
Handcrafted • N/A
250QFM1572 • **Value $21**

16

Mouse Caroler
Handcrafted • N/A
250QFM1655 • **Value $21**

17

Mr. Claus
Handcrafted • N/A
350QFM1595 • **Value $16**

18

Mrs. Claus
Handcrafted • N/A
350QFM1602 • **Value $15**

19

Owl
Handcrafted • N/A
250QSM1555 • **Value $18**

1989 Collection

	Price Paid	Value
1.		
2.		
3.		
4.		
5.		
6.		
7.		
8.		
9.		
10.		
11.		
12.		
13.		
14.		
15.		
16.		
17.		
18.		
19.		
Totals		

1

Pink King
(also avail. in Nativity Set, #3550QFM1685)
Handcrafted • N/A
300QFM1642 • **Value $14**

2

Raccoon
Handcrafted • N/A
350QFM1575 • **Value $14**

3

Raccoon Caroler
Handcrafted • N/A
350QFM1652 • **Value $18**

4

Teacher Elf
Handcrafted • N/A
300QFM1612 • **Value $15**

5

Train Car
Handcrafted • N/A
350QFM1562 • **Value $17**

6

Yellow King
(also avail. in Nativity Set, #3550QFM1685)
Handcrafted • N/A
300QFM1635 • **Value $15**

1988

7

Dog
Handcrafted • N/A
200GHA3524 • **Value $14**

8

Donkey
(also avail. in Nativity Set, #3550QFM1685)
Handcrafted • N/A
225QFM1581 • **Value $11**

9

Indian Bear
Handcrafted • N/A
325QFM1511 • **Value $17**

10

Jesus
(also avail. in Nativity Set, #3550QFM1685)
Handcrafted • N/A
250QFM1564 • **Value $22**

11

Joseph
(also avail. in Nativity Set, #3550QFM1685)
Handcrafted • N/A
250QFM1561 • **Value $13**

12

Kitten in Slipper
Handcrafted • N/A
250QFM1544 • **Value $19**

13

Koala & Hearts
Handcrafted • N/A
200VHA3531 • **Value $12**

14

Koala & Lollipop
Handcrafted • N/A
200VHA3651 • **Value $21**

15

Koala & Ruffled Heart
Handcrafted • N/A
200VHA3631 • **Value $62**

16

Koala with Bow & Arrow
Handcrafted • N/A
200VHA3624 • **Value $13**

17

Lamb
(also avail. in Nativity Set, #3550QFM1685)
Handcrafted • N/A
225QFM1574 • **Value $27**

18

Mary
(also avail. in Nativity Set, #3550QFM1685)
Handcrafted • N/A
250QFM1554 • **Value $16**

19

Mouse Angel
Handcrafted • N/A
250QFM1551 • **Value $27**

1989 Collection

	Price Paid	Value
1.		
2.		
3.		
4.		
5.		
6.		

1988 Collection

	Price Paid	Value
7.		
8.		
9.		
10.		
11.		
12.		
13.		
14.		
15.		
16.		
17.		
18.		
19.		
Totals		

1

Mouse in Cornucopia
Handcrafted • N/A
225QFM1514 • **Value $18**

2

Mouse/Pumpkin
Handcrafted • N/A
225QFM1501 • **Value $44**

3

Owl
Handcrafted • N/A
225QFM1504 • **Value $18**

4

Penguin
Handcrafted • N/A
375QFM1541 • **Value $23**

5

Santa
Handcrafted • N/A
375QFM1521 • **Value $42**

6

Shepherd
(also avail. in Nativity Set, #3550QFM1685)
Handcrafted • N/A
250QFM1571 • **Value $14**

7

Snowman
Handcrafted • N/A
350QFM1534 • **Value $19**

8

Stable
(also avail. in Nativity Set, #3550QFM1685)
Handcrafted • N/A
1400QFM1584 • **Value $17**

9

Tank Car
Handcrafted • N/A
300QFM1591 • **Value $26**

10

Train Engine
Handcrafted • N/A
300QFM1531 • **Value $16**

11

Unicorn
Handcrafted • N/A
350QFM1524 • **Value $34**

1987

12

Bear
Handcrafted • N/A
450XHA3709 • **Value $27**

13

Boy Lamb
Handcrafted • N/A
295EHA4197 • **Value $20**

14
Bunny
Handcrafted • N/A
200EHA4179 • **Value $145**

15
Bunny
Handcrafted • N/A
250XHA3729 • **Value $20**

16

Bunny Boy
Handcrafted • N/A
250XHA3737 • **Value $21**

17

Bunny Girl
Handcrafted • N/A
250XHA3749 • **Value $21**

18

Chick/Egg
Handcrafted • N/A
350EHA4199 • **Value $15**

19

Clown Teddy
Handcrafted • N/A
200VHA3507 • **Value $18**

1988 Collection

	Price Paid	Value
1.		
2.		
3.		
4.		
5.		
6.		
7.		
8.		
9.		
10.		
11.		

1987 Collection

	Price Paid	Value
12.		
13.		
14.		
15.		
16.		
17.		
18.		
19.		
Totals		

1

Fawn
Handcrafted • N/A
200XHA3757 • **Value $22**

2

Ginger Bear
Handcrafted • N/A
200XHA207 • **Value $24**

3

Giraffe
Handcrafted • N/A
350VHA3519 • **Value $92**

4

Girl Lamb
Handcrafted • N/A
295EHA4187 • **Value $22**

5

Mouse
Handcrafted • N/A
200SHA3467 • **Value $16**

6

Mouse
Handcrafted • N/A
295VHA3527 • **Value $29**

7

Puppy
Handcrafted • N/A
200XHA3769 • **Value $20**

8

Raccoon Witch
Handcrafted • N/A
200HHA3487 • **Value $22**

9

Santa
Handcrafted • N/A
350XHA3717 • **Value $40**

10

Sebastian
Handcrafted • N/A
200EHA4167 • **Value $52**

11

Turkey
Handcrafted • N/A
375THA49 • **Value $19**

1986

12

Boy Bunny
Handcrafted • N/A
295EPF4133 • **Value $20**

13

Bunny
Handcrafted • N/A
350EHA3476 • **Value $21**

14

Bunny Girl
Handcrafted • N/A
295EPF4106 • **Value $21**

15

Cat
Handcrafted • N/A
200HHA3486 • **Value $22**

16

Duck
Handcrafted • N/A
295EHA3463 • **Value $15**

17

Duck Sailor
Handcrafted • N/A
295EPF4113 • **Value $16**

18

Girl Bunny
Handcrafted • N/A
200EHA3503 • **Value $32**

19

Goose
Handcrafted • N/A
200EHA3516 • **Value $16**

1987 Collection

	Price Paid	Value
1.		
2.		
3.		
4.		
5.		
6.		
7.		
8.		
9.		
10.		
11.		

1986 Collection

	Price Paid	Value
12.		
13.		
14.		
15.		
16.		
17.		
18.		
19.		

Price Paid	Value

Totals

1

Katybeth
Handcrafted • N/A
200XHA3666 • **Value $45**

2
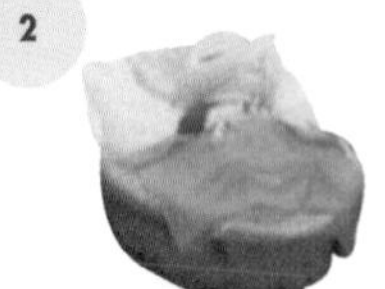
Mouse
Handcrafted • N/A
200XHA3533 • **Value $69**

3

Mr. Mouse
Handcrafted • N/A
200XHA3573 • **Value $30**

4

Mr. Squirrel
Handcrafted • N/A
200THA3403 • **Value $21**

5

Mrs. Mouse
Handcrafted • N/A
200XHA3653 • **Value $29**

6

Mrs. Squirrel
Handcrafted • N/A
200THA3416 • **Value $21**

7

Owl
Handcrafted • N/A
200GHA3456 • **Value $16**

8

Pandas
Handcrafted • N/A
350VHA3523 • **Value $21**

9

Penguin
Handcrafted • N/A
295XHA4413 • **Value $23**

10

Rhonda
Handcrafted • N/A
350XHA3553 • **Value $40**

11

Rodney
Handcrafted • N/A
350XHA3546 • **Value $27**

12

Santa
Handcrafted • N/A
350XHA3673 • **Value $40**

13

Sebastian
Handcrafted • N/A
200VHA3516 • **Value $75**

14

Sebastian
Handcrafted • N/A
200XHA3566 • **Value $85**

15
Sheep & Bell
Handcrafted • N/A
295EPF4126 • **Value $15**

16
Unicorn
Handcrafted • N/A
200VHA3503 • **Value $16**

17

Witch
Handcrafted • N/A
300HHS3473 • **Value $95**

18

Basket
Handcrafted • N/A
200EHA3495 • **Value $42**

19

Bears
Handcrafted • N/A
450XHA3392 • **Value $30**

1986 Collection

	Price Paid	Value
1.		
2.		
3.		
4.		
5.		
6.		
7.		
8.		
9.		
10.		
11.		
12.		
13.		
14.		
15.		
16.		
17.		
1985 Collection		
18.		
19.		
Totals		

1

Bunny
Handcrafted • N/A
200EHA3482 • **Value $36**

2

Cat
Handcrafted • N/A
200XHA3482 • **Value $32**

3

Ceramic Bunny
Handcrafted • N/A
(N/A)EPR3701 • **Value $14**

4

Goose
Handcrafted • N/A
250XHA3522 • **Value $18**

5

Horse
Handcrafted • N/A
350XHA3412 • **Value $11**

6

Kitten
Handcrafted • N/A
200VHA3495 • **Value $30**

7

Lamb
Handcrafted • N/A
350EHA3442 • **Value $20**

8

Mouse
Handcrafted • N/A
350EHA3455 • **Value $25**

9

Mouse
Handcrafted • N/A
350XHA3405 • **Value $25**

10

Mr. Santa
Handcrafted • N/A
200XHA3495 • **Value $21**

11

Mrs. Santa
Handcrafted • N/A
200XHA3502 • **Value $22**

12
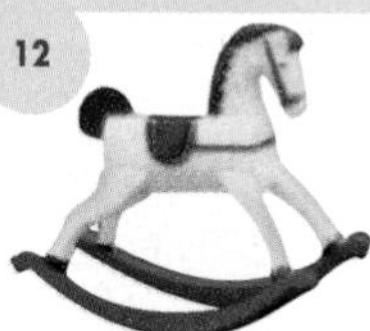
Rocking Horse
Handcrafted • N/A
200XHA3515 • **Value $30**

13

Shamrock
Handcrafted • N/A
200SHA3452 • **Value $19**

14

Skunk
Handcrafted • N/A
200VHA3482 • **Value $24**

15

Turkey
Handcrafted • N/A
295THA3395 • **Value $22**

1984

16
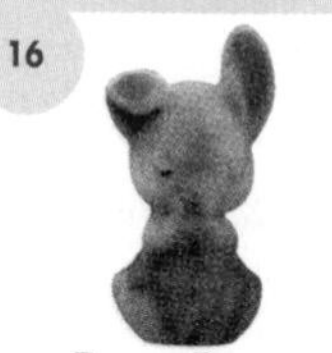
Brown Bunny
Handcrafted • N/A
350EHA3401 • **Value $16**

17

Chick
Handcrafted • N/A
200EHA3461 • **Value $30**

18
Dog
Handcrafted • N/A
200VHA3451 • **Value $58**

19

Duck
Handcrafted • N/A
200EHA3474 • **Value $32**

1985 Collection

	Price Paid	Value
1.		
2.		
3.		
4.		
5.		
6.		
7.		
8.		
9.		
10.		
11.		
12.		
13.		
14.		
15.		

1984 Collection

	Price Paid	Value
16.		
17.		
18.		
19.		

	Price Paid	Value
Totals		

1

Duck
Handcrafted • N/A
350EHA3434 • **Value $23**

2

Hedgehog
Handcrafted • N/A
200THA3444 • **Value $20**

3

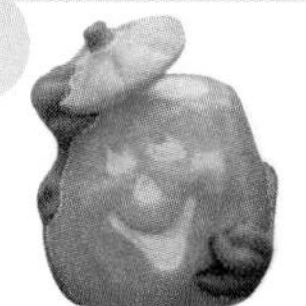

Jack-O-Lantern
Handcrafted • N/A
200HHA3454 • **Value $26**

4

Kitten
Handcrafted • N/A
200HHA3441 • **Value $24**

5

Koala
Handcrafted • N/A
295XHA3401 • **Value $29**

6

Mouse
Handcrafted • N/A
200THA3451 • **Value $42**

7

Panda
Handcrafted • N/A
200VHA3471 • **Value $26**

8

Penguin
Handcrafted • N/A
200VHA3464 • **Value $32**

9

Puppy
Handcrafted • N/A
200XHA3494 • **Value $54**

10

Redbird
Handcrafted • N/A
200XHA3501 • **Value $46**

11

Rodney
Handcrafted • N/A
295XHA3391 • **Value $40**

12

Soldier
Handcrafted • N/A
200XHA3481 • **Value $37**

1983

13

Angel
Handcrafted • N/A
200XHA3467 • **Value $52**

14

Animals
Handcrafted • N/A
750XHA3487 • **Value $40**

15

Betsey Clark
Handcrafted • N/A
350EHA2429 • **Value $32**

16

Bunny
Handcrafted • N/A
250EHA3457 • **Value $16**

17

Cherub
Handcrafted • N/A
350VHA3497 • **Value $26**

18

Chick
Handcrafted • N/A
250EHA3469 • **Value $195**

1984 Collection

	Price Paid	Value
1.		
2.		
3.		
4.		
5.		
6.		
7.		
8.		
9.		
10.		
11.		
12.		

1983 Collection

	Price Paid	Value
13.		
14.		
15.		
16.		
17.		
18.		

Totals

1

Cupid
Handcrafted • N/A
550VHA4099 • **Value $375**

2

Deer
Handcrafted • N/A
350XHA3419 • **Value $52**

3

Duck
Handcrafted • N/A
250EHA3477 • **Value $195**

4

Flocked Bunny
Handcrafted • N/A
350EHA3417 • **Value $16**

5

Kitten
Handcrafted • N/A
200XHA3447 • **Value $43**

6

Kitten
Handcrafted • N/A
350VHA3489 • **Value $110**

7

Mouse
Handcrafted • N/A
200XHA3459 • **Value $45**

8
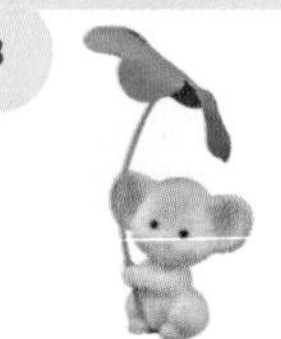
Mouse
Handcrafted • N/A
350SHA3407 • **Value $21**

9

Penguin
Handcrafted • N/A
295XHA3439 • **Value $70**

10

Polar Bear
Handcrafted • N/A
350XHA3407 • **Value $220**

11

Santa
Handcrafted • N/A
295XHA3427 • **Value $44**

12

Shirt Tales
Handcrafted • N/A
295HHA3437 • **Value $42**

13

Snowman
Handcrafted • N/A
300XHA3479 • **Value $42**

14

Turkey
Handcrafted • N/A
295THA207 • **Value $45**

1982

15

Ceramic Bunny
Handcrafted • N/A
300EPF3702 • **Value $49**

16

Duck
Handcrafted • N/A
300EHA3403 • **Value $32**

17

Kermit
Handcrafted • N/A
395VHA3403 • **Value $35**

18

Kitten
Handcrafted • N/A
395HHA3466 • **Value $57**

19

Miss Piggy
Handcrafted • N/A
395VHA3416 • **Value $36**

	Price Paid	Value
1983 Collection		
1.		
2.		
3.		
4.		
5.		
6.		
7.		
8.		
9.		
10.		
11.		
12.		
13.		
14.		
1982 Collection		
15.		
16.		
17.		
18.		
19.		
Totals		

1

Mouse
Handcrafted • N/A
450XHA5023 • **Value $66**

2

Pilgrim Mouse
Handcrafted • N/A
295THA3433 • **Value $218**

3

Rocking Horse
Handcrafted • N/A
450XHA5003 • **Value $95**

4

Santa (rigid)
Handcrafted • N/A
450XHA5016 • **Value $185**

5

Tree
Handcrafted • N/A
450XHA5006 • **Value $145**

6

Witch
Handcrafted • N/A
395HHA3456 • **Value $375**

1981

7

Cupid
Handcrafted • N/A
300VPF3465 • **Value $58**

8

Ghost
Handcrafted • N/A
300HHA3402 • **Value $290**

9

Lamb
Handcrafted • N/A
300EPF402 • **Value $31**

10

Leprechaun
Handcrafted • N/A
300SHA3415 • **Value $48**

11

Penguin
Handcrafted • N/A
300XHA3412 • **Value $97**

12

Raccoon Pilgrim
Handcrafted • N/A
300THA3402 • **Value $52**

13

Redbird
Handcrafted • N/A
300XHA3405 • **Value $39**

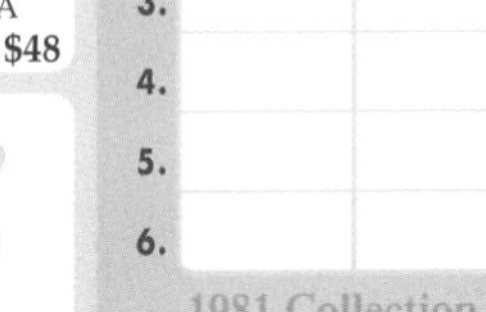

14

Squirrel Indian
Handcrafted • N/A
300THA3415 • **Value $49**

15

Turkey
Handcrafted • N/A
300THA22 • **Value $50**

1980

16

Angel
Handcrafted • N/A
300XPF3471 • **Value $42**

17

Kitten
Handcrafted • N/A
300XPF3421 • **Value $40**

18
Pipe
Handcrafted • N/A
75SPF1017 • **Value $65**

1982 Collection	Price Paid	Value
1.		
2.		
3.		
4.		
5.		
6.		
1981 Collection		
7.		
8.		
9.		
10.		
11.		
12.		
13.		
14.		
15.		
1980 Collection		
16.		
17.		
18.		
Totals		

1980

1

Reindeer
Handcrafted • N/A
300XPF3464 • **Value $94**

2

Santa
Handcrafted • N/A
300XPF39 • **Value $34**

3

Sleigh
Handcrafted • N/A
300XPF3451 • **Value $50**

4

Turkey
Handcrafted • N/A
200TPF3441 • **Value $80**

5

Turtle
Handcrafted • N/A
200VPF3451 • **Value $50**

1979

6
Bunny
Handcrafted • N/A
200EPF377 • **Value $91**

7

Duck
Handcrafted • N/A
200EPF397 • **Value $62**

8

Love
Handcrafted • N/A
150VPF1007 • **Value $120**

9

Mouse
Handcrafted • N/A
150XPF1017 • **Value $120**

1978

10

Joy Elf
Handcrafted • N/A
150XPF1003 • **Value $106**

11

Kitten
Handcrafted • N/A
150HPF1013 • **Value $25**

12

Mrs. Snowman
Handcrafted • N/A
150XPF23 • **Value $97**

13

Pilgrim Boy
Handcrafted • N/A
150TPF1003 • **Value $32**

14

Pilgrim Girl
Handcrafted • N/A
150TPF1016 • **Value $32**

15

Turkey
Handcrafted • N/A
150TPF12 • **Value $87**

1977

16

Barnaby
Handcrafted • N/A
125EPF12 • **Value $225**

17

Bernadette
Handcrafted • N/A
125EPF25 • **Value $215**

	Price Paid	Value
1980 Collection		
1.		
2.		
3.		
4.		
5.		
1979 Collection		
6.		
7.		
8.		
9.		
1978 Collection		
10.		
11.		
12.		
13.		
14.		
15.		
1977 Collection		
16.		
17.		
Totals		

1

Chick
Handcrafted • N/A
125EPF32 • **Value $215**

2

Mouse
Handcrafted • N/A
125XPF122 • **Value $110**

3

Pilgrims
Handcrafted • N/A
150TPF502 • **Value $240**

4

Witch
Handcrafted • N/A
125HPF32 • **Value $190**

1976

5

Betsey Clark
Handcrafted • N/A
125XPF151 • **Value $273**

6

Drummer Boy
Handcrafted • N/A
125XPF144 • **Value $262**

7

Owl
Handcrafted • N/A
100HPF515 • **Value $320**

8

Pilgrims
Handcrafted • N/A
100TPF502 • **Value $220**

9
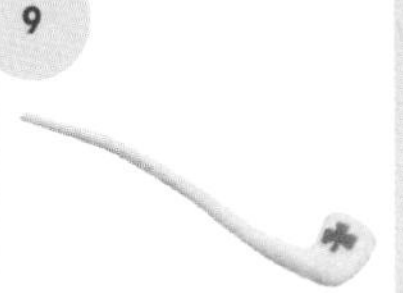
Pipe
Handcrafted • N/A
89SPF266 • **Value $148**

10

Santa
Handcrafted • N/A
125XPF131 • **Value $90**

11

Scarecrow
Handcrafted • N/A
100HPF522 • **Value $300**

12

Snowman
Handcrafted • N/A
125XPF44 • **Value $65**

13

Turkey
Handcrafted • N/A
100TPF512 • **Value $158**

1975

14

Bunny
Handcrafted • N/A
125EPF49 • **Value $675**

15
Devil
Handcrafted • N/A
125HPF29 • **Value $340**

16

Duck
Handcrafted • N/A
125EPF69 • **Value $680**

17

Girl
Handcrafted • N/A
125EPF57 • **Value $560**

18

Indian
Handcrafted • N/A
125TPF29 • **Value $55**

1977 Collection

	Price Paid	Value
1.		
2.		
3.		
4.		
1976 Collection		
5.		
6.		
7.		
8.		
9.		
10.		
11.		
12.		
13.		
1975 Collection		
14.		
15.		
16.		
17.		
18.		
Totals		

1974

1

Santa
Handcrafted • N/A
125XPF49 • **Value $285**

2

Angel
Handcrafted • N/A
125XPF506 • **Value $425**

3

Bunny
Handcrafted • N/A
59EPF186 • **Value $675**

4

Chick
Handcrafted • N/A
159EPF206 • **Value $665**

5

Child
Handcrafted • N/A
50EPF193 • **Value $665**

6

Jack-O-Lantern
Handcrafted • N/A
75HPF502 • **Value $47**

7

Pilgrims
Handcrafted • N/A
100TPF13 • **Value $300**

8

Raggedy Andy
Handcrafted • N/A
125PF1433 • **Value $112**

9

Raggedy Ann
Handcrafted • N/A
125PF1432 • **Value $114**

10

Reindeer
Handcrafted • N/A
125XPF493 • **Value $475**

11

Santa
Handcrafted • N/A
125XPF486 • **Value $365**

12

Scarecrow
Handcrafted • N/A
100HPF • **Value $425**

13

Snowman
Handcrafted • N/A
125XPF473 • **Value $275**

14

Turkey
Handcrafted • N/A
75TPF13 • **Value $350**

1975 Collection

	Price Paid	Value
1.		

1974 Collection

	Price Paid	Value
2.		
3.		
4.		
5.		
6.		
7.		
8.		
9.		
10.		
11.		
12.		
13.		
14.		
Totals		

Kiddie Car Classics

Since 1992, Kiddie Car Classics have been loved by both die-hard car enthusiasts and casual collectors alike. This year, the line incorporates several major changes. All available Kiddie Cars were retired on December 31, 2000 and future releases will be limited – both in the number of pieces produced in the line each year and in edition size for each piece.

2001

1

1928 Jingle Bell Express (LE-14,500)
Current
6000QHG9065 • **Value $60**

2

1935 American-National Fire Tower (LE-14,500)
Current
7500QHG9064 • **Value $75**

3

1935 Duesenberg (4th in the *Vintage Speedster* Series, LE-14,500)
Current
9000QHG7116 • **Value $90**

4

1935 Timmy Racer (LE-14,500)
Current
5000QHG7118 • **Value $50**

5

1936 Gillham™ "Birthday" Special (LE-14,500)
Current
2000QHG7115 • **Value $20**

6

1937 Steelcraft Auburn (LE-14,500)
Current
3000QHG2211 • **Value $30**

7

1950s Red Baron Airplane (LE-14,500)
Current
6500QHG7114 • **Value $65**

8

1957 Custom Chevy® Bel Air® (LE-14,500)
Current
5500QHG7117 • **Value $55**

2000

9

1924 Toledo Fire Engine #6 (1st in *Fire Brigade Series*)
Retired 2000
6500QHG9053 • **Value $68**

10

1926 Steelcraft Catalog Cover Tin Sign
Retired 2000
795QHG5601 • **Value $8**

11

1927 Gillham™ "Honeymoon Special"
Don Palmiter Custom Collection
Retired 2000
6000QHG7111 • **Value $70**

12

1934 Christmas Classic
Retired 2000
5000QHG9061 • **Value $53**

13

1935 American Tandem (LE-24,500)
Retired 2000
1QHG9058 • **Value $105**

14

1935 Gillham™ Auburn (3rd in *Vintage Speedster* Series, LE-24,500)
Don Palmiter Custom Collection
Retired 2000
9000QHG9059 • **Value $102**

15

1935 Toledo Duesenberg Racer (5th & final in *Winner's Circle Collector's Series*)
Retired 2000
5500QHG9057 • **Value $65**

2001 Kiddie Car Classics

	Price Paid	Value
1.		
2.		
3.		
4.		
5.		
6.		
7.		
8.		

2000 Kiddie Car Classics

	Price Paid	Value
9.		
10.		
11.		
12.		
13.		
14.		
15.		
Totals		

1

1937 Mickey Mouse Streamline Express Coaster Wagon (LE-24,500)
Retired 2000
4800QHG6322 • **Value $54**

2

1938 American Graham Roadster (LE-29,500)
Retired 2000
7500QHG9060 • **Value $78**

3

1938 Toledo Air King Airplane
Retired 2000
5000QHG9052 • **Value $58**

4

1943 Aviator Coloring Book Cover Tin Sign
Retired 2000
995QHG5602 • **Value $10**

5

1958 Custom Corvette (LE-29,500)
Don Palmiter Custom Collection
Retired 2000
6500QHG7112 • **Value $89**

6

"Asking for Directions" Tin Sign
Retired 2000
600QHG5603 • **Value $8**

7

Don's Sign
Retired 2000
1600QHG3623 • **Value $18**

8

Parking Sign
Retired 2000
800QHG3630 • **Value $10**

9

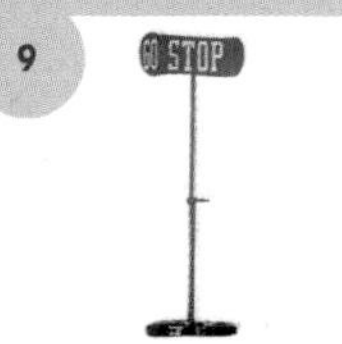

Stop Sign
Retired 2000
1000QHG3622 • **Value $11**

10

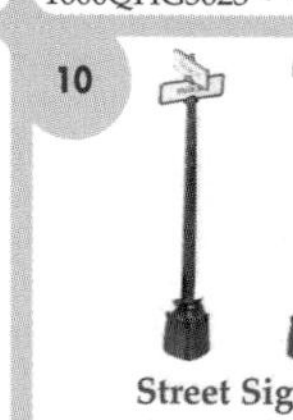

Street Signs
Retired 2000
1000QHG3629 • **Value $12**

11

Streetlamp
Retired 2000
1500QHG3624 • **Value $17**

12

1941 Steelcraft Spitfire Airplane
Retired 2000
2500QHG2206 • **Value $38**

13

1950 Murray® Torpedo
Retired 2000
2500QHG2209 • **Value $35**

14

1955 Murray® Fire Chief
Retired 2000
2500QHG2208 • **Value $38**

15

1956 Garton® Kidillac
Retired 2000
2500QHG2210 • **Value $45**

16

1968 Murray® Boat Jolly Roger
Retired 2000
2500QHG2207 • **Value $35**

1999

17

1926 Speedster (2nd in *Vintage Speedster Series*, LE-29,500)
Retired 2000
9000QHG9048 • **Value $93**

18

1934 Garton® Chrysler® Airflow
Retired 2000
5000QHG9056 • **Value $55**

19

1937 Steelcraft "Junior" Streamliner (LE-39,500)
Retired 2000
7000QHG9047 • **Value $72**

	Price Paid	Value
2000 Kiddie Car Classics		
1.		
2.		
3.		
4.		
5.		
2000 Kiddie Car Corner		
6.		
7.		
8.		
9.		
10.		
11.		
2000 Mini Kiddie Car Collection		
12.		
13.		
14.		
15.		
16.		
1999 Kiddie Car Classics		
17.		
18.		
19.		
Totals		

1

1941 Garton® Field Ambulance (LE-39,500)
Retired 2000
6500QHG9049 • **Value $68**

2

1941 Garton® Roadster (LE-39,500)
Retired 2000
7000QHG9050 • **Value $72**

3

1941 Garton® Speed Demon (4th in *Winner's Circle Collector's Series*)
Retired 2000
5500QHG9046 • **Value $63**

4

1949 Gillham™ Special
Don Palmiter Custom Collection
Retired 2000
5000QHG7108 • **Value $68**

5

1949 Gillham™ Sport
Don Palmiter Custom Collection
Retired 2000
6000QHG7109 • **Value $63**

6

1949 Gillham™ Sport with Golf Bag (Artists On Tour, yellow)
Retired 2000
(N/C) No stock # • **Value $72**

7

1950 Holiday Murray® General
Retired 2000
6000QHG9054 • **Value $63**

8

1950 Murray® General
Retired 2000
5000QHG9051 • **Value $85**

9

Call Box & Fire Hydrant (set/2)
Retired 2000
2500QHG3618 • **Value $26**

10

"Cinder" & "Ella" Dalmatians (set/2)
Retired 2000
1500QHG3619 • **Value $17**

11

"Cinder Says . . ." (3rd & final in *Bill's Boards Series*)
Retired 2000
3000QHG3621 • **Value $32**

12

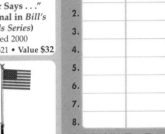

Corner Drive-In Sidewalk Signs (set/2)
Retired 2000
1500QHG3616 • **Value $16**

13

Fire Station #1 (LE-39,500)
Retired 2000
7000QHG3617 • **Value $74**

14

Flagpole
Retired 2000
2000QHG3620 • **Value $21**

15

Table & Benches (set/3)
Retired 2000
2000QHG3615 • **Value $21**

16

1941 Murray® Pursuit Airplane
Retired 2000
2500QHG2203 • **Value $27**

17

1953 Murray® Dump Truck
Retired 2000
2500QHG2201 • **Value $27**

18

1955 Murray® Champion
Retired 2000
2500QHG2202 • **Value $27**

19

1955 Murray® Fire Truck
Retired 2000
2500QHG2204 • **Value $27**

1999 Kiddie Car Classics

	Price Paid	Value
1.		
2.		
3.		
4.		
5.		
6.		
7.		
8.		

1999 Kiddie Car Corner

	Price Paid	Value
9.		
10.		
11.		
12.		
13.		
14.		
15.		

1999 Mini Kiddie Car Collection

	Price Paid	Value
16.		
17.		
18.		
19.		
Totals		

1998

1

1955 Murray® Tractor and Trailer
Retired 2000
2500QHG2205 • **Value $27**

2

1951 Hopalong Cassidy™ Velocipede (LE-24,500)
Retired 2000
4800QHG6325 • **Value $52**

3

1926 Steelcraft Speedster by Murray® (1st in *Vintage Speedster Series*, LE-29,500)
Retired 1998
9000QHG9045• **Value $150**

4

1929 Steelcraft Roadster by Murray® (LE-39,500)
Retired 1998
7000QHG9040 • **Value $90**

5

1930 Custom Biplane
Don Palmiter Custom Collection
Retired 2000
5500QHG7104 • **Value $82**

6

1930 Spirit of Christmas Custom Biplane
Don Palmiter Custom Collection
Retired 1998
6000QHG7105 • **Value $87**

7

1940 Custom Roadster with Trailer (LE-39,500)
Don Palmiter Custom Collection
Retired 2000
7500QHG7106 • **Value $79**

8

1941 Steelcraft Chrysler by Murray®
Retired 2000
5500QHG9044 • **Value $58**

9

1941 Steelcraft Fire Truck by Murray®
Retired 2000
6000QHG9042 • **Value $64**

10

1941 Steelcraft Fire Truck by Murray® (Convention, silver)
Retired 1998
(N/C) No stock # • **Value N/E**

11

1950s Custom Convertible
Don Palmiter Custom Collection
Retired 1999
6000QHG7101 • **Value $65**

12

1955 Custom Chevy®
Don Palmiter Custom Collection
Retired 2000
5000QHG7103 • **Value $72**

13

1958 Murray® Champion
Retired 2000
5500QHG9041 • **Value $60**

14

1960 Eight Ball Racer (3rd in *Winner's Circle Collector's Series*)
Retired 2000
5500QHG9039 • **Value $60**

15

1998 Nascar® 50th Anniversary Custom Champion
Don Palmiter Custom Collection
Retired 2000
6000QHG7110 • **Value $69**

16

Don's Street Rod
Don Palmiter Custom Collection
Retired 1999
5500QHG7102 • **Value $60**

17

Car Lift and Tool Box (set/2)
Retired 2000
2500QHG3608 • **Value $28**

18

Corner Drive-In (LE-39,500)
Retired 2000
7000QHG3610 • **Value $73**

19

Famous Food Sign (2nd in *Bill's Boards Series*)
Retired 2000
3000QHG3614 • **Value $32**

	Price Paid	Value
1999 Kiddie Car Classics		
1.		
2.		
1998 Kiddie Car Classics		
3.		
4.		
5.		
6.		
7.		
8.		
9.		
10.		
11.		
12.		
13.		
14.		
15.		
16.		
1998 Kiddie Car Corner		
17.		
18.		
19.		
Totals		

1

KC's Motor Oil
Retired 2000
1500QHG3609 • **Value $19**

2

Menu Station with Food Trays (set/3)
Retired 2000
3000QHG3611 • **Value $32**

3

Newspaper Box & Trash Can Set (set/2)
Retired 2000
2000QHG3613 • **Value $22**

4

1932 Keystone Coast-to-Coast Bus (LE-29,500)
Retired 2000
4500QHG6320 • **Value $48**

5

1934 Mickey Mouse Velocipede
Retired 2000
4800QHG6316 • **Value $50**

6

1937 De Luxe Velocipede
Retired 2000
4500QHG6319 • **Value $52**

7
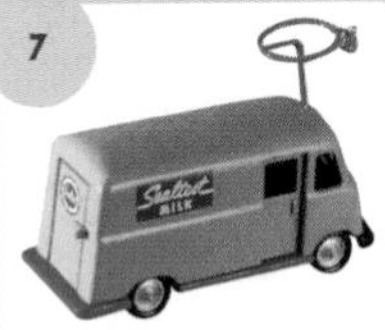
1960s Sealtest Milk Truck
Retired 2000
4000QHG6315 • **Value $43**

8

1937 GARTON® Ford (LE-24,500)
Retired 1997
6500QHG9035 • **Value $140**

9

1938 GARTON® Lincoln Zephyr (LE-24,500)
Retired 1997
6500QHG9038 • **Value $140**

10

1939 GARTON® Ford Station Wagon
Retired 1999
5500QHG9034 • **Value $88**

11

1939 GARTON® Ford Station Wagon (Artists On Tour, brown)
Retired 1997
(N/C) No stock # • **Value N/E**

12

1940 Gendron "Red Hot" Roadster (2nd in *Winner's Circle Collector's Series*)
Retired 1999
5500QHG9037 • **Value $92**

13

1941 Steelcraft Oldsmobile by Murray®
Retired 1999
5500QHG9036 • **Value $88**

14

1956 Murray® Golden Eagle (LE-29,500)
Retired 1997
5000QHG9033 • **Value $95**

15
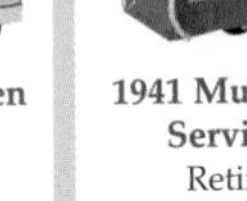
1941 Murray® Junior Service Truck
Retired 1999
5500QHG9031 • **Value $90**

16
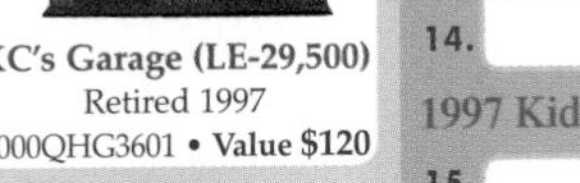
KC's Garage (LE-29,500)
Retired 1997
7000QHG3601 • **Value $120**

17

Pedal Petroleum Gas Pump
Retired 1999
2500QHG3602 • **Value $45**

18

Pedal Power Premium Lighted Gas Pump
Retired 1999
3000QHG3603 • **Value $48**

19

Sidewalk Sales Signs
Retired 1999
1500QHG3605 • **Value $28**

	Price Paid	Value
1998 Kiddie Car Corner		
1.		
2.		
3.		
1998 Sidewalk Cruisers		
4.		
5.		
6.		
7.		
1997 Kiddie Car Classics		
8.		
9.		
10.		
11.		
12.		
13.		
14.		
1997 Kiddie Car Corner		
15.		
16.		
17.		
18.		
19.		
Totals		

1

Sidewalk Service Signs
Retired 1999
1500QHG3604 • **Value $28**

2

Welcome Sign (1st in *Bill's Boards Series*)
Retired 1999
3000QHG3606 • **Value $63**

3

1937 Scamp Wagon (LE-29,500)
Retired 2000
4800QHG6318 • **Value $75**

4

1939 American National Pedal Bike
Retired 2000
3800QHG6314 • **Value $57**

5

1939 GARTON® Batwing Scooter
Retired 2000
3800QHG6317 • **Value $70**

6

1960 Murray® Blaz-O-Jet Tricycle
Retired 2000
4500QHG6313 • **Value $58**

1996

7

1935 Steelcraft Airplane by Murray® (LE-29,500)
Retired 1997
5000QHG9032 • **Value $133**

8

1935 Steelcraft by Murray® (LE-24,500)
Retired 1996
6500QHG9029 • **Value $160**

9

1937 Steelcraft Airflow by Murray® (Artists On Tour, red)
Retired 1996
(N/C) No stock # • **Value N/E**

10

1956 GARTON® Hot Rod Racer (1st in *Winner's Circle Collector's Series*)
Retired 1999
5500QHG9028 • **Value $80**

11

1961 Murray® Super Deluxe Tractor with Trailer
Retired 1998
5500QHG9027 • **Value $97**

12

1964-1/2 Ford Mustang
Retired 1999
5500QHG9030 • **Value $78**

13

1935 American Airflow Coaster (LE-29,500)
Retired 1998
4800QHG6310 • **Value $80**

14

1935 Sky King Velocipede
Retired 1999
4500QHG6311 • **Value $70**

15

1941 Keystone Locomotive
Retired 1998
4500QHG6312 • **Value $65**

16

1950 GARTON® Delivery Cycle
Retired 1999
3800QHG6309 • **Value $65**

17

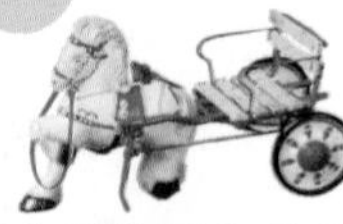

Late 1940s Mobo Sulky (LE-29,500)
Retired 1999
4800QHG6308 • **Value $100**

	Price Paid	Value
1997 Kiddie Car Corner		
1.		
2.		
1997 Sidewalk Cruisers		
3.		
4.		
5.		
6.		
1996 Kiddie Car Classics		
7.		
8.		
9.		
10.		
11.		
12.		
1996 Sidewalk Cruisers		
13.		
14.		
15.		
16.		
17.		
Totals		

1995

1

1937 Steelcraft Airflow by Murray® (LE-24,500)
Retired 1996
6500QHG9024 • **Value $130**

2

1937 Steelcraft Auburn (LE-24,500)
Retired 1996
6500QHG9021 • **Value $190**

3

1937 Steelcraft Auburn (Artists On Tour, dark green)
Retired 1995
(N/C) No stock # • **Value N/E**

4

1948 Murray® Pontiac
Retired 1998
5000QHG9026 • **Value $78**

5

1950 Murray® Torpedo
Retired 1996
5000QHG9020 • **Value $165**

6

1955 Murray® Royal Deluxe (LE-29,500)
Retired 1999
5500QHG9025 • **Value $80**

7

1959 GARTON® Deluxe Kidillac
Retired 1996
5500QHG9017 • **Value $115**

8

1961 GARTON® Casey Jones Locomotive
Retired 1996
5500QHG9019 • **Value $100**

9

1962 Murray® Super Deluxe Fire Truck
Retired 1997
5500QHG9095 • **Value $95**

10

1964 GARTON® Tin Lizzie
Retired 1997
5000QHG9023 • **Value $93**

11

1935 Steelcraft Streamline Velocipede by Murray®
Retired 1999
4500QHG6306 • **Value $72**

12

1937 Steelcraft Streamline Scooter by Murray®
Retired 1997
3500QHG6301 • **Value $62**

13

1939 Mobo Horse
Retired 1998
4500QHG6304 • **Value $77**

14

1940 GARTON® Aero Flite Wagon (LE-29,500)
Retired 1999
4800QHG6305 • **Value $70**

15

1958 Murray® Police Cycle (LE-29,500)
Retired 1999
5500QHG6307 • **Value $74**

16

1963 GARTON® Speedster
Retired 1999
3800QHG6303 • **Value $75**

17

1966 GARTON® Super-Sonda
Retired 1997
4500QHG6302 • **Value $68**

1994

18

1939 Steelcraft Lincoln Zephyr by Murray® (LE-24,500)
Retired 1996
5000QHG9015 • **Value $128**

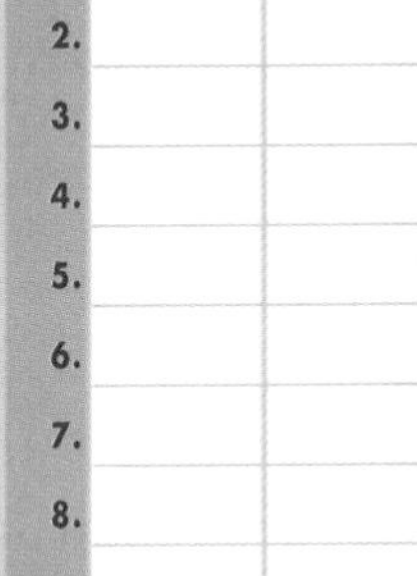

1995 Kiddie Car Classics	Price Paid	Value
1.		
2.		
3.		
4.		
5.		
6.		
7.		
8.		
9.		
10.		
1995 Sidwalk Cruisers		
11.		
12.		
13.		
14.		
15.		
16.		
17.		
1994 Kiddie Car Classics		
18.		
Totals		

Kiddie Car Classics

1

1941 Steelcraft Spitfire Airplane by Murray® (LE-19,500)
Retired 1996
5000QHG9009 • **Value $195**

2

1955 Murray® Dump Truck (LE-19,500)
Retired 1996
4800QHG9011 • **Value $145**

3

1955 Murray® Fire Truck (LE-19,500, white)
Retired 1996
5000QHG9010 • **Value $345**

4

1955 Murray® Ranch Wagon (LE-19,500)
Retired 1996
4800QHG9007 • **Value $135**

5

1955 Murray® Red Champion (LE-19,500)
Retired 1996
4500QHG9002 • **Value $130**

6

1956 GARTON® Dragnet® Police Car (LE-24,500)
Retired 1997
5000QHG9016 • **Value $83**

7

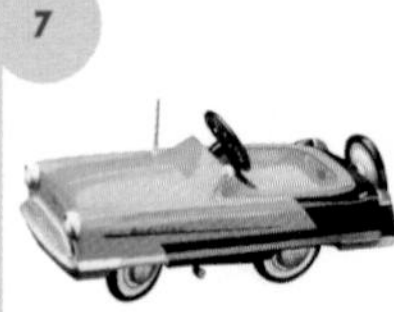

1956 GARTON® Kidillac
Retired 1994
5000QHX9094 • **Value $88**

8

1956 GARTON® Mark V (LE-24,500)
Retired 1997
4500QHG9022 • **Value $82**

9

1958 Murray® Atomic Missile (LE-24,500)
Retired 1997
5500QHG9018 • **Value $100**

10

1961 Murray® Circus Car (LE-24,500)
Retired 1997
4800QHG9014 • **Value $84**

11

1961 Murray® Speedway Pace Car (LE-24,500)
Retired 1997
4500QHG9013 • **Value $84**

1993

12

1955 Murray® Fire Chief (LE-19,500)
Retired 1996
4500QHG9006 • **Value $150**

13

1968 Murray® Boat Jolly Roger (LE-19,500)
Retired 1996
5000QHG9005 • **Value $105**

1992

14

1941 Murray® Airplane (LE-14,500)
Retired 1993
5000QHG9003 • **Value $440**

15

1953 Murray® Dump Truck (LE-14,500)
Retired 1993
4800QHG9012 • **Value $300**

16

1955 Murray® Champion (LE-14,500)
Retired 1993
4500QHG9008 • **Value $370**

17

1955 Murray® Fire Truck (LE-14,500)
Retired 1993
5000QHG9001 • **Value $425**

18

1955 Murray® Tractor and Trailer (LE-14,500)
Retired 1993
5500QHG9004 • **Value $375**

	Price Paid	Value
1994 Kiddie Car Classics		
1.		
2.		
3.		
4.		
5.		
6.		
7.		
8.		
9.		
10.		
11.		
1993 Kiddie Car Classics		
12.		
13.		
1992 Kiddie Car Classics		
14.		
15.		
16.		
17.		
18.		
Totals		

Future Releases

Use this page to record future releases and purchases.

Hallmark Ornaments	Item #	Status	Price Paid	Value

Page Totals:	Price Paid	Value

Total Value Of My Collection

Record the value of your collection here.

Keepsake Series

Page Number	Price Paid	Value
Page 43		
Page 44		
Page 45		
Page 46		
Page 47		
Page 48		
Page 49		
Page 50		
Page 51		
Page 52		
Page 53		
Page 54		
Page 55		
Page 56		
Page 57		
Page 58		
Page 59		
Page 60		
Page 61		
Page 62		
Page 63		
Page 64		
Page 65		
Page 66		
Page 67		
Page 68		
Page 69		
Page 70		
Page 71		
Page 72		
Subtotal		

Magic Series

Page Number	Price Paid	Value
Page 72		
Page 73		
Page 74		
Page 75		

Miniature Series

Page Number	Price Paid	Value
Page 76		
Page 77		
Page 78		
Page 79		
Page 80		
Page 81		
Page 82		
Page 83		
Page 84		

2001-1973 Collections

Page Number	Price Paid	Value
Page 85		
Page 86		
Page 87		
Page 88		
Page 89		
Page 90		
Page 91		
Page 92		
Page 93		
Page 94		
Page 95		
Page 96		
Page 97		
Page 98		
Page 99		
Subtotal		

	Price Paid	Value
Page Totals:		

Total Value Of My Collection

Record the value of your collection here.

2001-1973 Collections

Page Number	Price Paid	Value
Page 100		
Page 101		
Page 102		
Page 103		
Page 104		
Page 105		
Page 106		
Page 107		
Page 108		
Page 109		
Page 110		
Page 111		
Page 112		
Page 113		
Page 114		
Page 115		
Page 116		
Page 117		
Page 118		
Page 119		
Page 120		
Page 121		
Page 122		
Page 123		
Page 124		
Page 125		
Page 126		
Page 127		
Page 128		
Page 129		
Page 130		
Page 131		
Subtotal		

2001-1973 Collections

Page Number	Price Paid	Value
Page 132		
Page 133		
Page 134		
Page 135		
Page 136		
Page 137		
Page 138		
Page 139		
Page 140		
Page 141		
Page 142		
Page 143		
Page 144		
Page 145		
Page 146		
Page 147		
Page 148		
Page 149		
Page 150		
Page 151		
Page 152		
Page 153		
Page 154		
Page 155		
Page 156		
Page 157		
Page 158		
Page 159		
Page 160		
Page 160		
Page 161		
Page 162		
Subtotal		

Page Totals:	Price Paid	Value

Total Value Of My Collection

Record the value of your collection here.

2001-1973 Collections		
Page Number	Price Paid	Value
Page 163		
Page 164		
Page 165		
Page 166		
Page 167		
Page 168		
Page 169		
Page 170		
Page 171		
Page 172		
Page 173		
Page 174		
Page 175		
Page 176		
Page 177		
Page 178		
Page 179		
Page 180		
Page 181		
Page 182		
Page 183		
Page 184		
Page 185		
Page 186		
Page 187		
Page 188		
Page 189		
Page 190		
Page 191		
Page 192		
Page 193		
Page 194		
Subtotal		

2001-1973 Collections		
Page Number	Price Paid	Value
Page 195		
Page 196		
Page 197		
Page 198		
Page 199		
Page 200		
Page 201		
Page 202		
Page 203		
Page 204		
Page 205		
Page 206		
Page 207		
Page 208		
Page 209		
Page 210		
Page 211		
Page 212		
Page 213		
Page 214		
Page 215		
Page 216		
Page 217		
Page 218		
Page 219		
Page 220		
Page 221		
Page 222		
Page 223		
Page 224		
Page 225		
Page 226		
Subtotal		

Page Totals:	Price Paid	Value

Total Value Of My Collection

Record the value of your collection here.

2001-1973 Collections		
Page Number	Price Paid	Value
Page 227		
Page 228		
Page 229		
Page 230		
Page 231		
Page 232		
Page 233		
Page 234		
Page 235		
Page 236		
Page 237		
Page 238		
Page 239		
Page 240		
Page 241		
Page 242		
Page 243		
Page 244		
Page 245		
Page 246		
Page 247		
Page 248		
Page 249		
Page 250		
Page 251		
Page 252		
Page 253		
Page 254		
Page 255		
Page 256		
Page 257		
Page 258		
Subtotal		

2001-1973 Collections		
Page Number	Price Paid	Value
Page 259		
Page 260		
Page 261		
Page 262		
Page 263		
Page 264		
Page 265		
Page 266		
Page 267		
Page 268		
Page 269		
Page 270		
Page 271		
Page 272		
Page 273		
Page 274		
Page 275		
Page 276		
Page 277		
Page 278		
Page 279		
Page 280		
Page 281		
Page 282		
Page 283		
Page 284		
Page 285		
Page 286		
Page 287		
Page 288		
Page 289		
Page 290		
Subtotal		

Page Totals:	Price Paid	Value

Total Value Of My Collection

Record the value of your collection here!

2001-1973 Collections

Page Number	Price Paid	Value
Page 291		

Spring Ornaments

Page Number	Price Paid	Value
Page 292		
Page 293		
Page 294		
Page 295		
Page 296		
Page 297		
Page 298		
Page 299		
Page 300		
Page 301		
Page 302		

Merry Miniatures®

Page Number	Price Paid	Value
Page 303		
Page 304		
Page 305		
Page 306		
Page 307		
Page 308		
Page 309		
Page 310		
Page 311		
Page 312		
Page 313		
Page 314		
Page 315		
Page 316		
Page 317		
Page 318		
Page 319		
Subtotal		

Merry Miniatures®

Page Number	Price Paid	Value
Page 320		
Page 321		
Page 322		
Page 323		
Page 324		
Page 325		
Page 326		
Page 327		
Page 328		
Page 329		
Page 330		
Page 331		
Page 332		
Page 333		
Page 334		
Page 335		
Page 336		
Page 337		
Page 338		

Kiddie Car Classics

Page Number	Price Paid	Value
Page 339		
Page 340		
Page 341		
Page 342		
Page 343		
Page 344		
Page 345		
Page 346		

Future Releases

Page Number	Price Paid	Value
Page 347		
Subtotal		

Page Totals:	Price Paid	Value

A Look Back At 2000

Every year, there are a few special ornaments that capture the fancy of Hallmark collectors everywhere. Here's a look at just some of the ornaments that had collectors returning to their favorite gift stores again and again in 2000:

The recent passing of Charles Schulz in February of 2000 led to a renewed interest in the PEANUTS® characters. 2000's Open House Ornaments, which featured Charlie Brown, Linus, Lucy, Snoopy and Woodstock, were especially sought after by collectors wishing to honor the memory of the beloved comic strip creator.

Dr. Seuss is always able to put a smile on the face of even the "grinchiest" sourpuss. From "Gifts for the Grinch" to "Green Eggs and Ham™," no page was left unturned in bringing the wonderful books of Dr. Seuss to life.

Licensed products were not the only ornaments snapped up by collectors. The Li'l Blown Glass collection provided a nostalgic reminder of how ornaments were produced in simpler times. "Li'l Roly-Poly Penguin" and "Li'l Mrs. Claus" were just two of the friendly members of this well-received set.

The first edition to the *Toymaker Santa* ornament proved that collectors are still willing to invest in a brand-new series in addition to keeping up with their long-running favorites. With a new edition joining the series in 2001, all indications point to this series lasting a very long time.

The exquisite detail on the "Time for Joy" ornament had enthusiastic collectors searching around the clock for it. Both ornament and clock collectors felt they would be cuckoo to pass it up.

So which ornaments will be the "talk of the town" for 2001? We'll just have to wait and see!

Collector's Club News

We all know what happens the night before Christmas. Santa Claus takes off for his annual trek around the world as children wait in eager anticipation of morning, hoping that Santa left them all of the goodies they asked for. But have you ever wondered what happens the night before the night before Christmas?

When you join the Hallmark Keepsake Ornament Collector's Club in 2001, you'll find out as "The Night Before The Night Before Christmas" is the club's theme this year! And there's a whole new cast of characters for you to collect.

Of course, even Santa needs a little help sometimes, and his trusty elves "Globus" and "Lettera" are all set to help him find his way from Antarctica to Zimbabwe. (Let's just hope he doesn't take that wrong turn at Albuquerque again!). And, of course, "Mrs. Claus" is all set with that list of houses for her husband to visit. It's just like they say – behind every successful man, there's a great woman! This set of three charming pieces can be yours – they come free as "keepsakes of membership" when you sign up with the club.

If you think Santa's job is easy, think again! It takes lots of planning to travel the world in a single night, so Hallmark has built "Santa's Desk – 2001 Studio Limited Edition" to help him sort out all those last-minute flight plans before he takes off. Sculpted by the entire Keepsake Studio, "Santa's Desk" is truly a treasure, but it's only available through a special mail-in offer for club members, so don't miss out!

Hallmark On The Web

Jump on-line and click onto www.hallmark.com for up-to-the-minute information about the Keepsake line.

And be sure to also visit the virtual Hallmark community at www.CollectorsQuest.com for news briefs, contests and bulletin boards!

In addition to these great rewards, club members have the chance to purchase exclusive ornaments that are not offered anywhere else. This year's ornaments include "Santa Claus Marionette," sculpted by Ken Crow, the traditional five-piece "Nesting Nativity," sculpted by Linda Sickman and "1958 Custom Corvette," sculpted by Don Palmiter, for those with a "need for speed." Just be careful not to let it joy-ride around the branches!

Hallmark club members never turn down an opportunity to socialize with each other, so the company sponsors special events where members can get even more exclusive pieces to build their collection. "With Help From Pup," a two-piece miniature ornament set of an elf and his puppy stacking gifts for Santa's sleigh is offered exclusively at Keepsake Ornament events to members only. And Hallmark will reward all existing members who sign up a friend to the club with the "Gift For A Friend Teddy Bear," an adorable little buddy who will be an everlasting symbol of friendship and holiday cheer. This year's Jubilee events, held in celebration of the club's 15th anniversary, will offer even more special pieces for club members.

Annual membership in the Hallmark Keepsake Ornament Collector's Club is just $25. So don't just buy the ornaments – be one of the collectors nationwide who know just how much fun collecting can be! Contact your favorite retail store for membership, or you can reach the club at:

Hallmark Keepsake Ornament Collector's Club
P.O. Box 419824
Kansas City, MO 64141-6834
(800) 523-5839

Local Club Spotlight

Hallmark Keepsake Ornament enthusiasts are a breed apart from fans of other collectible lines. Although there is an official Hallmark Keepsake Ornament Collector's Club, countless other clubs have sprung up across the country. These local clubs give collectors in the same region a chance to meet, share their collections and have a lot of fun at the same time! The local clubs also give members an opportunity to take an active role in giving back to the community.

Connecticut

The long-standing New England Ornament Collector's Club has been getting together to discuss Hallmark ornaments for over a decade. Members meet once a month to participate in activities and listen to guest speakers. The group also works hard to help their area towns with civic-minded activities like collecting non-perishable food items to take to homeless shelters. As the holidays draw near, they also collect gifts that can be given to less fortunate children and host an annual charity auction. And, whenever they can, this hearty New England bunch embarks on bus trips to local events (and even one trip to the heart of Hallmark in Kansas City). Hopefully, they had a big bus – at one time the club numbered over 100 members and stands 50 strong today.

Members of the New England Ornament Collector's Club pose with Keepsake artist Joanne Eschrich (center).

Mississippi

The small town of Hattiesburg, Mississippi is best known as "Hub City," and the Hub's Can't Stop At One! Ornament Club is a hub of activity in the world of Hallmark collecting! Small in number, but big in spirit, the club helps out charitable organizations such as the Susan G. Komen Breast Cancer Foundation. At each month's meeting, the club also partakes in seasonal activities ranging from Easter egg decorating contests in the spring to wreath decorating contests during the holiday season.

Members from the Hub's Can't Stop At One! club share a laugh with Hallmark's crabby, but lovable, Maxine.

Missouri

Based in Joplin, Missouri, the Bright Christmas Dreamers Collector's Club formed in 1992 and meets the first Thursday of every other month. The popular club has 40 members from three different states! The Dreamers actively support the Joplin Ronald McDonald House. They also decorate and donate a Christmas tree for the annual YMCA Christmas auction.

When they're not busy helping the community, the club enjoys visiting other local clubs, hosting speakers, traveling to national events and holding their own weekend flea markets. These devoted Dreamers have also participated in every national Hallmark event since 1994 and look forward to many more.

Members of the Bright Christmas Dreamers pose as their favorite snowman ornaments.

Oklahoma

The Okie Keepsakers line up their gift baskets for inspection.

The Okie Keepsakers club keeps busy with trading display tips, hosting programs and participating in charitable events. The Keepsakers have chosen a domestic violence intervention charity as the recipient of their support. Members of the Tulsa-based club contribute diapers, school supplies and other necessities to the charity. The club also helps out the charity by assembling Easter baskets for children and Mother's Day baskets for women. When winter is at its harshest, the Keepsakers adopt families in need of Christmas cheer.

Wisconsin

The Bay Dreamers club (shown with artist Ed Seale) is just one of many local Hallmark clubs throughout the country.

Through the dedication of its 30 club members, the Bay Dreamers Club has raised over $5,000 since its inception in 1994 for various local charities. Each Christmas, many in the club participate in the "Letters from Santa" program that helps the U. S. Postal Service make sure that every child's letter to Santa Claus gets answered.

If you are interested in joining a local Hallmark club, ask your retailer if there are any in your area. If not, why not start your own?

A Tour Of Crown Center

Thousands flock to the Crown Center each year to experience Kansas City's greatest tourist attraction.

Before Joyce Hall envisioned the Crown Center in downtown Kansas City in 1968, the area was littered with deserted parking lots and run-down office buildings. Hall's idea to construct what is now an 85-acre complex on the fringes of the city transformed Kansas City's downtown area into a place where people can gather to shop, live, work and play. The Crown Center is an entertainment mecca complete with two hotels, dining for all occasions, a tri-level shopping plaza, an ice skating rink, a movie theater, two stages for live performances and so much more!

The Visitor's Center

Guests to the Hallmark Visitor's Center can see the success of the business chronicled from its humble beginnings to the billion-dollar company we know today. Through enlarged versions of the tools that the artists use in the Studio, you can learn about the details of sculpting Keepsake Ornaments . A museum of past and present greeting card designs is located here as well as an exhibit on how the cards are produced. Then, rest your feet for a while as you watch videos of"Hallmark Hall of Fame" specials. And before you leave, make sure to check out the decorated trees that were given to Joyce Hall as gifts by his artists!

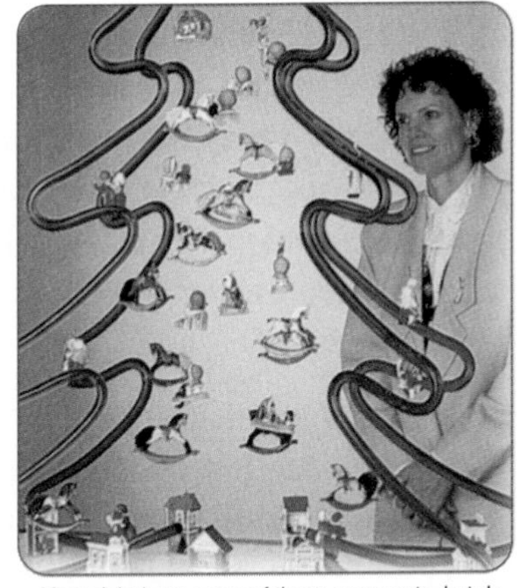

You might have some of these ornaments, but do you have a unique tree like this to hang them from?

Also in the Crown Center is Kaleidoscope, an interactive children's exhibit sponsored by Crayola. Both centers are free to the public.

Other Hallmark Collectibles

Once you've filled your tree to capacity with Keepsake Ornaments and sprinkled Merry Miniatures throughout your home, you might think that you've discovered all there is to the world of Hallmark collecting.

The truth is, you've only just begun! Throughout the years, Hallmark has offered an enticing array of products that devoted Hallmark collectors should not overlook. Some of these elusive pieces may be harder to locate than an early *Frosty Friends* or *Here Comes Santa* ornament. Here's a brief look at some of the more popular collections.

Cookie Cutters

There's nothing better than a batch of warm cookies that have just come out of grandma's oven – nothing that is, except cookies that have been made with Hallmark cookie cutters! Your grandma may even have used a Hallmark cookie cutter when she was a young girl, because the cutters predate even the long-running Keepsake Ornament Collection. Cookie cutters were produced in either hard or soft plastic, and some come with eyelets for hanging or displaying the cutters. Hallmark also produced cookie shapers, which are shaped to represent stars, trees and other popular designs.

Don't think that you have to wait until December 25th to bake your cookies, either! Hallmark made cutters for every occasion and holiday, including

Thanksgiving, Halloween, Easter, St. Patrick's Day and Valentines Day. These cutters will probably set you back a little more than the 75¢ they originally retailed for, but by spending just a little dough, you'll be jazzing up the cookie batter for your next get-together!

Lapel Pins

Wearing your Keepsake Ornaments around your neck might not be practical, and may draw some confused stares from others. If you're determined to wear some holiday cheer, however, hunt down a few Hallmark Lapel Pins and "Pin on a little holiday fun!," as their slogan suggests. Most lapel pins are affordable and can be found for around $5, but a few pricier pins will set you back a larger sum.

Little Gallery

Hallmark's Little Gallery line offered an eclectic mix of porcelain figurines, pewter plates and crystal accessories. Betsey Clark, known for her many appearances on Keepsake Ornaments, appeared in the Little Gallery collection as both a pewter figurine and a wood plaque. Other fondly remembered pieces in the line include the pewter donkey and elephant figurines that were released in commemoration of the 1980 presidential election.

Little Gallery was popular in the 1970s, but was eventually discontinued by Hallmark in 1984. But, don't despair! Little Gallery didn't disappear for good. The New England Pewter Company obtained the rights to continue producing some of the items, although not under the Little Gallery name.

Salt And Pepper Shakers

Worth Its Salt

How do you know that you have an authentic Hallmark salt and pepper shaker set in your collection? Just turn it upside down! Many of the sets are stamped "© Hallmark Cards, Inc." on the bottom. Just make sure that the shaker is empty before you flip it over!

While it might provide a steady surface, the dining room table isn't the proper place to put your Christmas tree. Why not dress up your table with a Hallmark salt and pepper shaker set instead? These shakers originally retailed for $6.99 and if you scour the secondary market, you might be able to find a pair for not much more. Themes include Santa and Mrs. Claus, an autumn acorns and wheat set and Thanksgiving pilgrims and turkeys.

Stocking Hangers

What do the characters of Santa Claus, BARBIE™ and Winnie the Pooh all have in common? Each is perfect for keeping your holiday stockings from falling into the fireplace! Licensed properties frequently appear as stocking hangers and characters such as Snoopy are always sought after.

From Santa's naughty and nice list to a kitten's curved candy cane, these whimsical holiday characters give your stocking plenty to hang on to. But don't just take them out at Christmas – they look terrific on the mantle any time of the year!

Tender Touches

Hallmark's Tender Touches collection leaves collectors with a warm, fuzzy feeling. Designed by master artist Ed Seale, these porcelain figures celebrate the arrival of spring and will put a spring in your step as well. An observant eye can occasionally spot a Tender Touches critter that has jumped into the regular line of Keepsake Ornaments. "High Hopes" is a 1995 Tender Touches entry into the Spring Ornaments line and the three furry "Glee Cub Bears" can be found caterwauling in the 1991 Keepsake Collection.

How do you know if you've spotted an original Tender Touches figurine? Check the box – the figurines were packaged in plain boxes that feature the Tender Touches logo above a ribbon design that has HALLMARK COLLECTIONS written on it. Other Tender Touches boxes depict two bunnies under a shady tree waiting for their furry friends to arrive. The Tender Touches logo on the box is written in script or a more woodsy tree ring design.

Tree Toppers & Tree Bases

After you've decorated your entire tree with Keepsake ornaments, no ordinary tree topper will do. Hallmark's large collection of tree toppers can cap off your tree perfectly. While many are still affordable, keep your eye out for older tree toppers at yard sales and collectible shows. Angels seem to be the most popular tree toppers, and those from the 1970s are especially popular. In particular, the beautiful translucent "Christmas Angel" from 1979 fetches a healthy sum on the secondary market. If you'd like something more affordable, there is a large selection (including a goose) from recent years to choose from.

But don't let the top of your tree have all the fun! In 1993, Hallmark introduced the "Holiday Express" miniature tree base. This handcrafted, battery operated tree base was just the right size for displaying Miniature Ornaments.

Meet Clara Johnson Scroggins

She's known throughout the country for her extensive collection of Hallmark Ornaments and is widely regarded as the nation's foremost ornament historian. These days, Clara Johnson Scroggins can be found giving talks about the joys of ornament collecting at Hallmark stores and collectibles shows across the country. She has been featured in several newspapers and magazines including the *New York Times*, *USA Today* and *Better Homes & Gardens* and has made appearances on such television shows as *Today* and *Good Morning America*. In addition, Clara travels the world to share her love of ornament collecting with fellow enthusiasts.

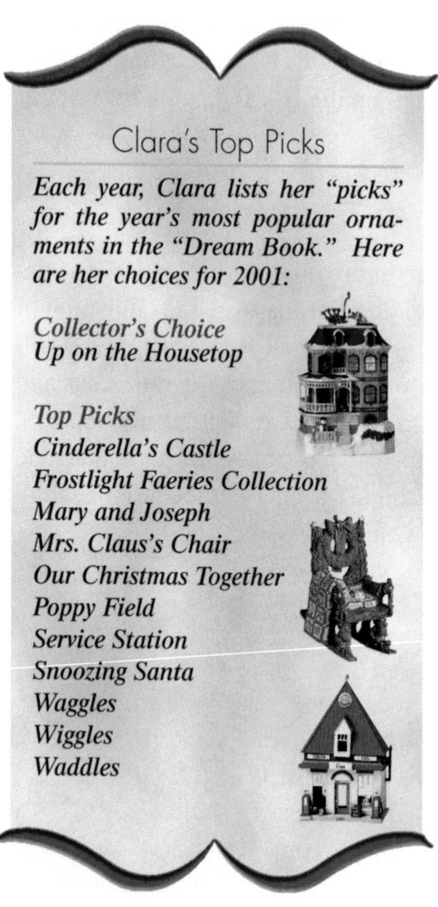

Clara's Top Picks

Each year, Clara lists her "picks" for the year's most popular ornaments in the "Dream Book." Here are her choices for 2001:

Collector's Choice
Up on the Housetop

Top Picks
Cinderella's Castle
Frostlight Faeries Collection
Mary and Joseph
Mrs. Claus's Chair
Our Christmas Together
Poppy Field
Service Station
Snoozing Santa
Waggles
Wiggles
Waddles

For Clara, the holiday season is about spending time with family and friends and, through ornament displays, remembering all the wonderful times and milestones in your life. Birthdays, weddings, special occasions – they can all be chronicled on the Christmas tree (or trees, as is the case in Clara's house!)

Clara's affection for ornaments began in a shopping mall over thirty years ago. While battling the depression that set in after her first husband died, Clara took a friend's advice to do something new each day. This led her to a local shopping plaza, where she spotted a silver cross ornament, the look of which gave her a new sense

Clara stores all of her ornaments in a climate-controlled room and she starts planning her Christmas decorations early! But with thousands of ornaments, it would be impossible to put them all up every year. And she doesn't do all the decorating herself, either. Instead, she puts baskets of extra ornaments under the trees and invites all of her holiday visitors to hang up ornaments that they like.

of peace. After purchasing the cross, she saw that it was a second edition. Thus, she began to scour the nation looking for the first edition of the piece. Her search led her to other special works of art and soon Clara amassed thousands of ornaments. Today, her collection numbers over 500,000 – it is believed to be the largest ornament collection in the world.

When she started writing the book "Hallmark Keepsake Ornaments: A Collector's Guide" in 1980, the ornament division of Hallmark was small. Now, after writing nine books, Clara is the foremost authority on collecting Hallmark ornaments and even serves as consultant and National Spokesperson for the Hallmark Keepsake Division.

Clara was born in Little Village, Arkansas and spent the majority of her childhood there. She now resides in Tampa, Florida. She and her husband of 25 years, Joe Scroggins, Jr., have one son, three grandchildren and a great-granddaughter.

Clara and her husband Joe enjoy Tampa's Festival of Trees.

Secondary Market Overview

While most collectible lines produce pieces limited to one production year, Keepsake Ornaments are available for only half that time (July through December), which makes it even harder to collect every piece from the "Dream Book." And since Hallmark has been designing ornaments since the early 1970s, new enthusiasts may be interested in adding older, already retired ornaments to their collections. So how do you go about obtaining these out-of-production pieces? You should look to the secondary market.

Secondary Market? What's That?

The secondary market is a meeting place for collectors all over the world who are looking to buy, sell or swap collectibles, or, in this case, Hallmark ornaments and figurines. Retired pieces often increase in value after they are out of production, so you'll most likely pay a higher price for your purchases than you would at a Hallmark store. The prices on the secondary market fluctuate depending on if the piece is rare, popular or otherwise in demand. Some ornaments, especially the initial release in a series, can sell for hundreds of dollars on the secondary market.

But Where Do I Start?

Since it's such a big place with so many possibilities, dealing on the secondary market might seem a bit foreboding, and you might be wondering where to start your search. Contact local retailers first to see if they know of any collector's events in the area. They might even know collectors who are willing to help you find the elusive ornament!

The best place to look for retired ornaments is the Internet. There, you can get a feel for how hard to find your piece is, which will help you determine how much you're willing to pay for it. Go to any search engine and type in words such as "Hallmark," "secondary market," "ornaments" or "collectibles" to find great sites to help you in your search! Use Internet bulletin boards to their full potential by posting information about your collection and what you're looking for. You never know who you'll meet!

Don't forget Internet auction sites, either. They can be a great place to find the ornaments you're looking for and can also put you in contact with other collectors who will help you with future forays into the secondary market. But buyer, beware. When purchasing merchandise off the Internet, be sure that you're using a secure server and that you're comfortable with the retailer or individual with whom you're doing business. If you're concerned, you might want to check with the Better Business Bureau (*www.BBBonline.org*) or ask the seller for references.

Specialists are also available (for a possible fee) to aid in your secondary market treasure hunt. These dealers usually offer newsletters and other information to put you in touch with the local collectibles happenings in your area. Also, think about taking out an ad in the classified section of your local newspaper to advertise what pieces you're looking for, or what pieces you have to sell.

The Total Package

Whether you're buying or selling, keep in mind that the condition of the packaging is very important. If the packaging is in bad condition, the value of the piece itself can be diminished. Likewise, if the packaging is missing, the ornament will decrease significantly in value. Often considered a part of the ornament itself, the packaging validates the authenticity of the ornament and without it, the piece is incomplete. Be sure to store all of your packages in a safe, dry place and keep them in mint condition, especially if you plan to sell any of your ornaments at any time.

Sure, the value of your collection is important, but above all, remember that ornament collecting is about sharing memories, spending time with friends and family, and celebrating the most glorious time of all – the holiday season!

Exchanges, Dealers & Newsletters

Angelic Seasons
Michelle Spicer
3334-2869 Battleford Rd.
Mississauga, Ontario
L5N 2S6
Canada
905-816-9221

Christmas in Vermont
Kathy Parrott
51 Jalbert Road
Barre, VT 05641
802-479-2024
katparrott@aol.com

The Christmas Shop
Shirley Trexler
P.O. Box 5221
Cary, NC 27512
919-469-5264

Collectible Exchange, Inc.
6621 Columbiana Road
New Middletown, OH 44442
800-752-3208 • 330-542-9646
www.colexch.com

Holiday Keepsakes
Tom Barker
500 W. Carpenter Street
McLeansboro, IL 62859
618-643-4704
fax: 618-643-3486
www.mcleansboro.com/keepsakes

Mary Johnson
P.O. Box 1015
Marion, NC 28752-1015
828-652-2910
maryjorn@wnclink.com

Morris Antiques
Allen and Pat Morris
2716 Flintlock Drive
Henderson, KY 42420
270-826-8378
prm@dynasty.net

The Ornament Shop
Beth Warnecke
P.O. Box 1071
Findlay, OH 45839-1071
419-427-8506
www.ornament-shop.com

The Ornament Trader Magazine
Judy Patient
P. O. Box 469
Lavonia, GA 30553-0469
800-441-1551 • 770-517-3694
fax: 770-517-2316
jpat721868@aol.com

Twelve Months of Christmas
Joan Ketterer
P.O. Box 97172
Pittsburgh, PA 15229
412-367-2352

From Paper To Finished Product

Keepsake artists such as Ken Crow play an important role in the journey an ornament takes from a drawing to the final product.

Collectors must wonder where the talented Keepsake Ornament artists find their inspiration for the beloved ornaments and figurines that Hallmark releases annually. Truth is, they find their inspiration in every day life – from friends and family, local and far away places, books and magazines, and even the great artists of the past. Though each artist brings something new and refreshing to the design table, the production process remains the same for every ornament.

The pieces in this year's "Dream Book" actually began production two years ago! The Keepsake artists submit drawings of their own ideas as well as offering artistic renderings of ideas presented to them by Hallmark. Those images are then reviewed and the best ones are chosen for development. Sometimes many ideas from various drawings are incorporated into a final sketch.

A model of the piece is then designed and photographed, and no less than seven sculptures are made by the many artists in the studio. Some of those figurines are used to experiment with different color schemes, while only one will become the mold for the final ornament. The ornament is then cast and mass manufactured in the Hallmark production facility.

Years ago, ornaments were made of yarn and glass, but today's artists have an unlimited array of materials and new technology at their disposal. Thanks to the hard work of the Hallmark staff, you're able to delight family and friends with a tree full of stunning ornaments each and every year.

Easy Decorating Tips

Even though you look forward to pulling out your Hallmark ornaments every Christmas season, there's no reason why you have to pack them away when the holidays are over. There are plenty of ways to display your favorite pieces around the house both during the holidays and throughout the year.

The Stockings Were Hung . . .

Mary's Angels make perfect stocking accessories!

Nearly everyone decorates their tree for the holidays but what about your stockings? This year, jazz up the traditional holiday stocking using themed ornaments. You can make the adorable display pictured at left by using pieces from the *Mary's Angels* series. Just glue some white cloud-shaped felt or cotton to a blue stocking, sprinkle some glitter and soon the *Mary's Angels* will be right at home floating in the clouds! Why not go a step further and create a personalized stocking for all of your family members using ornaments which reflect their interests and hobbies? You can even create a special present for the family pet by using pieces from the *Puppy Love* series and some of your furry friend's favorite doggy treats.

Help In The Kitchen

Many Hallmark Ornaments can move easily from the tree into the kitchen! "Creative Cutter – Cooking for Christmas," "Sweet Contribution – Cooking for Christmas" and "Kiss the Cook" are great kitchen companions year-round! Display them near your flour and sugar canisters or hang them from your cabinet door handles. You can even make a home for them on the ledge on your oven! No one will be brave enough to pilfer a cookie before dinnertime when "Fluffy™ on Guard" from the *Harry Potter*™ ornament collection is guarding your cookie jar!

Back To School

Crayola and Hallmark have had a long relationship and in each year's Keepsake Collection, there's something new from the people who gave us the colorful crayons! You can make this Crayola display simply by adding a few *CRAYOLA® Crayon* series ornaments to any holiday basket. And make sure to toss in a few *real* crayons and a coloring book to complete the look! Or, set up a basket of Crayola products with paper and other creative utensils (include child-safe scissors, non-toxic glue and other fun stuff!) for your child's work area at home. Be sure to decorate the basket with pieces like 2001's "Color Crew Chief CRAYOLA® Crayon," or even this year's new Merry Miniature – "Bee Bright!" Just make sure that your selections can not be easily broken by little hands!

This is a great way to display all of your Crayola® ornaments for the holidays!

Off To See The Wizard

You can make a great homage to the classic movie *The Wizard of Oz* by covering a piece of plywood or styrofoam with green felt and then adding gold or yellow fabric to create the Yellow Brick Road. With decorative mini-trees, shrubs, rocks and flowers (all available at

Why not create this great scene in your home with all of your *Wizard of Oz*-themed ornaments.

your local craft store), you can create many different scenes from the movie, including the romp through the poppy fields, meeting Glinda the Good Witch and arriving at the Emerald City. By painting some plastic tubing florescent green, it can look just like the Emerald City from the movie! And don't forget to hang "Witch of the West" and "The Wizard of OZ™" on your display for that final authentic touch!

Faerie Dust And Potting Soil

After the Christmas tree is on the curb (or back in its box!), there are other trees perfect for ornament display. Imagine a little faerie sprinkling magical dust on a summer topiary. Why not use one of the *Frostlight Faeries* to watch over your indoor plants, too? Either nestled in the leaves or hovering over the flowerpot (use a piece of wire grounded in the soil of the pot to hang your ornaments), you can keep the faeries busy all year long.

Spice up summer topiaries with Hallmark faeries.

The Need For Speed

With such detailed miniature reproductions of trains and automobiles in the *LIONEL® Train* series, the Kiddie Car Classics and the *Classic American Cars* series, why not keep them around all year long? With a few spare pieces of toy tracks from a train set or a toy racetrack, all of your transportation-themed ornaments can be transformed into a display that proudly presents the history of motion and the great vehicles of today.

You can display your trains in a basket, too. Just add some flowers and be creative!

Alphabetical Index

All Hallmark Keepsake Ornaments, Spring Ornaments, Merry Miniatures and Kiddie Car Classics are listed below in alphabetical order with the piece's location within the Value Guide section and the box in which it is pictured on that page.

Alphabetical Index

Alphabetical Index

Alphabetical Index

Acknowledgements

CheckerBee Publishing would like to extend a special thanks to Clara Johnson Scroggins, Tom Barker, Helen Cherry, Dee Ferry, Roberta Flanagan, Vicki Gilson, Mary Johnson, Terry Legrand, Debbie McAnneny, Kathy Parrott, Rita Randall, Alice Sandkuhl, Tom Schmidt, Van Tyner, Elaine Wibben and Diane Zimmer. And many thanks to the great people at Hallmark.